Manga
from the
Floating
World

Comicbook
Culture and
the *Kibyōshi*
of Edo Japan

Harvard East Asian Monographs 279

Manga

from the

Floating

World

Published by the Harvard University Asia Center

Distributed by Harvard University Press

Cambridge (Massachusetts) and London, 2006

Comicbook Culture and the *Kibyōshi* of Edo Japan

Adam
L.
Kern

Printed in the United States of America

The Harvard University Asia Center publishes a monograph series and, in coordination with the Fairbank Center for East Asian Research, the Korea Institute, the Reischauer Institute of Japanese Studies, and other faculties and institutes, administers research projects designed to further scholarly understanding of China, Japan, Vietnam, Korea, and other Asian countries. The Center also sponsors projects addressing multidisciplinary and regional issues in Asia.

Library of Congress Cataloging-in-Publication Data

Kern, Adam L.
    Manga from the floating world : comicbook culture and the kibyōshi of Edo Japan / Adam L. Kern.
       p. cm. --(Harvard East Asian monographs ; 279)
    Some kibyoshi items translated from Japanese.
    Includes bibliographical references and index.
    ISBN-13: 978-0-674-02266-9 (cloth : alk. paper)
    ISBN-10: 0-674-02266-1 (cloth : alk. paper)
    1. Kibyoshi-bon. 2. Comic books, strips, etc.--Japan. 3. Japanese fiction--Edo period, 1600–1868--History and criticism. I. Title.
PL747.4.K46 2006 741.5'95209—dc22

2006026130

Index by Ivan Grail

Last figure below indicates year of this printing
16 15 14 13 12 11 10 09 08 07 06

For

Mara Beth

Acknowledgments

My foremost debt of gratitude in the making of this book is owed to the fine mentors who have trained and inspired me over the years. Haruko Iwasaki introduced me during my graduate studies to Santō Kyōden, the *kibyō-shi*, and Edo Japan's world of popular literature. Ed Cranston, Howard Hibbett, and Jay Rubin have each in his own way rendered wise guidance, warm friendship, unflinching honesty, and unstinting support.

Aside from other colleagues at Harvard University in the Department of East Asian Languages and Civilizations, the least of whom are not Phil Kuhn, Stephen Owen, and Michael Puett, I wish to thank the accommodating and friendly administrative staff, Gus Espada, Frankie Hoff, Tom Johnson, Susan Kashiwa, Linda Thai, and Franklin Yates. The director, librarians, and staff at the Yenching Library have similarly provided essential assistance: Abe Nobuhiko, Matt Bilder, James Cheng, Horst Huber, Eddie Kuge, Ray Lum, Xiao-he Ma, Ellen McGill, Kuniko Yamada McVey, and Hilde De Weerdt. And thanks to those at affiliated institutions for kindly allowing me access to archived woodblock-printed materials: Anne Rose Kitagawa at the Arthur M. Sackler Museum; and Joe Earle, Anne Nishimura Morse, Jennifer Riley, Rachel Saunders, and Sarah E. Thompson at the Museum of Fine Arts, Boston.

My most inestimable institutional debt goes to the Edwin O. Reischauer Institute of Japanese Studies at Harvard for its liberal backing in multiple forms—a dissertation completion grant, a postdoctoral fellowship, a subvention for the present volume, and miscellaneous funds for travel, research, course development, and my junior leave. More personally, I wish to thank the Institute's directors and staff members for consistently going above and beyond their job descriptions, especially Galen Amstutz, Mary Amstutz, Margot Chamberlain, Ruiko Connor, Ted Gilman, Andy Gordon, Susan Pharr, and M. J. Scott.

Several other foundations and agencies displayed extreme munificence as well. The Japanese government's Ministry of Education fully sponsored my two years as a research student at the University of Kyoto. The American government provided a Foreign Language and Area Studies grant for advanced language training. Also at Harvard, the Faculty of Arts and Sciences furnished a Tenure-Track Faculty Publication Grant that covered the lion's share of my costs related to permissions and reproduction fees; the Satoh-

Artcraft Fellowship, thanks to the philanthropy of Satō Senju, sustained me as a Ph.D. candidate for several years; and the Clark and Cooke Funds enabled me to purchase the upmarket computer equipment used in this project.

I should also like to thank my erstwhile colleagues, staff, and students at the University of Washington, Seattle, particularly Andrew F. Jones, David Knechtges, and John Whittier Treat in the Department of Asian Languages and Literature; Eddy Harrison and Keiko Yokota-Carter of the East Asia Library; and Susan Hanley at the Jackson School. And thanks to the Japan Endowment for granting me an ad hoc travel grant when I most needed one.

My heartfelt appreciation goes to too many people and institutions in Japan to thank adequately. My major debt at the University of Tokyo is to Nobuhiro Shinji for facilitating my tenure as a Visiting Scholar in the Department of Comparative Literature, for allowing me to audit seminars, and for including me in his research group on Edo-period chapbooks. I also greatly value the kindness, patience, and indulgence of the frequenters of said group, particularly Futamata Jun, Iwata Hideyuki, Adam Kabat, and Kobayashi Fumiko.

At the National Institute of Japanese Literature in Tokyo, I have the many research librarians, staff, and director to thank, but especially: Robert Campbell, for graciously arranging my year as Visiting Professor; Suzuki Jun, for his kindhearted backing; Ida Tarō, for his congeniality; Ōtaka Yōji, for lending me his copy of a crucial picturebook; and Takahashi Noriko, who helped run my research group with Tanahashi Masahiro, Suzuki Jūzō, and others.

At the University of Kyoto, I am indebted to the staff, students, professors, and librarians in the Department of Japanese Literature, but mostly to Hamada Keisuke for his magnanimity in supervising my studies, encouraging my various travels off the beaten trail, even offering to share his own desk. I also want to thank Kondō Fumio of the Department of Economics and his family for their steady friendship.

I am eternally grateful to the late Kazuo Monane at Harvard and to numerous people at Kōdansha Publishers for setting up, overseeing, and extending an invaluable research internship: company president Noma Sawako; internship supervisor Ōtake Eiji; homestay hosts Hoshino Yūko and the recently deceased and much missed Tomonari; Marumoto Shin'ichi and the superb editorial staff in the Fine Arts department; and Andō Yuka, among others in the International Division; not to omit Yuri Kōichi and the gang at the *manga* weekly *Young Magazine*.

Many souls have been involved in this project at one stage or another in some manner, making editorial suggestions, providing materials, lending a friendly ear, posing provocative questions, or offering general camaraderie, intellectual or otherwise: Mikael "Mickey" Adolphson, Bob "Robert" Bock, Hal Bolitho, Jim Brandon, Bill Burton, Jeff Clayman, Stephen M. Forrest, Maria Heim, Charles Inouye, Regine Johnson, Sumie Jones, Sun Joo Kim, Jacquie Kern, Jennifer Kern, Larry Kominz, Ted Mack, Maeda

Kingorō, Emanuel Yi Pastreich, the members of the Platinum Comics online discussion group, Tonya Putnam, Paul Rouzer, John Rosenfield, Sue and Dick Salzman, John Solt, Ron G. Stewart, Matt Thorn, Royall Tyler, Akiko Walley, Kristin Williams, Richard Wright, Thelma Wolfe, and Lewis Wurgaft.

Although the solecisms of this book are my own, several people have been intimately involved with shaping and polishing it. I would particularly like to thank: two anonymous readers, for their genuinely insightful and constructive comments; three of my brilliant graduate students, for their indispensable aid and perspicacity—Will Fleming on proofing, Ivan Grail on indexing, and especially Glynne Walley on research and permissions; Jeff Cosloy, for his eye-catching cover art; and, of course, my trusty editors—the perfectly bilingual William M. Hammell and the sharp-eyed Susan Lumenello—for their diligence and savvy.

Most of all, I am grateful to my two sets of parents on either side of the Pacific—Hasegawa Makoto and Terumi, Judy and Eugene B. Kern—for their truly selfless love and support. Likewise my amazing wife, Kayo Tada, and our newborn daughter, Mikako Alana.

This book is dedicated to the memory of my Bodhisattva of a kid sister.

A.L.K.

Contents

Illustrations

Manga

from the

Floating

World

Comicbook

Culture and

the *Kibyōshi*

of Edo Japan

Part I

The *Kibyōshi*

(A Study)

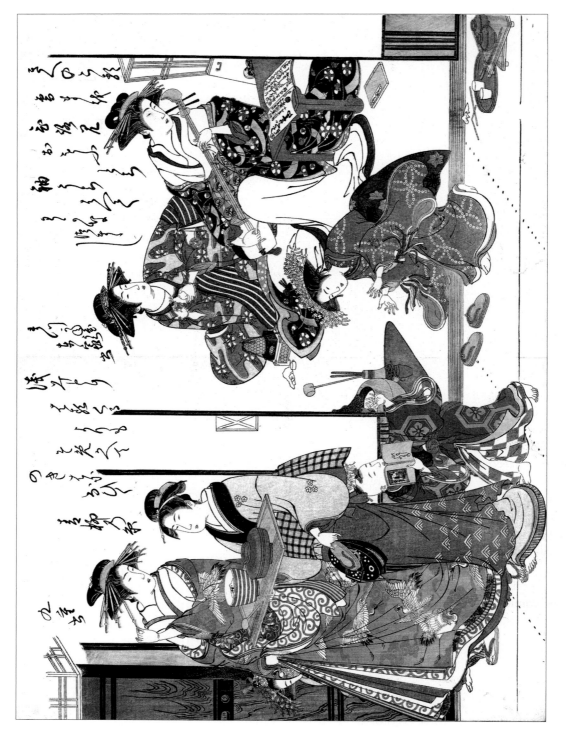

Fig. I.1 Two courtesans-in-training struggling over a yellow-covered comicbook (*kibyōshi*), as other women of the Yoshiwara pleasure quarter carry on with their affairs. From *A Pageant of the Latest Beauties, Their Calligraphy Mirrored* ([*Yoshiwara keisei*] *Shin bijin awase jihitsu kagami* [*New Beauties of the Yoshiwara in the Mirror of Their Own Script*], Japanese, Edo period, 1784), a book of woodblock prints; ink and color on paper; by Kitao Masanobu (Santō Kyōden, 1761–1816). Source unidentified. Photograph © 2006 Museum of Fine Arts, Boston.

*The reading of a comic book is an act of both
aesthetic perception and intellectual pursuit.*
—Will Eisner

Pageant of the Latest Beauties and Their Prized Possession

Behind the otherwise closed paper doors to the backroom of a bordello, deep within that foremost quarter of sophisticated adult entertainment throughout much of Edo-period Japan (1600–1868) known as the Yoshiwara, what should the contested object of desire above all others be but a little yellow comicbook? Or so one might gather from a scene in a celebrated series of woodblock prints of the late eighteenth century, entitled *Pageant of the Latest Beauties, Their Calligraphy Mirrored*. The jumbo-sized pictures of this lavishly colored album purport to provide an insider's glimpse of the private lives of various courtesans, collectively known in English, if too conveniently to be accurate, as geisha (**Figure I.1** and **Color Figure 4**).[1]

One young courtesan-in-training (*kaburo*), perhaps in her early teens, spreads open the comicbook even as she ambles on, holding her hand out to keep a slightly less junior assistant courtesan (*shinzō*) at bay. The assistant courtesan, straddling the threshold to the hallway, thrusts both hands out frantically, as though it were her *own* comicbook being pilfered. Judging by the imposing inscription on the back cover (**Figure I.2**)—"Property of Hanazono"—the comicbook most likely belongs not to this panicky assistant, let alone the impish trainee, but to the assistant's so-called elder sister.

---

1. Fully titled *Pageant of the Latest Beauties, Their Calligraphy Mirrored: Courtesans of the Yoshiwara (Yoshiwara keisei: Shin bijin awase jihitsu kagami)*, this series of seven oversized polychromatic prints (*nishikie*) was issued as an up-market album by publisher Tsutaya Jūzaburō in 1784. The preface is signed Shoku Sanjin (a.k.a. Ōta Nanpo). A few prints in this series bear the alternative title *Autograph Collection of Famous Ladies of the Blue Towers (Seirō meikun jihitsu shū)*, which must have been an incomplete project planned for release the previous year, as attested to by a veiled reference within to the year of the rabbit (1783).

Fig. I.2 Although not entirely legible, the title of this comic-book may be *Best Man in Japan* (*Koitsu wa Nippon*, 1784). The phrase "Property of Hana-zono" is scribbled onto the back cover. Detail from *A Pageant of the Latest Beauties, Their Calligraphy Mirrored* (*Shin bijin awase jihitsu kagami*, 1784). See Fig. I.1 for fuller information on the original. Photograph © 2006 Museum of Fine Arts, Boston.

That would probably be one of the two full-fledged, high-ranking courtesans (*oiran*) seated at ease, kimono draped casually, engrossed in her own particular divertissement. One courtesan, glancing at a songbook of music from the popular stage, plucks the *shamisen*, an instrument sounding anywhere from soulfully noisy to elegantly twangy. The other seems content stroking her pet, a rather overfed white mouse.

In contrast to the relaxed demeanor of these two high-ranking courtesans, a third scrambles down the corridor, apparently after having spent too long in such amusements herself. In some haste, judging by the swiftness with which she thrusts a hairpin into her elaborately coiffured hair, she must be running late for some eagerly awaiting client. Perhaps the maid busing dishes was dispatched a few moments earlier to gently remind the courtesan of her appointment? A second trainee, possibly appearing before a client for the first time, peeks out from behind the courtesan's skirts bashfully. Paying her no heed, the harried courtesan manages to throw back a glance, less to her fellow courtesans, already oblivious to her, than to the contest between the two underlings. This glance, which almost seems fixed on the comicbook, underlines the tension inherent in her transition from leisure to labor.

But what is it that makes this little yellow comicbook so irresistible that it seems destined to be the sole plaything smuggled into the workplace? The pivot between private and public spheres, this comicbook occupies more than the psychic and spatial centers of this particular picture. As one of the principal forms of the popular literature of late eighteenth-century Edo, the city that would become Tokyo, this type of comicbook also, arguably, was central to the Japanese popular imagination. This contention is based on more than a reading of this one woodblock print, which, in spite of some delightful realistic detail, remains an elegant fiction. Like all such fictions, this print can hardly be taken as an unadulterated portrayal of historical fact, even though its particular adulteration may point toward some interesting, even insightful, details about the represented historical moment.

Much of the appeal of *Pageant of the Latest Beauties* depends upon the conceit of the insider's behind-the-scenes view of the Yoshiwara pleasure quarter, a view that only a slim fraction of the male populace could ever hope to behold in real life, perhaps equivalent to the backstage dressing room of Vegas showgirls or Victoria's Secret supermodels. Some of the pictorial details thus are remarkably specific to that time and place. For instance, the chopsticks, saké cup, and crumpled paper that the maid seems to have forgotten on the hallway floor are probably the accoutrements of a parlor game of charades popular in Edo during the 1770s and 1780s.[2] The crowning touch, however, and one that imparted an exceptional vicarious thrill, is the inclusion of amorous verses hovering over the figures of each courtesan in imitation of her individual calligraphic style. Whether these exemplars are accurate facsimiles of real-life poems is almost beside the point. What this series really mirrors, perhaps inevitably, is the existence of certain fantasies about these refined ladies of the night as sex objects, fashion plates, even cultural icons.

Given the unabashed fictionality of this picture, it is possible that the artist, one of whose several pseudonyms was Kitao Masanobu (1761–1816), had ulterior motives for positioning the comicbook so conspicuously. Masanobu was an up-and-coming member of the Kitao School of woodblock prints, specializing in the detailed, faithful, "realistic" portrayal of individual human beings, as opposed to the often undifferentiated, indistinguishable, even more blatantly stylized idioms of most other schools. Still, he also happened to be on the verge of becoming one of the leading writers of these yellow comicbooks, albeit under yet another pseudonym by which he is best known to posterity—Santō Kyōden. Indeed, he had published his breakthrough work, *Those Familiar Bestsellers*, only a couple of years prior to *Pageant of the Latest Beauties*. And although the title of the depicted comicbook is practically illegible, thereby allowing the work to stand for all such comicbooks, it is possible that it reads *Best Man in Japan* (*Koitsu wa Nippon*, 1784), a work written by Ōta Nanpo (under the alias Yomo Sanjin) and issued by Tsutaya Jūzaburō, the men who, respectively, penned the preface to

---

2. The game, called "Bent Chopsticks" (*hissakibashi*), or more colloquially "How's that for it?" (*dōde gozansu*), involved arranging chopsticks and a cup to form a picture. For more on this, see Yamanaka, *Sunaharai*, pp. 15–21.

and published *Pageant of the Latest Beauties*. If so, then positioning this comicbook at center might have been a whimsical self-reference of sorts. At the very least, it was an act of product placement for the genre in which Masanobu was beginning to shine.

Should this reading exalt the little yellow comicbook unduly, it does so in part as compensation for the fact that most commentators on this and similar pictures have tended to treat the genre patronizingly, as a minor detail, an object hardly deserving mention, let alone elaboration. Too often the genre has been written off as some sort of amorphous "illustrated chapbook" (*ezōshi*) or "picturebook" (*ehon*)—or relegated to the status of some kind of premodern precursor of the *manga*, which is to say the modern Japanese comicbook. However, this was indeed a full-fledged comicbook in its own right—and one of the bestselling forms of woodblock-printed literature in its day, for that matter—known as the *kibyōshi*. Pronounced unaccentedly in three and a half rapid beats \kē byō-ō shē\, rhyming with *he oh-owes me*, the term means something like "yellow-covered" booklet.

Goals of the Present Study

The main purpose of the present volume is to introduce the *kibyōshi* to the informed general reader as well as to the student of Japanese literature and culture, to enter into its world, and to intimate why the young women in Masanobu's woodcut supposedly find the genre so beguiling. In so doing, this volume also amounts to a foray into the social milieu in which the *kibyōshi* was produced and consumed, which is to say the culture of the city of Edo during the mid-Edo period, specifically the An'ei-Tenmei era, roughly the 1770s and 1780s.

These decades, it should be observed, are perhaps the major casualties in the usual division of the Edo period into a first half, chiefly known for the Genroku era (1688–1704), and a second half, mostly defined as standing in the wake of the first. In a sense, this two-part periodization is reasonable, since Genroku epitomizes a monumental transformation. For the first time within the literary, dramatic, and poetic arts of Japan, commoner culture dazzlingly came to the fore. This transformation informs the works of what can be called the Genroku Triumvirate: the brilliant chronicler of commoner culture and ironist Ihara Saikaku (1642–1693) in prose fiction, especially the "novella of the Floating World" (*ukiyozōshi*); Chikamatsu Monzaemon (1653–1725), fancifully labeled "Japan's Shakespeare," in the kabuki but especially the puppet (*ningyō jōruri*) theater, who helped transform the popular stage into the main platform of mass entertainment; and Japan's poet laureate himself, Matsuo Bashō (1644–1694), in what is now termed "haiku," who brought something of the classic poetic tradition within the reach of contemporary commoners and effectively elevated what was then a lowbrow form of poetry to the top of the popular canon. The study outside Japan of Edo-period literature has tended to concentrate on the Genroku era, then, though this regrettably has resulted in the discounting of the two other cultural peaks.

Fortunately, some scholars reject this halving scheme and instead follow a tripartite periodization, which, it must be admitted, takes its own liberties and may not finesse a generalized understanding of the period by more than a fraction.[3] Nonetheless, its major advantage, by virtue of according each major cultural peak its due, resides in refusing to conflate the second peak—An'ei-Tenmei (specifically covering the reign eras 1772–1780 and 1781–1789, respectively)—with the third—Bunka-Bunsei (often abbreviated, taking the last parts of both words, to "Kasei," 1804–1817 and 1818–1829). Although Kasei holds its own particular fascination—and many of its representative authors like Takizawa (a.k.a. Kyokutei) Bakin (1767–1848), Shikitei Sanba (1776–1822), and Jippensha Ikku (1765–1831) had written *kibyōshi* earlier in their careers—the main focus of this study is An'ei-Tenmei, a period of time largely marked by the perception of the eastward swing of the cultural center of gravity away from western Japan (Kamigata), with its old imperial capital of Kyoto and other nearby cities (especially Osaka), toward the new shogun's capital of Edo.

An'ei-Tenmei Japan can lay claim to some wonderful and influential cultural figures, too, though their names are probably less familiar to the average educated Westerner than the Genroku Triumvirate. The best generally known might be Ueda Akinari (1734–1809), author of the ghostly *Tales of Moonlight and Rain* (*Ugetsu monogatari*, 1776), which garnered some notice a half century ago by virtue of *Ugetsu* (1953). On top of the fact that this film adaptation departs from Akinari's novella significantly, Akinari himself was a product of western Japan. So, although he dabbled in the popular literature associated with Edo, his literary works do not best emblemize the culture of that city.

Unfortunately, the major authors from Edo proper during this time have received even less attention in the West. Although there is little scholarly let alone popular consensus, one possible An'ei-Tenmei Trio, if one must be named, might easily be Hiraga Gennai (1728–1780), Ōta Nanpo (1749–1823), and Santō Kyōden (a.k.a. Masanobu)—all personalities who were influentially active in various literary, poetic, dramatic, and visual arts. The involvement in multiple arts may be one feature of Japanese culture in general, though it seems strikingly prominent in what could be termed An'ei-Tenmei culture. That said, there were other important players on Edo's cultural stage at the time, such as the actor Ichikawa Danjūrō V (1741–1806), whose artistic endeavors by no means were confined to the kabuki theater. Sakurada Jisuke (1734–1806) was an outstanding playwright, even if he has garnered less notice than Chikamatsu. Nor should one overlook the publishing titan Tsutaya

---

3. Nakano Mitsutoshi, for one, subscribes to the tripartite periodization. For more on this in English, see his article "The Role of Traditional Aesthetics."

Jūzaburō (nicknamed Tsutajū, 1750–1797), whose eye for talent and stomach for financial risk made him one of the pivotal arbiters of literary as well as artistic taste. Indeed, Tsutajū backed many of the leading polychromatic woodblock artists of the day, like Tōshūsai Sharaku (fl. 1794–1795) and Kitao Shigemasa (1739–1820), but especially Kitagawa Utamaro (1753–1806), who might also be mentioned as one of An'ei-Tenmei Edo's colorful emblems.[4]

These figures were so pivotal to the formation of a particular local identity that any study of the cultural history of Tokyo could easily commence with them and not just with the 1923 earthquake and conflagration—which undeniably necessitated a reinvention of the city—or even with just the nineteenth-century renaming of Edo to "the Eastern Capital." In some respects, the Edo that would become Tokyo as a cultural construct starts to take shape during An'ei-Tenmei, more so than when a small swamp village embarked on its physical and economic transformation into the shogunal capital at the very beginning of the seventeenth century.

An'ei-Tenmei culture saw a uniquely Edoesque brand of playful irreverence that went hand in hand with the commercial triumphs of the lower merchant class, though these triumphs never quite translated into social or political respectability. Edo during the 1770s and 1780s could also boast the rise to public consciousness of such things as the geisha, that professional male as well as female dancer or musician not to be confused with the courtesan (*yūjo*), the queen of the complex hierarchy of feminine entertainers. It should be noted that the vast majority of prostitutes (*jorō*) were not courtesans, and courtesans were not exactly considered mere prostitutes themselves, since the higher-ranking ones always had the right of refusal, even if it must be acknowledged that their arts were, in essence, sensual.[5] An'ei-Tenmei culture was also characterized by the popularity of madcap verse (*kyōka*), whose leading practitioners intermingled in demographically diverse social circles of townsmen, samurai, actors, artists, writers, courtesans, and so on. And then there was the *kibyōshi*, which this volume maintains not only mirrored and constructed urban commoner culture, but was also one of the major vehicles for the assertion of that culture in the political sphere.

The very assertion of an urban commoner culture in a country whose arts had historically been dominated by the court and its samurai aides qualifies as a political act of sorts. Yet the *kibyōshi* also became the most salient form of political satire. Thus, it was because the genre seemed poised to transform the uniquely Edoesque brand of townsmen culture into something more, perhaps even a national culture, thereby displacing traditional

---

4. For more on Utamaro and Tsutajū, see Julie Nelson Davis, *Utamaro Draws Their Ravishing Features: Ukiyo-e Images of Women in Late Eighteenth-Century Japan* (forthcoming from Reaktion Press).

5. For a detailed explanation of the differences among the various ranks and types of courtesans, geisha, and prostitutes over time and by place, see Seigle, *The Yoshiwara*.

culture, that the shogunal government intervened. During the far-ranging social, economic, and political reforms engineered by Matsudaira Sadanobu (1758–1829), chief regent and advisor to the shogun himself, the politically satirical strain within the *kibyōshi* was essentially banned and its authors hounded. As a result of this and similar actions, the Kansei Reforms, as they are known, effectively cut the An'ei-Tenmei cultural efflorescence off at the stem.[6]

This suppression is crucial to a second major goal of this volume: to suggest why the *kibyōshi* was relatively short lived. The genre is said to have flourished for just over three decades, beginning in 1775 with the publication of Koikawa Harumachi's (1744–1789) *Master Flashgold's Splendiferous Dream* (*Kinkin sensei eiga no yume*) and ending in 1806, the last year Kyōden published a work in this mode. The standard explanation among Japanese cultural and literary historians has long been that the genre abruptly fell victim to the reforms. Yet those critics of the *kibyōshi* among these historians are hard pressed to explain why Sadanobu would devote any attention to the likes of a comicbook ostensibly for children. Did the *kibyōshi* corrupt youth? If so, how? Was it considered injurious to public morals by virtue of its adulation of the multifarious dissipations of the so-called Floating World? In the course of considering these sorts of questions, this volume also explores that playful world of urban popular culture during An'ei-Tenmei as manifest in the kabuki theaters, sideshow spectacles, and demimonde, meaning the pleasure quarters and red-lantern "bathhouses" where (as in the "Soaplands" of present-day Tokyo's major red-light districts) male clients got clean as scrub maids got dirty.

This volume endeavors as well to show that the *kibyōshi*, although assuming the guise of children's comicbooks, was anything but silly kid stuff. As a rule, the *kibyōshi* is possessed of a sophisticated if entertaining content, dabbling often in social satire and occasionally in political satire. To add insult to injury, from the perspective of those being lampooned, the genre managed to flout the spirit of official sumptuary regulations and publishing edicts without ever breaking the letter of the law, at least not too overtly. This subtleness has meant that some commentators have denied that the *kibyōshi* ever engaged in "genuine" satire. Satire can be the more effective for its subtlety, but the larger point is that the genre's satire is not so subtle that it should have gone largely unacknowledged. In order to demonstrate as much, some relatively simple conventions of reading the pictures as well as the words will be addressed. Although many of these conventions are intuitively obvious, some are so specific to the literary and pictorial expression of Edo-period Japan, as well as to the particulars of its politics, that a modicum of explanation is necessary.

---

6. The Kansei Reforms were actually two related sets of edicts that did not perfectly coincide with the Kansei era (which should not be confused with the Kasei era).

The shogunal government for its part recognized that this seemingly playful genre was progressively becoming a more serious form of social resistance. To be clear: the *kibyōshi* was *not* a fatuous genre for the semiliterate, as some critics have charged—and perhaps even as Masanobu's woodcut itself implies. On the contrary, it was an extraordinarily developed visual-verbal form that was capable of genuine sociopolitical satire, satire that the shogunate appears to have perceived as a threat to the ideological foundations supporting the entire social structure and, hence, to its own political viability, if not legitimacy.

What the Kansei Reforms effectively destroyed, it must be emphasized, was the satirical strain within the *kibyōshi*, not the *kibyōshi* itself. Indeed, the genre carried on well after the last edict of the reforms had been issued, petering out over the next decade or two. Thus, while the Kansei Reforms figured significantly in the demise of the *kibyōshi*, ultimately other factors were involved, some of which were internal to the genre. It is possible that the *kibyōshi* would have imploded, in other words, even had there never been a Kansei Reforms.

Reference to the comicbook format of the *kibyōshi* brings us to a third major goal of this volume: to explore the nature of the highly refined visual-verbal imagination in Edo-period literature and art. This imagination was born of a millennium of profound interplay among the various literary, pictorial, and dramatic arts in Japan, not to mention the complicated visual-verbal aspect of the Japanese system of writing. This system employed both Chinese graphs and two Japanese syllabaries, effectively intermixing semantic, graphic, phonetic, and symbolic aspects in complex fashion. By any reckoning, in the final analysis the *kibyōshi* represents an adult form of visual-verbal narrative art.

"Adult," it should be clarified, not in the sense of pornographic, though some scholars (not all of whom are Westerners) have exhibited a pronounced tendency to group the *kibyōshi* together unreflectively with other forms of woodblock-printed literature and art that depict the Floating World and its various carnal delights. (This misunderstanding is natural, perhaps, since so many *kibyōshi* are set in this grown-up playpen.) Rather, "adult" because the *kibyōshi* on the whole addresses a variety of mature concerns and interests. As Tanahashi Masahiro, one of the major *kibyōshi* scholars, has proclaimed: "The world described by the *kibyōshi* is one of adult play."[7] This play embraces a variety of forms of humor, barbed sociopolitical satire, impishly promiscuous allusions to much of the Chinese as well as the entire Japanese cultural heritage, and puzzles engaging the rich Japanese visual-verbal imagination.

Consequently, most readers of the *kibyōshi*, not unlike its authors, were fully grown, well-educated townsmen—male urban members of the lower

---

7. Tanahashi, *Edo gesaku zōshi*, p. 17.

samurai class as well as merchants and artisans. The age, gender, and social standing of this readership may come as something of a surprise, especially since *Pageant of the Latest Beauties* would seem to provide visual evidence to the contrary. No doubt this was Masanobu winking at the knowing reader, pretending to take the ruse of the children's comicbook format literally in order to poke fun at those who believed the *kibyōshi* to be no more than a decadent pulp fiction for "women and children."

Since the *kibyōshi* indisputably reached a large audience, at least within Edo, and because it exemplifies the visual-verbal imagination, this volume also touches on the nature and history of the comicbook in Japan. Indeed, one major contention is that if the comicbook is defined as a medium of entertaining, sustained visual-verbal narrative, often with an emphasis on topical humor and social issues, mass-produced and sold on the cheap to a broad segment of the general population and not just a narrow privileged elite, then the *kibyōshi* should be considered one of the earliest if not *the* earliest comicbook for adults in Japanese literary history. It may even conceivably have been the "first" such comicbook in *world* literary history, for that matter, as some cultural commentators have claimed.[8]

What is clear is that, within Japanese literary history, few if any major precedents exist for the *kibyōshi*. Granted, some individual works in a similar mold but predating the *kibyōshi* came to appeal to a more adult readership. These works began appearing sporadically within genres of picturebooks, such as the "companion booklet" (*otogizōshi*) or the lightly illustrated "syllabary booklet" (*kanazōshi*), and within different sorts of "children's comicbooks," such as the "redbook" (*akabon*) and the "blackbook" (*kurohon*). And it must be admitted that the *kibyōshi* emanates directly out of this particular comicbook culture. By contrast, however, the *kibyōshi* was the first true comicbook genre to be written *exclusively* with the sophisticated adult reader in mind. Simply put, there had never been anything quite like it before.

The *kibyōshi* was also probably the most popular of these picturebooks and comicbooks, not to mention most other genres of literature up to its day, in terms of sales. The question of why this no doubt dubious distinction—which alone qualifies the *kibyōshi* for scholarly attention, in my estimation—should go to a comicbook for adults inevitably begs ready comparisons with the modern Japanese *manga*. After all, just over one third of all printed matter in Japan, accounting for about a quarter of total publishing sales, consists of comics and comic magazines, according to one recent study by the Japanese Research Institute for Publications.[9] Moreover, the *manga* undeniably has become a force to be reckoned with in literary markets outside Japan, particularly elsewhere in Asia.

---

8. Schodt, for one, hails works in the genre as "the world's first comic books." In *Dreamland Japan*, p. 22.

9. The figures for 2002 are 38.1 percent and 22.6 percent, respectively. Cited in Natsume, "Japanese Manga," p. 3.

There are copious similarities that make it tempting to rummage around for the roots of the modern *manga* within the *kibyōshi*. Both are products of consumer societies, though admittedly of vastly different stripes of capitalism—one early and preindustrial, the other advanced and perhaps *post*industrial. Consequently, both the *kibyōshi* and the *manga* are mechanically mass produced on an assembly line, one powered by hand, the other by electricity. Then again, if the *kibyōshi* is a precursor of the *manga*, it is not, as will be argued, the direct progenitor. Nor could it ever have been so. For one thing, too much epochal literary and visual history intervenes. Drawing a line to connect these two dots is simply too pat. For another thing, the early practitioners of the modern form seem to have had mostly Western comicbooks in mind and were no doubt oblivious, for all intents and purposes, to the very existence of the *kibyōshi*.

Paradoxically, however, it turns out that Kyōden, a major author of popular literature, including the three *kibyōshi* translated in this volume, largely introduced the term *manga*—at the time meaning something like "comic sketches"—into the popular lexicon through one of his bestselling pictorial works in 1798. Although others seem to have invented the term *manga* during An'ei-Tenmei, or possibly earlier, this etymology runs contrary to the conventional wisdom that the renowned artist Katsushika Hokusai (1760–1849) coined the term and made it famous in his amusing sketchbooks *Hokusai manga*, which began publication in 1814. Hokusai, I suggest, may have appropriated the term by virtue of his direct association with Kyōden, since he not only personally knew the author but also provided pictures for several of his *kibyōshi*. Is it remotely possible, then, that the *kibyōshi* was the "original" *manga*, albeit not in the modern sense of the word?

Accordingly, this volume rejects the notion that the *kibyōshi* merits attention merely for the light that it casts on what is referred to throughout, perhaps redundantly, as the "modern *manga*" (to differentiate it from the Edo-period variety). As appealing and instructive as it might be to compare and contrast these two comicbook forms, to treat one strictly in terms of its relationship with the other would be to risk robbing both of their dignity and distinctiveness. Bearing this caveat in mind, some preliminary observations about the relationship between the *kibyōshi* and the modern *manga* are called for. After all, although hardly embracing the same cluster of genres, the *kibyōshi* and the modern *manga* are indisputably similar media.

To summarize, the present volume serves as an introduction to the *kibyōshi*, its socioeconomic and historical contexts, readership, critics, narrative conventions, modes of visuality, history as a genre and a media and a format, relationship to the modern *manga* as well as to other genres of Edo's popular literature, comic spirit, and satire. Surely, the *kibyōshi* provides a superb source of insight into the popular imagination of the late eighteenth-century Japanese. Also, its often amusing pictorial presentation affords an immediately recognizable context that may appeal intuitively to the relatively uninitiated, as well as to the more experienced student of Japanese cultural history. In short, mostly to offset the genre's longstanding critical snubbing, I propose to take Masanobu's gag of placing the *kibyōshi* at the center of the scene, as it were, seriously.

In doing so, I argue that the *kibyōshi*, although not having spawned the modern *manga*, nevertheless offers a similarly informative, visually compelling, and perhaps even an ultimately meaningful glimpse into one of the world's most fascinating civilizations during one of that civilization's greatest cultural efflorescences. Deceptively garbed as a genre for children, this yellow-covered comicbook is actually exceedingly urbane, displaying a remarkable degree of allusivity to the whole range of literature and culture available for consumption in eighteenth-century Japan, a rich visual-verbal imagination, and a comic spirit that at times crosses over into the realm of sharp sociopolitical satire, against which the shogunal government acted to defend itself. Perhaps more than any other form of literature, the *kibyōshi* both captures and creates the popular cultural *zeitgeist* of late eighteenth-century Japan—and this it does with pizzazz.

State of the Field of Kibyōshi Studies

One of the ironies of the *kibyōshi* is that its enormity as a phenomenon of popular culture is rivaled only by the historical paucity of scholarly interest in it. Although speculating about the reasons for this risks devolving into a rather banal rehash of some of the usual objections to cultural conservatism, and no doubt might smack of apologia, a few words on this subject nonetheless will help shed light on the reception of the genre in historical terms, and can serve to introduce the reader to some issues and names referred to throughout this study.

First, the *kibyōshi* has suffered by virtue of its association with the Edo-period popular literature known as *gesaku*. Literally meaning "frivolous works," *gesaku* covered an assortment of often humorous popular genres. Independent scholar Mori Senzō has suggested that the *kibyōshi* has been disavowed as the object of academic inquiry because genres of *gesaku* do not fit neatly into Western categories of literature, foreign cookie cutters into which the Japanese have in general long been trying to squeeze their own letters.[10] And anyway, *gesaku* has habitually been taken at face value, dismissed as too "frivolous" and amateurish, not worthy of study (especially, one suspects, by those missing the essential irony gene). This dismissal amounts to folly as egregious as mistaking literary Nonsense for pure gibberish.

At the other extreme, some detractors have dismissed the *kibyōshi* and like genres as being too professional—a commercially produced, formulaic literature without soul, which is to say, a kind of pulp fiction. The elitist and

---

10. Mori, *Mori Senzō chosakushū zoku hen 7*, p. 369.

classist assumption behind such dismissals seems to have been that authors and readers of popular literature belonged to the ranks of plebes, especially those economically necessary but socially parasitical merchants. Comicbooks throughout their history, as Roger Sabin writes of a different cultural context, "have been perceived as intrinsically 'commercial,' mass-produced for a lowest-common-denominator audience and therefore automatically outside notions of artistic credibility."[11]

The *kibyōshi* and other genres of so-called pulp fiction, like the comicbook in the West, have indeed been maligned as mindless entertainment. Whatever one's opinion of the content of individual works, in point of fact, many major authors of the *kibyōshi* were intellectuals from the lower strata of the elite samurai class. Far from some Machiavellian ploy to provide a comic opiate for the masses, however, the fact of samurai authorship suggests a cultural movement that crossed class lines because of the nature of both the *kibyōshi* and the demographically diverse early modern city that it took as its overarching setting.

The notion that popular literature was a socially worthless if economically profitable diversion is a shibboleth that must also be dispelled in order to move beyond the characterization of Edo-period literature as embodying the "premodernity" against which Modernization and Westernization were deliberately constructed during the Meiji period (1868–1912), when Japan was "opening up" to the outside world. If contextualized in terms of Progress, one of the main buzzwords of the day, *gesaku* seemed directly at fault for Japan's cultural and thus technological backwardness. In spite of the fact that some major authors continued to read and be influenced by Edo's popular literature—one need only consider Natsume Sōseki's comic novel *I Am a Cat* (*Wagahai wa neko de aru*, 1905) or Akutagawa Ryūnosuke's satirical *Kappa* (1927), let alone the more recent works of Inoue Hisashi (1934–), to catch a whiff of the *gesaku* spirit in modern Japanese letters—it became fashionable to project all the presumed decadence, superficiality, and triviality of the past onto a single common scapegoat.

"The new literary program was set out most explicitly by Tsubouchi Shōyō," Joel Cohn writes of a pivotal articulation of this sort of sentiment, "especially in his [*Essence of the Novel* (*Shōsetsu shinzui*, 1885)], in which he stressed that fiction had a vital place in modern civilization, and could secure its claim to respectability by adhering to the principle of realism and at the same time avoiding all traces of vulgarity. In this respect, according to Shōyō, it could do no better than to make itself the diametric opposite of *gesaku*, which he assailed not only for its artificiality and didacticism, but also for the crudity and frivolity of its attempts at comedy."[12] No doubt the Meiji-period strategy of vilifying *gesaku* was part of a larger campaign of re-

---

11. Sabin, *Comics, Comix & Graphic Novels*, p. 8.
12. Cohn, *Studies in the Comic Spirit in Modern Japanese Fiction*, p. 21.

jecting traditional Japanese culture in one fell swoop. The Edo period itself, in Carol Gluck's terse formulation, became an "invented other in relation to which modernity posited itself."[13]

Now that Japan *has* modernized, less seems to be at stake in admitting that its late traditional period was unlike that of its early modern Euro-American counterparts in profound ways. Thus, the misleading rhetoric about *gesaku* can probably be dispensed with. The time is right, in other words, if not long overdue, for a critical reassessment of popular literary genres like the *kibyōshi*. This reassessment should be conducted not by the standard of European historical or Naturalist novels—a standard many scholars East and West seem to have set in accordance with the hindsight of what was emulated in Japan during the late nineteenth and early twentieth centuries—but by the late eighteenth-century standards of the *kibyōshi* itself.

Even Nakamura Yukihiko, one of the great twentieth-century scholars whose efforts have gone a long way toward legitimizing Edo-period popular fiction, has frowned upon the ethereality of genres like the *kibyōshi*: "What is lacking in *gesaku, when compared with modern literature,* is any serious confrontation with life."[14] It could be argued, however, that even the most frivolous aspects of the *kibyōshi* that the critics cite as proof of the genre's uselessness—things such as its visual-verbal riddles, daunting word games, and incessant punning—even these are intended not merely to entertain. Rather, by engaging them in such puzzles, the *kibyōshi* helped put readers in a skeptical frame of mind, encouraging them to question authority and to regard social reality as a text that is constructed and, consequently, that can be deconstructed. The *kibyōshi*, in other words, may mount a serious confrontation with life after all. This may not have been a confrontation in terms a Japanese Disraeli or Zola would have preferred, but in its role and reception as sociopolitical satire, it is a confrontation the *kibyōshi* mounted nonetheless—and one that the authorities took seriously.

The low esteem traditionally accorded to the *kibyōshi*, not to mention other forms of popular fiction, has no doubt adversely affected the genre's early reception outside Japan. Some Western scholars have taken their cues from Japanese scholars who ultimately took their cues from Western notions of what literature should be. Donald Keene, whose landmark *World Within Walls* virtually defined the field of Edo literary studies in the United States, justifies his disapproval of the *kibyōshi* as "glorified comic books for adults" by quoting none other than Nakamura himself.[15] Unable to ignore the vast popularity of the *kibyōshi*, though, Keene has written about such humorous popular literature, albeit begrudgingly: "These writings, despite

---

13. Gluck, "The Invention of Edo," p. 262.

14. Nakamura, *Gesakuron* (1966), p. 132. Quoted in Keene, *World Within Walls*, p. 410. Emphasis mine.

15. Keene, *World Within Walls*, p. 399.

the education of the authors, are almost totally lacking in intellectual content. Readers today seldom find *gesaku* fiction satisfying, even if they can admire the deftness of the style, or the lighthearted humor."[16] On the other hand, why should "readers today" expect that a genre of late eighteenth- and early nineteenth-century literature adhere to such modern standards as might obtain in the novel of the West?

The *kibyōshi* has also suffered from the deep-rooted stigma against the comicbook as a kind of childish medium. Part of this stigma has to do with the putative age of readers: "A publication for children designed to excite mirth" is how *The Oxford English Dictionary* (1965) defines "comics" in general. The other part has to do with the putative age of the medium. Scott McCloud, in his enlightening study of the comicbook (in comicbook form, no less), has suggested, "The art form of comics is many centuries old, but it's perceived as a recent invention and suffers the curse of all new media, the curse of being judged by the standards of the old."[17] Along these lines, David Kunzle, author of a substantial study of the history of the comicbook, opines, "Critics and scholars have by and large ignored the comic strip and its history. I do not think many sociologists or critics of the mass media have denied the social importance of the comic strip; but neither do they regret the lack of a history of the subject."[18] Accordingly, the myth of the comicbook's immaturity in Japan can hardly be dispelled without an historical study of its own.

Like all readers, students of Edo-period art, literature, religion, history, and so forth have their personal preferences and tastes. However, to ignore the *kibyōshi* simply because it reminds one of "children's" comicbooks is to neglect a rich source of cultural history. "One cheats oneself, as a human being," Susan Sontag has asserted, "if one has respect only for the style of high culture, whatever else one may do or feel on the sly."[19] When cultural conservatives take note of the comicbook, it is usually only to condemn it as a low-brow form complicit in the predicament of our Postliterate Age, when cultural literacy is grounded more in movies, television, and the Internet than in novels, essays, and poetry; and people can read but choose not to. If one must posit a zero-sum equation between reading and viewing (which is a false dichotomy to begin with), however, the comicbook would probably fall on the other side of the fence from the animated film. Besides, it may not be entirely fair to consign the comicbook to the status of a lowbrow form.

Precisely because enduring Western attitudes toward pictorial or illustrated literature began to influence the Japanese during the Meiji period, these attitudes are worth mentioning, even if only briefly. Henry James,

---

16. Keene, *World Within Walls*, p. 401.
17. McCloud, *Understanding Comics*, p. 151.
18. Kunzle, *The Early Comic Strip*, p. 1.
19. Sontag, "Notes on 'Camp,'" in *Against Interpretation and Other Essays*, p. 287.

Stéphane Mallarmé, and Mark Twain are among the literary lights who accused illustrators of somehow sabotaging the vitality of their words (though one hopes Twain would have softened his criticism had he lived to see Norman Rockwell's rendering of *Huckleberry Finn*). For such Western authors, who rely on alphabetic writing and not on Chinese graphs with their strong visual-verbal element, the activity of reading has by and large been conceptually limited over the past two centuries to the ability of the reader to transpose the textual world into one of images within his head. Illustrations, in such terms, have been condemned as corroding the reader's literary imagination.

Along these lines, Bruno Bettelheim, who has argued persuasively for the positive significance of fairy tales on childhood development, has nonetheless warned against pictures as stunting young intellectual growth: "[I]llustrated storybooks, so much preferred by both modern adults and children, do not serve the child's best needs. The illustrations are distracting rather than helpful." Bettelheim supports his point with a vague reference to scientific research: "Studies of illustrated primers demonstrate that the pictures divert from the learning process rather than foster it, because the illustrations direct the child's imagination away from how he, on his own, would experience the story."[20]

Aside from the immediate objection that visuality itself is an integral part of how most children (even adult children) experience the world—of which writing is also a part as well as a descriptive tool—the main problem with Bettelheim's position is that he effectively takes the image out of imagination. Especially in the Japanese case, where the writing system creatively combines pictures, semantics, and abstractions, verbal literacy and visual literacy are not so easily disentangled. The *kibyōshi* in particular suggests that the visual-verbal imagination can enrich, rather than impoverish, the nature as well as the experience of reading.

The reading of a comicbook is not the same thing as the reading of a novel, to be sure. Yet the inclusion of pictures in any narrative can add complexity in a positive way. Pictures need not dumb down literary material but can, in the right hands, augment it. In the wrong hands, even an entirely pictureless novel can be a mind-numbing affair. The "graphic novel"—a term coined in an effort to distance the comicbook from its lingering puerile and plebeian associations—and the novel itself both depend on the talents of their creators.[21] There is nothing intrinsic to either form that precludes genius. Thus have some of the great *littérateurs* in the West intuited the vast potential of the comicbook. Thomas Mann, in his introduction to a

---

20. Bettelheim, *The Uses of Enchantment*, pp. 59–60.

21. Eisner defines "graphic narrative" as a "generic description of any narration that employs image to transmit an idea. Film and comics both engage in graphic narrative." In Eisner, *Graphic Storytelling and Visual Narrative*, p. 6.

celebrated graphic novel by Belgian political cartoonist Frans Masereel (1889–1972), enjoined his reader to be "captivated by the flow of the pictures" and to experience a "deeper purer impact than you have ever felt before."[22] Goethe seems to have said of Rodolphe Töffler, who published what some have claimed to be the first known comicbook in the West, *Adventures of Obadiah Oldbuck* (1842): "If for the future he would choose a less frivolous subject and restrict himself a little, he would produce things beyond all conception."[23]

After nearly a century of such soothsaying and anticipating that the form would both achieve critical respect as a legitimate art and win popular admiration, there is some reason to suppose it has. The most obvious case in point to readers in the United Kingdom is American Chris Ware's graphic novel *Jimmy Corrigan: The Smartest Kid on Earth*, which earned the *Guardian* "First Book Award" in 2001. Marjane Satrapi's two-volume *Persepolis*, about her life as a young woman before, during, and after the Islamic revolution in Iran, has met with phenomenal critical and commercial success around the globe. In the United States, Art Spiegelman's *Maus*—a disquieting if poignant exposé of the author's tortured feelings about recounting his father's victimization during the Jewish holocaust in Nazi Germany—won a Pulitzer Prize in 1992. Spiegelman's Pulitzer was not for literature, however. The comicbook medium being *sui generis*, the prize committee devised a new category in order to accommodate Spiegelman's work if not the medium itself.

The Pulitzer Prize for literature did, however, go to Michael Chabon in 2001 for his novel, *The Amazing Adventures of Kavalier and Clay*, about two Jewish boys living in WWII-era New York City who decide to fight Nazis by writing comicbooks. There have also been several movies about comicbook artists in recent years including *Crumb* (1995), about R. Crumb, and *American Splendor* (2003), about Harvey Pekar, which took the Grand Jury Dramatic Prize at the Sundance Film Festival. This is not to overlook the unprecedented popularity of animation such as *The Simpsons*, the long-running television cartoon for adults as well as children, and Miyazaki Hayao's *Spirited Away*, which won the 2003 Academy Award in the recently established category of best animated feature film.

In spite of the current upsurge in interest in the comicbook and related media within academe—what is referred to as the "Visual Turn"—the comicbook continues to garner no more than modest respect. Even in the age of *Maus* and Miyazaki, comicbook writers and readers are, according to Sean Howe, "still battling the shame that's been heavily indoctrinated over the decades, still striving to be taken seriously."[24] Indeed, various forms of

---

22. Mann's statement, from the English version of Masereel's work (issued in 1919 as *Passionate Journey*), is quoted in Eisner, *Comics and Sequential Art*, p. 1.

23. Also sometimes rendered Töpffer. In McCloud, *Understanding Comics*, p. 7.

24. Howe, *Give Our Regards to the Atomsmashers!*, p. ix.

pictorial fiction have fallen between disciplinary cracks in Japan, at least until recently. The *kibyōshi* in particular has languished in the exquisite limbo of being neither exclusively art nor literature. Naoki Sakai has commented on an analogously paradoxical situation: "The copresence of visual and verbal elements within the same space of a work has implied either vulgarity or incompleteness in its mode of presentation . . . Hence, such a genre of artwork as the cartoon has been considered inferior both to verbal documents without illustration and to visual presentations containing no written words."[25] Which is to say, the comicbook, and forms like it, is damned if it does and damned if it doesn't. Apparently, even with all the superheroes, it just can't win.

These enduring biases against the comicbook form aside, Japanology has generally tended to shy away from public inquiries into the nature of the comic imagination in Japanese literature. Granted, Orientalist meditations upon "Zen" forms such as the comic haiku of the sort R. H. Blyth published had their day in the sun. Since then, however, few serious studies have appeared. "The world likes humor, but treats it patronizingly," E. B. White once noted wryly. "It decorates its serious artists with laurels, and its wags with Brussel sprouts."[26] Fortunately, Cohn's *Studies in the Comic Spirit in Modern Japanese Literature* and Howard Hibbett's masterly *The Chrysanthemum and the Fish* are the exceptions that prove the rule. There is also Marguerite Wells's book *Japanese Humor*, though it does not by and large deal with comic literature per se. In a fascinating and important article on Meiji political caricature, Peter Duus adopts the frame of argument that comic forms can have serious scholarly uses.[27] That Duus feels compelled to stipulate as much speaks to the skeptical reluctance on the part of many students of Japanese cultural history to accept such a premise, as though the mere presence of humor in a text somehow nullifies the potential for historiographical veracity.

That said, there is reason for optimism. A trickle of scholarly interest in the *kibyōshi* can be detected in the nineteenth century, beginning perhaps as early as 1834, with the publication of Takizawa Bakin's study of comicbooks and their authors.[28] Bakin, who had written in the by-then defunct *kibyōshi* genre (but ultimately moved on to more ponderous forms of popular literature), was not precisely a literary historian, though his impulse to make objective sense of historical material is nonetheless palpable. As part of the literary debate surrounding Westernization and Modernization, which had begun during the latter part of the nineteenth century and continued into the early part of the twentieth, popular literature such as the *kibyōshi* indeed

---

25. Sakai, *Voices of the Past*, p. 116.

26. White, "Some Remarks on Humor," p. 304.

27. Duus, "Weapons of the Weak, Weapons of the Strong."

28. Bakin's work can be found both in Takizawa Bakin, *Kinsei mono no hon Edo sakusha burui,* and in Naitō and Komiyama, *Onchi sōsho 10.*

became a kind of straw man against which the new vision of literature as promoting social progress was frequently measured. This meant that only a handful of Meiji intellectuals—author Kōdō Tokuchi (1843–1913) was one—overtly acknowledged that the *kibyōshi* had any literary value whatsoever.[29] Newspaper publisher, parodist, and postcard collector Miyatake Gaikotsu (1867–1955) was another, lending credence to the genre indirectly by virtue of his quirky but absorbing biography of Kyōden.[30]

During the first half of the twentieth century, however, scholars such as Yamaguchi Takeshi and Ebara Taizō effectively launched a critical reevaluation of the *kibyōshi* and related genres. This effort gained momentum after the Second World War, especially with Nakamura Yukihiko's *Discourse on Frivolous Literature* (*Gesakuron*, 1966), a magisterial work that laid the foundations for the rigorous study of popular literature in general and the *kibyōshi* in particular, inasmuch as Nakamura considered the *kibyōshi* to be the genre of *gesaku* par excellence. Hamada Giichirō, Nakano Mitsutoshi, and others have carried on more or less in this vein, grounding discussions of particular genres in the larger framework of *gesaku* studies.[31]

A couple of major studies devoted to the *kibyōshi*, both of which provide detailed synopses of individual works, have gone a long way toward mapping the vast terrain of the genre. In the early 1970s, Mori Senzō published a groundbreaking two-volume compendium, *Kibyōshi Précis* and *Kibyōshi Précis Continued* (*Kibyōshi kaidai* and *Zoku kibyōshi kaidai*), providing knowledgeable, if somewhat impressionistic, summaries of approximately 200 works arranged by author. To the extent that the present volume is indebted to Mori's work, a wish of his might be fulfilled in roundabout fashion: "The *kibyōshi*, a literature indigenous to Edo, does not exist in the West. Westerners are therefore completely oblivious to it . . ." Mori observed in his preface. "Which is why I would like to introduce the *kibyōshi* to them."[32]

More exhaustively, Tanahashi Masahiro, a product of the influential *gesaku* studies circle at Waseda University, has recently completed his indispensable, encyclopedic five-volume *Kibyōshi Overview* (*Kibyōshi sōran*, 1986–2004), which provides synopses and bibliographic notes, arranged chronologically, for approximately two thousand pieces.[33] Tanahashi has also pub-

---

29. Koike, *Edo no gesaku ehon 6*, p. 37.

30. Miyatake, *Santō Kyōden.*

31. See, for example, Nakano, *Gesaku kenkyū.*

32. Mori, "Kibyōshi kaidai josetsu," p. 333.

33. Tanahashi, *Kibyōshi sōran 1: Zenpen* (1986); *Kibyōshi sōran 2: Chūhen* (1989); *Kibyōshi sōran 3: Kōhen* (1991); *Kibyōshi sōran 4: Sakuin hen* (1994); and *Kibyōshi sōran 5: Zuroku hen* (2004). Inasmuch as Volume 4 contains several indexes to the authors, titles, and miscellaneous topics of the preceding three volumes, *Kibyōshi Overview* amounts to a rich, if sometimes uneven, encyclopedia of mid-Edo culture as well as of the *kibyōshi*. Unfortunately, being out of print, the first four volumes rarely are put on sale in used bookstores and, when they are, the price is prohibitively expensive. As of this writing, Tanahashi has no firm plans for a second printing.

lished *Kibyōshi Studies* (*Kibyōshi no kenkyū*, 1997) and *A Chapbook of Frivolous Edo Literature* (*Edo gesaku zōshi*, 2000), both of which have advanced the field considerably. Adam Kabat has recently issued two spellbinding volumes in Japanese on *kibyōshi* dealing with monsters, a subject the student of Edo culture can avoid only at his or her own peril.

Several foundational anthologies of *kibyōshi* have also appeared over the years, one of the earliest of which to include pictures was issued in the 1920s. This was the volume Yamaguchi devoted to the *kibyōshi* (though some of the pieces are slightly expurgated) within his multivolume compilation of the popular literature, poetry, and drama of the Edo period.[34] Three decades later, Mizuno Minoru began publishing several essential studies and collections of the *kibyōshi*, the most significant of which is surely *Collection of Kibyōshi and Fashionbooks* (*Kibyōshi sharebon shū*, 1958). Issued in the Iwanami anthology of classical Japanese literature (analogous to the Norton Critical Editions), this volume more than any other helped legitimize the genre as a serious topic of inquiry in the eyes of the Japanese academy if not actually admitting it into the canon of premodern literature.[35]

It took rival publisher Shōgakukan over a dozen years before including Hamada's *Kibyōshi, Comic Haiku, and Madcap Verse* (*Kibyōshi senryū kyōka*, 1971) in its multivolume anthology of premodern Japanese literature.[36] Tanahashi recently updated Hamada's work, which suggests at least sustained interest in the subject.[37] The most comprehensive anthology of *kibyōshi* to date, though, is that of Koike Masatane (son of Edo-literature scholar Koike Tō-gorō) at Waseda and his group. This six-volume work, titled *Edo's Frivolous Picturebooks* (*Edo no gesaku ehon*)—though glossed playfully, in a classic *gesaku*-like gag, to be read as *Edo's Parodic Picturebooks* (*Edo no parodī ehon*)—contains several dozen annotated pieces.

The publication of these works by Kabat, Koike, and Tanahashi, while grounded in solid scholarship, bespeaks the recent collective effort in Japan to introduce the *kibyōshi* to a readership wider than the merely academic. Over the past few decades, the study of the *kibyōshi* has started to flourish, culminating in a flurry of scholarly activity that has only intensified and, arguably, has begun attracting a more general audience, in part due to a seemingly temporarily piqued interest in things Edoesque, largely by virtue of the four hundredth anniversary in 2003 of the establishment of the Tokugawa shogunate. Even before the quadracentennial hoopla, however, the

---

34. Yamaguchi, *Kibyōshi nijūgoshū*.

35. Mizuno, *NKBT 59*. Mizuno also edited the two-volume *Kibyōshi shū* (1969 and 1973) and wrote the important *Kibyōshi sharebon no sekai*. Mizuno furthermore also began a projected 20-volume anthology, though unannotated, of Santō Kyōden's works, five volumes of which are devoted to the *kibyōshi*. Nobuhiro Shinji and Tanahashi Masahiro assumed editorial responsibilities for the project after Mizuno passed away.

36. Hamada, *NKBZ 46*.

37. Tanahashi, *SNKBZ 79*.

present "Edo boom" was already under way, having gained a powerful boost, as some social commentators have suggested, from a post-bubble nostalgia for an imagined golden age of social and economic prosperity.

There have been a few public exhibits of *kibyōshi*, such as the one held at the Hiraki Woodblock Museum in Yokohama in 1999, which made over three hundred works accessible for open viewing. A catalogue titled after the exhibit, *The World of the Kibyōshi: Flower of Gesaku* (*Gesaku no hana: Kibyōshi no sekai*), and an accompanying facsimile reproduction of one of Kyōden's *kibyōshi*, replete with colored frontispiece and yellow covers, were published to commemorate the occasion.[38]

Many institutions of higher learning in Japan, including most major universities, now feature in their curricula courses on Edo's playful literature. The University of Tokyo has had several eminent scholars of *gesaku* on its faculty, such as Mizuno Minoru and Nobuhiro Shinji. All around Japan, university, municipal, and public libraries carry modern reproductions and annotated versions of popular literature, and very often original editions. The Kaga Collection (Kaga bunko) at the Tokyo Metropolitan Central Library in Hibiya houses some 1,300 works. The National Diet Library and Toyo Bunko (Tōyō bunko) each have approximately 1,000 works. The Ebara Collection at the University of Kyoto, the Matsuura Museum of History in Hirado, and several other places have hundreds upon hundreds of titles.

It is sometimes said that modern Japanese art historians came to value the woodblock print of the Floating World (*ukiyoe*)—which, during the Edo period, had been considered a plebeian form of poster art—only after discovering that artists and collectors in Europe and America treasured the form. Awareness of the *kibyōshi*, by contrast, developed in Japan after the discovery of the woodblock print but prior to the full discovery of the *kibyōshi* in the West. Within the past decade in Japan, the increasing economic success of the modern *manga* has stimulated further interest in the *kibyōshi*. Since the *kibyōshi* has often, for better or worse, been touted as a premodern progenitor of the modern *manga*, this interest seems unlikely to vanish anytime soon.

In the West, the *kibyōshi* has only recently been discovered, at least in comparison to the woodblock print. Some of the preliminary discussions in English include Shunkichi Akimoto's chapter on the genre in his book *The Twilight of Yedo* (1952), Leon Zolbrod's synopsis of Bakin's "Fleacatcher" *kibyōshi* (1965), James T. Araki's article "The Dream Pillow in Edo Literature" (1970), and Keene's brief remarks in *World Within Walls* (1976).[39] In

---

38. The work contains a preface by Professor Suzuki Toshiyuki of Chūō University. The facsimile reproduction of Kyōden's *Hana no Oedo Yoritomo-kō on'iri* (1789) also contains a slightly annotated transcription into modern Japanese. Both volumes were published together in a single sleeve by Hiraki Ukiyoe Bijutsukan, 1999.

39. Akimoto's chapter, fully titled "Kibyoshi-bon [*sic*] or Yellow-cover Illustrated Story-Books of Latter Yedo Days," is in *The Twilight of Yedo*, pp. 107–231. Akimoto retains the old orthography for "Edo."

German, Martina Schönbein has an admirable study of a single *kibyōshi* by Kyōden, replete with full scholarly exegesis, annotation, transcription, and keys to reading the anomalous cursive script.[40] Stella Bartels-Wu, in her book on one of Bakin's *kibyōshi*, argues that the modern *manga* and the *kibyōshi* share much in common.[41] And Ekkehard May provides a broad contextualization of *kibyōshi* publishing in his study of the commercialization of *gesaku*.[42] Although there has hitherto never been a full-length study of the *kibyōshi* in English, the inclusion of three translations—two by Chris Drake and one by the late James Araki (gleaned from his original article)—in Haruo Shirane's cornerstone anthology, *Early Modern Japanese Literature* (2002), surely amounts to a milestone for integrating the *kibyōshi* into mainstream Edo studies in the West.

There have also been a number of inquiries into the popular literature of Edo, most notably Haruko Iwasaki's pioneering "The World of *Gesaku*." Several other works (aside from the previously mentioned books by Cohn and Hibbett) have dealt with this subject, too, either in whole or in part: Robert Leutner's *Shikitei Sanba and the Comic Tradition in Edo Fiction*; Andrew Markus's fine *Willow in Autumn*; and some noteworthy scholarly articles by Peter F. Kornicki and J. Scott Miller, among others. A few translations of *kibyōshi* are also to be found in the "episodic festschrift" in honor of Hibbett, edited by John Solt, and in the second of three planned volumes in an anthology of Edo and early Meiji literature currently being edited by Sumie Jones and others.

Generally speaking, however, the dearth of annotated, let alone typescript, versions of texts in Japan until very recently has adversely affected Western scholarship of the *kibyōshi* and other genres of Edo popular literature. Non-native speakers of Japanese have more or less tended to steer clear of original materials. And sensibly so, perhaps, for unannotated works written in the squiggly-looking anomalous script (*kuzushiji*) can be somewhat tricky to decipher. A more time-efficient strategy is to rely on edited versions, first handled by Japanese experts in the field, with their praiseworthy tradition of philological meticulousness. The cumulative result of this situation is that Western scholarship has tended to lag years if not decades behind that of the East.

Methodology

As a hybrid genre, the *kibyōshi* draws significantly from literature, poetry, woodblock prints, storytelling, and the theater—various media, in other words, as well as genres. Thus, any approach to the *kibyōshi* from the discipline of literature in

---

40. Schönbein, *Das Kibyōshi "Happyakuman ryō kogane no kamibana" von Santō Kyōden (1791)*.

41. Bartels-Wu, *Mitatemono und kibyōshi*. Thanks to Andreas Dierks for bringing this to my attention.

42. May, *Die Kommerzialisierung der japanischen Literatur in der späten Edo-Zeit (1750–1868)*.

the traditional sense, even buttressed by the field of Japanese studies, finds itself perforce limited. At the risk of diffuseness, then, the present volume also dips into visual culture, pop culture, and cultural studies. Passing reference is made to a growing corpus of work in the field of comicbook culture, especially the writings of comicbook creators themselves, the usual suspects being Will Eisner (the so-called "Leonardo of the comic-book form"), Scott McCloud, Roger Sabin, and Art Spiegelman, but also including some scholars and critics, such as Diana Donald, Sean Howe, Sharon Kinsella, David Kunzle, Susan Napier, Fred Schodt, and Shimizu Isao.

Although these fields do not share the same methodologies, let alone definitions of scholarly scrupulousness, this volume endeavors to back up some of its broader claims with something approaching a pale imitation of the philological rigor of Japanese studies as practiced in Japan. Such philology, the main methodology of the study of national literature (*kokubungaku*), is admittedly out of fashion elsewhere. However, the *kibyōshi* is complex enough a genre to warrant such rigor, for though just about anyone literate in Japanese can comprehend the surface meaning of a *kibyōshi*, getting at the deeper levels is far more challenging and fruitful an enterprise. Thus, this volume presents the kind of sustained close reading, in the form of introductory essays and heavy annotations to the three pieces translated herein, that is too often avoided, or at least deemphasized, in much of the work in the area of cultural studies. Furthermore, an attention to the vocabulary (if not the grammar) of the *kibyōshi* has the added benefit of providing a feel for the way that Edo-period Japanese varies from the modern language, though the inclusion of so many Japanese terms may seem superfluous to any but the most devoted student.

This volume also makes use of some basic comparative techniques. If the *kibyōshi* is to be taken as a central genre of mid-Edo cultural production, reading it against other media and genres is imperative. Situating it *vis-à-vis* some works of Western and earlier Japanese literature is likewise beneficial. Also, though no art historian, I am interested in such things as the visual idiom of the *kibyōshi* picture, the relationship of the visual and verbal texts, and the place of the *kibyōshi* in the history of Japanese caricatural arts. Consideration is accorded to the materiality of the *kibyōshi* as well, following the important work by Kornicki, among others. The issues of genre and format surrounding the *kibyōshi* cannot be untangled without at least a grounding in an understanding of the *kibyōshi* and its kindred forms as physical objects. My conviction that the *kibyōshi* should be translated to approximate as closely as possible the contemporaneous comicbook reading experience means that something of both the original format as well as the aesthetics must be sacrificed. Addressing issues of materiality thus might help to compensate for that portion of the format that ends up getting lost in translation.

Finally, an interest in the comic spirit of mid-Edo Japan lurks beneath the surface of this project. The *kibyōshi* is, after all, a *comic* genre—comedy not in the strict classic sense of the universe restored to the way it should be, but in the relaxed sense of the world turned upside down for fun, or even for sociopolitical satire, and left that way. Simply put, although I cannot explain exactly why, the best works of *kibyōshi*—like the cream of *MAD* magazine, *National Lampoon*, or *Punch*—make me laugh. In this regard I openly place myself in the same company as Leslie Fiedler when confessing: "I am surely one of the few people pretending to intellectual respectability who can boast that he has read more comic books than attacks on comic books. I do not mean that I have consulted or studied the comics—I have read them, often with some pleasure."[43]

What is more, the subject matter of the present study sometimes affects the prose of the present study. To do otherwise, out of some vague notion of scholarly objectivity, might actually be *unfair* to my material. To paraphrase Sontag on camp, to write about the *kibyōshi* too seriously would be "embarrassing."

In short, my methodology, with its multifaceted approach, may resemble a potpourri of pop culture, philology, visual culture, *histoire du livre*, and some other things thrown in for good measure, slightly inflected by the tone of the material itself. Admittedly, this may amount to less a meticulous methodology than an anarchy—though such might actually be warranted by the broadranging nature of the *kibyōshi* itself.

Organization of the Present Study

This study is organized into two main parts. The first consists of five chapters (including this one) introducing different aspects of the *kibyōshi*. Chapter 1, entitled "The Floating World in An'ei-Tenmei Edo," in addition to providing some essential facts about the *kibyōshi* and a little useful background information on Edo-period Japan for the uninitiated, argues that the *kibyōshi* can serve as a mirror of An'ei-Tenmei culture, which has been mostly overlooked in the English-language scholarship on the Edo period. Moreover, the *kibyōshi* was a crucial genre in the forging of a uniquely Edoesque identity *vis-à-vis* the traditional seat of political, economic, and cultural power in Kamigata. One of the principal means for achieving this identity was a strategy of Edo-centrism, which involved mapping Edo as the central cultural space against a variety of peripheries.

Chapter 2, "The Blossom of Pulp Fiction," situates the *kibyōshi* in its intergeneric and intermedia contexts. Discussed here is the influence upon the *kibyōshi* of a few important types of popular literature, such as the mock-sermon book (*dangibon*) and fashionbook (*sharebon*); the popular theater, meaning kabuki and the puppet stage; and several other related genres or arts, such as guidebooks (*annaisho*), critical reviews (*hyōbanki*), comic

---

43. Fiedler, "The Middle Against Both Ends," p. 122.

poetry (*kyōka*, *senryū*, and *hareku*), performance arts like comic storytelling (*rakugo*), and a range of what could be termed "theatrical texts." The argument is that the *kibyōshi* is worth studying because it is one of the most sophisticated and interesting forms of popular literature, but also because it is a central genre by virtue of the way it deliberately appropriates so much from so many other genres and media. This is also one of the reasons the *kibyōshi* can be difficult to master, as though tugging at a single thread that turns out to be interwoven into an entire tapestry of art and culture. To help isolate each strand, I also briefly touch on the compositional practice of modifying various themes (*sekai*) with set types of variation (*shukō*).

Chapter 3, "*Manga* Culture and the Visual-Verbal Imagination," explores the *kibyōshi* as a comicbook. This entails consideration of the visual-verbal imagination, cartoon art, imagistic allusivity, the issue of pornography, and especially the way that proponents of "*manga* culture" have tended to distort the premodern tradition, unsubstantiatedly claiming the *kibyōshi* as the progenitor of the modern form. Although I am interested in the relationship between these two, the modern *manga* is hardly the primary focus. This is not to suggest that the modern *manga* should merit little or no attention. On the contrary: along with Japanese animation (*anime* or Japanimation), the modern *manga* represents the vastest frontier of contemporary Japanese literature and art remaining to be explored. Rather, interest in the modern *manga* seems already to be gaining enough momentum to make its study in English more or less inevitable. Since such cannot necessarily be said of the *kibyōshi*, it is the *kibyōshi* upon which this chapter concentrates.

Chapter 4, "The Rise and Pratfall of the *Kibyōshi*," provides a rudimentary periodization of the *kibyōshi*, in lieu of a fuller history, though including some brief synopses of works that several major scholars in Japan take to be "representative." Additionally, I plumb the depths of the genre's origins in earlier comicbooks (*kusazōshi*) and picturebooks, and propose an explanation for its demise. A good deal of attention is also lavished upon the group of *kibyōshi* that engaged in political satire, especially those works that satirized Neo-Confucian tenets, since such satire has largely been overlooked or overtly denied. This chapter also suggests that the genre's increasing profitability may have undermined some of the qualities that made it compelling in the first place. Simply put, the *kibyōshi* seems to have been a victim of its own commercial success.

The second part of the book, Chapters 5 through 7, which begins from the "back" cover and is to be read in the "Japanese" order from right to left, contains annotated translations of and introductory essays to three *kibyōshi*. The first of these, to which Chapter 5 is devoted, is *Those Familiar Bestsellers* (*Gozonji no shōbaimono*, 1782). Not unlike Jonathan Swift's *Battle of the Books*, perhaps, this story describes a clash between genres of woodblock-printed pictures and booklets from Edo and Kamigata. These genres are personified as characters and granted human form within the pictures. So the hero of the *kibyōshi*—a *kibyōshi* himself—appears as a charming connoisseur of

Edo's pleasure quarters. In this way, *Familiar Bestsellers* complements existing scholarship on, and makes for a visually immediate and congenial introduction to, a variety of topics of interest, including: the rise of the commercial publishing industry in Edo and the competition with its Kamigata counterpart; the characteristics of many contemporary genres and works of art and literature associated with both regions; and the intensely hybrid and allusive character of the *kibyōshi* genre. *Familiar Bestsellers* can thus be read as a case study in the construction of a uniquely Edoesque cultural identity.

The second piece, *Playboy, Roasted à la Edo* (*Edo umare uwaki no kabayaki*, 1785) of Chapter 6, is widely considered to be a masterpiece of the *kibyōshi* genre. Concerned with the issue of propagandistic self-fashioning, this story details the efforts of an inexperienced rich kid named Enjirō to recast himself, through a sustained publicity campaign of sorts, as a sexy "player" in the Floating World. An ironic comment on the rise of the *nouveau riche* in late eighteenth-century Edo, *Playboy* also contains prodigious in-group references to some of the leading figures of popular culture of the day, including kabuki actors, rakes, playwrights, madcap poets, courtesans, and geisha. Furthermore, to the extent that Enjirō's misadventures are set in motion by his overly literal reading of works of popular literature, the story is a germane cautionary tale for students of Edo's popular literature. Although several translations and synopses of this piece are available in English, the translation in this volume (like the others here) integrates the visual and verbal texts within the same physical frame, more closely approximating the way that works in the genre were read in their own day.

The *kibyōshi* of Chapter 7, *The Unseamly Silverpiped Swingers* (*Sogitsugi gingiseru*, 1788), describes the life, loves, and career as geisha of a pair of conjoined twins. This may seem not to be the most suitable of pieces for a few reasons. For one, the topic is easily given to the kind of exoticization to which Orientalism has long been prone. For another, there is no reason to believe that this piece was a particular success. Nor has it been deemed worthy of annotation in Japanese.[44]

Still, *Swingers* provides an enthralling glimpse into the way that the mid-Edo popular imagination grappled with such topics as: the relationship between gender and sex, attitudes toward contemporary pornography and erotica, Buddhist eschatology—or at least folk beliefs about karmic retribution and hell—and the use of representations of the corporeal Other in fashioning a vision of "normal" bodily identity. This glimpse strikes me as visually irresistible. Furthermore, to the extent that the characters in the verbal story are depicted in the pictures as actors in the roles of namesake characters from the popular stage, this piece makes for a strong case study in both the tensions of the visual-verbal nexus and the impact of the

---

44. This is not entirely true, for there is one full annotation in Kern, "Santō Kyōden gasaku no kibyōshi *Sogitsugi gingiseru* no saikō to shichū."

kabuki theater upon the *kibyōshi*, a topic that is merely beginning to receive notice. Plus, it may be instructive to try to understand why this piece of popular fiction was not, relatively speaking, especially popular.

It must be acknowledged that these three pieces were in part selected on subjective grounds. Just because this study has scholarly pretensions does not mean that my personal response to the humor of my material should be completely disregarded. Yet there are some objective reasons informing these selections, too. Although they do not correspond to each distinct stage of development of the *kibyōshi* that some scholars in the field have delineated, and to which I basically subscribe, these pieces nonetheless represent certain tendencies within and features of the genre. For instance, *Familiar Bestsellers* illustrates the variational technique of pastiche (*fukiyose*), since the work is a veritable hodgepodge of genres of books, pictures, and even other forms of printed matter. And *Swingers* illustrates the variational technique of "intertwining" (*naimaze*), since it combines two well-known stories or "worlds" (*sekai*) of famed real-life lovers.

Finally, although all of these pieces were penned by Santō Kyōden, and therefore do not represent the full range of *kibyōshi* authorship, they nonetheless allow for comparisons among works within a single author's literary corpus. As such, the present study performs double duty, introducing the *kibyōshi*, but also paving the way for a more in-depth future exploration of the professionalization of literature that Kyōden epitomizes. Thus, this volume mostly defers discussion of the man whose works are herein translated. Suffice it to say that two centuries after his death, Kyōden is rising from the dead in Japan in much the same way that Genroku author Saikaku was resuscitated during the late nineteenth and early twentieth centuries. Facilitating this revival is the publication of the somewhat exaggeratedly titled *Complete Works of Santō Kyōden* (*Santō Kyōden zenshū*), a planned twenty-tome collection of his major pieces. Even so, aside from the breadth of his literary corpus, underpinning this project is a fascination with the multimedia brilliance of the man, one of the bestselling author-illustrators of the mid-Edo period, to which we now turn.

Chapter 1

The Floating World in An'ei-Tenmei Edo

Osaka's sophistication is Edo's gaucherie.
—Shiba Zenkō

Swamptown to Boomtown

The basic facts of life in Edo-period Japan are well known, having been studiously written about elsewhere.[1] Popular fictional representations outside Japan, while hardly beholden to historical veracity, have colorfully sketched the entire period in broad strokes, from the establishment of the shogunate in James Clavell's novel *Shōgun* (where he encodes the real-life Tokugawa into the fictional Toranaga), to its disintegration in Edward Zwick's fanciful film *The Last Samurai*. Nonetheless, a few basic words about the sociopolitical order are warranted, though these are by no means intended as a comprehensive overview.

Generally speaking, society was organized into four main classes—based on each group's supposed contribution to the commonweal, more or less according to Neo-Confucian precepts of usefulness[2]—as follows, in order of descending rank: (1) the aristocratic samurai (split up as *sam-u-rai* in English but *sa-mu-ra-i* in Japanese), immediate "servants" to the throne and, by extension, to all those involved in ruling the following three classes of commoners (*shōjin*); (2) the landed peasantry, valued for producing agricultural goods, especially since both goods and land became increasingly scarce relative to the sharply rising population; (3) artisans, who fashioned various articles, some of which actually had utilitarian value; and (4) merchants, who were frowned upon as virtual parasites for exploiting the hard labor of others, depleting raw materials, and dealing willingly in filthy lucre.

---

1. For sturdy introductions to the history of the Edo period, see Nakane and Ōishi, *Tokugawa Japan*, and Hall, *Early Modern Japan*.

2. In Japanese, the four classes (*shimin*) of samurai, peasant, artisan, and merchant are referred to as *shi-nō-kō-shō*. The use of this term to stratify society is conventionally associated with Toyotomi Hideyoshi (1536–1598).

These four classes in practice were not castes. Aside from mobility among the subdivisions within each class, there was more fluidity among the classes themselves than is oftentimes presumed. Some merchants were "promoted" to honorary samurai—and some samurai deliberately renounced their privileged status to become merchants. Those samurai who were cut loose from their stipends of rice, for one reason or another, became masterless drifters (*rōnin*). Essentially free agents, what they were free to do was starve to death unless they could secure some kind of gainful employment, which many of them sought in the metropolitan centers.

There was also a fifth class of sorts that, consisting of "non-humans" (*hinin*), was not considered a true class at all. Most occupants of this category were "hamlet people" (*burakumin*), so called because they were restricted to living in specific sections of town where they were less likely to "contaminate" members of respectable society. Historically earning their livelihood as butchers or by working leather, these untouchables—analogous to India's *harijan*—were considered unclean for having violated Buddhist law against the taking of life in any form. In fact, one of the most vile words in Japanese is probably the epithet for these hamlet folk, "great filth" (*eta*). However, a variety of other people were considered non-humans as well, such as those working as actors, courtesans, and in other "marginalized" professions. For some reason, however, a samurai who took human life was never similarly stigmatized and demoted into this category, at least as long as the murder was committed in the Neo-Confucian context of service to one's lord.

Buddhism itself was not the only system of thought or "religion" in Japan. Shinto, with its emphasis upon ritual purification and the worshiping of a pantheon of deities, and Neo-Confucianism, the state-sponsored ideology that emphasized values such as social utility and proper etiquette in a hierarchical social system, both coexisted more or less with Buddhism in a kind of precarious syncretic *détente*. Even Christianity was not unknown in Edo-period Japan. There is a long history of Westerners coming to peddle and purchase commodities. The headway of the proselytizers among them was one reason the shogunate acted to close the country off to most Westerners, largely confining an anointed but necessary few—primarily merchants of the Dutch East India Company—to the manmade island of Deshima (a.k.a. Dejima) in Nagasaki harbor.[3] Nonetheless, Christianity was met with more open hostility than the other organized ideologies. Untold hundreds if not thousands of underground Christians were rooted out and dealt with accordingly, meaning burned at the stake or crucified.

And like other world religions, Buddhism itself had a variety of sects, with adherents of Pure Land outnumbering most others within the general

---

3. In reality, Japan during the Edo period was hardly sealed off hermetically from the rest of the world, as has been supposed for a long time. For the classic article on this subject in English, see Toby, "Reopening the Question of *Sakoku.*"

population. Not to reduce the differences to a Zen-like minimum, but in general, Pure Land advocated that any sentient being could attain spiritual enlightenment in the world to come merely by uttering a prayer, called the *nenbutsu*, invoking the name of Amitabha Buddha. Zen itself advocated that one could attain as much in *this* world by ascetic practice such as seated meditation (*zazen*). Pure Land belief figures in two of the *kibyōshi* in this volume, whereas Zen figures in none.

In terms of the political system, the country was a motley collection of approximately 260 semi-sovereign fiefs or domains (*han*), headed by enfeoffed though still occasionally fiercely autonomous samurai lords known as daimyo (literally "big names"). Ultimately, these warlords were under the control of the Emperor (*tennō*), at least on paper.[4] Yet he or she—there was actually one Empress during the Edo period, Meishō (r. 1630–1643)—was more a paper tiger who never could hope to herd the various fat cats of the domains. During the period under study, only two sovereigns ascended the Chrysanthemum Throne: Gomomozono (r. 1771–1779) and Kōkaku (1780–1817). In reality, others ruled in their name: Tokugawa Ieharu (1737–1786; r. 1760–1786) and Tokugawa Ienari (1773–1841; r. 1786–1837), though the latter was so young when he was put in charge that someone *else* was put in charge of him. That was Matsudaira Sadanobu, who as Senior Councilor to the shogun from 1787 to 1793 was arguably the most powerful man in the land. Sadanobu was also the man who made it his personal mission to crack down on the leading authors of popular literature such as the *kibyōshi*.

Ieharu and Ienari, the tenth and eleventh *de facto* rulers, were members of the Tokugawa samurai clan. Under the leadership of Tokugawa Ieyasu (1542–1616; r. 1603–1605), the clan had, in the early part of the seventeenth century, finally unified the country after centuries of internecine warfare. Ieyasu revived the defunct office of shogun, or Military Overlord, though the holder of this title never directly controlled more than a quarter of the domainal lords at any given time. Ieyasu established his "tent government" (*bakufu*) in 1603. The so-called Tokugawa Peace that ensued brought some semblance of stability and prosperity to the realm. Accordingly, most historians, political scientists, and economists refer to these 265 years or so as the Tokugawa period, whereas most students of literature, art, and culture refer to them as the Edo period.

So that his clan would not fall under the sway of the *ancien régime*, Ieyasu shrewdly founded his headquarters in a marsh in the middle of nowhere,

---

4. Actually, the term *tennō* (not unlike the term *kibyōshi*) is a retrospective term. That is, it was just returning into vogue during the period under study after half a millennium of nonuse. "From the time of Juntoku *tennō* (r. 1210–1221) until its revival at the time of Kōkaku *tennō* (r. 1779–1817)," writes scholar Watanabe Hiroshi, "the posthumous title *tennō* was not officially used either before or after death . . . People of the Edo period would not have said something like 'Gomizunoo *tennō*.'" In Roberts, "About Some Japanese Historical Terms," p. 39.

which is to say on the opposite side of the main island of Japan from the historic seat of the imperial family in Kamigata to the West (present-day Kyoto, Nara, and Osaka). Situated near a formidable sound opening to the Pacific Ocean, this swamptown, called "Edo"—which means something like "Baydoor" or even "Portsmouth"—would eventually be renamed "Tokyo"— "Eastern Capital."

In order to whip the many daimyo into line from its remote outpost, the shogunate implemented in 1634 a policy of forced residence, known as "alternate attendance" (*sankin kōtai*). Under this system, it was incumbent upon each warlord and his chief retainers to split their time between his domainal base and an Edo domicile, where his loved ones—wife and any heirs—were to remain, in effect, urbanely caged hostages. In addition to providing corvée labor and other resources for public construction projects, as with the building of Edo Castle, this system accelerated the development of the main thoroughfare connecting Edo and Kyoto, the so-called East-Sea Highway (*Tōkaidō*), to accommodate the increased traffic (including Dutch and Ryūkyūan delegations). The system also afforded a significant portion of the population a tremendous degree of mobility, certainly unprecedented in Japanese history up to that point, and probably far greater than in contemporary European societies.

With daimyo and their extended retinues from all over the country residing in Edo, the city began growing exponentially. The conventional wisdom is that by An'ei-Tenmei (1772–1789), Edo boasted a population of over one million inhabitants, making it the largest metropolis in the world at the time. In some fundamental respects, it may have been one of the most advanced, too. Susan Hanley, as part of an effort to ground the cultural roots of Japan's twentieth-century "economic miracle" in the more quantifiable terms of material culture, has made the case that Edo was at least equal to contemporary London or Paris in terms of quality of life.[5] Hanley bases her work on such factors as the nutritional value of the diet of the average person, the strength of his clothing and housing, and even the effects of the advanced network of night soil removal upon agricultural output and public health. For this last reason alone, Edo unquestionably would have been a more pleasant metropolis in which to reside, since unlike its European counterparts, its denizens astutely did not dump their raw sewage into the main river running through town.

Aside from the enviable sanitation and newfound political stability, Edo-period Japan also underwent a remarkable series of positive socioeconomic transformations. An epochal nationwide shift from an agrarian to a market economy brought about a demographic landslide from rural periphery to urban centers. Yet there was also an eastward shift of *cultural* momentum (*bun'un tōzen*), following the political and economic shifts of the seventeenth

---

5. Hanley, *Everyday Things in Premodern Japan.*

century, away from the old imperial capital to the new shogunal one. This eastward cultural shift is visible down to such things as the easily overlooked trade of thumb-sized figurines: "The earliest Japanese *netsuke* were carved in Osaka and Kyoto . . . but in the late eighteenth century the production of netsuke began in Edo" and soon came to lead the market.[6]

The shift is especially evident in terms of the publishing industry, which had developed and thrived in Kamigata, but reached astounding new heights in Edo roughly during the period under study. Moriya Katsuhisa notes that throughout most of the seventeenth century, Kyoto dominated the publishing world, having 701 publishers to Osaka's 185 and Edo's 242. During the eighteenth century, Kyoto declined to 536 publishers, while Osaka and Edo more or less reached parity, boasting 564 and 493 publishers, respectively. The nineteenth century witnessed the reduction of Kamigata into a shade of its former grandeur: while Kyoto declined to 494 publishers and Osaka to 504, Edo more than doubled, reaching 917 publishing houses.[7] Konta Yōzō, a scholar of Edo-period publishing history, pinpoints Edo's eclipse of Kamigata publishing to the third quarter of the eighteenth century. While Edo publishers overtook their Kamigata rivals by the 1730s in terms of the number of books sold, it was not until An'ei-Tenmei that Edo surpassed the combined total output of the Kyoto and Osaka publishing industries.[8] What the statistics tell us—and what is captured imaginatively in *Familiar Bestsellers*—is that by the second half of the eighteenth century, Edo had clearly surpassed Kyoto and Osaka in terms of publishing if not in actual cultural output itself, at least insofar as Edo's popular imagination was concerned. As we will see, Edo's sense of itself as the new cultural center may be considered one of the defining characteristics of An'ei-Tenmei culture.

With even more people flocking to Edo from all over the country, the resultant intermixing of dialects and customs of members of various classes led to vibrant new cultural formations that were appreciably different than those of Kyoto-Osaka and other cultural regions of the country. The Floating World of commoner culture that informs the entire Edo-period began taking on an especially Edoesque cast. High and low rubbed elbows in public spaces such as bathhouses (even the legitimate kind), temples, markets, bazaars, and the popular theaters, not to mention the various pleasure quarters. A popular culture lively enough to satisfy the fussiest of epicureans as well as the masses evolved on its own terms. Many works of art and literature depict an assortment of people mingling freely. Lovers frolic intimately in bed. Shop owners and customers conduct business over tea and tobacco in sitting rooms. Men and women of various classes convene book clubs. Even samurai and untouchables share a passenger boat. The *kibyōshi* certainly reflects

---

6. Earle, *Netsuke*, pp. 17–18.

7. Moriya, "Urban Networks and Information Networks," p. 115.

8. See Konta, *Edo no hon'yasan*, p. 93. Also see Morita, "Edoki shoten no hassei dōkō."

this Floating World of An'ei-Tenmei Edo: it is a world pullulating with excitement, enthrallment, exuberance.

To the extent that this center began to be emulated nationwide, the shogun's capital was arguably transformed into Japan's first "early modern" metropolis. "To say that alternate attendance helped foster a national culture," historian Constantine Vaporis writes, "is a truism of sorts."[9] Proponents of modernization theory are quick to point out that it is only with the Westernization and the industrialization of the Meiji period (1868–1912) that a genuinely modern, Western-style, centralized nation-state was possible. Be that as it may, even if the new demographic mélange did not make Edo the flowerbed of a democratic revolution, it did help transform the metropolis into a cultural hothouse that increasingly would come to be juxtaposed—especially within the *kibyōshi*—against other major cities in Japan. The result was that Edo envisioned itself, and was increasingly coming to be envisioned by others, as *the* cultural center to be emulated.

A great deal of this cultural construction was carried out in literature. Surprisingly, perhaps, Edo is generally acknowledged as the most literate society in the eighteenth-century world, certainly compared to the major European metropolises. However, hard statistics are simply not available. Peter Kornicki, lamenting that the earliest reliable literacy rates go back only to the end of the nineteenth century, when Japan was modernizing, offers one scrap of data: "The figures commonly cited for literacy rates in the early 1870s are 40 percent for males and 15 percent for females."[10] Hanley points out that what is known of Japanese literacy during this period suggests it was several times greater than in England.[11] One certainly imagines that literacy was higher in Edo, owing to the greater concentration of schools and samurai there, than in the Japanese countryside.

The government, for its part, seems to have viewed literacy pragmatically. A literate peasantry would benefit from various mass-printed agricultural manuals—as well as the publication of Neo-Confucian teachings—and this, it was believed, would translate to increased productivity to meet the alarmingly rapid expansion of the population.[12] A relatively large portion of samurai and many peasants, artisans, and even merchants were probably educated in a variety of venues befitting their status, from officially sponsored domain schools, through local temple classrooms, to private academies.[13] Although the approach to teaching literacy in each of these was by all accounts nothing if not somber, turning even a lively book of creative fiction like *The Tale of*

---

9. Vaporis, "To Edo and Back," p. 27.

10. Kornicki, *The Book in Japan*, p. 275.

11. Hanley, *Everyday Things in Premodern Japan*, p. 190.

12. One such work, for instance, was Miyazaki Yasusada's (1627–1693) *Agricultural Compendium* (*Nōgyō zensho*, ca. 1697).

13. For more on education during the Edo period, see Dore, *Education in Tokugawa Japan*, and Rubinger, *Private Academies of Tokugawa Japan*.

Genji into an occasion for memorization, let alone into an ideological front, students were nonetheless able to apply their lessons to reading for pleasure on their own time. To the extent that the rise of mass-produced literature in the seventeenth century supported pleasurable reading among the masses outside of these formal educational environments, it may have represented an epochal transition in the very notion of reading as well as of writing.

Woodblock Printing Industry

Although xylographic or "woodblock" printing had been known in Japan for hundreds of years in the form of monastic publishing, it was not until the beginning of the seventeenth century that it became a viable commercial enterprise. Before long an industry trafficking in Floating World pictures (*ukiyoe*) and illustrated books (*eiri kanpon*) took shape. Technological advances were made by and by, as with the invention of alignment marks (*kentō*), which allowed for multiple printings with minimal bleed of color. New-and-improved vegetable dyes and more cost-effective paper were also developed, making printed matter cheaper to produce and more durable than ever. And it was more accessible, since there is some evidence to suggest that print runs increased from the hundreds to the thousands of copies. Indeed, what began in the seventeenth century as an increase in literary output and consumption had become by the eighteenth century a cultural phenomenon of astounding proportions. Although xylographic printing did not immediately supplant handwritten manuscripts, more titles were produced this way during the Edo period than there are extant titles for the preceding millennium.

Printing improved in terms not only of output and cost, but also of velocity of composition, reproduction, and dissemination. The turnaround time between event and publication diminished markedly during the Edo period. Asai Ryōi's *Musashi Stirrups* (*Musashi abumi*, 1658), an illustrated syllabary booklet about the Great Edo Fire of 1657, was a watershed for having been published within a year of the actual conflagration. Over a century later, during An'ei-Tenmei, by contrast, illustrated broadsheets—albeit much shorter than Ryōi's booklet—describing how Mt. Asama spewed heavy volcanic ash all over Edo in the seventh month of 1783 (Tenmei 3) were printed *en masse* and distributed throughout most of the country within only a few *days* of the actual eruption (**Figure 1.1**). Surely, this kind of improved turnaround time represented a paradigmatic shift in the spread of information in Japan.[14]

Such improvements were due largely to newer technologies and better materials but also to organizational advances in the division of labor. The average publishing house (*hanmoto*) was diversified into assembly line-like

---

14. For a discussion of the relationship of broadsheets and early Japanese newspapers, see Kinoshita and Yoshimi, *Nyūsu no tanjō*.

Fig. 1.1 Broadsheet depicting
the eruption of Mt. Asama in
1783, printed and widely distributed within a few days of
the actual event. Courtesy of
the University of Tokyo, Institute of Socio-Information
and Communication Studies,
Ono Hideo Collection.

stables of talent that included authors (*sakusha*), copyists (*hikkō*), printers (*hanzuri*), block carvers (*hangishi*), and artists (*gakō*). Publishers, who commissioned works, supplied the capital (**Figure 1.2**). Furthermore, the standardization of literary themes (*sekai*) and set compositional techniques of variation (*shukō*) also played an important role in the accelerated turnout of printed matter.

Ironically, however, this compositional standardization initially flourished in the world of the popular stage. This is probably what allowed Chikamatsu to craft one of the earliest "overnight pickles" (*ichiyazuke*), his puppet play *Love Suicides at Sonezaki* (*Sonezaki shinjū*, 1703), which debuted within about a month of the real-life incident that inspired it. Such quickly steeped pieces, being restricted to a single venue, obviously were debilitatingly limited in reach. Broadsides, ballad sheets, textiles, even paper fans, by virtue of their mass production, all became potently vendible cocktails concocted out of one part news, one part gossip, and one part pure invention. When genres of popular literature such as the fashionbook (*sharebon*) and the *kibyōshi* began dabbling in the representation of trends in apparel, the potential for literature to *stimulate* desire also became apparent.

Granted, earlier genres of literature, such as the syllabary booklet and Floating World novella of the late seventeenth and early eighteenth centuries, had been able to keep abreast of the latest vogues. However, the fashionbook and the *kibyōshi* must have made it feel as though a millennium of change was being compressed into a mere decade or two. It may even be possible that the acceleration of composition, reproduction, and dissemina-

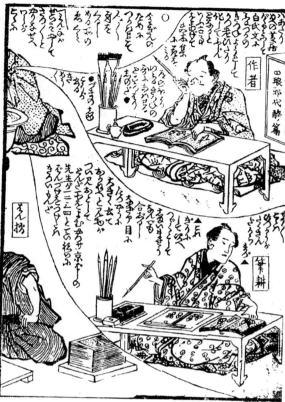

tion of woodblock-printed genres also contributed to the perception of an acceleration in the pace of style—and of urban existence itself.

What is clear is that the *kibyōshi* enjoyed a signal popularity. Of all the many genres of mass-printed literature, the *kibyōshi* may even have been *the* most widely read genre in its day. Bestsellers are thought to have been issued in the thousands of copies per run. It is conceivable that more readers among the common classes knew the loveably bumbling upstart Enjirō than his romantic foil from that other story, the Shining Prince Genji. This is not an argument for the literary quality of the *kibyōshi*, though it does speak to literary-historical value: the *kibyōshi* merits attention if for nothing else than its megalithic presence in the popular culture of late eighteenth-century Japan. The *kibyōshi* was so popular it could not have helped but influence people's perceptions, fantasies, dreams, and waking lives.

Fig. 1.2 Fanciful schematic of the publishing process as an assembly line of specialists (clockwise from upper right): a pugnosed author, a copyist, a printer, a bespectacled block carver, an artist, and (at top) a publisher—whose depiction with a gold ingot for a face suggests that what drives this process is capital. From *Takarabune kogane no hobashira* (1818), a multivolume comicbook written by Tōri Sanjin and illustrated by Katsukawa Shunsen. Courtesy of Hōsa bunko.

The *Kibyōshi* as Physical Object

The popularity of the *kibyōshi* largely depended upon its existence as a material object, so a few words on that subject are in order. Like many other genres of mass-produced literature during the Edo period, the *kibyōshi* assumed a mid-sized (*chūbon*) format, measuring roughly 13 × 18 centimeters (5 × 7 inches). While other genres vary in their standard page length, the *kibyōshi* typically consists of one to three separate volumes called fascicles (*kan* or *maki*). Each fascicle is composed of five double leaves, which is to say ten pages, for sheets of paper were printed on one side, then folded in half, blank sides together, forming two pages. Thus, a *kibyōshi* might have 10, 20, or 30 pages. The majority of works, however—including all those translated herein—boast three fascicles in 30 pages. The pages of each fascicle are loosely hand-stitched or "brochéd" together into pliant though sturdily lined soft covers, making the *kibyōshi* less a codex-form book, with hard covers and stiff binding, than a kind of floppy pamphlet or "chapbook."

Curiously, far from being sewn to each other, fascicles were often deliberately left loose. The existence of cover art on *each* loose fascicle—not just on the first one—suggests that fascicles may sometimes have been sold separately as well as in sets. This raises the intriguing possibility that the *kibyōshi*, if not other woodblock-printed popular literature, may have been a precursor to the serial story. There being no regularly issued newspapers or literary magazines at the time, let alone *manga*, at least not in the modern sense of these terms, there was no such thing as serialized literature or syndicated comic strips.[15] More to the point, though, the *kibyōshi* as a rule was not *issued* serially. Works were not published in installments, at different times during a publishing year, in other words. Rather, the *kibyōshi* was produced in individual fascicles in mock imitation of earlier types of children's comicbooks, which were typically issued that way. In fact, some *kibyōshi*, beginning with Harumachi's *Master Flashgold*, were sold in ultrathin coverslips called "bag stashers" (*fukurozashi*), presumably to keep the loose fascicles more or less together.[16] Regrettably, hardly any coverslips are extant. These were preposterously fragile affairs, less genuinely protective wrapping than delicately decorative shell, made of a too-easily tattered gossamer, bearing a title and sometimes a pleasant design of some sort, perhaps only lightly embossed (**Figure 1.3**).

The interior paper of the *kibyōshi*, though steely by coverslip standards, contrasted with acid-free paper is flimsy and slightly furry to the touch. Called Mino paper (*minogami*), it tends to be thin enough that especially thick printing is often visible from one page to its obverse side. Yet the high fiber content would have made this ragpaper resistant in its day to rough-thumbing, dog-earing, and early-onset brittleness. Over time, though, the absorbency made it susceptible to such blights as finger grease, moldering, worming, and dampstaining (see **Color Figure 8**). Like other woodblock-

---

15. Granted, some forms of critique literature, such as *The Yoshiwara, Detailed*, were issued biannually, though these do not seem to have contained running stories. And although there were broadsheets, these were issued sporadically.

16. The term could also apply to any book sold in a colorful cloth bag. See Mizuno, *NKBT 59*, p. 90, n. 14.

Fig. 1.3 Rare example of a "bag stasher" (*fukurozashi*), a flimsy coverslip used to hold together the separate volumes of a single *kibyōshi*. From *Thousand-Armed Goddess of Mercy, Julienned* (*Daihi no senrokuhon*, 1785), written by Shiba Zenkō and illustrated by Kitao Masanobu. Courtesy of Tokyo Metropolitan Central Library, Kaga Collection.

printed genres, the *kibyōshi* has proven perishable. At present it seems to be a frail, evanescent medium, one especially prone to these sorts of blemishes but also to printing dyes fading to the point of imperceptibility. That so many works have survived at all seems remarkable.

Those cultural commodities that Japanese society deemed "valuable" traditionally tended to be inscribed on silk, ceramic, iron, even stone. Needless to say, paper traveled better. The midsized format and resilient though lightweight pages spelled portability. Several *kibyōshi* could easily be carried about in one's sleeve, the equivalent of the modern pocket, or slipped beneath one's pillow without fear of incurring damage. The hand-stitched binding was surprisingly durable, too, at least relative to many a Western comicbook: "The fragility of the stapled pamphlet," as Sean Howe has put it, ". . . is testament to the medium's resignation that *there will be no exposure to the outside world*."[17] As one popular souvenir of Edo, the *kibyōshi* was perhaps actually meant to be transported and exposed abroad, meaning distant provinces.

Mino ragpaper was also fairly cheap, certainly when compared to paper produced in previous epochs. Centuries earlier, during the Heian period (794–1185), when Kyoto's court culture was at its peak, paper had been a precious, even rare commodity. Sei Shōnagon undertook writing her famed

17. Howe, *Give Our Regards to the Atomsmashers!*, p. ix. Emphasis in the original.

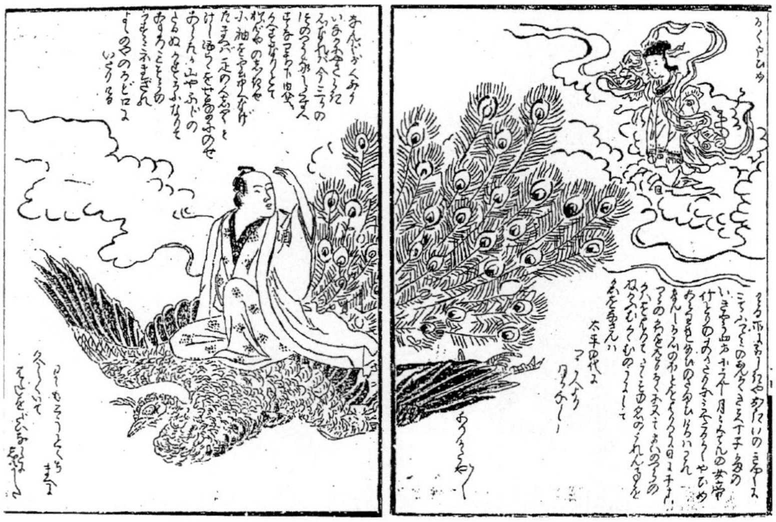

Fig. 1.4 Scene from *Party at the Yoshinoya!* (*Yoshinoya shuraku*, 1788), a *kibyōshi* written by Santō Kyōden and illustrated by Kitao Masayoshi. Reprinted in Mizuno, *SKZ 1*, p. 509. Courtesy of Perikansha.

Pillow Book (*Makura no sōshi*, ca. 990s) only after having received a bolt of paper as a gift bestowed upon her by the Empress herself. By the eighteenth century, the growth of the lumber industry, innovations in the production of paper mulberry, and increased demand all contributed to the greater availability of paper and, thus, to its less prohibitive cost.

The typical *kibyōshi* is thought to have been about as cheap as a lunch bowl of buckwheat noodles. Granted, the price of Mino paper rose sharply during the 1780s due to lumber shortages and famines.[18] The high estimates therefore say *two* bowls of noodles.[19] In either case, for those who could not afford a trip to one of the Floating World establishments, its vicarious thrills were available in the *kibyōshi* for a relative pittance. Today, however, a work can easily fetch thousands of dollars on the open market—even tens of thousands for a famous title—amounts perhaps even dearer than a night on the town with an actual geisha.

Like the modern *manga*, and as a scene from *Familiar Bestsellers* illustrates, the *kibyōshi* was a form of *recyclable* literature. It was so in the double sense of material recyclability, for the paper could be returned to pulp and then reconstituted as paper, and of conceptual recyclability, for its literary matter could be and usually was recast employing particular compositional conventions. The cherrywood blocks used in printing were also doubly recyclable. Aside from the rather mundane sense of erasing the surface impressions from a block so that a new composition could be carved, there was the frugal practice of reusing the pictorial portion of a woodblock shorn of its verbal element. For instance, some of the pictures in the *kibyōshi* titled *Party at the Yoshinoya!* (*Yoshinoya shuraku*) (**Figure 1.4**), written by Kyōden and illus-

---

18. For more on this, see Sorenaka, "The Kansei Reforms," p. 155.
19. Tanahashi, *Edo gesaku zōshi*, p. 12.

Fig. 1.5 Scene from the joke-book *Arrowroot Flower* (*Tarō-bana*, 1789), whose pictures recycled those in *Party at the Yoshinoya!* of the previous year. Written by Santō Kyō-den and illustrated by Kitao Masayoshi. Reprinted in Mutō, *Hanashibon taikei 13*, p. 347. Courtesy of Tōkyōdō shuppan.

trated by Kitao Masayoshi in 1788, are literally recycled in their *Arrowroot Flower* (*Tarōbana*), a jokebook (*hanashibon*) published the following year (**Figure 1.5**).[20] This means that the verbal text was erased from the original woodblocks so that completely different anecdotes could be poured into the same pictorial vessel. Since the verbal text of *Arrowroot Flower* has nothing to do with its own pictures, the recycling must have been done for commercial, rather than artistic or literary, purposes, economizing on the composition and carving of new wooden printing blocks as opposed to some kind of clever visual allusion to the earlier work.

All told, the durability, portability, and availability of the *kibyōshi* helped put it in the hands of readers. Extremely long works like the classic *Tale of Genji* would not have found a comparably large non-aristocratic readership during the mid-Edo period because they never could have been produced in the requisite quantity. They were simply too cumbersome. Much of the success of the *kibyōshi*, then, was derived by the brute facts of its materiality, specifically its brevity as well as the way that materiality dovetailed with the distribution of work within the publishing stable and the organization of literary material within the minds of its creators.

Back to the Frontispiece

Another important aspect of the materiality of the *kibyōshi* was the nature of its pictures. The internal ones were colorless affairs: black ink starkly set against pale off-white paper. What scattered few counterexamples remain, containing mostly inoffensive coloring, are limited to individual copies,

---

20. Mentioned in Iwanami, *Nihon koten bungaku daijiten 4*, p. 202. Kyōden's *kibyōshi* can be found in Mizuno, *SKZ 1*, pp. 493–510. His jokebook is in Mutō, *Hanashibon taikei 13*, pp. 337–384.

Fig. 1.6 The titular protagonist of the classic tale about a woman with a saucer fused to her skull. From *The Story of Lady Dishhead* (*Hachikazuki*, ca. 1624–1643), an anonymous hand-colored picturebook. Reprinted in Yoshida, *Tanrokubon*, p. 165. Courtesy of Kodansha International. Permission of Kurofunekan.

certainly not the entire print runs. Judging by the inferior quality of the hues and the occasional failure to stay within the lines, these must have been independently commandeered by younger readers as coloring books, rather than produced in some kind of deliberate mock imitation of earlier genres of hand-colored books like the *tanrokubon* of early seventeenth-century Kyoto, or the so-called Nara picturebooks that began appearing even earlier (**Figure 1.6** and **Color Figure 5**).[21] Acknowledging its own dull-as-February monochromes, one *kibyōshi*, Koikawa Yukimachi's *The Virtuous Prosperity-Boosting Specs* (*Sakaemasu megane no toku*, 1790), playfully called for the inclusion of "quintuple-hued viewers" (*goshiki megane*) that would artificially colorize the black-and-white illustrations (not completely unlike modern "3–D glasses," perhaps?)—and for only a modest additional charge (**Figure 1.7**).[22]

---

21. For more on the hand-colored *tanrokubon*—so called because of its reliance on orange-red (*tan*) and mineral green (*roku*)—and the *Nara ehon*, see Yoshida, *Tanrokubon*.

22. Illustrated by Kitao Masayoshi. Yukimachi was one of Harumachi's disciples. Mentioned in Screech, *Western Scientific Gaze and Popular Imagery in Later Edo Japan*, p. 183.

Fig. 1.7 Characters looking at printed matter through colorizing spectacles. From *The Virtuous Prosperity-Boosting Specs* (*Sakaemasu megane no toku*, 1790), a *kibyōshi* written by Koikawa Yukimachi and illustrated by Kitao Masayoshi. Courtesy of Tokyo Metropolitan Central Library, Kaga Collection.

Greater expense was lavished upon the colorful print gracing the front cover of each work's fascicles. The pragmatics of cost and limitations of technology meant that though color was excluded from the interior pictures, it was included on the covers. Publishers simply could not produce thirty pages of interior color on a massive scale for a reasonable price. One polychromatic print strategically placed on each fascicle, though, was not out of the question, especially if it caught the eye of the prospective buyer. This fact speaks to the commercial savvy of the publishers who tried to maximize their resources by marshalling color on the covers to sell copy. In this respect, the *kibyōshi* perhaps presages the modern *manga* weekly, whose splashy cover art too often belies the drab black-and-white of its interior pictures. Some *kibyōshi* covers at present seem to contain little if any color whatsoever. These must have been produced as cheap affairs, stinting on color altogether, or at the very least employing inferior pigments that over time have sallowed.

The typical "pasted-on frontispiece" (*hari edaisen*), as it was formally known, was a multicolored woodblock print—technically a brocade print (*nishikie*), albeit on a miniature scale.[23] As such, it ranks among the most opulent

---

23. The standard work on *kibyōshi* frontispieces has long been Hamada, *Kibyōshi edaisen shū*, which includes miniature black-and-white reproductions of innumerable frontispieces, arranged chronologically by publisher. More recently, Tanahashi issued *Kibyōshi sōran 5*, which

cover art in Japanese publishing history up to that point in time. Most works of popular literature, after all, simply bore a title strip; in rare instances, a light pattern might be embossed onto the cover.[24] The early genres of comicbooks (*kusazōshi*) began sporting frontispieces, though these are almost always monotonous, or at least monochromatic, affairs. Indeed, the frontispiece seems to have blossomed only with the *kibyōshi*.[25] How much more brilliantly the colors of the *kibyōshi* frontispiece must have shone in comparison—and especially in light of the repeatedly issued austerity measures of the period.

These measures, which culminated during the Kansei Reforms of the late 1780s and early 1790s, in effect, sought to drain the color from commoner existence, turning everything from clothing to architectural exteriors into various shades of gray. What pastels there were all but retreated from public life. One could still find brightness in the closed, shadowy private spheres of the pleasure quarter, where top courtesans wore sumptuous silk brocade, or on the kabuki stage, where actors served as powerful fashion plates, largely by dint of tint. Yet like the brocade print itself, the *kibyōshi* cover—more so than other genres of illustrated fiction, which typically did *not* contain frontispieces—must have provided a kind of easily concealed, portable compensation in its multicolored splendor.

Additionally, the frontispiece served as a visual-verbal colophon, indicating the title of the work, information about its publisher, author, and perhaps illustrator, and the year of issuance. In so doing, the frontispiece identified the individual work as part of a larger batch issued by a particular publisher in a given season. The written title often gestures toward the work's compositional principle. Many titles are deliberately baffling as part of the strategy of piquing the reader's interest, the result being that it is nearly impossible to make sense of them, much less translate them well, without first performing a close reading of the story. This is especially true because the Chinese graphs of the title are often playfully reinterpreted—some would say undermined—by a completely counterintuitive, even farfetched, Japanese gloss. Often a "supertitle" (*tsunogaki*) preceding the main title—analogous to the English subtitle following a colon in many academic books—lends an added humorous twist.

Information about the publisher was usually disclosed on the frontispiece by the inclusion of his name along with, on some occasions, his ad-

---

follows Hamada's organization, though it contains more generously sized examples and thankfully is cross-referenced to the other volumes in *Kibyōshi Overview*.

24. That said, Buddhist sutras have a long history of illustrated frontispieces in Japan. As Kornicki notes: "The earliest Japanese example is attached to a copy of the *Lotus sūtra* written in silver ink in the ninth century and is probably copied directly from a Tang exemplar. This frontispiece consists simply of stylized ornamentation, but later Japanese examples commonly illustrate variations on the theme of Śākyamuni Buddha preaching to disciples, albeit with increasing elaboration." In Kornicki, *The Book in Japan*, p. 89.

25. Hamada makes this claim in *Kibyōshi edaisen shū*, p. 2.

dress. Most *kibyōshi* publishers operated on Tōriaburachō, the Grub Street of late eighteenth-century Edo, though there were also other locations.[26] One almost always finds the publisher's crest incorporated into the frontispiece design, too. The three-peaked mountain-and-ivy seal of Tsutaya Jūzaburō is visible in the frontispieces to *Playboy*; the encircled cross of the Nishimiya in the frontispieces to *Unseamly Silverpiped Swingers*. The pseudonyms of the author and the artist may also be indicated, though these almost always appear in a cartouche at the end of the last fascicle if not at the end of each fascicle. Which of these were displayed on the cover depended on a variety of factors, such as the publisher's *modus operandi*, the degree of name recognition of the author and artist, and the content of the work in question. The producers of salacious works naturally tended to avoid displaying the specific details of their identities, lest the authorities hold them responsible for breaking one or more of the innumerable regulations against licentiousness.

The outlay of capital for color, and the fact that the compositions were often virtuoso works of art unto themselves, most conspicuously suggests that the *kibyōshi* frontispiece was fully recognized for its advertising potential (**Figures 1.8** and **1.9** and **Color Figure 7**). The cover was designed to

(*left*) Fig. 1.8 A bevy of beautiful spooks. From the frontispiece to the second fascicle of *Life of a Stretchy Monster* (*Mikoshi nyūdō ichidaiki*, 1782), a *kibyōshi* written by Iba Kashō and illustrated by Torii Kiyonaga. Courtesy of the Matsuura Historical Museum.

(*right*) Fig. 1.9 A mob of monsters. From the frontispiece to the third fascicle of *Life of a Stretchy Monster* (*Mikoshi nyūdō ichidaiki*, 1782), a *kibyōshi* written by Iba Kashō and illustrated by Torii Kiyonaga. Courtesy of the Matsuura Historical Museum.

---

26. For a list of publishers' addresses, see the front matter to Tanahashi, *Kibyōshi sōran 5.*

grab attention with a splash of vivid colors in some kind of humorous, silly, unlikely, puzzling, or otherwise allusive composition.[27] Accordingly, the typical frontispiece less faithfully depicts an actual scene from the ensuing story than it presents a loosely inspired image aimed to entice the prospective reader or buyer. As part of this strategy, some frontispieces deploy a logic of the surreptitious or even the libidinous gaze—though not as titillating as many of the covers to American pulp magazines circa the 1930s. The covers to the three volumes of Kyōden's *Familiar Bestsellers*, for instance, implicitly compare the story to something one might behold in a peepshow—then all the rage in Edo.

The frontispiece served as an imprint, then, pictorially announcing its genre (especially *vis-à-vis* earlier comicbooks) and, just as importantly, visually identifying a work as having been issued by a specific publisher in a particular year. A key feature of An'ei-Tenmei culture being the acceleration of faddishness through published materials, the *kibyōshi* displays a heightened sensitivity to cultural, if not chronological, time. As a rule, the frontispieces of all *kibyōshi* issued by a single publisher in one season, regardless of the author, employed the same visually distinguishable base motif. For instance, all the *kibyōshi* that Tsutaya Jūzaburō published at the beginning of 1785 employed the same picture scroll (*emakimono*) motif on their covers. This is true of Kyōden's *Playboy* (**Figure 1.10**), Tōrai Sanna's *Chop Not the Roots of the Money Tree* (**Figure 1.11**), and so on. The author's pseudonym and the title of each work, along with Tsutaya's mark, appear on the rolled-up portion of the scroll. The scene depicted on the unfurled portion is loosely based on a scene from the ensuing story.

Most *kibyōshi* were published at the beginning of the new year—which, by the old lunar calendar, marked the start of spring. This means, for one thing, that a work was technically written the year prior to its issuance. For *Playboy* to have been released at the beginning of 1785, then, it must have been written in 1784. Judging by the financial pressures on authors as well as publishers, it might be assumed that nobody was inclined to sit on a piece any longer than necessary after having written it.

For another thing, the timing of release typically affected the form as well as the content of a *kibyōshi*. Since most works were issued during the New Year, many stories refer to the season's festivities. Furthermore, the practice of presenting a *kibyōshi* in a paper coverslip, as useful as it was in keeping loose fascicles together, more importantly derived from the way that collections of madcap verse were issued in decorative wrappings in mock imitation of the presentation of serious *haikai* poetry as a New Year's

---

27. "Properly employed," Eisner says of the first page or "splash" of the Western comicbook—though this can apply to the *kibyōshi*'s frontispiece—"it seizes the reader's attention and prepares his attitude for the events to follow." Eisner, *Comics and Sequential Art*, p. 62.

gift (*oseibo*). Thus, just as *haikai* verse displayed a sensitivity to the particular season by the inclusion of a "seasonal word" (*kigo*), so too did the base motif of the *kibyōshi* frontispiece typically nod to its season. The frontispiece, therefore, sometimes contains a visual-verbal pun on the Chinese zodiac sign associated with that particular year. The jinglebell-like objects that figure prominently in the upper third of the frontispieces to Kyōden's *Swingers*, called "monkey fasteners" (*kukurizaru*), signal the year of the monkey (*sarudoshi*), 1788. Moreover, although these fasteners were used as children's bedding ornaments, they were also associated with the season's festivities in the pleasure quarters, since there was the practice among courtesans of using these fasteners as talismans to retain or "hold fast" their clients in the coming year.

The monkey fastener, thus, spells not only the year of issuance but, more subtly, the specific season. This was a useful distinction for a publisher to make, since during a particularly successful year, he might enjoy two or even three issuing seasons—though the main one always occurred at the beginning of the year. Accordingly, different visual base motifs were employed for *each* publishing season. Kyōden's *Playboy* makes for an interesting case study as it was one of the few works popular enough to be reissued with

(*left*) Fig. 1.10 Frontispiece employing the picture-scroll motif that graces the various *kibyōshi* issued by Tsutaya Jūzaburō in the New Year's publishing season of 1785. From the first edition of *Playboy, Roasted à la Edo* (*Edo umare uwaki no kabayaki*, 1785), a *kibyōshi* written by Santō Kyōden, illustrated by Kitao Masanobu, and published by Tsutaya Jūzaburō. Courtesy of Hōsa bunko.

(*right*) Fig. 1.11 Frontispiece employing a picture-scroll motif. From *Chop Not the Roots of the Money Tree* (*Kiruna no ne kara kane no naruki*, 1785), a *kibyōshi* written by Tōrai Sanna, illustrated by Kitagawa Chiyojo, and published by Tsutaya Jūzaburō. Courtesy of the University of Kyoto, Faculty of Letters Library.

Fig. 1.12 The second and third frontispieces from the third edition of Kyōden's *Playboy, Roasted à la Edo* (*Edo umare uwaki no kabayaki*), issued in 1793. Reprinted in Tanahashi, *Kibyōshi sōran 5*, p. 390. Courtesy of Seishōdō shoten.

newly commissioned cover art not once but twice—and both times within the same calendar year. The first reissue, which is to say the second edition of the work, appeared during the primary season, at the beginning of 1793. Its base motif was a mirrored vanity (*kyōdai*), supposedly reflecting a scene from the story (see **Figure 6.1**), though also playfully suggesting that it is the reader him-or herself who is reflected. Other *kibyōshi* issued by the Tsu-taya that season likewise employ the same mirror-stand motif. The second reissue of *Playboy*, which is to say the third edition, came out midyear and, thus, contains a completely different base motif (**Figure 1.12**). This differentiation among editions suggests that cover art boasted specialized conventions with which readers were expected to be more or less familiar.

At a more basic level, the parts of the *kibyōshi* cover add up to signify the whole. The humor of its title (often containing puns, parodies, and palindromes, as well as a playful gloss) and the particulars of the publishing information confirm the message conveyed instantaneously by the format (the middling size, the whimsicality of the illustration, and the once viridian, now yellowed, color of its cover); namely, that this is a *kibyōshi*.[28]

A Silent Yet Crowded Daydream

Little is known about the sociology of the *kibyōshi*'s readership, let alone that of mid-Edo period popular literature. Statistics about the composition of readers according to class, gender, age, geography, educational background, profession, and so on are rare to nonexistent. And though scholarship on the eighteenth-

---

28. In the early days of the *kibyōshi*, when its cover was still indistinguishable from that of the bluebook (*aohon*), its title must have carried more of the burden of indicating adult content.

century woodblock publishing industry is profuse, direct evidence about circulation numbers, let alone readership, is measly. Educated guesswork, speculation, and conjecture are, thus, the necessary if crude tools in playing the numbers game, a game that often yields less clarity and consensus than queries and disagreement. One is therefore compelled to give more credence to anecdotal evidence, secondary sources, and clues found within works themselves than one might otherwise prefer. Such an endeavor is naturally fraught with peril, for there can be worlds of difference among the addressed reader, the ideal reader, and the actual reader—especially when it comes to a genre of comic fiction. Since 43 percent of all statistics are worthless, as an old saw has it, the only firm conclusion is that there are no firm conclusions. Thus, just the most preliminary remarks are possible here.

Judging by such artifacts as publishing catalogues, government documents, and import lists, for instance, readers of the *kibyōshi* must have been *exclusively* uneducated "women and children" (*jochū-samagata onko-samagata*). One of the earliest English-language works on the *kibyōshi* seems to have taken such frequently occurring phrases literally, calling the genre the "undisputed queen" of comicbooks.[29] Indeed, the visual evidence of Masanobu's *Pageant of the Latest Beauties*, as well as many other contemporary woodblock prints, appears to imply a female readership—and a young one at that (**Figure 1.13** and **Color Figure 1**).

On the other hand, to the extent that the ideal reader—who can be surmised if not actually reconstructed through such things as the various literary allusions in a work—more closely approximates the actual reader than does this addressed reader, it is likely that actual readers were primarily well educated, worldly, theatergoing, pleasure-quarter-frequenting townsmen (*chōnin*) of Edo—low-ranking samurai as well as merchants (and possibly even some artisans)—mostly in their twenties and thirties, with leisure time and disposable income aplenty. This is because the kind of sophisticated reader who had ideally mastered nothing less than the entire literary, dramatic, and visual imagination of traditional Japan—for the range of allusions in the *kibyōshi* is that sweeping—was predominantly male. Aside from the fact that men were far more likely to be literate than women, since men attended school in greater proportion to women, men were also the primary frequenters of the sorts of Floating World establishments routinely represented in the *kibyōshi*.

If the average *kibyōshi* readers were adult males, why do so many *kibyōshi* refer to them as "women and children"? Surely this is in jest. When the narrator of *Familiar Bestsellers* addresses his readers as "you kids," for instance, he probably does so kiddingly (not unlike the way late-night TV talk show host David Letterman, say, humorously addresses his audience). Kyōden

---

29. Akimoto, *The Twilight of Yedo*, p. 143.

Fig. 1.13 A young geisha engrossed in a *kibyōshi*. The inscription reads "Ochie of the Koiseya at Kobikichō, Shin'ya-shiki" (*Kobikichō shin'yashiki koiseya Ochie*). From the multicolored woodblock series "Edo's Celebrated Beauties" (*Edo kōmei bijin*) by Kitagawa Utamaro, ca. 1792–1793. At the time, Ochie would have been just under twenty years old. Courtesy of the Chiba City Museum of Art.

thereby perpetuates the "wink-wink-nudge-nudge" running joke about the genre's tongue-in-cheek pretense of being no more than a comicbook for the semiliterate. Mizuno has suggested that this gag was also a clever means of forestalling governmental wrath, effectively preempting censorship by self-mockingly dismissing such works as "silly kid stuff—nothing to get exercised over."[30]

That said, it goes without saying that the ideal reader would have been no younger than an adolescent, for he needed to be old enough to have been both initiated into the Floating World of pleasure as well as thoroughly schooled in the various literary traditions. Some actual readers, on the other hand, may have been considerably younger, for several *kibyōshi* seem to have been used as coloring books for aspiring artists unable to stay between the lines. And some authors and illustrators of the *kibyōshi* began their work in their teens.

Still, if a fictional protagonist is any indication, Enjirō in Kyōden's *Playboy* begins reading about the romantic heroes of the stage when he is around nineteen or twenty. Being so sheltered and inexperienced, though, his readings turn out to be comical misreadings. Beneath the surface of this comedy looms the suggestion, perhaps, that the *kibyōshi* and other like theatrical texts may have sometimes served as a bridge spanning the worlds of juvenile and adult reading. Could the young courtesan trainee in *Pageant of the Latest Beauties* be interested in the *kibyōshi* as a guidebook to learn about the adult world around her? Something similar may pertain to the modern *manga* and even the Western comicbook, incidentally. No small number of Japanese adults today will privately admit that they taught themselves Chinese graphs in some measure by reading the Japanese gloss to such graphs within modern *manga*. Similarly, Art Spiegelman claims to have learned to read closely by virtue of his early exposure to comics.[31]

When Enjirō pores over his theatrical texts at the very beginning of *Playboy*, he is shown lying on the floor near a lantern, alone in the privacy of his own room. In fact, there are scenes of such solitary reading in many *kibyōshi*, even if only parodic. Kyōden's *Rosei's Dream—The Night Before* (*Rosei ga yume sono zenjitsu*, 1791), for instance, opens with the Chinese character Lu Sheng (Rosei, in Japanese) engrossed in a perhaps secret stash of Japanese comicbooks. These scenes, parodic though they might be, depict reading for pleasure as something inducing a trance-like absorption, transporting the depicted reader into "a silent yet crowded daydream," as Jean Marie Goulemot so memorably put it.[32] Or, as Yoshida Kenkō said centuries earlier, "The pleasantest of all diversions is to sit alone under the lamp, a book spread out before you, and to make friends with people of a distant past

---

30. Mizuno, *Kibyōshi sharebon no sekai*, p. 164.
31. Interview on National Public Radio, December 21, 2001.
32. Goulemot, *Forbidden Texts*, p. viii.

you have never known."[33] What is striking about such scenes in the *kibyōshi*, however, is that they depict individual readers less laboring over impenetrable classics than engaged in the leisurely pursuit of contemporary literature. *Familiar Bestsellers* portrays the members of a book club gathered to chat about their literary opinions of the latest works. All in all, these *kibyōshi* celebrate the pleasures of reading as something that can be enjoyed by the masses, not just the aristocratic elite, even the masses who are on the verge of adulthood. This suggests that the *kibyōshi* was conscious of itself as a comicbook in the sense I have defined it, as an entertaining, mass-produced, visual-verbal genre for adult readers, especially among the common people.

Another frequently addressed reader within the *kibyōshi* is that of the average—though not necessarily particularly literate—member of the theatergoing public. *Familiar Bestsellers*, for instance, begins with the grandiose theatrical salutation "Ladies and gentlemen!"[34] In fact, later within the same work, Kyōden casts his net even wider, portraying the *kibyōshi* genre itself as appealing to the broadest possible readership—"regardless of their social standing," as the narrator puts it. Although this portrayal must have been wishful thinking on Kyōden's part, a ploy to "write" his own success in the genre, it may also have been meant as a call to other authors to cater to a cross-section of the general populace—a kind of manifesto of a popular readership. Still, it may also have been a truthful description of actual readers, for Kyōden tried his hand at the *kibyōshi* believing it to possess exactly this kind of broad appeal.

Indeed, the *kibyōshi* depicted and aimed for a general audience. Granted, the most famous Edo-period work of comic literature to portray members from every level of society in their naked quiddity is probably Shikitei Sanba's (1776–1822) funnybook *Bathhouse to the Floating World* (*Ukiyoburo*, 1809–1813), but the *kibyōshi* of previous decades had already sufficiently warmed the waters. It is possible that Sanba's cross-section of society trope was less a bolt from the blue than a natural progression, in other words, since not only did he write in the *kibyōshi* genre before helping to forge the funnybook genre, but one of his mentors was none other than Kyōden.

Regarding size, although it would be impossible to plot changes in the numbers of readers over the heyday of the *kibyōshi*, it is axiomatic that the genre's readership was substantial. The fact that the cover art of the *kibyōshi* was typically multicolored suggests that works were indeed reaching a mass audience, for color was costly. It certainly would not have been lavished upon works unless the publisher was confident or at least reasonably hopeful that a significant return could be made upon his capital investment.

More concretely, there must have been enough readers to consume the titles that were being produced. Mori estimates that more than 2,000 works

---

33. In Keene, *Essays in Idleness*, p. 12.
34. Literally "East and West! East and West!" (*Tōzai tōzai*).

were issued in the three decades of the genre's heyday.[35] Likewise, Tana-hashi lists over 2,000 works in his *Kibyōshi Overview*. Since Mori and Tanahashi count only extant works, and it is reasonable to assume that some works have been lost to posterity, a less conservative estimate of 2,500–3,000 works might not be drastically misguided. This would mean that perhaps as many as 100 *kibyōshi* were, on average, published annually. If spread out over the course of a year, one could read almost two new works per week. This fig-ure is hardly trifling. It certainly surpasses the output of a single modern *manga* magazine, which tends to be issued weekly.[36]

But what of the numbers of copies produced? Again, there is a paucity of information. Still, during the second half of the eighteenth century, suc-cessful works of popular literature seem to have sold in the thousands of copies per run. Gennai's *Rootless Grass* (*Nenashigusa*, 1763), an important early mock-sermon book, is said to have sold over 3,000 copies in its first year. A couple of decades later, successful works in the multivolume comicbook—a slightly longer but exponentially more complicated genre to produce than the *kibyōshi*—typically sold between 5,000 and 8,000 copies per run, according to Konta.[37] This jibes perfectly with the figures for the average multivolume by Kyōden or Bakin, said also to have sold between 5,000 and 8,000 copies.[38] Bakin, a fiction author himself who nonetheless aimed at accuracy, reckoned that a smash hit during this period might sell between 10,000 and 15,000 cop-ies per run.[39] And sales of Harumachi's bitingly satirical *The Twin Arts, Par-roted* (*Ōmugaeshi bunbu no futamichi*, 1789) reputedly soared over 15,000 copies—perhaps making it the all-time bestselling *kibyōshi* in a single edition.[40] Overall, these numbers portray a sizable market, which seems entirely plausible *vis-à-vis* rising literacy rates and the growing number of publishers.

Assuming these estimates are not wildly exaggerated, then, averaging the low estimate of 5,000 copies per run with the high of 15,000, the greatest bestsellers, such as Kyōden's *Playboy*—issued in *three* editions—might con-ceivably have enjoyed a total print run of anywhere from 15,000 to as many as 45,000 copies. Taking the middle road, perhaps some 30,000 copies were floating around in a city with approximately one million inhabitants. This is quite amazing when one considers that the mega-hits at the top of the *New York Times* Bestseller List rarely reach 3 percent of the American population. It may well be that in the age before television in Japan, the *kibyōshi* and the kabuki theater delivered the most popular forms of entertainment.

---

35. Mori, *Mori Senzō chosakushū zoku hen 7*, p. 368.

36. Even if one considers the dozens of *manga* titles issued weekly in all of Japan, if the difference in the scale of populations is taken into consideration, the *kibyōshi* still holds it own.

37. Konta, *Edo no hon'yasan*, p. 144.

38. Nakamura, *Nakamura Yukihiko chojutsushū 14*, pp. 158–161.

39. Takizawa Bakin, *Kinsei mono no hon*, p. 58.

40. Matsuki, *Tsutaya Jūzaburō*, p. 83.

Admittedly, the number ten thousand, like "a zillion" in English, is a general expression of uncountable quantity. Thus, there was probably less output than contemporary sources estimate. Still, if only 5,000 copies were produced per run, there were about three copies of *Playboy* for every 200 denizens of Edo. But even in the case of the lower numbers, there still were probably more copies of *Playboy* than printed versions of *The Tale of Genji*. And anyway, there is no reason to suppose that exactly the same readers bought copies of every *kibyōshi* that was published. It is more likely that a larger set of readers than 3 percent of the population purchased fewer titles than were issued each year. A completely unsubstantiated though not completely unreasonable figure, therefore, might be that 10 percent of the population of Edo either read or owned a *kibyōshi*. Unless otherwise proven, this might be a convenient rule of thumb, if one must be proffered.

That said, until more precise statistics come to light, and more is known about the scale and nature of circulation networks to other parts of Japan, let us assume that Edo's *kibyōshi* drain is roughly offset by the extension of lingering copies through various means. There was a sizeable industry of lending libraries (*kashihon'ya* or *kashibon'ya*), not to mention secondhand booksellers who peddled their goods on foot, at flea markets, even in *bouquinistes* along major rivers.[41] Also, there seem to have been informal networks of friends—perhaps like the reading groups of the sort depicted in *Familiar Bestsellers*—who shared copies of books among themselves, a practice known as "circulating reads" (*mawashiyomi*). Unauthorized handmade facsimiles are known to have been made of various books, too, so it is not unrealistic to think that this practice extended to the *kibyōshi*.[42]

One complication to any speculation about the scale of readership based on the number of copies produced per title is that these figures do not necessarily translate into consumption. The number of copies produced in Edo cannot be the exact number of copies consumed there, since not all copies of a *kibyōshi* remained within the metropolis. Some are known to have journeyed to outlying regions.

Take the case of Hirado, an island-peninsula about as far flung from Edo geographically as one could get and still be on one of the major islands

---

41. In Edo alone there were twelve guilds of booklenders, and while individual lenders went from neighborhood to neighborhood hauling their merchandise in pack loads (*furoshiki*), they also sometimes set up shop at places such as the Yanagiwara flea market (*Yanagiwara no hoshimise*), located on the south bank of the Kanda River (near Asakusa, in close proximity to the Yoshiwara), and in small riverbank stalls. Typically, books were rented in five-day periods for one tenth the actual price. For a brief discussion in English of the history of these book lenders, see Kornicki, "The Publisher's Go-Between," and Moriya, "Urban Networks and Information Networks." In Japanese, see Konta, *Edo no hon'yasan*, and Nagatomo, "Hon'ya kashihon, kashihon'ya no shuppan."

42. Kornicki notes that ". . . it was surprisingly common in the Tokugawa period for manuscript copies to be made of printed books." In Kornicki, *The Book in Japan*, p. 103.

of Japan.[43] Although one might imagine that the *kibyōshi* never reached Hirado in significant numbers, the personal collection of the local daimyo Matsuura Seizan (1760–1841) that survives in the Matsuura Museum of History contains just under 340 titles, including Kyōden's *Familiar Bestsellers, Playboy,* and *Swingers.*[44] Seizan, admittedly something of a literatus, no doubt collected these during his required residence in Edo, though he does not seem to acknowledge as much anywhere in his massive diary (at least from the little of it I thumbed through).[45] One therefore wonders if, once back in Hirado, Seizan kept his collection to himself or shared it with others as a sign of his putative urbanity? The very fact that his collection has been preserved not only speaks to Seizan's enthusiasm for the *kibyōshi* but also raises the possibility that he may have regarded the genre as a kind of cultural capital.

One also wonders if authors in Edo were even aware that their works were being read abroad. Rural folk are not infrequently the butt of jokes in the *kibyōshi,* so authors certainly did not particularly cater to those residing outside the city. On the other hand, works such as Harumachi's *Master Flashgold's Splendiferous Dream,* which describes a rural samurai coming to Edo in the hopes of striking it rich, no doubt afforded a vicarious thrill to those who had never been to the shogun's capital, let alone to its glamorous pleasure quarters. Just because the *kibyōshi* was devoted to the people, fads, places, slang, and styles of Edo and its Floating World, in other words, does not mean that the genre's readership was limited to that city. Readers may have viewed the *kibyōshi* as a fun guidebook of sorts, even if they had no intention of ever actually visiting. There was certainly no industry-wide restriction, let alone any governmental policy, about keeping the genre inside Edo's city limits. In short, there is no telling how many *kibyōshi* migrated. It is possible that dozens if not hundreds of hitherto undiscovered titles are locked away, along with swords and other personal treasures, in family storehouses throughout Japan, just waiting to be discovered.

Even less is understood of the possible production of the *kibyōshi* outside the shogun's capital. This probably has to do with the fact that it has long been an article of faith that the *kibyōshi* was autochthonous to Edo. "The *kibyōshi,*" writes Mori, typifying the conventional thinking, "is a literature local to Edo."[46] Indeed, most *kibyōshi* are set there. All *kibyōshi* seem to have been written, illustrated, and published there, too. The *kibyōshi* is even taken to be one of the only major genres of mid-Edo period popular literature

---

43. Today Hirado is most quickly accessible from Hakata by speedboat, or from Nagasaki by car over a recently constructed bridge.

44. The author wishes to express his gratitude to the National Institute of Japanese Literature for a generous traveling grant that allowed him to survey the collection at the Matsuura shiryō hakubutsukan.

45. Nakamura and Nakano, *Kasshi yawa,* in six volumes.

46. Mori, "Kibyōshi kaidai josetsu," p. 333.

that did not originate even in part in Kamigata.[47] But if the *kibyōshi* was read outside Edo, is it not also conceivable that it was produced outside Edo as well? After all, composition of the closely allied fashionbook started in Edo and spread to Kamigata, where it was especially popular in Osaka during the early decades of the nineteenth century (since the Kyōhō Reforms that curtailed the Kasei cultural efflorescence were not as strictly enforced there as in Edo)—why did the same thing not happen with the *kibyō-shi*? Publishing centers in other important castle towns and metropolitan areas like Kyoto, Nagoya, and Osaka mass produced their own popular literatures, and most of the major publishers in these cities maintained outlets and even branch offices in Edo, where they might have produced *kibyōshi*. So why does it seem they did not?[48] Could there have been such a thing as the Himeji *kibyōshi*? Intriguing a prospect though this might be, until evidence to the contrary comes to light, the *kibyōshi* can only be defined in terms of Edo. Thus, to the conundrum, "If a *kibyōshi* is produced in the backwoods, and nobody from Edo can be read about in that story, is it still a *kibyōshi*?" the answer must be in the negative.

In conclusion, what this brief foray into readership tells us, and what the numbers suggest, is that the *kibyōshi* may have been one of the most widely read forms of popular literature—if not literature in general—up to that point in Japanese literary history. The best conjecture is that the addressed readership of women and children had little if anything to do with the ideal readership, to say nothing of actual readers, who were probably a sizable proportion of the educated, adult townsmen of Edo. This is certainly true of the *authors* of the *kibyōshi*, as we will see presently. Still, since the complexion of the actual readership has yet to be established with anything resembling certainty, more questions have been raised than answered. How did readership in various cities differ in terms of such things as age, class, and background? Were texts read out loud as well as silently? Were they read in groups, as some scholars have speculated, as well as by solitary readers? Would a shop clerk, say, have been as likely as a samurai intellectual to read such comicbooks? Did young courtesans in training actually squabble over *kibyōshi*?

Author, Artist, Auteur

One class of *kibyōshi* reader about whom a little more is known is the writer. All writers are by definition readers, though this pertains especially to the case of the *kibyōshi*, since aside from the genre's intense intertextuality, writers often portray themselves within their works as readers of previous literary works. So who wrote *kibyōshi*? What was his class? Was he always a

---

47. Genres of *gesaku* that originated in Kamigata include: the *hanashibon*, the *akabon*, the *kyōka*, and probably even the *dangibon*.

48. See, however, the groundbreaking collection of Nagoya *gesaku* in Hino, *Kyōto daigaku zō daisōbon kisho shūsei 14.*

he? How many of her or him were there? Was there a particular stereotypical personality who was presumed to be most suited to the task, like the "nerd" of Western comicbooks or the *otaku* of modern *manga*?

Like so many other genres of popular literature, the *kibyōshi* was written under a pseudonym. This has slightly complicated investigations into authorship. Until relatively recently, it was not unheard of for an eminent scholar to slip, writing about the artist Kitao Masanobu and the author Santō Kyōden, to cite an infamous case, as though these were not simply two appellations used by the same person, but two different people entirely. Accordingly, lingering questions remain about such basic facts as how many discrete authors wrote in the genre. Mori singles out a couple dozen major writers for special treatment without providing an exhaustive list. Tanahashi, on the other hand, enumerates over a hundred pseudonyms in his five-volume compendium. Since it is known that some authors used multiple pseudonyms even within a single genre, how many actual human beings this boils down to is anyone's guess.

Authors of the *kibyōshi*, no doubt like those of other forms of popular literature, were almost exclusively adult males. This is more or less clear from what little is known about the real-life identities of authors. Furthermore, aside from the fact that the majority of educated denizens of Edo were men, authorial pseudonyms were overwhelmingly masculine. Granted, some women could have written under such pseudonyms, though no evidence to that effect—certainly not on any significant scale—has, to the best of my knowledge, come to light. Also, the scarcity of feminine pseudonyms itself suggests that female authorship of the *kibyōshi* tended to be rare if not actually nonexistent, or at least not regarded as a viable marketing ploy.

One exception would seem to be Kyōden's younger sister, Yone (ca. 1771–1788), who prior to her untimely death at age seventeen, was poised to become more than a minor presence in the world of playful literature. Under the penname Kurotobi Shikibu, or "Lady Blackhawk" (a takeoff on *Tale of Genji* author Murasaki Shikibu, "Lady Lavender"), she had already glided onto the *gesaku* scene by producing a small but respectable corpus of madcap poems and a *soupçon* of *kibyōshi*—most notably *The Well of Secret Love* (*Hito shirazu omoi somei*, 1784). Some scholars express doubt about the authenticity of Yone's authorship at such a tender age, insinuating that Kyōden himself ghostwrote her works as a kind of bid for publicity, the novelty of a female *kibyōshi* writer calculated to grab attention.[49] Yet this dismissal ignores the fact that mid-Edo saw plenty of precociously talented authors, poets, and artists. Ōta Nanpo published his celebrated *Collected Works of*

---

49. Tanahashi, for instance, characterizes the attribution of Yone's authorship of this *kibyōshi* as dubious on the stated grounds that she would have been only about fourteen years old at the time of its composition; see Tanahashi, *Kibyōshi sōran 1*, pp. 562–563. Mori states a similar opinion in *Mori Senzō chosakushū zoku hen 7*, p. 346.

Fig. 1.14 Comicbook authors Santō Kyōden and sister Kurotobi Shikibu in the opening scene of *Tale of the Two Tambours* (*Jidai sewa nichō tsuzumi*, 1788), a *kibyōshi* written by Santō Kyōden and illustrated by Kitagawa Yukimaro. Courtesy of Tokyo Metropolitan Central Library, Kaga Collection.

Master Sleepyhead (*Neboke sensei bunshū*, 1767) when he was in his late teens.[50] And Kyōden began illustrating *kibyōshi* in his early teens—slightly younger than Yone would have been when penning *Secret Love*.

Kyōden wryly comments on the ostensible absence of female writers by including a scene in one of his *kibyōshi* in which his younger sister consents to reticence vociferously (**Figure 1.14**):

[Narrative] "There are hardly any women in comicbooks!" complains Kyōden's kid sister, Lady Blackhawk. So it is she upon whom the curtain opens, little more than a prop really, seated idly like some inert puppet.

[Kyōden] You're probably dying to speak up, but there's too much inserted text here, so keep quiet.

---

50. For a transcribed edition, see Hamada, *Ōta Nanpo zenshū 1*, pp. 341–366.

[Lady Blackhawk] I really *would* like to chime in, but I won't make so much as a peep![51]

A woman may also have illustrated several *kibyōshi*. This was Kitagawa Chiyojo. Although this penname implies that she was a female disciple of the *ukiyoe* master Kitagawa Utamaro, next to nothing is known about her (including her dates).[52] Some scholars believe that Utamaro—perhaps following the lead of his friend Kyōden?—concocted the Chiyojo name himself as a feminine cover for his own compositions.[53] If not actively determined to debunk the slightest indication of female literary or artistic creativity, male-dominated scholarship itself in Japan regrettably has been mostly mute on the sexual politics of artistic self-fashioning within Edo-period popular literature. Until there is more solid evidence to the contrary, the existence of a couple of feminine pseudonyms alone cannot be taken as indicative of some kind of short-lived Edo-period renaissance of the female hand in Japanese letters. Clearly, there needs to be additional work (to borrow Virginia Woolf's notion of an imaginary sibling of Shakespeare) on all Kyōden's Sisters.

In terms of social class, most of the early *kibyōshi* writers were samurai. This may come as something of a surprise, since one might expect that only merchants or artisans would have sullied their hands in creating commercial, mass-produced "pulp fiction." The mental image of a deadly serious warrior dashing off comicbooks, perhaps chuckling good-naturedly to himself in the process, might even strike some people as jolting. Yet samurai were the ones with the regular stipends, higher education, and leisure for such amateurish pursuits. Many of the *kibyōshi* greats, like Koikawa Harumachi (1744–1789) and Ōta Nanpo, were in fact members of the lower echelons of the samurai class whose bureaucratic responsibilities were petty enough to allow them ample free time. Some, however, cut slightly less undistinguished figures. Hōseidō Kisanji (1735–1813), for one, was deputy to his daimyo, serving in Edo as the High Commissioner (*rusuiyaku*) of Akita domain.

One of the monumental ironies of the *kibyōshi*, if not mid-Edo popular fiction in general, is that arguably the most powerful samurai in the land and the chief architect of the draconian Kansei Reforms—which among other things censured the leading *kibyōshi* authors—is believed to have *possibly* written one such frivolous piece himself. Granted, this haughty lion of

---

51. The piece is *Tale of the Two Tambours: An Historical-Domestic Drama* (*Jidai sewa: Nichō tsuzumi*, 1788), written by Kyōden and illustrated by Kitagawa Yukimaro. For an annotated edition, see Koike, *Edo no gesaku ehon 6*, pp. 133–146.

52. Chiyojo seems to have illustrated several celebrated *kibyōshi*, such as *Kiruna no ne kara kane no naruki* (1785) by Tōrai Sanna; *Nenshi onnrei chō* (1784) and *Kinpira kodomo asobi* (1784) by Ōta Nanpo (under the pseudonym Yomo no Akara); and *Ganri yasuri no kogiri akinai* (1785) by Koikawa Sukimachi. See Mizuno, *NKBT 59*, p. 133; Koike, *Edo no gesaku ehon 6*, p. 40; and Tanahashi, *Kibyōshi sōran 5*, pp. 523–526, pp. 611–612, and passim.

53. Tanahashi, *Kibyōshi sōran 5*, p. 123.

Shirakawa domain, whose name is known to every student of Tokugawa history, composed his satirical *The Seigneurial Type* (*Daimyō katagi*, ca. 1784) on the sly, under an alias (Kyokuhō), and prior to assuming the mantle of Chief Senior Counselor to the Shogun.[54] Nonetheless, that Matsudaira Sadanobu may have dabbled clandestinely in comicbook writing certainly stands in stark contrast with the fact that two centuries later, when former Prime Minister Miyazawa Kiichi agreed to publish an opinion column in a nationally syndicated newspaper, he did so openly in comicstrip form.[55] Clearly, attitudes about using cartoons to express political views have come a long way from Sadanobu's satire to Miyazawa's *manga*.

In the early years of the *kibyōshi*, only the most successful merchants could afford to pursue such extracurricular activities. Kyōden is the prime example. Even before becoming self-sufficient as a *kibyōshi* author, which allowed him to launch his own tobacco shop in the heart of swanky Ginza and ransom not one but two courtesans (though not at the same time), he helped manage his father's thriving pawnshop. As the *kibyōshi* genre became more demonstrably lucrative, however, merchants and artisans began putting pen to paper in droves—though none of them seems to have quit his day job: Kishida Tohō (d. 1788), who penned *The Kabuki-Crazed Uncouth Grandee* (*Kyōgenzuki yabo na daimyō*, 1784), like Ichiba Tsūshō (1739–1812) for that matter, earned his keep mounting pictures; Yoneyama Teiga (dates unknown) scraped by as a scribe; Koikawa Yukimachi (dates unknown), a disciple of Harumachi, made a killing as a physician, though this did not prevent him from applying some of his scientific know-how to *The Virtuous Prosperity-Boosting Specs* (*Sakaemasu megane no toku*, 1790); Sensa Banbetsu (dates unknown) somehow subsisted on his activities in Dutch Studies (*Rangaku*), which is to say Western science; and Shitchin Manpō (dates unknown) sweetened his coffers as a confectioner.[56]

It is no secret that the shogunal government granted some merchants honorary rank as samurai for financial services rendered. What is less widely known is that a few samurai went so far as to become merchants in order to take up writing popular literature professionally, as their chief occupation, as was the case with Bakin, one of Kyōden's disciples, who would become the preeminent author in the reading book (*yomihon*) genre. Another prominent case in point is that of Hanasanjin (1790–1858), who legally renounced his samurai status in order to devote himself to writing fashionbooks, multivolume comicbooks, and melodramatic "sentiment books" (*ninjōbon*) especially. Among *kibyōshi* authors, one deliciously immoderate case is that of

---

54. Iwasaki makes the case for Sadanobu's authorship of this piece in "Portrait of a Daimyo." Strictly speaking, this piece is something of a hybrid *kibyōshi*, as Iwasaki points out. And although it was never actually published, four of Sadanobu's retainers seem to have copied it separately.

55. Mentioned in Schodt, *Dreamland Japan*, p. 19.

56. Seigle, *Yoshiwara*, p. 143.

Tōrai Sanna (1744–1810). Barely making ends meet as a low-ranking samurai, Sanna turned to more profitable endeavors, such as running a bordello and writing comicbooks. Little wonder that one of his most celebrated and, thus, profitable pieces was titled *Chop Not the Roots of the Money Tree (Kiruna no ne kara kane no naruki,* 1785).[57]

Sanna does not seem to have renounced his status as a samurai outright, though his various extracurricular activities probably placed him on the far side of acceptable warrior behavior. In fact, some scholars have suggested that it was no accident that so many authors of genres of playful literature like the *kibyōshi* were low-ranking samurai who felt acutely disenfranchised from the sociopolitical system. The standard thinking is that these men wrote as a form of escapism from the tedium and frustrations of their lot. Aside from standing to gain more financially relative to their merchant counterparts, most of these samurai were unconscionably talented individuals who were unable to bring their various gifts fully to bear. The samurai may have been on top of the class heap, but within that uppermost crust, many a brilliant individual went undervalued. These men tended not to rise to their level of *in*competence, so to speak, but to remain frozen in dead-end positions for which they were exasperatingly overqualified.

The prototype of this "marginalized talent" theory was Hiraga Gennai (1728–1779), a samurai with ties to the remote domain of Takamatsu on Shikoku, the least sizable of the major islands of Japan. The word "polymath" is invariably mentioned in the same breath as "Gennai," for he was a da Vinciesque character. In science, Gennai distinguished himself by his encyclopedic state-sponsored botanical cataloguing, notable mining ventures, the discovery and application of a homespun Japanese asbestos, and experimentation with electrostatic generators (*erekiteru*), to name but a few sparkling examples (**Figure 1.15**). He also participated in Dutch Studies, which no doubt positioned him to become one of the pioneers of Western-style oil painting (*aburae*) in Japan. In literature, Gennai wrote everything from treatises to puppet plays. But it was his success in the mock-sermon book (*dangibon*) that won him the reputation as one of the early inventors of playful literature (*gesaku*), though he hardly created either from scratch. Still, for all Gennai's wide-ranging activities and obvious flamboyance, he nonetheless felt thwarted by bureaucratic restrictions. Something of this frustration is said to come across in his writings (and was a key factor in his

---

57. For annotated versions of this *kibyōshi*—which was one of the works that female artist Chiyojo illustrated—see both Mizuno, *NKBT 59*, pp. 115–133, and Koike, *Edo no gesaku ehon 6*, pp. 5–40. Sanna also wrote about brothels, as in *Those Amorous Three Religions (Sankyō shiki,* 1783), a fashionbook about Confucius, Laozi, Buddha, and a Shinto sun god disporting themselves in a Yoshiwara establishment. For a transcribed edition, see Mizuno, *Sharebon taisei 12*, pp. 119–138. For more on Sanna in English, see Johnson, "Tōrai Sanna and the Creation of Difference."

Fig. 1.15 An electrostatic generating box (*erekiteru*) used to what at the time must have seemed to readers like shocking effect. From *Trilateral Babble* (*Wakaran monogatari*, 1803), a *kibyōshi* written by Kanwatei Onitake and illustrated by Kakō (Hokusai). Courtesy of Tokyo Metropolitan Central Library, Kaga Collection.

decision to become a *rōnin*). A few scholars have even speculated that Gennai was marginalized for his open homosexuality, though that assumes a homophobia among Edo-period Japanese that other scholars have contested. Certainly he ended up on the fringes of respectable society, for he died in jail, the apparent victim of a lovers' quarrel.[58]

Although none of the other *gesaku* authors quite matches Gennai's sweeping scope or colorfulness, he seems to have become the chief model whom Nakamura and others have in mind when claiming that the majority of authors wrote as a form of escapism. It is certainly true that many of the samurai writers came to Edo from other provinces, and so may have felt geographically marginalized. And Hino Tatsuo has proposed that the madcap verse coterie served as a kind of utopian space that allowed such dis-

---

58. For the standard work on Gennai, see Haga, *Hiraga Gennai*.

affected intellectuals temporary solace from the strictures of an essentially feudalistic society.[59] Hibbett wryly describes Nanpo as "a samurai of high aspirations but low rank."[60] What better way to come to terms with, if not to symbolically resist, the malaise of marginalization than to write humorous works employing such devices as exaggeration and inversion?

It is certainly true that many commentators have opined that not just satire but humor in its multifaceted forms is often used for psychological venting. In what could be described as an expressive theory of joking (reminiscent of Ki no Tsurayuki's influential expressive theory of Japanese poetry), Ted Cohen has argued that human beings naturally jest in order to provide "relief from certain oppressions."[61] Similarly, in an apparent positive spin on Freud's intimation that incessant punning is the obsession of a neurotic personality, Harvey Mindess has argued that such may actually be a form of constructive verbal resistance: "Punning at any level excites expanded ideation, a creative escape from the inhibiting rigors of words."[62] Victor Raskin has put the matter most simply in observing that people joke "instead of getting angry."[63]

While these theories and observations and opinions mostly seek to explain the motives of authors, less has been forwarded about the motives and responses of actual readers. If authors really wrote to vent, would this have helped readers to vent as well? What is the relationship between the cathartic whimsy of authors and readerly catharsis? Fans as well as authors of modern *manga* are often said, perhaps unfairly, to use the genre to escape into their own fantasy world. Keene has applied a similar logic to authors of pop literature as well. Writing of the poets of madcap verse, he maintains: "Their fascination with trivialities, shared by the authors of the *kibyōshi* and *sharebon*, was clearly the result of a disinclination or inability to face the world seriously."[64] Even if true, can this be said to pertain to the *readers* of the *kibyōshi*? To the extent that a number of works present a kind of social or political satire, thereby allowing readers as well as authors to focus their frustrations on a target, it perhaps can. Those *kibyōshi* in a satirical vein, just like those modern *manga* whose psychic center resides in an adolescent counterculture, seem to present their own kind of symbolic resistance to authoritarian society. However, such *kibyōshi* refrain from the sort of escapism found in those modern *manga* that truck in the explicit portrayal of sex and violence. The main obscenity dealt with in the satirical *kibyōshi*, as we will see, tends to be governmental incompetence, hypocrisy, and corruption.

---

59. See Hino, *Edojin to yūtopia*.
60. Hibbett, *The Chrysanthemum and the Fish*, p. 104.
61. Cohen, *Jokes*, p. 10.
62. Mindess, *Laughter and Liberation*, p. 87.
63. Raskin, *Semantic Mechanisms of Humor*, p. 28.
64. Keene, *World Within Walls*, p. 519.

In a comicbook form such as the *kibyōshi*, no consideration of the author would be complete without a look at the artist. The relationship between author and artist is a central issue in understanding the creative process as well as the institutional context of the publishing house. It is an issue that begs several questions: What was the professional relationship between the author and the artist within the stable? Did author and artist work together in stages, at the same time, physically together? Did one exercise greater creative control over the finished product than the other? If so, which one? In the many known cases in which the same person served as both artist and author, did he use different pseudonyms for each task and, if so, why? How common was it for a *kibyōshi* to be written and illustrated by the same person as a kind of *auteur*? Who were the artists, anyway? And what can any of this tell us about the visual-verbal imagination of An'ei-Tenmei Edo?

A survey of principal *kibyōshi* artists amounts to a who's who list of the premier woodblock artists of the period. Foremost among these would have to be Kitagawa Utamaro (1753–1806), Eishōsai Chōki (fl. ca. 1790s), Torii Kiyonaga (1752–1815), and Utagawa Toyokuni (1769–1825). This is not to omit the leading members of the popular Kitao School of *ukiyoe*: Kitao Masanobu (1761–1816), Kitao Masayoshi (1764–1824), and probably the most prolific artist in the *kibyōshi*, Kitao Shigemasa (1739–1820). Other notable though perhaps less familiar artists to the informed Western reader might include Kitagawa Chiyojo (fl. ca. 1781–1801), Kitagawa Yukimaro (fl. 1780s), Katsukawa Shun'ei (1762–1819), Tokakutei Kimō (dates unknown), and Utagawa Toyohiro (1773–1829). Finally, there was the indefatigable giant Katsukawa Shunrō (1760–1849), whose so-called "Great Wave"—that global icon of Japanese woodblock printing if not of Japan itself—was composed under the *nom de plume* by which he is remembered to posterity, Katsushika Hokusai.

As might be expected of any comicbook, several authors also illustrated their own *kibyōshi* under their established authorial penname. The most obvious examples are probably Koikawa Harumachi, Shikitei Sanba, and Jippensha Ikku. As for Kyōden, he tended to use his artistic style Kitao Masanobu for those works he both wrote and illustrated early in his career, though after his initial successes, he began increasingly to use the Kyōden pseudonym.

Regarding the professional and creative relationships between the author and the artist, the internal evidence yields a few minor clues. Most *kibyōshi* are careful to treat the composition of the words and the pictures as two discrete activities, reserving terms like "playfully written by" (*gesaku*) or "composed by" (*saku*) for the author, and "illustrated by" (*gakō*) or "pictures by" (*ga*) for the artist. In those cases in which the same historical person performed both roles under the same pseudonym, he tended to use the apparently interchangeable bylines "written and illustrated by" (*sakuga*) or "illustrated and written by" (*gasaku*). *Familiar Bestsellers*, for example, was "illustrated and written by Masanobu" (*Masanobu gasaku*) early in Kyōden's career.

Yet there are also innumerable instances in which the same historical person performed both roles under *different* pseudonyms.[65] *Playboy*, for instance, was "playfully written by Kyōden" (*Kyōden gesaku*) but "illustrated by Masanobu" (*Masanobu gakō*). In those cases when only the pseudonym of an author is stipulated, the artist is either the same person as the author, or possibly an in-house artist. In the final analysis, these designations do not significantly illuminate the real-life relationship between author and artist, though they do suggest that both roles were regarded as discrete even when the same person performed them under the same style.

The Draft-Manuscript Book

A significant source of insight into the relationship between the *kibyōshi* author and artist—and, thus, into the nature of *kibyōshi* composition—is to be found in the "draft-manuscript book" (*sōkōbon*). Analogous to the storyboard of today's film industry—or, closer still, to the so-called "dummy" of the Western comic-book assembly-line process—it provides an author's rough sketches and preliminary notes to be used by the artist in illustrating a *kibyōshi*.[66] Thus, the draft-manuscript book was not a series of trial sketches by an artist, or even an author's own pre-visualization drawings. Rather, it was an author's nuts-and-bolts instructions to his artist on how to compose the pictures.

The draft manuscript might not have been an isolated phenomenon. Texts serving a similar function existed in other areas of cultural production. For instance, Sanba wrote the funnybook *Portraits of Drunkards* (*Namaei kata-gi*, 1806), which the comic-story raconteur Sakuragawa Jinkō appropriated as a "performance text" (*daibon*) upon which to base his skits.[67] Thus, the use of something like the draft manuscript may have been part of the wider cultural practice of providing artistic instructions to be implemented by someone else.

Be that as it may, it was not known that draft manuscripts for the *kibyōshi* existed at all until fairly recently, with the serendipitous unearthing of one at a rare book sale in Tokyo's Mitsukoshi department store by members of a study group in 1975. In this document, author Santō Kyōden provides notes to his illustrator Kitao Shigemasa for the *kibyōshi* titled *Blowdart Targets of Countless Human Affairs* (*Ningen banji fukiya no mato*, 1803). A comparison of

---

65. Throughout much of Japanese cultural history, people have tended to dabble in a multiplicity of arts. Assuming a different pseudonym for each art—or even several pseudonyms within the *same* art—may have been a way of stimulating creativity. An author might change his nominal style in order to change his artistic style.

66. "The term 'storyboard' refers to a draft used for planning films in which the action is shown in a series of sketches and is accompanied by explanation and dialogue . . ." In Spaulding, *The Page as a Stage Set*, p. 9.

67. For more on this, see Leutner, *Shikitei Sanba*, p. 64.

Fig. 1.16 Scene from
*Nine Months Inside an
Author's Womb, Illus-
trated* (*Sakusha tainai
totsuki no zu*, 1804), a
kibyōshi written by
Santō Kyōden and
illustrated by Kitao
Shigemasa. Courtesy
of Tokyo Metropoli-
tan Central Library,
Kaga Collection.

Shigemasa's final pictures in the published *kibyōshi* against Kyōden's preliminary sketches and instructional jottings in this draft manuscript demonstrates a remarkable degree of fidelity.[68] The same pertains to the few other
draft manuscripts that have since been discovered—miraculously, one feels,
since every scrap of paper during the Edo period was a candidate for recycling, even fair copies of bestselling works being fair game. Kitao Shigemasa's pictures in *The Goldenrod Hue of Chikusai's Treasure* (*Chikusairō takara
no yamabuki iro*, ca. 1794) match author Tsukiji Zenkō's draft manuscript brilliantly.[69] And the pictures in Kyōden's *kibyōshi* titled *Nine Months Inside an
Author's Womb, Illustrated* (*Sakusha tainai totsuki no zu*, 1804) (**Figure 1.16**) follow the rough contours in the author's draft manuscript (**Figure 1.17**).[70]

The fidelity between these draft manuscripts and their final, published
kibyōshi suggests that the responsibility for the visual-verbal nexus—if not
the final *kibyōshi* itself—fell squarely upon the shoulders of the author, not
the artist. The artist no doubt added the occasional artsy flourish, though it
was the author who seems to have coordinated the process of fashioning
the visual-verbal text. Unless a draft manuscript comes to light in which an
artist gives instructions to an author, it must be concluded that in the case
of two different people fulfilling the authorial and artistic functions of a
kibyōshi, it was the author who exerted creative control.

68. Mentioned in Suwa, *Shuppan koto hajime*, p. 95.

69. For pictures, see Tanahashi, *Kibyōshi no kenkyū*, p. 344.

70. See Tabako to shio no hakubutsukan, *Kansei no shuppankai to Santō Kyōden*, p. 86 and
passim.

Fig. 1.17 Draft manuscript for *Nine Months Inside an Author's Womb, Illustrated,* with instructions from Santō Kyōden to artist Kitao Shigemasa. Courtesy of the National Diet Library.

It is, therefore, tempting to refer to the author of the *kibyōshi,* following the lead of film theory on the director, as the *auteur.* For even if an author provides "only" the verbal but not the visual text, ultimately it is he who is responsible for the composite whole. And in the mid-Edo popular imagination—judging by passages in reviewbooks of *kibyōshi,* as well as in *kibyōshi* themselves—it does indeed seem as though the author was conceived of as actually having been the primary creator.

That said, it is nonetheless useful to retain the terms "author" and "artist" to refer to the actual activities of creating verbal and visual texts, even if these roles are at times performed by the same historical person. It is less a matter of how these activities were represented to readers within a *kibyōshi* than of how these roles were divided within a publishing stable. Eisner makes a similar point about the Western comicbook: "In order to consider, separately, the role of the writer, it is necessary to arbitrarily limit the 'writing' for comics to the function of conceiving the idea and the story, creating the order of telling and fabricating the dialogue or narrative elements."[71]

Along these lines, the *auteur* label might on the one hand best be reserved for he who is responsible for composing the draft manuscript, which then becomes the basis for the author to craft his verbal text and the artist to craft his visual text. On the other hand, to refer to the "author" of a

71. Eisner, *Comics and Sequential Art,* p. 122.

finished *kibyōshi* might inadvertently privilege the verbal over the visual text. Furthermore, to the extent that the *auteur* of the draft manuscript is creating a visual-verbal text, which later is merely fleshed out by an author and an artist, the author himself *is* a kind of artist. Eisner, who as a comicbook "creator" devotes no small amount of attention to this sort of issue, in one of his how-to books advised his readers to "Think of your function as a visualizer rather than an *illustrator*."[72] Although subordinating the role of author to that of illustrator in this context, Eisner's characterization of the creative process as "visualization" seems apt for the *kibyōshi auteur*. This is one lesson that the draft manuscript has to offer, that the *auteur* is a kind of visualizer.

A second lesson of the draft manuscript is that part of the professionalism of the *kibyōshi* (and, therefore, perhaps, other mass-produced popular literature) was bound up in the attention devoted to careful planning and, it follows, editing. Good writing involves rewriting, as seems to have been Bashō's ideal nearly a century earlier. Yet this notion flies in the face of the representation, within many a *kibyōshi* story or prologue, of the author's lot as the harried amateur who must resort to unprofessional means to meet his publisher's deadlines. In *Familiar Bestsellers*, for instance, the fictional author / illustrator-*cum*-narrator admits to exploiting his own silly dreams as the material for the *kibyōshi*. The representation of the overworked author is, thus, largely a pose of feigned humility (*higeman*), covering up both the careful editorial process and, more to the point, the commercial nature of the *kibyōshi*.

Literary Coteries

Authors and artists worked together on their draft manuscripts in the context of the professional publishing stable. Authors, artists, publishers, actors, politicians, courtesans, geisha, shop owners, doctors, and many other creative souls representing various classes, professions, and interests intermingled freely in various Floating World venues. Here, the differences among these classes and professions, and perhaps even commercial interests, which is to say the normal hierarchical and economic dynamics of society at large, were set aside, opening up an unencumbered space that had creative potential. Anthropologist Victor Turner has observed a similar kind of *communitas* within the liminal setting of the initiation rite in many societies.[73] Literary scholar Ogata Tsutomu has written about temporarily closed communities producing *haikai* poetry and other kinds of "coterie literature" (*za no bungaku*), which he takes as significant to poetic and dramatic praxis.[74] Taking her cue from the work of these two scholars (among others), Haruko Iwasaki has cogently argued that such liminal spaces, primarily in the form of the literary coterie (*za*), were a key feature of Edo's world of playful litera-

---

72. Eisner, *Comics and Sequential Art*, p. 153.
73. Turner, *Dramas, Fields, and Metaphors*.
74. Ogata, *Za no bungaku*.

ture.[75] More specifically, these collaborative spaces may be considered one of the keystones of An'ei-Tenmei culture and of the *kibyōshi*; for if nothing else, one often encounters a number of in-group jokes and references to other members of the same coterie within a work. This applies to each of the three *kibyōshi* published herein. Sometimes, the point of an entire scene may be less a matter of plot furtherance than making such esoteric allusions.

The literary coterie most germane to the *kibyōshi* was the "madcap poetry" (*kyōka*) circle, though there were other spaces, as well, such as book clubs (like the one represented in *Familiar Bestsellers*) and even amateur theatrical groups. A few worth mentioning here are the theme parties thrown by members of these madcap poetry circles. The famous "Handtowel Competition" (*tanagui awase*), in which partygoers submitted fanciful designs for handtowels involving clever visual-verbal puns, exerted a profound influence on the composition of Kyōden's *Playboy* (as we will see in the chapter on that work). There was also the "treasure competition" (*takara awase*), which one might easily mistake for some patrician pastime of the Heian Court, like the "poetry competition" (*uta awase*) or the "picture competition" (*e awase*) mentioned in *The Tale of Genji*. However, the Edo variety was really a *mock-heroic* form. Partygoers would find some everyday item or found object and concoct an outrageously fanciful, convoluted story, often involving visual-verbal puns, about its origins and ownership, as though it were some truly rare jewel.

The artistic intermingling of these spaces was in some ways a microcosm of the social fluidity that was increasingly transforming metropolitan centers around Japan, though at the vanguard of this phenomenon was Edo. People from all walks of life intermingled there on street corners, at temple fairs, on pilgrimages, within the bathhouses, and in the Floating World hotspots of the pleasure quarters, theaters, and street spectacles. These were demographically diverse spaces, but they were hardly democratic, for while they might temporarily suspend the hierarchical relations that pertained in society at large, they nonetheless invented their own new hierarchies. The women of the pleasure quarters, for instance, had a steep grade of ranks, from top courtesan, through the lowliest of apprentices, down to the humblest of scullery maids. Likewise, in the world of kabuki, the stage star might easily be dismissed outside the theater as a non-human. It is not that liminal spaces have no structure, in other words, but that their structure is really an Anti-Structure in terms of Society at large. This kind of symbolic inversion also informs many a *kibyōshi*, especially in its moments of sociopolitical satire. It is even possible that one motivation for the shogunal crackdown on the *kibyōshi* and its authors was precisely the way the genre reflected the social intermingling that seemed to be threatening the maintenance of the Neo-Confucian social hierarchy.

---

75. Iwasaki, "The World of *Gesaku*." Ikegami makes a similar argument in *Bonds of Civility*.

**Paradox of
Interrelatedness**

The close teamwork of author and artist in publishing stables, the phenomenon of literary coteries, and the fact that it was not uncommon for a
single person to dabble in a variety of arts under
different pseudonyms all suggest a fundamental truth about the *kibyōshi*. A
thoroughly collaborative enterprise, the *kibyōshi* is radically interrelated to a
variety of genres, media, arts, and texts, often to a dizzying degree. The
kibyōshi can be said to be promiscuously allusional, intertextual, hybrid. So
much so that some works in the genre seem barely to cohere, approaching
what art historian James Elkins has termed, in a different context, the "inas-
similably complex."[76]

Indeed, the *kibyōshi* embodies the radical cross-fertilization among literary, pictorial, dramatic, and even musical genres that informs many Japanese
arts. Writing on poetry competitions of the Heian period, Setsuko Ito has
argued that there was a "close relationship between poetry, music, and the
fine arts at the court [poetry contest]."[77] Likewise, some scholars feel that
such cross-fertilization characterizes Japanese popular culture even at present.[78] The *kibyōshi* may be the quintessential manifestation of this interrelatedness in its day.

The *kibyōshi* alludes to a staggeringly wide range of literary and extra-
literary material. It might even be easier, perhaps, to catalogue that to which
the *kibyōshi* does *not* allude than that to which it does. The *kibyōshi* looks to
no less than the entire historical range of the literary and cultural imagination in Japan, everything from the highbrow, through the lowbrow, down to
otherwise overlooked *quotidiana*. This range includes things such as children's
stories, elementary textbooks, copybooks, dictionaries, encyclopedias, theatrical libretti, popular song, advertisements, street signs, Buddhist sutras,
Neo-Confucian tracts, printed board games, lucky charms, lottery tickets,
maps, guidebooks, paper caulking, the city of Edo itself, the cluster of genres
of playful literature, and so on *ad infinitum*.

This is not to omit the hallowed classics of the already thousand-year-old
Japanese literary tradition and the even longer and more hallowed one of
China. Such works must have been widely available at booksellers, as well as
in schools around the country and certainly in the major metropolises.[79] The
Japanese "classics" would include such works as: the two national "mytho-

---

76. Elkins uses this phrase in his discussion of Leonardo's *Last Supper* in *Why Are Our
Pictures Puzzles?* p. 115.

77. Ito, "The Muse in Competition," p. 205.

78. Timothy J. Craig, among others, holds that such hybridity "between old and new, native and foreign, one genre and another . . . is a hallmark of Japanese culture." In Craig, *Japan
Pop!* p. 8.

79. That said, some works now considered canonical may not be mentioned in the *kibyōshi* at all, and some classical works the *kibyōshi* refers to regularly have now been relegated to
footnotes.

histories," the *Record of Ancient Matters* (*Kojiki*, ca. 712) and the *Chronicles of Japan* (*Nihon shoki*, 720); folk or fairy stories (*tsukuri monogatari*) like *The Tale of the Bamboo Cutter* (*Taketori monogatari*, ca. late ninth or early tenth century); poem-tales (*utamonogatari*) like *The Tales of Ise* (*Ise monogatari*, ca. 880–950); psychologically astute, fictional tales (*monogatari*) epitomized by Murasaki Shikibu's incomparable *The Tale of Genji* (*Genji monogatari*, ca. 1000); the writer's commonplace or creative notes, like Sei Shōnagon's *Pillow Book*; the great collections of short stories and anecdotes (*setsuwa*), like *Tales of Times Now Past* (*Konjaku monogatari*, ca. late eleventh century), *A Collection of Gleanings from Uji* (*Uji shūi monogatari*, ca. 1190–1242), and *The Miscellany of Ten Maxims* (*Jikkinshō*, 1252); the essay or miscellany, especially Kamo no Chōmei's *Account of My Hermitage* (*Hōjōki*, 1212) and Yoshida Kenkō's *Essays in Idleness* (*Tsurezuregusa*, ca. 1331); the grand military epic of lute-playing minstrels (*biwa hōshi*), *The Tales of the Heike* (*Heike monogatari*, ca. thirteenth century); the canon of performed noh plays (many of which were available in printed form); the imperial poetry collections (*chokusen shū*), such as *Japanese Verse Old and New* (*Kokin wakashū*, ca. 920); and many, many, many others at once too numerous to mention but too important *not* to mention without embarrassment.

Most formally educated men would have been exposed to the classics of Chinese letters by Confucius, Mencius, Zhuangzi, Laozi, and so on as part of their basic training in reading and writing. Indeed, the *kibyōshi* often alludes to such things as the Confucian *Analects*; *The Classic of Filial Piety*; *The Great Learning*; the Four Books; the Taoist classic of the *Yijing*; the *Thousand Character Classic* (Ch. *Qianziwen*, J. *Senjimon*); and the *Wenxuan* (J. *Monzen*). One also finds mention of the *Mengqiu* (J. *Mōgyū*), a three-volume compendium of anecdotes from ancient China that was not only an important primer of Chinese poetry, but one of the top two texts of some fifty used for literary studies during the Edo period.[80] Other Chinese works that were an integral part of the traditional curriculum in Japanese schools, like *Tang Poetry Anthology* (Ch. *Tangshi xuan*, J. *Tōshisen*)—which figures as a character in *Familiar Bestsellers*—seem to have been of only minor significance in China at the time.[81] A wide swath of other Chinese works, from Sima Qian's (ca. 145–85 BCE) *Records of the Grand Historian* (*Shiji*), through the more or less contemporaneous vernacular novel (*baihua xiaoshuo*), to popular classics such as *Water Margin* (Ch. *Shuihu zhuan*, J. *Suikoden*), are also referenced in many a *kibyōshi*.

The *kibyōshi* can be said to stand at the center of the contemporary popular imagination, then, not merely by virtue of its vast popularity, but

---

80. The *Mengqiu* was compiled by Li Han (J. Rikan), who was active during the Five Dynasties period (907–960) of the Tang. According to Ishikawa Ken, *Gakkō no hattatsu*. Cited in Dore, *Education in Tokugawa Japan*, p. 143.

81. For more on this, see Yoshikawa, et al., *Tōshisen*.

because of its deliberate hybridity, allusivity, even intertextuality.[82] This feature results in what could be termed the "paradox of interrelatedness." On the one hand, this radical interrelatedness among genres, texts, media, and people makes the *kibyōshi* a daunting genre to study, sometimes perversely so, since in order to move beyond a banal surface reading, one must grapple with a complex network of these interconnections. It is often difficult to discuss a single work *meaningfully* without getting sucked into a vertiginously amorphous swirl of visual and verbal allusions, genres, and energies. The little yellow comicbook, in other words, is a kind of black hole into which many things get sucked, never to emerge in quite the same form again. All of Edo culture becomes collapsed within it. The *kibyōshi* almost seems to take pleasure in devouring other genres whole, as does the novel, according to Bakhtin.

The *kibyōshi*, then, is a genre of synthesis, even more self-consciously so than other genres that partake of *ars combinatorial*. Something similar of course pertains to many forms of cultural production, but the *kibyōshi*—at least throughout most of its brief history—places a premium upon such interplay. It is almost as though the story is the excuse—the text is the pretext—for the author to playfully tease his friends within the same literary coterie while challenging other readers with a staggering array of allusive references so oblique as to be genuine puzzles. The *kibyōshi* not only privileges such interconnections, because it is the only one of the adult genres of Edo's popular literature to be *heavily* pictorial, but it also provides an excellent window onto the rich visual-verbal imagination of the period in a way that perhaps no other genre can. Without a knowledge of the entire range of the literary imagination of Japan and perhaps China, one risks missing not only an allusion or two, but the very point of the story itself. Indeed, it is primarily for this reason that, as Nakamura maintains, Japanese scholars widely acknowledge the *kibyōshi* as being "among the most difficult works in Japanese literature."[83]

This radical interrelatedness is probably not just a projection of the scholarly interests of those who study the *kibyōshi* but also a genuine feature of the genre *itself*, for so many of the punch lines and solutions to the allusional puzzles can be solved only with recourse to related texts. Since the stories of the *kibyōshi* were assembled out of literary formulae according to set variational procedures, it may be the networks of meanings, associations, and reverberations that determine a piece's distinctive freshness. Something

---

82. Kamens, in his study of intertextuality in classical Japanese poetic praxis, defines the term as a discursive practice that was "not wholly beyond the reach of agency, but rather something toward which poets, among others, may strive, perhaps even through such obvious gestures as allusion, as well as through yet subtler means—in addition to the fact that it may exist regardless of what poets do." In Kamens, *Utamakura, Allusion, and Intertextuality in Traditional Japanese Poetry*, p. 8.

83. Nakamura, "Modes of Expression in a Historical Context," p. 11.

similar may pertain to some Western comicbooks: "Readers are exposed to other mediums, each of which has its own rhythm," writes Eisner. "There is no way of measuring it, but we know that these different media influence each other."[84] Yet it is this interrelatedness of the *kibyōshi* that occasions, in J. Thomas Rimer's apt phrase, the "central act of recognition."[85]

To the skeptic for whom no amount of assertion backed by the evidence of the translations themselves will suffice, it should be pointed out that the *kibyōshi*, like kabuki and the woodblock print, is a useful point of entry into a culture like that of An'ei-Tenmei Edo, in which the poetic, literary, dramatic, artistic, and even musical arts are intimately interconnected. And although it might be objected that the average real-life reader was capable of appreciating only a fraction of the allusive play that the ideal reader would theoretically appreciate, it should be observed that the greater one's understanding, the deeper one's appreciation. "The total riches," writes Cohen on the multiplicity of levels of meaning in jokes, "are available only to those who know."[86]

On the other hand, even if one *can* identify the many various sorts of allusions, it is often difficult to discuss any *kibyōshi* in isolation. Indeed, the paradox of interrelatedness entails that since the arts and literatures of the Edo period are so closely interrelated, it is pointless to discuss any of them in perfect isolation. Yet without doing so, one can never get to know that wider context in the first place. To me, this paradox speaks to one of the major surprises of the *kibyōshi*. The complexity and depth of its allusions, while not as time-honored as the intertextual strategies of the thousand-year old tradition of classical poetry, nonetheless seem equally advanced. Indeed, the *kibyōshi* displays a remarkable degree of allusive sophistication.

To summarize, the interconnectedness of the little yellow comicbook presents a golden opportunity. Its hybridity, allusivity, and interplay among producers qualify it as an unsurpassed vortex through which many other genres, media, texts, and authors can be studied. For the student of Japanese literature who enjoys a challenge, reading a *kibyōshi* can be a useful but fun exercise in identifying references to many of the great works, high and low, of Chinese as well as Japanese letters. Moreover, the *kibyōshi* can serve as a kind of skeleton key to a variety of cultural practices of the mid-Edo period, if not to other periods as well. The same can be said of *haikai*, kabuki, or many other cultural forms for that matter, since so much crossover occurs among the arts. However, the *kibyōshi* has the advantage of visual immediacy, providing a frame of reference that can more or less be understood by people who read not one word of Edo-period Japanese.

---

84. Eisner, *Graphic Storytelling and Visual Narrative*, p. 69.
85. In the Foreword to Jordan and Weston, *Copying the Master and Stealing His Secrets*, p. xxi.
86. Cohen, *Jokes*, p. 23.

The vastness of the *kibyōshi* phenomenon, then, as well as its myriad allusions and generic hybridity, qualifies the genre for the attention of anyone interested in Japanese literature, art, culture, and history, among other fields. Simply put, just as the little yellow comicbook resides at the center of our picture from *Pageant of the Latest Beauties*, so too was it a central genre of mid-Edo cultural production, if not *the* central genre. In pulling all the various genres of art, drama, poetry, history, mythology, and literature into its often chaotic pages, the *kibyōshi* achieved a centrality not just to lowbrow or "frivolous" literature but to contemporary life in An'ei-Tenmei Edo itself.

Transversion, Subversion, and Indiscriminate Anarchy

The radical interrelatedness of the *kibyōshi* raises at least two points. First, the mixing of what *at the time* would have been identified as highbrow and lowbrow cultural elements means that the *kibyōshi* cannot adequately be described either as a lowbrow genre or, conversely, in light of its sophistication, as a highbrow genre. By plopping elements of both highbrow and lowbrow culture together on the same plane, the *kibyōshi* sinks the former to new lows and elevates the latter to new highs, thereby symbolically turning social hierarchies on their heads.

This inversion, or at least this entangling, spells cultural upheaval. "The tendency of the humor, in its insistent violence," wrote New York intellectual Robert Warshow about *MAD* magazine, "is to reduce all culture to indiscriminate anarchy."[87] The *kibyōshi* communicated social anarchy in its deployment of highbrow and lowbrow elements in a double structure related to variational techniques, and also in its very *look*—words and pictures jumbled together, not only mirroring the haphazardly growing boomtown, but challenging the putatively "normal" procedures of reading. These palpable aspects of the *kibyōshi*'s "indiscriminate anarchy" must have constituted much of the symbolic threat to the hierarchical order that the shogunate found alarming. And what better way to challenge shogunal hegemony than through textual disorder? To the government, the apparent inversion of what it deemed to be classics and trash may have signaled an alarming dissolution of the distinction between patricians and plebes.

If this link seems somewhat tenuous, it should be pointed out that the designations highbrow (*ga*) and lowbrow (*zoku*) were not just a matter of literary taste in eighteenth-century Japan. They were also intimately aligned with notions of social class. To categorize the *kibyōshi* today as lowbrow merely because the format *resembles* children's comicbooks for commoners, or because it was categorized as a genre of "frivolous literature," then, is to

---

87. Warshow, "Paul, the Horror Comics, and Dr. Wertham," p. 54.

accept the eighteenth-century elitist denunciation of the *kibyōshi* unthinkingly. Rather, it makes more sense to consider the genre in terms of *transversion*, which is to say the fusion of highbrow and lowbrow cultural elements into a new (though hardly midbrow) composite.[88] The little yellow comic-book was, to borrow a metaphor from its pages, neither "clouds nor mud," but a butterfly, flitting playfully in-between.

A second point about the *kibyōshi*'s radical interrelatedness is that it calls into question the blithe categorization of the genre as a genre in the first place. Merely by labeling the *kibyōshi* as a *kibyōshi*, scholars have invoked a certain generic completeness that may run counter to its transgressive inter-generic hybridity. Although lines between genres were never clear-cut during the first few centuries of Japan's mass-publishing industry, they seem to have been especially permeable in parodic forms like the *kibyōshi*. Thus, the application of the term "genre" to the *kibyōshi* effectively hides the radical-ness of its interrelatedness. In other words, there can and should be some debate about whether the *kibyōshi* is a genre, a format, a medium, or some combination of these.

This issue is potentially complicated by the fact that at least one other "genre" is known to have essentially assumed the *kibyōshi* format. Not everything with a yellow cover, in other words, *is* a yellow cover. As might be expected of a vastly popular literature, other genres inevitably copied its format, imitation being the sincerest form of profitability. The most salient example of this can be seen in the format of the jokebook. Many a joke-book resembles the *kibyōshi* closely in terms of size, layout, illustration style, splash art, and even cover color. In fact, some works traditionally categorized as *kibyōshi* may actually be jokebooks—such as Sakuragawa Jihinari's *Sakuragawa's Notebook of Old Chestnuts* (*Sakuragawa hanashi no chōtoji*, 1801).[89] Perhaps the only immediate tell-tale sign that this is a "*kibyōshi*-style joke-book" (*kibyōshi-jitate hanashibon*) and not a *kibyōshi* per se is that each anec-dote is contained in its own section marked by a discernible section title that is otherwise absent in the *kibyōshi* (**Figure 1.18**).

Some books of comic haiku (*senryū*) were made to resemble *kibyōshi*, too. For instance, there is Harumachi's *Year-End Parade* (*Sekki yagyō*, 1783), a kind of "greatest hits" compilation of comic haiku masquerading as a *kibyōshi*, which was later pirated as a *kibyōshi*-style jokebook (**Figure 1.19**).[90] Along these lines, Bakin took seventeen haiku (*hokku*) about fleas and shepherded them into *The Vendetta of Mr. Fleacatcher Managoro, the Fifth* (*Katakiuchi nomitori manako*, 1791), a booklet that is probably a *kibyōshi* but may well be some-

---

88. For more on transversion, see Lecercle, *Philosophy of Nonsense*, p. 186.

89. The library at Waseda University, Tanahashi (in *Kibyōshi sōran*), and Iwanami shoten, *Kokusho sōmokuroku 3* (p. 685) categorize Sakuragawa's jokebook (illustrated by Utagawa Toyokuni) as a *kibyōshi*.

90. For more on this, see Ebara, "Kibyōshi *Sekki yagyō*."

Fig. 1.18 The presence of a section title at extreme right—"The Fart" (*He*)—suggests that this is less a *kibyōshi* than a *kibyōshi*-style jokebook (*kibyōshi-jitate hanashibon*). From *Sakuragawa's Notebook of Old Chestnuts* (*Sakuragawa hanashi no chōtoji* (1801), written by Sakuragawa Jihinari and illustrated by Utagawa Toyokuni. Courtesy of the University of Tokyo, Bungakubu kokubungaku kenkyūshitsu.

thing else.[91] Likewise, Kyokuhō's *The Seigneurial Type* (*Daimyō katagi*, ca. 1784) was a hybrid piece, just as much beholden to the mock-sermon book as to the *kibyōshi*.[92]

On the other hand, it is impossible to judge some *kibyōshi* by their covers. At times, certain works seem to have been privately repackaged, though often with a new frontispiece—or none at all—into "compound booklets" (*gōseibon*). Not to be confused with the "multivolume" comicbook (*gōkan*), which presents a single story in multiple fascicles, the compound booklet was really a kind of personal *collectanea*.[93] In conclusion, materiality or, more to the point, format alone did not the *kibyōshi* genre make. Rather, its success also depended greatly upon its content.

---

91. Translated, with a brief introduction, in Zolbrod, "The Vendetta of Mr. Fleacatcher Managoro." For an annotated version, see Iwata, "*Katakiuchi nomitori manako*." Zolbrod uses the term "haiku," though these were really comic *hokku*—not to be confused with *senryū*. While all three are seventeen-syllable verses, haiku and *senryū* were written to stand on their own, whereas the *hokku* was written to participate in a longer sequence.

92. Iwasaki, "Portrait of a Daimyo," p. 11.

93. I am indebted to Adam Kabat for his views on this subject.

The *Kibyōshi* as Map and Mirror

It is self-evident that the *kibyōshi* reflects the Floating World of An'ei-Tenmei Edo down to its glittering quiddity. Yet this reflection can only be significantly warped. The genre's refusal to engage in psychological realism, plus the preponderance of verbal pyrotechnics, fantastic plots, contrived situations, parody, irony, satire, and humor—not to mention the commercial pressures exerted upon its producers—intensify this warp. Still, it is precisely because of this warp, let alone in spite of it, that contemporary life in Edo, especially its demimonde, somehow emerges in the pictures and stories with just as much wonderfully distorted vividness as Paris's Moulin Rouge in the poster art of Henri de Toulouse-Lautrec, or as the society of *précieuses* in the farces of Molière. Aside from the pleasurable idiosyncrasy of its warp, then, not unlike a funhouse mirror, perhaps making it the more compelling, the *kibyōshi* nonetheless can at times provide sharply focused insight into the popular imagination.

Indeed, the *kibyōshi* is a treasure trove of dreams, delusions, rumors, urban myths, anxieties, shocking peccadilloes, erotica, exotica, and trivia that provide valuable clues to the private yet collective lives of the ordinary people of Edo during one of the peak moments in Japanese cultural history. As is the case with so much Edo-period literature, the *kibyōshi* chronicles the

Fig. 1.19 Illustration from *Hyaku fukuja ōtoshibanashi* (1789), a *kibyōshi*-style jokebook by Koikawa Harumachi pirated from his *Year-End Parade* (*Sekki yagyō*, 1783), a collection of comic haiku masquerading as a *kibyōshi*. Reprinted in Miyao, *Eiri Edo kobanashi jisshu 7*.

fantasies, if not the realities, of the day. The reader of Kyōden's *Swingers*, for instance, encounters such things as the sex life of conjoined twins, a mixed crowd at a street spectacle, a public urinal on the exterior of a private house, and veiled references to superstitions about straddling the seams of tatami mats. Similarly, the reader of *Playboy* encounters the "bedwetting hustle" (*shōbengumi*), a putatively notorious scam, in full swing during An'ei-Tenmei, in which a gold-digging woman would ingratiate herself with a wealthy mark, maneuvering him into providing the usual trappings of a kept woman—spending money, a wardrobe, even a suite of apartments. Each time her gullible sugar daddy would come by to consummate the costly affair, the conniving hustler would feign incontinence, deliberately urinating in bed, thereby dampening the man's sexual desires.

Whether such a scam actually took place is beside the point, for urban myths can powerfully affect people's perception of reality. "A wild story tells something about the mentality of the age," John Brownlee writes, "and can be exploited by a historian who does not believe a word of it to be 'true.'"[94] The *kibyōshi*, whose stock in trade is such wild stories, reflects some aspect of people's inner lives, then, even if it does not accurately convey "reality." Thus, the *kibyōshi* might not satisfy the fundamental demand of the historian for verifiably objective truth, but it does at least capture what authors felt readers might find worth writing about, and what many readers actually found interesting enough to purchase. And if what is depicted in the pictures of the *kibyōshi* can and *should* not be assumed to accurately reflect reality the way a photograph would come to supposedly reflect it, at least those pictures provide a hint of how everyday objects may actually have appeared to the artist, even if that vision was mediated by the artist's hunches about what his audience wanted to see.

Although it would seem that there is little danger in reading the *kibyōshi* as a transparent window onto a realistic world, since the pictures and stories are so playfully outrageous, there is a danger in mining a genre of popular art and literature like the *kibyōshi* for historical fact. As long as it is kept in mind that the *kibyōshi* reflects less Reality than what that society may have wanted to believe was real, thereby forging social reality, the *kibyōshi* can supplement the study of Edo-period culture that relies on more self-evidently veracious modes of historical evidence.

This notion that in reflecting social reality the *kibyōshi* forges Reality is nothing new. Over half a century ago, Edo-literature scholar Koike Tōgorō characterized the genre as a kind of "periodical magazine of the community" (*gurūpu no kikan zasshi*), shaping as well as reflecting attitudes about the fashions, tastes, lingo, personalities, and sentiments of fashionable society in Edo.[95] The *kibyōshi*, it might be said, prescribes as well as describes.

---

94. Brownlee, "*Jikkinshō*," p. 125.
95. Koike, *Santō Kyōden no kenkyū*, p. 211.

This is part and parcel of the advent of mass publishing, since merely by representing something in print, that something acquires a certain degree of normative force. As one of the most popular genres of mid-Edo period literature to mirror Edo, then, the *kibyōshi* contributed significantly to the act of mapping Edo.

At first blush, this kind of constructivist argument may not seem to apply to a *comic* genre. For even if one admits that comedy can reflect society, the claim that it helps construct society might itself seem ludicrous. However, it is largely through the threat of ridicule, even the subtle threat, that comedy exerts a particularly robust normative force—perhaps even more so than shogunal edicts. And in its potential to turn the represented world upside down through its tropes of reversals, inversions, and transversions, comedy harbors the capacity to wreak symbolic havoc with the sociopolitical order. Part of what must have distressed the government about the *kibyōshi* was that, being issued in such obvious volume and enjoying such massive popularity, the genre was capable not only of reflecting the rise of the merchant class that was threatening the stability of the sociopolitical hierarchy, but also of influencing a mass readership's perceptions about the shogunate's own ability to handle the looming crises.

In more tangible terms, one way that the *kibyōshi* helped write Edo was by delineating its cultural landscape. Indeed, Inoue Takaaki has contended that the *kibyōshi* renders the physical space as well as the particular historical moment of An'ei-Tenmei Edo.[96] More recently, Marcia Yonemoto has argued that genres of Edo literature, such as the *kibyōshi* and the fashionbook, can be said to *literally* map mid-Tokugawa Edo.[97] Indeed, in surveying the hotspots, commercial establishments, key players, and specialty goods of Edo, the *kibyōshi* helped provide readers with a cognitive map, if not actually a literal one, of the increasingly convoluted metropolis. To the extent that this could only have affected the way that its readers went about conducting much of their lives in their city, the *kibyōshi* served as a kind of imaginative guidebook to the indiscriminate anarchy that it itself invoked in its format as well as its radical interrelatedness. If the crazy layout of the *kibyōshi*, intermixing images and words in complex arrangement, somehow mirrored the craziness of the city, the *kibyōshi* also compensated by helping readers to make sense of it all.

Similarly, the *kibyōshi* helped attire the city. The *kibyōshi* tailored as well as took the measure of the "clothing community" of late eighteenth-century Edo.[98] The same is true of the fashionbook, though since that genre was also produced in Kamigata, it did not wardrobe Edo exclusively. Through-

---

96. Inoue, *Edo gesaku no kenkyū*, p. 19.
97. Yonemoto, *Mapping Early Modern Japan*.
98. Davis writes of the "clothing community" in *Fashion, Culture, and Identity*, p. 13 and passim.

out much of premodern literature, illustrated or not, depictions of clothing served as a kind of characterization, instantaneously communicating nuances of personal taste as well as the basic facts of class. In the literature of such a hierarchical society, clothing *is* character. The prescriptiveness of such descriptions becomes more powerful when that literature is produced in bulk and circulated *en masse*. Thus, genres of popular literature and art served, much like courtesans and kabuki actors themselves, as fashion plates for the people.

Even more influentially, in representing the language of the city, the *kibyōshi* participated in the construction of Edo's "speech community."[99] The *kibyōshi* certainly captured various accents, which is to say the spoken language as it might actually have been spoken, full of quirks and agrammatical constructions, and registering differences in gender, class, profession, regional dialect, mood, and so on. Like the fashionbook, the mock-sermon book, and other dialogue-heavy genres of pop literature, the *kibyōshi* is polyphonic.[100] It is a veritable rattlebag of voices. Although these voices are difficult to convey in translation, in the original one can almost *hear* the speech of country hunters, townsmen, urbane sophisticates, poseurs, proud samurai, and shameless hucksters, the sales patter of showmen, vendors hawking their goods, the headlines of broadsheet salesmen, the cant of ruffians, the affectations of the precious, people speaking to each other as marks as well as friends, shop clerks greeting unannounced visitors, passersby cursing a couple apparently making love, sons begging forgiveness of fathers, mothers intervening on behalf of sons, and the words of maids, kept women, courtesans, and geisha.

The *kibyōshi*, in other words, aimed for a kind of linguistic realism. In portraying a demotic language—speech the way that it was spoken by the various classes and types of people in Edo at the time—works give the impression of stylistic diversity, at least in the speech of the different characters. This diversity helps imbue the genre with its stylistic tang. Actually, the literary style of the *kibyōshi* might best be characterized as the *lack* of style. That is, although many works are clearly beholden to the narrative voice of earlier modes of storytelling, in its dialogue the *kibyōshi* exhibits what Bakhtin terms the "carnivalesque" by virtue of its rejection of stylistic unity. Even if it is conceded that some of this linguistic realism is stereotypical, deriving from humorous character types well established in literature, the *kibyōshi* presents what one might indeed have actually heard on the street corners, in the public baths, and at the teahouses of the Floating World of An'ei-Tenmei Edo.

---

99. For more on the speech community, see Hawkes, *Structuralism and Semiotics*, pp. 23–28.

100. Araki contends that the "full use of realistic dialogue in fiction is an innovation for which the writers of the *sharebon* can be given credit." In Araki, "*Sharebon*: Books for Men of Mode," p. 32.

What might therefore be oxymoronically dubbed the stylized linguistic realism of the *kibyōshi* also seems to have participated in a rudimentary form of linguistic leveling, meaning the erasing of differences in regional dialects and the invention of a new common language. This the *kibyōshi* did by mocking certain forms of language and lionizing others—specifically the Kamigata brogue and the Edo vogue. *Familiar Bestsellers* and *Swingers* have their fun with language from Kyoto's countryside, for instance. Samurai actually coming from the countryside to Edo who wanted to avoid getting ridiculed for their regional dialect actively emulated the prestigious Mikawa dialect, according to Ōta Nanpo.[101] Since language is an integral part of social formation, it is not hard to understand how a mass-circulating genre like the *kibyōshi* might possibly have exerted this kind of normative force. The invention of Edo as a cultural space, then, probably had just as much to do with the erasing of regional dialects in devising a new common language of Edo as did the establishment of the Tokugawa shogunate there at the beginning of the seventeenth century.

To summarize, the *kibyōshi*, like the fashionbook and other genres of Edo's popular literature, represented in writing a vernacular, natural, even demotic language. In so doing, the *kibyōshi* helped narrow the longstanding gap between the written representation of language and something approaching actual speech. Its vast popularity allowed it to project its version of a developing common Edo language to its readers who had come from the various provinces to the shogunal capital. Thus, within Edo at least, the *kibyōshi* participated in the construction of a central linguistic imaginary. Outside Edo, however, people probably went about their business as usual.

Edo-Centrism and Symbolic Annihilation

It was through the valorization of such things as the fashion, language, and behavior of the Edo sophisticate, then, that the *kibyōshi* and related genres of popular culture participated in constructing as well as reflecting Edo's cultural sophistication. And yet this construction and reflection were part of an even larger, more far-reaching social process: the swing of cultural gravity from Kamigata toward Edo. The concomitant project of forging a uniquely Edoesque identity became an increasingly self-conscious, prominent feature of that city's arts. It was a collaborative project, joining authors, illustrators, and publishers, not to mention readers themselves, in writing a creation myth of sorts that took Edo as the hub of the cultural universe.

Edo, according to this logic, was the key component in several recurring binaries, the center against which a variety of peripheries were contrasted on geographical, temporal, cultural, even national axes. Edo was made to stand

---

101. In Mizuhara Akito, *Edogo Tōkyōgo hyōjungo* (Heibonsha, 1994), pp. 22–24. Cited in Vaporis, "To Edo and Back," p. 39.

for eastern vs. western Japan, urban vs. rural, urbane vs. uncouth, modern vs. ancient, Japan vs. China, even Asia vs. the West. Hardly the antithesis of these secondary, allegedly lesser terms, Edo was the pivotal Self around which innumerable Others were made to pivot obsequiously. This can be seen in one way that the denizens of Edo used to refer to their city. The honorific prefix *o* is rarely used in Japanese to refer to oneself or to one's own group, though it was sometimes affixed to Edo to show due veneration for the shogun's capital but also no small sense of pride. *Oedo* was *Our Edo.*[102] Such "Edo-centrism," as it is called, which figures in the *kibyōshi* translated herein, characterizes much of the popular literature of the period and therefore may be considered one of the hallmarks of An'ei-Tenmei culture.

So powerful was Edo's cultural centripetalism that Gennai in one of his stories expressed astonishment that people actually could be found inhabiting the houses on the outskirts of town—as though all humanity should really be congregated in the center of the center, at Nihonbashi, Edo's "Bridge of Japan." Such hyperbole reflects less any verifiable trend in demographic distribution, needless to say, than it does the powerful cultural suction that Edo as concept exerted upon the popular imagination. The *kibyōshi* and like genres indeed helped to map the cultural space of Japan as Inoue and others have claimed. In one of his other works, a fashionbook, Gennai ranked the nation's top licensed districts as mere outposts with respect to Edo's own: "The pleasure quarters of the various provinces are innumerable—from Kyoto's Shimabara, Osaka's Shinmachi, and Nagasaki's Maruyama on down—and each has its own local appeal, with something to find pleasing. Of these our own Edo's Yoshiwara is the finest—though saying as much renders the fact as trite as repeating it over and over."[103]

To the extent that only a few places other than Edo typically merit mention—foremost among them being Kamigata, which serves just as much as a foil for identity forging as the butt of various jokes—this mapping, in representing the world according to a native son of Edo, can be said conversely to symbolically annihilate most other places on earth. Something similar is evident in Saul Steinberg's widely imitated *New Yorker* cover, which accords more graphic space to Manhattan from 9th Avenue to the Hudson than it does the rest of the world from New Jersey, through the continental U.S. and Pacific Ocean, to a blotch off on the distant horizon representing Japan.[104] Whereas Steinberg pokes self-reflexive fun at the tendency among readers of his magazine to take New York as the center of the universe, Edo during the second half of the eighteenth century does

---

102. This is not to be confused with that other popular term "Grand Edo" (*Ōedo*).

103. Gennai's fashionbook is *Yoshiwara saiken sato no odamaki hyō* (1774). In Nakamura, *Fūrai Sanjin shū*, p. 290.

104. Steinberg's cover is titled "View of the World from 9th Avenue." In *The New Yorker*, March 26, 1976.

not seem to have been secure enough yet with its own claim to cultural supremacy—which was but a blink compared to the millennium of Kamigata's established history—to poke fun at its provincialism with quite the same abandon.

If Edo's popular literature could write off most other metropolitan centers—Nagoya, Kagoshima, Himeji, Kanazawa, and so on—through a strategy of minimization, marginalization, and omission, Kamigata it could never completely ignore. The best that could be done to Kyoto-Osaka, and the western region that these cities were made to represent, was to displace them ever so slightly. This is because Kamigata had been the original Japanese model for Edo. That is to say, Edo-centrism replicated the form of Kamigata-centrism, which had in turn ultimately replicated the ancient China-centrism. As is well known, Kyoto was modeled on the grid plan of the capital in China—whose very graphs spell *Central Kingdom*. Edo, thus, simply displaced the object, not the venerable process, of center making. In this regard, because Edo's popular literature up to and including the An'ei-Tenmei era can be said to maintain the status quo, perpetuating the old system of binaries rather than replacing it with something radically new, it would seem to have been more late traditional than early modern.

More than any of the other binaries, the Edo-Kamigata one, far from being cut-and-dried, was polyvalent. It therefore appeared frequently within the popular literature of the day. Dozens of contemporary plays, too, were set in Edo as a deliberate reaction against Kamigata's domination of the theater. This binary thus sometimes reflected a real-life commercial rivalry. Kyōden's *Familiar Bestsellers*, to name a familiar example, took Edo's eclipsing of Kamigata's publishing industry as its theme. In their campaign against Kamigata, other Edo-centric *kibyōshi* commandeered anything at hand as a weapon, even noodles. The commercial success of Edo's thin buckwheat noodle over Kamigata's thicker flour variety informs Harumachi's *kibyōshi* of personified victuals, *The Monstrous* Udon *and* Soba *Noodles of Mt. Ōe* (*Udon soba: Bakemono Ōeyama*, 1776) (**Figure 1.20**).[105]

It should be noted that the *kibyōshi* and other heavily Edo-centric works of Edo's popular literature sometimes referred to Osaka in particular, without conflating this great metropolis with Kyoto into one monolithic "Kamigata." Indeed, many a work counterpoised Osaka's brand of "elegance" against Edo's "urbanity." "I'm a playboy from Edo—not *Osaka*!" one fictional author-narrator insists, before noting the decline of Osaka's Tatsumatsu hairdo vs. the rise of Edo's Honda topknot. In reflecting the cultural shift from Osaka to Edo that was taking place, this fashionbook, Hōseidō Kisanji's *Today's Fashionable Chic* (*Tōsei fūzoku tsū*), by virtue of influencing the first *kibyōshi*, Harumachi's *Master Flashgold*, would have a profound effect

---

105. For an annotated edition, see Koike, *Edo no gesaku ehon 1*, pp. 35–60.

Fig. 1.20 The personified protagonists of *The Monstrous* Udon
and Soba *Noodles of Mt. Ōe* (Udon
soba: Bakemono Ōeyama, 1776), a
kibyōshi written and illustrated by
Koikawa Harumachi. Courtesy
of Tokyo Metropolitan Central
Library, Kaga Collection.

on the entire *kibyōshi* genre.[106] The subtitle to a *kibyōshi* published later tell-
ingly runs "Osaka's sophistication is Edo's gaucherie."[107]

Edo-centrism is not infrequently inflected with the rhetoric of the old
city vs. country antithesis, too, constructing Edo's urban sophistication
against the "rural" uncouthness of even other urban centers. Kyoto and
Osaka types are, thus, referred to as though they *themselves* were "country
bumpkins" (*yūdeku*)—a term that came to be applied in the Fukagawa unlicensed quarter to anyone, even city dwellers, whose knowledge of Edo's
demimonde was crassly superficial. The rural periphery in many a *kibyōshi*,
therefore, turns out to be more stylized than substantive, as we see in *Swingers*. This stylization contributes to the comic nature of these narratives too.
"The *agroikos*," as Eric Segal has observed in a different context, "is an archetypal comic figure."[108]

Deeper down, however, this rhetoric may project the anxiety many authors of popular literature themselves may have felt, or assumed a large part
of their readerships felt, coming to Edo from the provinces as part of the

------

106. Mizuno, *Sharebon taisei 6*, pp. 65–82.

107. The line in Japanese is *Naniwa no tsū wa Edo no yabo*. The work in question is *Kō no
mono no o* (1783), a *kibyōshi* written by Shiba Zenkō and illustrated by Kitao Masanobu. Cited
in Tanahashi, *Kibyōshi sōran 1*, p. 451.

108. Segal, *The Death of Comedy*, p. 4.

system of alternate attendance. In this sense, perhaps the *kibyōshi* helps to work out the anxieties of different kinds of unevenness. Before he transforms himself into the playboy Master Flashgold, Harumachi's protagonist is just such a lowly samurai from the hinterlands. His transformation somehow mirrors the demographics of contemporary migration from rural periphery to urban centers that was part of the shift from agrarian to commercial base. One can only imagine that it stimulated such a desire in readers.

Edo-centrism also frequently has a temporal aspect, alluding playfully to noticeable aspects of contemporary metropolitan life, especially current fashions of speech, dress, music, literature, and so forth, not to mention the latest gossip. Edo thereby emerges not just as the geographic center of the domainal collectivity, but as the chronological center. Many a work of Edo literature pits the present against the decaying past—a contrast that had its place in the debates among serious scholars of National Learning (*Kokugaku*), Chinese Studies, and so on, as well as in the heated Edo-Kamigata rivalry. Edo is repeatedly portrayed as the Quintessential Now against which all possible Thens are implicitly contrasted, if not explicitly juxtaposed. Often, the past is ridiculed as *démodé*, as in *Familiar Bestsellers*, in which previous genres are made to dress and to speak in the fashions of yesteryear, not in the trendy manner of the Edo present. This was more than an exaltation of contemporary chic as a strategy to overtake the Kamigata tradition. It also amounted to a commercial ploy, since one form of expression of contemporary metropolitan life that appears frequently within the *kibyōshi* is the latest commercial product for sale, as we see in the pieces translated in this volume.

If the *kibyōshi* wrote its own popularity by passing itself off as *au courant*, the flip side was a proportionately rapid obsolescence. Since the *kibyōshi* is all about immediacy, the minutiae of the moment that would be forgotten a moment later, the radical topicality of the genre may have doomed it to obscurity. Today, many of the references in the *kibyōshi* seem dismayingly arcane, the artifacts of a bygone century as remote to us as Heian Japan must have seemed to the denizens of An'ei-Tenmei Edo. For this reason, the *kibyōshi* comes across at times as completely impenetrable. The *kibyōshi* does not concern itself directly with such things as universal truths or grand statements about the human condition, let alone the meaning of life. For such answers, one must extrapolate to the point of hallucination.

A domestic-foreign axis may also inform Edo-centrism. Edo often is made to symbolize Japan *vis-à-vis* China, Korea, India, or even the West, not to mention other fantastic realms such as the fabled Isle of Women, the country of Hollow Chests, and the land of Longlegs. Sometimes, national differences are represented graphically by physiognomic or bodily signifiers, no doubt as part of the construction of Japaneseness as some putative human "normalcy." Several works, thus, portray a veritable menagerie of

Fig. 1.21 In an imagined "Kingdom of Blacks" (*Kuronbō no kuni*), a woman scrubs her skin "whiter than snow" (*yuki yori shiroku*) with washing powder ordered from the Tamaya—an actual beauty shop in Japan—as her husband looks on in amazement. From *Cosmetics for Seven Female Masakados* (*Onna Masakado hichinin geshō*, 1792), a *kibyōshi* written by Santō Kyōden and illustrated by Kitao Masayoshi. Courtesy of Waseda University Library, Special Collections.

freaks (*katawa*), monsters (*bakemono*), and what to the Japanese at the time must have seemed like exotic creatures, including African slaves, who had been brought to Japan to serve Western whites (**Figure 1.21**).[109] The principle of "difference projected" often is at work in these examples, shrugging off cultural attributes that are uncomfortable if not painful to recognize in one's own self or group and casting them onto a convenient Other.

Of course, Japanese literature had long dealt with freaks and foreigners. Yet it was becoming increasingly difficult to pretend that no other peoples existed out there in the world. Although the Tokugawa shogunate had endeavored to confine Westerners to Deshima, interlopers sporadically ap-

---

109. A transliterated version of this *kibyōshi*, Kyōden's *Cosmetics for Seven Female Masakados* (*Onna Masakado hichinin geshō* [*sic*], 1792), can be found in Mizuno, *SKZ 3*, pp. 155–168.

peared, breaking whatever illusion of homogeneity was otherwise being maintained. In 1771, for instance, the Hungarian adventurer Moric Aladar Benyowsky (1746–1786) landed unexpectedly on the Japanese coast, causing something of a stir. More monumentally, in 1785 the Japanese themselves, out of a desire to expand, dispatched missions of enquiry to Ezo (present-day Hokkaido), inhabited by the un-Japanese-looking Ainu. Yet it was these various foreign and physiological Others who, through their representation in the *kibyōshi* and other forms of popular literature, were beginning to colonize the popular imagination of An'ei-Tenmei Edo.

Along these lines, the foreign Other was also represented in the *kibyōshi* linguistically, in the form of a limited number of both "loanwords" derived from Western languages and even Western writing. Shiba Zenkō, in *Thousand-Armed Goddess of Mercy, Julienned* (*Daihi no senrokuhon*, 1785), puns on the Portuguese-derived word for the main ingredient in turpentine (*terementeina*).[110] The "Dutch" alphabet even appears in Kanwatei Onitake's appropriately titled *Trilateral Babble* (*Wakaran monogatari*, 1803).[111] In his preface, Onitake exhibits the writing of Japan, China, and Holland along with representative figures from each country (**Figure 1.22**). Novelty gag though it surely was, *Trilateral Babble* also may have been one of the first instances in which the representation of Western writing found a wide popular audience in Japan. Furthermore, the Dutch letters are used to more than decorative effect. When read aloud, they actually make sense to the Japanese ear. However, so as not to *completely* exclude readers as yet unschooled in Dutch (meaning just about everybody in Edo), the letters are glossed with Japanese phonetic guides for anyone to decipher.

Edo-centrism in popular literature was not merely a reflection of social reality, then, or even an absolute construction of it. Rather, if not an attempt at reconciling a seismological clash of cultures—the Edo-Kamigata shift being the undeniable epicenter—Edo-centrism was, at minimum, a bid for cultural supremacy, a kind of fictional confutation in which, as Evelyn B. Tribble has put it, "one's opponents were invited onto the page, there to be confronted and, it [was] hoped, defeated . . ."[112] The *kibyōshi*, like several related genres of popular literature, took Edo and its Floating World as the measure of just about everything: the urban center against which even Kyoto and Osaka measured only as a rural periphery; the modern, new, faddish paragon of style (linguistic as well as sartorial) against which the hackneyed fell flat; and the quintessential exemplar of Japaneseness against which other Asian and non-Asian groups were strikingly counterpoised. In

---

110. Inoue makes this point in *Edo gesaku no kenkyū*, p. 350.

111. For a transcribed though unannotated version of this text, see Tōkyō gakugei daigaku kokugo kokubungakkai kinsei bungaku bunkakai daigakuin dōjin, *Kusamura*, vol. 20 (1998), pp. 233–254.

112. Tribble, "The Peopled Page," p. 109.

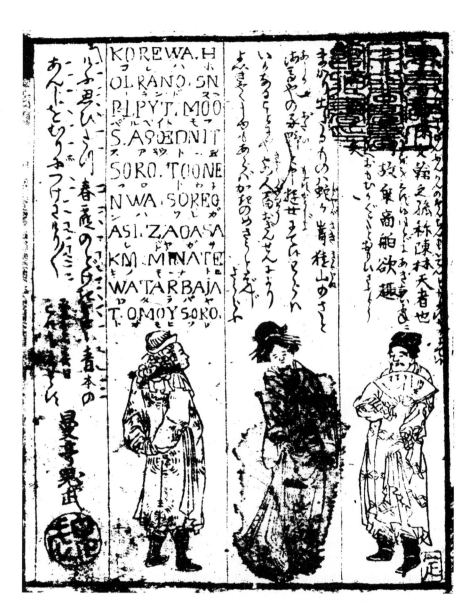

Fig. 1.22 Specimens of Chinese, Japanese, and Dutch persons and writing. From the Preface to *Trilateral Babble* (*Wakaran monogatari*, 1803), a *kibyōshi* written by Kanwatei Onitake and illustrated by Kakō (Hokusai). Courtesy of Tokyo Metropolitan Central Library, Kaga Collection.

short, the *kibyōshi* played with difference, though the stakes of this game were far from lighthearted.

On the other hand, Edo-centrism—especially its valorization of a common Edo language—can be said to have participated in a larger strategy of generating a readership by drawing the line between insiders and outsiders. The many forms of puns, puzzles, allusional challenges, code words, word games, special argot, secret languages, rebuses, and so on that the *kibyōshi* genre mobilizes obsessively do something similar, sorting out those who "get" the answer from those who do not. Thus, in the final analysis, the use of Edo-centrism in the *kibyōshi* reflected and constructed Edo as a cultural space only among its readers in Edo who caught all the esoteric references and could solve the various forms of puzzles. The *kibyōshi* never projected the Edo culture or language effectively to the *actual* rural periphery, in other words, not only because of the limits of woodblock printing, but also because of the way that the genre itself was conceived.

Some twentieth-century thinkers such as Yanagita Kunio and Orikuchi Shinobu have argued that modernization began during the Meiji period largely as a result of a center-periphery dynamic played out on a national scale. If the *kibyōshi* and other forms of Edo popular literature, by symbolically annihilating competing urban centers and projecting that city as the center of the emerging nation, served as precedent to this process, then perhaps the *kibyōshi* was indeed early modern in a sense. Granted, by that logic, the establishment of the Central Kingdom of China itself would have to mark the beginning of early modernity eons earlier. But in the case of eighteenth-century Edo, the central city was beginning to undergo linguistic and social leveling that, by virtue of the new and ever-improving print media, was affecting the popular imagination in increasingly profound and fast ways. Although the *kibyōshi* might be regarded as late traditional in that its content represents the literary culmination of everything that came before it, it might be said to be early modern in its will toward social and linguistic leveling, a will that was backed up by a growing commercial industry, and one that somehow set the pattern of increasing centralization that would most typify Tokyo.

Underwriting Desire

Mention of the people, places, and things of Edo that were a part of the process of identity construction in widely disseminated genres like the *kibyōshi* naturally has a promotional effect. Pay tribute to a clothing store within a *kibyōshi*—the Nakaya, say—and business there might get a welcome boost. The advent of mass publishing, then, advanced the practice of advertising, which can be thought of as the stimulation of desire to buy something. Granted, as a form of mass entertainment, the popular stage had already begun to realize the potential of product placement, of effectively retailing commercial goods within its plays. Yet print could bring the message to the people rather than require that the people come to the message. In a larger sense, then, the advertising potential of the *kibyōshi* was a natural byproduct of the capacity of mass-produced literature to reach and *influence* a broad audience beyond the physical limitations of the stage. Thus, it should come as no surprise that the *kibyōshi* contained a range of advertisements, from the subtle winking nod, through simple notices in the form of publisher's lists or colophons at the end of a work, to actual cases of product placement within the fabric of stories.

The colophon graces many a *kibyōshi*, announcing other works in a variety of genres issued by the publisher of the *kibyōshi*. Such is visible in the colophon at the end of Kisanji's *A Treasury of Loyal Sophisticates (Ana dehon*

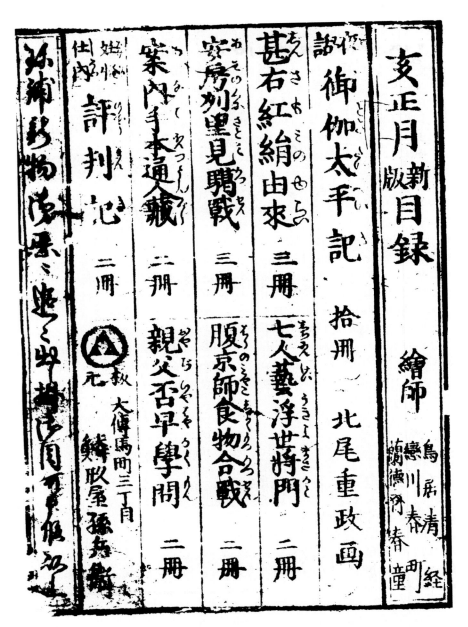

Fig. 1.23 Colophon announcing various titles in print. From *A Treasury of Loyal Sophisticates (Ana dehon tsūjingura*, 1779), a *kibyōshi* written by Hōseidō Kisanji and illustrated by Koikawa Harumachi. Courtesy of Tokyo Metropolitan Central Library, Tokyo Collection.

tsūjingura, 1779) (**Figure 1.23**). There were advertisements for *kibyōshi* within the colophons of other genres, too, of course, since advertising was by no means restricted to the *kibyōshi*. The colophon at the end of the 1785 New Year's edition of *The Yoshiwara, Detailed (Yoshiwara saiken)*, for instance, a kind of guidebook to Edo's most celebrated pleasure quarter, contains announcements for about 50 works in different genres closely tied to the Yoshiwara, some of which were previously published, but others of which were being published at the same time as *The Yoshiwara, Detailed* itself. These include such things as woodblock albums like Masanobu's *New Pageant of*

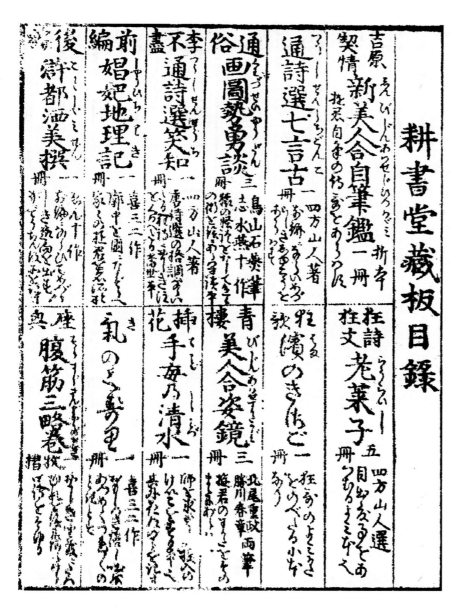

Fig. 1.24 First of four pages of a publishing announcement. From the New Year's edition of *The Yoshiwara, Detailed* (*Yoshiwara saiken*, 1785). The entry at top right is for *A Pageant of the Latest Beauties*. Reprinted in Hanasaki, *Tenmeiki Yoshiwara saiken shū*.

Beauties (1784); fashionbooks like Kyōden's *The Rookie's Room* (*Musukobeya*, 1785); madcap prose and poetry; and *kibyōshi* like Zenkō's *Thousand-Armed Goddess* (**Figure 1.24**). The colophon suggests that publishers of popular literature were well aware of the advertising potential of their printed media.

Sometimes advertisements of the sort appearing within a colophon are worked into the main narrative of the *kibyōshi*. In *Familiar Bestsellers*, for instance, Kyōden praises several *kibyōshi* and their authors associated with Tsuruya Kiemon (fl. ca. 1780s), the proprietor of the Senkakudō publishing house that issued *Familiar Bestsellers* itself. Of course, to the extent that the hero of *Familiar Bestsellers* is a *kibyōshi*, this piece might also be engaged in underwriting the very genre.

Fig. 1.25 In an early example of product placement, the text of an advertisement for Kyōden's real-life tobacco store is embedded smack in the middle of the left panel of this *kibyōshi*, *Nenashigusa fude no wakabae* (1794). Written and illustrated by Santō Kyōden. Courtesy of Tokyo Metropolitan Central Library, Tokyo Collection.

Advertisements for other kinds of commercial goods on sale in Edo are also to be found. Kyōden provides one of the best case studies, plugging his own tobacco paraphernalia store (which he ran under his merchant name, Kyōya Denzō) within several of his *kibyōshi*. For instance, he slips the following ad into the main narrative of one piece (**Figure 1.25**):

Here, allow me to present an announcement. Kyōden has just recently opened a new store specializing in the latest paper tobacco-pouches and in sundry rare goods. This has been a message humbly requesting the kind favor of your patronage![113]

Likewise, in another piece:

And now, allow me to present an announcement. Santō Kyōden has just recently opened a new store specializing in paper tobacco-pouches of the latest style—possessed of a simple elegance, resembling those made of cloth, and convenient to use. I humbly request the kind favor of your patronage. Signed: Kyōya Denzō of Kyōbashi in the Ginza.[114]

---

113. Mentioned in Tani, *Edo no kopīraitā*, p. 55. A transliterated version of the text can be found in Mizuno, *SKZ 3*, pp. 497–524. For more on this, see Kern, "Blowing Smoke."

114. *Mikenjaku sannin namaei* (1794). Mentioned in Tani, *Edo no kopīraitā*, p. 54. A transliterated version of the text can be found in Mizuno, *SKZ 3*, pp. 475–496.

Such advertisements of one's non-literary commercial goods seem to have found their way into the works of other authors and into other genres of popular literature, too. It is known that Kyōden disciple Shikitei Sanba promoted his medicine shop at the end of the volumes in his funnybook *Bathhouse to the Floating World*. Yet a *kibyōshi* might plug commercial products that apparently had little if anything to do with that *kibyōshi*, its author, or its publisher per se. The washing powder (*araiko*) used to whiten the African lady in Kyōden's *Cosmetics for Seven Female Masakados* (*Onna Masakado hichinin geshō*, 1792), for instance, which was on sale in Edo at the Tamaya, does not seem to have any demonstrable connection to Kyōden. Tempura restaurants, according to Mori, are promoted in this way within some works, too.[115]

Occasionally a kind of food rather than a specific eatery might be advertised. Like many cartoon monsters (*bakemono*), "Tofu Boy" (*Tōfu Kozō*) was the offspring of the mass market, conceived as a commercial tie-in—the Edo version, Adam Kabat opines, of some well-known modern advertising cartoon characters:

Sometimes new monsters were created specifically for the mass market. These were often linked to current gossip, theater productions, or sideshow attractions. This process, in which a certain monster was promoted through various media simultaneously, is strikingly similar to the promotion campaigns that are carried on today. A case in point is . . . Tofu Boy, a cherubic, rotund creature who wanders about town carrying a tray of tofu. Nothing much ever happens to Tofu Boy. He may follow somebody home at night, or inadvertently drop his tofu, more scared than scary. Tofu Boy is a true "character monster" in that with his trademark tray of tofu he is instantly recognizable even though he doesn't do anything per se or have any story—an Edo version of Hello Kitty.[116]

In a similar kind of marketing gimmick, Sanba timed the release of some of his multivolume comicbooks that he based on kabuki plays with the actual staging of those plays: "Something over 40 percent of his *gōkan*—28 titles in all—are based closely on kabuki or *jōruri* dramas," writes Leutner, "works . . . whose publication seems often to have been timed to coincide with the openings of new plays or new mountings of old favorites."[117] In a sense, comicbook and kabuki play were mutually reinforcing, for those who read Sanba's multivolumes would have wanted to see the play (if they had not done so already) and, conversely, audience members wanting a written version of the play might have been tempted to purchase Sanba's piece.

Naturally, the *kibyōshi* also often includes advertisements for goods that only exist within the fictional world of the story. So, for instance, "menu

---

115. For more on the tempura plug in Kyōden's *kibyōshi*, titled *Hana no emi shichi fuku mōde* (1793), see Mori, "Tenpura no senden o shiteiru kibyōshi."

116. Kabat, "Monsters as Edo Merchandise," p. 75.

117. Leutner, *Shikitei Sanba*, p. 45.

boards" in several *kibyōshi* announce imaginary products not vendible outside the fictional frame in the real world. The characters in Kisanji's *Dreamers the Winners* (*Miru ga toku issui no yume*, 1781) rent magic "dream pillows" that supposedly allow one to see a specifically requested dream. There is reason to believe that some real-life entrepreneurs had the vision to market products based on such fictional goods, too. If anything demonstrates the advertising potential of the *kibyōshi*, it is this. We know that the *netsuke* used to accessorize one's tobacco pouch (perhaps not unlike tiny plastic creatures dangling from cell phones today) imbibed deeply of the wellspring of popular culture, including specific works of *kibyōshi*.[118] The imaginary handtowel featuring a pug-nosed character that would eventually become the visual model for Enjirō in Kyōden's *Playboy* may be an example, too. Although it is not clear precisely when the make-believe handtowel was turned into an actual commercial good, it is still on sale as a novelty item in the Asakusa section of Tokyo, a brief jaunt from where the Yoshiwara pleasure quarter was situated during An'ei-Tenmei.[119]

Those who subscribe to the dubious notion that the *kibyōshi* was the direct progenitor of the modern *manga* no doubt will take the existence of such commercial tie-ins, product placement, and commercial crossover as further evidence of a strong link between the two. The modern *manga* is even more extensively shot through with commercialism: "The most striking aspect of *CoroCoro* is not the quality of its stories," Schodt writes of Shōgakukan's *manga* magazine for young boys, to take but one case, "it is the number of tie-ins with other industries."[120]

If it could be proved that *CoroCoro* or some other modern *manga* derived this tactic *directly* from the *kibyōshi*, that would be one thing. Absent that, however, what can be said is that advertisements within the *kibyōshi* and related genres were the natural product of the logic of mass printing. If it sometimes seems difficult to differentiate between product placement and local color, especially since there is often no evidence to demonstrate how an author might have benefited financially by plugging some commercial good, in the larger context of constructing an Edo identity, such trivial distinctions disappear. Not to overstate the case, but the *kibyōshi* was a key utensil in the underwriting of Edo. In conclusion, if the *kibyōshi* as a vastly popular genre can be read as an advertisement for the Floating World of An'ei-Tenmei Edo, its people, language, commercial establishments, and genres, not to mention the city itself, then any kind of product placement or local color can be said to have painted the popular imagination.

---

118. For more on this, see Iwasaki, "Speak, Memory!"
119. The shop, the Fujiya, is located in Taitō-ku at Asakusa 2–2–15.
120. Schodt, *Dreamland Japan*, p. 85.

Chapter 2

The Blossom of

Pulp Fiction

PULP (pulp) n. 1. A soft, moist, shapeless mass or matter. 2. A magazine or book containing lurid subject matter and being characteristically printed on rough, unfinished paper. —American Heritage Dictionary, New College Edition, as cited by Quentin Tarantino in the film Pulp Fiction

The Kibyōshi as the Flower of Gesaku

The radical interrelatedness of the *kibyōshi* to other genres, as well as its capacity to map and mirror the world of An'ei-Tenmei Edo, qualifies it as an excellent entrée into that world's popular culture. Indeed, the *kibyōshi* has on occasion been hailed as the consummate genre of *gesaku*, that assortment of popular literary forms epitomizing the efflorescence of Edo's sophisticated culture during the mid- and late Edo period. Many major scholars of Edo-period literature consider the *kibyōshi* to represent the acme of popular literature. A recent exhibit of *kibyōshi* in Yokohama characterized it as the "flower of *gesaku*."[1] At first blush, this phrase seems overwrought, an oxymoronic cliché mindlessly describing in organic terms something mass-produced by machines. However, the metaphor is peculiarly apt—perhaps in ways unbeknownst to the exhibit's organizers?—for something like it has enjoyed perennial life. As far back as the earliest extant writings in Japan, such as the eighth-century *Record of Ancient Matters*, laughter has been said to "burgeon forth" (*saku*) like some uncommon blossom.

The word *gesaku* literally means frivolous (*ge*) composition (*saku*). It can be interpreted to mean "playful writing," suggesting that such works were tossed off half in jest. Looking at the Chinese graphs, one might easily suppose they should be read *gisaku*, since *gi* is the more common

---

1. So called by curator of the Hiraki Ukiyoe Museum, Satō Mitsunobu. In the preface to Satō, *Gesaku no hana*, p. 1.

pronunciation. The less common one, however, puns on the homonym *ge* in words like "vulgar" (*gehin*), so that *gesaku* might also suggest "lowbrow blooms" of laughter. In either case, the word is redolent with ironic self-denigration, as though its fruits were merely the whimsical divertissements of amateur writers, or else the "pulp fiction" of commercial hacks. This does not mean that the genres subsumed by the term *gesaku* should be taken at face value, for many works in this mode were complex literary and artistic creations.

Be that as it may, *gesaku* is a catchall term, covering a constellation of loosely allied genres of typically humorous popular literature. These genres mostly consist of prose fiction, such as the mock-sermon book, collections of humorous anecdotes, the "funnybook," various forms of comicbooks—like the adult *kibyōshi* and the more serious-minded multivolume chapbook that tended to revel in stories of cold revenge—madcap Chinese prose, melodramatic "sentiment books," fashion books, and the oft-times moralistic "reading book."[2] Several kinds of comic poetry are also closely related to *gesaku* as well, though these are not typically subsumed under the term. These include such things as madcap verse, madcap Chinese poetry, a hybrid form of madcap Chinese prose and poetry, comic haiku, and even a kind of haiku so bawdy as to be all but unprintable.

It might be observed from this abbreviated inventory that not all genres of *gesaku* are expressly comic. The multivolume chapbook, the sentiment book, and the reading book can hardly be described, after all, as predominantly lighthearted. Generally speaking, though, by the early years of the nineteenth century when these particular genres flourished, the label that had previously been reserved exclusively for those works peddling in playfulness had come to indicate more broadly anything written as a form of mass entertainment—even if that entertainment was flavored by mercilessness, melodrama, or moralism. Yet it is the comic element in particular that sets *gesaku* apart and qualifies it for consideration, in the opinion of many, as a literary phenomenon. In his noteworthy study of the comic spirit in modern Japanese literature, Cohn singles out *gesaku* for special mention as "one of the supreme comic high points in Japanese cultural history."[3]

Whether or not the *kibyōshi* best epitomizes mid-Edo popular literature, what is certain is that since the former is such an intensely hybrid affair, it cannot be fruitfully studied without at least a general understanding of the latter. It would be difficult to appreciate the *kibyōshi* fully without situating it in its most immediate generic context. And yet a rehearsal here of all the various genres comprising *gesaku* would be a fool's errand, fraught with

---

2. Those genres that assumed booklet format, like the *kibyōshi*, might also be described by the related term "playful chapbooks" (*tawarezōshi*)—*taware* being the Japanese reading of the Chinese graph *ge* of *gesaku*.

3. Cohn, *Studies in the Comic Spirit in Modern Japanese Fiction*, p. 18.

innumerable chances to inadvertently mislead, since Japanese let alone Western scholarship has only barely begun to consider this massive literature, which numbers maybe in the thousands if not tens of thousands of titles. Thankfully, other scholars have gone out on a limb to get at these genres already.[4]

Still, few if any of these scholars have concerned themselves with exploring the interconnections among *gesaku* genres with respect to the *kibyōshi* in particular. This chapter therefore briefly touches upon a few such genres that seem exceptionally germane. These include the mock-sermon book, the fashionbook, and the jokebook. Some others that are not typically subsumed under the *gesaku* rubric but nonetheless exert a palpable influence upon the *kibyōshi* are also considered, such as various forms of guidebook literature, the *kibyōshi* reviewbook, comic poetry like the madcap verse and comic haiku, and even kabuki and its associated theatrical texts.

Two caveats are in order. First, although earlier forms of "children's" comicbooks such as the redbook and blackbook also shaped the *kibyōshi*, discussion of these incunabula is deferred until a later chapter. Second, and more significantly, it should be kept in mind that the paradox of interrelatedness complicates any consideration of literary influence, for the interplay among the tapestry of these genres makes them virtually impossible to disentangle from one another. So, for the sake of simplicity, only the most salient features of each genre are focused upon here.[5]

The Mock-Sermon Book

One of the archetypal genres of Edo *gesaku*, from which the *kibyōshi* drew some inspiration in its portrayal of the Edo vernacular if not its sense of humor, was the *dangibon*. Although literally meaning "sermon book," this was actually a genre of *mock* address, typically consisting of one or more humorous stories that had little if any seriously religious or moralizing content.[6] *A*

---

4. In English, see especially Hibbett, *The Chrysanthemum and the Fish*; Iwasaki, "The World of *Gesaku*"; Keene, *World Within Walls*; Leutner, *Shikitei Sanba*; Shirane, *EMJL*; and Ueda, *Light Verse From the Floating World*.

5. This is not to imply either that any given genre influenced the *kibyōshi* only in a single way, or that other genres did not influence the *kibyōshi* considerably. The *kibyōshi* may have appropriated its brand of sophistication primarily from the fashionbook, for example, though the fashionbook contributed other things, too, just as the *kibyōshi* looked to other genres for its conception of sophistication.

6. The genre's name indicates not the content of individual works per se, but rather its origins in soapbox oratory (*dangi*). Originally, this oratory was a kind of public sermon employing earthy humor and simple terms in order to popularize Buddhist teachings, especially those of the Nichiren, Ritsu, and Jōdo sects, though it quickly came to be appropriated as a vehicle of popular street entertainment. When set to print—and absorbing humorous content from the *otogizōshi*, the *kyōgen* stage, Chinese vernacular tales (*baihua*), the "character sketches" (*katagimono*) of Ejima Kiseki, and so forth—the mock sermon book itself was born.

Treatise on Flatulence (*Hōhiron*, 1774) and *Biographies of Limp Dicks in Seclusion* (*Naemara in'itsuden*, 1768), for instance, can hardly be described as sermons, at least not in the *bona fide* sense.[7] Nor can *The Funeral Director's Blowout-Sale Circular* (*Sōshichi yasuuri no hikifuda seshi koto*, 1752), for that matter, a darkly comic short story describing a bungled attempt at an advertising blitz.[8]

The roots of the mock-sermon book, like many other genres of *gesaku*, ultimately may extend back to works published in Kamigata, such as Issai Chozan's *Hickish Zhuangzi* (*Inaka Sōshi*, 1717).[9] By mid-century, however, a homegrown Edo variety, emphasizing that city's customs, people, places, and, especially, the colloquial speech of its commoners, had become massively popular. So much so that the mock-sermon book is retrospectively taken to be one of the earliest major representative genres of Edo's popular literature. The first such work of consequence, and no doubt the most celebrated exemplar, is widely considered to be Jōkanbō Kōa's *Newfangled Spiels* (*Imayō hetadangi*, 1752). This was an immediate bestseller, garnered critical hosannas, and inspired a sequel issued within the year.[10]

Although the mock-sermon book reached its pinnacle of popularity over the next decade or two, it remained a vibrant form throughout the latter half of the eighteenth century. Its heavy use of the Edo vernacular set a precedent for the fashionbook, the *kibyōshi*, the funnybook, and other heavily dialogue-based genres of popular literature.[11] Since its expanse of cursive scrawl was relieved by only one or two rather simple illustrations per story, however, the mock-sermon book cannot be considered a "comic-book" per se. Granted, some of its occasional illustrations can be quite lively, as with those in Hiraga Gennai's smash hit *Rootless Grass* (*Nenashigusa*, 1763) (**Figure 2.1**).[12] Still, one often finds references to the content of particular mock-sermon books within individual *kibyōshi*. Kyōden's *Unsavorily Mismatched Jiffy Shanks* (*Fuanbai sokuseki ryōri*, 1784), a fanciful takeoff of sorts on Gennai's story from two decades earlier, presumes a detailed knowledge of Gennai's illustrations as well as his verbal text (**Figure 2.2**).[13]

---

7. For translations of these pieces, respectively, see Drake, "A Theory of Farting," or Sibley, "On Farting"; and Marceau, *Biographies of Limp Dicks in Seclusion*.

8. For a translation, see Kern, *The Funeral Director's Blowout-Sale Circular*.

9. Here, *Sōshi* refers to Zhuangzi as well as to the chapbook format. An annotated version of the text is in Nakano, *SNKBT 81*, pp. 1–68. Nakano reads the term *sōji*.

10. *Newfangled Spiels* (which contains the story about the funeral director) was praised in the reviewbook *Sengoku dōshi* (1754). Its sequel was *Moralizing Spiels* (*Kyōkun hetadangi*), which was billed in advertisements and in its subtitle as *Spiels, Continued* (*Zoku hetadangi*). No doubt these works, which were issued in Edo, contributed the word that defined the genre, which may be why the *dangibon* is not associated with Kamigata per se.

11. See the brief history of the *dangibon* in the explanatory essay in Nakano, *SNKBT 81*, pp. 359–418.

12. For an annotated version of *Nenashigusa*, see Nakamura, *Fūrai Sanjin shū*, pp. 33–94.

13. A transcribed but unannotated version of this *kibyōshi* can be found in Mizuno, *SKZ 1*, pp. 149–168.

(*left*) Fig. 2.1 A goofy-looking water sprite (*kappa*). From *Rootless Grass* (*Nenashigusa*, 1763), a mock-sermon book by Hiraga Gennai. Reprinted in Nakamura, *Fūrai Sanjin shū*, p. 89. Courtesy of Iwanami shoten.

(*below*) Fig. 2.2 A goofy-looking water sprite (*kappa*), modeled on the one in Gennai's *Rootless Grass* of two decades earlier. From *Unsavorily Mismatched Jiffy Shanks* (*Fuanbai sokuseki ryōri*, 1784), a *kibyōshi* written and illustrated by Santō Kyōden. Courtesy of Tokyo Metropolitan Central Library, Kaga Collection.

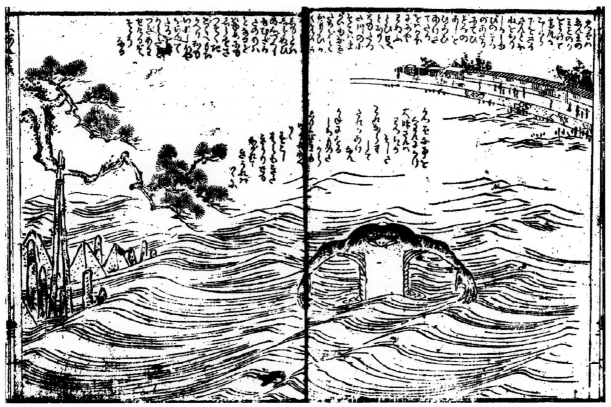

The Fashionbook   The genre of *gesaku* to exert the most influence upon the *kibyōshi*, if just one must be named, is probably the fashionbook (*sharebon*).[14] A mainstay of Edo *gesaku*, this urbane brand of popular fiction, as a rule sparsely illustrated, is largely devoted to the latest and swankest *haute couture*, etiquette, and colloquialisms of the day. The word *share* means "smart" in two senses—nattily dressed (as in modern Japanese *oshare*) as well as wittily or even punningly worded. To the extent that the licensed districts served as the ever-gushing font of such fashionableness, most fashionbooks naturally concern themselves with the Floating World of pleasure quarters. Most but not all, for there was a variety of other formulae and even settings, such as: "meetings, travel, banquets, the boudoir, the morning after, and so on."[15] Kyōden's *Three Madames and Their Dirty Tale* (*Kokei no sanshō*, 1787), for instance, traces the domesticated lives of courtesans after their retirement from the major pleasure quarters of Edo.[16]

The two most salient features of the fashionbook to impact the *kibyōshi*, though, are arguably the emphasis placed upon this sort of sophistication and the implementation of an everyday conversational style as narrative. Earlier genres of literature like the companion booklet, syllabary booklet, and Floating World novella, as well as forms of popular theater such as *kyōgen* and especially kabuki, employed the contemporary dialogue of the common folk to varying degrees of effectiveness. However, the authors of mid-Edo genres of playful literature like the mock-sermon book and the fashionbook became unprecedentedly preoccupied with the narrative possibilities of the realistic rendering of language as it was spoken outside the aristocracy. More so than the mock-sermon book, even, the fashionbook—or at least its main "conversational" form (*kaiwatai sharebon*)—gave itself over completely to this preoccupation. In many such works, the dialogue *was* the story. The only narrative intrusions of descriptive prose were the occasional "stage directions," usually rendered in a smaller hand—the premodern equivalent of italics—or with symbols or boxed names indicating the different speakers (**Figure 2.3**). Such works certainly contain little if anything in the way of interior monologue. As such, the fashionbook represents one of the earliest efforts at *sustained* realistic conversation in the vernacular within Japanese letters, an effort that clearly carried over into the dialogic sections of the *kibyōshi*.

14. For more on the fashionbook in English, see Araki, "*Sharebon*: Books for Men of Mode"; Kornicki, "*Nishiki no Ura*"; Miller, "The Hybrid Narrative of Kyōden's *Sharebon*"; and Martin, "Santō Kyōden and His *Sharebon*." In German, see Schamoni, *Die Sharebon Santō Kyōden und ihre Literaturgeschichtliche Stellung.*

15. Nakamura, *Gesakuron*, p. 144.

16. For an annotated version, see Nakano, *SNKBT 80*, pp. 79–102. For a translation, see Campbell, *Three Madames and Their Dirty Tale.*

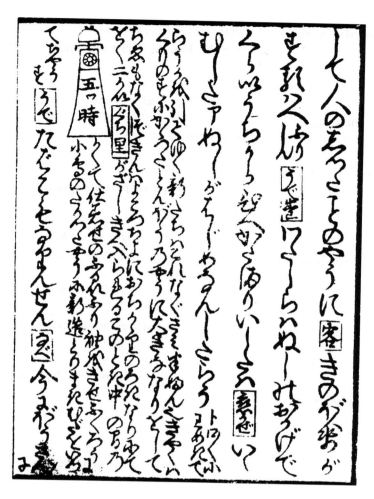

Fig. 2.3 Representative
page from *Behind Silk Brocade*
(*Nishiki no ura*, 1791), a
conversational fashionbook
by Santō Kyōden. Courtesy
of Tokyo Metropolitan
Central Library, Special
Acquisitions Collection.

Although there are many interesting exceptions, the *kibyōshi* and the fashionbook also generally share an abiding fascination with the world of the pleasure quarters, its rules of etiquette, characters, fashionable garb and lingo, and, above all, the Edo brand of sophistication. Kamigata had long boasted its own ideal of classiness (*sui*) and stylishness (*iki*).[17] It was only natural that, with the swing eastward, Edo developed its homegrown variety as a major part of the assertion of its own cultural identity. Thus, the terms sophistication (*tsū*), sophisticate (*tsūjin*), and great sophisticate (*daitsū*)— which had collectively evolved from the frequenter (*tōribito* or *tōrimono*) of the pleasure quarters in Edo—became household words in the shogun's capital around the An'ei-Tenmei era.[18] The hallmark of this brand of Edo

---

17. Pincus renders *iki* as "bordello chic" in *Authenticating Culture in Imperial Japan*, p. 119.

18. The term "sophistication" (*tsū*)—which sometimes is an abbreviation of the term "sophisticate" (*tsūjin*)—seems to go as far back as *A Guide to Love in the Yoshiwara* (*Yoshiwara koi no michibiki*, 1678). The earlier term "frequenting" (*tōri*) had often been suffixed to another word, as in the "frequenter" (*tōribito*) of, or the "regular" (*tōrimono*) in, the pleasure

sophistication was not only "cool," meaning a casual indifference to all that was required in the pursuit of pleasure—even squandering a vast fortune—but a kind of "penetrating" (*tōru*) understanding of the "world's loopholes" (*seken no ana*). This was less cynicism than *savoir-faire*. Thus, sophistication in Edo often took the form of an ironic detachment that was nonetheless grounded in a mastery of the particular details of Edo's cultural hotspots. Indeed, *tsū* might well be defined as the Edo brand of decadent urbanity that held sway in the Floating World of pleasure quarters, kabuki theaters, sideshow spectacles, and urban life at large.

Some fashionbooks consisted entirely of discussions among various sorts of characters desperate to acquire—or pretending to already possess—this brand of Edo sophistication. These characters include the rookie or youngster (*musuko*) not yet fully initiated into the ways of the Floating World; the poseur or half-baked sophisticate (*hankatsū* or *hanka tsūjin*), who tries too hard; and the out-and-out cultural philistine or boor (*yabo*), who is oblivious to the fact that his efforts will never quite pay off. Most readers would no doubt identify to one degree or other with these characters even if only privately, since few people were—or are—perfect sophisticates. Just as these characters serve as a vehicle for the reader to learn about the demimonde, then, so too do these characters themselves typically engage a "drumbearer" (*taikomochi*) or drum doctor (*taiko isha*), a kind of amiable escort for hire in the pleasure quarters whose role it was to keep a client company, provide comic relief, relieve tedium (especially while waiting for the chronically late courtesans to appear), and otherwise smooth over any awkward moments or breaches in decorum with light banter.

Many a fashionbook is concerned with the education of the aspiring sophisticate, and with the machinations of the professional guides, courtesans, and various entertainers or performers who earn their livelihood off of him. These are stock figures who find their home away from home in the *kibyōshi* as well—one certainly recognizes their likes in the playboy wannabe and his opportunistic sidekicks in Kyōden's *Playboy*. The kind of fashionbook that does as much has built into its very structure a way of including the less than perfectly sophisticated reader without offending him.

It is often said that the major strain of fashionbook follows the pattern of Inaka Rōjin Tadanojijii's *The Playboy's Idiom* (*Yūshi hōgen*, 1770), in which a sophisticate instructs a rookie on proper pleasure-quarter deportment.[19] The laughs in such works typically come at the cost of the boor, who not

---

quarters. Likewise, there was such a thing as the "frequenting boor" (*tōriyabo*). However, when *tōri* came to stand on its own, it was read as *tsū*. For more on this etymology, see Nakao, *Sui, tsū, iki*, pp. 145–164. Nakao cites the pronouncement in *Morisada's Trivia*: "In Kamigata it's *sui*, whereas in Edo it's *tsū*" (p. 145). Also, Teruoka notes that the term *daitsū* first appeared in 1770 but had become commonplace by 1777. In Teruoka, "The Pleasure Quarters and Tokugawa Culture," p. 26.

19. For an annotated edition, see Mizuno, *NKBT 59*, pp. 269–294.

infrequently hails from the provinces but is always inept. Sometimes it is the poseur who, only pretending to sophistication, is bound to have his humorous comeuppance. The comedy in this sort of fashionbook, then, typically resides in the pretensions of these stock comic types and how they fall laughably short of the ideal of sophistication. Edo's sartorial and linguistic styles, in other words, are constructed chiefly through the negative example of men behaving badly. In this sense, the fashionbook reminds one of those English pamphlets in the age of George III (1738–1820) that, according to Diana Donald, expounded "the rules of conduct through ironic presentations of their *opposites*. Every social solecism, from boorish table manners to garrulity, uncouth posture and impoliteness to ladies is illustrated here."[20] It is this tendency in the fashionbook to ridicule the departure from the notion of fashionable behavior it constructs that must have imbued the genre with much of its normative force.

This sophistication à la Edo is not the only major concern of the *kibyōshi*, or the fashionbook for that matter. Yet it is what separates the *kibyōshi* from earlier genres of comicbooks. In fact, the *kibyōshi* might functionally be defined as a kind of sophisticated Edo-period comedy of manners, with plenty of colloquial and witty repartee, in the guise of children's comicbooks. In this sense, the fashionbook is more fundamental to the *kibyōshi* than just about any other genre of *gesaku*.

Guidebook Literature

To the extent that the Edo fashionbook and the *kibyōshi* provided a kind of insider's view of Edo's sexiest contemporary cultural landscape, these genres can be said to have participated in the phenomenon of guidebook (*annaisho*) literature. Consisting of such things as travel guides to famous spots (*meishoki*) in urban centers but also in the country, etiquette manuals on connoisseurship in the pleasure quarters (*showake hidensho*), and various breeds of *vade mecum* to particular houses of pleasure (*annaiki*), the guidebook—although not a genre of *gesaku* per se—represented an important slice of the mass-publishing industry's pie of activities.

The guidebook that exerted the most profound influence upon the *kibyōshi* was arguably *The Yoshiwara, Detailed* (*Yoshiwara saiken*), in part because one of the major *kibyōshi* publishers, Tsutaya Jūzaburō, got his start peddling it himself. First published around 1684, subsequently revised periodically, though becoming issued regularly from about 1725 on, this guidebook provided a wealth of factual details about Edo's most storied licensed district that even the actual connoisseur would no doubt find of use.

Yet the roots of *The Yoshiwara, Detailed* seem to run deep within fiction, as with the imaginative *Tales of the East* (*Azuma monogatari*, 1642)—the "East" here referring to the Yoshiwara pleasure quarter "out east" in Edo. It might

---

20. Donald, *The Age of Caricature*, p. 96.

seem odd that a factual guidebook drew its inspiration from a fictional one. Guidebook literature, however, did not fall under any kind of obligation to be stringently truthful. Indeed, such works often delighted in embellishment, sometimes for the sake of advertising particular establishments, sometimes because local color sold copy, and sometimes because fiction was stranger than fact. "We read these works today as fiction," opines Richard Lane, "but at the time they were obviously written with very practical considerations in mind, as witness the inclusion of notations regarding mileage between stopovers and of other detailed travel information."[21]

This fictional vein runs throughout guidebook literature, almost as though verity and invention were viewed not as mutually exclusive but as two sides of the same strategic coin of stimulating the desire for travel—and for travel literature. One sees this certainly from the early seventeenth century, when travel was being transformed into tourism—pleasure jaunts, in other words, albeit largely under the cover of a "religious" purpose. The characters in one of Saikaku's yarns, for instance, set off on a supposedly holy pilgrimage in order to fulfill their own secret amorous desires.[22] Entire books based on similar road-trip misadventures can be found early on in works such as *Chikusai's Saga* (*Chikusai monogatari*, ca. 1620s), a syllabary booklet attributed to Karasumaru Mitsuhiro (1579–1638) describing the eponymously named quack doctor and his sidekick Niraminosuke as they bumble along from Kyoto to Nagoya on the country's main thoroughfare.[23] *Chikusai* helped establish the general pattern, if not the specific itinerary, of subsequent fictional travelogues, everything from Asai Ryōi's *Famous Sights Along the East-Sea Highway* (*Tōkaidō meishoki*, 1659) to Jippensha Ikku's funnybook *Hoofing It Along the East-Sea Highway* (*Tōkaidōchū hizakurige*, 1802–1822), which has been touted as "Japan's great comic novel."[24]

Guidebook literature helped the popular imagination map and, thus, increasingly interconnect the historically disconnected country. Whatever "factual" details were provided therein no doubt found their users, but the point of the literature probably had more to do with the construction of a social imaginary. Such literature became a kind of advertisement not just for the places mentioned but also for their very interconnectedness. Not everyone could afford to indulge their wildest fantasies in the Yoshiwara, no more than could everyone afford a fun-filled outing down the East-Sea Highway supposedly to worship at the Grand Shrines at Ise (though no doubt many did). In this sense, guidebook literature provided the

---

21. Lane, "The Beginnings of the Modern Japanese Novel," p. 676.

22. Translated as "The Barrelmaker Brimful of Love," in de Bary, *Five Women Who Loved Love*, pp. 72–113.

23. Karasumaru is thought to have written *Chikusai* during the 1620s but published it later, sometime between 1635 and 1645. See Putzar, "*Chikusai monogatari*."

24. For a translation that renders the colloquial dialogue into Cockney, see Satchell, *Shanks' Mare*.

antidote to the fever-inducing toxin it slyly administered. If guidebook literature contributed anything to the *kibyōshi*, then, it was this lesson about how to open up the Floating World to the popular imagination as well as to the popular consumer, vicariously satisfying some of the desire it aroused.

Reviewbooks   A kind of guidebook to the terrain of the *kibyōshi* itself, known as the *kibyōshi* reviewbook (*kibyōshi hyōbanki*), also existed.[25] This was a minor strain within the much larger corpus of reviewbook (*hyōbanki*) literature that broadly overlaps with guidebook literature, and therefore is not ordinarily classified as a genre of *gesaku*. Since the *kibyōshi* critique was closely associated with the reception of the *kibyōshi*, it probably influenced the composition of the *kibyōshi* as well, for surely authors must have written increasingly with reviewers in mind.

The reviewbook shares much in common with literary criticism, too. There was a venerable tradition in Japan of such criticism, as one might expect, going back at least as far as *Nameless Sheaves* (*Mumyōzōshi*), an early twelfth-century critique of fiction, in the form of a dialogue among several women, that ranked *The Tale of Genji* at the top of some 200 works.[26] It was not until the Edo period that this tradition seems to have coalesced into a mass-produced and widely circulated genre of reviewbook that trained its critical eye on any number of popular topics, such as storytellers and seafood. There was also the courtesan reviewbook (*yūjo hyōbanki*), which has obvious similarities to *The Yoshiwara, Detailed* and other guidebooks to the pleasure quarters. One of the classics of this subgenre was Fujimoto Kizan's *Great Mirror of the Way of Love* (*Shikidō ōkagami*, 1678), an encyclopedic tome detailing everything from the latest coiffures, through various sorts of demonstrations of one's supposed sincerity in affection (*shinjū*), down to how to *laugh* properly in different social settings.[27]

There was also the critique of kabuki stars, which in its early days tended to focus more on the physical charms of young male actors than on their acting skills per se—as with the provocatively titled *Bed Buggers* (*Yarō mushi*, ca. 1660). It was only with later works, such as Ejima Kiseki's *The Versatile Actor* (*Yakusha kuchijamisen*, 1699), that the kabuki critique offered authentic criticism of performances on the actual theatrical stage. By the early nineteenth century, the actor reviewbook (*yakusha hyōbanki*) had become such a

---

25. Actually, this is a retrospective term. At the time, it was variously referred to as the picturebook critique (*ezōshi hyōbanki*), comicbook critique (*kusazōshi hyōbanki*), or bluebook critique (*aohon hyōbanki*).

26. Only twenty of these works are extant. For more on *Mumyōzōshi* in English, see Marra, "Mumyōzōshi."

27. See Fujimoto Kizan, *Shikidō ōkagami*.

fixture that Sanba was able to turn the tables, publishing a spoof titled *Critique of Theatergoers* (*Kyakusha hyōbanki*, 1811).[28]

The typical *kibyōshi* reviewbook consisted of several parts, in the fashion of these earlier reviewbooks: itemized rankings of recently published works, a freewheeling dialogue among fictional critics, and light illustration. One of the best-known examples, Ōta Nanpo's *Flowery Felicitations* (*Kikujusō*, 1781), helped confer a kind of canonical pop status upon the forty-seven pieces it evaluated.[29] The preface invokes both the classic "rainy night conversation" from *The Tale of Genji* (in which Genji and his chums rank the various assets of women) and the contemporary "face showing" (*kaomise*) performance on the kabuki stage—as if to say that classification is both a timeless human activity and of keen timely interest. Indeed, following the designation of the "Six Poetic Immortals" of classic verse, reviewers eventually anointed "Six *Kibyōshi* Immortals" (*kusazōshi rokkasen*)—Hōseidō Kisanji, Ichiba Tsūshō, Koikawa Harumachi, Shiba Zenkō, Shinra Banshō, and Tōrai Sanna.

Another of Nanpo's reviewbooks, *Bystanders See It Better* (*Okame hachimoku*, 1782), is germane to *Familiar Bestsellers* (see **Figure 5.1**). Providing an itemized ranking of authors, artists, and works issued at the beginning of that publishing year, Nanpo acclaimed Kyōden's piece as the most excellent in the category of self-executed artwork.[30] Conversely, *Familiar Bestsellers* contains an evaluative discussion of various *kibyōshi* that could easily have taken place within a *kibyōshi* reviewbook—many of the titles Kyōden mentions in fact appeared in *Flowery Felicitations* the previous year. Although the *kibyōshi* reviewbook is not, strictly speaking, a kind of *gesaku*, it is nonetheless so dependent upon *gesaku*, and influential upon at least this particular *kibyōshi*, that it might be fruitful to consider it as an honorary member of the club.

Another *kibyōshi* reviewbook of interest is Onajiana Nokitsune's *Memento Edo* (*Edo miyage*, 1784).[31] Nokitsune evaluates each *kibyōshi* as though it were a kabuki play, which suggests how much the *kibyōshi* reviewbook is indebted to the actor reviewbook—and how much the *kibyōshi* genre itself has in common with the stage. More to the point, the souvenir representing Edo turns out to be none other than the *kibyōshi*. To the extent that an author

---

28. Sanba modeled his work on Utei Enba's humorous critique of brothel-goers *Kyakusha hyōbanki* as well as on Kiseki's *Yakusha hyōbanki*. See Raz's fascinating article "The Audience Evaluated."

29. Nanpo wrote his picturebook critique in three fascicles under the pseudonym Shoku Sanjin. In the first part, following conventions of the actor reviewbook, he ranks forty-seven *kibyōshi* published at the beginning of that year. In later fictional sections, he touches upon the world of comicbook publishing. The auspicious title refers to a design of chrysanthemums arranged into the graph for congratulations (*kotobuki*). A transliterated version can be found in Hamada, *Ōta Nanpo zenshū 7*, pp. 220–252. For a discussion of this text, see Wada, "*Kikujusō* zengo."

30. *Okame hachimoku* is transliterated in Hamada, *Ōta Nanpo zenshū 7*, pp. 253–273.

31. Nakano, *Edo meisho hyōbanki shūsei*, pp. 231–244. Also see Hayakawa, *Edo miyage*.

who stood to gain financially by promoting the genre his book reviewed can be trusted, at least, this suggests that just as the woodblock print of the Floating World (*ukiyoe*) had been nicknamed the "Edo print" (*Edoe*), the *kibyōshi* had, by the mid-1780s, become the city's representative genre of comic fiction.

Madcap Verse The *kibyōshi* was also heavily indebted to genres of popular comic poetry, specifically the madcap verse (*kyōka*), the madcap Chinese poem (*kyōshi*), and the comic haiku (*senryū*), all of which were closely related to *gesaku*. The most influential form of popular poetry was undoubtedly the first of these. Just as the *kibyōshi* can be read as a kind of parody in the guise of children's comicbooks, or the mock-sermon book a kind of parody of serious religious homily, the *kyōka* is a kind of humorous poem in the form of the short verse (*tanka*), that longstanding *sine qua non* of cultural sophistication in thirty-one syllables (conventionally rendered in alternating lines of 5–7–5–7–7). The "madcap *tanka*," as the *kyōka* might technically be rendered, dispenses with the rules, lexicon, and topics of classical poesy, occasionally groping at the ludicrous.

According to the headnote to one verse, for instance, after a certain man passed gas, those around him, in an excess of laughter, pressed him for a poem on the subject as a way for him to make amends for his *faux pas*. This he does by a composing a bit of doggerel that can be read as a string of individual farts (*he*), as the embarrassed laughter of the farter (*he he*), as the derisive chortle of those around him (*he he he*), or as any combination thereof:

He he he he he	Hee hee hee hee hee
He he he he he he he	Har har har har har har har
He he he he	Hee hee hee hee hee
He he he he he he	Far far far far far far far far
He he he he he he	He hee-hee far-far farted![32]

Not to reduce the entire poetic tradition to a cliché, but this type of verse is certainly a far cry from the kind of *tanka* scattering cherry blossoms in the spring breeze in order to symbolize life's bittersweet evanescence.

The madcap poem became so wildly popular in late eighteenth-century Edo that it must be considered a central feature of An'ei-Tenmei culture. Indeed, the "*kyōka* boom," largely associated with Ōta Nanpo and his Edo circle—many of whom were the greatest *kibyōshi* authors of the day—often overshadows the fact that the madcap verse actually began in Kamigata with poets such as Taiya Teiryū (1654–1734). One of the members of Nanpo's circle, as a matter of fact, Mitsui Karitsu, who was head of the Mitsui

---

32. Nakamura, *Gesakuron*, p. 150. This verse is also a palindrome (*kaibun*)—an added feather in the poet's cap.

family that ran the governmental money exchange (*kawase*), was himself a Kamigata poet who had relocated to Edo.

The madcap poem undeniably influenced the content of specific works of *kibyōshi*. In this volume, one scene from Kyōden's *Familiar Bestsellers* largely depends upon knowledge of a particular verse. Yet it was the centrality of the *kyōka* circle within the world of *gesaku* that perhaps had the most indelible, if intangible, impact. The *kyōka* circle provided the main venue in which the creators of various types of popular literature and allied genres and media most freely and artistically and imaginatively and consequentially intermingled. Although authors no doubt came to know each other through each other's writings if not through their participation in the same publishing stable, the *kyōka* circle was arguably a far more vital, immediate, and personal locus of social and creative interaction.

To put this slightly more concretely, the *kyōka* circle was a kind of literary coterie that fostered cross-media influence among its participants—warlords, vassal samurai, kabuki idols, woodblock artists, scriveners, fabulously wealthy merchants, celebrated courtesans, and others who otherwise might never have interacted so freely and so artistically meaningfully. Understanding the interconnections among members of a particular coterie helps to make important as well as interesting connections among the superabundance of oft-seemingly disparate figures peopling Edo literature, drama, and life. This kind of understanding is therefore an indispensable key to artistic production during An'ei-Tenmei. Reading works produced by members of a *kyōka* circle in dialogue allows for the kinds of insights one might gain by meditating upon the works by the various members of Virginia Woolf's Bloomsbury group, for instance or of Natsume Sōseki's "Thursday Meeting Club" (*Mokuyōkai*). Indeed, Haruko Iwasaki has argued that the participation of various authors, artists, and poets in Edo's *kyōka* circles imbued their works in multiple genres with a particular group dynamic that is fundamental to understanding the individual works of each author.[33] Simply put, the *kyōka* circle was the primary cite of *gesaku* creativity.

The *kyōka* circle is essential to understanding the *kibyōshi*, moreover, since its members routinely inscribed a variety of in-group jokes and allusions to each other within their works. This is evident in the *kibyōshi* translated here. To take the most salient case, Kyōden's *Playboy* makes several oblique references to Suzuki Uemon, Ichikawa Danjūrō, and other members of the *kyōka* circle in which Kyōden participated, so that the work cannot be fully appreciated without recourse to that circle—or at least to a particular banquet for circle members known as the Handtowel Competition. While some scholars have occupied themselves with trying to locate a real-life model for the comic hero Enjirō—even though he seems to be the

---

33. Iwasaki draws upon Ogata Tsutomu's argument for the centrality, in poetic and dramatic praxis, of "coterie literature" (*za no bungaku*). See Iwasaki, "The World of *Gesaku*."

stock-comic rookie who habitually inhabits the fashionbook—the more abiding real-life center of this piece, if one must be named, is probably the nexus of relationships among these *kyōka*-circle participants.

Comic Haiku   Aside from the madcap verse, a number of related poetic genres also influenced the *kibyōshi*. The "madcap *shi*" (*kyōshi*), a comic version of Sino-Japanese verse (*kanshi*), became increasingly satirical and popular from the middle of the eighteenth century on. During An'ei-Tenmei, *kyōshi* collections such as *Songs of the Northern Quarter* (*Hokurika*, 1786), a series of thirty quatrains on the Yoshiwara by Ichikawa Kansai (1749–1820), were certainly in vogue.[34] Nanpo's *Collected Works of Master Sleepyhead* (*Neboke sensei bunshū*, 1767) epitomized the related hybrid genre of "madcap poetry and prose" (*kyōshibun*). The subversion in these "madcap" forms of traditional genres of poetry and prose-poetry—which no doubt goes back to the "madcap play" (*kyōgen*) of the noh stage, if not earlier, and which had their analogue in the form of "madcap prose" (*kyōbun*)—is a paradigmatic key to *gesaku*, which can be thought of by and large as a parodic enterprise.

The most popular form of comic poetry intimately connected to the *kibyōshi* as well as *gesaku* in general was the *senryū*. In fact, the *senryū* was at times referred to as "playful verse" (*zareku*), suggesting an affinity with "playful literature" (*gesaku*), the graph for "playful" being the same in both terms (though pronounced differently). This was a pithy little verse that, for the sake of simplicity, can be thought of as a comic poem in the seventeen-syllable haiku form. Just as the madcap *tanka* assumed the form of the *tanka* to spoof its contents, likewise the *senryū* assumed the form of the haiku (*hokku*).[35] True, a few "comic haiku" parodied specific haiku, but most merely assumed the haiku form in the course of making some sly if cheeky observation. Some of these comic haiku are as memorable as the best epigrams in the Western literary tradition for the way their wit shines through the brevity of the form.

Although the *senryū* can be rendered loosely as "comic haiku," it should be pointed out that some haiku could themselves be rather humorous. In fact, the haiku was originally conceived of as an amusing (*hai*) departure from the

---

34. Markus has written about this in his paper, "Itinerary of a Useless Man."

35. Strictly speaking, the terms haiku and *senryū* were not widely used during the eighteenth century, and came into vogue only during the nineteenth and early twentieth centuries. During An'ei-Tenmei, the seventeen-syllable poem was called a *hokku* and was often used as the opening verse in a game deriving from the art of linked poetry (*renga*). Although the haiku is now written to stand on its own as an independent verse, the *hokku* was typically written as part of a longer sequence. There were some genuinely funny *hokku*—the *hokku* on fleas that Bakin harnesses in one of his *kibyōshi* comes to mind—yet the *senryū* was written to stand on its own. Thus, the *senryū* can be described as a comic haiku as long as this caveat is kept in mind.

forbiddingly serious strictures of the poetic tradition of linked verse (*renga*). In his earlier moments, the great haikai poet Matsuo Bashō employed a lexicon in his poetic prose and poetry all but inconceivable in previous epochs, referring to such things as sleeping whores and pissing horses. The comic haiku was even less beholden to orthodoxy, poetic or otherwise, dwelling instead on topics that would have made even Bashō blush.

Moreover, a significant number of comic haiku came to take joy in the shock of the scatological and the obscene. This culminated in a subgenre in its own right, an Edo analogue of the dirty limerick or the Greek *obscaena*, known as the transgressive verse (*bareku*), which might be rendered simply as "bawdy haiku."[36] Works in this vein almost make the madcap verse on farting seem refined. Some commentators find the comic haiku's bawdier brethren offensive to the point of not uttering its name. In his otherwise fine book on the comic haiku, Makoto Ueda holds that "there is a multitude of senryu peppered with slang words for male and female genitals as well as for various bedroom practices used by courtesans. . . .Many of these senryu violate our sense of decency."[37] Although the *kibyōshi* tends to avoid out-and-out raunchiness, in its bolder moments it shares with the more risqué comic haiku, if not with the bawdy haiku itself, a delightful propensity to titillate with erotic or scatological innuendo, as is evidenced in the *kibyōshi* translated in this volume.

The comic haiku and other contemporary genres demonstrated dramatically that the relaxing of literary conventions could result in mass popularization of a literary form. Such was an important precedent for the *kibyōshi* and other forms of Edo's playful literature. The *senryū* relaxed the complex, strict compositional rules of classic linked poetry, such as the observation of seasonal words (*kigo*), cutting words (*kireji*), a restricted lexicon (relative to the classical *tanka*), and so on. This meant that even people lacking extensive poetic training could participate in the fun. As long as a genre had relatively simple rules, even if it mocked the complex rules of its antecedents, it could find a mass following. One need not be a haiku master, in other words, to write comic haiku.

Indeed, with the publication of Karai Senryū's (1718–1790) *Senryū's Annotated Collection of Myriad Verses* (*Senryū hyō manku awase*) in 1759, reading and writing in the namesake genre became something of a craze. Although its popularity had ebbs and flows, the comic haiku tradition continues and even thrives in Japan to this day, as is evidenced by the phenomenon of

---

36. For a meditation upon the *bareku* in Japanese, see Shimoyama, *Senryū no erotishizumu*. "As the distinction between haiku and *senryū* became more pronounced," writes Solt, "a division emerged in *senryū* itself which opposed the usual variety of comic *senryū* with the more risqué '*bareku*.' Bareku, literally 'violating propriety verse' was, by definition, taboo in polite society." In Solt, "Willow Leaftips," p. 129.

37. Ueda, *Light Verse from the Floating World*, p. 26. In introducing the *senryū* into English, Ueda dispenses with the macron.

"salaryman *senryū*"—comic haiku sent in by the general reader and published in regular columns in many of the national as well as regional newspapers.[38]

The comic haiku and the *kibyōshi* both partake of the popular culture of their day, so their mutual compatibility is hardly surprising. Both arguably reached their apogee during the 1780s. Some writers were active in both genres as well. Kyōden, for instance, in addition to his *kibyōshi*, fashion-books, and so forth, is thought to have compiled at least one comic haiku collection.[39] The *kibyōshi* and the comic haiku also both assume relatively succinct forms. Mori classifies the *kibyōshi* as a genre of short, highly dense literature, placing it in the same category as the comic haiku, the comic *tanka*, and the *tanka* itself.[40] Although Mori does not embellish, it is clear that from the reader's perspective the *kibyōshi*, like these other genres, requires a good deal of unpacking. The brevity of these forms allows no room for contextualization, let alone excess information. Accordingly, the *kibyōshi* and the comic haiku share some similarly abbreviated modes of humor. Kyōden ratifies this position when, in *Familiar Bestsellers*, he remarks that the *kibyōshi* is imbued with the "wit of the comic haiku."[41]

Likewise, Ebara Taizō long ago suggested that the comic haiku can be viewed as a *kibyōshi* in miniature, and conversely that the *kibyōshi* can be viewed as a comic haiku writ large, shot through with the same comic spirit.[42] Ebara did not elaborate, though one characteristic must surely be the way the comic haiku and the *kibyōshi* alike delight in exposing human foibles (*ana o ugachi*). R. H. Blyth was not exaggerating when he contended that the comic haiku "cannot bear the slightest untruth, whether of hyperbole, hypocrisy, self-deception, affectation, or . . . sentimental sexuality."[43] Thus, although many genres of Edo popular literature employ the digging remark (*ugachi*), laying bare the loopholes (*ana*) in the façade of a person or a society, the comic haiku and the *kibyōshi* share a special propensity for this kind of highly condensed mode of satire.

A less ethereal connection can be found in the allusions to particular comic haiku within works of the *kibyōshi*. Oftentimes these allusions enrich the reading experience. In Kyōden's *Playboy*, for instance, a reference to kept women prone to bedwetting might have called to mind a popular comic haiku on the subject. Granted, since the *kibyōshi* and the comic haiku both

---

38. For more on this, see Gardner, "The Blessing of Living in a Country Where There Are *Senryū*."

39. This is the *Kokon maekushū* (1796), a reissue of the *Gleanings of the Haikai-Styled Yanagidaru* (*Haifū yanagidaru shūi*).

40. Mori, *Kibyōshi kaidai*, p. 11.

41. Actually, Kyōden uses the term *haikai*, referring to the freewheeling wit of what would come to be known as haiku—though his contemporaries would have understood this to refer to those comic *haikai* that later would come to be known as *senryū*.

42. Ebara, "Kibyōshi *Sekki yagyō*," p. 407.

43. Blyth, *Edo Satirical Verse Anthologies*, p. xxvi.

had their fingers on the pulse of popular culture in all its sometimes wonderfully tasteless glory, it is impossible to know with any certainty if such allusions were intentional. Nonetheless, there are instances in which certain *kibyōshi* scenes seem to depend upon a knowledge of a specific comic haiku. When Kyōden refers to the Mimeguri Embankment in a later scene from *Playboy*, for instance, the "sunken" shrine gate in the picture makes sense as soon as one recalls a comic haiku—in vogue at the time—comparing said gate to a water taxi. Thus, this comic haiku may serve here as a "think-for-yourself punch line" (*kangae ochi*), a kind of missing link that the reader must supply for himself in order to "get" the joke. If the reader fails to make the connection, something vital is lost. To the extent that individual verses of comic haiku had widespread currency—perhaps like the lyrics to a Beatles song of some two centuries later?—*kibyōshi* authors evidently counted upon a familiarity among a significant portion of their educated urban readers.

Performance Arts

A variety of different types of oral and literary performance arts impacted upon the *kibyōshi* as well. The average denizen of Edo during the 1780s would certainly have been familiar with street-corner oration (*tsuji-dangi* or just *dangi*), attention-grabbing public lectures (*kōdan*), storytelling with visual aids (*etoki*), and the epic-length compositions performed by zither-wielding jongleurs (*biwa hōshi*) in gathering places such as temple fairs and open markets. In fact, along with the *kibyōshi* and kabuki, these sorts of performance arts collectively amounted to a major form of popular entertainment throughout An'ei-Tenmei. There was also the impersonation of kabuki dialogue, often drawn from a particular performance, replete with the exact gestures and "vocal mannerisms" (*kowairo*) of individual stars. Some impressionists, like Matsukawa Tsuruichi, no doubt would have given Rich Little a run for his money. The conjoined geisha protagonists of Kyōden's *Swingers* perform such a routine to *shamisen* accompaniment for guests in a private partyroom. Reputedly first performed at the entrance to playhouses as a means of drumming up audience members, vocal impersonation swept Edo as a craze during the 1780s, a tribute to the emerging celebrity culture as much as it was to individual actors.

The most enduring form of performance art, one not entirely unrelated to vocal impersonation, was comic storytelling (*rakugo*). Unlike vocal impersonation, however, which found its main niche as a casual pastime performed by and for kabuki fans at parties, comic storytelling was a highly polished craft performed by more than just avid amateurs. The solo professional raconteur would typically dazzle his audience with meticulously crafted and rehearsed routines in a veritable choir of sonorous voices and choreographed gestures to match his fictional characters in a way that might rival the art of Ruth Draper, Spalding Gray, even Garrison Keillor. Such a choir of voices plays a key role in the fashionbook as well as the *kibyōshi*.

Fig. 2.4 An impish Dream Creature, garbed in pajamas, taunting a slumbering man with the "Dream Gold" routine. From *Rosei's Dream—The Night Before* (*Rosei ga yume sono zenjitsu*, 1791), a *kibyōshi* written by Santō Kyōden and presumably illustrated by Kitao Shigemasa. Courtesy of Tokyo Metropolitan Central Library, Kaga Collection.

Although not typically labeled *gesaku*, comic storytelling and its analogous written forms (such as the jokebook), were nonetheless closely allied with a variety of genres of popular literature and drama. The think-for-yourself punch line, in fact, is just one of the many set categories of comic dénouement in *rakugo* of which the *kibyōshi* makes substantial use. It is well attested that comic storytelling routines, including specific gestures and voices, were inserted into kabuki and puppet plays.[44] Likewise the *kibyōshi*. One such bit, "Dream Gold," describes a boatman who, counting gold ingots covetously in his sleep, wakes up to find himself grabbing his own family jewels.[45] Kyōden makes sly reference to this comically gripping climax in one of his *kibyōshi*, titled *Rosei's Dream—The Night Before* (*Rosei ga*

---

44. Brandon, *Kabuki*, p. 29.

45. Yano, *Rakugo*, p. 11. Also see Yano's essay on "Dream Gold" (*Yumekin*) in Haniya, *Yume*, pp. 99–104.

yume sono zenjitsu, 1791). The story is set in the Jumbled-Up Land of Dreams (*Muchara koku*), where Dream Creatures produce dreams as puppet or kabuki plays and then export them to earth to be shown to slumbering human beings. Since some of these Dream Creatures turn out to be quite mischievous, not all of their staged dreams can be described as sweet (**Figure 2.4**).

The Jokebook

Comic raconteurs frequently looked to "jokebooks" (*hanashibon*) for material. Inasmuch as some such jokebooks must have been written with performance in mind, it is difficult to determine if the *kibyōshi* drew exclusively upon the one or the other. The *kibyōshi*, in other words, seems to have appropriated both actual performances of comic storytelling as well as the printed texts that either served as scripts for or else were bootleg transcripts of such performances. The mutual interconnections between—or rather the interchangeability of—comic storytelling and the jokebook come across dramatically in a scene from *Familiar Bestsellers* in which one of the characters, a personified jokebook, provides entertainment at a party as though he himself were a comic raconteur.

The typical jokebook was a loose collection of comic anecdotes, sketches, and stories (*hanashi, kobanashi, otoshibanashi*) that tended to run much shorter than those of the mock-sermon book.[46] Unlike the mock-sermon book, moreover, which employs many Chinese graphs, the jokebook practically engenders verbal punning and other sorts of wordplay by virtue of its heavy reliance on the Japanese phonetic syllabary (*kana*).[47] The jokebook provided an important precedent in this regard for the *kibyōshi*.

The jokebook was published in two major formats, one of which in fact is easily mistaken for the *kibyōshi*.[48] The first of these, chronologically speaking, is that of the syllabary booklet, which tended to be sparsely illustrated, containing perhaps only one illustration of a key comic moment gleaned from a dozen or more stories. In fact, this type of jokebook is even sometimes referred to as a comic syllabary booklet. Anrakuan Sakuden (1554–1642) compiled one of the earliest in this mode, *Slumber-Rousing Laughs* (*Seisuishō*), in 1623. Many a *rakugo* skit extracts its material directly from Sakuden, as does many a *kibyōshi* for that matter, since the stories are short enough to be readily exportable. To take one old chestnut, a man visits a Buddhist monk to ask for help in warding off a menacing local dog. "Paint the word

46. Generally speaking, the *hanashibon* is the written version of various sorts of oral anecdotes (*otoshibanashi*), both of which drew their material from *setsuwa* and *otogizōshi* and became the stock in trade of *rakugo*.

47. Since *kana* is a phonetic system, it remains open to punning, whereas Chinese graphs interject a visual element to the sound and thereby specify a meaning.

48. Mutō Sadao actually divides the illustrated *hanashibon* into four major categories spanning the years 1613–1856: (1) early works; (2) *kibyōshi*-style works; (3) *gōkan*-style works, and (4) miscellaneous works. See Mutō, *Eiri kobanashi o yomu*.

'tiger' on your hand," the monk advises. The man complies and sets off, only to return not long after, complaining that the dog bit him after all. "Hmmm," the monk replies. "I guess that dog can't read."

The existence of the earlier jokebook in syllabary book format calls into question the received wisdom that the mock-sermon book is the first genre of *gesaku*. The jokebook actually extends back much further in time, perhaps by as much as a century. However, it was not until the jokebook assumed the mid-sized guise of the densely pictorial comicbook (*kusazōshi*) that it came to be labeled as a kind of *gesaku*. In fact, a number of jokebooks are physically indistinguishable, for all intents and purposes, from the major comicbooks—the redbook, blackbook, bluebook, and multivolume chapbook as well as the *kibyōshi*. Occasionally, some *kibyōshi* are misidentified as jokebooks and some jokebooks misidentified as *kibyōshi*. However, whereas even the *kibyōshi*-style jokebook (*kibyōshi-jitate hanashibon*) gathers together otherwise unrelated comic anecdotes, the actual *kibyōshi* weaves such anecdotes—which often are traceable to specific jokebooks—into the fabric of an entire story.

Aside from content, however, and a reliance upon the Japanese syllabary, the jokebook contributed to the *kibyōshi* by providing a model rich in wordplay, irony, and even social satire. Just as many a *kibyōshi* observes an allegorical double structure, so too does the early anonymous jokebook *Today's Tales of Yesterday* (*Kinō wa kyō no monogatari*, ca. 1615), which relies on a classic-contemporary dichotomy, as its title makes explicit by spoofing the formulaic opening "Now it is long ago!" (*Ima wa mukashi*) of older humorous collections. And just as one of the hallmarks of the *kibyōshi* is its interrelatedness with other genres and media, Sakuden's thousand-plus stories are too, for Sakuden himself was heavily steeped in the arts, especially pictorial storytelling and the tea ceremony, not to mention various other sorts of literature (like the *setsuwa*).[49]

Later jokebooks, such as Kimuro Bōun's *Dappled Rice Cakes* (*Kanokomochi*, 1772) or Nanpo's *Pickled Red Snapper* (*Tai no misozu*, 1779), present more up-to-date anecdotes, emphasizing familiarity with the life and lingo of contemporary Edo.[50] This sort of emphasis in the jokebook (and other forms of *gesaku*) can only have influenced the *kibyōshi*. It is no coincidence that many important *kibyōshi* authors—Harumachi, Bakin, Sanba, and Ikku come to mind—were also active in the jokebook. These authors dismissed some of the comicbook-style jokebooks they themselves penned as "frivolous works," which raises the possibility that the jokebook itself was

---

49. Sakuden was clearly conversant with the great *setsuwa* collections, such as *Fukuro zōshi* (ca. late 1150s), *Uji shūi monogatari* (ca. 1190–1242), *Kokon chomon jū* (1254), *Otogizōshi* (sixteenth century), *Shaseki shū* (thirteenth century), *Genkō shakusho* (compiled by Kokan Shiren, 1278–1346), and so on, as well as a variety of other sources.

50. See Odaka, *NKBT 100*.

considered at the time to be a kind of *gesaku*.[51] Although this can be explained away as the jokebook's tendency to assume the format and thus the rhetoric of the most popular genres of the day, if not an effort on the part of these authors to extend their success in *gesaku* genres to their jokebooks, it cannot be denied that the jokebook was a significant tributary to the mighty river that was playful literature.

Popular Stage and Comicbook Page

The main form of public entertainment for a significant portion of Edo's denizens during An'ei-Tenmei was the popular stage, meaning the puppet theater (*ningyō jōruri* or *bunraku*) and kabuki. To the extent that this popular stage and popular literature were manifestations of the same popular imagination, they could not help but be profoundly interrelated, even if their outward expression at first glance seems drastically different. Indeed, the popular stage is so central to *gesaku* that Edo literature scholar Maeda Kingōrō once counseled that in order to appreciate the *kibyōshi* fully one must first study kabuki for no less than twenty years.[52] Similarly, Mizuno has lamented the stage's influence on much Edo popular literature as inordinate.[53] And in a valuable article on their interconnections, C. Andrew Gerstle has observed: "*Gesaku* writers borrowed content and styles from *kabuki* and *ningyō jōruri* books, and certain writers—Kyōden and in particular Sanba—seem to have kept their eyes on the theatre."[54] Inoue Takaaki has even gone so far as to suggest that *gesaku* in essence amounts to a "send-up of the stage" (*butai no modoki*).[55]

The influence of the theater upon Edo's popular literature in general and the *kibyōshi* in particular is so overwhelming, then, that few if any scholars seem to have plumbed the converse—in what ways did popular genres affect both the composition of popular drama and its *reception* among theatergoers? How did the various parodies of the forty-seven *rōnin*, for instance, affect people when they watched any number of kabuki or puppet versions of *Treasury of Loyal Retainers*? And were actors and playwrights themselves affected?

Such queries are beyond the purview of the present study. One question that cannot be so readily deferred, though, has to do with why the *kibyōshi* appears to be more beholden to the kabuki than the puppet theater. Each of the three pieces translated here is conspicuously indebted to the former though hardly to the latter. Is this a coincidence, born of the fact that Kyōden

---

51. For instance, the *hanashibon* titled *Sato sodachi hanashi suzume* identifies itself as a *gesaku*. See Mutō, *Eiri kobanashi o yomu*, p. 113.

52. Personal conversation, Cambridge, MA 1992.

53. Mizuno, *Edo shōsetsu ronsō*, p. 59.

54. Gerstle, "Flowers of Edo," p. 103.

55. Inoue, *Edo gesaku no kenkyū*, p. 19.

was a kabuki enthusiast who participated in amateur kabuki circles himself? The unevenness is curious, especially in light of the popularity of both stages. True, the puppet theater had long been on the wane—at least in Kamigata: "After the death of Chikamatsu Hanji (1725–1783)," Karen Brazell notes, "no other great playwrights wrote for the puppets, and their popularity declined. The two major puppet theaters in Osaka folded in 1765 and 1767, handing over their facilities to kabuki actors, and for a century the puppet tradition was kept alive only in small urban theaters and in the countryside."[56] This is not to say that the puppet theater became completely dormant in the shogun's capital. As Gerstle points out, "In Edo, *gidayū* puppet theatre flourished particularly from the 1770s, when Hiraga Gennai and others wrote new plays for Edo theatres, giving further impetus to amateur devotees."[57] Kabuki may have been more vibrant, then, but the puppet theater was being kept alive in Edo, if not actually experiencing something of a revival.

Furthermore, the kabuki and the puppet theaters were inextricably linked to each other. Aside from all the shared conventions, styles, and stories, playwrights like Chikamatsu wrote for both, and even then, kabuki often staged adapted pieces (*maruhonmono*) based on scripts of hit puppet plays, usually with only slight modification. In this sense, it is hard to claim that a *kibyōshi* referred only to a kabuki play when that play itself had puppet precedents. Nonetheless, the mutual interrelatedness of kabuki and the puppet stages makes this apparent unevenness even more curious.

As odd as it sounds, perhaps the *kibyōshi* looked more to kabuki than to the puppet stage because actors participated in madcap poetry circles whereas puppets did not. That is to say, actors were cultural icons in a way that puppet playwrights, chanters, puppeteers, not to mention puppets, never were. The cult of the kabuki actor has to do with the rise of a celebrity culture during the Edo period that could only have been largely the product of mass publishing. Even Enjirō, to the extent that he can be said to be savvy, is savvy to this, for he hires groupies to throng to his home as though he were a kabuki star. The actor as celebrity is of paramount importance to the relationship between the *kibyōshi* and kabuki in at least one important way, since it joins the two in the same enterprise.

How, then, does the kabuki stage specifically impact the *kibyōshi* page? First, there is the *kibyōshi*'s overt appropriation of such things as specific plots, characters, scenes, settings, snippets of dialogue, lyrics, music, sounds, gestures, and so on—the surface of the performances themselves, things that would be obvious to just about anyone watching a kabuki play. Some works of *kibyōshi* allude to more in-depth aspects, such as personal details of the actors portraying roles associated with certain characters—something that only the more sophisticated theatergoer would be capable of appreciating.

---

56. Brazell, *Traditional Japanese Theater*, p. 19.
57. Gerstle, "Flowers of Edo," p. 105.

Not all *kibyōshi* are beholden to the particulars of kabuki in this subtle way, to be sure. Yet even those that are not nonetheless are indebted to a variety of less obvious aspects of the popular stage, such as conventions of playwriting.

Comic business, especially in the form of wordplay, outwardly graces stage and page alike. Japan certainly provides a rich case study in the long tradition of paronomasia in Asia. One finds all sorts of "playful writings" (*gisho*) in Book 16 of the eighth-century *Anthology for Myriad Ages* (*Man'yō-shū*)—a term that suggests the possibility that *gesaku* (the *ge* of which is the same graph as the *gi* of *gisho*) has some spiritual antecedents as far back as a millennium. Nonetheless, it is worth mentioning that the *kibyōshi* (along with most other forms of *gesaku*) and kabuki share a penchant for various types of verbal wordplay and humor, such as simple puns (*jiguchi*), strings of puns (*monozukushi*), palindromes (*kaibun*), tongue twisters (*hayakotoba*), far-fetched etymologies (*kojitsuke*), pivot words (*kakekotoba*), and associative words (*engo*). "Verbal humor is a striking feature of kabuki scripts" as James Brandon puts it, "taking the form of innumerable puns, rhyming games, and wordplay of other kinds."[58] Moreover, both stage and page share a propensity for close parody (*modoki*), which may be ironic given that the *kibyōshi* frequently pokes fun at the melodramatic tone of many a kabuki play, most notably the domestic dramas (*sewamono*) and, arguably its most concentrated form, the double-suicide piece (*shinjūmono*). Two of the three *kibyōshi* translated here, for instance, contain mock travel songs (*michiyuki*) of lovers supposedly on the way to their self-inflicted deaths.

The *kibyōshi* also shares with kabuki a similar kind of conventionalized irrealism. By no means is verisimilitude the primary concern of stage or page. Theatrical time, for instance, is especially elastic. "The action of the plays easily leaves the dramatic present and readily overflows the confines of the physical stage," writes Brazell on traditional Japanese theater, including kabuki. "Theatrical time may be contracted and expanded to match plot requirements or aesthetic values, and a given locale may disappear as quickly as it is invoked."[59] Likewise, the anecdotal nature of many *kibyōshi* may be just as much the result of this kind of temporal elasticity as the physical format of the chapbook, which breaks up the plot into frames, the largest of which is the double-page spread.

Along these lines, the *kibyōshi* and kabuki also share a certain amount of play with narrative frame. Such play implicitly differentiates between the scripted text and the transitory moment of a performance. Actors on stage sometimes step out of character puckishly in a way that one accustomed only to "realistic" theater might find jolting (though such self-reflexivity is certainly not unknown in modernist and postmodern drama as well as literature). This they do through a variety of asides to the audience, im-

---

58. Brandon, *Kabuki*, p. 39.
59. Brazell, *Traditional Japanese Theater*, p. 27.

promptu speeches, and ad-libbed embellishments (*sutezerifu*). These contain comments about recent events in Edo, puffery about the fame of the particular play in which they are acting, even references to characters on stage by the personal name of the actors, including *themselves*.

Sometimes actors ribbed each other during a performance by referring to details of one another's private lives. Such in-group verbal jabbing is known as "dressing-room punch lines" (*gakuya ochi*), the kabuki equivalent of locker-room humor, perhaps, though not quite as crude. At other times, a stage star might advertise a commercial product on sale. The most well known early example of this was an unscripted spiel Ichikawa Danjūrō II delivered in 1718 and which an audience member transcribed. Dressing as a vendor of an expectorant medicine (*uirō*), Danjūrō laced his speech with various sorts of wordplay cleverly advertising the Ichikawa acting house as well as the drug. The kabuki stage in fact came to embrace such product placement. Playwrights wove advertisements into the very fabric of stories in the so-called advertisement plays (*kōkoku geki*).[60] No doubt this was an important inspiration for the many embedded advertisements in the *kibyōshi*.

Yet the *kibyōshi* delights in such self-reflexivity in general as well. In *Familiar Bestsellers*, the narrator adopts the persona of a stage actor delivering a prologue directly to an audience in his own name. Also, *kibyōshi* authors took subtle swipes at members of their inner circle, as we will see in all three pieces translated here. Such dressing-room humor no doubt existed in the culture at large and may have been the natural outgrowth of any highly structured narrative art. Yet one wonders if it entered the *kibyōshi* by virtue of the participation of actors in the same madcap poetry circles as *kibyōshi* authors. One of the kabuki stars during the heyday of the *kibyōshi*, Ichikawa Danjūrō V (1741–1806), frequented the *kyōka* circle of Nanpo, Kyōden, and other leading *kibyōshi* authors, composing verse under the pseudonym Hakuen. Hino Tatsuo has even suggested that Hakuen may have been a central figure of this coterie, second only to Nanpo himself.[61]

The *kibyōshi* also sometimes takes a cue from the old theatrical switcheroo of wardrobing a character in disguise only to reveal his secret identity dramatically. "Lo and behold that stern samurai from Kawashō 'in reality' (*jitsu wa*) turns out to be none other than our hero's merchant brother!" audience members might have thought during Chikamatsu's play *Love Suicides at Amijima* (*Shinjū ten no Amijima*, first performed as a puppet play in 1721). Although this kind of melodramatic bombshell certainly figures in enough *kibyōshi* stories to be more or less predictable, some works ingeniously draw their characters to resemble not simply stage characters but certain actors in particular roles—sometimes even particular roles performed during one

---

60. For more on Danjūrō's performance in the play *Wakamidori ikioi Soga*, and on "advertising plays" in general, see Matsumiya, *Edo kabuki to kōkoku*, pp. 149–151.

61. Hino, *Edojin to yūtopia*, pp. 63–64. Cited in Gerstle, "Flowers of Edo" p. 103.

specific performance years earlier. Such play with double or multiple frame can be seen in Kyōden's *Swingers* (1788), as with its representation of the character Seijūrō as the actor Ichikawa Monnosuke in the role of Seijūrō in an illustrious three-day performance in 1781. The reader who fails to connect the dots misses a large part of the fun.

Theatrical Texts　　This phenomenon suggests the grip of the theater on the popular imagination in Edo as the *kibyōshi* catered to it. It also raises the possibility that Kyōden expected his readers were aware of some kind of secondary source closer to the publication of his *kibyōshi*. Indeed, there existed a variety of woodblock printed texts associated with the stage that might collectively be termed "theatrical texts." Any performance of a kabuki or puppet play can be viewed as a "text" in the larger sense. I intend a slightly more restricted (though still broad) meaning of any printed matter that is used to represent some aspect of a staged play, be it the plot, a visual image, or even, perhaps, the aura of a particular actor's fame.

The theatrical text, thus, can be a verbal text, such as the playbook used by performers during rehearsals and performances called the recital libretto (*shōhon*, *nagauta shōhon*, *jōruri shōhon*, etc.) of songs from the puppet theater. Versions of these books were also available for public consumption.[62] In fact, it is the playbook Enjirō is shown reading in the opening scene of *Playboy* that impresses him with the heroic ideal, thereby setting him off on his comic misadventures. Plot books (*sujibon*) and dialogue books (*serifubon*) were also accessible, as were books that catered to the various imitative arts "parroting" actors (*ukiyomonomane*, *monomane*, and *kowairo*) and that were subsumed under the rubric of "libretto parroting" (*shōhon ōmuseki*).[63] These arts relied not only upon direct quotation from plays, but also upon the comic voice inflections and gesticulations associated with specific actors in particular roles. One certainly sees the influence of these arts upon the *kibyōshi* in general—and upon each piece translated herein.

The theatrical text can also assume a primarily pictorial form, as with various types of sometimes overlapping woodblock-printed actor prints (*yakushae*), actor books (*yakusha ehon*), "likeness prints" of actors (*yakusha nigaoe*), close-up facial portraits (*ōkubie*), and single-sheet prints (*ichimaie* or *ichimaizuri*). The last of these is personified in *Familiar Bestsellers* as a kabuki-esque character. In one scene, he is involved in a finger-slicing demonstration of affection. In another scene, he is depicted in the sort of dramatic pose (*mie*) that actors hold on stage for several intense seconds in a kind of

---

62. Koyama differentiates between the widely for-sale *shōhon*, which contained everything from dialogue and stage directions to details of actors' wardrobes and stage properties, and the on-stage *shōhon*, containing musical scores for *shamisen* players and lyrics for reciters. In Koyama, *Jōkyoku no shinkenkyū*, p. 21.

63. For a discussion of stage-related publications, see Akama, *Kabuki bunka no shosō*.

visual equivalent of the sound bite. Such poses are also the stuff of innumerable pictorial theatrical texts.

Furthermore, many *kibyōshi* seem to follow the tendency in such prints to position the viewer as analogous to the theatergoer seated before the stage. The *kibyōshi* reader and theatrical-text viewer see the depicted characters as an audience member might see actual actors—from a similar vantage point. Thus, they are seen on a scale comparable to that of how actors would appear in proportion to their backdrop interior or landscape stage set and objects that, in some *kibyōshi*, look uncannily like stage props. The heavily theatrical *kibyōshi* represents, then, not *just* the *mise-en-scène* of the actual stage (which is to say the positioning of actors, scenery, and props), but the representation of that *mise-en-scène* within pictorial theatrical texts. In this sense, such *kibyōshi* present a kind of doubly mediated vision.

The theatrical text could also assume visual-verbal form, as with the illustrated playbook (*eiri kyōgenbon*) or the digest comicbook for puppet plays (*jōruri shōroku kusazōshi*).[64] Works in such modes allowed one to read a play without actually having to set foot in the theater—or a play that was never actually staged at all—in addition to helping audience members follow along during actual performances (**Figure 2.5**). In Osaka, similarly short, illustrated scripts (*nehon*) were popular from around 1784 on.[65] And many a blackbook can be considered essentially a retelling of a play. These texts influenced the *kibyōshi* in profound ways, too. To take the most obvious example, the layout of verbal and pictorial text is often very similar. That is to say, the convention in these theatrical texts of placing narrative text (*ji*) at the top of the page and dialogic text (*kotoba*) near the figures of the characters carries over into the *kibyōshi*.

Since the theatrically inflected *kibyōshi* shares so much with the many types of theatrical text, one wonders if the differences are significant. Is a work like Kyōden's *Swingers*, which certainly does not purport to be a "serious" retelling of its antecedent kabuki material, to be disqualified as a theatrical text simply by virtue of the playful liberties it takes? Adopting a wider view, it seems that kabuki plays, serious theatrical texts, and even genres like the *kibyōshi* that parody these two all participate in the construction of a kabuki actor's stardom within the context of celebrity culture.[66] Perhaps the *kibyōshi* was the most potent form of advertisement for the actor as celebrity, since those pieces that play with frame in this way effectively equate the ability of the reader to identify the actor behind a character with an insider's knowledge of the stage. In so doing, the *kibyōshi* constructs the actor as the object of sophistication.

---

64. Throughout the period under study, the term *kyōgen* referred primarily to kabuki plays and less to the *kyōgen* plays associated with the noh theater.

65. Brandon and Leiter, *Villainy and Vengeance*, p. 8.

66. For more on this topic, see Kominz, *The Stars Who Created Kabuki*.

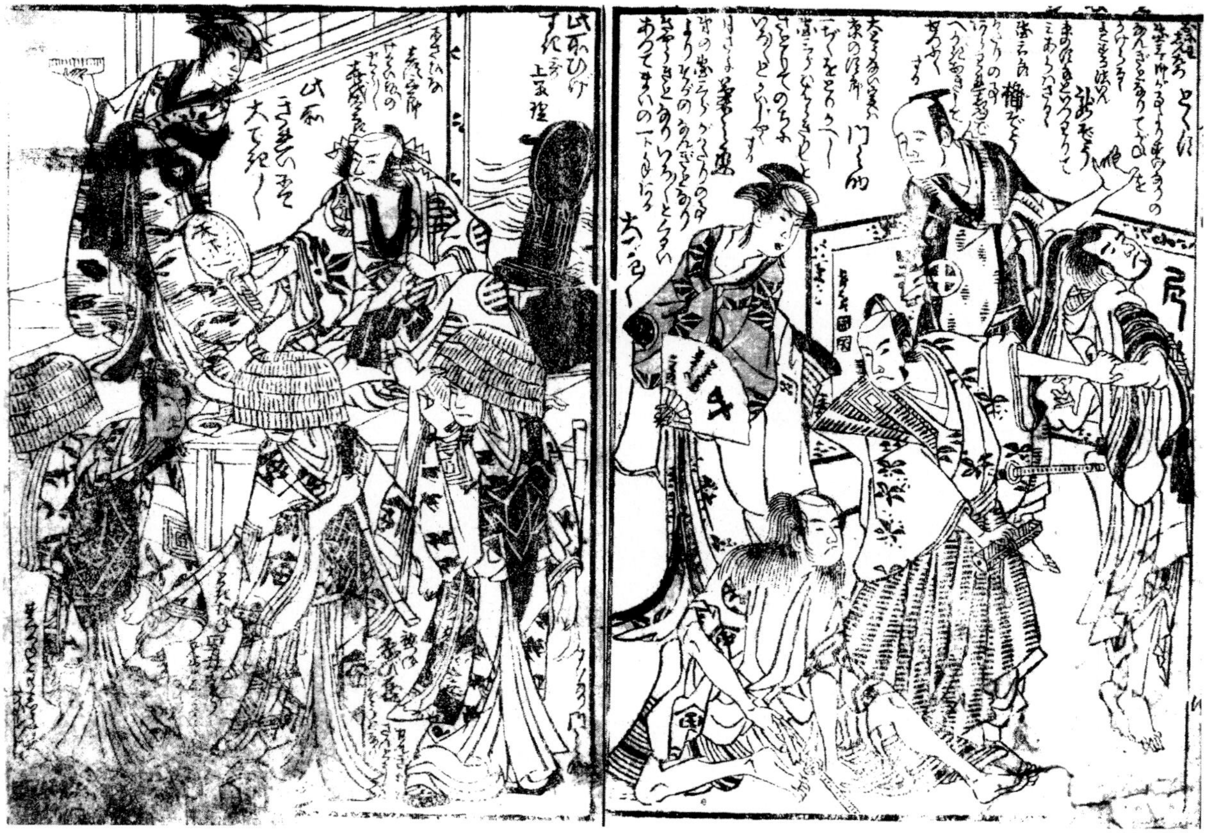

Fig. 2.5 Illustrated program to the 1792 production of the kabuki play *Pale Purple Soga, Edo Style* (*Waka murasaki edokko Soga*), featuring the actors Ichikawa Ebizō, Ichikawa Monnosuke II, and Ichikawa Omezō I. Reprinted in Clark and Ueda, *The Actor's Image*, p. 295. *Courtesy of the University of Tokyo, General Library.*

It is therefore possible that the theatrical text may influence the *kibyōshi* as much as the kabuki theater itself influenced the *kibyōshi*, since not only is each of these involved in the mutual enterprise of valorizing the kabuki actor, but they are also entangled in a complex intertextual web with each other. Even the most seemingly blatant of references in a *kibyōshi* to a scene from a particular kabuki play may have been mediated through a theatrical text such as the recital libretto available to audience members watching a play—or even through another *kibyōshi* that parodies a *related* kabuki play. How such a nexus of interconnections affected audience members watching a kabuki play is a matter of conjecture.

The participation of the *kibyōshi* in this kind of nexus raises another interesting issue. When Edo kabuki troupes took to the road, which they are known to have done occasionally, what sort of printed matter would have traveled too? Aside from woodblock prints serving as posters and various forms of illustrated playbooks that might be hawked in conjunction with performances, is it possible that commercially savvy publishers tried to peddle *kibyōshi* outside Edo this way? Whatever the case may be, the influence of the popular stage and its associated theatrical texts upon the *kibyōshi* suggests that a major segment of the *kibyōshi* readership consisted of the literate members of the theatergoing public.

All the Stage Is 275
Worlds and a Few
Variational Procedures

The *kibyōshi*, like other forms of *gesaku*, also importantly shares with the popular stage a similar array of compositional techniques involving the sophisticated manipulation (*shukō*) of literary formulae (*sekai*). A book-length study could be devoted to this topic alone, though here a few points will have to suffice. First, these terms can be thought of, for the sake of convenience, as variation and theme, respectively. Although literally meaning "world," the second of these (*sekai*) is an amalgam of elements from one or more stories, consisting of such things as characters, settings, situations, conflicts, motives, tropes, and so forth, which most people were presumed to know. Yet there were so many various worlds available to kabuki—Izuka Tomoichirō counts some 275; others count many times more—that there was need of enumerating them in handbooks such as *Worlds, Classified* (*Sekai kōmoku*, ca. Tenmei era).[67] One way of understanding An'ei-Tenmei culture—if not the psyche of Edo-period Japanese—would be to conduct a detailed study of these worlds, since, like literary formulae in the West, such themes reveal foundational mythical archetypes.

The manner in which these various themes are manipulated is called the variation (*shukō*). Literally meaning something like "device" or "invention," *shukō* is a kind of varying operation that, at its best, pushes these set themes in unprecedented directions. The significance of the variational procedure to Edo's cultural production cannot be overemphasized.

In his *magnum opus* on the comic literature of the Edo period, Nakamura Yukihiko makes the astounding claim that the composition of Edo-period art, literature, and drama can be discussed meaningfully, without being oversimplified, in terms of this single concept.[68] A scholar of eminent prudence, Nakamura does not make this claim lightly. Over the course of several chapters, he methodically explicates the structure of various genres of *gesaku* (especially the fashionbook, the madcap verse, and the comic haiku), theater (kabuki and puppet plays), and even *haikai* poetry, all in terms of this single concept. Nakamura concludes that the genre to best exemplify this technique of compositional variation is none other than the *kibyōshi*. The *kibyōshi*, according to Nakamura, is the genre of variational procedure *extraordinaire*. To the extent that the variational procedure can truly be said to occupy the center of literary and cultural production during the Edo period, then, the *kibyōshi* provides a superb medium for study.

---

67. Brandon, *Kabuki*, p. 31. Brandon cites Izuka Tomoichirō, *Kabuki saiken* (Daiichi shobō, 1926).

68. Nakamura, *Gesakuron*, pp. 142–178. Other Japanese scholars of *gesaku* agree with Nakamura. See, for example, Inoue, *Edo gesaku no kenkyū*, especially the chapters on *kibyōshi*, composition, humor, and *shukō*.

Several types of variational procedures work their magic at the level of plot, some of which Haruko Iwasaki has discussed in English in an informative, condensed overview.[69] Therefore, only a couple major examples of variational procedure frequently encountered in the *kibyōshi* shall be mentioned here.

The simplest to explain—and one of the most prevalent—is probably a kind of "intertwining" (*naimaze*). This usually involves the combination of two worlds. Hollywood has no shortage of films that work along similar lines—*Dracula vs. Frankenstein* (1971) and, more recently, *Freddy vs. Jason* (2003) come to mind. Kyōden's *Unseamly Silverpiped Swingers* conjoins, through the figure of conjoined twins, two worlds of ill-fated couples, both of which were the basis of hundreds of works of prose fiction as well as kabuki dramas. Sometimes the world of a classic story might be crossed with the world of contemporary An'ei-Tenmei Edo, as with Harumachi's *Master Flashgold*, which juxtaposes Zeami's *Kantan* with the Floating World of Edo's major pleasure quarters. At other times, a Chinese world might be intertwined with or rewritten into a Japanese one, in a kind of cross-cultural "acclimation" (*hamemono*), like *Loyal Water Margin* (*Chūshin suikoden*, 1799), which combines the worlds of the Japanese forty-seven loyal retainers (*Kanadehon chūshingura*, first performed in 1748) and the Chinese *Water Margin*.[70] More than two worlds can be threaded together into a single story, too. The kabuki play *Scarlet Princess of Edo* (*Sakura hime azuma bunshō*, 1817) deftly interweaves three separate strands: (1) the love affair between the priest Seigen and Princess Sakura (a world popular from as far back as 1674), (2) the Sumida River world, and (3) the gangster world (*kizewamono*) of Tsurigane Gonsuke.[71]

Sometimes, multiple worlds—even *dozens* of worlds—were combined or "blown together" (*fukiyose*) into a single complex. This potpourri is a second example of a major variational procedure. Its worlds typically share a single, easily identifiable common denominator. Otherwise, they would devolve into a frustratingly chaotic gallimaufry. Kyōden's *Familiar Bestsellers* is a carnival of various sorts of woodblock-printed matter. His *Playboy* can be read as a pastiche of high-flying playboys. And in the case of Zenkō's *Thousand-Armed Goddess of Mercy, Julienned* (*Daihi no senrokuhon*, 1785), characters from a mélange of otherwise unrelated worlds—drawn from literature, legend, history, and the contemporary Edo cultural scene—are gathered together on account of their each missing an arm. The story is accordingly interlaced with strings of puns (*monozukushi*) on armlessness. Literary pastiche and wordplay not only go together hand in hand, therefore, but are also actually manifestations of the same principle on different levels. The pastiche is a

---

69. Iwasaki, "The Literature of Wit and Humor in Late-Eighteenth-Century Edo."
70. Iwasaki calls *hamemono* "fitting in."
71. Written by Tsuruya Nanboku V, Sakurada Jisuke II, and Tsuuchi Genshichi. In Brandon, *Kabuki*, p. 242.

kind of string of puns writ large on the narrative level, and the string of puns is a kind of verbal—or visual-verbal—pastiche writ small on the verbal (or visual-verbal) level. In this sense, the variational procedure also informs more than the plot of a story.

Thus, any given text can allude to its worlds in different ways, and on assorted levels. Of course, any world itself can contain multiple aspects. The world of one of the couples in *Swingers*, Onatsu and Seijūrō, for instance, encompasses the many different versions of their story, its performance by certain actors on the kabuki stage, representations of those actors within theatrical texts (including a variety of woodblock pictures), common associations with the personal lives of those actors, songs associated with various performances of that story but also with those actors and even possibly the playwrights, and so forth. (In this sense, it should be noted, the term "world" is quite apropos, because it suggests the wide-ranging breadth of these "themes.") Accordingly, variational procedures can be used to combine worlds on many levels other than mere plot. In addition to the linguistic level of strings of puns and other sorts of wordplay, there is also the visual level. Many *kibyōshi* (not to mention other kinds of woodblock pictures) employ a kind of visual irony or pun (*mitate*) in which images from two different worlds are juxtaposed to witty if not humorous effect. The best *kibyōshi*, then, play with worlds on several of these different levels. Such multiple implementation of variational procedures is more or less evident in each of the three *kibyōshi* translated within this volume.

A literature based on such a small set of variational procedures and a limited number of themes naturally risks becoming terribly formulaic, derivative, tedious. A key requirement of any variational procedure, therefore, is novelty. Novelty is one of the major features of all mid-Edo playful literature. Its emphasis helps imbue the *kibyōshi* with its penchant for trendiness. This requirement is built into many definitions of variational procedure too, so that it is often rendered as an "*innovative* variation" on a set theme. It goes without saying that the innovativeness depends upon the particular skills of the author. Kyōden was widely considered to be one of the best. His *Familiar Bestsellers* and *Playboy* have been acclaimed as masterpieces of the genre. *Swingers*, as has been noted, seems *not* to have been a particular success, however. That said, most other *kibyōshi* are still not as original in their execution as the works in this volume. Many works in the genre come across as jejune, to say the least. Mori singled out only about 10 percent of all titles as meriting serious attention.[72] Some commentators,

---

72. Mori, in *Kibyōshi kaidai* and *Zoku kibyōshi kaidai*, addresses 200–250 *kibyōshi* that he considers superior works. Since as many as 2,500–3,000 works may have been published, it might be said that Mori finds that no more than 10 percent of the total number of *kibyōshi* worth his attention. He argues that the majority of *kibyōshi* fall more under the rubric of the early bluebooks, which is to say works of less-than-adult satisfaction.

incidentally, have dismissed 90 percent or more of all modern *manga* as fluff, so one wonders if there is some kind of glass ceiling or hidden threshold governing the appraisal of comicbooks in Japan.

Perhaps the best way to regard the variational procedure is as the creative treatment of a literary formula. The *shukō* pays homage to set themes by using them as its basic material, though at the same time, it does not serve those themes obsequiously. The variational procedure is a celebration of novelty in the handling of old themes rather than in the devising of new plots. Prior to the introduction of Western Romanticism during the late nineteenth century, it certainly seems that in popular Japanese literature and theater, originality had everything to do with the skillfulness of the execution of variational procedure rather than with "brand-newness" of the theme. Something analogous separates the master from the novice on the stage of improvisational jazz. And it is this brand of originality of implementation that separates the trash from the classics within the *kibyōshi*. If the prefaces to many a *kibyōshi* are any indication, authors strained to develop new twists on familiar themes. And if the various *kibyōshi* reviewbooks are not wildly distorted, readers delighted in seeing how an author extemporized on such themes, wringing new ideas out of old stories.

One advantage of this kind of variational procedure is that relying upon familiar themes could help overcome the sometimes profound differences in cultural background of readers who came to Edo from various regions. Thus, to be successful, an author needed to balance familiarity with novelty, the conservative element of theme with the progressive element of variation. A slight imbalance in one direction might result in stagnation or, in the other direction, chaos. The potential for narrative anarchy, however, had genuine political applications: what better way to engage in cultural identity building if not to tear down the corpus of classical literature that had previously held sway? The variational procedure need not be parodic, though like parody it entails the imitation and transformation of antecedent material. The tendency toward parody of the *kibyōshi*—and toward sociopolitical satire—may thus be latent in, if not a natural outcome of, the very structure of the compositional technique of *shukō*.

Along these lines, it must be observed that many a variational procedure "updates" a classic tale into a contemporary setting. Indeed, many *kibyōshi* do as much, too. This is because such updating is an intrinsic—though hardly *necessary*—byproduct of manipulating *classic* antecedent texts, whose worlds are by definition set in the past. *Master Flashgold* thus modernizes the classic noh story *Kantan* into the Edo present the way that *West Side Story* recasts Shakespeare's *Romeo and Juliet* in 1950s Manhattan. But it is possible to intertwine two contemporary worlds—or two timeless worlds—too. One can see this in a visual pun (*mitate*) that presents what appears to be a silhouette of a flower, only to reveal it (in kabukiesque manner) as a pair of acrobatic men in loincloths, neither one of these images being a particular chronological "updating" of the other (**Figure 2.6**).

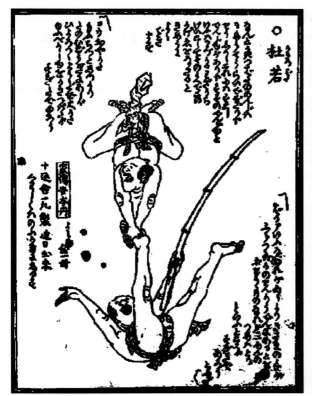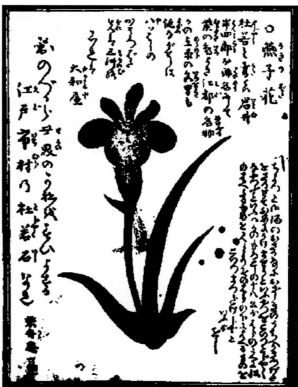

Furthermore, the stories of many *kibyōshi* were set deliberately in the past less to take pleasure in an updating dynamic, or even to exploit the potential for fun with contrasts, than to couch their political satire. That is, just because a *kibyōshi* seems to juxtapose a former world with a present one does not mean that the story is intended *primarily* to bring some old tale up to date. Rather, what appears to be a modernizing variational procedure is actually a kind of defamiliarization—a "backdating," as it were, as a pretext to address contemporary events, printed discussion of which the government forbade vehemently.

Another advantage of this kind of artistic production, then, is that it enabled authors to dovetail the mechanical reproduction of the woodblock process with the creative literary production of stories. The variational procedure was just as much a part of the assembly-line process of textual production as carving wooden blocks and printing images on paper. Yet it was also a means of overcoming the stasis, the automated feel of a popular literature assembled according to literary formulae. The variational procedure was, in other words, a way of manufacturing literary and cultural products in a way that did not feel manufactured. It was a seamless integration of material and nonmaterial aspects of the text.

In the final analysis, the *kibyōshi* was truly a form of recyclable literature. Just as the variational procedure allowed for the quick "recycling" of worlds into new literary material, so too was the paper itself not infrequently

Fig. 2.6 Silhouette of a flower revealed as two acrobatic loincloth-garbed commoners. From *Otsuriki* (1810), a picturebook of visual puns (*mitate ehon*) written by Jippensha Ikku and illustrated by Kitagawa Tsukimaro. Courtesy of Waseda University Library.

recycled. As illustrated in *Familiar Bestsellers*, popular literature was often made from—and eventually returned to—rough, low-grade recycled paper (*suki-gaeshi no kami*). Or it might be scrapped for wadding or wall caulking (*koshi-bari*), or for a protective layer for storing lacquer and other breakables. This two-ply recyclability informs the modern *manga*, too. It is conceivable, then, that the *kibyōshi* and other genres of *gesaku*, as throwaway forms of mass entertainment, perhaps prefigured today's "read-and-toss" (*yomisute*) comic-book in Japan. Disposable entertainment for people with disposable income. And yet the fact that so many *kibyōshi* and other forms of playful literature remain extant is a tribute to the value readers must have placed on these works. One of the many ironies of the *kibyōshi*, then, is that in spite of the fact that it was intended as ephemera, it nonetheless remains one of the mid-Edo period's most enduring legacies.[73]

---

73. Art Spiegelman, in an interview on National Public Radio on September 16, 2004, made a similar point about American comic strips of the early twentieth century.

It's only lines on paper, folks!
—R. Crumb

**Manga
Culture**

The modern *manga* is said to have emerged in Japan sometime during the 1920s, though since little consensus exists as to what constitutes the modern *manga*, a wide range of alternative dates has also been proffered. One of the earliest is 1895, when Imaizumi Hidetarō applied the term *manga* to his Western-style cartoon strips that ran in Fukuzawa Yukichi's newspaper *Jiji shinpō*.[1] However, many commentators subscribe to the view that the *manga* "began in Japan with the serialization of *Shōchan's Adventure* (words by Oda Nobutsune [a.k.a. Shōsei] and pictures by Kabashima Katsuichi), alongside the Japanese translation of *Bringing Up Father*, originally drawn by George McManus, in the *Asahi Graphic Weekly*, in January 1923."[2]

Whatever date one opts for, the birth of the modern *manga* as a form falls well outside the chronological purview of the present study. Nonetheless, to the extent that the *kibyōshi* is often characterized as *the* progenitor of the modern *manga*, and since no small number of cultural commentators have tried to ground the modern *manga* in Japan's premodern tradition of visual culture, an exploration of the relationship between the two forms is in order.

Yumoto Kōichi, among others, has posited the existence of a pervasive "*manga* culture" (*manga bunka*) that he claims began in and flowed *continuously* from the Edo period.[3] Shiokawa Kanako has similarly argued that the

---

1. Miyamoto "The Stratifying Process of the Notion of 'Manga,'" p. 324. Miyamoto quotes Shimizu Isao.

2. Tsurumi, "Edo Period in Contemporary Popular Culture," p. 750.

3. Yumoto, *Edo mangabon no sekai*, p. 7.

aesthetics of the *kibyōshi* and allied genres of mid-Edo literature "govern comic books today," supposedly by virtue of an *uninterrupted* technological progression in the comicbook form itself.[4] Shimizu Isao, in his sweeping history of the *manga*, locates its origins as far back as the early eighteenth-century Toba cartoons of Osaka if not the early twelfth-century Toba scrolls.[5] Taking a reader-centered approach, Okada Toshio, in his book *Introduction to Otakuology*, has imaginatively tried to link the culture of obsessive fans of *manga* and *anime* (*otaku bunka*) to Edo's burgeoning consumer culture.[6] And Susan Napier, author of a landmark English-language study of Japanese animation, has more cautiously opined: "Certainly Edo period works have images that appear to have direct links to both manga and anime, particularly with the *kibyōshi* . . ."[7]

Too many others espouse variations on this theme to be listed, let alone adequately addressed here. What can be said is that the prevailing notion of a monolithic and transhistorical *manga* culture tends to represent the *kibyōshi* as either a major immediate influence upon the modern *manga*, or even the primary progenitor by virtue of its comicbook format. Although it cannot be denied that the premodern tradition of visual culture influenced the modern visual tradition in ways that must have also *somehow* affected the modern *manga*, to maintain that the *kibyōshi* influenced it *directly*, as though the originators and practitioners of the modern form actually took their cues from the *kibyōshi*, is certainly problematical, and would seem to smack of overgeneralization, ahistoricism, and wishful thinking. Until proof to the contrary comes to light, if anything occasioned the advent of the modern Japanese *manga*, it was the Western comic strip and comicbook, not the *kibyōshi*.

The very fact that the *kibyōshi* phenomenon terminated in the first decade or so of the nineteenth century (even though some individual works may have straggled on) suggests that, just as Edo-period comicbooks for children did not metamorphose directly into the modern children's story, the *kibyōshi* did not empty unremittingly into the modern *manga*, which at the earliest appeared at the very end of that century.[8] The first comic-strip *manga* to be published in Japanese newspapers certainly were inspired by foreign caricature, not the native tradition. "Historians usually trace the cartoon's introduction into Japan," writes historian Peter Duus, "to Charles Wirgman (1832–91), a former British army officer turned correspondent for

---

4. Shiokawa, "'The Reads' and 'Yellow Covers,'" p. 27.

5. Shimizu makes this argument in "Japan's Rich Tradition of Cartoons & Comics," as well as in *Manga no rekishi*. Thanks to Ron Stewart for bringing a couple of these sources to my attention.

6. Okada, *Otaku gaku nyūmon*.

7. Napier, *Anime from* Akira *to* Princess Mononoke, p. 21.

8. For more on the unrelatedness of Edo-period children's stories and modern children's stories in Japan, see Ozaki, *Kodomo no hon no hyakunenshi*.

the *London Illustrated News*, who settled in Yokohama shortly after its opening and began publishing *Japan Punch*, a comic magazine that poked fun at life in the port and caricatured its prominent residents. Copies soon found their way into the hands of curious Japanese readers, as did other caricatures, satirical prints, and humor magazines imported from the West."[9]

Although some artists who issued both picturebooks (*ehon*) during the Taishō period (1912–1925) and the early Western-influenced Japanese comicbooks may have looked to Edo's visual tradition for inspiration, it would seem that such inspiration is, at best, nominal. A close link between the advent of the modern *manga* and the *kibyōshi* remains to be demonstrated.

Furthermore, the very notion that a monolithic visual culture continued unchanged from the Edo period, if not earlier, into modern times is itself not without complications. Significant historical upheavals in visuality—occasioned by paradigmatic shifts in the nature of media, not to mention phenomenal improvements in their reach—separate the late eighteenth and the early twentieth centuries in Japan no less than in America. Thus, a more moderate position is called for. Tsuji Nobuo is probably on the right track when arguing that the modern *manga* does not derive *entirely* from the Western comicbook.[10] Timothy Craig puts the matter aptly: "Japanese comic artists have taken a physical form imported from the West, combined it with a centuries-old Japanese tradition of narrative art and illustrated humor, and added important innovations of their own to create what amounts to a totally new genre."[11] Likewise, Schodt is justified in drawing parallels without insisting upon causation when remarking: "In the early 19th century, *kibyōshi*, 'yellow-cover' booklets, were produced by the thousands. Like modern comics, *kibyōshi* evolved from illustrated tales for children and gradually encompassed more and more sophisticated adult material. Most pages consisted of a drawing combined with the text in a block above it to form an illustrated, running story."[12]

Be that as it may, why do so many cultural commentators, in trying to trace the modern *manga* back to traditional forms, end up exaggerating the role and distorting the nature of the *kibyōshi*? No doubt there are just as many motivations as there are commentators, including Orientalist motivations even among the Japanese themselves, for the myth of cultural uniqueness sells copy everywhere. That said, the culture wars in Japan surely play a considerable role. In *Adult Manga*, her sociology of the modern Japanese comicbook industry, Sharon Kinsella suggests: "The opposition to the manga and animation industries by conservative elements in postwar society has encouraged

---

9. Duus, "Weapons of the Weak, Weapons of the Strong," p. 968.
10. Tsuji, "Early Medieval Picture Scrolls as Ancestors of *Anime* and *Manga*."
11. Craig, *Japan Pop!* p. 8.
12. Schodt, *Dreamland Japan*, p. 138. See also Schodt, *Manga! Manga!*, p. 37.

the defenders of manga, namely professional manga critics, to emphasize or even invent stylistic origins for manga in ancient Japanese history."

Kinsella goes on to pooh-pooh the resultant tendency: "The majority of cultural criticism has so far associated *manga* not with the international phenomenon of popular culture, but with far earlier forms of Japanese graphic art. *Manga* has been compared repeatedly to the twelfth century illustrations of Bishop Toba (*Tobae*), or the wood block print (*ukiyoe*) culture of the eighteenth and nineteenth centuries."[13] Thus, it would seem as though the attempt to ground the modern *manga* in some amorphous Japanese tradition—into which the *kibyōshi* would be subsumed as part of *ukiyoe* culture—is part of a reactionary ploy to legitimize *manga* by downplaying the otherwise incontestable influence of global but especially Western popular culture.

Whatever other motivations might be at play, the main danger in positing the existence of a monolithic, transhistorical *manga* culture is that it risks distorting both the modern as well as the premodern forms. That is, in trying to impart an air of legitimacy to the modern *manga* by claiming that it partakes in some putatively venerable and unbroken tradition, proponents of *manga* culture perceive strong connections where there are few if any. And they end up, inadvertently perhaps, patronizing the premodern tradition, treating it as though it were valuable *only* by virtue of its relationship to the modern *manga*—and as though it were some kind of static single entity, which is surely a vexed proposition since that tradition encompasses a full millennium of dynamic literary and visual history.

The notion that the modern *manga* has its roots in the *kibyōshi*, and thereby can be legitimized as emanating from a "traditional" Japanese genre, may unintentionally consign the *kibyōshi* to the status of neglectable precursor, not as something that demands sustained attention in its own right. Furthermore, to the extent that the *kibyōshi* participated in the revolution that was the application of mass printing to popular literature, there would seem to be reason to question its status as a "traditional" genre. That is, mass printing may be considered one of many harbingers of early modernity, at least in literary terms, since it allowed for the effective extension of a central culture to the periphery in an unprecedented way that lent itself to the eventual emergence and maintenance of the modern nation-state.

Goals of the Present Chapter

Such speculation aside, this chapter provides a couple of examples of ways in which the notion of a monolithic, transhistorical *manga* culture has distorted the premodern tradition, thereby affecting the reception and understanding of the *kibyōshi*. In keeping with the overarching purpose of the present study to introduce the *kibyōshi*, these examples naturally reveal more

---

13. Kinsella, *Adult Manga*, p. 19.

about the *kibyōshi* than the modern *manga*. The first example is the characterization of the *kibyōshi* as pornographic, a characterization that seems to be a projection of a similar strain within the modern *manga*. The second example is the claim that the modern *manga* somehow traces its origins back to Hokusai's sketchbooks. While arguing that the notion of a transhistorical *manga* culture flattens out the premodern tradition into a one-dimensional entity, a practice that can be discerned in the way that *Hokusai manga* is enlisted to stand for just about the entire tradition, this chapter also observes that during An'ei-Tenmei it was not Hokusai but Kyōden who popularized the term *manga*. This leads to the question: could the *kibyōshi* itself have been the "original" *manga*? And in the broadest possible sense that it was the first comicbook for adults in Japan, it could well have been.

After that, this chapter suggests ways in which some pictorial conventions in both the *kibyōshi* and the modern *manga* may appear at first glance to be identical, thereby lending credence to the claim that the two genres are directly connected, though upon closer inspection they turn out to be dissimilar in origin if not use. These conventions are the so-called text balloon or bubble, the speed line, and panelization. This discussion leads to a consideration of the nature of the visual-verbal imagination as manifest in the *kibyōshi*. In particular, it is argued that this visual-verbal nexus benefits immensely from the nature of Japanese writing itself as well as from the calligraphic tradition. It might seem as though the relationship between the words and the pictures within the *kibyōshi* is a relatively simple affair, something grasped intuitively by anyone familiar with comicbooks, graphic novels, or *manga*. The complexity of the situation, however, is suggested by outlining a few positions that see this relationship from diametrically opposite perspectives.

Admittedly, the present chapter might seem to dismiss the modern *manga* along the same lines that the *kibyōshi* itself has been dismissed—defining one as important only for the light it casts upon the other. Yet this slight is hardly perpetrated out of the conviction that the modern *manga* merits no serious attention. On the contrary, solid work on the modern *manga* is desperately called for since its phenomenon is vast, its subject matter compelling, and its visual-verbal imagination remarkable. To the extent that interest in the *kibyōshi* depends upon interest in the modern *manga*, the importance of the *manga* to any inquiry into the *kibyōshi* cannot be completely denied. Furthermore, the modern *manga* is too broad a phenomenon, and its study still too embryonic, for meaningful comparisons to be made at the present juncture. Besides, any discussion of the particular ways in which the visual-verbal imagination is manifest in the *kibyōshi* should not be unduly influenced by a consideration of the modern form. Thus, only the most tentative comments on the connections between the two are possible at this stage, and these will be made mostly in passing here while discussing the visual-verbal imagination within the *kibyōshi*.

Kibyōshi, Manga, and Pornography

One example of how the *kibyōshi* too often gets squeezed into *manga* culture is the way in which it is not infrequently represented as erotic or even pornographic. The assumption seems to be that the modern *manga* itself is largely characterized by portrayals of graphic sex (to say nothing of gratuitous violence), a characterization that is not entirely fair.[14] The *kibyōshi* is a form for adult readers, to be sure, perhaps even an Edo analogue of what Kinsella calls the "adult manga," but hardly bearing the implied explicit content that might easily be read into this term. Simply put, the *kibyōshi* is not fundamentally pornographic. It is *not* some kind of X-rated woodblock-printed genre. Its works almost never aim at stimulating sexual desire through the graphic representation of such things as oversized genitalia and comely lovers locked in acrobatic positions impracticable for the most limber of contortionists, even those putatively idealized in the *Kama Sutra*.

The mistaken impression of the *kibyōshi* as pornographic, not to mention the attendant stigma sometimes attached to the form in polite society, is widespread and longstanding, and thus requires no small amount of debunking. Such impressions are perpetuated regularly in works attempting to force the *kibyōshi* to fit into the cookie cutter of *manga* culture. Napier, for instance, in her landmark study, defines the *kibyōshi* as "illustrated books with an often humorous and/or erotic content."[15] Kanako Shiokawa, in bending over backwards to ground the modern *manga* in the *kibyōshi*, characterizes the latter as "adult (and often erotic)."[16] And one major scholar of modern Japanese literature seems to be under the sway of something like *manga* culture when he claims in passing that genres of playful literature such as the *kibyōshi* and the fashionbook were "frequently banned by the authorities for obscenity."[17]

Such distortion may stem from the conflation of illustrated books *like* the *kibyōshi* with X-rated woodblock prints, or from the presumption that works deriving their energy if not their setting from the Floating World inevitably depict that world graphically in all its unadulterated carnality. Yet this is precisely how the notion of a monolithic *manga* culture flattens out the premodern tradition. One of the earliest works on the *kibyōshi* in English certainly has not helped matters by describing the genre in shockingly fallacious terms—or perhaps not so shocking, given that Japanology has at times been prone to eroticizing as well as exoticizing traditional Japan—as catering to a readership that was "under the spell" of a "pornocrasy."[18]

---

14. For more on sex in modern *manga*, see Allison, *Permitted and Prohibited Desires*.
15. Napier, *Anime from Akira to Princess Mononoke*, p. 21.
16. Shiokawa, "'The Reads' and 'Yellow Covers,'" p. 25.
17. Washburn, *The Dilemma of the Modern in Japanese Fiction*, p. 55.
18. Akimoto, *The Twilight of Yedo*, p. 148.

Fig. 1 A young geisha engrossed in a *kibyōshi*. The inscription reads "Ochie of the Koiseya at Kobikichō, Shin'yashiki" (*Kobikichō shin'yashiki koiseya Ochie*). From the multicolored woodblock series "Edo's Celebrated Beauties" (*Edo kōmei bijin*) by Kitagawa Utamaro, ca. 1792–1793. At the time, Ochie would have been just under twenty years old. Courtesy of the Chiba City Museum of Art.

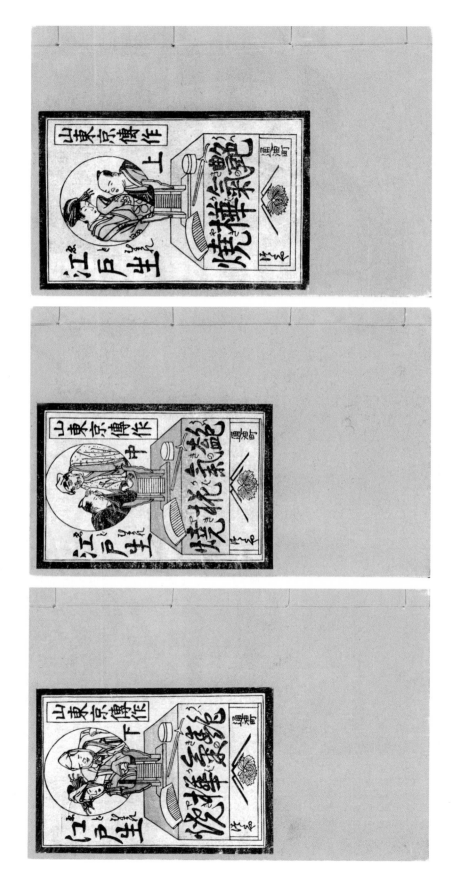

Fig. 2 The three frontispieces to the 1793 deluxe second edition of *Playboy, Roasted à la Edo* (*Edo umare uwaki no kabayaki*; originally published in 1785), a *kibyōshi* written and illustrated by Santō Kyōden. Reprinted in Kisho fukuseikai, *Shinseiki* 35.

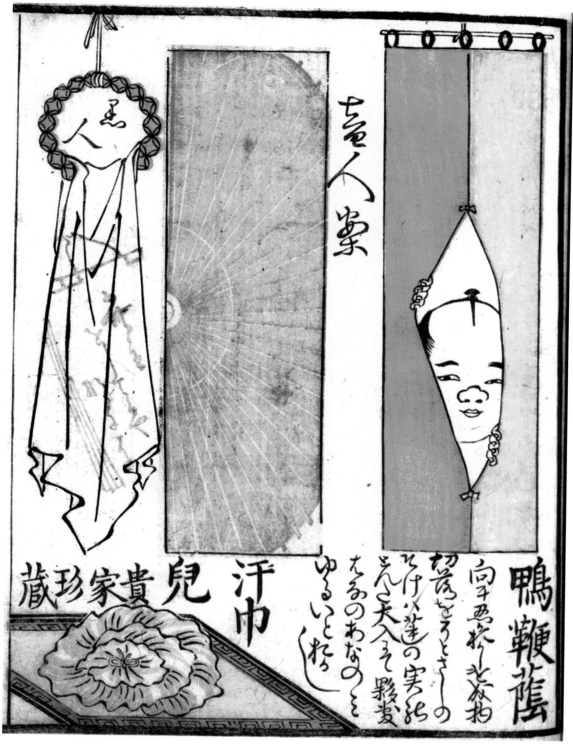

蔵珍家貴 兒 汗巾

喜人案

鴨鞭�

Fig. 3 Kamo no Muchikage's unnamed pug-nosed character who would become the model for Enjirō. From *The Handtowel Competition* (*Tanagui awase*, 1784), a humorous picturebook (*kokkei mitate ehon*) written and illustrated by Santō Kyōden. Courtesy of the National Institute of Japanese Literature.

Fig. 4 Two courtesans-in-training struggling over a yellow-covered comicbook (*kibyōshi*), as other women of the Yoshiwara pleasure quarter carry on with their affairs. From *A Pageant of the Latest Beauties, Their Calligraphy Mirrored* ([*Yoshiwara keisei*] *Shin bijin awase jihitsu kagami* [*New Beauties of the Yoshiwara in the Mirror of Their Own Script*], Japanese, Edo period, 1784), a book of woodblock prints; ink and color on paper; by Kitao Masanobu (Santō Kyōden, 1761–1816). Source unidentified. Photograph © 2006 Museum of Fine Arts, Boston.

Fig. 6 Cover of the redbook *Monkey vs. Crab* (*Saru kani gassen*). Written by Nishimura Shigenaga. Reprinted in Kisho fukuseikai, *Kisho fukuseikai sōsho* 4.

Fig. 5 The titular protagonist of the classic tale about a woman with a saucer fused to her skull. From *The Story of Lady Dishhead* (*Hachikazuki*, ca. 1624–1643), an anonymous hand-colored picturebook. Reprinted in Yoshida, *Tanrokubon*, p. 165. Courtesy of Kodansha International. Permission of Kurofunekan.

Fig. 7 The two extant frontispieces from *Life of a Stretchy Monster* (*Mikoshi nyūdō ichidaiki*, 1782), a *kibyōshi* written by Iba Kashō and illustrated by Torii Kiyonaga. Courtesy of the Matsuura Historical Museum.

Fig. 8 Master Wetdream making love behind a standing screen to a daimyo's daughter—"A sixteen-year-old, as yet untouched by any man, and so starved for love!" From *Master Wetdream's Fantasy Pillow* (*Isei sensei yume makura*, ca. 1789). Courtesy of Ritsumeikan University, Art Research Center.

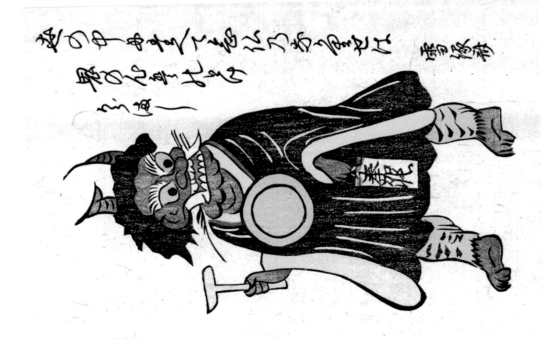

Fig. 10 Ōtsu print (Ōtsue) of a demon with mallet, gong, and list of temple donors. From *Souvenirs of Ōtsu* (*Ōtsu miyage*, 1780), a madcap-poem picturebook (*kyōka ebon*). Reprinted in Kisho fukuseikai, *Kisho fukuseikai sōsho 1.*

Fig. 9 In a scene from one of the only known surviving "smallpox picturebooks" (*hōsō ebon*), a child performs an inspiring feat. Since such books were presented to children in their sickbeds as protective amulets—the vermillion color of the ink being believed to fend off all manners of evil as well as illness—they were normally burned after use. From *Children's Acrobatics to Keep Safe from Smallpox* (*Hōsō anzen kodomo no karuwaza*, date unknown). Written by Tamenaga Shunsui (1790–1843) and illustrated by Sadashige. Reprinted in Hanasaki, *Hōsō ebon shū*, p. 27.

What is within the realm of the reasonable is that the yellow of the *kibyōshi*'s covers connoted something naughty, for traditionally this was the color of passion rendered graphically—of "blue" love.[19] It was also the hue of the Hachijō silk that most discriminating playboys preferred, if contemporary fashionbooks are any gauge. The pseudonym of the *kibyōshi* progenitor, Koikawa Harumachi—"Loveriver Springtown"—in playing off the associations of sexual passion with spring (*haru* or *shun*) and with some watery gushing of pleasure, mischievously implies that his books overflow with eroticism. Thus, the view of the *kibyōshi* as smutty may have been deliberately propagated from its very inception—well before the misguided tendency now to regard the form as some kind of precursor to present-day Japanese "depraved" comics (*hentai manga*) or "mangerotics" (*ero manga*).

Along these lines, it is also sometimes erroneously said that the shogunate censured Kyōden for his supposed violation of the "absolute ban on pornography."[20] It is true that he produced a handful of risqué works. His *Erotic Dream Puzzles* (*Shikidō yume hanji*, ca. 1786), for one, contains a self-portrait of the author engaged in an act of autoeroticism while eyeballing a likeness of the courtesan Kikuzono (whom in real life he would eventually wed). Yet this work was in no way a *kibyōshi*. Rather, it was a "pillowbook" (*makurabon*)—something to be hidden within easy reach while lying in bed.[21] Besides, as we will see in the next chapter, in point of fact Kyōden was technically prosecuted for having issued three fashionbooks without having obtained the proper stamps of approval from the Publishing Association.

That said, some *kibyōshi* can be quite randy. Hardcore porn was such a basic fact of life in a city like Edo, where there was no shortage of fully grown single men (among other interested parties), that some reference to it within popular literature was almost to be expected. A significant portion of the publishing industry was dedicated to concupiscence, to "libidinous representation"—as Timon Screech has expediently formulated it—catering primarily to male sexual fantasies.[22] Indeed, "spring pictures" (*shunga*) or "underground images" (*higa*) were widely and readily and cheaply available. During An'ei-Tenmei, though, these were referred to by a variety of terms: "pillow prints" (*makurae*), "risqué sheets" (*abunae*), and "giggle pix" (*waraie*), not to overlook the louche illustrations in "erotica" (*kōshokubon*), "vernal

---

19. This equation is complicated by the fact that the *kibyōshi* was originally termed bluebook (*aohon*) and that in English the color yellow, aside from its use in some negative terms, is associated with one of the earliest comic-strip characters—Richard Felton Outcault's *Yellow Kid*, which began appearing in Joseph Pulitzer's newspaper *The New York World* in 1895.

20. Najita, "History and Nature in Eighteenth-Century Tokugawa Thought," p. 469.

21. For a discussion of *Shikidō yume hanji*, see Ujiie Fuyumi, "Masanobu no na iri makurabon," in *Kikan ukiyoe 65* (April 1976). According to Hayashi Miichi, Kyōden produced four pornographic books. Cited in Nobuhiro, "Santō Kyōden's *Sharebon*," p. 144.

22. Screech, *Sex and the Floating World*, p. 16.

Fig. 3.1 Master Wetdream making love behind a standing screen to a daimyo's daughter—"A sixteen-year-old, as yet untouched by any man, and so starved for love!" From *Master Wetdream's Fantasy Pillow* (*Isei sensei yume makura*, ca. 1789), an anonymous *kibyōshi*-style pillow-book. Courtesy of Ritsumeikan University, Art Research Center.

volumes" (*shunpon*), and "flesh books" (*ehon*).[23] That a playful form like the *kibyōshi* would poke fun at this nubile, indeed fertile, discursive space, then, was inevitable. Kyōden's *Swingers* manages to do so while leaving enough to the imagination so as not to devolve into that which it spoofs.

What would have been truly scandalous, though, is if in the course of playing with the conventions, characters, and situations of hardcore porn, a few *kibyōshi* did not occasionally cross the line into decidedly non-virgin territory. Indeed, it must be acknowledged that a rare few works *seem* to qualify as lubricious. For instance, the anonymously penned *Master Wetdream's Fantasy Pillow* (*Isei sensei yume makura*, ca. 1789) does unto *Master Flashgold's Splendiferous Dream* something as equally perverse—and, it must be said, enjoyable—as what R. Crumb's *Fritz the Cat* does unto *Felix the Cat* (**Figure 3.1** and **Color Figure 8**).[24] Such is the exception that proves the rule, however. If ranked by the standards applied to present-day American movies, it might be conjectured that about 90 percent of *kibyōshi* would be rated PG-13; 9 percent NC-

23. The *e* of *ehon* here is a different Chinese graph than the one in "picturebook." For a valuable article on the terminology of pornography during the Edo period, see Smith, "Overcoming the Modern History of Edo 'Shunga.'"

24. For more on this in Japanese, see Hayashi, *Enpon Edo bungakushi*, pp. 284–310. Araki discusses and partially translates this piece—the title of which he renders "Mr. Wet-Dozer's Dream Pillow"—in his seminal article, "The Dream Pillow in Edo Fiction," pp. 98–105.

17; and only 1 percent, perhaps, XXX. Such ratios, by modern *manga* terms, are uninspiringly modest.

The definition of "wet stuff," in the contemporary idiom, being notoriously slippery, it might be objected that the pornography standards of Edo's Tōriaburachō are not comparable to those of present-day Hollywood. Like any other signifying practice, porn is, to some measure, culturally bound. Contrary to his famous definition, chances are that Justice Potter Stewart would *not* have recognized every single type of Japanese pornography even if he had seen it. Something like the "whose sleeves?" (*tagasode*) was a category of erotic print that supposedly stimulated fetishistic, if not sexual, desires merely by depicting rich sultry fabrics hanging suggestively from a wardrobe rack.[25] One therefore wonders if some *kibyōshi* may have included this kind of libidinous representation that today might go all but undetected.

Judging by such things as extant wish-lists and itemized catalogues of the contents of bridal trousseaus (*yomeiri dōgu*), many a blushing bride of even middle-class families was the blissful recipient of various sorts of comic-book as well as of pornography—allegedly to bone up on the ways of the world prior to the wedding night.[26] Although it is likely that genres such as the *kibyōshi* were requested by virtue of their entertainment or even literary or artistic value, they seem to have subsequently been misrepresented, for better or worse, because of a kind of guilt by association—association with flesh books, which women may have desired for reasons beyond sex education, after all. In a latter day, novelist Izumi Kyōka (1873–1939) would confess to stumbling upon a stash of Edo-period woodblock printed matter in his mother's bridal chest, at least if one of his fictional stories is any indication.[27] And good thing that he did, too, for surely Kyōka's sensibilities owe something to genres of Edo's popular fiction.

Furthermore, the Japanese associated laughter with sex well before Freud came along. That which could bring a "grin" to one's face, or send one into paroxysms of "laughter"—the Japanese term *warai* covers both meanings—was loosely associated with sexual *jouissance*. The sense of connection among these sorts of pleasurable dissipations is ratified linguistically in terms like "giggle pix" and "leer books." One therefore wonders if at the time any kind of humorous literature evoking titters was considered even slightly titillating.

---

25. There is a long history in Japan of eroticizing someone sight unseen through the merest peep of his or her fabrics, poetry, handwriting, etc., all of which, surely, are visual markers of social class. For more on the "whose sleeves?" in English, see Tanaka, "Erotic Textiles."

26. For more on bridal trousseaus, see Kokuritsu rekishi minzoku hakubutsukan, *Otoko mo onna mo sōshingu*.

27. These were mostly polychromatic prints (*nishikie*) and blackbooks (*kurobyōshi*). This story, *Illustrated by Kunisada* (*Kunisada egaku*, 1912), is reprinted in Izumi Kyōka, *Izumi Kyōka shū*, pp. 39–69.

Still, since the comic spirit of the vast majority of *kibyōshi* seems to outweigh any apparent prurience, those scant few dirty works may qualify less as *kibyōshi* per se than as porno-satirical takes on—or, more likely, rip-offs of—the *kibyōshi* genre. The *kibyōshi* aims to arouse comic laughter rather than sexual desire, let alone release; the double vision inherent in parody would seem to blur the single-minded focus incumbent upon viewers of pornography.[28] Accordingly, the very notion of a sleazy *kibyōshi* is oxymoronic. Something like this, if not a pious consensus against discussing such matters as pornography, explains why most scholars of the *kibyōshi* per se, including Tanahashi in *Kibyōshi Overview*, refrain from classifying *Master Wetdream* as a *kibyōshi*. (Another reason might be that unlike all extant examples of the *kibyōshi*, the interior pictures of *Master Wetdream* appear to have been printed in color.) What is clear is that if such an erotic work really is a *kibyōshi*, it certainly occupies the immoral minority.

Some gags in the *kibyōshi*, not to mention its language, cannot help but be described as off-color. More than one work touches on spousal abuse, visually impaired people, differently physiognomied individuals, and many other sensitive topics in a trifling manner that today would for good reason be deemed offensive. Some works disturbingly make light of the molestation of children. On the one hand, this sort of thing needs to be taken in context. The manhandling of a young teenage courtesan-in-training in *Familiar Bestsellers*, for instance, was probably understood as part of the fetishization of the incipient sexuality of such young women in the pleasure quarters—the deflowering (*mizuage*) of whom was peddled as a special treat for the client (though it could only have been a brutal rite of passage for the young woman). On the other hand, the abuse of servant girls even outside the quarter was apparently so widespread that Teshima Toan (1718–1786), in his standard primer *Early Lessons* (*Zenkun*, 1773), warned against it vehemently.[29] That said, while children are hardly immune from violence even within children's literature, they are not usually sexually assaulted there the way they sometimes are *said* to be in the *kibyōshi*—though such sexual assault is never depicted graphically in the *kibyōshi* as it tends to be in the modern *manga*.

All things considered, then, the *kibyōshi* is not essentially pornographic, though at times it does flirt with the notion. Thus, if the *kibyōshi* must be likened to a modern comicbook form for the sake of comparison, instead of the adult *manga*, it might be considered as a kind of Edo-period analogue of the "comix" in the sense Spiegelman intends, referring to the sophisticated "co-mixing" of visual and verbal elements in the best of comicbooks:

---

28. Goulemot, writing on erotic literature in eighteenth-century France, has argued that since "pornographic literature requires a strict focus" and "parody requires a reading on two registers," the two are inherently at odds. In Goulemot, *Forbidden Texts*, p. 71.

29. Sawada, *Confucian Values and Popular Zen*, p. 112.

"Rather than comics," he writes, "I prefer the word comix, to mix together, because to talk about comics is to talk about mixing together words and pictures to tell a story."[30] Spiegelman's use of "x" playfully misleads, referencing those explicit underground works where "X" marks the spot. "Comix," thus, has recently begun to gain general acceptance as a term referring to any comicbook appealing to adult readers without signifying pornography. As Charles McGrath observes in a recent article in the *New York Times*, "Many practitioners of the form prefer the term 'comix,' with that nostalgic 'x' referring to the age of the underground comics, which were sold in head shops along with bongs and cigarette papers."[31] To the extent that the yellow of the *kibyōshi* covers must have similarly suggested something uninhibited, the term "comix" might not actually be inexcusably inapt.

Thus, the typical characterization of the *kibyōshi* as obscene suggests how *manga* culture commonly conflates the premodern tradition. It also suggests how one conspicuous feature of the modern *manga* may be projected backwards onto the *kibyōshi*. Although some individual works fool around with the conventions of pornography (as with Kyōden's *Swingers*), and some works can be offensive for other reasons, the genre itself cannot be described as pornographic. All told, it might be said that the misrepresentation of the *kibyōshi* demonstrates how facilely proponents of *manga* culture would contort the premodern tradition to satisfy their own desires.

Manga's Mangled Etymology

Almost all accounts of the birth of the Japanese comicbook attribute the coining of the term *manga*, meaning something like "impromptu pictures" or "doodles," to the artist Katsushika Hokusai (1760–1849).[32] So much so that this etymology has acquired the force of fact. Otherwise trusty lexicons in Japan and in the West (like the *Oxford English Dictionary*) have subscribed. Some commentators have even gone so far as to proclaim Hokusai the father of the modern *manga* itself, which is surely an example of *manga* culture gone wild. Yet there is a vast difference between Hokusai's sketchbooks and the modern comicbook— or even the *kibyōshi* as an Edo-period comicbook. *Hokusai manga* is more of a sketchbook of comic figures in fifteen volumes (published piecemeal from 1814 to as late as 1878) than a sequential visual-verbal narrative per se, even though some of its compositions dabble in sociopolitical satire (**Figure 3.2**).

---

30. Spiegelman, "Commix [*sic*]: An Idiosyncratic Historical and Aesthetic Overview," in *Print*, vol. 42, no. 6 (November-December 1988), p. 61. Quoted in Levine, "Necessary Stains," p. 99, no. 1.

31. McGrath, "Not Funnies," p. 26.

32. To cite but one recent example, Kinko Ito minces no words in claiming that "Hokusai was the first to coin the term *manga*." In Ito, "A History of *Manga* in the Context of Japanese Culture and Society," p. 460.

Fig. 3.2 Samurai underlings grimacing as their master squats in an outhouse. From *Hokusai manga*. Courtesy of the Arthur M. Sackler Museum, Harvard University.

Such quibbles can be set aside, some *manga* culture proponents might object, for genres inevitably develop over time in spite of their original designations. What is significant is that *Hokusai manga* stands today as the most illustrious early example of a work to incorporate the term *manga* conspicuously into its title.[33] Thus, although Hokusai did not invent the *form* of the modern *manga*, or even devise its style, he can at most be credited with having bequeathed the *term* that ultimately would come to identify the modern Japanese comicbook.

33. For a discussion in English and reproductions, see Michener, *The Hokusai Sketchbooks*.

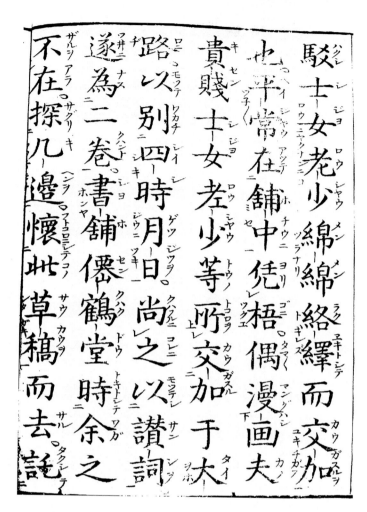

Fig. 3.3 One of the early appearances of the word *manga* in print (second column from right at bottom), albeit glossed in the traditional orthography as *mangwa*. From the Preface to *Seasonal Passersby* (*Shiki no yukikai*, 1798), a picturebook written by Santō Kyōden and illustrated by Kitao Shigemasa. Private collection of Professor Ōtaka Yōji.

Still, strictly speaking, Hokusai did not invent the term *manga*. For one thing, it graces the title of Aikawa Minwa's *Doodles of a Hundred Women* (*Manga hyakujo*) of 1814—the same year *Hokusai manga* began publication.[34] For another, the term appears within works predating Hokusai's caricatures by a couple of decades, if not more. It can also be found, for instance, within the preface to one of Kyōden's picturebooks, the bestselling *Seasonal Passersby* (*Shiki no yukikai*), published in 1798 (**Figure 3.3**).[35] The illustrations in this book, provided by Kitao Shigemasa, cannot be said to have foreshadowed the whimsicality of *Hokusai manga*, since their style cannot really

---

34. I am indebted here to the discussion in Shimizu, *Manga no rekishi*, pp. 17–19. Shimizu also dispels the myth that the word *manga* was a Japanese invention. While it is true that the Japanese applied the word to caricature, the Chinese seem to have used it much earlier to describe the spoonbill duck.

35. Also called *Shiji no yukikai*, this work is reprinted in Yamaguchi, *Fūzoku zueshū*, pp. 385–402.

be described as comical (see **Figure 3.7**). Yet Kyōden's work apparently went far in lodging the term in the popular idiom: "Because *Seasonal Passersby* was a hit," Shimizu opines, "the word *manga* gained public visibility."[36] Curiously, Shimizu also maintains that the first *known* usage of the word *manga* within a work is to be found in Suzuki Kankyō's *Miscellany of Impromptu Drawings (Mankaku zuihitsu)* of 1771—though Shimizu fails to explain why he feels this work was not sufficiently popular to have introduced the term into widespread circulation.

Nonetheless, the word must have been trendy enough to be deployed in a comic haiku (*Yanagidaru 96*) written prior to 1790, for that is when Karai Senryū (the compiler of the collection in which the poem appeared) died:

Manga to wa	Dubbed "sketchy comics"
Iedo midari de	They're still inadvertently
Nai tehon	Decent portrayals.[37]

Whatever the case may be, none of these specimens fixed the word *manga* permanently in the popular imagination. Even Kyōden's ostensibly influential usage did not set the term in his *own* mind; for he fails, it would seem, to reprise it anywhere else, certainly not in any of his *kibyōshi* in the years immediately following *Seasonal Passersby*. Nor did he use the term to refer to the *kibyōshi*. Nor do other authors for that matter.[38] In fact, in the preface to one of his *kibyōshi* published the year prior to *Seasonal Passersby*, that is, in 1797, Kyōden employed the similar term *mange*—"impromptu frivolities"—in describing his comic pictures.[39] What this suggests is that the term *manga* existed in the language during mid-Edo to refer to a doodle or caricature of some sort, but this it did alongside several terms, enjoying no privileged position.

Until earlier appearances of the word *manga* are unearthed—perhaps even in Chinese sources (though Shimizu and other Japanese scholars insist not)—one wonders, in the meantime, how Hokusai came to appropriate the term *manga* over other available choices. Hokusai was almost certainly familiar with many of the above-mentioned works, including Kyōden's *Seasonal Passersby*. Yet he also knew Kyōden personally, for at the beginning of his career, Hokusai (albeit under the pseudonym Shunrō) had collaborated di-

---

36. Shimizu, *Manga no rekishi*, p. 19.

37. Cited in Nakamura, *Kogo daijiten 5*, p. 453. The play on words in the original yields two meanings: "Although they're called doodles, they're still inadvertently an accurate handbook to life," and "Although they're called crude pictures, they're hardly obscene."

38. These claims are based both on the nonappearance of the word *manga* in the extensive index volume to Tanahashi's *Kibyōshi Overview* and on my reading of the *kibyōshi* in the first four volumes of Mizuno, *Santō Kyōden zenshū*, which run until 1802—five years past his initial use of the term *manga*. The fifth and final volume has not yet, at the time of this writing, been published.

39. Kyōden employed the *man* of *manga* and the *ge* of *gesaku* in his *Wasōbyōe gonichibanashi* (1797), as can be seen in Mizuno, *SKZ 4*, p. 105.

rectly with Kyōden, then at the end of *his* career, on a number of projects, most notably illustrating three *kibyōshi*.[40]

It may also be possible—though this is admittedly speculation—that Hokusai not only was exposed to the word *manga* by virtue of his association with Kyōden, but somehow came to associate it with the Toba cartoon style that Kyōden had employed in some of his earlier works, including the rendering of Enjirō, the protagonist of his most successful *kibyōshi*. If true—and this is doubly speculative—then the *kibyōshi*, while not the original *manga* per se, at the very least may have played a supporting role in Hokusai's appropriation of the term, an appropriation that seems ultimately to have influenced the naming of the modern Japanese form.

What this suggests is that neither Hokusai nor the *kibyōshi* gave birth to the modern *manga*. The connection between the modern *manga* and the *kibyōshi* is extremely tenuous. However, it is conceivable that the early practitioners of the modern Japanese comicbook might not have been able to appropriate the term *manga* for their enterprise had Hokusai not illustrated some *kibyōshi* under the man who supposedly popularized the term during the mid-Edo period. And if one defines *manga* loosely as a *comicbook medium* in the widest sense (as proponents of *manga* culture are wont to do), then the *kibyōshi* probably *was* the original adult *manga*.

What is incontestable, though, is that the *kibyōshi* seems to have been the first comicbook genre for adults in Japanese literary history. To be clear about this claim, several narratives with strong visual-verbal elements in Japan predate the *kibyōshi*. The picture scroll (*emakimono*), for instance, existed as a major visual-verbal narrative form from the classical, throughout the medieval, and into the Edo period itself. However, this was anything but a low-priced, mass-printed affair consumed by a wide readership under and beyond the aristocracy. With the establishment of a commercial woodblock-printing industry during the first half of the seventeenth century, though, genres of mass-printed illustrated books for adults, such as the syllabary booklet (*kanazōshi*), the Floating World novella (*ukiyozōshi*), and the companion booklet (*otogizōshi*), began to reach a significantly broad popular audience. Yet these too were hardly comicbooks, since their illustrations were few, far between, and not integral to the story itself. In such lightly illustrated narratives, the pictures were secondary, perhaps utterly incidental, both to the experience of reading and to the meaning of the story.

Sometime around the middle of the eighteenth century, a few genres of visual-verbal narrative came to be issued in significant numbers. The red-

---

40. The works in question—*Jitsugokyō osana kōshaku* (1792), *Momotarō hottan banashi* (1792), and *Hinpuku ryō dōchū no ki* (1793)—are reproduced in Mizuno, *SKZ 3*, pp. 9–33, 35–58, and 193–212, respectively. Hokusai continued to illustrate for Kyōden in other genres into the early nineteenth century. It was not until 1797, a few years after the death of his master Katsukawa Shunshō, that Shunrō assumed the more famous pseudonym by which he would be remembered as one of the great "six immortals" of the woodblock print.

book, the blackbook, and the bluebook thus should be given full credit as the earliest true comicbooks in Japan, at least in the sense that I have defined the term. Yet these early comicbooks seem to have been written primarily for a semiliterate readership. It is only with the *kibyōshi* that one finds a genuine genre of *adult* comicbook, something that, with its combination of humor and sociopolitical satire, was more or less written *exclusively* for literate adults.

Similarly, it might be observed that in world literary history, visual-verbal narratives go back several millennia, to Egyptian hieroglyphic narratives and to pre-Columbian pictorial texts like the so-called Mexican Codex, brought to light in Europe by Cortés himself.[41] However, these were obviously not comicbooks as such either. Nor was the illuminated manuscript of Europe in the Middle Ages, for that matter, for though it enjoyed a glorious tradition (sometimes in early printed form), its proselytizing or at least religious aims would seem to disqualify it from consideration as *primarily* a kind of entertainment widely available to the masses.[42] Indeed, it appears as though the earliest European example of a *comic* narrative of sorts that was mass printed and widely disseminated is to be found in a city and culture and time similar to that of An'ei-Tenmei Edo: namely, the single-sheet comic strip of 1780s London. It would take the English a few more decades, however, before mass-printed *booklets* anything remotely like the *kibyōshi* became a staple of the reading public.[43]

Thus, the *kibyōshi* may well be the earliest known genre of adult comicbook in world history. Even if this proposition is eventually dispelled, though, the *kibyōshi* will arguably remain one of the most appealing embodiments of the visual-verbal imagination in An'ei-Tenmei Edo.

Manga vs. Kibyōshi

In a sense, the *kibyōshi* and the *manga* share much in common. They certainly seem to be similar media, which is to say they bear certain resemblances in format, modes of production, and reception. In terms of the first of these, the *kibyōshi* and the modern *manga* are inherently visual-verbal narratives. Both employ a number of similar pictorial conventions. And both seem visually associated with other forms of culture by virtue of their role as meta-media, parts of a larger network of closely aligned genres, commercial goods, and advertising mechanisms comprising virtual industries unto themselves.

In terms of production, the *kibyōshi* and the modern *manga* are mass-fabricated in assembly-line-like processes that exert vaguely similar pressures on authors and artists to produce, often to the point that earlier

---

41. For a brief discussion of this, see McCloud, *Understanding Comics*, p. 10.
42. For more on what she terms "pictorial hagiography," see Hahn, *Portrayed on the Heart*.
43. For more on this, see Kunzle, *The Early Comic Strip*, p. 1 and passim.

material—even the material of one's competitors—is, in one form or another, recycled. Both rely on the availability of disposable income in a capitalist society in some stage of industrial development. Both the *ki-byōshi*, by virtue of the woodblock printing process, and the modern *manga*, by virtue of the modern printing press, are products of mechanical reproduction, even if the former was powered by hand and the latter by electricity.

In terms of reception, the *kibyōshi* and the modern *manga* have enjoyed a comparable degree of broad-based appeal, gripping the mainstream popular imagination in ways that at the time of their emergence must have felt genuinely unprecedented. A case could be made that the majority of readers of both forms tended or tend to consist of "middle-class" men in their twenties and thirties. And if the modern *manga* industry has made significant headway in diversifying its readership, the same might be said of the *kibyōshi*, which over time seems to have broadened its own base to the point that it lost some of its unique qualities. Indeed, if the *kibyōshi* was one of the top-selling genres of its day, so too is the *manga* at present. One is hardly surprised to see the proverbial impeccably attired middle-aged businessman on the Tokyo subway briskly thumbing through the latest issue of *Young Magazine*, or a schoolgirl in the far-flung fishing village of Noboribetsu, Hokkaido, poring over *Nakayoshi*, one of several "comicbooks for girls" (*shōjo manga*). "Japan is the first nation in the world," Schodt notes, waxing idealistic only slightly, "to accord 'comic books' . . . nearly the same social status as novels and films."[44]

It is therefore natural to draw comparisons between the *kibyōshi* and the modern *manga*. It is also understandably tempting for those with a vested interest in overcoming the conservative cultural criticism of the latter to argue for an historical continuity with the former. Still, political agendas aside, the *kibyōshi* and the modern *manga* would seem to share a number of superficial similarities owing to the nature of the comicbook medium itself, rather than to any direct causal or historical link between the two forms or between their corresponding visual cultures. If the *kibyōshi* and the modern *manga* can be said to emanate from a common ground of Japanese visual culture, they certainly do not emanate from the same wellspring.

As shall be argued at more length in what follows, the visual regime of the *kibyōshi* seems to derive primarily from the representation of the popular stage in woodblock prints, whereas the visual regime of the modern *manga* derives primarily from Western genres like the comicbook and the cinema. Any apparent similarity or overlap between the two is, more often than not, coincidental, an epiphenomenal effect of the comicbook medium itself that one might just as easily observe in comicbooks appearing in

---

44. Schodt, *Dreamland Japan*, p. 19.

isolation anywhere around the world, not evidence that the *kibyōshi* poured continuously into the modern *manga*. Both are types of comicbooks, to be sure, though their respective visual idioms are just about completely unrelated. In the final analysis, the *kibyōshi* and the modern *manga* are similar media but different genres. Thus, many of the putative similarities between the two turn out to be flukes, hardly educing a more profound cultural homology, or common origin, let alone a verifiable direct influence. At a deeper level, dissimilarities become glaringly apparent.

Bubbles on the Surface

One example of such a superficial similarity that turns out to have sharply different origins and even uses is to be found in the example of the text "balloon" or "bubble." When this device appears in the modern *manga*, as in the Western comicbook, it generally tends to encapsulate text representing the speech or thoughts of a character. The *kibyōshi* makes frequent use of the bubble, too, though almost never in this same way. Such text typically gets positioned near the figure of the character without being demarked by enclosing lines, as though simply hovering in the ether. Rather, the *kibyōshi* uses the bubble to enclose scenes, replete with figures of characters and perhaps some written narrative text, that are most often associated with some other realm, particularly that of dreams. The *kibyōshi* has dream bubbles, in other words, not speech or thought bubbles.

The bubble in the *kibyōshi* and other genres of illustrated Edo literature can also sometimes convey a fictional character from one realm to another. In one of Akinari's ghost stories from *Tales of Moonlight and Rain* entitled "The Dream-Inspired Carp" (*Muō no rigyo*), published during An'ei though not a *kibyōshi*, the Priest Kōgi returns from an underwater kingdom in a wisp of smoke emanating from a fish about to be sliced open and devoured (**Figure 3.4**). Similarly, in one of Kyōden's *kibyōshi*, a courtesan trapped in the underworld appears before her lover within billows of incense (**Figure 3.5**). The bubble functions this way in other *kibyōshi* too, as evidenced by the pieces translated herein.

Furthermore, the tail of the bubble sometimes points toward some spot "offstage"—or "offpage"—completely outside the pictorial frame, as though to indicate that the bubble's contents are conveyed telepathically or supernaturally or spiritually from the Beyond. More frequently, the tail emanates from a character's midsection. This reflects the longstanding popular belief in Japan that the soul is reposed in the center of the body, just below the navel. However, by the twentieth century, the locus of individuality in the modern *manga* had shifted to the head—which would seem to suggest direct influence from the Western comicbook as opposed to the *kibyōshi*.

There are two major theories about the origins of the bubble convention in premodern Japanese visual culture. The first holds that the bubble

Fig. 3.4 Priest Kōgi magically transported from the underwater kingdom through a wisp of smoke emanating from a fish about to be devoured. From *Tales of Moonlight and Rain* (*Ugetsu monogatari*, 1776), a reading book by Ueda Akinari. Courtesy of Niigata University Library.

derives from the folk belief that a departed soul can appear as a vision within graveside incense fumes (*hangonkō*).[45] To the extent that the actual fumes of such incense appear to connect earth and heaven visually, its appropriation as a pictorial device to connect earthly and otherworldly realms could hardly have been more apropos. The *kibyōshi* scenario just cited is a case in point. Ultimately, this convention probably traces back to the Chinese pictorial trope of Emperor Wu (r. 141–87 BCE) gazing upon the image of his departed wife Li who appears before him within incense billows.

The other major theory holds that the bubble derives from the pictorial convention of representing dreams within a mist band (*suyarigasumi*), a kind of stylized cusped cloud with pictorially narrative weight, apparently a practice connected to the tropic rendering of the Buddha's dreamlike visitation to mortals. Although the use of the mist band as a pictorial device goes back to Heian-period picture scrolls, if not earlier, and can be spotted throughout premodern Japanese visual culture, it seems as though it is only during the

---

45. See Natsume, "Kibyōshi o manga kara miru," pp. 196–197.

Fig. 3.5 The courtesan Takao appearing from the underworld to her lover Tadanobu via incense billows. From *Unsavorily Mismatched Jiffy Shanks (Fuanbai sokuseki ryōri,* 1784), a *kibyōshi* written and illustrated by Santō Kyōden. Courtesy of Tokyo Metropolitan Central Library, Kaga Collection.

early Edo period that the mist band is made to convey dreams: the "earliest-known unambiguous use" of this kind of dream balloon, according to Kenji Kajiya, "occurs in 'The Flute' (*Yokobue*) scene in [the woodblock-printed book] *Illustrated Tale of Genji (Eiri Genji monogatari*), published in Kyoto by Yamamoto Shunshō (1610–1682) in 1654. A simplified version of the smoke-shaped outline is used to distinguish the dream from the dreamer."[46] Kajiya maintains that dream-conveying mist bands appear no earlier: "Before the device of balloons was invented in the early Edo period, dream figures are represented in the same scenes, and in essentially the same forms, as humans."[47]

Whichever theory of the origins of the dream bubble to which one subscribes, it must be said that neither one informs the modern *manga,* which indubitably appropriates its text balloon from the Western comic-

46. Kajiya, "Reimagining the Imagined," p. 91.

47. Kajiya, "Reimagining the Imagined," p. 89. Kajiya dismisses the rival theory on the grounds that the incense-fume device "has sometimes been depicted in Japan but does not seem to have been popular enough to become a forerunner of the balloon" and refers the reader to "*Gadai: Setsuwa, densetsu, gikyoku* (Subject matter: Narratives, legends, and dramas), vol. 4 of *Genshoku ukiyoe dai hyakka jiten* (Tokyo: Taishūkan shoten, 1981), p. 123." In Kajiya, "Reimagining the Imagined," p. 104, n. 14.

book. Needless to say, the Western comicbook probably did not derive its text balloon from premodern Japan. Furthermore, it should be clear that the *kibyōshi*'s dream bubble and the modern *manga*'s text bubble fulfill different functions. Therefore, while the materialization of the bubble in both the *kibyōshi* and the modern *manga* might at first seem to suggest a direct pictorial link, if the premodern bubble reveals anything, it is that the dream of *manga* culture proponents of direct influence between the two is itself illusory.

Yet it is hard to believe that the use of the bubble in both genres is entirely coincidental. It is possible that the nature of the comicbook engenders a balloon-like device. Once a medium of visual-verbal narrative begins to depict more than a straight or linear progression of narrative time, some kind of narrative pictorial device like the bubble becomes useful. The bubble helps to render temporal complexity pictorially because it is essentially a form of mini-panelization—a smaller panel that can represent one moment in narrative time within a larger panel representing another moment (usually representing the visual if not narrative present). Thus, it is plausible that the bubble is a natural effect of the comicbook medium itself. If so, then this might help explain why various cultures around the world seem to have invented something like the bubble device independently—as a function of the medium, not because there was some kind of synchronized global cabala of comicbook creators. Surely there is no direct causal link among the Jewish *tefillin* (phylactery), the American balloon, and the early Edo-period mist band.[48] It is by virtue of the comicbook medium itself, then, that the Japanese have their incense fumes and the Italians their *fumetti* (puffs of smoke).

Mention of the bubble as a form of mini-panelization raises the issue of panelization itself, which, although present in both the modern *manga* and the *kibyōshi*, upon closer inspection also turns out to be a superficial similarity. The modern *manga* customarily employs multiple panels on each page, allowing for moment-to-moment transitions of the sort one might find in a comic strip or on the movie screen. The *kibyōshi* as a rule tends to take the page as its primary panel, engendering transitions that are almost always scene-to-scene. Granted, it could be argued that the dream bubble, the corner picture (*komae*), and other sorts of mini-panelization in Edo-period visual culture each are a form of multiple panelization, though these certainly do not amount to the primary unit of visual-verbal narrative as the multiple panel is in the modern *manga*. Absent moment-to-moment transitions, which can be said to facilitate if not actually to encourage the depiction of physical movement, there was little if any need for the *kibyōshi* to develop

---

48. There is some speculation that in Europe the bubble developed from the Jewish prayer practice of strapping leather cases (*tefillin* in Hebrew) containing written law to the forehead.

expressionist or synaesthetic lines, which figure prominently in many modern *manga*. Furthermore, the absence of multiple panels on the typical *kibyō-shi* page precludes the cinematographic technique one not infrequently finds in the modern *manga* of the "bleed," a panel that hemorrhages into timeless space.

The third and last example here of a superficial similarity in a pictorial convention may be provided by a kind of expressionist line, in fact, the so-called speed line, which the Japanese refer to as the motion line (*dōsen*). Although it appears ubiquitously in the modern *manga* and only sporadically in the *kibyōshi*, the more significant difference resides in the type of action conveyed with it. In the modern *manga*, the motion line covers a vast range, from characters ripping off each other's clothes, through the emphasis of well-endowed body parts, to facial expressions of rapture. In the rare instances in which the motion line is used within the *kibyōshi*, according to Natsume Fusanosuke in his study of the subject, it is restricted to the conveyance of water, wind, light, and little else.

This is surprising since motion lines had been used in Japan prior to the *kibyōshi* in a way more in keeping with the modern *manga*. One finds them in earlier picturebooks (*ehon sōshi*) and picture scrolls, where they might animate a toy wheel rolling down a hill, carriage wheels spinning round, a halberd being twirled, even the slapping down of a token in the game of travel Parcheesi (*sugoroku*).[49] What this quick survey suggests, then, is that if modern *manga* artists discovered the motion line in their native tradition rather than in Western comicbooks, they did not do so in the *kibyōshi*. And even if they did, they must have applied it to a wider range and different order of action than can be found there. In the case of the motion line, then, the modern *manga* bypassed the *kibyōshi*.

It should be observed that for each superficial similarity between the *kibyōshi* and the modern *manga*, there are probably many more profound differences. During the century or so dividing the two forms, the nature of the socioeconomic infrastructure in Japan changed dramatically. The remarkable transformation from a proto-bourgeois economy into one of advanced capitalism—a transformation that arguably has had its most conspicuous manifestation in the so-called postwar Japanese "economic miracle"—could not but affect the nature of visuality, since the technologies of mechanical reproduction, delivery, and consumption were themselves completely transformed. It was not simply a matter of the modern printing press displacing woodblock printing, in other words, but new kinds of media that changed the way people looked at the world.

---

49. Natsume draws these examples from *Shigisan engi emaki* (twelfth century), *Heiji monogatari ekotoba* (thirteenth century), *Ishiyamadera engi emaki* (tenth century), and *Haseo sōshi* (thirteenth-fourteenth century), respectively. In Natsume, "Kibyōshi o manga kara miru," pp. 198–200.

Generalizing grossly, the *kibyōshi* derived its visual idiom from the then-available woodblock-printed representation of the kabuki stage, whereas the modern *manga* has so far found its visual idiom in radically new forms of foreign media unknown during An'ei-Tenmei, such as the Western comic strip, the Western comicbook, the animated film, the photographic frame, the silver screen, the small screen, the computer screen, even the video-game screen. This is not to imply that the modern *manga* has *completely* disregarded premodern Japanese visual culture. However, compared to these new media, premodern modes of visuality pale badly. How, then, could the visual regime of the modern *manga* not but differ paradigmatically from that of the *kibyōshi*?

To refine this slightly, the modern *manga* can be described in the main as a kind of visual analogue of the film, since the serial nature of its multiple panels within each page either takes its inspiration from, or else closely resembles, the sequential unfolding of frames on the celluloid spool. One might generally view the modern *manga* as a sequence of images that, were the gaps only *slightly* filled in, would effortlessly amount to an *anime* or some other kind of movie. The multiple panelization on the average page allows the *manga* to pan wide, zoom in, flash back, fade out, all in accordance with the cinematographic storyboard. The *anime* is less an animated film in this sense than it is an animated *manga*, though both ultimately are indebted to motion pictures. And as one would expect, many *manga* are closely linked to *anime*, which according to Napier, draws upon "worldwide artistic conventions of twentieth-century cinema and photography."[50]

The *kibyōshi*, which cannot be described as a serial narrative in quite the same way since its basic panel tends to be the single page, takes most of its visual cues from representations of the popular theater in theatrical texts, which is to say both woodblock-printed books as well as pictures. Being a woodblock-printed genre itself, and its artists being woodblock print artists themselves, the *kibyōshi* naturally obeys—or at least plays off—many of the visual conventions of the woodblock print in general, not just those concerned with the stage; for instance, scenes in some *kibyōshi* resemble maps, board games, encyclopedia pages, and so forth. That said, the *kibyōshi* is particularly beholden to the kabuki theater as manifested in such things as the actor picture (*yakushae*), the kabuki star portrait (*nigaoe*), the beauty picture (*bijinga*), the illustrated playbook (*eiri kyōgenbon*), and theatrically inflected works in earlier genres of comicbooks, principally the blackbook.

The moment-to-moment transition between panels in the modern *manga*, then, suggests an affinity with the cinema, whereas the scene-to-scene transition of the *kibyōshi* suggests an affinity with the *mise-en-scène* of the kabuki stage as represented in some form of woodblock-printed theatrical text. Thus, the *kibyōshi*, like the theatrical text, positions the reader in the per-

---

50. Napier, *Anime from* Akira *to* Princess Mononoke, p. 4.

spective of the audience member with respect to the stage and its actors, which is to say at the bottom of the page looking up. In fact, when a *kibyō-shi* depicts a fictional audience, it tends to be situated this way, as evidenced by the depictions of the Dutch-style peepshow in *Familiar Bestsellers* and the freakshow in *Swingers*. Furthermore, the *kibyōshi*, like the theatrical text, represents the stage chanter's narrative (*ji*) and the stage character's dialogue (*kotoba*) by laying out these utterances on different parts of the page, which is to say at the top and near the figures below, respectively, since the chanters and actors are analogously separated on stage.

In conclusion, the few apparent similarities between the *kibyōshi* and the modern *manga* surveyed here—as well as the tendency mentioned previously of both genres to include commercial tie-ins, product placement, and mass marketing—would seem to be flukes, only superficially related, products of the comicbook medium as it was conceived and produced in isolated moments in time, rather than indicative of some putative historical continuity. Phenomenal advances in the technology of mechanical reproduction and in capitalism itself fundamentally changed the nature of visuality and continue to separate the visual regimes of the *kibyōshi* and the modern *manga*. Thus, contrary to the intimations of the proponents of *manga* culture, the modern *manga* was *not* the inevitable culmination of the *kibyōshi*. Nor did the *kibyōshi* entail the *manga*. The modern *manga* would have come into existence even without the *kibyōshi*. Furthermore, even if it could be demonstrated that the modern *manga* borrowed this or that convention or style or trope from the *kibyōshi*, the *kibyōshi* cannot be meaningfully described as a major influence, let alone as the direct progenitor. A distant, even long-lost uncle, perhaps. Certainly not the father.

The most that can be said of premodern influence, then, is that the *kibyōshi* provided the precedent of a vastly popular comicbook for adults—conceivably even a comicbook that was close to reaching its potential as a medium of visual-verbal narrative. One may be able to track adult comicbooks over time from the *kibyōshi*, into the multivolume (*gōkan*), through Meiji satirical prints, up to the modern *manga*, in other words, not in terms of visual-verbal conventions, artistic styles, literary tropes, let alone stories or their *auteurs*, but in terms of an adult readership. In this sense, it is possible that this precedent of an adult comicbook in An'ei-Tenmei Edo may have helped predispose the Japanese to the eventual reception of the modern Western comicbook.

No diary or record or other evidence has come to light, to the best of my knowledge, demonstrating that a *kibyōshi* author or artist became involved in the production of the modern *manga*. Nor could there be, of course, for too much time separates the two. Since the *kibyōshi* as a phenomenon more or less ended in 1806 (though individual works continued to be issued for a couple more decades), even if one defines the *manga* liberally, placing its origins in 1895 instead of the 1920s, upwards of ninety years separate the *kibyōshi*'s demise and the *manga*'s rise.

Still, one suggestive correlation between the *kibyōshi* and the modern *manga* is that both seem to have attained phenomenal popularity at crucial technological turning points in cultural history: the *kibyōshi*, during the transition from a handwritten manuscript culture to a woodblock print culture that was also tied up with the decline of the *ancien régime* in Kamigata and the rise of a centralized culture in Edo-Tokyo; and the modern *manga*, during the transition from woodblock-print and even print culture to an electronically driven, fast-paced, modern culture under the spell of Western influence.

Visuality itself, it might be suggested, was being challenged in fundamental ways in the heyday of both genres. As Screech and others have argued, it was during the mid-Edo period when Japanese proponents of Western science (*Rangaku*—literally "Dutch Studies") helped introduce the microscope, the telescope, even the *optique*, to the public, and this not only radically altered how many Japanese artists literally saw the world, but how the popular imagination visualized the world as well.[51] This is evident in the way that Kyōden in his book of mock-designs, *The Latest Word on Fine Patterns* (*Komon shinpō*, 1786) microscopically enlarged the common flea to the scale of artistic visibility—the first time anything like this had been done, I would hazard to guess, in the history of Japanese visuality. This is also evident in the way that one of Andō Hiroshige's (1797–1858) woodblock prints would, decades later, reveal the world from the perspective of an eagle soaring high over the landscape, shrinking human beings to the minuscule scale of insects.[52] When technological advances and paradigmatic shifts in society alter the way people look at the world, it is only natural for people to look to visual genres to assess the new and to reassess the old scopic regimes.

Thus, it is possible that the meaning of the superficial similarities between the *kibyōshi* and the modern *manga* is not merely that the efforts of the proponents of *manga* culture to demonstrate influence are insupportably overstated. That much seems obvious. Rather, the visual-verbal imagination in Japan achieves its greatest inspiration during moments of intense technological, economic, and social upheaval that challenge fundamental notions of visuality.

The Visual-Verbal Imagination

What, then, was visuality like during the late eighteenth century? How did one read a comic-book such as the *kibyōshi*? "Most of the talents required for the understanding of this volume," writes Chris Ware on the inside cover flap to his graphic novel *Jimmy Corrigan*, "are essentially intuitive." The same might be said of the *kibyōshi*; for any discussion of reading its words and pictures may seem so readily apparent or natural—even to the

---

51. For more on this, see Tani, *Asobi no dezain*.
52. For more about the influence of the Western regime of visuality on Japanese art, see Screech, *The Western Scientific Gaze*.

non-initiate who has never so much as glanced at a Western comic strip, a graphic novel, or a modern Japanese *manga*—as to be superfluous.

However intuitive the reading process of the *kibyōshi* might seem, though, it is by no means automatic. Nor should it be comfortably written off. And even if it were a simple matter, as a means of getting at the visual-verbal imagination, a discussion of such a reading is warranted. Even when there is little or no difference between the ways of reading a *kibyōshi* and a graphic novel or a modern Japanese *manga*, similarities, as we have seen, may prove to be superficial. Not to explore the reading of the *kibyōshi* would be to treat as facile a rich visual-verbal imagination, one that is worth exploring in full, even if this volume admittedly represents the most rudimentary of beginnings.

To begin with the obvious, as a visual-verbal narrative the *kibyōshi* is constituted of words and pictures. This applies even to those few works making use of the rebus, a puzzle in which the reader must decode pictures and other signs as though they were words—a little like reading the heart in "I ♥ NY" as "love." One such *kibyōshi* is *A Diverting View of A Treasury of Loyal Retainers* (*Onagusami chūshingura no kangae*, 1797) by Takizawa Bakin (1767–1848).[53] Bakin's narrative and dialogic texts are "written" mostly with pictures (though a few syllabary graphs sneak in here and there) (**Figure 3.6**). Aside from the fact that Bakin employs actual words on his frontispiece, which is still part of the story after all, and that the pictures are to be decoded verbally, such rebus works are the exception that proves the rule. For all intents and purposes, the *kibyōshi* is composed of both verbal and pictorial texts.

But what is the relationship between these two types of text? Do the words illustrate the pictures or do the pictures illustrate the words? Although the safe answer, and the one to which the present author subscribes, is a little bit of both, in fact, opinions span the full spectrum of possibilities. At one extreme, what might be called the "exclusively literary," the story is held to consist of the words. Pictures are mere illustrations—nice embellishments, perhaps, but incidental, expendable, and superfluous to the meaning of the story itself. Although nobody, to the best of my knowledge, advocates this position in its purest form, some—especially literary scholars—come close. Kōdō Tokuchi, one of the first intellectuals to appreciate the literary value of Edo-period playful literature, included in his late Meiji-period volume of one hundred *kibyōshi* transcriptions only a dozen or so pictures, as though these were simply charming accoutrements.[54] More recently, Mori, who is well aware of the indispensability of pictures to the *kibyōshi*, aside from including relatively few pictures in

---

53. For an annotated edition, see Hayashi, *Zashikigei chūshingura*, pp. 89–112. For an English translation, see Inouye, *A Diverting View of Loyal Retainers*.
54. Kōdō, *Kibyōshi hyakushu*.

Fig. 3.6 Scene from a rebus-style *kibyōshi* in which the narrative text consists mostly of pictures to be puzzled out and read as words. Here, the honorable Lord En'ya Hangan Takasada commits ritual disembowelment (*seppuku*). From *A Diverting View of* A Treasury of Loyal Retainers (*Onagusami chūshingura no kangae*, 1797). Written by Takizawa Bakin and illustrated by Kitao Shigemasa. Reprinted in Hayashi, *Zashikigei chūshingura*, p. 103. Courtesy of Kawade shobō shinsha.

his two-volume collection of *kibyōshi* précis, in the course of an otherwise laudable effort to admit the genre into the academy as a topic of serious inquiry, claims that the *kibyōshi* should be considered a form of *literature* since "its verbal text can stand on its own without pictures."[55]

The converse of this position might be termed the "exclusively pictorial," the notion being that the story essentially consists of the pictures, with the words playing a minor or supplementary role. Nobody has proposed this reading in its purest form, though some art historians and cultural studies historians (not to mention the present author) have mined the *kibyōshi* (to say nothing of the *ukiyoe*) for its pictorial elements without due attention to the verbal text. What is more, some scholars have suggested that the

---

55. Mori, *Kibyōshi kaidai*, p. 12.

pictures command the main interest of visual-verbal texts. Charles Shirō Inouye, for instance, in a pair of provocative articles has raised the possibility that what he terms "pictocentrism"—essentially, the historic pride of place that pictures can claim within the Japanese storytelling imagination—may be a definitive feature of Japanese culture in general. Even if true, though, this is such a sweeping proposition that it is hard to see how it might be convincingly demonstrated.[56]

Such a position may also inhere in the remarks of cultural critic Yōrō Takeshi that the way the words seem to comment upon the pictures in the modern *manga* is analogous to the function of the phonetic guide (*furigana*) in glossing Chinese graphs—the implication being that meaning in the modern *manga* is primarily generated through the pictures, not the words, which are seen as playing an auxiliary role.[57] Along these lines, cultural historian Tanaka Yūko observes: "Every page [of the *kibyōshi*] was filled with pictures, and letters were packed in blank spaces as if they were footnotes to the pictures."[58] Certainly, the mind's eye registers the pictures more immediately than it absorbs the meaning of the difficult-to-decipher squiggly lines of verbal text. Still, underwriting these different flavors of pictocentrism is probably a general skepticism of written or verbal language, which some commentators no doubt might be tempted to attribute to some Zen-like privileging of actual experience over textual representation. Yet to the extent that even the rebus *kibyōshi* must be "read" as words, the notion of a *purely* pictorial reading of the *kibyōshi* seems untenable.

Occupying the middle ground is the view that word and picture play equally important roles in generating meaning. Both constitute the story. The pictures are not mere illustration or decoration. The words are not merely verbal gloss or footnotes. The *kibyōshi* story *is* the words and the pictures in tandem. The words and the pictures are mutually reinforcing, synergetic, symbiotic, synaesthetic. It is less the case that the pictures illustrate the words, or the words illustrate the pictures, then, than both the words and the pictures, in illustrating each other, participate in the construction of the whole text, the story, the meaning. Keene puts it aptly: "The *kibyōshi* can be properly appreciated only when read with their illustrations, as a special genre halfway between literature and art."[59] To finesse this slightly, however, it might be said that the inclusion of both words and pictures in the *kibyōshi* qualifies it as a genre of literary and artistic potential that—in my opinion—is neither less literary nor less artistic for the double-edged nature of that potential. The *kibyōshi* is less "halfway," in other words, than it is twice as far.

---

56. See Inouye, "Pictocentrism" and "Pictocentrism—China as a Source of Japanese Modernity."

57. Yōrō, *Suzushii nōmiso*, p. 38.

58. Tanaka, "The Creation of Culture through the Printing Media," p. 64.

59. Keene, *World Within Walls*, p. 400.

To refine this even further, the visual-verbal nexus of the *kibyōshi* is a kind of dynamically integrative conglomeration. It is not just that the visual and verbal texts are interlocked, unable to stand on their own. Rather, the words and the pictures somehow add up to something greater than the sum of their parts. In his thought-provoking study of eighteenth-century Japanese discourse, Naoki Sakai characterizes this kind of visual-verbal text as observing what he terms a *gestalt* relationship: "It is impossible to extract the meaning of the whole text from either the pictorial or the verbal text alone, since their copresence creates a surplus of signification that does not exist in either text alone."[60]

Within this middle ground, however, there is a range of interpretations about *how* the words and the pictures add up to a third meaning. Haruo Shirane, an eminent scholar of premodern Japanese literature outside Japan, has suggested, albeit in passing, that the relationship between pictures and words in the *kibyōshi* is characterized by a "harmonious balance."[61] There are many instances in which the words and the pictures indeed complement each other harmoniously in the construction of the story. In *Familiar Bestsellers*, for instance, the word "pine" (*matsu*), which like the English can refer either to the tree or to the act of longing for someone, is merrily planted near the image of a pine tree.

Such examples notwithstanding, the visual-verbal relationship itself in any given work can be a more complex and at times contentious matter. As Earl Miner observed of the *kibyōshi* on precisely this point: "Both the harmony and the variance [between visual and verbal texts] call for interpretation by the reader."[62] Thus, although the words and pictures of the *kibyōshi* may be more or less equal partners in contributing to the overall story, working in symbiosis, the power dynamic also can shift one way or the other within a single panel: sometimes the pictures serve the words, in other words, and sometimes the words serve the pictures. Indeed, the visual-verbal nexus in the *kibyōshi* enjoys many disharmonies, gaps, omissions, and discrepancies. The dynamic is less harmonious than discordant, a matter of some tension, or even just of irrelevance.

Far more absorbing than harmony, at any rate, is jaggedness. Witnessing the overlapping or the dovetailing of words and pictures can be a good deal of fun, though the way that they disagree, run up unevenly against each other, even threaten to tear the story apart amounts to the greater challenge—and *thrill*—of reading the *kibyōshi*. Such disjunctions often reinforce the satirical aims of a particular work, for as with irony or Sakai's *gestalt*, the reader must generate a transcendent third meaning. By highlighting the tensions between verbal utterances and visual appearances, the *kibyōshi*

---

60. Sakai, *Voices of the Past*, p. 176. Sakai's discussion appears on pp. 172–176.
61. Shirane, *EMJL*, p. 672.
62. Miner, "The Grounds of Mimetic and Nonmimetic Art," pp. 91–92.

effectively puts the reader-viewer in a frame of mind to dig for loopholes (*ana o ugatsu*). This trope informs much of the popular literature of the Edo period, though it was especially crucial to the *kibyōshi* and therefore by extension to An'ei-Tenmei culture. Thus, if readers were not already glaring at society or politics through this kind of skeptical lens, they certainly would have been schooled in doing so through the *kibyōshi*. The sociopolitical satires in particular may have helped train the reader to view Social Reality as a textual ground in which various sorts of loopholes are to be exposed.

To take a few examples of such ironic visual-verbal disjunctions, the first line of the narrative in Kyōden's *Playboy* describes Enjirō as the son of a wealthy merchant. The picture, by contrast, portrays a laughably boorish slouch. The composite amounts to a rather unflattering portrait of the *nouveau riche*. The words of *Familiar Bestsellers* tell a story of the ebb and flow of printed matter, though the pictures reveal human beings drawn from contemporary Edo and Kamigata, the suggestion perhaps being that the people of Edo are on the rise just as its genres are. The verbal text of *Swingers* depicts stage characters, though the pictorial text reveals actors in the role of those stage characters.

The Pictorial Storytelling Theory

One of the more stimulating theories to address the visual-verbal nexus within the *kibyōshi*—and one that depends upon the jaggedness of words and pictures playfully at odds—likens the relationship between the *kibyōshi* narrator and the pictures to that of the public storyteller and his or her visual aids. Before turning to this theory, a brief word is in order on pictorial storytelling (*etoki*) itself, a practice that has a venerable tradition throughout Asia, according to Victor Mair, who has traced its trajectory from its Indian genesis, through its gradual transmission in China (via a popular Buddhist folk-literature known as *bianwen*), to its eventual appearance in places like Indonesia and Japan.[63]

Pictorial storytelling persisted in Japan across the centuries. Gorai Shigeru has speculated that the early twelfth-century frolicking animal scrolls (*chōjū giga*) of the abbot Toba Sōjō (1053–1140)—often touted as one of the foundational texts of Japanese caricature—may have functioned as "a kind of children's book or collection of pictures to accompany the telling of folk tales among commoners."[64] Barbara Ruch, in arguing that such pictorial storytelling during the fourteenth through sixteenth centuries played a role in the development of a national literature, describes the practitioners of

---

63. Mair, *Painting and Performance*.
64. Gorai Shigeru, "Chōjū giga ken to minzoku," p. 57 in Tani Shin'ichi, ed., *Chōjū jinbutsu giga*, and in *Shinshū Nihon emakimono zenshū 4* (1976), pp. 49–66. Quoted in Yiengpruksawan, "Monkey Magic," p. 83.

pictorial storytelling as "men and women who used paintings and illustrated texts as visual props and whose narrative performances played a crucial role in introducing the emaki and ehon to all levels of society."[65] And Virginia Skord has asserted that some companion booklets were used this way as well: "The composition and transmission of *otogi-zōshi* were but part of a larger vocal performance tradition that arose during the medieval period. Vocal performance was a literary rather than an oral art and was therefore dependent on a written text or libretto. In the case of *otogi-zōshi*, a performer might display an illustrated manuscript to an audience as he recited the stories with appropriate gestural and musical accompaniment."[66]

It is possible that some *kibyōshi* made use of pictorial storytelling praxis in one way or another by virtue of the genre's association with the companion booklet (if not other similar genres), which contributed something of its subject matter and visual-verbal conventions to the *kibyōshi*. This is not to say that the *kibyōshi* itself was used as a visual aid in pictorial storytelling, for if it was, it could only have accommodated a couple of private audience members on account of its diminutive size, especially relative to the easel-sized visual aids depicted in pictures from the period. The authors of the *kibyōshi*, though, were undoubtedly aware of the phenomenon of public pictorial storytelling, which thrived during An'ei-Tenmei, even if they did not come to it through the companion booklet or some other form of popular literature. A few years later, Kitao Shigemasa depicted such a scene when illustrating Kyōden's *Seasonal Passersby* (**Figure 3.7**).

The chief proponent in this country of the pictorial storytelling thesis as applied to the *kibyōshi* is Sumie Jones, who has articulated her position in an article comparing and contrasting the visual-verbal texts of William Hogarth and Kitao Masanobu (Kyōden). Jones argues that the *kibyōshi* appropriated the manner in which some blackbooks modeled the relationship between their narrative writing and pictures upon the relationship between the pictorial storyteller's spiel and his visual aids. "Although [*kibyōshi*] were written for a far more educated audience, they consistently imitated the superficiality, oversimplification, and indifference to logic of the 'black cover' style. The combination of thematic and artistic sophistication with a careless and inarticulate narrator was the chief charm of [the *kibyōshi*]."[67] Jones goes on to claim, "The reading of a [*kibyōshi*] on a sophisticated level consists in bemusement with the inadequate narrator."[68]

---

65. Ruch, "Medieval Jongleurs and the Making of a National Literature," especially pp. 288–299.

66. Skord, *Tales of Tears and Laughter*, p. 4. Skord seems to take her cue from Ruch's discussion of the distinction between vocal literature (*onsei bungaku*)—"the art of voice projection or the intoning of a prose/poetry text"—and oral literature (*kōshō bungaku*)—"[which is] a product of and flourishes in a world of illiteracy." See Ruch, "Medieval Jongleurs," p. 286.

67. Jones, "William Hogarth and Kitao Masanobu," p. 49.

68. Jones, "William Hogarth and Kitao Masanobu," p. 52.

Fig. 3.7 A pictorial storyteller performing with a visual aid to a small crowd in a public space. From *Seasonal Passersby* (*Shiki no yukikai*, 1798), a picturebook written by Santō Kyōden and illustrated by Kitao Shigemasa. Private collection of Professor Ōtaka Yōji.

Thus Jones, who specifically takes up Kyōden's *Playboy* but not other *kibyōshi*, seems to imply that the relationship of the "inadequate" narrator in the *kibyōshi* to its pictures is analogous to that of a putatively inadequate pictorial storyteller to his visual aids. The pictorial storytelling theory, then, implicitly maintains that the *auteur* of the *kibyōshi* constructs a humorously unreliable *narrator* and thrusts him into the awkward position of having to comment on the spur of the moment upon a preexisting pictorial story he has never seen before and does not adequately comprehend. Under this theory, the inadequate narrator concocts what to him seems like a reasonable-sounding narrative, though to the discerning reader it is one that comes across as transparently farfetched. Simply put, the unreliable narrator is a kind of unprepared pictorial storyteller whose act is one of "unintentionally" comical confabulation.

The spatial layout of the average *kibyōshi* certainly *looks* as though this might be the case. The way that the writing is crowded into the nooks and crannies of the pictures, as if the pictures preceded the words, would appear to support the pictorial storytelling theory, which, after all, holds that the pictures precede the words of the narrator (as distinct from the author and *auteur*). The narrator, the layout of the *kibyōshi* page insinuates, must concoct his fatuous explanation *around* the pictures just as he must physically squeeze his written words into the empty spaces *within* the pictures. This effect is a complete fiction, of course, for it would seem that, in the case of the draft manuscript at least, the *auteur* initially articulates the visual and verbal texts at more or less the same time, in a single creative stroke. The apparently haphazard scattering of the written words upon the *kibyōshi* page thus belies the painstakingly orchestrated real-life process of composing the *kibyōshi*.

It should be observed that the pictorial storytelling theory is not a form of pictocentrism. Although the theory might seem to propose that the *kibyōshi* pretends that the pictures precede the words, in point of fact, such was hardly the case, for the theory depends upon the existence of a competent *auteur*. The theory tacitly acknowledges the comic visual-verbal imagination of the *auteur*, in other words, as opposed to the incompetent confabulation of the narrator-*cum*-storyteller, since ultimately it is the *auteur* who can be credited with having coordinated words and pictures to yield such an artful illusion in the first place.

As compelling as this theory might be, and even if it could be proven to pertain to Kyōden's *Playboy*, it is difficult to see how it informs most other *kibyōshi*. It certainly does *not* pertain to *Swingers*, since the discrepancies between the visual and verbal representations of the characters are alluded to, if not actually spelled out, within the narrator's verbal text itself. For instance, although the verbal text describes the character Seijūrō though the pictures portray the actor Ichikawa Monnosuke in the role of Seijūrō, the narrative *also* contains sly references to that actor, thereby confirming to the sophisticated reader that the narrator is indeed cognizant of the apparent discrepancy between his visual and verbal texts. Thus, the narrator of *Swingers* cannot be described as inadequate. Likewise, the many discrepancies between the pictorial and verbal texts in *Familiar Bestsellers* result not from an inept fictional narrator but from a clever, real-life artist personifying an otherwise abstract story in obvious coordination with the narrator (to say nothing of the author or the *auteur*). Based on a reading of the *kibyōshi* in this volume, then, it would seem that the pictorial storytelling thesis has limited general applicability.

In conclusion, whether or not one subscribes to the pictorial storytelling theory, its main contribution probably resides in emphasizing the jaggedness of the visual-verbal nexus within the *kibyōshi*. This jaggedness need not entail the existence of an inadequate narrator, in other words, but it always suggests the presence behind the text of a masterminding *auteur*.

It might be added that the gimmick of the confabulating narrator has its analogue in other cultural practices that were prevalent during An'ei-Tenmei. One can certainly see how the efforts of the unreliable narrator to concoct an ostensibly reasonable-sounding explanation for pictures that all but baffle him—an explanation which the discerning reader can see through readily—parallels the patently outrageous claims of the half-baked sophisticate within the fashionbook. Confabulation was also the operative principle in a widespread game of sorts of constructing deliberately farfetched but humorous etymologies (*kojitsuke*), often involving some kind of wordplay. The humorous etymology runs throughout Japanese literature, but it appears with exceptional regularity and puckishness, one feels, during An'ei-Tenmei. Along the same lines, the previously mentioned mock-heroic treasure competition was all the rage at the time, too. This was essentially a party game involving the concoction of some fabulous verbal history for some everyday physical object, the more banal the better.

Curiously, each of these three confabulatory practices informs Kyōden's *Playboy*. As we will see, Enjirō as a character can be read as a half-baked sophisticate who cannot quite make sense of the Floating World into which he desperately wants to break; Enjirō's story provides a farfetched etymology of *itself*; and the key point of reference for many of the veiled allusions was a real-life treasure competition, wherein contestants concocted imaginative designs on handtowels involving some kind of visual-verbal pun. Thus, if the pictorial storytelling theory pertains to Kyōden's *Playboy*, it does so in a more complex manner than the theory itself might suggest. Or rather, it would seem that confabulatory practice is the larger principle underwriting the inadequate narrator. The pictorial storytelling theory, then, is based on one instance of the manifestation of a more widely obtaining compositional practice of confabulation. Insofar as Edo-centrism itself is a kind of imaginative rewriting of its own origins, it might be hypothesized that one of the hallmarks of An'ei-Tenmei Edo was nothing less than this sort of comic confabulation in the service of deeper agendas.

Wherever one falls on the spectrum from the exclusively literary to the exclusively pictorial, it must be acknowledged that one must read both the words and the pictures against each other as well as together in order to grasp the entire story. In this sense, it might be said that an integrated reading of the *kibyōshi* depends upon a synaesthetic visual-verbal imagination. One must apply verbal thinking to the pictures as well as to the words, and visual thinking to the words as well as to the pictures. The presence of visual-verbal humor throughout the genre suggests that authors intended such synaesthesia and readers were on the same page.

Image as Word

Up to this point I have treated word and picture separately, as though these were two discrete entities. However, the words and pictures in the *kibyōshi* are interlocked in another significant respect that cannot be ignored, since it gets to the heart of the contemporary visual-verbal imagination. Namely, in the *kibyōshi*, the pictures have an inherent verbal dimension, and the words have an inherent pictorial dimension.

To take these assertions in order, the pictures in the *kibyōshi* have a verbal dimension in at least a few rudimentary respects. First, the pictures can be read as a kind of writing, even the pictures in *non*-rebus pieces. That is to say, several images within the works translated here, when "read" verbally or in conjunction with the verbal text, yield a visual-verbal pun. When in *Playboy* Enjirō has his comeuppance, the pictures show him wrapped in a mat. The phrase "to wear a mat" was an idiomatic expression meaning something like "to eat humble pie." Most *kibyōshi* would seem to contain this kind of visual-verbal play.

Second, many of the pictures in the *kibyōshi* in their day acquired the force of pictorial tropes or icons, carrying with them associated *verbal* texts as well. The *kibyōshi* invokes the verbal aspect of a visual-verbal text by referencing that text pictorially, as we see throughout the history of the genre (and, indeed, as is specified in the annotation to each of the translations in this volume). This is not just "simple" pictorial allusion, in other words, of pictures alluding to other pictures for the sake of visual playfulness, but literary allusion working through pictures to refer to the *verbal* aspect of other stories.

Finally, the pictures in the *kibyōshi* have a verbal element by virtue of the most banal sense of containing writing, even if that writing itself is in the form of pictures meant to be read as writing (as with the rebus *kibyōshi*). Writing pervades the *kibyōshi* picture. Some of this writing, like the narrative block that tends to hover at the top of the page, supposedly exists *outside* the fictional world, imperceptible to the depicted characters. Even reported speech or reported thought embedded within that narrative would not be perceptible *as writing* to the characters doing the speaking or thinking. Some other writing, however, exists within the depicted fictional world, perceptible to the characters themselves one way or another: either *visually*, as with street markers, shop signs, signboards, notice boards, love letters, pamphlets, and so on; or *aurally*, as with the writing inscribed near characters and used to represent dialogue, which the characters can supposedly "hear" even if they cannot "see" it as written representation.

It might also be noted in passing that there are differences in language and its written representation in the narrative and dialogic blocks. Generally speaking, the narrative block employs more Chinese graphs and assumes a more "literary" narrative voice, utilizing such devices as the storyteller's authoritative past tense (signaled by the grammatical suffix *-keri*), which brings the reader up to the narrative "present" of the pictures and dialogue. The dialogue itself is usually rendered in the non-past "tense" and tends to bear few if any Chinese graphs, thereby minimizing the pictorial dimension to promote the illusion of being somehow closer to an orality of the characters in their spoken language.

That said, this model has any number of complications, though only three shall be mentioned here. First, there are many instances in which characters cross established, conventional lines, showing awareness of the world of pictures or of writing outside their fictional frame. This is to be expected, in fact, since one hallmark of the *kibyōshi* is its innovation with framing, which may be primarily indebted to self-reflexivity on the popular stage. In a scene from Kyōden's *Rosei's Dream*, one character, a pajama-clad Dream Creature, confides to another such character about a pictorial detail of the *kibyōshi* in which they appear: "I hear our author had a terrible time costuming us Dreams!"

Second, the house crests included on the clothing of depicted characters for the reader's ease in keeping the various characters straight represent a gray area. Would such crests also have been visible to the characters them-selves within the fictional realm? Depending upon the particular piece, the answer to this conundrum could be argued either way.

Finally, the Western alphabet as it appears in Kanwatei Onitake's *Trilateral Babble* (*Wakaran monogatari*, 1803), while easily recognizable to us today as writing, probably appeared to early nineteenth-century Japanese readers of the work as ciphers communicating foreignness, not as an actual system of writing (see **Figure 1.22**). This is an example of actual writing exploited less for its textual iconicity than as a symbol that serves a different function for its readers than it was "originally" intended (assuming, of course, that the Dutch on Deshima were not reading *kibyōshi*, too).

Word as Image   This last example, which is surely *sui generis*, nonetheless sug-gests the complementary assertion to the notion that the pic-tures in the *kibyōshi* have a verbal dimension: namely, the written word in the *kibyōshi* is inherently pictorial. Although such textual iconicity is patently obvious in the case of Western writing in the *kibyōshi*, which presumably had no verbal meaning to contemporary Japanese readers, as well as in the case of Chinese pictographs, which are by definition pictorial, it nonetheless also pertains to the Chinese ideographs and to the two Japanese syllabaries that are also part of the Japanese writing system. Aside from the fact that *all* writing is at its most basic level pictorial by virtue of assuming visual form, both Chinese ideographs and the Japa-nese syllabaries ultimately trace their origins back to pictographs. That is, Japanese writing of the period had a palpable pictorial dimension, though there is some reason to suspect that this is less apparent to readers today.

For the sake of those not familiar with the Japanese writing system, and at the risk of overgeneralization, this system consists of: (1) a pair of sylla-baries (*kana*), a bit like the English alphabet except that each syllabary set uses signs to represent the sounds of syllables. There is a cursive-looking syllabary (*hiragana*) and a straight-edged one (*katakana*) that more or less re-semble each other (though their differences seem slightly more pronounced than those between cursive and straight-hand scripts in English); (2) Chi-nese graphs (*kanji*), ranging from simple "pictographs," essentially pictures resembling the object they are assigned to represent (e.g., a single line repre-sents a finger counting "one"); to highly abstract "ideographs," essentially symbols representing ideas with little or no pictorial correspondence; with a range of combinations in-between.[69]

Both Chinese ideographs and the twin Japanese syllabaries might not seem to bear any distinct pictorial quality, then, though in actuality both ultimately trace their origins back to pictographs. Furthermore, Japanese

---

69. For an accessible yet more thorough introduction to the basics of Chinese graphs, see Henshall, *A Guide to Remembering Japanese Characters*, pp. xiii–xxiii.

writing—by combining pictographs, ideographs, and syllabaries—mixes visual and verbal elements as a matter of course. It is thus a complex synthesis of different orders of representation, not unlike the pictures and the words within the *kibyōshi* itself. This similarity suggests that the *kibyōshi* may be a kind of literary-artistic manifestation of the Japanese writing system, though the nature of this relationship has admittedly yet to be worked out systematically.

Although the *kibyōshi* is written in the hybrid style blending Japanese syllabary and Chinese graphs (*wakan konkōbun*), it tends to emphasize the Japanese syllabary and downplay Chinese graphs, certainly relative to most other forms of Edo's popular literature. This it does by using syllabary in places where many other genres would normally employ Chinese graphs. Thus, from a distance, the *kibyōshi* tends to look as though it were composed primarily of Japanese syllabary with few if any Chinese graphs to speak of.

If the *kibyōshi* is indeed as sophisticated as the present study claims, why does the genre refrain from using the more sophisticated Chinese graphs, opting instead for the comparatively simple-to-read syllabary? For one thing, the syllabary cleverly would have aided less literate readers while simultaneously helping to perpetuate the gag that the genre was a kind of comicbook for children and for women, since traditionally *kana* was called the "woman's hand." Indeed, earlier comicbooks tend to be written almost exclusively in the Japanese syllabary (which means that even a beginning student of Japanese today can read a transcribed version of such works with little difficulty).

For another thing, the Japanese syllabary facilitates wordplay, especially puns, since Chinese graphs visually specify a meaning among two or more different homonyms, whereas a phonetic syllabary does not, since it represents sounds. Thus, the *kibyōshi*, by virtue of its preponderance of syllabary, was able to more fully realize the potential of wordplay that remained latent in more blatantly "adult" genres using more Chinese graphs. Ironically, then, simple writing allows for—perhaps even *engenders*—complicated verbal pyrotechnics. And so the joke is on those who would dismiss the *kibyōshi* on the grounds that its writing appears simplistic, something befitting children, for this appearance is profoundly deceptive.

The *kibyōshi* also sometimes plays with visual aspects of the Japanese syllabary. For instance, in the title of the first *kibyōshi* in this volume, the term familiar (*gozonji*) puns aurally on booklets (*gosōshi*) only by a stretch of the imagination. However, this pun comes across orthographically, which is to say *visually*; for in the premodern syllabary (*rekishiteki kanazukai*), these terms were written as *kosonshi* and *kosoushi*, respectively, which, when calligraphically rendered, can be made to resemble each other to no small degree.

That said, the *kibyōshi* also delights in playing on some pictorial aspect of its Chinese graphs. One common trick is to chop up a graph into smaller units and present these to the reader as a kind of puzzle. Virtually every schoolchild in Japan today knows a fossilized form of this game that has become a mnemonic device for remembering how to write the graph for "spring" as "three" (*san*) "people" (*nin*) under the "sun" (*hi*). Such play can of course be terribly recondite. For instance, in one scene from *Rosei's Dream*, Kyōden puns on the reading of a disarticulated graph to invoke the forbidden name of the monomaniacal warlord Toyotomi Hideyoshi (1536–1598). This Kyōden does by drawing attention to the graph for "this" (*kore*). When broken down into its constituent parts, said graph can be read as "person under the sun" (*hi no shita no hito*), which, in turn, plays on the phrase "Man from Kinoshita" (*Kinoshita no hito*)—one of Hideyoshi's nicknames. Just in case the reader cannot perform the visual-verbal gymnastics to solve this riddle, Kyōden provides another clue within the verbal text, invoking the name Mashiba Hisayoshi. This was an established code word punning on the warlord's erstwhile name, Hashiba Hideyoshi.[70] Thus, the visual text says one thing, the verbal text another, though both add up to yield a third politicized meaning.

Another common type of play with Chinese graphs is the use of an impish Japanese phonetic gloss. One often sees this kind of bilingual or macaronic play in the titles of *kibyōshi* (as well as of other forms of playful literature).[71] One example of a title employing such play is Onitake's *Trilateral Babble*: the Chinese graphs literally mean "Japanese" (*wa*) "Sino" (*kan* or *ka*) "Dutch" (*ran*) "miscellaneous talk" (*zatsuwa*), though when read aloud, the Japanese words spell something like "incomprehensible chatter."[72]

This double structure of pitting a formal, Chinese layer of text against an informal, playful, Japanese layer has its analogue in the variational technique of acclimation (*hamemono*) in which a Chinese story or world is transposed or intertwined with a Japanese one. More to the point, perhaps, the way that this kind of macaronic play undermines official discourse is similar to the exposing of some loophole or contradiction, most often between social norms and reality, often to ironic or satirical effect. Such play is all

---

70. Kuwata notes that the imperial court awarded Hideyoshi the surname Toyotomi in 1586. For a while prior to that he styled himself Kinoshita and then Hashiba. See Kuwata, *Toyotomi Hideyoshi kenkyū*, pp. 121–127.

71. Strictly speaking, such play is more diglossic than bilingual. For two important articles on this subject, see Ariga, "The Playful Gloss," and Jones, "Language in Crisis."

72. Regarding whether the title should be read *Wakaran monogatari* or *Wakaran zatsuwa*, the Chinese graphs are unglossed in the title of some versions of this *kibyōshi*. However, not only are they glossed as *monogatari* in other versions, but also Onitake himself sanctioned that reading in an advertisement for *Trilateral Babble* embedded in the text of another of his *kibyōshi* (entitled *Aa shinkirō*) published the same year. See Tanahashi, *Kibyōshi sōran 3*, p. 200 and *Kibyōshi sōran 5*, p. 597. That said, the *zatsuwa* reading may suggest that Onitake's work spoofed a popular corpus of scientific treatises epitomized by Dutch Studies scholar Morishima Chūryō's illustrious catalogue of things Western, *A European Miscellany* (*Kōmō zatsuwa*, 1787).

about jaggedness, about the way that two texts generate a *gestalt* meaning by illustrating each other unevenly. One modern example of this, which can be spotted as a bumper sticker in Japan, is actually something of a trilingual pun: the Japanese syllabary gloss reads *Ai rabu yū*, which is how the English phrase "I love you" is rendered, though the meaning of the actual Chinese graphs is something like "I 'love' (*ai*) 'nude' (*ra*) 'dancing' (*bu*) because it's 'excellent' (*yū*)." When these levels of meaning are read against each other, the tensions become highly provocative.

Brush with the Tradition Macaronics, disarticulated graphs, orthographic play with syllabary—these manifestations of the visual-verbal imagination are impossible to render in translation. Furthermore, the possibilities for these types of visual-verbal play are limitless, and lest this discussion devolve into a taxonomy of the inexhaustible, it should also be pointed out that the written word in the *kibyōshi* is also inherently pictorial because the Japanese system of writing takes on an additional "pictorialness" in the context of the venerable calligraphic tradition.

The most abstract Chinese ideograph, even a theoretically pure abstraction of a graph, while assuming pictorial form merely by being rendered in writing, would nonetheless become a form of art when written with a brush. The strong calligraphic tradition of premodern Japan arguably transforms all writing into art, in other words, even writing that is not calligraphically rendered, simply by virtue of the fact that readers were acculturated to calligraphic practice. Calligraphy, after all, must have shaped the way people both wrote and *read*. Throughout most of premodern Japanese history, reading was an intensely visual activity by virtue of this calligraphic tradition. Indeed, in Edo-period Japan, according to Kornicki, printed books were so "profoundly visual" that "a reader's encounter with a work of fiction encompassed not only an engagement with a text and the conventions and expectations aroused by that, but also with a calligraphic style reproduced in the printed text and with a visual style in the illustrations."[73]

This calligraphic tradition, as is often observed, somehow survived the advent of woodblock printing. Even after the introduction of moveable-type printing into Japan in 1593, xylographic printing was retained largely because of the weight accorded to calligraphic aesthetics. Since the point of moveable-type printing is to have a readymade set of graphs at hand, any sense of a living hand is annihilated; for even if the moveable type is made to mimic calligraphy, any given graph will appear the same way each time it is deployed. The result is something that appears stiff, unnatural, mechanical, and too standardized. As we have seen in the *Pageant of the Latest Beauties*, the individual hand was highly prized, even fetishized. Little wonder that

---

73. Kornicki, *The Book in Japan*, p. 58.

there was a strong disinclination toward the impersonal effect of moveable-type printing.

Woodblock printing, by contrast, allowed something of the quirkiness and thus the sensuality of an individual style to shine through. A calligrapher put brush to paper that was then pressed to a wooden printblock, leaving inky outlines that were subsequently carved around. Granted, this process was theoretically possible in the case of copperplate printing, though in the days before electric engraving, carving even a pliant metal by hand was prohibitively formidable, time consuming, and expensive. Wood, by virtue of its malleability, could convey the flowing beauty of calligraphy, imparting the illusion of handwriting even in a printed medium. Perhaps woodblock printing was retained because the handwritten "human" feel of its rendering of calligraphy helped offset (no pun intended) the psychic loss of manuscript culture (even though this was more a perceived than an actual loss, since xylographic printing by no means immediately displaced manuscript culture).

The calligraphic tradition impacts the visual-verbal imagination, then, by treating words as pictures, even in a mass-printed genre like the *kibyōshi*. And by elevating pictures and words onto the same plane of readerly awareness, text can be synaesthetically played with. The larger point, however, is that the calligraphic treatment of the Japanese writing system, in its intermixing of words and pictures, shapes the very nature of that visual-verbal imagination. Like the comicbook in the West, or even the modern *manga*, the *kibyōshi* devotes attention to the visual treatment of words as graphic art. The *kibyōshi* habitually brings the pictorial aspect inherent in Japanese writing, and its calligraphic treatment, to the fore, delighting especially in visual-verbal play, as is witnessed by each of the pieces translated herein, though more in the annotations than in the translations proper, since this kind of play is unachievable in an alphabetic system of writing.

This aspect of the visual-verbal imagination as manifested in the *kibyōshi* appears to perform a less significant role in the modern *manga*, since not only has the calligraphic tradition seemingly become diminished in modern Japan, but the visual-verbal connection of the syllabaries to Chinese graphs themselves has also, with the modern standardization of the syllabaries, been mostly forgotten. Although calligraphy continues to be offered in Japanese schools, the continual erosion of the calligraphic tradition as a result of the rise of moveable-type printing, computers, the Internet, and so on has also arguably impaired much of the visual pleasure that calligraphy traditionally has imparted. On the other hand, television, movies, the Western comicbook—these have arguably contributed to the visual-verbal imagination in Japan, enriching the modern *manga* in new ways. If such a thing as visual-verbal IQ could be measured, there might not be any appreciable change between the average reader of the *kibyōshi* in late eighteenth-century Edo and the average reader of a *manga* in early twenty-first-century Tokyo. These visual-verbal imaginations might have different complexions, in other words, but one probably cannot be said to be superior to the other. Yet it cannot be denied that the nature of these two visual-verbal imaginations varies significantly.

To summarize what has been said thus far about the visual-verbal dynamic within the *kibyōshi*, then: the "pictures" always have a verbal component, since pictures have the potential to become a form of writing (as with the rebus), but more pragmatically, because all *kibyōshi* include writing as part of the visual plane apparent not just to the reader but to the fictional characters themselves. Furthermore, the "words" in the *kibyōshi* are pictorial in several respects: in that *all* written representation is pictorially derived and represented; in that writing, within the general context of the calligraphic tradition, tends to become artistically read even when it is not especially artistically written; in that the spatial arrangement of words on the page makes some writing a part of the picture in a way that would have been appreciable to characters within that pictorial plane; and finally and paradoxically, in that the verbal and pictorial texts both comprise the bigger "picture," which is to say the overall surplus of signification that the ideal reader constructs and takes away as the "meaning" of the story.

To the extent that word and picture overlap, it might be argued that there is no real difference between the two. Theoretically, even if the *kibyōshi* contained no pictures whatsoever, the interrelatedness between the words and pictures would still pertain, since on the linguistic level, like the male dot in the female spiral of yin, and the female dot in the male spiral of yang, words always contain a pictorial aspect. Anything written down, even pure gibberish, is by virtue of its being written down, pictorial. Thus, word and image dissolve into each other, not just within the *kibyōshi*, but also within their very essence. This perspective would render the functional distinction between word and image meaningless were it not for the fact of an analogous division of labor between author and artist within the publishing industry (even when the same historical person performed both roles). That the *auteur* managed both visual and verbal texts does not seem to have altered the structure of the industry. Thus, it is possible to speak of visual and verbal texts as discrete entities in theory only as long as it is kept in mind that this is really a false distinction at the level of creation and reception *outside* the context of the publishing stable.

On the level of physical layout, the *kibyōshi* page tends to be divided into several parts. Usually the narrative block floats across the top of the page. Within this picture, the figures of the characters and their represented dialogue can be seen. Although this layout would seem to imply that there is a set order for reading any given *kibyōshi* page, in practice, the reading process is probably a lot messier. The visual-verbal nexus of the *kibyōshi* entails that this process is a dialectic. The eye needs to jump between word and image. One needs to do more than merely read words in the "usual" order which, in the case of Edo Japan, was top to bottom, right to left. One also needs to skip around from one level or order of signifier to another, reading the objects in the pictures, becoming conscious of the shape of the writing, its spacing, and its resonances with the verbal text. "Comics take this reading experience to a more primal level," writes Aimee Bender, "we graze from a picture, down, to the side, up the diagonal, merging imagery and words effortlessly."[74]

Such a dialectic resists skimming. If one were to speed read the *kibyōshi* the way that many modern *manga* seem meant to be read, in a kind of rapid-fire page-flipping mode, one would miss much of the fun. Granted, many readers lavish attention upon their modern *manga* or Western comicbooks, and some works in these genres indeed tempt readers to such careful savoring. And yet modern *manga* and Western comicbooks do not, on the whole, demand quite the same intensity of effort and playful imagination intrinsic to the reading of the visual-verbal nexus in the *kibyōshi*.

Pictorial Allusion

Although reference has already been made to simple pictorial allusion and to visual irony (*mitate*) in passing, it is worth revisiting these here. Taking these in order, pictorial allusion also informs the visual-verbal imagination during the Edo period, as well might be expected. The pictures in the *kibyōshi* allude to anything and everything—even other *kibyōshi* from years earlier. Sometimes pictorial allusion to a particular *kibyōshi* can be misleading, as we have seen in the case with certain works that simply appropriated the wood printblocks to a *kibyōshi* and added a new story that had nothing whatsoever to do with the pictorial text. However, at other times, pictorial allusion plays an important role in decoding a story. Consider the figure of Rosei in Hōseidō Kisanji's *Dreamers the Winners* (*Miru ga toku issui no yume*, 1781) (**Figure 3.8**). Years later, Kitao Shigemasa (if he was in fact the artist) would copy this figure almost exactly within Kyōden's *Rosei's Dream* (1791) (**Figure 3.9**). Granted, the verbal text in the preface to *Rosei's Dream* invokes Kisanji's *Dreamers the Winners*, but at the point in the story where this picture appears, there is no verbal clue. For the reader to "get" the allusion he must recognize the picture from a work published a decade earlier. This practice is prevalent enough that one supposes authors could safely expect readers possessed a high degree of visual literacy in terms of the *kibyōshi* as well as other forms of texts available in An'ei-Tenmei Edo.

One of the remarkable kinds of pictorial allusion operative in much Edo-period visual representation was the *mitate*, which, for the sake of convenience, can be thought of as a kind of *visual pun*. It is also possible to contextualize the *mitate* as a kind of variational procedure (*shukō*) for manipulating images in entertaining ways. This was the visual equivalent of intertwining (*naimaze*), in which two or more worlds (*sekai*) are combined. The more disparate these images (and thus worlds), the more surprising—

---

74. Bender, "Flat and Glad," p. 48.

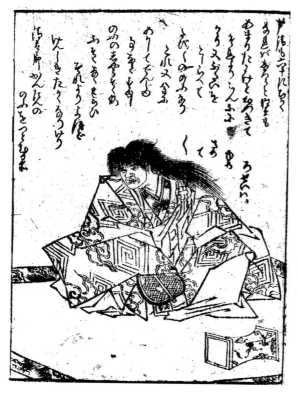 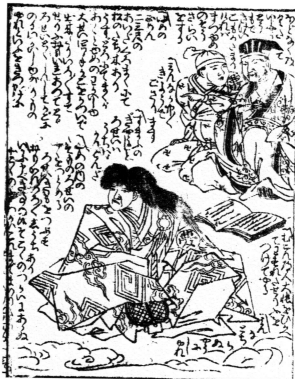

and, therefore, according to much humor theory, the *funnier*—the effect. Much of the fun of the visual pun is the unexpectedness of the revelation— a lot like the theatrical trope of the disguise unmasked or the loophole revealed.

Many genres of popular literature engaged in such visual-verbal allusive play. Even some children's comicbooks (*kusazōshi*) employ *mitate*, suggesting that the practice was widespread enough to be understood and enjoyed from an early age.[75] There was also a wide range of *mitate* pictures, such as the shadowgraph (*kagee*), which presents a silhouette of what appears to be one object and then is "revealed" to be another object entirely (as with **Figure 2.6**); and the "projection picture" (*utsushie*), which similarly presents the viewer with a "projection" or shadow on a wall or paper screen, only to reveal it as something completely different.

This kind of imagistic or figurative pun has a long history in Japan (though ultimately coming from the continent) as part of a wider cultural practice. In fact, the *mitate* as a poetic concept had already existed for over a thousand years by the time of the first *kibyōshi*, as is evidenced by the following poem by Ōtomo no Tabito (665–731):

(*left*) Fig. 3.8 Rosei as pictured in *Dreamers the Winners* (*Miru ga toku issui no yume*, 1781), a *kibyōshi* written and illustrated by Hōseidō Kisanji. Courtesy of the National Diet Library.

(*right*) Fig. 3.9 Rosei as modeled on the Rosei in Kisanji's *Dreamers the Winners* of a decade earlier. From *Rosei's Dream—The Night Before* (*Rosei ga yume sono zenjitsu*, 1791), a *kibyōshi* written by Santō Kyōden and presumably illustrated by Kitao Shigemasa. Courtesy of Tokyo Metropolitan Central Library, Kaga Collection.

---

75. For some examples of such *mitate* books for children, see Suzuki and Kimura, *Kinsei kodomo no ehonshū*.

Wa ga sono ni	In my arbor now
Ume no hana chiru	Petals scatter from the plum—
Hisakata no	Or is it snow
Ame yori yuki no	That floats down drifting over us
Nagarekuru ka mo	From the boundless sky?[76]

It is highly unlikely that Tabito in real life mistook snowflakes for plum blossoms; for this was a recognized conceit called "elegant confusion." The poet merely pretends to mistake one image for another.

Moreover, several games of charades employed *mitate*. The chopsticks and saké cup discarded on the hallway floor of Masanobu's *Pageant of the Latest Beauties* are the implements of one such game. Sometimes a person would masquerade as somebody else, and try to have opponents guess the alluded-to identity. The treasure competition and the humorous etymology may also be conceived of as kinds of *mitate*, provided that the two worlds being juxtaposed are being referenced *visually*.

To summarize the discussion of the visual-verbal imagination, at least three overarching points can be made. First, the words and the pictures in the *kibyōshi* must be read against each other as well as in tandem in order to grasp the *gestalt* of the story. This double structure has its analogue in macaronic play, in various forms of variational procedure at the level of plot, such as acclimation (*hamemono*) and even intertwining (*naimaze*), and perhaps even at the level of visuality, in the trope of visual irony (*mitate*) that also presents two pictorial "texts" that must be read against each other in order to generate an overarching "third" meaning. Although the theory of pictorial storytelling may possibly obtain in the case of Kyōden's *Playboy*, it does not seem to do so widely in the genre as a whole, though the underlying principle of confabulation, which informs everything from humorous etymologies to so-called treasure competitions, certainly invites the reader to see a chasm between the text and pretext. At the most basic level, then, the relationship of the words and pictures in the *kibyōshi* participates in the satirical construction and deconstruction of texts. When this trope would come to be applied in the works of political satire, as with the so-called *reductio ad absurdum* pieces, this deconstructing mode (*ugachi*) invited the reader to look for the loopholes in the text that was Society.

Second, it should be noted that many of the tropes through which this imagination is manifest—pictorial allusions, visual puns, macaronic play, the manipulation of calligraphy and other pictorial aspects of Chinese graphs and of the Japanese syllabary, etc.—can be found in other genres in premodern Japan, to be sure. And no doubt there are many other manifestations of this imagination not mentioned here, for the list could go on *ad infinitum*. Yet it certainly seems as though the visual-verbal imagination is

---

76. *Man'yōshū* #822. Translated by Cranston, *The Gem-Glistening Cup*, p. 543.

brought to the foreground within the *kibyōshi*. Simply put, the *kibyōshi* represents the epitome of such visual-verbal play.

Finally, the calligraphic tradition of handling Japanese writing, and the hybrid nature of Japanese writing itself, with its use of Chinese graphs and Japanese syllabaries, would seem to predispose the Japanese visual-verbal imagination to an especially rich synaesthetic faculty. The interrelatedness of picture and word within the Japanese writing system and the calligraphic tradition have enriched the visual-verbal imagination, positioning *auteurs* to play with the language in a highly sophisticated way. Alphabetic-based languages do not similarly predispose the visual-verbal imagination in the West as imaginatively, which is not to say that the Western visual-verbal imagination itself is unimaginative. It simply derives its idioms from a different source.

Caricatural Aesthetics of the *Kibyōshi*

There is another aspect of the visual-verbal imagination of the *kibyōshi* that needs to be addressed, even if only sketched in rough contours, and that is the relationship between the *kibyōshi* and the cartoon. It has been widely observed that Chinese graphs somehow resemble cartoon images. As Schodt puts it, "*Manga* pictures are not entirely unlike Japanese ideograms, which are themselves sometimes a type of 'cartoon,' or a streamlined visual representation of reality."[77] This notion of a "streamlined visual representation" concurs with E. H. Gombrich's classic formulation of the cartoon as "the condensation of a complex idea into one striking and memorable image"—a formulation that can also be said to apply to Chinese graphs.[78] To the extent that *kibyōshi* pictures acquire an iconographic status, perhaps it is possible for certain scenes within the *kibyōshi* to have become like Chinese graphs in not only their streamlined representation of some comic situation, but also in terms of their widespread recognition by virtue of the genre's popularity.

Eisner shrewdly observes that calligraphy is similar "to the modern comic strip if one considers the effect the cartoonist's style has upon the character of the total product."[79] Bender makes a similar point from the perspective of the enjoyment afforded by the writing in comicbooks as well as by the pictures: "Comics also seem to be acknowledging, overtly, the visual pleasure in reading that happens with text, too, but doesn't seem to be talked about enough."[80] However one conceives of the cartoon, then, let alone calligraphy, the notion of some kind of streamlined representation

---

77. Schodt, *Dreamland Japan*, p. 26.
78. Gombrich, *Meditations on a Hobby Horse*, p. 130.
79. Eisner, *Comics and Sequential Art*, p. 14.
80. Bender, "Flat and Glad," p. 47.

for the sake of visual pleasure seems integral to both, and thus also would seem to inform the *kibyōshi*. Hence, just as the Japanese writing system can be said to affect the visual-verbal imagination, so too would it seem to predispose the Japanese toward the delights of caricature.

The visual pleasure of the *kibyōshi*, let alone its relationship to the history of cartoon art in Japan, has been neglected as a subject by Japanese literary scholars (as well as those in art history and cultural studies). The two chief works that comment upon the visual as well as the verbal texts tend to limit their comments to the task at hand.[81] This may help explain why the major annotators of Kyōden's *Playboy* mistakenly interpret a comment in the text about Toba cartoons of eighteenth-century Osaka as being about the Toba pictures of twelfth-century Kyoto. Thus, more work must be done on the specific relationship of the *kibyōshi* pictures to the tradition of caricatural art in Japan. Since much of the existing work on the history of Japanese caricature has been conducted by proponents of *manga* culture, there may be a tendency to draw causal relationships between different moments in that history and the *kibyōshi* too casually.

That said, the various types of comic pictures in the *kibyōshi* did not just pop out of a peach floating down a river. They derived from a rich tradition of caricature widely available in Edo (and other major metropolises) during the eighteenth century in woodblock-printed form. Thus, it seems reasonable to suppose that the artists of the *kibyōshi* were passively aware of such caricature, though there is also reason to suppose that some of those artists actively participated in that same tradition themselves. Thus, although this assertion may smack of the same kind of assumption informing *manga* culture's assertion of an historical continuity between the modern *manga* and the premodern tradition, in the case of the *kibyōshi* it can be demonstrated that there were close links between the *kibyōshi* and many forms of premodern caricature.

Indeed, the *kibyōshi* artist seems to have had at his disposal a palette felicitously smeared with a variety of colorful caricatural styles and modes. These include such things as the early eighteenth-century Toba cartoons (*Tobae*) from Osaka, madcap drawings (*kyōga*), funny pictures (*kokkeiga*), frivolous pictures (*giga*), and so forth.[82] The makeup (*kumadori*) of kabuki actors, which gains its dramatic effect through the stylized exaggeration of facial features, might also partake of this tradition. In so doing, it may have, in some ways, influenced the *kibyōshi*, especially in its woodblock prints of actors (epitomized by one of Tsutajū's greatest artists Sharaku)—but also especially *parodies* of such actor prints (*nigaoe giga*). One such collection,

---

81. These are Tanahashi, *SNKBZ 79*, and the six volumes of Koike, *Edo no gesaku ehon*. Although some cultural and art historians have addressed the topic of visual pleasure in the *kibyōshi*, they tend not to consider it in relationship to the verbal story.

82. Shimizu, *Manga no rekishi*, p. 21.

蓮生

市川團十郎

三舛

Fig. 3.10 The kabuki star Ichikawa Danjūrō, rendered with
an exaggeratedly prominent
nose. From *Picturebook of Water
and Sky* (*Ehon mizu ya sora*, 1780),
a collection of actor caricatures
by Matsuya Nichōsai. Courtesy
of Hōkoku bunko.

Picturebook of Water and Sky (*Ehon mizu ya sora*, 1780), by Matsuya Nichōsai
(fl. 1781–1788, a.k.a. Jichōsai), contains comic, streamlined portraits of actors that certainly look as though they could have appeared within a *kibyōshi*
(**Figure 3.10**).

Fleshing out this history of these styles and genres is beyond the scope
of the present chapter, let alone this study and the expertise of this author.
And, not to reduce this history to the bare bones of caricature itself, it
might be observed that cartoons and anthropomorphism have been closely
connected in this history—and within the *kibyōshi* itself.

The earliest extant funny figures in Japan are said to be those drawn as a
kind of graffiti beneath the eaves of a famed temple in Nara, the Hōryūji,
dating to the eighth century. It was not until several centuries later, however,
that the earliest known example of cartoons used in telling a story are said
to have assumed literary form. This was the *Frolicking Critters* (*Chōjū giga*), the
celebrated late Heian-period illustrated scroll attributed to the Buddhist abbot Toba Sōjō (1053–1140). Often referred to as the Toba pictures (*Tobae*),
this scroll depicts cartoon-like images of animals in dignified human activities, including rolling around on the ground in paroxysms of laughter (**Figure 3.11**).

While the Toba pictures are said to have exerted a profound influence on
subsequent caricature in Japan, they indisputably partake of a pervasive

Fig. 3.11 Rabbit and frogs laughing convulsively. From *Frolicking Critters* (*Chōjū giga*, ca. late twelfth century), an illustrated scroll by Toba Sōjō. Courtesy of Kyoto National Museum. Permission of Kōzanji.

anthropomorphism in the serious literature and arts of Asia, especially those associated with Buddhism. On the one hand, it is possible that this traces all the way back to theriomorphism in India—the belief that each Hindu god is manifested in his own individual "animal vehicle" (*vāhana*).[83] Thus, Baudelaire's dictum, "the first business of an artist is to substitute man for nature," while perhaps germane enough in the West, would have carried less weight in the Eastern tradition. On the other hand, it is also possible that anthropomorphism was intrinsically linked to comic drawings from the beginning because together they allow authors and artists even in disparate cultures to treat sensitive political and cultural issues by virtue of its ability to defamiliarize human affairs into the realm of non-realistically portrayed animals. It may therefore be no coincidence that what some scholars take to be the earliest extant cartoons in world history, those written on papyrus during Egypt's New Kingdom (ca. 1580–1090 BCE), are also heavily anthropomorphic, depicting "the breakdown of an old social order—lions are happily playing checkers with gazelles, wolves are protectively watching goats, and a cat is tending a flock of geese," as Susan Stewart has observed. "The cartoon reconciles [these] antinomies . . . by turning 'natural enemies' into social allies, and in the case of the first picture, the disequilibrium brought about by the checkers match will be determined by a game order rather than a natural order."[84]

In either case, the interchangeability of nonhuman and human beings seems to have continued in the arts into the Edo period. Anthropomorphic

---

83. Hyers, *Zen and the Comic Spirit*, p. 27. Maria Heim, a specialist of Indic religions, explains in a private communiqué to the present author: "Each god has a particular animal as his 'mount' or 'vehicle' that is symbolically and iconographically associated with him. Shiva has a bull, Vishnu a gander, Durga has a lion, Ganesha has a rat, etc. There are myths about these animals in the literature and they are useful when identifying a deity in art, because they will always be depicted with their animal."

84. Stewart, *Nonsense*, p. 66.

play certainly can be found in some works of ink painting that associate certain zany Zen figures with particular animals. In the inscription to his sketches of frogs, to take one celebrated example, the artist Sengai (1750–1837) reversed the polarity of the usual symbolism by observing that if one can become a Buddha through seated meditation, then all frogs must be Buddhas.

Just as playfully, though less overtly philosophically, Edo-period literature often employed anthropomorphic devices as a vehicle less to pacify opposites (as with the New Kingdom cartoons) than to serve as a kind of fictional confutation, as we have observed in the case of Edo-centric works. The creature battle (*irui gassen*), as this anthropomorphic confutation was known, featured opposing groups of monsters, animals, or inanimate objects (such as noodles) representing different human social groups. In the syllabary booklet *Tale of Chickens and Rats* (*Keiso monogatari*, ca. 1636), for instance, bird and beast scuffle over rations of rice. Such was the stuff of various genres of children's books, too.[85] One folk tale became the basis for the redbook *Monkey vs. Crab* (*Saru kani gassen*) by Nishimura Shigenaga (d. 1756) (**Figure 3.12**).[86] This, in turn, would inspire works even in the

Fig. 3.12 The namesake protagonists of *Monkey vs. Crab* (*Saru kani gassen*), a redbook by Nishimura Shigenaga. Reprinted in Kisho fukuseikai, *Kisho fukuseikai sōsho 4*.

---

85. For more on the creature battle in comicbooks, see Koike, *Edo no ehon 2*, pp. 17–18.

86. Suzuki and Kimura, *Kinsei kodomo no ehonshū*, pp. 46–56.

kibyōshi genre, such as Harumachi's *Old Yarn of Monkey vs. Crab* (*Saru kani tōi mukashibanashi*, 1783). Many a *kibyōshi* adopted this kind of anthropomorphic confutation as its framework—*Familiar Bestsellers* being one obvious example—yet this was no doubt also part of the ploy of having the genre masquerade as a children's comicbook.

Shoddy Chic

Although the creature battle informs only a small percentage of *kibyōshi*, it would be easy to dismiss the art of the genre as so much silly kid stuff. This is because from a distance, the black-and-white interior pictures appear to be a shoddy affair. Indeed, when compared to the highly refined, lavishly colored prints like the one from *Pageant of the Latest Beauties*, the black-and-white internal pictures of the *kibyōshi* appear downright primitive. This primitiveness largely owes to the fact that the pictures are executed in a clear-line style. On the one hand, this style is somewhat indebted to the quick-sketch technique (*byōsha*) of much Buddhist iconography, lending an impression of speed outstripping artistry—of impromptu execution as opposed to deliberation and craft. Yet the pictures in the *kibyōshi* cannot boast quite the same devil-may-care air of spontaneity.

On the other hand, the clear-line style of the *kibyōshi* does not register the same fine detail as many of the larger-format genres of *ukiyoe*. Nor does it have the etched depth, ornate design, crosshatch stippling, or chiaroscuro shadings of contemporaneous Georgian caricature, for that matter (unknown in Japan at that time though it may have been). Shadows appear rarely in the *kibyōshi*, and even then only as solid black silhouettes representing figures perhaps hidden behind a paper door (as with one scene in *Playboy*). The clear line pertains to ground and figure, throwing both into equal focus. And although there may be the occasional Chinese ink-style background on screen paintings decorating rooms, most of the scenery does not stick out as having been executed in a different style—as do the realistic backgrounds of Hergé's *Tintin*, for instance, which contrast noticeably with the cartoonish figures.[87]

That said, many of the *kibyōshi* illustrators were the finest woodblock artists of the day. Hokusai, Utamaro, Toyokuni, Kiyonaga, Kitao Masanobu, Shigemasa, Masayoshi—the list goes on. Thus, it is impossible to say that the impromptu appearance was the miscarriage of mere hacks. Rather, this was an intentional effect. The pictorial style of the *kibyōshi*, if such a unitary entity may be said to exist, can be described as a kind of deliberately calcu-

---

87. Incidentally, it must be observed that Hergé's clear-line style has been traced back to Japanese prints. "This method of rendering the world accurately, sensuously, and yet very simply by distilling every sight down to its primary linear constituents derives most obviously from the eighteenth- and nineteenth-century Japanese popular woodblock-print style called *ukiyoe*, and its masters Hiroshige and Hokusai." In Sante, "The Clear Line," p. 30.

lated *shoddy chic*. That this was a matter of deliberate calculation and not just incompetence or indifference is self evident, and not merely because the evidence of the draft manuscript suggests as much. But why go to all the trouble to carefully plan pictures that end up looking completely unplanned?

There were probably a variety of closely interrelated payoffs. For one thing, this deception perpetuates the running gag of the *kibyōshi* as a genre of children's comicbook. The relaxed, unfastidious appearance suggests an amateur hand, a literatus (*bunjin*) tossing off casual compositions before resuming his putatively serious scholarship. This plays into the way that mass-produced commercial literature tried to pass itself off as a kind of dilettantish pursuit—as anything but pulp fiction. Paradoxically, the shoddiness of the pictures may also have spelled just the opposite, a jaded professional, a beleaguered commercial artisan struggling to meet a publisher's deadline—which may have actually been the case in real life with some artists, for that matter, who might have found some comfort in pretending to adopt a style that they perforce had to adopt in order to meet real deadlines. Certainly many *kibyōshi* present a fictional author-illustrator as a bewildered figure, who (as in *Familiar Bestsellers*) must resort to his own act of confabulation, such as mining his very dreams for literary material.

By depicting himself as one stripe or other of buffoon, the *kibyōshi* author-artist could avert criticism for any carefully couched political satire by having the authorities think this really was silly kid stuff. The workmanlike, economical, almost frugal lines also help to insulate the artist against the charge that the genre delighted in depicting Floating World extravagance.

Moreover, the tossed-off appearance in simple lines aids the overall humor of the pictures. "The cartoon is the result of exaggeration and simplification," Eisner writes, apparently following Gombrich's formulation. "The elimination of some of the detail in an image makes it easier to digest and adds to the humor. . . ."[88] And here, perhaps, is where one finds the most salient feature of the pictorial style of the *kibyōshi*. What allows the best works to achieve this kind of effect is the way that the genre's artists were able to join calligraphy and the cartoon in a simple idiom that *humorously* belied the otherwise sophisticated nature of the visual-verbal dynamic.

Much of the visual pleasure of the *kibyōshi* resides in how the apparent shoddiness of the clear-line style hides a variety of crepuscular pictorial minutiae. For instance, the easily overlooked dotted lines along the collar and beltline of the young protagonists in *Swingers* represent a specific kind of stitching that can be let out for growth, suggesting the advancement of narrative time. The *kibyōshi* picture is a kind of visual paradox in this sense, presenting the reader with the spectacle of subrealism in its sketchiness and hyperrealism in its obsessive attention to trivia drawn from everyday life.

---

88. Eisner, *Comics and Sequential Art*, p. 151.

For someone hoping to find photorealistic detail, the *kibyōshi* may actually therefore just as easily delight as disappoint.

Although such detail work can be technically impressive, especially in such a small format, the details themselves often reinforce the puzzle-like quality of the *kibyōshi*. That is, the couching of fine pictorial details within a broader, more slapdash frame—which one also sometimes finds in *MAD* magazine (though perhaps rarely to the same impressive degree)—is part of the larger satirical structure of encouraging readers to find loopholes within the surface text. To the extent that sophistication was largely defined during An'ei-Tenmei as the ability to see through façades—and this lies at the heart of the visual-verbal imagination as well—the shoddy chic style of the *kibyō-shi* comes across as shoddy only to those not in the know. To those in the know, the style is satisfyingly chic indeed.

The *kibyōshi* picture, then, has by and large been neglected as an aesthetic object. Although there have been some forays into the nature of the visual-verbal dynamic within the *kibyōshi*, to the best of my knowledge there has not been a single serious study of the aesthetics of its pictures. On the one hand, this is hardly surprising, since serious art critics routinely undervalue comicbook art. Furthermore, most mere mortals (including this one) simply do not possess the expertise to deal with the complexities of the visual-verbal imagination as both literature and art. On the other hand, it is slightly surprising, since one would think that there would be some interest in the handiwork of the greats of woodblock printing, especially since these artists provided sometimes exquisitely wrought, multicolored frontispieces in addition to the black-and-white interior pictures.

What, then, might such a study of *kibyōshi* aesthetics achieve? For one thing, it would be useful in identifying the work of the occasionally un-named artist. Also, it would be fascinating to understand stylistic differences within the oeuvre of a single author over time, or perhaps among his different genres. Such a study might also help cast some light on the relationship of the gaze of characters in the pictures of a *kibyōshi* with its verbal narrative flow, and how these things affect the compositional layout of words and pictures on the page. Eventually, such stylistic analysis might provide a basis of comparison with the modern *manga*.

Furthermore, however useful it is to compare and contrast *kibyōshi* pictures to woodblock prints, ultimately, the pictures in the *kibyōshi* should be judged according to the goals of the *kibyōshi* genre. This means assessing how well the pictures work with the words in adding up to the overall story. A study of *kibyōshi* aesthetics therefore might help disengage the genre's interior pictures from the standards of the polychromatic woodblock print or even the modern *manga*, depositing in their place standards more in keeping with the goals of the *kibyōshi* itself—such as the synergy of narrative text and pictures with the overall story, especially its structures of humor and satire.

Chapter 4
The Rise and Pratfall of the Kibyōshi

As our government deteriorates,
our humor increases.
—Will Rogers[1]

Periodization in Lieu of a Proper History

Only a fraction of extant *kibyōshi* having been studied, a history of the genre remains to be written. During the three decades of its vogue, beginning with Koikawa Harumachi's *Master Flashgold's Splendiferous Dream* (*Kinkin sensei eiga no yume*, 1775) and fizzling out, some two or three thousand titles later, in the first decades of the nineteenth century, perhaps later, the *kibyōshi* underwent innumerable transmogrifications, rendering even the finest periodization dubious at best. Characterizations of the genre as "satirical fiction" or "parodist literature," or "didactic works," for instance, overlook the exuberant, good-natured early works, not to mention several rather dreary, formulaic vendetta pieces of later years—though by the same logic these characterizations themselves are equally suspect.

Although no single schema could ever adequately describe the genre's vast and diverse corpus, then, this has not deterred some scholars from trying to bring this bulk of material under rein. After all, such periodizations, like all generalizations, have some usefulness as heuristic devices, provided one keeps in mind their provisional nature. Mori largely set the prevailing thinking, or at least encapsulated it, by observing, "The *kibyōshi* was born during the 1770s, flourished in the 1780s, declined during the 1790s, and vanished during the first decade or so of the 1800s."[2] Koike Masatane and others have fleshed out Mori's dictum, proposing a four-stage periodization: an incipient period (1775–1783); a golden age (1784–

---

1. Sterling and Sterling, *Will Rogers' World*, p. 57.
2. Mori uses the era names An'ei, Tenmei, Kansei, and Bunka, respectively (though he skips Kyōwa, 1801–1803). See Mori, "Kibyōshi sharebon mangen," p. 367.

1787); the period of the Kansei Reforms (1788–1790); and a final epoch (1791–1806).[3]

In a slightly fuller manner still, according the first few *kibyōshi* their own period, Uda Toshihiko has tendered a five-part periodization: (1) the first batch of *kibyōshi*, initiated by Harumachi's *Master Flashgold* (1775–1779); (2) the early works, epitomized by the likes of those by Hōseidō Kisanji; (3) the "gossip pieces," about contemporary personalities, happenings, and scandals (1784–1787); (4) the "protest pieces" (1788–1790), satirizing the repressive social and fiscal policies under the regimes of shogunal regents Tanuma Okitsugu and Matsudaira Sadanobu; and (5) the "late pieces" (1791–1806), pale imitations of those works issued before the Matsudaira regime institutionalized the sweeping Kansei Reforms.[4]

In lieu of a full-fledged history, this chapter follows a combination of these periodizations, albeit with some revision. At the risk of considerable lopsidedness, more attention is paid to those periods *not* represented by the pieces included for translation, specifically the period of the so-called protest *kibyōshi*. Also, this preliminary history commences not with the first *kibyōshi*, but its antecedents in what has often been dismissed as illustrated "fairy tales" and "children's comicbooks." If anything, the Visual Turn suggests that it is no longer possible to deny this comicbook culture that the *kibyōshi* epitomizes its place within Japanese cultural history.

Incunabula: Companion Booklets and Early Comicbooks

"The *kibyōshi*," suggests Mori, "may be called children's stories for adults, or even picturebooks for grownups."[5] One of the earliest genres to influence the *kibyōshi* was in fact the so-called companion booklet (*otogizōshi*), long held to be just such a collection of children's stories. This was a lightly illustrated genre that, deriving from the confluence of the fictional tale (*monogatari*) and short-story collection (*setsuwa*) following the dissolution of the Heian court, began to flourish from the twelfth through the seventeenth centuries, during which time some four hundred such pieces were issued.

Throughout most of its early history, the companion booklet was produced by hand in illustrated-scroll format (*emakimono*). During the Muromachi period (1333–1573), some works were issued in a hand-illustrated booklet format known as the Nara picturebook (*Nara ehon*). By the early part of the Edo period, however, with advances in woodblock-printing technology,

---

3. Koike adopts this four-part periodization in organizing the *kibyōshi* of the first four of the six volumes of *Edo no gesaku ehon*. The last two volumes do not add new periods.

4. See Uda, "Kibyōshi no sekai." Although Uda's periodization is numbered one through six, the number four seems to have been skipped.

5. Mori, *Mori Senzō chosakushū zoku hen 7*, p. 325.

Fig. 4.1 A demonic snake-woman wraps herself around the Dōjōji temple bell, inside of which the priest Anchin is hiding. From the companion booklet *The Tale of Dōjōji (Dōjōji monogatari,* ca. 1660). Reprinted in Skord, *Tales of Tears and Laughter,* p. 146. Courtesy of the University of Hawaii Press.

the companion booklet began to assume the form of the woodblock-printed picturebook (*eiri kanpon*) with which the genre is still generally associated today (**Figure 4.1**).

Afflicted by the chronic categorization as "fairy tales" for the semiliterate, the companion booklet nonetheless boasts a wide variety of material, much of which was clearly intended for a more literate—and therefore, presumably, a more adult—readership. "*Otogi-zōshi* have long suffered from what we would now call 'bad press,'" contends Skord in her study of the genre. "Early in the eighteenth century, a small and not very representative sampling of the stories was published under the title *Otogi bunko,* and advertised as appropriate reading material for women and children. Ever since, the public mind has identified *otogi-zōshi* with fairy and folktales."[6]

In reality, the more grown-up companion booklet sports many of the same characteristics as the *kibyōshi*—a marked intertextuality, a penchant for wordplay fostered by the use of the phonetic Japanese syllabary (*kana*) instead of the mixed Japanese-Chinese hybrid (*wakan konkōbun*), witty repartee, verbal puzzles, scatological humor, and an irreverence toward the usual conventional pieties of those in political or moral authority. Both the *kibyōshi* and the companion booklet tend to combine stories in similar fashion,

6. Skord, *Tales of Tears and Laughter,* p. 9.

what Skord calls "narrative splicing," but which writers of playful literature called intertwining (*naimaze*).[7] In the final analysis, the companion booklet seems to have provided the *kibyōshi* with the precedent of a successfully mass-produced picturebook—though hardly a *comicbook* per se—that was not just for kids anymore.

The primordial sludge from which the *kibyōshi* more or less directly emerged, however, was a cluster of murkily differentiated genres of woodblock-printed, illustrated popular fiction, published in Edo and flourishing roughly from the seventeenth through the nineteenth centuries. These genres were collectively known as grass booklets (*kusazōshi*), after the squiggly-looking "grass" (*kusa*) script in which such chapbooks (*-zōshi* or *sōshi*) were typically written. Decades later, *littérateur* Takizawa Bakin, by then an erstwhile *kibyōshi* author himself, offered the counter explanation that the term originally meant "stinky booklet" (*kusai-zōshi*), owing to the way that its dyes, when initially printed at least, gave off a pungent odor. This claim of course is not without its own strong whiff of the humorously specious etymology.[8]

Whatever the source of the terminology, the grass-script chapbooks are significant because they were among the first *bona fide*, mass-produced *comicbooks* in Japanese literary history. That is, although the case could be made for earlier types of illustrated comic fiction like the companion booklet, not to mention the syllabary booklet (*kanazōshi*) and the novella of the Floating World (*ukiyozōshi*), these were only lightly illustrated genres, including perhaps one picture per ten, if not more, pages of writing. And even then, the illustrations mostly occupied their own pages and thus were separated spatially from the main body of writing. The grass booklet, on the other hand, intermixed words and pictures on just about every page, so that the main body of writing inhabited the same pages as the pictures and often the same narrative space. For the purposes of this study, then, the term *kusazōshi* is rendered functionally as "comicbook" rather than "grass booklet."[9] This is the comicbook culture from which the *kibyōshi* evolved and which, perhaps, the *kibyōshi* most vividly epitomizes.

The woodblock-printed comicbook, to generalize crudely, can be divided into two major groups. The first consists of the early genres—the redbook, blackbook, and bluebook. The longstanding consensus among scholars has been that these works were intended primarily for those with only a modicum of literacy, especially "women and children." As if to confirm this,

---

7. Skord, *Tales of Tears and Laughter*, p. 57.

8. Takizawa Bakin, *Kinsei mono no hon Edo sakusha burui*, pp. 25–26. Also mentioned in his *Iwademo no ki*, in Hayakawa, *Shin enseki jisshu 4*, p. 186. Bakin seems to have used the character for stinky (*kusai*) instead of grass (*kusa*) in the word *kusazōshi* throughout his writings.

9. More generally, however, the term "grass booklet" describes any heavily illustrated or pictorial chapbook as opposed to those books that contain few if any illustrations whatsoever, and are therefore termed reading books (*yomihon*).

most of these works employ a simplistic visual as well as verbal idiom. Nonetheless, some early comicbooks seem to have made use of more grown-up material. In her recent book, Takahashi Noriko convincingly argues that no small number of these works borrow significantly from both the popular stage and theatrical texts—chiefly the recital libretto, the illustrated playbook, and the portrait print of kabuki actors—and not infrequently in ways that only a sophisticated adult reader would fully have appreciated.[10] It is conceivable, in other words, that some early woodblock-printed comicbooks, like some companion booklets before them, may actually have been intended for and read by readers of most ages and literacy levels, if not solely by adult readers. If true, as seems likely, then the *kibyōshi*'s gimmick of disguising sophisticated material in juvenile form probably had its precedent in these earlier genres. In either case, though, the first purely adult comicbook in Japanese literary history was the *kibyōshi*.

The second major group of woodblock-printed comicbook, consisting of the *kibyōshi* and the multivolume chapbook, while appropriating many features of the earlier genres, is unmistakably—even *exclusively*—meant for adult readers. In fact, the division between early and late comicbooks may even be appreciable visually. Generally speaking, in terms of space, in the redbook, blackbook, and bluebook, the pictures predominate; the words are plopped down in blank spaces almost as an afterthought. In the *kibyōshi* and the multivolume chapbook, by contrast, the pictures are either balanced with, or even dominated by, the words.

Furthermore, there are subtle visible differences in the writing itself, specifically in the proportion of cursive syllabary to Chinese graphs. This may be difficult to perceive for someone unfamiliar with the Japanese writing system, since all genres of the woodblock-printed comicbook employ an anomalous squiggly script (*kuzushiji*) that may appear to render both Chinese graphs and the cursive syllabary visually indistinguishable. As a rule, though, the early genres of woodblock-printed comicbooks tend to be written almost entirely in the easy-to-read cursive syllabary, with few Chinese graphs and certainly no complicated ones, as might befit a semiliterate readership. The *kibyōshi* and the multivolume comicbook, by contrast, employ more Chinese graphs, even some demanding ones, though admittedly this increase is sometimes only marginal.

Extremely slight technical differences are present among genres, and even authors within genres, in terms of both the style of the squiggly script and the base Chinese graphs upon which individual syllabary graphs are derived. Such differences tend to go unnoticed by modern Japanese readers, and might not have been consciously noticed during the mid-Edo period, for that matter, except by the most attentive of readers. Still, stylistic and

---

10. Takahashi, *Kusazōshi to engeki*.

script-related differences do in fact exist. The *kibyōshi* employs its own standard set of syllabary graphs that differs subtly from those of other genres. Hamada Keisuke and others have compiled tables of these graphs that can be useful in reading the average *kibyōshi*.[11]

The use of a standard set of syllabary graphs represents a major innovation of sorts. This is because historically speaking there was a variety of ways of rendering any particular syllabary graph based on different Chinese base graphs. The situation is somewhat analogous to—though far more complex than—English in the period before any kind of provisional consensus was reached about Capitalization, ye conventions of printing, and orthographie *efpecially*. The regulation of script and the minimization of base graphs in these woodblock-printed comicbooks, then, was part of a larger process of standardization concomitant with the woodblock-printing revolution in seventeenth-century Japan. This standardization tended to make reading easier, faster, and more accessible, thereby encouraging a broader readership and stimulating the growth of the commercial publishing industry. Thus, xylographic formats and genres such as the Edo comicbook, and the syllabary booklet well before it, cumulatively helped transform reading from a form of primarily hard study into a genuine pastime that even adults could enjoy. Perhaps this is the real difference being alluded to by the gendered and ageist distinction between adult male readers and "women and children"—serious versus playful readers.

The genres of woodblock-printed comicbook were also differentiated visually by the color of their covers, which would have been evident to even the less-than-perfectly literate. Because these genres overlapped in convoluted ways, it is possible that the cover colors indicated more the general comicbook nature of these works as a whole than anything else. That is, the colors of the redbook, blackbook, and bluebook covers are probably more descriptive of a general juvenile content than prescriptive of fine distinctions among "genres." The selection of color might well have been an arbitrary decision, left to the whim of the publisher, or a matter of what hues happened to be at hand. Generic lines among these early comicbooks were, in other words, fuzzy at best.

In fact, these lines seem to have been blurred in the minds of the government, if not in the popular imagination. Thus, one of the publishing edicts condemned sophisticated genres such as the *kibyōshi* in terms of all comicbooks as juvenile genres: "Recently some wicked children's books have appeared which are ostensibly set in ancient times; henceforward these are to be regarded as undesirable. . . ."[12] And yet the often tremendous overlap among genres has not dissuaded efforts to tease out clusters of particular characteristics.

---

11. Hamada, "Hankō no kana jitai."
12. Translated in Kornicki, "*Nishiki no ura,*" p. 156.

Fig. 4.2 Woman discovering a peach (floating down the river), out of which will emerge the story's superhero protagonist. From *The Old Yarn of Peach Boy* (*Momotarō mukashibanashi*), a redbook illustrated and presumably written by Nishimura Shigenobu ca. the early 1770s. Published by the Uroko-gataya. Courtesy of Tokyo Metropolitan Central Library, Kaga Collection.

The Redbook

Dating from the early half of the seventeenth century, the redbook (*akabon* or *akahon*) is considered to be the oldest genre of woodblock-printed comic-book.[13] Its name derives from the characteristically monochrome sanguine of its covers (**Color Figure 6**). Its works tend to be chintzily illustrated, easy-to-read adaptations of children's stories, folk legends, fairy tales, and so forth, such as *The Old Yarn of Peach Boy* (*Momotarō mukashibanashi*, ca. early 1770s), a piece attributed to artist Nishimura Shigenobu.[14] Its minimum of writing was typical of most redbooks (**Figure 4.2**).

Not all redbooks are given to juvenile content, however. Some draw on kabuki and puppet plays, though the retelling is still noticeably simpler than in an analogous stage libretto.[15] Others draw on ghost stories, historical tales, revenge pieces, instructional works, even guides to the famous places and products of Edo—as though they were a form of guidebook themselves.[16] In fact, having been first popularized in Edo during the Genroku period and then chiefly produced there in subsequent years, the redbook is closely associated with that city. Consequently the genre's Edo origins have been taken for granted and, for a long time, have remained largely unexamined. As it turns out, however, there is some reason to believe that the Edo red-

---

13. The redbook became popular during the Genroku period. See Tanahashi, *Edo gesaku zōshi*, p. 6.

14. This attribution should be questioned, however, since Nishimura was mostly active during the 1730s and 1740s. For a transcribed and annotated version of this redbook, see Suzuki and Kimura, *Kinsei kodomo no ehonshū*, pp. 57–67.

15. This according to the discussion in Akama, *Kabuki bunka no shosō*, pp. 211–214.

16. For more on this, see Hirose, *Gesaku bungeiron*, p. 23.

book traces its origins back to a type of small-sized, illustrated children's storybook (*dōwabon*) with blood-red covers from Kamigata.[17] It is likely that this connection was not entirely forgotten during Kyōden's day, for the redbook personified as a character within *Familiar Bestsellers*, though associated with Edo, sympathizes with the Kamigata camp.

The first known redbooks published in Edo were the "mini reds" (*aka-kobon*), measuring only 4 × 5 inches (making them similar to Kamigata storybooks), which flourished during the seventeenth century.[18] By the early eighteenth century, this format had, for whatever reason, given way to a larger one. Perhaps this was to accommodate an increasingly older readership with diminishing eyesight, or to allow more space for visual-verbal play, or a testament to the genre's profitability? This was the mid-sized (*chūbon*) format, measuring approximately 5 × 7 inches, and running from one to three fascicles (*maki* or *kan*) in length.[19] Each fascicle consisted of five leaves broché together with string into ten pages. This mid-sized, five-leaves-per-fascicle format became the standard size and length of subsequent genres of woodblock-printed comicbook. The *kibyōshi* may therefore ultimately owe its general physical dimensions and form to the redbook.

The Blackbook

The blackbook (*kurohon* or *kurobon*), so named for its sooty-looking covers, was the redbook's younger sibling, coming into its own in Edo mid-century, perhaps by the 1740s. Although it assumed the mid-sized format of the redbook, its stories tended to be somewhat more complicated retellings of kabuki and puppet plays, heroic legends, and military accounts, though still rendered in easy-to-comprehend language and writing. This would be the closest Edo analogue, perhaps, of the penny dreadful and the proverbial half-penny dreadfuller—to say nothing of the action comics of an even later day. Although the *kibyōshi* freely draws upon the subject matter of both the redbook and the blackbook, its strong theatrical element is more clearly beholden to the latter. "The *kibyōshi*," opined Mori, "was born of the blackbook's womb."[20] Many a blackbook observes the playbook convention of placing narrative (*ji*) text, usually written in the traditional poetic meter of alternating "lines" of five and seven syllables, at the top of the page, and dialogue (*kotoba*) text, normally lacking meter, near the pictures of the

---

17. See Nakamura, "Kamigata ni okeru dōwabon" and Okamoto, "Shoki Kamigata ko-domo ehon o megutte."

18. *Shoshun no iwai* (1678) and *Momotarō* (ca. mid-seventeenth century) are two extant works in the smaller format.

19. Most mid-Edo comicbooks run from one to three fascicles, with the exception of the multivolume (*gōkan*) genre, which became popular in the early nineteenth century. However, these comicbooks seem never to have had four fascicles, no doubt because the Sinified reading of that number is homophonous with the graph for death (*shi*).

20. Mori, *Mori Senzō chosakushū zoku hen 7*, p. 328.

Fig. 4.3 Swashbuckling scene from the blackbook *A Rundown of Kinpira's Exploits* (*Kinpira tegarazukushi*, authorship and date unknown). Courtesy of Tokyo Metropolitan Central Library, Kaga Collection.

characters (**Figure 4.3**). Thus, the *kibyōshi* most likely appropriates—even if it also mocks—this particular convention from the blackbook, if not other sorts of illustrated theatrical text.[21]

Bluebook unto Yellowbook

The early bluebook (*aohon* or *aobon*) is virtually indistinguishable, in terms of format, content, and language, from the blackbook (**Figure 4.4**).[22] Many commentators therefore understandably minimize dissimilarities between the two.[23] Bakin maintained that because the particular pigment used in the red-

---

21. The puppet play may have appropriated the *ji/kotoba* convention from noh libretti, though the blackbook is not considered to be directly related to noh. Matsuwara Hidetada treats the similarities and differences among blackbook, bluebook, and *rokudanhon*—illustrated *jōruri* books—in Matsuwara, "Otogizōshi kanazōshi ni okeru iwayuru rokudanhon ni tsuite," pp. 237–253. Also see Takahashi Mitsuko's discussion of the confluence among illustrated "stage books" for kabuki (*kyōgen ehon*), blackbooks, and redbooks, in "Kurobon, aohon *Sakenomi dōshi* ni tsuite."

22. *Ao* is actually a blue-green. The choice of "blue" is made for the sake of both simplicity and puns in one of the translations to follow.

23. See Koike Tōgorō, "Akabon, kurohon, aohon, kibyōshi naka no Sogamono." Mizutani Futō, in *Kuzazōshi to yomihon no kenkyū*, concurs. Other scholars, however, differentiate sharply between the blackbook and the bluebook. See Takaki Yoshiji, "*Kinkin sensei* ni anji o

Fig. 4.4 Chikusai bursting into a shop with his sword drawn. From the bluebook *Chikusai* (authorship and date unknown). Courtesy of Tōhoku University, Main Library.

book cover had become prohibitively expensive, the blackbook and the early bluebook were essentially redbooks dressed down with cheaper dyes.[24] Although this might be slightly overstated, to the extent that any splash of color on the cover provided a gross indication of juvenile content, differences among genres were never simply a matter of black and blue.

To complicate matters slightly, though perhaps interestingly, the bluebook is customarily separated into those works that can be presumed to have catered to younger or less literate readers, and those catering to cultured adults. A greater gap may actually divide these two types of bluebook than the one dividing the early bluebook from the blackbook. The later bluebook probably even came to be called the *kibyōshi* in order to differentiate itself from its earlier, less urbane doppelgänger. Generally speaking, the early bluebook tends more toward the juvenile end of the spectrum, whereas the later bluebook, the more adult end. The *kibyōshi* may be considered the first true comicbook for adults, then, only to the extent that readers were aware that the bluebook had splintered in two in a way that the

---

ataeta sakuhin," or Sakamoto Shūji, "Kusazōshi ni okeru Edo shorin no dōkō," for a discussion of each genre in terms of publishing history.

24. Takizawa Bakin, *Kinsei mono no hon Edo sakusha burui*, pp. 25–26.

adult proclivities within the companion booklet, the redbook, and the blackbook had never entailed.

In order to explain how the bluebook came to be called the "yellow-covered book" (*kibyōshibon*)—or more casually just the "yellow covers" (*kibyōshi*)—it should be observed that the genre was not intentionally manufactured yellow from the start. Originally, the covers of the bluebook were an almost bright viridian, or bluish-green (*ao*), made by mixing the saffron yellow of turmeric and the deep indigo dye extracted from the flowers of a spiderwort (*tsuyukusa*).[25] These organic dyes over time proved fugitive, especially with exposure to sunlight, fading to various shades of pale yellow. The term *kibyōshi* thus may have been devised to refer deploringly to those bluebooks whose covers had regrettably sallowed. Although translated into English variously as "yellowbook," "yellowback," and "yellow jacket" (which may only work for certain pieces packing a satirical sting), the term might even be rendered "yellowed booklet."

Just how quickly viridian faded is not entirely clear. If the *kibyōshi* depicted in the hands of the courtesan-in-training in *Pageant of the Latest Beauties* really is supposed to be *Best Man in Japan*, then the real-life *kibyōshi*, which was published in 1784 (the same year as the print in which it is depicted), must have either yellowed immediately after publication, or was published with yellow covers deliberately. Then again, Kyōden might have colored his book yellow in anticipation of its eventual yellowing, to coincide with the viewing of the print at some future date.[26] Since the first *kibyōshi* was issued in 1775, this yellowing process could not have taken more than a decade at most.

Whatever the case may be, at its own zenith, at least, in spite of the fact that some works had already yellowed, the *kibyōshi* does not seem to have been generally called the *kibyōshi*. This is why Kyōden refers to the genre, within *Familiar Bestsellers* and elsewhere, as a bluebook, *not* as a yellowbook. Shikitei Sanba still calls the *kibyōshi* the bluebook as late as 1802 (see **Figure 4.23**). In the final analysis, the word *kibyōshi* is a retrospective designation, the nomenclature of a latter day, a neologism coined perhaps as late as the early nineteenth century to account for a genre that had most likely already passed its prime. It is even possible that when enough covers had faded to necessitate renaming the genre, the genre itself was in danger of fading from memory. But before condemning the *kibyōshi* to oblivion quite yet, let us turn to the first of its incipient works.

---

25. Tanahashi, *Edo gesaku zōshi*, p. 14.

26. It is not unreasonable to wonder if Kyōden originally depicted the *kibyōshi* in *New Pageant of Beauties* in a viridian that, like the real-life *kibyōshi*, sallowed over time. However, since the viridians and the other delicate tints in the version of the print used in this volume have *not* degraded, it can be concluded that Kyōden rendered the courtesan-in-training's bluebook with yellowed covers because that is how it appeared to the eye at the time.

Incipient Works, 1775–1779

The occasional vein of sophisticated moments in the early comicbooks crystallized into full-fledged mature form in 1775 with the publication of Harumachi's *Master Flashgold*. This is widely regarded as an epochal moment in the history of popular illustrated fiction, and therefore mid-Edo literary history, since it marked the birth of the woodblock-printed, mass-produced chapbook—which is to say the genuine comicbook—for an adult readership.[27] The event can be considered the An'ei-Tenmei counterpart of that monumental break between the syllabary booklet and the Floating World novella that occurred nearly a century earlier with the publication of Saikaku's *Life of an Amorous Man* (*Kōshoku ichidai otoko*, 1682).

On the one hand, it is probable that the growing tendency in the early comicbooks toward adult material would eventually have culminated in something like the *kibyōshi* anyway, even if Harumachi had not come along. Perhaps commercial pressures in the up-and-coming publishing industry drove juveniles of any stripe into more adult concerns, as was the case with the companion booklet during the early part of the eighteenth century. On the other hand, Harumachi took the imaginative leap of imbuing the bluebook with the urbane wit and subject matter of the fashionbook. Since none of the more adult examples of the early comicbooks or companion book do as much, this can be said to be what qualifies Harumachi's contribution to the *kibyōshi* as unique.

Harumachi was heavily involved in the production of the fashionbook, so it was virtually inevitable that he drew upon the genre in fashioning the *kibyōshi*. He took the prologue (*jo*), for instance, which while exceedingly rare or non-existent in the earlier genres of comicbooks was not uncommon in the fashionbook, and added it to his adult comicbooks.[28] This became standard operating procedure in the *kibyōshi*, and is one telltale sign in differentiating it from the redbook, the blackbook, and even the earlier bluebook.

One fashionbook in particular, however, informs *Master Flashgold*. That is *Today's Fashionable Chic* (*Tōsei fūzoku tsū*, 1773), the classic guide for the aspiring connoisseur of the Yoshiwara on the latest sartorial and tonsorial dos and don'ts.[29] Although written by Hōseidō Kisanji, Harumachi himself is

---

27. The complete picture is more complex. The supposed leap from childish to adult content was most likely a gradual process, by no means occurring overnight. Some early bluebooks bore adult themes; some later bluebooks did not outgrow their childishness. Strictly speaking, while most bluebooks now appear to have yellowed covers, only some of the books with yellowed covers would be categorized as bluebooks, provided their content was sufficiently unsophisticated.

28. Koike, *Edo no gesaku ehon 1*, p. 36.

29. For a transliterated edition of *Today's Fashionable Chic* see Mizuno, *Sharebon taisei 6* (1979), pp. 66–82. For a discussion in English of the similarities in fashion between it and *Master Flashgold,* see Iwasaki, "The World of *Gesaku*," pp. 87–93.

believed to have provided the illustrations. Harumachi's *Master Flashgold* updates Zeami's famed noh play *Kantan*, then, by using his own illustrations in Kisanji's *Today's Fashionable Chic* as a template.[30] That is, *Master Flashgold* recasts the classic story of *Kantan* in terms of contemporary Edo fashionableness, juxtaposing the highbrow world of the Chinese court with the lowbrow world of the contemporary scene of Edo's many pleasure quarters. In terms of variational procedures, *Master Flashgold* might be considered a kind of intertwining (if not an "acclimation") of a Chinese story.

The noh play *Kantan* describes the adventures of Rosei (Ch. Lu Sheng), a man who sets out to find spiritual enlightenment only to fall asleep on a magic dream pillow at a refreshment stand while waiting for his order of dumplings to cook. He is whisked away in a royal litter to the palace where the Emperor names him heir to the throne. Rosei thereupon lives out his life in idle luxury, frolicking in the many pleasures at court, but suddenly awakening to discover that his lifetime of revelries had been a dream taking no more than a few minutes of "real time."

In *Master Flashgold*, a backwoods samurai named Kinbyōe sets out to make his fortune in the shogun's capital, only to drift asleep on, again, a magic dream pillow while waiting at a roadside stand for his millet dumplings—an Edo specialty—to be cooked. He is escorted in a palanquin to a mansion where a wealthy merchant names him heir to untold riches. Kinbyōe makes himself over as an Edo playboy and has several outrageous adventures in various pleasure quarters. His unrestrained extravagance earns him the nickname Flashgold (*Kinkin*). Literally "gold gold," this term evokes the visual dazzle of the coins that, in the world of the pleasure quarters idealized in such fiction, any self-respecting sophisticate strews about liberally (**Figure 4.5**). *Kinkin* is also the first name of the putative author of the preface, Kinkin Saeru. The term may additionally be vaguely echoic of the arriviste (*narikin*), one who presumes that sudden economic prosperity can somehow translate into dramatically improved social respectability. In the end, however, Flashgold runs out of gold in a flash, and with it fades his attractive sheen. Suddenly *persona non grata* in fashionable society, Kinkin snaps out of his dream chop-chop, abandons his plans for worldly wealth, and promptly returns to the countryside whence he came.

The language of *Master Flashgold* is trendy, consisting of various argot and contemporary slang expressions, such as "thanks a heap" (*arigatayama*). Many of the chichi styles appearing in its pictures (**Figure 4.6**) are clearly beholden to those in the illustrations for *Today's Fashionable Chic* (**Figure 4.7**), such as the Honda topknot, clothes made of velvet (*birōdo*), and a sleek, black, "eyes-only cowl" (*mebakari zukin*) used to disguise the identity of

---

30. Written by Zeami (ca. 1364–1443). For an English translation, see Tyler, *Japanese Nō Dramas*, pp. 133–141.

Fig. 4.5 Master Flashgold strewing gold coins liberally about the pleasure quarter. From *Master Flashgold's Splendiferous Dream* (*Kinkin sensei eiga no yume*, 1775), a *kibyōshi* written and illustrated by Koikawa Harumachi. Courtesy of Tokyo Metropolitan Central Library, Kaga Collection.

important personages in the pleasure quarter—the eighteenth-century equivalent of movie-star sunglasses. What in particular separated Harumachi's adult comicbook from earlier bluebooks, then, was its appropriation of the realistic dialogue, customs, and trendy fashions of the Edo sophisticate that had hitherto been most evidently the provenance of the fashionbook.

In both spoofing the pretensions of the *nouveau riche* while providing readers with the vicarious thrills of the pleasure-quarters, *Master Flashgold* seized the grown-up popular imagination as no other comicbook ever had. It is no exaggeration to say that the combination of Harumachi's new take

Fig. 4.6 Master Flashgold dressed in a chic black halfcoat (*haori*) over a striped robe, flanked by a young assistant. From *Master Flashgold's Splendiferous Dream (Kinkin sensei eiga no yume,* 1775), a *kibyōshi* written and illustrated by Koikawa Harumachi. Courtesy of Tokyo Metropolitan Central Library, Kaga Collection.

on the old bluebook, Edo's moneyed and leisured adult readership, and entrepreneurial publishers such as Urokogataya Magobei and Tsutaya Jūzaburō resulted in the creation of not just a new genre, but a new market. One study estimates that between 50 and 60 *kibyōshi* were published in the two or three years immediately following *Master Flashgold's Splendiferous Dream.*[31] The themes and styles of the companion booklet and blackbook were coalescing into a new form. Although print runs initially were limited,

---

31. Hirose, *Gesaku bungeiron,* p. 75.

じゃうのむすとやう
上之息子風

Fig. 4.7 Sophisticate dressed in a chic black halfcoat (*haori*) over a striped robe, flanked by a young assistant. From the fashionbook that provided *Master Flashgold's Splendiferous Dream* with much of its visual idiom, *Today's Fashionable Chic (Tōsei fūzoku tsū,* 1773). Written by Hōseidō Kisanji and illustrated by Koikawa Harumachi. Courtesy of Tokyo Metropolitan Central Library, Tokyo Collection.

the demand for this exhilarating new kind of literature was extraordinary. The number of copies per run and the number of titles per year both increased. Ultimately, the result was the "*kibyōshi* craze" of the late 1770s and the 1780s—and a publishing boom of unprecedented dimensions.

Another one of the first *kibyōshi* was Harumachi's *Travelogue of Snobby Atelier (Kōmansai angya nikki,* 1776).[32] Not unlike a farce from the *kyōgen* stage

32. For annotated versions of the text, see Mizuno, *NKBT 59,* pp. 47–67 and Koike, *Edo no gesaku ehon 5,* pp. 5–40.

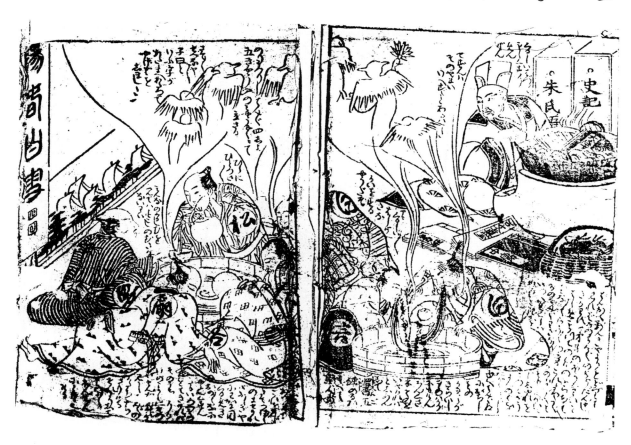

depicting the antics of the servants Tarō and Jirō when their master has left them to look after the manor, this *kibyōshi* describes the happenings at a school of *haikai* poetry called the Kōmansai—"Snobby Atelier"—when its master, Ban'oku, takes a trip. Fowl-like goblins with long beaks, known as *tengu* and associated with pomposity, use the master's absence as their chance to seize control of the school. This they do by demonically possessing the students, beginning with the one who has been put in charge, the result being that anarchy reigns: students are permitted to frequent the various pleasure quarters, break the formal rules of *haikai* composition, dabble in such decadent activities as Japanese "footbag" (*kemari*) and—heaven forbid!—even attend flower-arrangement parties. In the end, Ban'oku returns, realizes what has happened, and administers an emetic derived from didactic texts, whereupon the dastardly fiends are *literally* disgorged **(Figure 4.8)**.

Fig. 4.8 Students vomiting out avian spooks (*tengu*) as Master Ban'oku (upper right-hand corner) prepares more emetic from classic texts. From *Travelogue of Snobby Atelier* (*Kōmansai angya nikki*, 1776), a *kibyōshi* written and illustrated by Koikawa Harumachi. Courtesy of Tokyo Metropolitan Central Library, Kaga Collection.

Early Works, 1780–1783

On the heels of his own success, Harumachi next issued several other noteworthy *kibyōshi*, such as *The Monstrous* Udon *and* Soba *Noodles of Mt. Ōe* (*Udon soba: Bakemono Ōeyama*, 1776), *New Roots of Verbal Jousting* (*Kotoba tatakai atarashii no ne*, 1778), and *A Gratuitous Account* (*Mudaiki*,

Fig. 4.9 Two samurai dressed for excess. Note their elongated topknots, baggy outfits, and extra thick footwear. From *A Gratuitous Account* (*Mudaiki*, ca. 1781), a *kibyōshi* written and illustrated by Koikawa Harumachi. Courtesy of Tokyo Metropolitan Central Library, Kaga Collection.

1781).[33] Scores of later *kibyōshi* would hark back to these instant classics. Kyōden's *Modish Pattern of a Confucian Stripe* (*Kōshijima toki ni aizome*, 1789), his *Buffing Up Aoto's Loose Coins* (*Tama migaku Aoto ga zeni*, 1790), and Ōta Nanpo's *Absent White Lies* (*Teren itsuwari nashi*, 1786), to cite a few examples,

33. In Koike, *Edo no gesaku ehon 1*, pp. 35–60, pp. 87–112, and pp. 113–148, respectively. Hamada Giichirō speculates that *Mudaiki* might have been written as late as 1781 (in Koike, *Edo no gesaku ehon 1*, p. 114).

mostly owe the way their futuristic settings soften contemporary social and political criticism to one such work.[34] This was Harumachi's *A Gratuitous Account*, which took the fashionable tendency to excessiveness and exaggerated it even more in order to demonstrate how sartorial fashion itself is absurd—a technique that would become the mainstay of political satire (**Figure 4.9**).

Other authors followed Harumachi's lead. One to emerge as a major force was Hōseidō Kisanji (1735–1813), whose first major *kibyōshi*, titled *Peach Boy—A Present-Day Sequel* (*Momotarō gonichibanashi*, 1777), took the titular legend as it appeared in the redbook (see **Figure 4.2**) and updated it into a more adult, contemporary, and Edoesque visual as well as verbal idiom (**Figure 4.10**).[35]

But it was his *Dreamers the Winners* (*Miru ga toku issui no yume*, 1781) that helped propel Kisanji into the popular literary limelight. This story, which unequivocally harks back to *Master Flashgold*, is set in the Asakusa section

Fig. 4.10 After making his way home from Ogre Island of the classic legend, a modern Peach Boy shakes out a cascade of gold coins with his magic wish-fulfilling mallet. From *Peach Boy—A Present-Day Sequel* (*Momotarō gonichibanashi*, 1777), a *kibyōshi* written by Hōseidō Kisanji and illustrated by Koikawa Harumachi. Courtesy of Tokyo Metropolitan Central Library, Tokyo Collection.

---

34. In Koike, *Edo no gesaku ehon 6*, pp. 127–164; Mizuno, *SKZ 2*, pp. 209–227; and Wada, *Shoku Sanjin kibyōshi shū*, pp. 112–143 (and 146–156), respectively.

35. For an annotated edition of *Momotarō gonichibanashi*, see Koike, *Edo no gesaku ehon 1*, pp. 61–86.

of Edo, where a certain merchant by the name of Eigaya Yumejirō—
"Dreaming Second Son of the House of Splendor"—leases a variety of
dream pillows for a living, the quality of dream being directly proportional
to the pillow's rental fee.[36] In one scene, two stingy, low-ranking samurai
hire inexpensive dream pillows in order to watch a kabuki play and visit a
prostitute, rather than pay full price for the actual experiences. But the joke
is on them, for one samurai in his dream finds himself in a standing-room-
only section at the back of the theater from where he can barely see the
play. The other samurai ends up with a "riverboat dumpling" (*funamanjū*),
the cheapest sort of whore, who plies her trade, precariously, near the water's edge (**Figure 4.11**).

Since these gags come at the expense of samurai, Kisanji—himself a
samurai—may have been aiming to appeal predominantly to a merchant
readership, which was, after all, where the really big money was. And poking
fun at vicarious thrill-seekers may have been a way of teasing those readers
who visited the Floating World primarily through playful literature. Broadly
speaking, though, one senses a genuine exuberance in many of these early
kibyōshi beyond the profit motive, as though the authors themselves thrilled
to be taking part in the new cultural sensation. Harumachi and Kisanji remained active throughout this period, but many future luminaries were also
getting their start, including Shiba Zenkō (1750–1793), Iba Kashō (1747–
1783), Ichiba Tsūshō (1739–1812), Kitao Shigemasa (1739–1820), Nansenshō
Somahito (1749–1807), Nandaka Shiran (1757–1820), Tōrai Sanna (1744–
1810), and Kitao Masanobu (Kyōden), to name a few.

Among works produced in these years by these authors, Uda singles out
Kyōden's *Familiar Bestsellers* as exemplary, which is one of several reasons it is
included in the present study.[37] Another reason is that *Familiar Bestsellers* features many of the genres of comicbook and popular literature presently under discussion. As the title itself suggests, the *kibyōshi* genre during its first
decade had taken root, budded, even burgeoned forth in great quantity as
genuine "bestsellers." Between 65 and 84 titles were issued annually during
the period of the early *kibyōshi* (1780–1783), which, if apportioned over the
course of a year, means that a reader could savor at least one title per week.

One important distinction of these early *kibyōshi* is the way that some of
them differ from their comicbook antecedents. *Familiar Bestsellers* casts a
personified *kibyōshi* (though referred to as a bluebook) as the hero against
villains that include not only genres from Kamigata but also earlier genres
of comicbooks from Edo. The *kibyōshi* version of *Peach Boy*, for example, is
not merely a retelling of the folk legend, or even an updating of the folk
legend as per the redbook into modern-day Edo, but also a recasting of the

---

36. For an annotated edition of *Miru ga toku issui no yume*, see Mizuno, *NKBT 59*, pp. 69–
86. Araki has a translation in "Dream Pillow," pp. 78–98.
37. Uda, "Kibyōshi no sekai," p. 104.

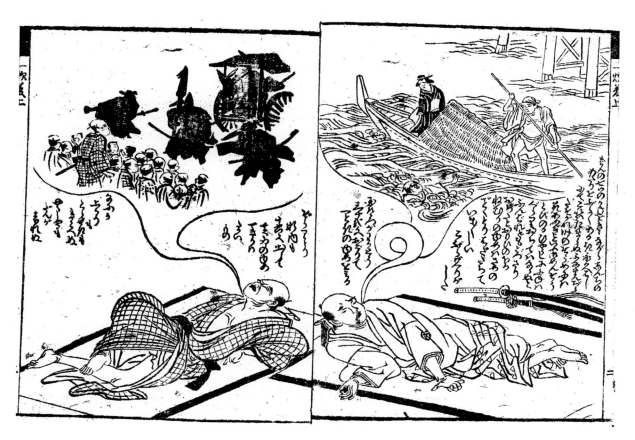

redbook genre itself in a sense. It might be added that in both representatives of the first batch of *kibyōshi* touched on too briefly here, *Flashgold* and *Travelogue of Snobby Atelier*, Harumachi draws upon the by-then old-fashioned noh and *kyōgen* theaters. And in the preface to *Familiar Bestsellers*, the narrator appears as if an actor on the *kyōgen* stage. Later *kibyōshi*, however, as the kabuki dream in *Dreamers the Winners* presages, would tend to be far more beholden to Edo's own kabuki stage.

Fig. 4.11 Two samurai getting less than they bargained for in their respective dreams. The one at left can hardly see the action on stage. The one at right gets no action with a streetwalker known as a "riverboat dumpling." From *Dreamers the Winners* (*Miru ga toku issui no yume*, 1781), a *kibyōshi* written and illustrated by Hōseidō Kisanji. Courtesy of the National Diet Library.

The Golden Age of the Gossip Pieces, 1784–1787

The golden age of the *kibyōshi* began around 1784, a year in which a record 92 titles were supposedly issued. Some scholars, however, take the following year as the benchmark because of the publication of Kyōden's megahit, *Playboy*.[38] As we will see from the chapter on that work, the characterization of the *kibyōshi* of this period as "gossip pieces" is not without warrant. Although most *kibyōshi* contain some reference to contemporary persons, places, events, and so forth, even if only in passing, many of the gossip pieces seem to do so with a certain zest. Harumachi's

---

38. Matsuki argues for 1785 on these grounds in *Tsutaya Jūzaburō*, pp. 74–75 and 79.

Manzaishū chobi raireki (1784), for example, contains various allusions to the poems and authors included in the *Manzaishū*, a collection of madcap verse compiled by Nanpo.[39] Nanpo's *Pat-a-Cake! Pat-a-Cake! (Atama tenten ni kuchi ari,* 1784) transposes warring samurai to the no-less competitive battlefield of Edo's contemporary restaurant scene, which allows for a certain dash of local spice.[40] Kyōden's *Horned Words of a Dishheaded Demoness (Hachikazuki hannya no tsuno moji,* 1785), a send-up of the legend of Lady Dishhead (see **Figure 1.6**), transports the entire story from its original courtly setting to the world of the Yoshiwara. Visually juxtaposing classical and contemporary worlds, the dish affixed to the heroine's head is depicted as resembling the wicker hat (*fuka amigasa*) typically worn as a disguise in Edo's celebrated pleasure quarter (**Figure 4.12**).[41]

Kyōden's masterpiece, *Playboy, Roasted à la Edo (Edo umare uwaki no kaba-yaki,* 1785), is laden with innumerable references to contemporary courtesans, kabuki actors, poets, authors, and so forth. Like many gossip pieces, *Playboy* pokes fun at the folly of social pretension, particularly that of its protagonist Enjirō, a presumptuous upstart. Within this kind of social satire that appears within the gossip pieces, it is possible to detect the seeds of political satire, especially since the venerable Japanese literary and dramatic tradition of ribbing the grandiose, upon which the *kibyōshi* indisputably draws, is itself by definition political. In a rigidly conceived class system, any discussion of high and low could not help but be so. A country samurai like Flashgold or a spoiled rich kid like Enjirō can become a playboy and temporarily "crash" fashionable circles, but he must always be hammered back into his place. Moreover, to the extent that *Playboy* can be said to have based its bungling protagonist on a local bureaucratic figure—the Fire Marshal of Edo Castle—the piece may have had a subtly irreverent edge. For every nine parts social satire in gossip pieces like *Playboy*, then, there was probably one part political satire. During the next period, these proportions must have felt as though they were reversed.

The Political Satire of the "Protest Pieces," 1788–1790

Although the *kibyōshi* parodied the format of the early comicbooks as well as the content of just about all cultural production, the gossip pieces added to this mix a dash of tart irony, if not scalding social satire. A few authors in the mid-1780s began gradually to extend this recipe from the realm of the social to that of politics. With the initial success of such

---

39. Koike, *Edo no gesaku ehon 2*, pp. 9–34.
40. Koike, *Edo no gesaku ehon 2*, pp. 61–96.
41. For a transliterated version of Kyōden's *kibyōshi*, see Mizuno, *SKZ 1* pp. 203–212. My thanks to Charo D'Etcheverry for bringing this pictorial touch to my attention.

Fig. 4.12 Lady Dishhead—updated from the classic legend into an Edoesque character—exhibited on stage as a freak. From *Horned Words of a Dishheaded Demoness* (*Hachikazuki hannya no tsuno moji*, 1785), a *kibyōshi* written and illustrated by Santō Kyōden. Courtesy of Tokyo Metropolitan Central Library, Kaga Collection.

endeavors, in terms both of getting past censors as well as of sales (not to mention the ever-increasing popularity of the genre as a whole), authors could only have felt emboldened. The rare punishment for violating the various publishing edicts was, thus far, merely a slap on the wrist—the proverbial "three-day ban" (*mikka hatto*) as some *kibyōshi* and comic haiku called it—and could only have fueled authorial cockiness. Swipes at contemporary political figures soon became *de rigueur*.

And so during the last few years of the decade, a pack of *kibyōshi* were set loose satirizing the policies of the Tokugawa regime, especially the fiscal measures of Tanuma Okitsugu and the increasingly hard-line reforms of Matsudaira Sadanobu. These works Uda refers to in terms of satire, resistance, and protest. Since there is some question about whether these pieces are "genuinely" satirical—and because the subject is important to any understanding of why the *kibyōshi* became a forbidden literature—comparatively more space is devoted here to this topic.

The protest pieces were very much a product of their particular time and place. It is no accident that *kibyōshi* in this mode were written during the mid-Edo period's most intense social disquiet. To begin with, celestial events like unscheduled comets did not bode well. They were feared to reflect poorly upon the government, whose responsibilities included supposedly keeping both cosmos and country in whack. The latter was stricken with an unrelenting series of natural catastrophes—droughts here, floods there, earthquakes, volcanic eruptions, and unseasonably cold weather everywhere. Not to mention blights of near biblical proportion. And the great famines of 1786 and 1787, which followed on the heels of lesser famines, resulted in some of the highest commodity prices in history.[42] Rice, observes historical economist Sorenaka Isao, soared to *triple* the usual rate virtually overnight.[43] As many as one million people nationwide are thought to have starved to death—a staggering figure if true, especially considering that this was roughly equal to the entire population of the city of Edo at the time.

The government, for its part, did not particularly help matters. Corruption, fiscal mismanagement, a disregard for the growing gap between rich and poor, indifference to the reasons underlying the threat of class warfare, preoccupation with factional infighting—the perception of these and more marred the regime of Senior Counselor Tanuma Okitsugu (1719–1788).[44] The political authority of the shogunate itself was becoming dangerously eroded. Tanuma's tenure as chief advisor ended abruptly in 1786 after Tokugawa Ieharu, the tenth shogun and Tanuma's benefactor, died mysteriously. There was even a rumor he had been poisoned.

By the time Matsudaira Sadanobu (r. 1787–1793) assumed the helm as Senior Counselor, he had a genuine social as well as an economic crisis on his hands. For one thing, the peasants were revolting. Of the 95 incidents of violent rural uprisings recorded during the eight years of the Tenmei era, according to Herbert Bix, over half—50—were concentrated during both years of the great famines.[45] Additionally, urban "house smashings" (*uchikowashi*) broke out in Edo proper, where enormous mobs stormed between five hundred to one thousand rice shops, according to Takeuchi Makoto,

---

42. Cullen, *A History of Japan*, p. 104. Cullen cites the table of retail prices in the diary of Motoori Norinaga (1759–1799), in Matsumoto, *Motoori Norinaga*, p. 122.

43. Sorenaka, "The Kansei Reforms," p. 152.

44. For more on the Senior Counselor's rise and fall, see Hall, *Tanuma Okitsugu*.

45. Bix, *Peasant Protest in Japan*, pp. 111–112.

in 1787 alone.[46] Perhaps the only thing *not* in short supply during the late Tenmei era, besides rebellions and shogunal anxiety, was grist for the satire mill.

The satire of the protest pieces undoubtedly reflects popular sentiment that was otherwise not being expressed peaceably. Although it is likely that these satires somehow contributed to public outrage, it has never been proven that they directly incited violence. From the government's perspective, of course, such distinctions must have appeared preciously fine. What was patently evident even to the dullest of bureaucrats was that the protest pieces spoofed a variety of sensitive topics that were, not to mince words, *verboten*.

Some such topics, based on a sampling of major works, include: the infamous corruption of the Tanuma regime (*Tanuma wairo seiji*); Tanuma's fiscal mismanagement and unfair devaluation of currency in the silver coin (*nanryō nishugin*); the bad blood between Tanuma Okitsugu and Sano Zenzaemon Masakoto (*Sano Masakoto jiken*) after Masakoto assassinated Okitsugu's son Mototomo; Tanuma's Hokkaido policy (*Ezochi seisaku*); and the state-sponsored Neo-Confucian policies that were advocated even more strenuously during Matsudaira Sadanobu's draconian Kansei Reforms, especially the exhortation of the "literary and martial arts" (*bunbu shōrei saku*) and the myriad sumptuary regulations (*ken'yaku rei*). One constant leitmotif is the conviction that the government's overzealousness in trying to dictate human behavior was at odds with human nature itself. This is why Mizuno refrains from using the term "protest" pieces, instead describing them as works "ironizing" the shogunal system.[47]

For an author to broach these topics, never mind to lampoon them, was not necessarily the safest of endeavors. Writing about Chikamatsu's more provocative puppet plays, Donald Shively concisely described the overall climate:

In seventeenth- and eighteenth-century Japan few forms of activity were as hazardous as the writing of political satire. The regime of the Tokugawa shoguns was a military dictatorship which considered its survival to depend upon preserving the political monopoly of the family and its adherents and maintaining the social privileges of the samurai class. It ruthlessly suppressed political criticism; it safeguarded itself with a network of censors, secret police, and informers; it even forbade private authors to discuss events involving the ruling class more recently than the sixteenth century.[48]

The network of censors to which Shively refers consisted primarily of the City Magistrate (*machibugyō*), which was the local body through which the shogunate acted, and the Publishing Association, which was one of the few

---

46. Takeuchi, "Kansei kaikaku to kibyōshi," p. 102.

47. For more on these targets of political satire, as well as this terminology, see the chapter "Bakusei fūshi no kibyōshi," in Mizuno, *Kibyōshi sharebon no sekai*, pp. 163–186.

48. Shively, "Chikamatsu's Satire on The Dog Shogun," p. 159.

guilds during the mid-Edo period to be permitted to exist—but only for so long as it proved effective in policing authors and publishers.

In order for a satirical work to make its way through this gauntlet without drawing blood from its author and publisher, then, it had to content itself with stirring up political undercurrents beneath an otherwise placidly portrayed surface of a work *seemingly* about the Floating World. The art of the protest *kibyōshi*, in other words, was one of overtones, not of overtness. It was a tightwire act between obscurity and objectionableness. If too subtle, readers would fail to catch the satire. If too flagrant, the authorities would take grave offense, and it would be the authors who would be caught. For this reason, the satire never became particularly strident. There is nary a whiff of moral outrage. "Discretion, rather than subversion," as Hibbett has memorably put it, "is the dominant characteristic of Edo humor."[49]

Granted, some authors must have felt incredulous about the mismatch between the government's harsh rhetoric and overzealous jeremiads on the one hand, and its offensive corruption, indifference, and ineffectualness on the other. Yet judging by their often chirpy tone alone, it is not easy to appreciate what was satirical about the protest *kibyōshi*. Furthermore, since most of the references are acutely topical, and the satire almost always carefully couched, readers at the remove of two or more centuries can easily miss the point. For this reason, social satire is less difficult to spot than political satire, which is not to deny that there is a close connection, if not an overlap, between the two. What cannot be denied, however, is that the stock in trade of the protest pieces was political satire.

To play devil's advocate, it might be objected that what politically inflected satire is present in the protest *kibyōshi* is pressed into the service of entertainment—satire not for the sake of satire but for the sake of fun. Perhaps such satire provides a temporary, symbolic defiance that never amounts to a genuine invitation to political rebellion? These pieces were hardly formal protests, after all. Nor were they the sort of petitions submitted to suggestion boxes in various domains throughout the Edo period.[50] And they certainly were not a revolutionary battle cry to be punctuated by the "sincerity blood" that their authors would shed in some kind of suicidal paramilitary gesture, as would be the case with Ōshio Heihachirō (1798–1837) and his *Call to Action* (*Gekibun*, 1836).[51] Even the most scathing protest piece, accordingly, cannot be considered a full-throated satire.

Along these lines, Keene has commented that *gesaku* in general lacks the "intensity" of true satire.[52] And "[i]nstead of being an effective critique,"

---

49. Hibbett, *The Chrysanthemum and the Fish*, p. 89.

50. The petition box in Tosa, for instance, was operative from 1759 to 1873. For more on this, see Roberts, "The Petition Box in Eighteenth-Century Tosa."

51. The text of *Gekibun* can be found in Miyagi, *Nihon no Meishō 27*. My thanks to Jeffrey Newmark for this reference.

52. Keene, *World Within Walls*, p. 411.

writes Sakai of *gesaku* genres like the *kibyōshi*, "parodist literature became a form of flirtation."[53] If true, then it would follow that flirtatious playboy-authors like Kyōden actually were prosecuted for their minor infractions of publishing regulations only, not because their works symbolically threatened the government. By this logic, the *kibyōshi* was merely a hodgepodge of fun and games with a pinch of social or even political cheekiness thrown in to zest things up. Silly kid stuff. Hardly genuine satire.

There are several problems with this sort of dismissal. For one thing, it assumes that entertainment, in the form of comic fiction, and satire are mutually exclusive. Not only can satire be entertaining, certainly, but many comic genres also function satirically. What is more, in the police-state-like climate of Tokugawa Japan, an author not wishing to hand his head on a platter to the shogunate had little choice but to dress his satire in clowns' clothing. Under an ideological regime that can be described as a state-sponsored Neo-Confucian brand of aggressive utilitarianism, which insisted that literature must be socially redeeming (and which no doubt had its homegrown counterpart in what could be termed the "cult of sincerity"), the simple act of being silly itself may have acquired the force of defiance. Perhaps this is one reason that so much playful literature dwells on the socially purposeless—things that point to the inevitable loopholes in the structure of contemporary common sense, like belly buttons or farts.

For another thing, this kind of dismissal, by turning the effectiveness of satire into a litmus test for its presence, seems to insist that Japanese satire be focused according to some sort of idealized Western standard. The protest pieces may come across as mere "flirtation," but this does not, in my opinion, disqualify them as satire. In their political irreverence, these pieces tapped into a popular impulse to protest a government run amok, an impulse that never materialized into an organized movement but was nonetheless palpable. What is more, the putative lack of focus of the protest pieces in fact characterizes one of the classic, and perhaps most common, modes of Western satire—Menippean satire, the seemingly disorganized structure of which coincides with the scattershot diffuseness of its various targets. Such a mode more or less describes many works of Edo's playful literature, for that matter, the least of which is not the "indiscriminate anarchy" of the *kibyōshi*.

The protest pieces are probably more highly focused than that, anyway. Works in this mode veiled their satire by employing a set number of identifiable techniques not unknown in Western satire, such as allegory, code words, *reductio ad absurdum*, asides, and other seemingly minor moments. Nonetheless, judged by *contemporaneous* Japanese standards, the protest pieces must have seemed like withering attacks.

---

53. Sakai, *Voices of the Past*, p. 181.

Generally speaking, authors of the protest pieces couched their political satire in allegory. According to Susan Klein, allegory is "a mode of structuring narrative in such a way that the reader is encouraged to discover a unifying meaning for an apparently disparate series of tropes by means of correspondences with an external religious or political discourse."[54] The protest pieces often aimed for just that, referring obliquely to especially political discourse through a variety of couching or defamiliarizing techniques. Such allegorical ploys complied with the letter, though not the spirit, of the edicts restricting mention of contemporary political figures, for instance.[55] And to the extent that a story set in the past in order to satirize some aspect of the present was known to readers, these ploys helped create (as well as played off) a common ground among readers from a variety of geographical regions in Japan.

For readers who needed additional help in making the connection between a story set in the past and the real-life drama of the present, authors often provided additional hints. It had long been a convention in the popular theater to select an historical figure who would call to mind the contemporary person through some thinly disguised personality quirk, similarity, or association. One regular method is a slight shift in register that, incidentally, also appears in the West. This can be over-the-top blatant, as with the "Razis" in *The Amazing Adventures of Kavalier and Clay* standing for the Nazis; or it can be slightly more subtle, as with the malevolent computer HAL in Arthur C. Clarke's *2001: A Space Odyssey* cleverly one-downing the acronym of that then-colossal American computer conglomerate, IBM. It can even involve an anagrammatic encoding, as with Baron Scarpia, the villainous police chief in Puccini's *Tosca*, standing for the real-life Baron Sciarpa.

An example of this variety of transposition is to be found in Zenkō's *Thousand-Armed Goddess of Mercy, Julienned*, a *kibyōshi* already mentioned briefly in connection with the variational procedure of pastiche (*fukiyose*).[56] Published in 1785, several years before the period of the full-fledged protest *kibyōshi* as defined by both Uda and Koike, this work nonetheless contains elements of political satire. Although set in the past, the story describes an economic crisis that should have been glaringly familiar to any of Zenkō's informed contemporary readers. The thousand-armed Goddess of Mercy (*Senju Kannon*), who herself suffers from the same sort of fiscal hardships besetting Japan, decides to make ends meet by having some of her extra arms chopped off and rented out—like so much radish julienne for handmade soup—to those in need of a handout (**Figure 4.13**). Renters include not only

---

54. Klein, *Allegories of Desire*, p. 19.

55. Beginning in 1644, the Tokugawa government had issued regulations against mentioning politically sensitive names or contemporary persons in materials to be published or performed in public.

56. For an annotated version, see Koike, *Edo no gesaku ehon 2*, pp. 133–146. For an annotated translation, see Kern, "Shiba Zenkō's *Thousand-Armed Goddess of Mercy, Julienned*."

Fig. 4.13 Merchants amputating some of the Goddess's extra hands. From *Thousand-Armed Goddess of Mercy, Julienned* (*Daihi no senrokuhon*, 1785), a *kibyōshi* written by Shiba Zenkō and illustrated by Kitao Masanobu. Courtesy of Tokyo Metropolitan Central Library, Kaga Collection.

those who are literally missing an arm—the warrior Taira no Tadanori (1144–1184), for instance, wants to replace the one he lost at the Battle of Ichi-no-Tani so that he can write the verse for which he is noted—but those whose armlessness is figurative, as with a maladroit or "unhandy" (*te ga nai*) courtesan (**Figure 4.14**).

Fig. 4.14 Armless characters—and one legless beggar—hoping for a helping hand. From *Thousand-Armed Goddess of Mercy, Julienned (Daihi no senrokuhon,* 1785), a *kibyōshi* written by Shiba Zenkō and illustrated by Kitao Masanobu. Courtesy of Tokyo Metropolitan Central Library, Kaga Collection.

Unfortunately for the Goddess, some of the renters inadvertently damage her arms through a variety of underhanded behavior—everything, we are told (but not shown), from fisticuffs and insect squishing to handjobs. The result being that she must take a loss when renting out her goods secondhand. At the beginning of the story, the arms fetch one gold coin each, though in the end, when renting to Tamuramaru—the protagonist of the noh play *Tamura,* who needs to "arm" himself against a rebelling demon—the Goddess must accept one eighth that rate.

Readers were expected to make the short leap from "Tamura" to "Tanuma" on their own. For those who needed an extra boost, there was that specific rate of exchange. As part of the effort to ease samurai indebtedness, then-regent Tanuma Okitsugu had imposed upon the merchants a silver coin (the *nanryō nishugin*)—its value notoriously set at one eighth a gold piece. Although this coin first entered into circulation in the preceding decade, in 1772, the protests against its implementation, beginning in Kyoto and Osaka but then spreading to Edo, continued through the 1780s. Just as the fictional Tamura compels that reluctant saleswoman, the Goddess of Mercy, to repossess her arms and let him have them for a pittance, so too did the real-life shogunal advisor Tanuma impose currency devaluations upon a peeved merchant class. More ominous, though, is the inconclusive-

ness of Zenkō's story. The outcome of Tamura's mission to quell the demonic rebellion is left unresolved, as though to ponder, "What sort of trouble will Tanuma encounter when trying to squelch peasant uprisings with rented hands?"

Another piece making use of allegory, though minus the close resemblance in names, is Kyōden's *Tale of the Two Tambours* (*Jidai sewa nichō tsuzumi*, 1788).[57] On the surface, this story is a whimsical updating of an historical confrontation between Taira no Masakado (d. 940) who, boldly declaring himself "Taira New Emperor" (*Heishin'ō*), led a revolt against the throne, and Fujiwara no Hidesato, the man whom the throne appointed to lead the retaliatory expedition.[58] The whimsicality is unmistakable—their duel takes the form of a radish-slicing showdown. Playing off the saying that Masakado had seven lives (his own plus half a dozen more), Kyōden gives Masakado six extra kitchen knives—"shadow chefs" (really body doubles) who lend their services "invisibly" behind him (**Figure 4.15**). But victory is Hidesato's,

Fig. 4.15 The ridiculous radish-slicing showdown. Hidesato, wielding a Super Eight Slice-O-Matic, defeats Masakado and his six shadow chefs. From *Tale of the Two Tambours* (*Jidai sewa nichō tsuzumi*, 1788), a *kibyōshi* written by Santō Kyōden and illustrated by Kitagawa Yukimaro. Courtesy of Tokyo Metropolitan Central Library, Kaga Collection.

57. Illustrated by Kitagawa Yukimaro. The "two tambours" of the title referred to the big and little drums of the pit orchestra of the popular stage. As a contemporary slang term, however, it referred disparagingly to Tanuma Okitsugu and his father. For an annotated version, see Koike, *Edo no gesaku ehon 6*, pp. 103–128.

58. These events are detailed in *Account of Masakado* (*Shōmonki*, ca. 940). For a translation, see Rabinovitch, *Shōmonki*.

for he calmly whips out a "Super Eight Slice-O-Matic" (*Hayawaza hachi-nin-mae*), thereby gaining the decisive edge.[59] Readers at the time would probably have been expected to connect this fanciful fight with the real-life political rivalry between Tanuma Okitsugu and his adversary, Sano Masakoto. The piece was so successful that it was republished even immediately after the Kansei Reforms were in full swing, when it was probably not safe to do so. (Then again, Matsudaira Sadanobu was no arch supporter of Tanuma Okitsugu.)

Sometimes the satire in these pieces is couched even more obscurely, in asides and other seemingly minor moments *vis-à-vis* the main "plot." One example is to be found in an offhanded remark in Kyōden's *Swingers* (1788). A huntsman and his wife, after having given birth to a two-headed child, wonder out loud how they will be able to feed the extra mouth with rice prices being so exorbitant. Had *Swingers* been published in any other decade, this remark would have to be read as a throwaway gag, a rather silly twist on the old cliché about country folk having too many children to support in light of the scarcity of food even out in the hinterlands. However, the timing of *Swingers*—published in the immediate wake of the two great famines—would have made this remark a thinly disguised firecracker of an attack on the administration's inability to prevent the birth of freaks or to provide food for its citizens.

Reductio Ad Absurdum Redux

The *least* obscure means by which the protest pieces couched their political satire, however, was undoubtedly *reductio ad absurdum*. This was a relatively bold satirical technique, employing inversion and exaggeration, which took some tenet of thought or argument to its logical extreme in order to reduce it to absurdity. Although this technique of skewing to skewer was present even in the early *kibyōshi*, as we have briefly seen in the case of Harumachi's *Gratuitous Account*, it became a key feature of the protest pieces.[60] A well-known Western example of this technique can be found in *A Modest Proposal*, in which Jonathan Swift rhetorically calls for cannibalism of the young. Many protest *kibyōshi* mobilize *reductio ad absurdum* (though the term was never articulated in precisely the same way in Edo-period Japanese) in attacking Neo-Confucian ideology in this sort of modest fashion. This may seem like an indirect or roundabout way of satirizing the sho-gunate, but to the extent that Neo-Confucianism underwrote the class sys-

---

59. A pure concoction on Kyōden's part. "Quick action" (*hayawaza*) was long associated with nimbleness in hand-to-hand combat, and valorized in war tales such as *Account of Masakado*, the very one describing Masakado's uprising. "Servings for eight" (*hachinin-mae*) puns on "eight-man act" (*hachinin-gei*), a street spectacle in which a solo performer single-handedly plays innumerable parts, not unlike a one-man band.

60. I am indebted to the discussion of "exaggeration and inversion" in the *kibyōshi* in Sitkin, "Upside-Down Topos."

tem upon which Tokugawa society itself was based, it was perilous enough a proxy.

On the other hand, inasmuch as authors were conveying something of the teachings of Neo-Confucianism, they could profess to extol the proper ideology, as opposed to any number of banned heterodoxies. After all, how could one be accused of contesting Neo-Confucian precepts by seemingly espousing them? This move allowed authors to identify the target of their satire while claiming the barest sanctuary under the banner of the very Neo-Confucian moralism that they sought to lampoon. It may also have afforded them a feeling of provisional security in broaching otherwise taboo subjects on the preposterously thin pretext of moral edification—though the real intent was, of course, to mock the underlying morals. These works therefore cannot be described as "didactic" or "moralistic," at least not in the usual, Neo-Confucian sense. Whatever thin veneer of Neo-Confucian didacticism these works possess turns out to be patently ridiculous.

The standard comic premise of these works can be described as the literalization or realization of some Neo-Confucian precept. One day everyone in Japan wakes up, lo and behold, the model citizen, the true believer, more Confucian than Confucius himself. Individuals miraculously abide by ethical considerations. Society actually runs according to moral principles. This premise, in light of the Tokugawa shogunate's incessant exhortations during the period, may itself have been read as satirical, in that it pokes fun at the very notion that doctrine can chisel human nature. This was the author thumbing his nose at Neo-Confucian finger-wagging. Be that as it may, these works took some Neo-Confucian vision of virtuous behavior and pushed it to its logical extreme in order to suggest how ridiculous that virtue actually is to begin with. Those protest pieces employing *reductio ad absurdum* this way, in other words, tend to ridicule the Neo-Confucian vision of a perfect society. Utopia is rendered as a darkly comic Dystopia.

One of the early major *kibyōshi* in this mode was Nanpo's *Absent White Lies* (*Teren itsuwari nashi*, 1786).[61] In taking aim at the virtue of truthfulness, a central concept in Neo-Confucianism, Nanpo shows how dysfunctionally society would run if this virtue were realized, which is to say put into universal practice. As the title suggests, one day people become utterly incapable of uttering anything but the total, unadulterated, literal truth—no matter how self-defeating or impolite the effect (a little like Jim Carrey's character in the movie *Liar Liar*—a lawyer who becomes magically dispossessed of the ability to prevaricate, much to his chagrin). Naturally, along with mendacity, there is no longer any use for the social lubricants previously necessary in keeping society running smoothly—seasonal greetings, conventional pleasantries, basic niceties, even artistic and dramatic contrivances.

---

61. For a transliterated version of Nanpo's *kibyōshi*, see Wada, *Shoku Sanjin kibyōshi shū*, pp. 112–143 and 146–156.

Fig. 4.16 A two-man stage horse, which an actor mounts with the assistance of a stagehand. From *Illustrated Encyclopedia of the Theater* (*Shibai kinmōzui*, 1803), a funnybook written by Shikitei Sanba and illustrated by Utagawa Toyokuni. Courtesy of Hōkoku bunko.

So, for instance, since stage props depend upon the sort of deception that is illusionism, a kabuki troupe dispenses with its usual stage horse manned by two assistants (**Figure 4.16**).[62] In the stage steed's stead, Nanpo's troupe employs an *actual* horse, the result being unscripted pandemonium (**Figure 4.17**). And rather than using the traditional potted pines as New Year's decorations, the suddenly unscrupulously honest denizens of Edo use *real* trees, turning their fair city into an overgrown forest (if not an urban jungle)—an ironic comment, no doubt, on Edo's lumber shortages.

Some protest *kibyōshi* reduce Neo-Confucian morality to absurdity in a more roundabout fashion. One group of works inverts the basic fact of life in an early capitalistic, urban society—that spending money comes all too easily. Although there are numerous rags-to-riches tales in the *kibyōshi* and in earlier genres (as with the companion booklet), *these* stories describe people who yearn for riches-to-rags. On the surface, this inversion almost seems to champion the Neo-Confucian condemnation of greed as unraveling the social fabric. On a deeper level, though, in light of the fact that the government sought to deal with its fiscal crises largely by trying to legislate extravagance out of existence with a string of sumptuary edicts, these pieces can only spoof Neo-Confucian values. One of the chief targets of the edicts was the philandering playboy whose profligacy in the pleasure quarters depleted the family fortune. This had certainly long been a favorite

---

62. For a color facsimile reprint and discussion of *Illustrated Encyclopedia of the Theater* (*Shibai kinmōzui*, 1803), a funnybook written by Sanba and illustrated by Utagawa Toyokuni, see Kokuritsu Gekijō, *Shibai kinmōzui*.

topic of the popular stage, since it allowed playwrights to pit the playboy's social obligations to his wife and parents against his personal love for a courtesan or geisha. Such behavior was condemned on the Confucian grounds that such a man was not fulfilling his proper familial responsibilities—he was either a bad husband or an unfilial son.[63] In the riches-to-rags version, however, the filial son tries to get rid of his riches to no avail.

One of the most commercially successful works in this mode was Kyōden's *One Spring Night in Edo, One Thousand Gold Pieces* (*Edo no haru ichiya senryō*, 1786).[64] The story describes the predicament of a rich merchant named Mochimaruya Chōjaemon—"Hangsontoit Everlastingly"—who must decide to whom he should bequeath his vast fortune. Since tycoons are known to spend, Everlastingly reasons, how better to determine who should get his life's savings than by holding a spending contest? After all, what good is money if it cannot be conspicuously squandered! He gives each member of his household, from the lowest servant to his own son, a

Fig. 4.17 A real horse wreaking havoc on stage, as theatergoers run for their lives. From *Absent White Lies* (*Teren itsuwari nashi*, 1786), a *kibyōshi* written by Ōta Nanpo and illustrated by Kitao Masayoshi. Courtesy of Tokyo Metropolitan Central Library, Special Acquisitions Collection.

---

63. It is a telling rebuke of Neo-Confucianism that for many lovers, the only way out of their Confucian dilemma of personal feelings versus social obligations was a double suicide, conducted in keeping with a belief in rebirth in Nirvana according to the competing ideological system of Buddhism.

64. For an annotated edition, see Mizuno, *Santō Kyōden no kibyōshi*, pp. 99–122.

tidy sum of gold ingots (*ryō*), which they are to deplete within one night during the New Year's celebrations (hence the "spring" of the title). The contestants fail spectacularly to droll effect, each for her or his own particular reason. The wife gets carried away shopping and loses track of time (a stereotype perpetuated in *Familiar Bestsellers*). Another character brings on a burglary, but when the burglar is apprehended and made to return the loot, it includes the original sum—and then some.

Other pieces in this vein similarly bestow upon their characters more funds than they know what to do with. Tōrai Sanna's profitable and palindromatically titled *Chop Not the Roots of the Money Tree* (*Kiruna no ne kara kane no naruki*, 1785) begins by inverting the old truism that poverty is an affliction. The wealthy merchant Manman *sensei*—"Master Fullyloaded" (a takeoff on Kinkin *sensei*, Master Flashgold)—reasons that since it is *wealth* that afflicts him (*motta ga yamai ari*), he needs to get rid of his in order to find respite, even if for only a few days. Of course, the harder Manman tries to disburden himself of his riches the more riches he ends up burdened with (**Figure 4.18**).

Along the same lines, Kyōden's *Modish Pattern of a Confucian Stripe* (*Kōshijima toki ni aizome*, 1789), presents a Japan whose now-virtuous citizenry rejects avariciousness to the extent of aspiring to poverty: customers haggle with merchants to get the shoddiest goods at the steepest prices; farmers plea with government bureaucrats to raise taxes prohibitively; the proprietor of a benevolent noodle restaurant dispatches his henchmen to chase down patrons who eat and run having paid in full; "putpockets" slip their own purses into the sleeves of unwary passersby; and highway bandits strip *themselves* naked, forcing their clothes, longswords, and moneybags on hapless travelers (**Figure 4.19**). By the final scene, several of the characters are in over their heads in an avalanche of gold coins, much to their consternation.[65]

The success of works published during the mid-1780s that couched their satire of governmental policies through some kind of allegorical structure, as in Zenkō's *Thousand-Armed Goddess*, or that satirized Neo-Confucian principles by reducing them to absurdities, like Nanpo's *Absent White Lies*, set a precedent for their ability to excite readers without inciting censors. Most of the major protest pieces appeared during the last two years of the 1780s, right before Matsudaira Sadanobu began cracking down on authors as part of the Kansei Reforms. Among the most eminent of these pieces (in addition to some of those mentioned above) are Kisanji's *Twin Arts Threshing Device* (*Bunbu nidō mangokudōshi*, 1788), Ran Tokusai's *Junior Turtle Emerges!* (*Kamenoko ga deta yo*, 1788), Kyōden's *Tale of the Two Tambours* (*Jidai sewa nichō tsuzumi*, 1788) and his *Probing the Human Cavities of Mt. Fuji* (*Fuji no hitoana*

---

65. For an annotated version, see Koike, *Edo no gesaku ehon 6*, pp. 127–164. My thanks to Kristin Williams for the coinage "putpockets."

Fig. 4.18 Cases of ten thousand gold ingots crowd out Manman and wife. From *Chop Not the Roots of the Money Tree* (*Kiruna no ne kara kane no naruki*, 1785), a *kibyōshi* written by Tōrai Sanna and illustrated by Kitagawa Chiyojo. Courtesy of Tokyo Metropolitan Central Library, Special Acquisitions Collection.

kenbutsu, 1788), as well as Harumachi's best-selling *Twin Arts, Parroted* (*Ōmugaeshi bunbu futamichi*, 1789).[66]

Several of these major works—which are among the most virulent, or at least the most transparent, of all the protest pieces—ridiculed Matsudaira Sadanobu's sloganeering campaign to encourage samurai to regard the literary (*bun*) and martial (*bu*) arts as two sides of the same cultured coin. This concept had originally emerged centuries earlier, in classics such as *The Miscellany of Ten Maxims* and *The Tale of the Heike*. It had been revived, however,

---

66. Many of these pieces are included in Koike, *Edo no gesaku ehon 3*. Some of the works by Kyōden can be found in Mizuno, *SKZ*. Some other titles that are frequently mentioned in this connection: Harumachi, *Yorokonbu hiiki no ezōshi* (1788); Tōrai Sanna, *Tenka ichimen kagami no umebachi* (1789); Ishibe Kinkō, *Kokubyaku mizukagami* (1789); Waka Rinsen, *Yo no naka shōchi Shigetada* (1789); and Kyōden, *Kiji mo naka zuwa* (1789).

Fig. 4.19 Having tied up and forced his own clothes, longswords, and moneybag on a hapless traveler, a highway bandit flees in nothing but a loincloth—and a huff. From *Modish Pattern of a Confucian Stripe* (*Kōshijima toki ni aizome,* 1789), a *kibyōshi* written and illustrated by Santō Kyōden. Courtesy of Tokyo Metropolitan Central Library, Kaga Collection.

during the early Edo period in the warrior code of 1615 (*Buke shōhatto*). And one of the most popular children's primers of the early seventeenth century, which was based on the testament of the warrior Imagawa Ryōshun (1325–1420), opens with the grand pronouncement, "He who knows not the literary arts shall prevail not in the martial arts."[67] By the mid-eighteenth century, then, the "Twin Arts!" (*bunbu nidō*) motto must have sounded as platitudinous to the urbane population of Edo as Nancy Reagan's "Just say 'No'!" must have seemed to inner-city drug addicts.

There is no evidence that samurai addicted to *haikai* gave it up *en masse* merely because Sadanobu urged them to return to classic versifying. Sadanobu himself may have privately poked fun at the Twin Arts ideal in his putatively penned *The Seigneurial Type* (*Daimyō katagi,* ca. 1784) prior to launching his public campaign. The most celebrated articulation of just how vacuous the Twin Arts phrase sounded, though, came in the form not of a *kibyōshi* but of a madcap poem attributed to Shoku Sanjin (a.k.a. Nanpo). Many of the protest pieces that lampooned the Twin Arts derive their inspiration directly from this *kyōka*. Like the best of madcap poems, Nanpo's suffers no shortage of wordplay.[68] The pun with the most bite, however,

---

67. For an English translation, see Steenstrup, "The Imagawa Letter."

68. The phrase *yo no naka ni* can mean "in the middle of the night" as well as "in all the world"; *ka hodo* means "like a mosquito" as well as "as much as this."

circles around the word *bunbu*—not only the government's catchword for the promotion of literary and marital arts, but the onomatopoetic drone of a mosquito, which was, after all, a standard metaphor for something fatuous as well as aggravating:

Yo no naka ni	Nothing in the world
Ka hodo urusaki	Bugs in the quiet of night
Mono wa nashi	So much as that buzz-buzzing
Bunbu to iute	About the so-called "Twin Arts"
Yoru mo nerarezu	You can hardly get to sleep!

It can only be sheer coincidence that in a later age Ambrose Bierce, in his *Devil's Dictionary,* puckishly explains the word "politics" as deriving from "poly," meaning "many," and "tics," meaning "blood-sucking creatures." Yet Nanpo's squib is sharper still by virtue of fact that the very form of the madcap verse parodies the classic verse that the Twin Arts policy was exalting. Had Nanpo expressed his parody in a madcap Chinese verse, say, or even in a comic haiku (the form of which parodies the *hokku* that the government wanted to discourage), it would not have carried quite the same sting.

Kisanji took up the *bunbu* theme in his *Twin Arts Threshing Device.*[69] Set during the Kamakura period, the shogun Minamoto Yoritomo and his chief general Hatakegawa Shigetada—who clearly represent Tokugawa Ienari and his Chief Councilor Matsudaira Sadanobu—decide to sort out samurai into those disposed toward the literary arts, those disposed toward the martial arts, and those who are disposable on account of being useless good-for-nothings. Exploiting the "human caverns" at the base of Mt. Fuji as a kind of makeshift threshing machine, to separate figuratively the wheat from the chaff, Shigetada has the samurai choose their own caves, unaware that their choices will determine their fates. Kisanji, on the other hand, was well aware of the apparent rise of an educated merchant culture and the demise of samurai, as evidenced by massive samurai debt to moneylenders: "My only concern," Yoritomo tells Shigetada, "is that in a peaceful realm one day, real warriors will be overwhelmed by literary types!" Kyōden, it should be noted, also wrote of the human caverns in his protest piece *Probing the Human Cavities of Mt. Fuji* (*Fuji no hitoana kenbutsu,* 1788). Likewise, Harumachi followed suit with *The Twin Arts, Parroted* (*Ōmugaeshi bunbu no futamichi,* 1789, illustrated by Kitao Masayoshi), in which he likened Matsudaira Sadanobu's hardheaded catchwords to a parrot's empty-headed squawking.[70]

Although Sadanobu had already begun cracking down on some of the major authors of the *kibyōshi,* madcap verse, and other forms of playful literature, the last major batch of protest pieces was published as late as 1790.

---

69. For an annotated edition, see Koike, *Edo no gesaku ehon 3,* pp. 45–80. For more on this piece, utopias, dystopias, and satire, see Burton, "In a Perfect World."

70. For more on this, see Minami, *Edo no fūshiga.* For an annotated edition of the *kibyōshi,* see Koike, *Edo no gesaku ehon 3,* pp. 107–142.

This date is worth mentioning, since it is sometimes assumed that political satire disappeared from the *kibyōshi* completely at the beginning of the Kansei era in 1789, or with the first round of the purges associated with the Reforms in 1788, or even when Sadanobu took office in 1787. However, it was in 1790 that the portion of the Reforms that specifically legislated against genres of playful literature such as the *kibyōshi* was issued. Perhaps this is why Kyōden's *Fast-Dyeing Mind Study* (*Shingaku hayasomegusa*, 1790) has been described as having been written for "didactic" purposes, as though Kyōden had finally turned away from satire for good?[71] He had not. For one thing, Kyōden's piece treats its subject lightly. This is Mind Study (*Shingaku*), a syncretic doctrine that swirled together Confucian, Shinto, and Buddhist ideas in a kind of pragmatic hodgepodge. At the very least, Kyōden dumbs down some tenets of Mind Study in an attempt to popularize it—the analogue of *Derrida for Dummies*.

More to the point, that same year Kyōden published other protest pieces, one of which is *Buffing Up Aoto's Loose Coins* (*Tama migaku Aoto ga zeni*, 1790).[72] Although this work does not scoff at the Twin Arts per se, it nonetheless is a classic example of a *reductio ad absurdum* spoof of another Neo-Confucian precept dear to Sadanobu, that of usefulness.[73] The story is set in the Kamakura period, during the reign of the regent Hōjō Tokiyori (1227–1263) and his legendary chief advisor Aoto (Aotozaemon no Fujitsuna)—virtually undisguised stand-ins for the Edo-period shogun and his Chief Councilor. Under Tokiyori's supreme leadership, everyone in the land miraculously becomes socially useful. So that the suddenly diligent populace—who now toil 'round the clock—never has to spend the unnecessary few moments away from their work stations venturing to the outhouse, artisans convert production from flowerpots to chamberpots. "The only useless things left over," the narration remarks sardonically, "were belly buttons and spare change for the dead." Even kabuki actors and courtesans, of all people, comply with the Confucian classics. However, with these various performers applying themselves to utilitarian purpose, nobody is left over to provide entertainment—nobody, that is, except for people with disabilities.

The story goes on to describe, in politically incorrect fashion and language, how various handicapped folk struggle to fill roles for which they are obviously not fit. In producing kabuki plays, for instance, a stutterer halt-

---

71. "The result of the *bakufu*'s pressure was that after 1790 the nature and content of the *kibyōshi* quickly changed," writes Shirane. "The obvious political and social satire of the earlier works was replaced with a thick layer of ethical didacticism, as evidenced in Santō Kyōden's *Fast-Dyeing Mind Study*." In Shirane, *EMJL*, p. 711.

72. Another piece is *Enma's Crystal Mirror* (*Kagami no jōhari*, 1790), which spoofs the policies of Matsudaira Sadanobu in no uncertain terms. For an annotated version, see Koike, *Edo no gesaku ehon 3*, pp. 213–248.

73. Illustrated by Kitagawa Utamaro. For an annotated version, see Mizuno, *SNKBT 85*, pp. 49–72. For a précis and brief discussion, see Mori, *Zoku kibyōshi kaidai*, pp. 215–220.

ingly delivers the opening monologue, a paralyzed man desperately tries to draw open the stage curtain, and deaf and mute actors have an insufferable time cuing each other. In another segment, a blind masseur and a syphilitic prostitute have a go at grappling in the sumo ring (**Figure 4.20**). Others making brief appearances in the story are a tone-deaf street singer (*mugei no goze*), an armless wonder (*tenbō*), a cripple (*izari*), a dwarf (*issun bōshi*), a hunchback (*semushi*), a one-eyed fellow (*ganchi*), and a macrocephalic "giant head" (*ōatama*).

Fig. 4.20 Sumo match between a blind masseur and a syphilitic prostitute. From the politically incorrect *Buffing Up Aoto's Loose Coins (Tama migaku Aoto ga zeni,* 1790), a *kibyōshi* written by Santō Kyōden and illustrated by Kitagawa Utamaro. Courtesy of the National Diet Library.

If any *kibyōshi* is likely to offend, it is this one. Indeed, it must be acknowledged that Kyōden's piece (like his *Swingers*) participates in the long and repugnant tradition in Japan—and elsewhere—of exploiting people with some kind of physical disability or deformity in the name of humor. In *The Tale of Genji*, Genji and his chum Tō-no-Chūjō make sport of a lady with a bulbous red proboscis. Similarly, a long-nosed priest gets scoffed at in *A Collection of Gleanings from Uji*. And there are any number of playlets within the *kyōgen* repertoire poking fun at the blind (*zatō*). Kyōden undeniably stoops to such lows for the sake of cheap laughs.

On the other hand, Kyōden may have had an ulterior motive in mind. There were certainly enough voices raised against such mockery of someone for something beyond his control, so Kyōden would have been aware that such stories were in terribly bad taste. Mind Study thinker Teshima Toan (1718–1786), with whose works Kyōden was familiar, says as much in his influential primer *Early Lessons* (*Zenkun*, 1773), urging his young readers against making fun of the handicapped.[74] It is possible that Kyōden deliberately risked public opprobrium for humiliating his disabled characters, then, for the sake of indirectly protesting an ideological system that seemed capable of putting even its least able members to hard labor. In this way, Kyōden mobilizes the supposedly socially useless to the constructive use of political satire.

From the preceding discussion of the protest pieces, a few overarching points can be made. First, it should be clear that these pieces indeed are politically satirical. Some of them are even quite focused in their satire, targeting specific tenets of the Kansei Reforms themselves, rather than relying strictly on innuendo. However, this satire was never too vitriolic. Nor could it be, for that matter. It was, to borrow Roger Sabin's memorable phrase about some Western comicbooks, "satirical to a point, but no further."[75] It is true that while these *kibyōshi* seem to delight in pointing out inconsistencies (*ana o ugachi*) in the ideological constructs of Neo-Confucianism, they do not offer up any programmatic solutions. In this sense, the *kibyōshi* resembled the proponents of National Learning who "rejected the Chinese tradition of Confucian formalism, but [who] had little to substitute for it except an unstructured naturalism and an intuitive appreciation."[76] Indeed, the *reductio ad absurdum* of the *kibyōshi* is essentially a contrarian tactic, working within existing social binaries, rather than something intellectually revolutionary or radically innovative—as in dispensing with those binaries and implementing out-of-the-blue new cognitive categories. The protest pieces *merely* turn the world upside down. Rags-to-riches becomes riches-to-rags, the Twin Arts metamorphose into a mosquito, and Utopia gives way to Dystopia. To the government, though, this sort of symbolic inversion— even if failing to posit a different world turned right-side up according to "heterodox" principles—must have seemed to contribute to the sense of its own crisis of legitimacy.

Second, the fact that the protest pieces offer no concrete solutions should not be mistaken as a lack of literary skillfulness. Their allegorical techniques can be quite sophisticated—sophisticated enough, at least, to have stumped some modern readers. In the various précis and annotated notes to Zenkō's *Thousand-Armed Goddess*, for instance, none of the commentators has suggested that Tamura is a stand-in for Tanuma. And while these pieces may indeed be entertaining, surely that does not diminish the power or quality of

---

74. Mentioned in Sawada, *Confucian Values and Popular Zen*, p. 112.
75. Sabin, *Comics, Comix and Graphic Novels*, p. 19.
76. Jansen, *Japan & Its World*, p. 28.

their satire. True, binary thinking is not necessarily the most imaginative form of political rebellion. Yet it supplies powerful enough symbolic resistance, and in An'ei-Tenmei Edo, symbols mattered. Moreover, in a literary tradition already a thousand years old, the use of satire, parody, and nonsense in this way may itself be read as groping for something new. Even though the protest pieces do not propose concrete original answers to societal woes, then, tearing down the structure of reverence for the past alone is an immense first stride. "Don't destroy the idols in anger," the Marquis de Sade shrewdly counseled, "break them up in play."[77]

It follows that, third, the protest *kibyōshi* may be one of the earliest examples in Japanese literary history of a group of works collectively engaging in political satire to dramatic effect. Satirical works appear here and there over the preceding millennium, to be sure. Prior to the Edo period, works might poke fun at the aristocracy as a class, or even boldly take aim at one of its figures in particular. Among the suitors for the Shining Princess's hand in the *Tale of the Bamboo Cutter* (*Taketori monogatari*, ca. late ninth or early tenth century), for instance, was a certain Prince Kuramochi, who is depicted rather unflatteringly. Since Kuramochi was a real-life descendent of Fujiwara no Yoshifusa (804–872), one of the powerful aristocratic figures of the late ninth century, this part of the story might have been read at the time as political satire. Nevertheless, such works were, owing to the relatively puny reach of hand-written manuscripts, of limited circulation and, therefore, social impact.

Although it is possible that many pre-Edo-period satires were published that have since been lost to posterity for one reason or another, it certainly appears that, with the mass printing of commercial literature, satire began to thrive in the Edo period from the seventeenth century onward even in spite of the tremendous personal risk to those involved in producing it. During the Genroku cultural efflorescence, works in the genres of the syllabary booklet, the novella of the Floating World, and the character sketch (*katagimono*) satirized a number of topics and people. Chikamatsu's puppet play *The Sagami Lay Monk and the Thousand Dogs* (*Sagami nyūdō senbiki no inu*, first performed in 1714) went so far as to spoof the by-then-dead shogun Tokugawa Tsunayoshi (1646–1709) and his infamous law aimed at preventing cruelty to animals—which ironically prescribed that offenders be meted out cruel and unusual punishment.[78] Several decades later, in the middle of the eighteenth century, Andō Shōeki (1703–1762) published his remarkable *Tale of the World of Law* (*Hōsei monogatari*, 1755), a political fable couched thinly in anthropomorphic terms.[79] And many of Gennai's mock-sermon books contain undeniably sardonic elements.

---

77. Quoted in Gorer, *The Life and Ideas of the Marquis de Sade*, p. 153.
78. See Shively, "Chikamatsu's Satire on The Dog Shogun."
79. See Yasunaga, *Ando Shoeki*.

However satirical such works might have been, though, they represent isolated phenomena. The protest pieces, by contrast, represent a unified corpus, collectively engaging in political satire leveled at a number of policies and politicians who were alive and, in many cases, still active in office. Since these works were mass produced, this satire must have reached a much broader readership than earlier individual efforts. In this sense, the protest pieces represent something new in the history of Japanese satire. Furthermore, they embody one of the defining features of An'ei-Tenmei culture: the hyper-skepticism of an age that was marked by a seemingly schizophrenic disconnect between oppressive Neo-Confucian rhetoric on the one hand and governmental corruption, hypocrisy, unfairness, and incompetence on the other. Although couched, the satire of these works could only have presented a bold challenge to the state-sponsored view of Reality. From this perspective, the question is not how *kibyōshi* authors were able to successfully mask their satire from the censors, but why the shogunate took so long in declaring these works unfit for publication (*zappan*)—and in penalizing the offending authors and publishers.

Post-Kansei Reforms Works, 1791–1806

The beginning of the end for the *kibyōshi* came in 1791. On this point, Uda and Koike concur. Their thinking is based largely on the observation that the last batch of protest pieces was published in 1790. Although a rare few works after that contain some minor moments of political satire, these moments are exponentially hard to pinpoint. Uda, Koike, and others have speculated that the underlying reason behind the demise of the genre was the suppression of the protest pieces. However, it seems clear that while a contributing factor, the Kansei Reforms cannot be blamed for everything. There are other factors, too, in particular internal ones that have hitherto been given short shrift. Furthermore, the very contention that the Kansei Reforms obliterated the protest pieces needs some unpacking, since the Reforms began much earlier than 1791, as far back in fact as 1788 or even 1787.[80] Thus, two related questions pose themselves: why did it take the Kansei Reforms so long to excise political satire from the *kibyōshi*, and did this excision really sound the death knell for the genre?

The apparent lag between the inauguration of the Kansei Reforms and the suppression of the protest pieces can be attributed to the fact that Sadanobu did not turn his attention in earnest to popular literature until 1789, when he began to harass some of the major authors of the *kibyōshi* and other forms of *gesaku*. And it was not until 1790 that the major portion

---

80. It should be noted that the dates of the Kansei Reforms (1787–1793) do not coincide perfectly with those of the Kansei era itself (1789–1800/1801). As with so many other aspects of the Edo period, this was a retrospective term.

of the reforms regulating the publication of popular literature was issued. Thus, the first crop of *kibyōshi* to be affected was those that were scheduled to be published at the beginning of 1791, which helps explain why some straggling elements of political satire can be found that year, though on a smaller scale than before. Kyōden himself was punished sternly in 1791, probably for his various protest pieces, though the official pretext had nothing to do with these *kibyōshi* per se.

Sadanobu waited until 1789 to crack down on popular literature because when he took office a couple of years earlier, he had bigger fish to fry, namely, purging the government of the remnants of the Tanuma regime. Accordingly, historians customarily divide the Kansei Reforms into two major phases. The first consisted of these purges, but also the implementation of a number of other policies, particularly financial measures such as relieving the samurai of their debts to money-lending merchants. There was also the exhortation that samurai should take up the Twin Arts by devoting themselves to letters as well as to arms. This was a double-edged sword, however, drawn not just to dissuade samurai from engaging in the popular arts such as *haikai* composition (instead of classic versifying), but also to encourage them to sharpen their skills in swordsmanship itself, which had, during the Tokugawa Peace, grown relatively rusty. Additionally, the first set of reforms included sumptuary regulations, though these amounted to little more than the usual nostrums for the various ills that were perceived as afflicting the body politic. Yet there were some new targets—in 1789, Sadanobu even outlawed the silver pipe, since it was a conspicuous sign of extravagance (as we will see in Kyōden's *Unseamly Silverpiped Swingers* of 1788).[81]

The second set of reforms began to be issued in 1790. These edicts aimed both to contain ideological dissent and, even more germanely for the *kibyōshi*, to regulate publishing stringently. The "Prohibition against Heterodoxy" (*Igaku no kin*) sought to defend the state-sponsored orthodoxy of Zhu Xi Neo-Confucianism against rival systems of thought, such as the Ancient Learning School. In this climate, any kind of satirical attack on Neo-Confucianism, even the seemingly light-hearted *reductio ad absurdum* of the *kibyōshi*, might well be labeled heterodox.

Be that as it may, it was the Kansei publishing edicts (*Ofuregaki Tenpō shūsei*) that gave Sadanobu the cudgel he needed to pulverize whichever utterance or work or genre he deemed malefic. These edicts were largely a rehashing of the Kyōhō-era publishing edicts of 1722, which commanded that: no new books were to be published without special prior permission; current events were not to be depicted in any form; gorgeous and extravagant works were to be avoided; erotica and pornography should be phased out; and all publications must clearly stipulate the names of the author, the

---

81. Mizuno, *SNKBT 85*, p. 52, n. 5.

artist, and the publisher.[82] The Kyōhō edicts also forbade works of fiction and drama from including the word *shinjū* in their titles since there had been a spate of double suicides almost immediately following performances of Chikamatsu's *Love Suicides at Sonezaki* (*Sonezaki shinjū*, first performed in 1703)—*The Great Mirror of Love Suicides* (*Shinjū ōkagami*, 1704) describes some seventeen copycat incidents—and in the ensuing years the trend showed no signs of abating.[83] People hurting themselves seems to have been less of a concern for Sadanobu.

Although the Kansei Reforms in general called for a "return to the Kyōhō Reforms," Sadanobu had his reasons for reiterating certain parts of the earlier publishing edicts, such as the bit aimed at curtailing anonymity, since unsigned works were free to criticize the government openly. In fact, there was a profusion of anonymous public graffiti during these years, most of which was openly hostile toward the government.[84] One can only imagine that such pasquinades contributed to the popular unrest of the day.

Sadanobu also included a few new twists in his publishing edicts, though. For one, all printed matter—including the *kibyōshi*—had to pass the scrutiny of a government-appointed censor. This entailed that all printblocks (*hangi*) be submitted for inspection and a corrected version (*kiyogaki*) made, if necessary, though in either case the blocks needed to be stamped "inspected" (*kiwame*). And since wholesale booksellers (*serihon'ya*) and lending libraries (*kashihon'ya*) were to be regulated, an unexamined protest piece could not be snuck into widespread circulation through these main points of entry without grave risk for the merchants. Furthermore, the *kibyōshi* itself—although referred to as a comicbook (*kusazōshi*)—was no longer permitted to touch on current political or social events at all, even if couched in the past. This was the "smoking gun," so to speak, demonstrating that the shogunate saw through the smokescreen of allegorical techniques that were the mainstay of the protest pieces. It was this clause, too, that effectively terminated the publication of the protest pieces.

Sadanobu was also determined to back up the various paper edicts with more than the ineffectual three-day bans that had, under the Tanuma regime, permitted authors a feeling of relative invulnerability. Thus was the authoritarian put back into shogunal authority. Official punishments for authors and publishers who violated any part of the publishing edicts entailed a range of humiliation and inconvenience: sequestration (*oshikome*), usually in the convenience of the offender's own home—a "convenience" for the authorities, that is, since offenders were often shackled into handcuffs or neck irons; localized banishment (*tokorobarai*), in which one was permitted

---

82. Kornicki has written about this topic extensively in both *The Book in Japan* and "*Nishiki no Ura*."

83. Fiorillo, "Tragedy and Laughter in the Floating World," p. 7.

84. See Yano, *Edo jidai rakusho ruiju*.

to remain in Edo, though restricted tantalizingly from certain sections of town—especially the Yoshiwara, other pleasure quarters, and Publisher's Row; and, perhaps most severely, exile from Edo itself (*Edo kamai*), which, for the dyed-in-the-wool sons of Edo who were the typical authors and publishers of the *kibyōshi*, might have seemed like a fate worse than death.

As for capital punishment itself, the most striking case of an Edo-period author to lose his head that comes to mind is that of public lecturer (*kōdanshi*)-cum-author Baba Bunkō (1715–1759). Although Bunkō had several run-ins with the authorities for his outspokenness, the proverbial final straw was his public oration *Raindrops in the Forest* (*Mori no shizuku*), which had criticized the daimyo Kanamori Yorikane (1713–1763) by name for mistreating the poor of his domain. Only a couple hundred people attended that particular lecture, though Bunkō had sold an abbreviated transcript of his spiel in pamphlet form, written in the cursive syllabary for a broad readership, that seems to have made its way into the book-selling circuit. With such incontrovertible written evidence of the alleged slander, the authorities could hardly ignore the matter. Bunkō was arrested, tried, and in 1759 publicly beheaded in Asakusa, where he had delivered his seditious lecture—an irony that surely was not lost upon the government.[85]

Not one *kibyōshi* author, however, seems to have been executed point blank. While this speaks to the success of the various allegorical techniques in insulating satire, these techniques ultimately did not provide complete immunity. A mere summons to appear before an official board of inquiry was enough to terrorize a few poor souls into swearing off literary insouciance—or even possibly into self-immolation. Some authors vanished from the publishing scene under unclear circumstances. By the end of 1791, virtually no major *kibyōshi* author had got by unscathed.

The first casualty was Hōseidō Kisanji, whose sarcastic *Twin Arts Threshing Device* did not exactly tickle Sadanobu. Shortly after this piece was released, in the beginning of 1789, Sadanobu apparently expressed his displeasure to Kisanji's immediate superior, the daimyo of Akita domain, who—if hearsay can be trusted—ordered Kisanji to disappear from Edo in a kind of involuntarily self-imposed exile.[86] Kisanji was never heard from again, at least not in the *kibyōshi*, or in any other work of playful literature, for that matter.

Likewise, Koikawa Harumachi, progenitor of the *kibyōshi*, ran into trouble on account of his *Twin Arts, Parroted*, which, in directly mocking Sadanobu's "parrot words" (*ōmu no kotoba*), could not have helped but rankle.[87] That summer, Harumachi was summoned to appear before Sadanobu

---

85. See Konta, *Edo no kinsho*, pp. 31–39. For more on this in English, see Farge, "Violating Censorship."

86. Although no official record of this incident is extant, Sadanobu's close attendant Mizuno Tamenaga recorded it in *Yoshino zōshi*, reprinted in Mori, *Zuihitsu hyakkaen 7*, p 357. Cited in Iwasaki, "Portrait of a Daimyo," p. 18 n. 49.

87. See Minami, *Edo no fūshiga*, pp. 69–70.

himself, though he never complied. At first he declined on medical grounds, but it is unclear if he had a preexisting condition or if the prospect of the looming inquisition incurred some kind of psychosomatic breakdown. His illness may not have been concocted, however, for Harumachi got out of having to present himself to Sadanobu by abruptly dying. Rumors flew that this ultimate escape had been self-inflicted.[88]

Even Edo's *kyōka* kingpin, Ōta Nanpo, seems to have been affected. Not long after composing his *kibyōshi Absent White Lies* and that buggy madcap poem of his, Nanpo unexpectedly gave up writing in the genres he had helped make so central to Edo popular literature. He wrote few if any *kibyōshi* after that, too. Almost nothing concrete is known about his reasons. One theory holds that a superior reproached him.[89] If true, it is not hard to imagine that none other than the Senior Councilor was the one pulling the strings (as he had probably done in the case of Kisanji). However, it is also possible, if somewhat less dramatic, that chastened by the examples of Kisanji and Harumachi, Nanpo simply took it upon himself to renounce playful literature preemptively.

The object of the most notorious rebuke in the history of eighteenth-century popular literature was undoubtedly Santō Kyōden. This is certainly true with the benefit of hindsight, since the records of the official proceedings are among the only ones involving a *kibyōshi* author that are still extant.[90] Yet it was probably also true at the time as well, for Kyōden's affair was, unlike those of the other authors, a decidedly public one. At the intense urging of his publisher, Tsutaya Jūzaburō, Kyōden in 1791 published three fashionbooks without having properly secured the official imprimaturs.[91] This was a technicality, really. A relatively minor matter of publishing protocol and by no means a grave offense. But it was one that the authorities could seize upon as a pretext in order to make an example of a leading author who had come to symbolize the genre in which the protest pieces were written. Sadanobu must have been licking his chops for this opportunity. Kyōden was hauled before the City Magistrate, forced to recant, summarily shackled, and placed under house arrest for fifty days.

Others also were implicated in the matter. Kyōden's father Denzaemon was interrogated for having supplied his son with the studio where the offending works were fabricated. Moreover, for his pivotal role, Tsutaya Jūzaburō had half his assets confiscated. This is a notable moment in Japa-

---

88. Bakin relates this story in his study of Edo-period authors, *Kinsei mono no hon Edo sakusha burui*. In Naitō and Komiyama, *Onchi Sōsho 10*, p. 17. Mizutani mentions the rumor of Harumachi's suicide in *Kusazōshi to yomihon no kenkyū*. Cited in Iwasaki, "'Portrait of a Daimyo,'" p. 18, n. 50.

89. Hamada, *Ōta Nanpo*, pp. 128–137. Cited in Iwasaki, "'Portrait of a Daimyo,'" p. 19, n. 51.

90. The classic article in English on Kyōden's brush with the authorities, which includes a translation of the official proceedings themselves, is by Kornicki, "*Nishiki no Ura*."

91. The three offending works were *Nishiki no ura*, *Shikake bunko*, and *Shōgi kinu burui*.

nese literary history, for Tsutajū was arguably the most influential publisher of popular literature and art in his day. It is no coincidence that Tsutajū issued many of the protest pieces, including Kyōden's *Probing the Human Cavities of Mt. Fuji*, Kisanji's *Twin Arts Threshing Device*, and Harumachi's *Twin Arts, Parroted*. Tsutajū's reprimand meant that the three-day ban had become a thing of the past, not just for authors of *kibyōshi* but for publishers too.

There may be more to the Kyōden-Tsutajū incident, however, than meets the eye. The record of the official proceedings also indicates that a couple of guild representatives (*gyōji*) were questioned before being banished from Edo. This seemingly insignificant detail lends credence to the notion that some publishers of illustrated popular literature and their representatives were conspiring to break off from the Publishing Association and form a splinter group of their own. If true, then it is possible that the main body of the Publishing Association deliberately did nothing to shield Kyōden from the wrath of the City Magistrate so that the renegade publisher Tsutajū could be kept in line. This would jibe with the fact that the Kansei publishing edicts *directly* mention the publishers of comicbooks (*kusazōshiya*), as opposed to those trucking in other genres. Under this reading, then, Kyōden's transgression was less being the poster child of a popular literature that had criticized state-sponsored Neo-Confucianism, let alone the trivial violation of publishing protocol, than it was working with a publisher who posed a threat to the authority of the Publishing Association—which was the shogunate's self-regulated instrument of controlling the publishing industry. In other words, Kyōden and Tsutajū seem to have been caught in the crossfire between conservative forces within the publishing world and a more progressive and increasingly profitable comicbook culture.

Class also may have played a role in Sadanobu's implementation of the Kansei publishing edicts. Of the many authors whom Sadanobu hounded, all were samurai except for Kyōden. One therefore wonders if it was the not-infrequent samurai authorship of the *kibyōshi* that the shogunate found particularly objectionable. The Twin Arts policy was, after all, aimed at turning samurai away from composing (and presumably reading) genres of playful literature. So how it must have infuriated Sadanobu to see samurai prolifically composing *kibyōshi*. It was one thing for merchants to publish works poking fun at the growing fissure between the increasingly beleaguered Neo-Confucian world order and economic reality. It was quite another thing for samurai to be doing as much.

Ironically, in light of the fact that Kyōden was punished for his protest *kibyōshi* on the pretext of his fashionbooks, he never published another fashionbook for as long as he lived, though he continued writing *kibyōshi* for another fifteen years (albeit shorn of political satire).[92] Furthermore,

---

92. Most other authors in Edo gave up writing fashionbooks after the Kansei Reforms, too.

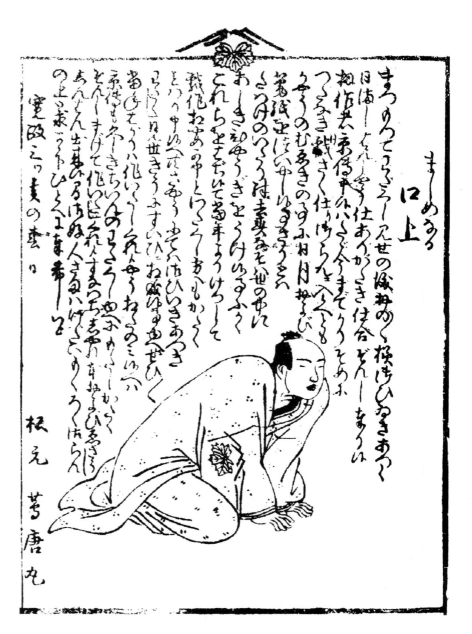

Fig. 4.21 Tsutajū (with his trademark ivy crest) kowtowing his apologies to the reader for having violated censorship regulations. From *Hako'iri musume men'ya ningyō* (1791), a *kibyōshi* written by Santō Kyōden and illustrated by Utagawa Toyokuni. Courtesy of Tokyo Metropolitan Central Library, Kaga Collection.

Kyōden managed to turn his inquisition and incarceration into an opportunity for publicity. In perhaps the only self-proclaimed "somber preface" (*majime naru kōjō*) to a *kibyōshi*, he has a fictional Tsutajū kowtowing his apologies for his role in the affair before the reading public (**Figure 4.21**).[93] By addressing the serious incident within one of his light works, Kyōden effectively passed himself off as the *enfant terrible* of Edo literature, almost

93. For more on Tsutajū's involvement in this incident, see Matsuki, *Tsutaya Jūzaburō*, pp. 94–100.

as though he were imitating one of his comic fool Enjirō's publicity stunts. When rumors began flying that Kyōden intended to give up writing playful literature completely, sales of his works soared.[94]

In this respect, Kyōden may have provided an example of someone who had not only survived Sadanobu, but who had ultimately profited from the experience. Thus, while no more protest pieces were written after 1791, some authors occasionally went too far and were reprimanded accordingly. For instance, Shikitei Sanba (1776–1822), one of Kyōden's most successful protégés and one of the great authors of post-Kansei Reforms popular fiction, was shackled for fifty days because of a *kibyōshi* he wrote. However, whereas the supposed misbehavior of Sanba's mentor can only be suspected of having degraded public morals, Sanba's *kibyōshi* directly incited physical violence (though not a popular uprising per se).

The piece in question, *Swaggering Headbands: A Chronicle of Urban Knight-Errantry in a Peaceful Realm (Kyan taiheiki mukō hachimaki,* 1799), lambasted the "petty squabbles and proud bravado" of Edo's "hotdog" fire brigades (**Figure 4.22**).[95] The members of an actual fire brigade took grave offense and—as though to prove Sanba *right*—assailed the residences of Sanba and his publisher, Nishimiya Shinroku (who had issued Kyōden's *Swingers*). To add insult to injury, Nishimiya was heavily fined for publishing the inflammatory piece. Although other writers and publishers of popular literature would continue to have their brushes with the authorities, Sanba's case represents the last time a major author was castigated specifically for a *kibyōshi*.

All told, the Kansei publishing edicts, backed up by the censure of leading authors, exerted a profound cumulative effect on the *kibyōshi* as a whole. Gone—or at least fading fast—was the playful irreverence that marks the finest *kibyōshi*. The works from 1791 on tend to lack that freewheeling spark of earlier works, even those that were not coruscating satires. Only rarely do the later pieces seem to display the imaginative crispness of bygone years.

As though in tacit acknowledgment of this tendency, many *kibyōshi* seem to have begun turning to the history of the *kibyōshi* genre itself for material. Sanba's *Spurious History of Comicbooks (Kusazōshi kojitsuke nendaiki,* 1802), to take a salient example, provides a fancifully meta-textual account of several of the great *kibyōshi*, including Kyōden's *Familiar Bestsellers*.[96] The last page of Sanba's work consists of his personal catalogue of favorite *kibyōshi* (though Sanba uses the word "bluebooks")—as in a *kibyōshi* reviewbook—arranged by author, some of which include: Harumachi's *Master Flashgold, Travelogue of Snobby Atelier,* and *Twin Arts, Parroted*; Kisanji's *Peach Boy—A*

---

94. Matsuki, *Tsutaya Jūzaburō*, p. 99.

95. This incident is described (and the title of Sanba's *kibyōshi* translated this way) in Leutner, *Shikitei Sanba*, pp. 29–30. For an annotated edition, see Koike, *Edo no gesaku ehon 4*, pp. 193–228.

96. For an annotated version, see Koike, *Edo no gesaku ehon 4*, pp. 229–266.

Fig. 4.22 Competing fire brigades, famed for their high-ladder acrobatics. The real-life members of one of these brigades were so affronted by their treatment in this story that they ransacked the homes of the author and the publisher. From *Swaggering Headbands: A Chronicle of Urban Knight-Errantry in a Peaceful Realm (Kyan taiheiki mukō hachimaki,* 1799), a *kibyōshi* written by Shikitei Sanba, illustrated by Utagawa Toyokuni, and published by Nishimiya Shinroku. Courtesy of Tokyo Metropolitan Central Library, Tokyo Collection.

Present-Day Sequel and *Twin Arts Threshing Device*; Zenkō's *The Unusual Treasure Ship* and *Thousand-Armed Goddess of Mercy, Julienned*; and Sanna's *Chop Not the Roots of the Money Tree* (**Figure 4.23**).

Kyōden published the self-reflexive *Nine Months Inside an Author's Womb, Illustrated (Sakusha tainai totsuki no zu,* 1804), which describes a desperate writer's attempt to "hatch" an idea for a new *kibyōshi* (**Figure 4.24**).[97] But he produced many other works, too, some of which make significant use of earlier *kibyōshi* as well as classics of Japanese literature. These *kibyōshi* include: *Rosei's Dream* (1791), *Monstrous Essays in Idleness (Bakemono tsurezuregusa,* 1792), *Master Flashgold's Abiding Dream (Kinkin sensei zōka no yume,* 1794), and *Some Strange Sideshow and Tales of Ise (Kowa mezurashii misemonogatari,* 1801),

---

97. Reprinted in Hirose, *Enshū kibyōshi 1,* pp. 39–74.

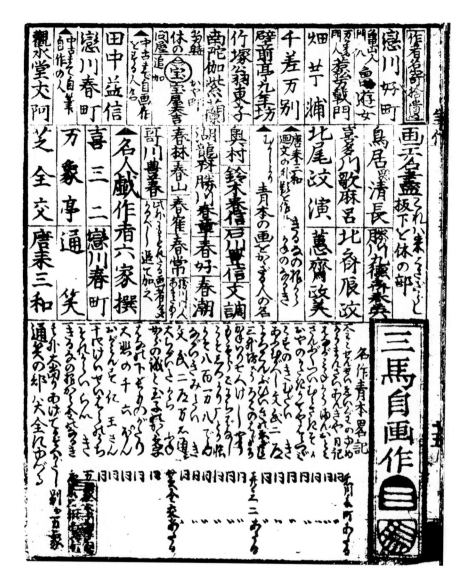

Fig. 4.23 "Abbreviated Catalogue of Bluebook Classics" (*Meisaku aohon ryakki*). From *Spurious History of Comicbooks* (*Kusazōshi kojitsuke nendaiki*, 1802), a *kibyōshi* written and illustrated by Shikitei Sanba. Reprinted in Kisho fukuseikai, *Kisho fukuseikai sōsho 1*.

among others.[98] While these works possess a definite charm, some critics and scholars have condemned the humor as comparatively stale.

Kyōden's *Some Strange Sideshow and Tales of Ise*, for instance, although having an ingenious format that played with visual-verbal puns between the main pictures and embedded corner pictures, was a rather timid send-up of the freakshow (which Kyōden had already mined in such works as *Swingers*, if not *Buffing Up Aoto's Loose Coins*).[99] For example, an advertisement

---

98. For more on *Master Flashgold's Abiding Dream* in English, see "Kinkin Sensei's Second Dream," in Akimoto, *The Twilight of Yedo*, pp. 219–231.

99. For transcribed editions of Kyōden's *kibyōshi*, see Fujisawa, *Kowa mezurashi* [sic] *mise-monogatari*, and Mizuno, *SKZ 4*, pp. 375–396.

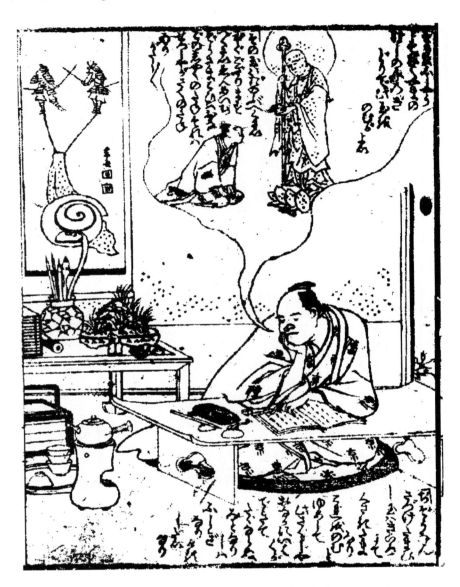

Fig. 4.24 Fictional author Kyōden trying to dream up a *kibyōshi*. From *Nine Months Inside an Author's Womb, Illustrated* (*Sakusha tainai totsuki no zu*, 1804), a *kibyōshi* written by Santō Kyōden and illustrated by Kitao Shigemasa. Courtesy of Tokyo Metropolitan Central Library, Kaga Collection.

accompanying the spectacle of the Coin Lady (*koban musume*), a woman whose face resembles an oblong gold coin (*koban*), depicts a young lady with a Japanese chessboard (*goban*) for a chest, leading one of the spectators to remark: "Now *there's* a woman who knows what it means to be well endowed!" (**Figure 4.25**).

One also sees Kyōden returning to familiar territory with *Rosei's Dream*, which nonetheless is considered to be one of the last masterpieces of the genre.[100] The story is a behind-the-scenes glimpse of Dreamland, where Dream Creatures, under the guidance of one Master Dream Spirit, pro-

---

100. For a transcribed though unannotated version, see Mizuno, *SKZ 2*, pp. 409–430.

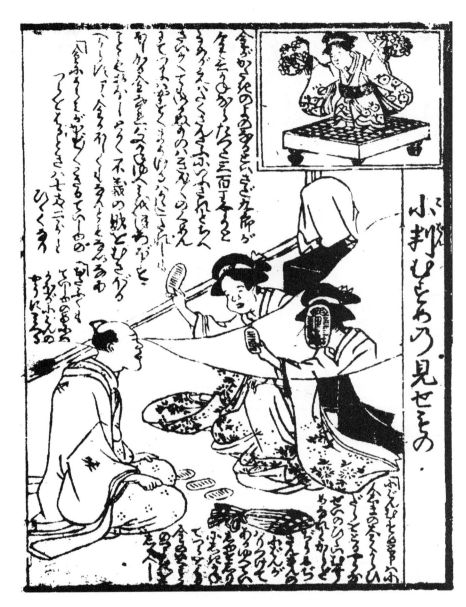

Fig. 4.25 Coin Lady (*Koban musume*) and Chessboard Lady (*Goban musume*). The spectator, whose perception is contained within a kind of thought balloon, exclaims: "Now *there's* a woman who knows what it means to be well endowed!" From *Some Strange Sideshow and Tales of Ise (Kowa mezurashii misemonogatari,* 1801), a *kibyōshi* written by Santō Kyōden and illustrated by Kitao Shigemasa. Courtesy of Tokyo Metropolitan Central Library, Kaga Collection.

duce kabuki and puppet plays that are shown to slumbering mortals on earth as dreams—mortals like Rosei in the noh play *Kantan,* Master Flash-gold in Harumachi's *kibyōshi,* and many others. Much of the interest of the piece for contemporary readers must have resided chiefly in how Kyōden provides fanciful creation stories (*kojitsuke*) of well-known dreams from literature, history, and drama. In this sense, his *kibyōshi* is a kind of prequel to many popular *kibyōshi*-related tales.

However, *Rosei's Dream* is also compelling because Kyōden wrote it in 1790 (and published it the following year), after Kisanji, Nanpo, and Haru-machi had been hounded out of Edo, out of *kyōka,* and out of existence,

Fig. 4.26 A mythological dream-devouring beast (*baku*) about to execute a Dream Creature for having produced unauthorized wet dreams. From *Rosei's Dream—The Night Before* (*Rosei ga yume sono zenjitsu*, 1791), a *kibyōshi* written by Santō Kyōden and presumably illustrated by Kitao Shigemasa. Courtesy of Tokyo Metropolitan Central Library, Kaga Collection.

respectively, but *before* Kyōden himself had been prosecuted for his fashionbooks. Thus, while Kyōden avoids the relatively overt political satire of the *reductio ad absurdum* pieces, he does not shrink from political satire altogether. His criticism is couched deep in the recesses of this work, in nooks and crannies and asides barely noticeable in the otherwise chaotic intermingling of visual-verbal play and textual associations. For instance, there is an offhanded remark implying that dreams—contrary to the protestations of Neo-Confucian moralists—are quite natural, as if to belittle any ideology maintaining otherwise. Kyōden also mocks the shogunate's monetary policies, implicitly comparing the silver coin foisted upon merchants to bags of sand used to immobilize prisoners as they get executed (**Figure 4.26**).

Demise, 1806–?

The end of the end for the *kibyōshi*, by most accounts, came in 1806, when Kyōden published his last work in the genre. Uda and Koike terminate their periodizations that year, as does Tanahashi in *Kibyōshi Overview*. Accordingly, it can be said that the *kibyōshi* was a relatively short-lived phenomenon, lasting little more than three decades in a literary tradition that had already spanned a millennium. For a brief, shining moment, during the last quarter of the eighteenth and the first decade of the nineteenth century, the *kibyōshi* was *the* genre of playful literature, arguably rivaling all others in terms of popularity, output, and influence. It was seemingly the most widely read genre up to that point in time in Edo and perhaps even in Japan. Then suddenly, almost overnight, the genre lost its cachet and, shortly thereafter, was gone forever.

Just why this should be the case—not to mention how long "shortly" was—is something of a mystery. Premodern Japanese literature tends to be highly conservative; hardly anything is allowed to turn fallow, let alone be forsaken. It is less the case that new genres simply appear out of nowhere than that they grow incrementally out of old ones that somehow persist. In this tradition, the notion of sudden death is conspicuous—and dubious.

At the risk of unfairly flattening out the conventional wisdom, it runs something like this. The *kibyōshi* disappeared primarily because the Kansei Reforms effectively outlawed the protest pieces, crushed several leading authors, and destroyed the *joie de vivre* of the Floating World way of life. People sobered up. The party was over. Readers as well as writers turned *en masse* from frivolous writings to more "serious" literary pursuits, such as the vendetta stories (*katakiuchimono*), sometimes also referred to as revenge pieces (*adauchimono*). These often contain scenes of extreme violence that presage certain modern *manga* in their goriness. Although the *kibyōshi* was turning more towards such stories, these were featured heavily in the developing "combined sheaf" or multivolume comicbook (*gōkan*) (**Figure 4.27**).[101]

Recent technological advances in mass printing and loose binding allowed the multivolume to be issued in a more extended format than its comicbook predecessors, including the *kibyōshi*. The enhanced page length, by providing more room for the kinds of twists and turns and vicissitudes of plot that suited the vendetta story, effectively widened narrative possibilities. The *kibyōshi* tried to retool itself in its final years, but its format proved too abbreviated, and its visual-verbal whimsicality too cumbersome, to compete with the seriousness and relative complexity that the multivolume afforded. And to the extent that the vendetta multivolume described a more heroic age—or at least provided a solid vehicle for symbolically working out social injustices—readers could forget the troubles of the present day. It was less a matter of multivolume authors playing off the sour mood of a populace in an age bereft of extravagance, though, than it was the way these authors catered to the growing interest in the popular theater. The *kibyōshi* disappeared, then, according to this logic, because of a combination of ideology, technology, and escapist nostalgia.

There are several possible objections to this narrative: it accords too much weight to the Kansei Reforms; it posits a zero-sum game between the *kibyōshi* and the multivolume as though the two genres were mutually

---

101. For a transcribed version of Kyōden's *Asaka no numa gonichi no adauchi* (1807), see Mizuno, *SKZ 6*, pp. 103–144.

Fig. 4.27 Head on a platter. From *Itoguruma kyūbi no kitsune* (1808), a multivolume comic-book written by Santō Kyōden and illustrated by Ichiryūsai Toyohiro. Courtesy of Hōsa bunko.

exclusive, as though readers would *completely* abandon succinct frivolity for longish vendetta themes as their preferred form of escapism (though without explaining why one form of escapism is more efficacious than the other); and it neglects internal developments within the *kibyōshi* itself, developments that have to do with the changing nature of readership and commercial pressures.

Regarding the first of these objections, the explanation of the demise of the *kibyōshi* as owing to the Kansei Reforms would seem to be overdetermined. The proposition that a genre could be decreed out of existence seems peculiar for several reasons, the least of which is not that if the publishing edicts had truly been effective, why were they continuously reissued throughout the eighteenth and nineteenth centuries? Such a proposition ironically smacks of the same ilk of fantasy that served as the comic premise of many of the protest pieces themselves. The very notion that the government could destroy a genre by dint of *diktat*, in other words, is almost as naive as the overzealously idealistic notions that the *reductio ad absurdum* pieces attacked in the first place—as if one day the citizens of Edo woke up and, lo and behold, gave up the *kibyōshi* along with uselessness and materialism and white lies.

Granted, Mizuno has pointed out that the efficacy of the Reforms was just as much a matter of the prosecution of authors like Kyōden as it was the promulgation of publishing and sumptuary laws (though surely these are not unrelated). Be that as it may, the general thrust of the conventional wisdom remains that it was the Kansei Reforms—their edicts buttressed by actions—that most effectively took the oomph out of the *kibyōshi* and the popular literature industry at large. To the extent that the sociopolitical satire of the *kibyōshi* was a form of resistance, as Will Rogers would have appreciated, it would seem that the harder the shogunate tried to get rid of the *kibyōshi* the more entrenched it would actually have become; for are not humor, satire, and nonsense needed most at precisely those moments of intense emotional or spiritual angst?

One result of the retrospective overemphasis given to the Kansei Reforms is that some commentators have ended up conflating the termination of the protest pieces with that of the *kibyōshi* genre as a whole. The Kansei Reforms may have at most rooted out political satire from the *kibyōshi*, but they did not lay waste to the genre itself. As Iwasaki has cannily put it: "What Sadanobu struck down from 1789 on was . . . not the established tradition of *gesaku* but the newly surging forces of political satire occasioned largely by his reforms."[102]

Furthermore, such a conflation occasions the neglect of the post-Reforms works. This neglect is unfair, in my opinion. It furthermore jibes with the disappointing tendency to foreclose interest in later works simply because the *kibyōshi* supposedly reached its zenith of popularity in the 1780s. As long as one seeks to evaluate the *kibyōshi* on its own merits and not merely as a fascinating "premodern" precursor to the modern *manga*, then why displace the same kind of generalization onto the different periods of the *kibyōshi*'s history, favoring the golden age of gossip pieces or the era of protest pieces— fascinating though works in these periods might be—to the exclusion of everything else? To relegate the significance of the late pieces to mere illustrations of the effect of the Kansei Reforms, what is more, is to commit the same sort of projection of highbrow vs. lowbrow stereotyping that has traditionally forestalled scholarship on the *kibyōshi* and other genres of playful literature themselves.

---

102. Iwasaki, "The World of *Gesaku*," p. 358.

From a less idealistic view, however, the conclusion that the *kibyōshi* disappeared soon if not immediately after the crackdown is not borne out by the evidence. In point of fact, the *kibyōshi* hardly evaporated overnight—certainly not in 1791—as a direct result of the Kansei Reforms. Rather, it hung on for another fifteen years, until 1806, at least. The genre clearly fell into general desuetude after that, though it does not seem to have done so categorically. A trickle of individual pieces continued to be issued sporadically throughout the first quarter of the nineteenth century—perhaps even as late as 1828.[103] This might be expected, for with the genre's contours being fuzzy, how could the dates of its lifespan not be so as well?

Along similar lines, if one accords format a primary place in the definition of Edo-period comicbooks, it must be acknowledged that the "standard" *kibyōshi* arrangement of three fascicles in yellow covers carried on in the *kibyōshi*-style jokebook (*kibyōshi-jitate hanashibon*) a couple of years beyond the 1806 cutoff date.[104] Or if one includes reprints of *kibyōshi* under different titles as part of the *kibyōshi* phenomenon, then the genre would have to be said to have continued long after that, well into the last quarter of the nineteenth century.[105] And anyway, since the multivolume comicbook emerged directly out of the *kibyōshi*, there is significant overlap of form and content, so it may be fruitful to explore the possibility that the multivolume is a subgenre of the *kibyōshi*. Or, the vendetta theme is a genre that survived in the shorter comicbook (*kibyōshi*) but thrived in the longer format (*gōkan*), whereas the various other themes one finds in the *kibyōshi* were genres that came under the sway of commercial pressures for a broader readership, and continued on in the less visual-verbal format of the funnybook. Any way one views it, however, the *kibyōshi* did not simply vanish into oblivion in 1791, though after 1806 it began to deliquesce, disintegrating and dissolving into other genres or modes or impulses.

This suggests a second objection to the traditional explanation about the demise of the *kibyōshi*; namely, that it seems to imply that the multivolume comicbook supplanted the *kibyōshi* as if readers could only chose one or the other, not both. Indeed, the traditional explanation seems to suggest that all multivolume comicbooks were monolithically devoted to revenge, which is one way of unfairly reducing an entire genre. And while it may appear retrospectively as though the two genres were locked in a winner-take-all contest, at the time it never could have been so tidy. In the rich literary marketplace that was early nineteenth-century Edo, it is hard to believe that readers

---

103. Markus, *Willow in Autumn*, p. 66.

104. For instance, *An Edo-Style Eel Story* (*Edomae hanashi unagi*), written by Ikku and illustrated by Harumachi II, was published in 1808.

105. Kyōden's *Enma's Crystal Mirror* (*Kagami no jōhari*, 1790), for example, was reissued during the Meiji period under the title *Ono no Takamura jigoku ōrai* (*Ono no Takamura's Pilgrimage Through Hell*).

would limit themselves to any single genre because one supposedly trafficked in frivolity and the other in vengeance. The reading public was far too pluralistic, as evidenced by the astounding diversification of the publishing market itself, to expect that *all* readers might give up one genre for the other at precisely the same time.

Since the multivolume comicbook grew organically out of a particular strain of the *kibyōshi*, there is considerable overlap between the two. Indeed, while it is tempting to characterize them as similar media but belonging to different genres, in practice it is sometimes difficult to sort out certain pieces into one or the other genre. The vendetta theme that the multivolume comicbook supposedly embodied also appears in many mid- and late-Edo media and genres, from the popular stage and its associated theatrical texts, to earlier comicbooks such as the blackbook.

More to the point, the vendetta theme runs unwaveringly throughout the entire history of the *kibyōshi*, too: at least one vendetta title was published just about every year from 1776 on.[106] Granted, most vendetta *kibyōshi* are comical takeoffs, as with Bakin's story about a feud between Mr. Fleacatcher Managoro and a pesky flea (**Figure 4.28**).[107] *Familiar Bestsellers* may be read as a vendetta piece *kibyōshi* style, for that matter, since the Kamigata camp wages its war against the Edo camp out of resentment for having been made obsolete. However, sometime during the beginning of the nineteenth century, the *kibyōshi* vendetta turned somber, and it is this somberness that is said to best characterize the multivolume comicbook (**Figure 4.29**).[108] Sanba, who wrote in both genres, lamented that the vendetta story within the *kibyōshi* had effectively "robbed" the genre of its hallmark humor.[109] Such overlap in content between the late *kibyōshi* and the early multivolume comicbook suggests that for a half dozen years, at least, the only appreciable difference between the two genres might have been one of format, not content.

Then again, there is also considerable overlap between the two in terms of format. Although most of the early vendetta *kibyōshi* assume the usual three volumes of five leaves (or ten pages) per volume form, a number of works from the mid-1780s on began expanding to *five* volumes. By the early nineteenth century, Kyōden was publishing vendetta *kibyōshi* in *six*

---

106. A glance at Tanahashi, *Kibyōshi sōran 5*, for instance, reveals that during An'ei-Tenmei alone, extant vendetta pieces issued in consecutive years include: *Katakiuchi yaguchi no rishō* (1776), *Katakiuchi shi no buzuri* (1777), *Katakiuchi onna hachinoki* (1778), *Katakiuchi kurama tengu* (1779), *Katakiuchi Edo no meibutsu* (1780), *Katakiuchi Suruga no hana* (1781), *Katakiuchi ume to sakura* (1782), *Katakiuchi samisen no yurai* (1783), *Katakiuchi futaba no matsu* (1784), *Katakiuchi ukiki no kameyama* (1786), *Katakiuchi sue no katsuyama* (1787), and *Katakiuchi ato no matsuri* (1788).

107. For a transcribed and annotated version of Bakin's *kibyōshi*, see Iwata, "*Katakiuchi nomitori manako.*"

108. For a transcribed version of this *gōkan*, Kyōden's *Itoguruma kyūbi no kitsune* (1808), see Mizuno, *SKZ 6*, pp. 235–303.

109. Leutner, *Shikitei Sanba*, p. 60.

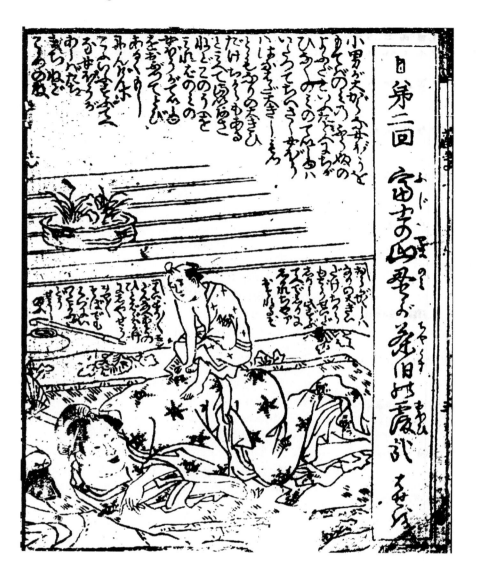

Fig. 4.28 Fleacatcher Managoro and the flea that gnaws at him. From *Vendetta of Mr. Fleacatcher Managoro, the Fifth (Katakiuchi nomitori manako,* 1791), a *kibyōshi* written by Takizawa Bakin and illustrated by Kitao Shigemasa. Courtesy of Tokyo Metropolitan Central Library, Kaga Collection.

volumes.[110] Thus, in some cases, the difference between a vendetta *kibyōshi* and a vendetta multivolume is marginal. In terms of contemporary terminology, readers at times referred to both simply as "mid-sizeds" (*chūbon*), as though no generic distinction could be made in terms of theme since the two shared the same format. Eventually, the average multivolume would become considerably longer, running four or more volumes of ten leaves (twenty pages) per volume. But for a decade, perhaps, the formats were virtually indistinguishable. It may even be possible to regard the two "genres" as a single genre that was growing in size. The *kibyōshi* may have naturally expanded its format, even if it had not turned toward vendetta themes.

---

110. The works in question—*Katakiuchi futatsu guruma, Katakiuchi Magotarō mushi,* and *Katakiuchi oinu kawara*—were all published in 1806.

Fig. 4.29 Violent scene from *Asaka no numa gonichi no adauchi* (1807), a multivolume comicbook written by Santō Kyōden and illustrated by Utagawa Toyokuni. Courtesy of Hōsa bunko.

A third objection to the standard explanation of the *kibyōshi*'s demise is that it does not really take into account a variety of other factors, such as internal trends within the *kibyōshi*, pressures of the publishing industry, and the rapidly changing composition of readership. Even though most of the major writers were hounded out of the genre, if not out of Edo, there still seems to have been a modest market for humorous works. The cumulative effect of the Kansei Reforms may have been to dissuade authors from taking personal risks merely for some bits of gold and scraps of irony. Yet the Reforms hardly legislated the taste and reading habits of *readers*. People did not simply give up popular literature and limit themselves to edifying Neo-Confucian tracts. Nor did the Reforms convince publishers to disinvest themselves of their commercial interests, for that matter. As long as readers turned the pages, and the *kibyōshi* turned a profit, publishers would engage authors for new pieces. Why suddenly discontinue what had been a lucrative venture for at least a dozen years even after the implementation of the Reforms? Surely the publishing industry as a whole would have trimmed those branches of the genre that were no longer viable, heeding the advice of one of its own in chopping not the roots of the money tree.

Some publishers resorted to reissuing earlier successful works, even if that entailed purchasing the rights from competing publishers. Enomoto Kichibei, for instance, paid an undisclosed sum to reissue four of Kyōden's *kibyōshi*.[111] Interestingly, one of these pieces was the infamous satire, *Modish Pattern of a Confucian Stripe (Kōshijima toki ni aizome, 1789)*. This suggests that Enomoto enjoyed living dangerously, or was financially hard up. Surely he could not have failed to appreciate the risks involved. Tsutaya Jūzaburō, by contrast—and as might be expected of someone who had experienced trouble firsthand—was slightly more cautious in his choice of pieces to reissue. In 1792, he began devoting some energy to bringing out second editions of several best-selling gossip pieces written prior to the Kansei Reforms, including Kyōden's *Playboy*.[112] To the extent that some of the newly penned late works seem to have tried to return to these sorts of themes, too, Sanba's punishment for his fire-brigade *kibyōshi* of 1799 must have sounded the general alarm that even gossip pieces were no longer acceptable. If there was a single breaking point, it was not the *original* Kansei Reforms per se, but their continued enforcement even after Sadanobu had left office.

After all, what was the *kibyōshi* without satire? Not only did the satirical impulse pick up steam from the gossip pieces to the protest pieces, but the very format of the genre itself was a kind of satire on earlier comicbooks, too, and the compositional technique of variational procedure was especially prone to parody. Without social or political satire, the genre had nowhere to go but to its roots—to satirize itself, in other words. Just as the proverbial paper on how one spent one's summer vacation trying to write a paper on how one spent one's summer vacation grows tedious and fast, so too the self-reflexivity of the *kibyōshi* during its painful last gasps. Compared to the thrills of the gossip and protest pieces, the post-Kansei works must have seemed bland. Bakin turned his back on the *kibyōshi* to take up writing the sparsely illustrated reading book in large part because he was more temperamentally suited to serious moralistic fiction than the light-hearted jokey stuff. Yet he himself says that he switched because the *kibyō-*

---

111. Enomoto reissued Kyōden's *Ippyaku sanjō imo jigoku* (1789), *Kōshijima toki ni aizome* (1789), *Kyōden ukiyo no eizame* (1790), and *Shingaku hayasomegusa* (1790). In Koike, *Edo no gesaku ehon 6*, p. 192.

112. In addition to *Playboy*, the Tsutaya published second editions of the following works by Kyōden in 1792: *Triple-Striped Ueda Silk, Woven with Playboy's Whims (Misujidachi kyaku no ki Ueda, 1787)*; and *One Spring Night in Edo, One Thousand Gold Pieces (Edo no haru ichiya senryō, 1786)*.

shi had lost its novelty.[113] For a genre like the *kibyōshi*, which was constantly reinventing itself in the most up-to-date fashions, and that went so far as to ridicule other genres for being passé—for a genre like *that* to grow passé itself effectively undermined its own *raison d'être*.

In order to understand how the *kibyōshi* pulled the rug out from beneath its own feet, it is necessary to observe the trajectory of its readership. It seems likely that massification eroded the unique qualities that had made the *kibyōshi* special. Generally speaking, the early *kibyōshi* was written by members of the intelligentsia for like-minded friends and published in relatively small runs. However, the broader that readers became in terms of class and education, the more the author lost sight of his readership, the result being that the allusions, the visual-verbal play, the in-group jokes became increasingly dumbed down. Much of the thrill of the *kibyōshi* had to do with its air of exclusivity. This is true on the level of wordplay, visual-verbal play, allusional puzzles, and so on. But this also pertains to the targets of satire. The gossip and protest pieces drew the line sharply between the knowing reader and the unknowing reader, which presumably included members of the government as well as the censors who had let such pieces be published. The paradox confronting the producers of the *kibyōshi* was this: how to open up the references in order to appeal to a broader public without jettisoning the "dressing-room" humor that had imbued the genre with its singular character. In bending over backwards to cater to an expanded readership, the *kibyōshi* lost its esoteric uniqueness. In this sense, the *kibyōshi* fell victim to its own success.

As commercial pressures drove publishers and authors to mark these in-jokes and references to antecedent texts more explicitly in pursuit of a less-educated readership, the pleasure for the more-educated reader of recognizing the allusions sorely diminished. As the genre became ever more popular, and as publishers started issuing copies in runs of thousands—and, if we are to believe Bakin, in tens of thousands—the readership must have far exceeded the number of members in all literary coteries in eighteenth-century Edo combined. The genre inevitably fizzled out, in other words, *not* because of the Kansei Reforms, but because the commercial pressure of reaching a larger, more common audience meant that writers eventually had to dispose of the very sort of in-group jokes and specialized puzzles that had characterized the *kibyōshi* to begin with.

To push this a step further, it is entirely possible that the *kibyōshi* may have imploded even if the Kansei Reforms had never taken place. To the extent that the allegorical structure of the *kibyōshi* engendered a kind of skeptical reading of social narrative, readers would also have applied that skepticism to the *kibyōshi* narrative itself. The yellowbook, in other words, planted the seeds of its downfall by jaundicing its own consumer base.

---

113. Mentioned in Zolbrod, "The Vendetta of Mr. Fleacatcher Managoro," p. 121.

In conclusion, it can be said that the *kibyōshi* ended not with the bang of the Kansei Reforms, but with the whimper of a literature that was struggling to remain fresh in its matter. Although the *kibyōshi* thrived during the last quarter of the eighteenth century, it did not simply disappear after the Reforms, or even in the first decade of the nineteenth century; it hobbled on, perhaps even in the considerably darker but no less visual-verbal form of the multivolume comicbook. The Kansei Reforms undoubtedly played a role in the demise of the *kibyōshi* by thwarting the genre's tendency toward satire. But there were other important factors in the genre's transmogrification.

As the *kibyōshi* eventually receded into the background, other genres that were more open to a wider audience came to the forefront. The *kibyōshi* cannot be said to have directly spawned the funnybook (*kokkeibon*), the reading book (*yomihon*), or the "human sentiment book" (*ninjōbon*), as it did the multivolume comicbook. After all, only the last of these can be considered a comicbook per se, since the other genres, being merely lightly illustrated, do not involve themselves in the visual-verbal imagination as richly as the *kibyōshi* or the multivolume. Nor do these other genres aim for Edo-centrism the way that the *kibyōshi* did. If anything, the funnybook was written for a broad enough readership even outside Edo to be considered among the first "national" genres in Japanese literary history.

Nonetheless, the funnybook seems to have inherited many features characterizing the *kibyōshi* other than the visual-verbal nexus. It is therefore possible that the *kibyōshi* bequeathed to it such traits as its increasingly earthy humor, its trope of exposing human foibles, and its emphasis on everyday speech and on storyteller's cadences. This makes a certain amount of sense, especially given that many of the progenitors of the funnybook were also *kibyōshi* authors themselves. Such is true of Sanba, who, in addition to composing *kibyōshi* penned well over one hundred funnybooks, including representative ones like *Bathhouse to the Floating World* (*Ukiyoburo*, 1809–1813) and *Barbershop to the Floating World* (*Ukiyodoko*, 1813–1814).[114] The same pertains to Jippensha Ikku (1765–1831), whose *Hoofing It Along the East-Sea Highway* (*Tōkaidōchū hizakurige*) is said to have elevated the funnybook to literary significance. Furthermore, Ikku was writing in both genres at the same time. Although he would not conclude *Hoofing It* until 1822, the first installment was published in 1802, when he was working on post-Kansei Reforms *kibyōshi* such as *A Monstrous Chronicle of Great Peace* (*Bakemono taiheiki*, 1804) (**Figure 4.30**), among others.[115]

---

114. Some of Sanba's other notable funnybooks include: *Illustrated Encyclopedia of the Theater* (*Shibai kinmōzui*, 1803); *Ono no Takamoron's Bogus Character Dictionary* (*Ono no Bakamura usojizukushi*, 1806); *Portraits of Drunkards* (*Namaei katagi*, 1806); and *Critique of Theatergoers* (*Kyakusha hyōbanki*, 1811).

115. For an annotated edition, see Koike, *Edo no gesaku ehon 4*, pp. 267–298.

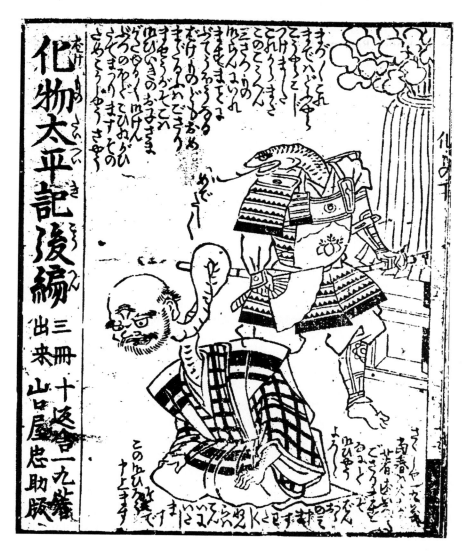

Fig. 4.30 Illustration from *A Monstrous Chronicle of Great Peace* (*Bakemono taiheiki*, 1804), a *kibyōshi* written and illustrated by Jippensha Ikku. Courtesy of Tokyo Metropolitan Central Library, Kaga Collection.

To the extent that the *kibyōshi* did in fact exert an influence upon the funnybook, as well as give birth to the multivolume comicbook, it is possible that the *kibyōshi*'s "demise" spells less failure than success. Had it not been for the *kibyōshi*, some of these other genres arguably might never have come into existence as quickly—or succeeded as phenomenally—as they did.

The Kibyōshi Legacy

Although the production of the *kibyōshi* ebbed during the first decades of the nineteenth century as other genres surged, the *kibyōshi* does not seem to have been completely abandoned by readers. One occasionally finds reference to its works in journals, novels, and personal correspondences. The toymaker Bon'un'an Kangetsu (a.k.a. Awashima Kangetsu, 1859–1926), for instance, mentions in his memoirs his fondness for Kyōden's *kibyōshi*, as well as the works of Saikaku and other Edo-period greats. Seeing that his father Awashima Chingaku was an Edo-period aesthete, it is possible that Kangetsu had inherited an uninterrupted tradition of such sentiments.[116]

During the Meiji period some of the authors calling for the unification of written and verbal expression (*genbun itchi*) within literature denounced playful literature as pulp fiction. If nothing else, this denunciation means that these authors themselves were reading it. Just as it is possible that Matsudaira Sadanobu wrote a *kibyōshi* under a pseudonym, it is also very likely that some advocates of *genbun itchi* may actually have been steeped in *gesaku*. Even Natsume Sōseki, one of the influential modernizers of Japanese literature, privately waxed nostalgic about the *kibyōshi* and the *akabon* (though using a less common term for it) in a poem composed in the last decade of the nineteenth century:

Fuyugomori	Holed up for winter—
Kibyōshi aru wa	It's either yellowbooks
Akabyōshi	Or else redbooks.[117]

Since Sōseki penned this verse in the 1890s at about the same time that the earliest comic-strip *manga* appeared, one wonders if those cartoonists included similar verses in their diaries?

The impact of the *kibyōshi* and other forms of mid-Edo popular literature, comicbooks or otherwise, upon Meiji-period satirical caricature (*fūshiga*), let alone upon literature in general, has yet to be adequately assessed. In his otherwise superb article on the Meiji political cartoon, which is sensitive to the Edo past, Peter Duus seems to overlook the *kibyōshi*:

But it is also true that the Japanese had little trouble understanding what political cartoons were all about. During the eighteenth century, anonymously drawn and mostly wordless comic books called *Toba-ehon* ("Toba picture books"), named after the putative artist of the humorous *Chōjū giga* ("frolicking birds and beasts") scroll, circulated widely, and by the early nineteenth century leading print artists such as Kuniyoshi and Hokusai were producing comical pictures and visual puzzles in great number and variety.[118]

Duus here cites the work of Inagaki Shin'ichi, who among others has tried to generalize *manga* culture widely enough to include Toba cartoons.[119] Thus, Duus understandably restricts the scope of his enquiry to the visual arts, since that is the hole into which political cartoons are often pigeoned. However, the conventions informing these political cartoons extend to the stage and to works of popular literature, especially the *kibyōshi*. Future

116. Awashima, *Bon'un'an zatsuwa*, p. 39 and passim.
117. Natsume Sōseki, *Sōseki zenshū 17*, p. 83, poem #421 (written in Meiji 28 / 1895).
118. Duus, "Weapons of the Weak, Weapons of the Strong," p. 968.
119. See Inagaki, *Edo no asobie*.

Fig. 4.31 Cover of a *kibyōshi*-inspired *manga* titled *Tales of Foxes at Flower-Viewing Time* (*Hanageshiki kitsune kōdan*) by Sugiura Hinako. Reprinted in *Sugiura Hinako zenshū 1*, p. 261. Courtesy of Chikuma shobō.

explorations of political caricature, whether during Meiji or beyond—Taishō also had a rich tradition of political caricature—might well benefit from a grounding in the further study of Edo's visual-verbal nexus as seen in the *kibyōshi*, particularly its protest pieces, and in other related genres.

More recently, self-styled Neo-Pulp Fictionist (*Shin gesakusha*) Inoue Hisashi has written a prize-winning send-up of Kyōden's *Playboy* (to be briefly touched upon in that chapter). Sugiura Hinako (1958–2005) took visual cues

Fig. 4.32 The Chinese Rosei poring over Japanese comicbooks in the privacy of his own hovel. From *Rosei's Dream—The Night Before (Rosei ga yume sono zenjitsu,* 1791), a *kibyōshi* written by Santō Kyōden and presumably illustrated by Kitao Shigemasa. Courtesy of Tokyo Metropolitan Central Library, Kaga Collection.

from the *kibyōshi,* as can be seen in her story *Tales of Foxes at Flower-Viewing Time (Hanageshiki kitsune kōdan)* (**Figure 4.31**).[120] However, these works—not to mention a few others, such as Yamada Murasaki's adaptations of Edo-period companion booklets—are isolated instances, novelty items more than anything else, and certainly do not constitute a full-fledged revival of Edo-period playful literature.

Be that as it may, in the opening scene of his last masterpiece in the *kibyōshi* genre, *Rosei's Dream* (1791), Kyōden whimsically depicted the protagonist in his ramshackle hut somewhere in China, engrossed, perhaps secretly, in poring over imported yellow comicbooks (**Figure 4.32**). In hindsight, now that the *manga* has become a global phenomenon—reaching a mass audience not just in the West but also in Asian countries harboring deep-seated misgivings toward Japan—this scene of unabashed fandom seems less whimsical than uncannily prescient. For to the extent that the *kibyōshi* may have been the original adult *manga,* Kyōden's dream of readers coveting Japanese comicbooks even in far-flung lands has indeed come to pass.

---

120. Reprinted in *Sugiura Hinako zenshū I,* pp. 261–272.

Reference Matter

The place of publication for all Japanese works is Tokyo, unless otherwise specified.

Abbreviations:

EMJL	*Early Modern Japanese Literature*
HJAS	*Harvard Journal of Asiatic Studies*
JJS	*Journal of Japanese Studies*
MN	*Monumenta Nipponica*
NKBT	*Nihon koten bungaku taikei*
SKZ	*Santō Kyōden zenshū*
SNKBT	*Shin Nihon koten bungaku taikei*
SNKBZ	*Shinpen Nihon koten bungaku zenshū*

Akai Tatsurō. "The Common People and Painting." In Nakane and Ōishi, eds., *Tokugawa Japan*, pp. 167–191.

Akama Ryō et al., eds. *Kabuki bunka no shosō*. In *Iwanami kōza kabuki bunraku 4*. Iwanami shoten, 1998.

Akimoto, Shunkichi. *The Twilight of Yedo*. Tokyo: Tokyo News Service, 1952.

Allison, Anne. *Permitted and Prohibited Desires: Mothers, Comics, and Censorship in Japan*. Boulder, CO: Westview Press, 1996.

Araki, James. "The Dream Pillow in Edo Fiction: 1772–81." In *MN*, vol. 25, no. 1 (1970), pp. 43–105.

———. "*Sharebon*: Books for Men of Mode." In *MN*, vol. 24, no. 1 (1969), pp. 31–45.

Ariga, Chieko. "The Playful Gloss: *Rubi* in Japanese Literature." In *MN*, vol. 44, no. 3 (1989), pp. 309–335.

Asakura Kamezō. *Misemono kenkyū*. Shibunkaku, 1977. First published by Shun'yōdō in 1928.

Asano Hidetaka, ed. *Kondō Kiyoharu gasaku* Dōke hyakunin shu *sanbu saku*. In *Taihei bunko 17*. Taihei shooku, 1985.

Atsumi Seitarō et al., eds. *Soga kyōgen gappeishū*. In *Nihon gikyoku zenshū 14*. Shun'yōdō, 1929.

Awashima Kangetsu. *Bon'un'an zatsuwa*. In *Iwanami bunko 31-159-1*. Iwanami shoten, 1999.

Bartels-Wu, Stella. *Mitatemono und kibyōshi: Edition, Bearbeitung und Übersetzung "Myōkinako kogome Dōmyōji" (1805) von Takizawa Bakin*. Wiesbaden: Harrassowitz Verlag, 1994.

Bender, Aimee. "Flat and Glad." In Howe, ed., *Give Our Regards to the Atomsmashers!*, pp. 44–50.

Bergson, Henri. "*Laughter.*" In Sypher, ed., *Comedy*, pp. 60–190.

Berry, Mary Elizabeth. *Japan in Print: Information and Nation in the Early Modern Period.* Berkeley: University of California Press, 2006.

Bettelheim, Bruno. *The Uses of Enchantment: The Meaning and Importance of Fairy Tales.* New York: Vintage Books, 1989. First published by Alfred A. Knopf, 1976.

Bix, Herbert P. *Peasant Protest in Japan, 1590–1884.* New Haven: Yale University Press, 1986.

Blyth, R. H. *Edo Satirical Verse Anthologies.* Tokyo: Hokuseido Press, 1961.

Bowen, Barbara C. "Rabelais's Unreadable Books." In *Renaissance Quarterly*, vol. 48, no. 4 (winter 1995), pp. 742–758.

Brandon, James R., trans. *Kabuki: Five Classic Plays.* Cambridge, Mass.: Harvard University Press, 1975.

Brandon, James R. and Samuel L. Leiter, eds. *Villainy and Vengeance, 1773–1799.* Volume 2 of *Kabuki Plays on Stage.* Honolulu: University of Hawaii Press, 2002.

Brazell, Karen, ed. *Traditional Japanese Theater: An Anthology of Plays.* New York: Columbia University Press, 1998.

Brownlee, John. "*Jikkinshō*: A Miscellany of Ten Maxims." In *MN*, vol. 29, no. 2 (1974), pp. 121–161.

Burton, William James. "In a Perfect World: Utopias in Modern Japanese Literature." Ph.D. dissertation, University of Washington, 2002.

Campbell, Robert, trans. *Three Madames and Their Dirty Tale.* In John Solt, ed., *An Episodic Festschrift for Howard Hibbett 10.* Hollywood, CA: Highmoonoon, 2002.

Clark, Timothy T. "The Rise and Fall of the Island of Nakazu." In *Archives of Asian Art*, vol. 45 (1992), pp. 72–91.

Clark, Timothy T. and Osamu Ueda with Donald Jenkins. *The Actor's Image: Print Makers of the Katsukawa School.* Chicago: Art Institute of Chicago and Princeton University Press, 1994.

Cohen, Ted. *Jokes: Philosophical Thoughts on Joking Matters.* Chicago: University of Chicago Press, 1999.

Cohn, Joel R. *Studies in the Comic Spirit in Modern Japanese Fiction.* Cambridge, Mass.: Harvard University Asia Center, Harvard University Press, 1998.

Conlan, Thomas D., trans. *In Little Need of Divine Intervention: Takezaki Suenaga's Scrolls of the Mongol Invasion of Japan.* Ithaca, NY: East Asia Program, Cornell University, 2001.

Craig, Timothy J., ed. *Japan Pop! Inside the World of Japanese Popular Culture.* Armonk, NY: M. E. Sharpe, 2000.

Cranston, Edwin A. *The Gem-Glistening Cup.* In *A Waka Anthology 1.* Stanford: Stanford University Press, 1993.

Cullen, L. M. *A History of Japan, 1582–1941: Internal and External Worlds.* Cambridge, Eng.: Cambridge University Press, 2003.

Davis, Fred. *Fashion, Culture, and Identity.* Chicago: University of Chicago Press, 1992.

Davis, Julie Nelson. *Utamaro Draws Their Ravishing Features: Ukiyo-e Images of Women in Late Eighteenth-Century Japan.* London: Reaktion Press, forthcoming.

De Bary, William Theodore, trans. *Five Women Who Loved Love.* Rutland, VT: Charles E. Tuttle, 1956.

Dällenbach, Lucian. *The Mirror in the Text*. Chicago: University of Chicago Press, 1989.

Dentith, Simon. *Parody*. London: Routledge, 2000.

Donald, Diana. *The Age of Caricature: Satirical Prints in the Reign of George III*. New Haven: Yale University Press. Published for the Paul Mellon Centre for Studies in British Art, 1996.

Dore, Ronald P. *Education in Tokugawa Japan*. Berkeley: University of California Press, 1965.

Drake, Chris, trans. "*A Theory of Farting*." In Shirane, ed., *EMJL*, pp. 512–519.

Duus, Peter. "Weapons of the Weak, Weapons of the Strong—The Development of the Japanese Political Cartoon." In *Journal of Asian Studies*, vol. 60, no. 4 (November 2001), pp. 965–997. Originally presented as the Presidential Address to the 53rd Annual Meeting of the Association for Asian Studies, Chicago, March 23, 2001.

Earle, Joe. *Netsuke: Fantasy and Reality in Japanese Miniature Sculpture*. Boston: Museum of Fine Arts, 2001.

Ebara Taizō. "Kibyōshi *Sekki yagyō*." In *Ebara Taizō chosakushū 17*. Chūō kōronsha, 1980, pp. 407–410. Originally published in the journal *Kosenryū kenkyū* (January 1940).

Eisner, Will. *Comics and Sequential Art*. Tamarac, FL: Poorhouse Press, 1985. 21st edition, 2001.

———. *Graphic Storytelling and Visual Narrative*. Tamarac, FL: Poorhouse Press, 1996. 5th edition, 2001.

Elkins, James. *Why Are Our Pictures Puzzles? On the Modern Origins of Pictorial Complexity*. New York and London: Routledge, 1999.

Enoyama Jun'ichi. "Yume no shukō to *Edo umare uwaki no kabayaki*." In Aoyama gakuin daigaku nichibun insei no kai, *Ryokkō shirin*, vol. 18 (1994), pp. 1–10.

Farge, William J. "Violating Censorship: Humor and Virulence in the Popular Writings of Baba Bunkō (1718–1759)." Talk presented at the Southern Japan Seminar in Panama City Beach, Florida, September 23, 2000.

Fiedler, Leslie. "The Middle Against Both Ends." In *Encounter*, August 1955, pp. 16–23. Reprinted in Heer and Worcester, eds., *Arguing Comics*, pp. 122–133.

Fiorillo, John. "Tragedy and Laughter in the Floating World: *Shinjū* in the Works of Utamaro and Kyōden." In *Andon*, vol. 54 (1996), pp. 3–23.

Fujimoto Kizan. *Shikidō ōkagami*. Yagi shoten, 1974.

Fujisawa Morihiko, ed. *Kowa mezurashi [sic] misemonogatari: kibyōshibon*. Kokon kisho kankōkai, 1935.

Fukuoka, Maki. "Contextualising the Peep-Box in Tokugawa Japan." In *Early Popular Visual Culture*, vol. 3, no. 1 (May 2005), pp. 17–42.

Furuhashi Nobuyoshi, ed. *Hyōgen no nagare—Kinsei*. In *Nihon bungeishi 4*. Kawade shobō shinsha, 1988.

Gardner, Richard A. "The Blessing of Living in a Country Where There Are *Senryū*: Humor in the Response to Aum Shinrikyō." In *Asian Folklore Studies*, vol. 61 (April 2002), pp. 35–75.

Geinōshi kenkyūkai, ed. *Kabuki*. In *Nihon shomin bunka shiryō shūsei 6*. San'ichi shobō, 1973.

Geis, Deborah R., ed. *Considering* Maus: *Approaches to Art Spiegelman's "Survivor's Tale" of the Holocaust*. Tuscaloosa: University of Alabama Press, 2003.

Gerstle, C. Andrew. "Flowers of Edo: Eighteenth-Century *Kabuki* and Its Patrons." In Samuel A. Leiter, *A Kabuki Reader: History and Performance*, Armonk, NY: M. E.. Sharpe, 2002, pp. 88–111.

Gerstle, C. Andrew, ed. *Eighteenth-Century Japan: Culture and Society*. Sydney: Allen & Unwin, 1989.

Gerstle, C. Andrew, trans. and annot. *Chikamatsu: Five Late Plays*. New York: Columbia University Press, 2001.

Gluck, Carol. "The Invention of Edo." In Stephen Vlastos, ed., *Mirror of Modernity: Invented Traditions of Modern Japan*. Berkeley: University of California Press, 1998, pp. 262–284.

Gombrich, E. H. *Meditations on a Hobby Horse and Other Essays on the Theory of Art*. Chicago: University of Chicago Press, 1963.

Gorer, Geoffrey. *The Life and Ideas of the Marquis de Sade*. New York: Norton, 1963.

Goulemot, Jean Marie. *Forbidden Texts: Erotic Literature and Its Readers in Eighteenth-Century France*. Philadelphia: University of Pennsylvania Press, 1994. First published in France as *Ces livres qu'on ne lit que d'une main*, 1991.

Groemer, Gerald. "Singing the News: *Yomiuri* in Japan during the Edo and Meiji Periods." In *HJAS*, vol. 54, no. 1 (June 1994), pp. 233–261.

Grosz, Elizabeth. "Intolerable Ambiguity." In Rosemarie Garland Thomson, ed., *Freakery: Cultural Spectacles of the Extraordinary Body*. New York: New York University Press, 1996, pp. 55–66.

Gunji Masakatsu and Sekiyama Kazuo. *Misemono zasshi*. San'ichi shobō, 1991.

Haga Tōru. *Hiraga Gennai*. Asahi shinbunsha, 1981.

———. "Precariousness of Love, Places of Love." In Jones, ed., *Imaging/Reading Eros*, pp. 97–102.

Hahn, Cynthia. *Portrayed on the Heart: Narrative Effect in Pictorial Lives of Saints from the Tenth through the Thirteenth Century*. Berkeley: University of California Press, 2001.

Hall, John Whitney. *Tanuma Okitsugu, 1719–1788: Forerunner of Modern Japan*. Cambridge, Mass.: Harvard University Press, 1955.

Hall, John Whitney, ed. *Early Modern Japan*. In *The Cambridge History of Japan 4*. Cambridge, Eng.: Cambridge University Press, 1991.

Hamada Giichirō. *(Hanmoto betsu nendai jun) Kibyōshi edaisen shū*. In *Shoshi shomiku shirīzu 8*. Yumani shobō, 1979.

———. *Ōta Nanpo*. Yoshikawa Kobunkan, 1963.

Hamada Giichirō, ed. *Tenmei bungaku—Shiryō to kenkyū*. Tōkyōdō shuppan, 1979.

———. *Ōta Nanpo zenshū*. Iwanami shoten, 1985–1990. 20 volumes.

Hamada Giichirō et al., eds. *Kibyōshi senryū kyōka*. In *NKBZ 46*. Shōgakukan, 1971.

Hamada Keisuke. "Hankō no kana jitai." In *Kokugogaku* (University of Kyoto), vol. 118, pp. 1–9.

Hanasaki Kazuo. *Edo kawaya hyaku sugata*. Miki shobō, 2000.

———. *Edo kawaya zue*. Taihei shooku, 1978.

———. *Hōsō ehonshū*. In *Taihei bunko 3*. Taihei shooku, 1981.

Hanasaki Kazuo, ed. *Tenmeiki Yoshiwara saiken shū*. Kinsei fūzoku kenkyūkai, 1977.

Haniya Yutaka, ed. *Yume*. In *Nihon no meizuihitsu 14*. Sakuhinsha, 1984.

Hanley, Susan B. *Everyday Things in Premodern Japan: The Hidden Legacy of Material Culture*. Berkeley: University of California Press, 1997.

Hattori Nankaku, comp. and annot. *Tōshisen kokujikai*. Ed. by Hino Tatsuo. Heibonsha, 1982.

Hawkes, Terence. *Structuralism and Semiotics*. Berkeley: University of California Press, 1977.

Hayakawa Junzaburō, ed. *Edo miyage*. In *Tokugawa bungei ruijū 12*. Kokusho kankōkai, 1924.

———. *Shin enseki jisshu 4*. Kokusho kankōkai, 1913.

Hayashi Yoshikazu. *Enpon Edo bungakushi*. Yūkō shobō, 1964.

Hayashi Yoshikazu, ed. *Zashikigei chūshingura*. Kawade shobō shinsha, 1985.

Heer, Jeet and Kent Worcester, eds. *Arguing Comics: Literary Masters on a Popular Medium*. Jackson: University Press of Mississippi, 2004.

Henshall, Kenneth G. *A Guide to Remembering Japanese Characters*. Tokyo: Charles E. Tuttle, 1988.

Hibbett, Howard. *The Chrysanthemum and the Fish: Japanese Humor Since the Age of the Shoguns*. Tokyo: Kodansha International, 2002.

———. *The Floating World in Japanese Fiction*. New York: Oxford University Press, 1959. Reprinted in Rutland, VT, by Charles E. Tuttle, 1975.

Hino Tatsuo. *Edojin to yūtopia*. Asahi shinbunsha, 1977.

———. "*Edo umare uwaki no kabayaki*: Kaisetsu." In *Kokuritsu gekijō jōen shiryōshū 164*. In Kokuritsu gekijō geinō chōsashitsu, ed. *Jōen shiryōshū*, vol. 309, no. 1 (1991), pp. 181–237.

Hino Tatsuo, ed. *Kyōto daigaku zō daisōbon kisho shūsei 14*. Kyōto daigaku bungakubu kokugogaku kokubungaku kenkyūshitsu, 1996.

Hirose Tomomitsu. *Gesaku bungeiron—Kenkyū to shiryō*. Kasama shoin, 1982.

Hirose Tomomitsu, ed. *(Eiinbon) Enshū kibyōshi 1*. Kasama shoin, 1971.

Hiyama Jun'ichi. "*Gozonji no shōbaimono* to hyōbanki." In Aoyama gakuin daigaku Nihon bungakukai, ed., *Aoyama gobun 24* (March 1994), pp. 63–72.

Hoffmann, Yoel, comp. *Japanese Death Poems: Written by Zen Monks and Haiku Poets on the Verge of Death*. Tokyo: Charles E. Tuttle, 1986.

Howe, Sean, ed. *Give Our Regards to the Atomsmashers! Writers on Comics*. New York: Pantheon, 2004.

Hyers, M. Conrad. *Zen and the Comic Spirit*. London: Rider, 1974.

Ikeda, Yoshiko. "Paternal Attitude toward Twins in Japan." In Takie Sugiyama Lebra and William P. Lebra, eds., *Japanese Culture and Behavior: Selected Readings*. Honolulu: University Press of Hawaii, 1974, pp. 313–322.

Ikegami, Eiko. *Bonds of Civility: Aesthetic Networks and the Political Origins of Japanese Culture*. Cambridge, Eng.: Cambridge University Press, 2005.

Inagaki Shin'ichi. *Edo no asobie*. Tōkyō shoseki, 1988.

Inagaki Tatsurō, ed. *Tsubouchi Shōyō shū*. In *Meiji bungaku zenshū 16*. Chikuma shobō, 1969.

Inoue Takaaki. *Edo gesaku no kenkyū—Kibyōshi o shu toshite*. Shintensha, 1986.

Inouye, Charles Shirō. *A Diverting View of Loyal Retainers*. In John Solt, ed., *An Episodic Festschrift for Howard Hibbett 11*. Hollywood, CA: Highmoonoon, 2003.

———. "Pictocentrism." In *Yearbook of Comparative and General Literature*, vol. 40 (1992), pp. 23–39.

———. "Pictocentrism—China as a Source of Japanese Modernity." In Jones, ed., *Reading/Imaging Eros*, pp. 148–152.

Ishikawa Ichirō. *Edo bungaku zokushin jiten*. Tōkyōdō shuppan, 1989.

Ishikawa Matsutarō, ed. *Nihon kyōkasho taikei 7: Ōraihen*. Kōdansha, 1972.

———. *Ōraimono taikei*. Ōzorasha, 1992–1994. 100 volumes.

Ito, Kinko. "A History of *Manga* in the Context of Japanese Culture and Society." In *The Journal of Popular Culture*, vol. 38, no. 3 (2005), pp. 456–475.

Ito, Setsuko. "The Muse in Competition: *Uta-Awase* through the Ages." In *MN*, vol. 37, no. 2 (summer 1982), pp. 201–222.

Iwanami shoten, ed. *(Hoteiban) Kokusho sōmokuroku*. Iwanami shoten, 1989–1991. 9 volumes.

————. *Nihon koten bungaku daijiten*. Iwanami shoten, 1983–1985. 6 volumes.

Iwasaki, Haruko. "The Literature of Wit and Humor in Late-Eighteenth-Century Edo." In Jenkins, ed. *The Floating World Revisited*, pp. 47–61.

————. "Matsudaira Sadanobu: Portrait of a Daimyo, Comic Fiction by Matsudaira Sadanobu." In *MN*, vol. 38, no. 1 (Spring 1983) pp. 1–48.

————. "Speak, Memory! Edo Netsuke in Their Literary Context." In *International Netsuke Society Journal*, vol. 21, no. 4 (Winter 2001), pp. 27–49.

————. "The World of *Gesaku*: Playful Writers of Late Eighteenth-Century Japan." Ph.D. dissertation, Harvard University, 1984.

Iwanami shoten Nihon koten bungaku daijiten henshū iinkai. *Nihon koten bungaku daijiten*. Iwanami shoten, 1983–1985. 6 volumes.

Iwata Hideyuki. "*Katakiuchi nomitori manako*: Honkoku, ryakuchū." In *Atomi gakuen joshi daigaku kokubungakka hō*, vol. 15 (1987), pp. 1–27.

Izumi Kyōka. *(Shinpen) Izumi Kyōka shū 2*. Iwanami shoten, 2004.

Jansen, Marius B. *Japan and Its World: Two Centuries of Change*. Princeton: Princeton University Press, 1980.

Jenkins, Donald, ed. *The Floating World Revisited*. Portland, OR: Portland Art Museum; and University of Hawaii Press, 1993.

Johnson, Regine. "Tōrai Sanna and the Creation of Difference." In *Japan Review*, vol. 7 (1996), pp. 83–97.

Jones, Sumie. "Comic Fiction in Japan During the Later Edo Period." Ph.D. dissertation, University of Washington, 1979.

————. "Language in Crisis: Ogyū Sorai's Philological Thought and Hiraga Gennai's Creative Practice." In Earl Miner, ed. *Principles of Classical Japanese Literature*. Princeton: Princeton University Press, 1985, pp. 209–256.

————. "William Hogarth and Kitao Masanobu: Reading Eighteenth-Century Pictorial Narratives." In *Yearbook of Comparative and General Literature*, no. 34 (1985), pp. 37–73.

Jones, Sumie, ed. *Imaging / Reading Eros*. Bloomington: The East Asian Studies Center, Indiana University, 1996.

Jones, Sumie et al., eds. *Edo Pop: An Anthology of Late Edo Literature, 1750–1850* (tentative title). Honolulu: University of Hawaii Press, forthcoming.

Jordan, Brenda G. and Victoria Weston. *Copying the Master and Stealing His Secrets: Talent and Training in Japanese Painting*. Honolulu: University of Hawaii Press, 2003.

Kabat, Adam. *Edo bakemono sōshi*. Shōgakukan, 1999.

————. "Monsters as Edo Merchandise." In *Japan Quarterly*, vol. 48, no. 1 (January-March 2001), pp. 66–77.

————. *Ōedo bakemono saiken*. Shōgakukan, 2000.

Kajiya, Kenji. "Reimagining the Imagined: Depictions of Dreams and Ghosts in the Early Edo Period." In *Impressions*, vol. 23 (2001), pp. 86–107.

Kamens, Edward. *Utamakura, Allusion, and Intertextuality in Traditional Japanese Poetry*. New Haven: Yale University Press, 1997.

Kaplan, Joel H. and Sheila Stowell. *Theatre and Fashion: Oscar Wilde to the Suffragettes.* Cambridge, Eng.: Cambridge University Press, 1994.

Kasuya Hiroki, ed. *(Shinpen) Senryū daijiten.* Tōkyōdō shuppan, 1995.

Katō Ikuya. *Edo no fūryūjin.* Ozawa shoten, 1980.

Kawazoe Yū. *Edo no misemono.* Iwanami shinsho, 2000.

Keene, Donald. *World Within Walls: Japanese Literature of the Pre-Modern Era, 1600–1867.* Tokyo: Charles E. Tuttle, 1978. First published by Holt, Rinehart, and Winston, 1976.

Keene, Donald, trans. *Chūshingura (The Treasury of Loyal Retainers).* New York: Columbia University Press, 1971.

Kern, Adam L. "Blowing Smoke: Tobacco Pouches, Literary Squibs, and Authorial Puffery in the Pictorial Comic Fiction (*Kibyōshi*) of Santō Kyōden (1761–1816)." Ph.D. dissertation, Harvard University, 1997.

———. "Santō Kyōden gasaku no kibyōshi *Sogitsugi gingiseru* no saikō to shichū." In *Chōsa kenkyū jikoku,* no. 22 (2001), pp. 17–62.

———, trans. *The Funeral Director's Blowout-Sale Circular.* In John Solt, ed., *An Occasional Festschrift for Howard Hibbett 17.* Hollywood, CA: Highmoonoon, forthcoming 2007.

———. "Shiba Zenkō's *Thousand-Armed Goddess of Mercy, Julienned.*" In Jones, *Edo Pop.*

Kinsella, Sharon. *Adult Manga: Culture and Power in Contemporary Japanese Society.* Honolulu: University of Hawaii Press, 2000.

Kinoshita Itoko and Yoshimi Shun'ya, eds. *Nyūsu no tanjō: Kawaraban to shinbun nishikie no jōhō sekai.* Tōkyō daigaku sōgō kenkyū hakubutsukan, 1999.

Kisho fukuseikai, ed. *Kisho fukuseikai sōsho 1.* Yoneyamadō, 1918.

———. *Kisho fukuseikai sōsho 4.* Yoneyamadō, 1926.

———. *(Kisho fukuseikai sōsho) Shinseiki 35–37.* Yoneyamadō, 1938–1939.

Kitahara Aiko. *Edo fūkyōden.* Chūō kōronsha, 1997.

Kiyoshi Seike. *The Japanese Art of Joinery.* Trans. Yuriko Yoboku and Rebecca M. Davis. New York: Weatherhill, 1977.

Klein, Susan Blakeley. *Allegories of Desire: Esoteric Literary Commentaries of Medieval Japan.* Cambridge, Mass.: Harvard University Asia Center, Harvard University Press, 2002.

Kōdō Tokuchi, ed. *Kibyōshi hyakushu.* Hakubunkan, 1907.

Koike Masatane. *Hankotsusha Ōta Nanpo to Santō Kyōden.* In *Edo Tōkyō raiburarii 2.* Kyōiku shuppan, 1998.

Koike Masatane, ed. *Edo no ehon 1: Shoki kusazōshi shūsei.* Kokusho kankōkai, 1987.

———. *Edo no ehon 2.* Kokusho kankōkai, 1988.

———. *Edo no ehon 3.* Kokusho kankōkai, 1989.

Koike Masatane, Uda Toshihiko, Nakayama Yūshō, and Tanahashi Masahiro, eds. *Edo no gesaku [parodī] ehon 1: Shoki kibyōshi shū. Gendai kyōyō bunko 1037.* Shakai shisōsha, 1980.

———. *Edo no gesaku [parodī] ehon 2: Zenseiki kibyōshi shū. Gendai kyōyō bunko 1038.* Shakai shisōsha, 1981.

———. *Edo no gesaku [parodī] ehon 3: Henkakuki kibyōshi shū. Gendai kyōyō bunko 1039.* Shakai shisōsha, 1982.

———. *Edo no gesaku [parodī] ehon 4: Makki kibyōshi shū. Gendai kyōyō bunko 1040.* Shakai shisōsha, 1983.

———. *Edo no gesaku [parodi] ehon 5: Zokkan 1. Gendai kyōyō bunko 1107.* Shakai shisōsha, 1984.

———. *Edo no gesaku [parodi] ehon 6: Zokkan 2. Gendai kyōyō bunko 1108.* Shakai shisōsha, 1985.

Koike Tōgorō. *Santō Kyōden no kenkyū.* Iwanami shoten, 1935.

———. "Akabon, kurohon, kibyōshi naka no Sogamono." In *Kokugo to kokubungaku,* no. 4 (1933).

Kokuritsu gekijō, ed. *Shibai kinmōzui—Kyōwa sannen shohonbon.* In *Kabuki no bunnan 3.* Kokuritsu gekijō geinō chōsashitsu, 1976.

Kokuritsu rekishi minzoku hakubutsukan, ed. *Otoko mo onna mo sōshingu: Edo kara Meiji no waza to dezain.* NHK puromōshon, 2002.

Kominz, Laurence R. *The Stars Who Created Kabuki: Their Lives, Loves and Legacy.* Tokyo, New York, London: Kodansha International, 1997.

Konta Yōzō. *Edo no hon'yasan.* Nippon hōsō shuppan kyōkai, 1983.

———. *Edo no kinsho.* Yoshikawa kōbunkan, 1981.

Kornicki, Peter F. *The Book in Japan: A Cultural History from the Beginnings to the Nineteenth Century.* Leiden, Boston, and Köln: E.J. Brill, 1998.

———. "The Enmeiin Affair of 1803: The Spread of Information in the Tokugawa Period." In *HJAS,* vol. 42, no. 2 (December 1982), pp. 503–533.

———. "*Nishiki no Ura*: An Instance of Censorship and the Structure of a *Sharebon.*" In *MN,* vol. 32, no. 2 (1977), pp. 153–188.

———. "The Publisher's Go-Between: *Kashihonya* in the Meiji Period." In *Modern Asian Studies,* vol. 14, no. 2 (April 1980), pp. 331–344.

Koyama Tadashi. *Jōkyoku no shinkenkyū.* Nihon gakujutsu shinkōkai, 1962.

Kunzle, David. *The Early Comic Strip: Narrative Strips and Picture Stories in the European Broadsheet from c. 1450 to 1825.* In Kunzle, *History of the Comic Strip I.* Berkeley, Los Angeles, and London: University of California Press, 1973.

Kuwata Tadachika. *Toyotomi Hideyoshi kenkyū.* Kadokawa shoten, 1975.

Lane, Richard. "The Beginnings of the Modern Japanese Novel: *Kana-Zōshi,* 1600–1682." In *HJAS,* vol. 20 (1957), pp. 644–703.

———. "Saikaku's Five Women." In de Bary, *Five Women Who Loved Love,* pp. 233–242.

———. "The Young Man from Edo Who Was Punished for Loving Too Daringly." In Michel Beurdeley et al., eds., *Erotic Art of Japan: The Pillow Poem.* Hong Kong: Leon Amiel, no date, pp. 227–242.

Laqueur, Thomas. *Making Sex: Body and Gender from the Greeks to Freud.* Cambridge, Mass.: Harvard University Press, 1990.

Lecercle, Jean-Jacques. *Philosophy of Nonsense: The Institutions of Victorian Nonsense Literature.* London: Routledge, 1994.

Legge, James. *Confucius: Confucian Analects, The Great Learning and The Doctrine of the Mean.* New York: Dover Publications, 1971. Republication of the 2nd revised edition, as published by the Clarendon Press, Oxford, in 1893 as vol. I in "The Chinese Classics" Series.

Leutner, Robert W. *Shikitei Sanba and the Comic Tradition in Edo Fiction.* In Harvard-Yenching Institute Monograph Series 25. Cambridge, Mass.: Council on East Asian Studies, Harvard University, and Harvard-Yenching Institute, 1985.

Levine, Michael G. "Necessary Stains: Art Spiegelman's *Maus* and the Bleeding of History." In Geis, ed., *Considering* Maus, pp. 63–104.

Mair, Victor H. *Painting and Performance: Chinese Pictorial Recitation and Its Indian Genesis.* Honolulu: University of Hawaii Press, 1988.

Marceau, Lawrence E., trans. *Biographies of Limp Dicks in Seclusion, "Naemara in'itsu den" (1768) by Hiraga Gennai.* In John Solt, ed., *An Episodic Festschrift for Howard Hibbett 8.* Hollywood, CA: Highmoonoon, 2001.

Markus, Andrew. "The Carnival of Edo: *Misemono* Spectacles from Contemporary Accounts." In *HJAS*, vol. 45, no. 2 (December 1985), pp. 499–541.

———. "Itinerary of a Useless Man: Terakado Seiken's (1796–1868) Literary Prosecution and Exile." Unpublished paper delivered at the Western Conference of the Association for Asian Studies, October 4–5, 1991.

———. *Willow in Autumn: Ryūtei Tanehiko, 1783–1842.* Cambridge, Mass.: Council on East Asian Studies, Harvard University, 1992.

Marra, Michele. "*Mumyōzōshi*: Introduction and Translation." In *MN*, vol. 39, no. 2 (summer 1984), pp. 115–145.

Martin, Nobuko Jo. "Santō Kyōden and His *Sharebon*." Ph.D. dissertation, University of Michigan, 1979.

Matsuki Hiroshi. *Tsutaya Jūzaburō: Edo geijutsu no enshutsusha.* Nihon keizai shinbunsha, 1988.

Matsumiya Saburō. *Edo kabuki to kōkoku.* Tōhō shobō, 1973.

Matsumoto, Shigeru. *Motoori Norinaga, 1730–1801.* Cambridge, Mass.: Harvard University Press, 1970.

Matsuwara Hidetada. "Otogizōshi kanazōshi ni okeru iwayuru rokudanhon ni tsuite." In *Gobun sōshi.* Toyonaka-shi: Tanaka Yutaka sensei no gotaishoku o kinensuru kai, 1981, pp. 237–253.

Matsuzaki Hitoshi, Hara Michio, Iguchi Hiroshi, and Ōhashi Tadayoshi, eds. *Chikamatsu jōrurishū 2.* In *SNKBT 92.* Iwanami shoten, 1995.

May, Ekkehard. *Die Kommerzialisierung der japanischen Literatur in der späten Edo-Zeit (1750–1868): Rahmenbedingungen und Entwicklungstendenzen der erzählenden Prosa im Zeitalter ihrer ersten Vermarktung.* Wiesbaden: Otto Harrassowitz, 1983.

Mayama Seika. *Mayama Seika zenshū 3.* Dai Nihon yūbenkai kōdansha, 1940.

McCloud, Scott. *Understanding Comics: The Invisible Art.* New York: Harper Perennial, 1994. First published by Kitchen Sink Press, 1993.

McCullough, Helen Craig. *Kokin Wakashū: The First Imperial Anthology of Japanese Poetry.* Stanford: Stanford University Press, 1985.

McCullough, Helen Craig, comp. and ed. *Classical Japanese Prose: An Anthology.* Stanford: Stanford University Press, 1990.

McGrath, Charles. "Not Funnies." In *The New York Times Magazine*, Sunday, July 11, 2004, pp. 24–33, 46, 55–56.

Mekada Makoto. *Tōshisen.* In *Shinshaku kanbun taikei 19.* Meiji shoin, 1964.

Mezur, Katherine. "Undressing the *Onnagata*: Kabuki's Female Role Specialists and the Art of Costuming." In Stanca Scholz-Cionca and Samuel L. Leiter, eds., *Japanese Theatre and the International Stage.* In Brill's Japanese Studies Library 12. Leiden: E. J. Brill, 2001, pp. 193–211.

Michener, James A., ed. *The Hokusai Sketchbooks: Selections from the Manga.* Rutland, VT: Charles E. Tuttle, 1958.

Miller, J. Scott. "The Hybrid Narrative of Kyōden's *Sharebon*." In *MN*, vol. 43, no. 2 (summer 1988), pp. 133–152.

Minami Kazuo. *Edo no fūshiga*. In *Rekishi bunka raiburarii 22*. Yoshikawa kōbunkan, 1997.

Mindess, Harvey. *Laughter and Liberation*. Los Angeles: Nash Publishing, 1971.

Miner, Earl. "The Grounds of Mimetic and Nonmimetic Art: The Western Sister Arts in a Japanese Mirror." In Richard Wendorf, ed., *Articulate Images: The Sister Arts from Hogarth to Tennyson*. Minneapolis: University of Minnesota Press, 1983, pp. 70–97.

Ming Wangqi. *Sancai tuhui 2*. Chengwen chubanshe, 1970.

Mitani Kazuma. *Edo Yoshiwara zushū*. Rippū shobō, 1977.

Miyagi Kimiko, ed. *Nihon no meicho 27*. Chūō kōronsha, 1978.

Miyamoto Hirohito. "The Stratifying Process of the Notion of 'Manga': From the Early Modern Age to the Modern Age in Japan." In *Bijutsushi: Journal of the Japan Art Society*, vol. 52, no. 2 (March 2003), pp. 319–334.

Miyao Shigeo, ed. *(Mihonkoku) Eiri Edo kobanashi jūnishu 11*. Kinsei fūzoku kenkyūkai, 1966.

Miyatake Gaikotsu. *Santō Kyōden*. In *Miyatake Gaikotsu chosakushū 6*. Yoshikawa kōbunkan, 1916.

Mizuno Minoru. *Edo shōsetsu ronsō*. Chūō kōronsha, 1974.

———. *Kibyōshi sharebon no sekai*. In *Iwanami shinsho 986*. Iwanami shoten, 1976.

———. *Santō Kyōden nenpukō*. Perikansha, 1991.

———. *Santō Kyōden no kibyōshi*. Yūkō shobō, 1976.

Mizuno Minoru, ed. *Kibyōshi sharebon shū*. In *NKBT 59*. Iwanami shoten, 1958.

———. *Kibyōshi shū 1*. In *Koten bunko 264*. Koten bunko, 1969.

———. *Kibyōshi shū 2*. In *Koten bunko 313*. Koten bunko, 1973.

———. *Yone manjū no hajimari, Shikake bunko, Mukashigatari inazuma byōshi*. In *SNKBT 85*. Iwanami shoten, 1990.

Mizuno Minoru et al., eds. *SKZ 1: Kibyōshi 1*. Perikansha, 1992.

———. *SKZ 2: Kibyōshi 2*. Perikansha, 1993.

———. *SKZ 3: Kibyōshi 3*. Perikansha, 2001.

———. *SKZ 4: Kibyōshi 4*. Perikansha, 2004.

———. *SKZ 5: Kibyōshi 5*. Perikansha, forthcoming.

———. *SKZ 6: Gōkan 1*. Perikansha, 1995.

———. *Sharebon taisei*. 30 volumes. Chūō kōronsha, 1978–1988.

Mizutani Futō. *Kusazōshi to yomihon no kenkyū*. Okugawa shobō, 1934.

Mori Senzō. *Kibyōshi kaidai*. Chūō kōronsha, 1972.

———. "Kibyōshi kaidai josetsu." In *Mori Senzō chosakushū zoku hen 7*, pp. 327–340.

———. "Kibyōshi sharebon mangen." In *Mori Senzō chosakushū zoku hen 7*, pp. 367–370.

———. *Mori Senzō chosakushū zoku hen 7—Kinsei*. Chūō kōronsha, 1993.

———. "Tenpura no senden o shiteiru kibyōshi." In *Mori Senzō chosakushū zoku hen 7*, pp. 363–367.

———. *Zoku kibyōshi kaidai*. Chūō kōronsha, 1974.

Mori Senzō, ed. *Zuihitsu hyakkaen 7*. Chūō kōronsha, 1980.

Morita Seigo. "Edoki shoten no hassei dōkō." In *Bungaku*, vol. 42, no. 9 (September 1974), pp. 76–85.

Moriya, Katsuhisa. "Urban Networks and Information Networks." In Nakane and Ōishi, eds., *Tokugawa Japan*, pp. 97–123.

Morohashi Tetsuji, ed. *Daikanwa jiten*. Taishūkan shoten, 1966–1968.

Mostow, Joshua S. *Pictures of the Heart: The* Hyakunin Isshu *in Word and Image*. Honolulu: University of Hawaii Press, 1996.

Mutō Motoaki. "Futari no Enjirō: *Edo umare uwaki no kabayaki* kara *Sōmagaki* e." In *Kokugo to kokubungaku*, vol. 72, no. 6 (1995), pp. 1–12.

Mutō Sadao. *Hanashibon taikei 13*. Tōkyōdō shuppan, 1979.

———. *(Edo no parodī) Mojiri hyakunin isshu o yomu*. Tōkyōdō shuppan, 1998.

Mutō Sadao, ed. *(Edo fūzoku) Eiri kobanashi o yomu*. Tōkyōdō shuppan, 1994.

Nagatomo Chiyoji. "Hon'ya kashihon, kashihon'ya no shuppan." In *Bungaku*, vol. 49, no. 11, (1981), pp. 83–94.

Naitō Chisō and Komiyama Yasusuke, eds. *Onchi sōsho 10*. Hakubunkan, 1910.

Najita, Tetsuo. "History and Nature in Eighteenth-Century Tokugawa Thought." In Hall, ed., *Early Modern Japan*, pp. 596–659.

Nakamura Yukihiko. "(Edo jidai) Kamigata ni okeru dōwabon." In *Bungaku kenkyū*, vol. 59, no. 3 (1960).

———. *Gesakuron*. Kadokawa shoten, 1966. Republished by Chūō kōronsha, 1982.

———. "Modes of Expression in a Historical Context." In Tōhō Gakkai, *Acta Asiatica: Bulletin of The Institute of Eastern Culture*, vol. 28 (March 1975), pp. 1–19.

———. *Nakamura Yukihiko chojutsushū 14*. Chūō kōronsha, 1983.

———. "*Edo umare uwaki no kabayaki* sadan." In *Kokubungaku*, vol. 50 (1974), pp. 35–41.

Nakamura Yukihiko, ed. *Fūrai Sanjin shū*. In *NKBT 55*. Iwanami shoten, 1961.

Nakamura Yukihiko and Nakano Mitsutoshi, eds. *Kasshi yawa*. Heibonsha, 1977–1978. 6 volumes.

Nakamura Yukihiko, Okami Masao, Sakakura Atsuyoshi, eds. *(Kadokawa) Kogo daijiten*. Kadokawa shoten, 1982–1999. 5 volumes.

Nakane, Chie and Shinzaburō Ōishi, eds. *Tokugawa Japan: The Social and Economic Antecedents of Modern Japan*. Tokyo: University of Tokyo Press, 1991.

Nakano Eizō. *Edo higo jiten*. Kyōyūsha, 1993.

Nakano Mitsutoshi. *Edo meisho hyōbanki shūsei*. Iwanami shoten, 1987.

———. "*Edo umare uwaki no kabayaki*: Sakuhin kanshō." In *Kyōden Ikku Shunsui*. In Jinbō Kazuya et al., eds., *Zusetsu Nihon no koten 18*. Shūeisha, 1980, pp. 80–91.

———. *Gesaku kenkyū*. Chūō kōronsha, 1981.

———. "The Role of Traditional Aesthetics." In Gerstle, ed., *Eighteenth-Century Japan*, pp. 124–131.

Nakano Mitsutoshi, ed. *Inaka sōshi, Imayō hetadangi, Tōsei anasagashi*. In *SNKBT 81*. Iwanami shoten, 1990.

———. *Sharebon kokkeibon ninjōbon*. In *SNKBZ 80*. Shōgakukan, 2000.

Nakao Tatsurō. *Sui, tsū, iki—Edo no biishiki kō*. Miyai shoten, 1984.

Napier, Susan J. *Anime from Akira to* Princess Mononoke: *Experiencing Contemporary Japanese Animation*. New York: Palgrave (for St. Martin's Griffin), 2001.

Natsume Fusanosuke. "Japanese Manga: Its Expression and Popularity." In *ABD*, vol. 34, no. 1 (2003), pp. 3–5.

———. "Kibyōshi o manga kara miru." In Tanahashi, ed., *Edo gesaku zōshi*, pp. 196–205.

Natsume Sōseki. *Sōseki zenshū 17*. Iwanami shoten, 1996.

Nobuhiro Shinji. "Santō Kyōden's *Sharebon*: Private Life and Public Art." In Jones, ed., *Imaging/Reading Eros*, pp. 142–145.

Odaka Toshio, ed. *Edo shōwa shū*. In *NKBT 100*. Iwanami shoten, 1966.

Ogata Tsutomu. *Za no bungaku*. Kadokawa shoten, 1973.

Okada Toshio. *Otaku gaku nyūmon*. Shinchōsha, 1996.

Okamoto Masaru. "Shoki Kamigata kodomo ehon o megutte." In *Bungaku*, no. 8 (1981) pp. 85–98.

Ōkubo Tadakuni and Kinoshita Kazuko, eds. *Edogo jiten*. Tōkyōdō shuppan, 1991.

Ōta Nanpo. *Neboke sensei bunshū* (1767). Reprinted in Hamada, ed., *Ōta Nanpo zenshū 1* (1985), pp. 341–366.

Ozaki Hotsuki et al., eds. *Kodomo no hon no hyakunenshi*. Meiji tosho shuppan, 1973.

Pincus, Leslie. *Authenticating Culture in Imperial Japan: Kuki Shūzō and the Rise of National Aesthetics*. Berkeley: University of California Press, 1996.

Putzar, Edward, trans. "*Chikusai monogatari*: A Partial Translation." In *MN*, vol. 16, nos. 1–2. (April-July 1960), pp. 161–195.

Rabinovitch, Judith. *Shōmonki*. Tokyo: Sophia University Press, 1986.

Raskin, Victor. *Semantic Mechanisms of Humor*. Boston: D. Reidel Publishing, 1985.

Raz, Jacob. "The Audience Evaluated: Shikitei Sanba's *Kyakusha Hyōbanki*." In *MN*, vol. 35, no. 2 (summer 1980), pp. 199–221.

Roberts, Luke S. "The Petition Box in Eighteenth-Century Tosa." In *JJS*, vol. 20, no. 2 (summer 1994), pp. 423–458.

Roberts, Luke S., trans. "About Some Japanese Historical Terms." In *Sino-Japanese Studies*, vol. 10, no. 2 (April 1998), pp. 32–42.

Rosenfield, John M. "The Anatomy of Humor in Hokusai's Instruction Manuals." In John T. Carpenter, ed., *Hokusai: Ukiyo-e Painting, Printmaking, and Book Illustration in Late Edo Japan*. Amsterdam: Hotei Publishing, 2005, pp. 298–327.

Rosenfield, John M. with Fumiko E. Cranston. *Extraordinary Persons: Works by Eccentric, Nonconformist Japanese Artists of the Early Modern Era (1580–1868) in the Collection of Kimiko and John Powers*. Ed. Naomi Richard. Cambridge, Mass.: Harvard University Art Museums, 1999.

Ruch, Barbara. "Medieval Jongleurs and the Making of a National Literature." In John W. Hall and Toyoda Takeshi, eds., *Japan in the Muromachi Age*. Berkeley: University of California Press, 1977, pp. 279–309.

Rubinger, Richard. *Private Academies of Tokugawa Japan*. Princeton: Princeton University Press, 1982.

Sabin, Roger. *Comics, Comix & Graphic Novels: A History of Comic Art*. London: Phaidon Press, 1996.

Sakai, Naoki. *Voices of the Past: The Status of Language in Eighteenth-Century Japanese Discourse*. Ithaca: Cornell University Press, 1992.

Sakamoto Shūji. "Kusazōshi ni okeru Edo shorin no dōkō." In *Shoshigaku 11* (1965).

Sante, Luc. "The Clear Line." In Howe, ed., *Give Our Regards to the Atomsmashers!*, pp. 24–32.

Satchell, Thomas, trans. *Shanks' Mare: Being a Translation of the Tokaido volumes of Hizakurige, Japan's Great Comic Novel of Travel and Ribaldry by Ikku Jippensha (1765–1831)*. Rutland, VT: Charles E. Tuttle, 1960. Reprint of the 1929 edition published by subscription in Kobe.

Satō Mitsunobu. *Gesaku no hana: Kibyōshi no sekai*. Hiraki ukiyoe bijutsukan, 1999, p. 1.

Satō Yōjin, ed. *Seirō wadan shinzō zui*. Miki shobō, 1976.

Sawada, Janine Anderson. *Confucian Values and Popular Zen: Sekimon Shingaku in Eighteenth-Century Japan*. Honolulu: University of Hawaii Press, 1993.

Schamoni, Wolfgang. *Die Sharebon Santō Kyōden's und ihre Literaturgeschichtliche Stellung.* Bonn: Rheinische Friedrich-Wilhelms Universität, 1970.

Schodt, Frederik L. *Dreamland Japan: Writings on Modern Manga.* Berkeley: Stone Bridge Press, 1996.

———. *Manga! Manga! The World of Japanese Comics.* New York: Kodansha International, 1983.

Schönbein, Martina. *Das Kibyōshi "Happyakuman ryō kogane no kamibana" von Santō Kyōden (1791): Ein Beitrag zur Edition japanischer Texte der Edo-Zeit.* Wiesbaden: Otto Harrassowitz, 1987.

Screech, Timon. *Sex and the Floating World: Erotic Images in Japan 1700–1820.* London: Reaktion Books, 1999.

———. *The Western Scientific Gaze and Popular Imagery in Later Edo Japan: The Lens Within the Heart.* Cambridge, Eng.: Cambridge University Press, 1996.

Segal, Eric. *The Death of Comedy.* Cambridge, Mass.: Harvard University Press, 2001.

Seigle, Cecilia Segawa. *Yoshiwara: The Glittering World of the Japanese Courtesan.* Honolulu: University of Hawaii Press, 1993.

Shimizu Isao. "Japan's Rich Tradition of Cartoons & Comics." In *Echoes of Peace: Quarterly Bulletin of the Niwano Peace Foundation* (January 1993), pp. 13–15.

———. *Manga no rekishi.* In *Iwanami shinsho 172.* Iwanami shoten, 1991.

Shimoyama Hiroshi. *Senryū no erotishizumu.* Shinchōsha, 1995.

Shiokawa Kanako. "'The Reads' and 'Yellow Covers': Pre-Modern Predecessors of Comic Books in Japan." In *Journal of Asian Pacific Communication,* vol. 7, nos. 1 and 2 (1996), pp. 19–29. Special Issue: *Comic Art in Asia: Historical, Literary and Political Roots.*

Shirane, Haruo, ed. *EMJL: An Anthology, 1600–1900.* New York: Columbia University Press, 2002.

Shively, Donald H. "Chikamatsu's Satire on The Dog Shogun." In *HJAS,* vol. 18, nos. 1–2 (June 1955), pp. 159–180.

———. *The Love Suicide at Amijima (Shinjū Ten no Amijima): A Study of a Japanese Domestic Tragedy by Chikamatsu Monzaemon.* In *Michigan Classics in Japanese Studies 5.* Ann Arbor: University of Michigan, 1991. First published in Cambridge, Mass. by the Center for Japanese Studies, Harvard University Press, 1953.

Sibley, William F., trans. "On Farting." In *Readings in Tokugawa Thought.* In *Select Papers 9.* Chicago: The Center for East Asian Studies, 1998, 3rd ed, pp. 167–174.

Sitkin, David A. "The Upside-Down Topos: Exaggeration and Inversion in the *Kibyōshi* of Santō Kyōden." In *Nagoya daigaku sōgō gengo sentā gengo bunka ronshū,* vol. 2, no. 1 (1980), pp. 269–283.

Skord, Virginia, trans. *Tales of Tears and Laughter: Short Fiction of Medieval Japan.* Honolulu: University of Hawaii Press, 1991.

Smith, Henry. "Overcoming the Modern History of Edo 'Shunga.'" In Jones, ed., *Imaging / Reading Eros,* pp. 26–34.

Solt, John. "Willow Leaftips." In Jones, ed., *Reading / Imaging Eros,* pp. 129–134.

Solt, John. ed. *An Episodic Festschrift for Howard Hibbett.* Hollywood, CA: Highmoonnoon, 2000–present. 15 volumes and ongoing.

Sontag, Susan. *Against Interpretation and Other Essays.* New York: Picador, 2001. First published by Farrar, Straus and Giroux, 1966.

Sorenaka, Isao. "The Kansei Reforms—Success or Failure?" In *MN,* vol. 33, no. 2 (summer 1978), pp. 151–164.

Spaulding, Amy E. *The Page as a Stage Set: Storyboard Picture Books.* Metuchen, NJ: Scarecrow Press, 1995.

Spiegelman, Art. Interview on National Public Radio, December 21, 2001.

———. Interview on National Public Radio, September 16, 2004.

———. *Maus I: A Survivor's Tale: My Father Bleeds History.* New York: Pantheon Books, 1991.

———. *Maus II: A Survivor's Tale: And Here My Troubles Began.* New York: Pantheon Books, 1991.

Steenstrup, Carl. "The Imagawa Letter: A Muromachi Warrior's Code of Conduct Which Became a Tokugawa Schoolbook." In *MN*, vol. 28, no. 3 (1973), pp. 295–316.

Sterling, Bryan B., and Frances N. Sterling. *Will Rogers' World: America's Foremost Political Humorist Comments on the Twenties and Thirties—and Eighties and Nineties.* New York: M. Evans and Company, 1989.

Stewart, Susan. *Nonsense: Aspects of Intertextuality in Folklore and Literature.* Baltimore: Johns Hopkins University Press, 1980.

Sugiura Hinako. *Edo e yōkoso.* Chikuma bunko, 1989.

———. *Sugiura Hinako zenshū 1.* Chikuma shobō, 1995.

Suwa Haruo. *Shuppan koto hajime—Edo no hon.* In *Edo shirīzu 11.* Mainichi shinbunsha, 1978.

Suzuki Jun. *Tachibana Chikage no kenkyū.* Perikansha, 2006.

Suzuki Jūzō and Kimura Yaeko, eds. *Kinsei kodomo no ehonshū: Edo hen.* Iwanami shoten, 1993. First published in 1985.

Suzuki Takeo. *Palaeopathological and Palaeoepidemiological Study of Osseous Syphilis in Skulls of the Edo Period.* Tokyo: University of Tokyo Press, 1984.

Sypher, Wylie, ed. *Comedy.* Baltimore: Johns Hopkins University Press, 1980. First published by Doubleday, 1956.

Tabako to shio no hakubutsukan, ed. *Kansei no shuppankai to Santō Kyōden: 200 nenmae ga omoshiroi!* Tabako to shio no hakubutsukan, 1995.

———. *Kiseru.* Tabako to shio no hakubutsukan, 1988.

Takahashi Mitsuko. "Kurobon, aohon *Sakenomi dōshi* ni tsuite." In *Kinsei bungei*, vol. 37, no. 11 (1982), pp. 16–34.

Takahashi Noriko. *Kusazōshi to engeki: Yakusha nigaoe sōshiki o chūshin ni.* Kyūko shoin, 2004.

Takaki Yoshiji. "*Kinkin sensei* ni anji o ataeta sakuhin." In *Edo bunka 4* (1929).

Takano Tatsuyuki, ed. *Nihon kayō shūsei 10.* Shunjūsha, 1929.

Takeno Seio. "Onatsu Seijūrō mono no rinkaku—Kinsei ki." In *Geinō*, vol. 30, no. 8 (1988), pp. 12–20.

———. "Tajimaya Onatsu no zōkei—*Onatsu Seijūrō* no hensen." In *Geinō*, vol. 31, no. 1 (1989), pp. 18–27.

Takeuchi Makoto. "Kansei kaikaku to kibyōshi." In *Edo no shuppan bunka.* In *Tabako to shio no hakubutsukan kenkyū kiyō 4.* Tabako to shio no hakubutsukan, 1991, pp. 101–111.

Takizawa Bakin. *Kinsei mono no hon Edo sakusha burui.* Ed. Kimura Miyogo. Yagi shobō, 1988.

Tanahashi Masahiro. *Kibyōshi no kenkyū.* Wakakusa shobō, 1997.

———. *Kibyōshi sōran 1: Zen hen.* In *Nihon shoshigaku taikei 48.* Seishōdō shoten, 1986.

———. *Kibyōshi sōran 2: Chū hen.* In *Nihon shoshigaku taikei 48.* Seishōdō shoten, 1989.

———. *Kibyōshi sōran 3: Go hen.* In *Nihon shoshigaku taikei 48.* Seishōdō shoten, 1991.

———. *Kibyōshi sōran 4: Sakuin hen.* In *Nihon shoshigaku taikei 48.* Seishōdō shoten, 1994.

———. *Kibyōshi sōran 5: Zuroku hen.* In *Nihon shoshigaku taikei 48.* Seishōdō shoten, 2004.

Tanahashi Masahiro, ed. *Edo gesaku zōshi.* Shōgakukan, 2000.

Tanahashi Masahiro, Suzuki Jūzō, Uda Toshihiko, eds. *Kibyōshi senryū kyōka.* In *SNKBZ 79.* Shōgakukan, 1999.

Tanaka Ichimatsu and Ienaga Saburō, eds. *Jigoku sōshi, gaki sōshi, yamai no sōshi.* In *Shinshū Nihon emakimono zenshū 7.* Kadokawa shoten, 1976.

Tanaka Yūko. "The Creation of Culture through the Printing Media." In Printing Museum, Tokyo, ed., *Printing in the Edo Period—Ieyasu: Typographic Man.* Printing Museum, Tokyo, 2000, pp. 60–64.

———. "Erotic Textiles." In Jones, ed., *Imaging/Reading Eros,* pp. 63–68.

Tani Minezō. *Asobi no dezain: Santō Kyōden Komongawa.* Iwasaki bijutsusha, 1984.

———. *Edo no kopīraitā.* Iwasaki bijitsusha, 1986.

———. *Share no dezain: Santō Kyōden ga Tanagui awase.* Iwasaki bijitsusha, 1986.

Teruoka Yasutaka. "The Pleasure Quarters and Tokugawa Culture." In Gerstle, ed., *Eighteenth Century Japan,* pp. 3–32.

Toby, Ronald. "Reopening the Question of *Sakoku*: Diplomacy in the Legitimization of the Tokugawa Bakufu." In *JJS,* vol. 3, no. 2 (1977), pp. 323–366.

Togasaki, Fumiko T. "Santō Kyōden's *Kibyōshi*: Visual-Verbal and Contemporary-Classic Intercommunications." Ph.D. dissertation, Indiana University, 1995.

Tōkyō gakugei daigaku kokugo kokubungakkai kinsei bungaku bunkakai daigakuin dōjin, ed. *Kusamura: Kinsei bungaku enshū nōto.* Tōkyō gakugei daigaku kokugo kyōiku gakka kokubungaku daisan kenkyūshitsu.

Torigoe Bunzō et al., eds. *Chikamatsu Monzaemon shū 1.* In *SNKBZ 74.* Shōgakukan, 1997.

Tribble, Evelyn B. "The Peopled Page: Polemic, Confutation, and Foxe's *Book of Martyrs.*" In George Bornstein and Theresa Tinkle, eds., *The Iconic Page in Manuscript, Print, and Digital Culture.* Ann Arbor: The University of Michigan Press, 1998, pp. 109–122.

Tsuchida Mamoru et al., eds. *Suga Sensuke zenshū 5.* Benseisha, 1993.

Tsuji, Nobuo. "Early Medieval Picture Scrolls as Ancestors of *Anime* and *Manga.*" In Nicole Coolidge Rousmaniere, ed., *Births and Rebirths in Japanese Art.* Leiden: Hotei Publishing, 2001, pp. 53–82.

Tsurumi, Shunsuke. "Edo Period in Contemporary Popular Culture." In *Modern Asian Studies,* vol. 18, no. 4 (1984), pp. 747–755.

Turner, Victor. *Dramas, Fields, and Metaphors: Symbolic Action in Human Society.* Ithaca: Cornell University Press, 1974.

Tyler, Royall, ed. and comp. *Japanese Nō Dramas.* London: Penguin, 1992.

Uda Toshihiko. "Kibyōshi no sekai: Hyōgen ga daiichigi no kimyō na bungaku kūkan." In *Yurīka,* vol. 10, no. 4 (April 1978), pp. 101–107.

Ueda, Makoto, comp. and trans. *Light Verse from the Floating World: An Anthology of Premodern Japanese Senryu.* New York: Columbia University Press, 1999.

Utagawa Toyokuni. *Kokon haiyū nigao taizen: Zōho.* In Waseda daigaku Tsubouchi hakase kinen engeki hakubutsukan, ed., *Yakushae kenkyū shiryō 1.* Waseda daigaku Tsubouchi hakase kinen engeki hakubutsukan, 1998.

Vaporis, Constantine N. "To Edo and Back: Alternate Attendance and Japanese Culture in the Early Modern Period." In *JJS*, vol. 23, no. 1 (winter 1997), pp. 25–67.

Wada Hiromichi. "*Kikujusō* zengo." In Hamada, ed., *Tenmei bungaku*, pp. 55–71.

Wada Hiromichi, ed. *Shokusanjin kibyōshi shū*. Koten bunkō, 1984.

Warshow, Robert. "Paul, the Horror Comics, and Dr. Wertham." In Robert Warshow, *The Immediate Experience: Movies, Comics, Theatre and Other Aspects of Popular Culture*. Cambridge, Mass.: Harvard University Press, 2001, pp. 53–74.

Washburn, Dennis. *The Dilemma of the Modern in Japanese Fiction*. New Haven and London: Yale University Press, 1995.

Wells, Marguerite. *Japanese Humor*. London: Macmillan Press, 1997.

White, E. B. "Some Remarks on Humor." In E. B. White, *Essays of E. B. White*. New York: Harper Perennial, 1999. First published in 1972.

Yamaguchi Takeshi. *Edo bungaku kenkyū*. Tōkyōdō shuppan, 1933.

———. *Yamaguchi Takeshi chosakushū 3*. Ed. Teruoka Yasutaka and Jinbō Kazuya. Chūō kōronsha, 1972.

Yamaguchi Takeshi, ed. *Fūzoku zueshū*. In *Nihon meicho zenshū: Edo bungei no bu 30*. Nihon Meicho zenshū kankōkai, 1929.

———. *Kibyōshi nijūgoshū*. In *Nihon meicho zenshū: Edo bungei no bu 11*. Nihon Meicho zenshū kankōkai, 1926.

Yamanaka Kyōko. *Sunaharai*. Shun'yōdō, 1926.

Yang, X. Jie, with Sadako Ohki. *kanaCLASSIC: An Electronic Guide to Classical Kana Writing*. CD-ROM published by The Institute for Medieval Japanese Studies, Columbia University, 1998.

Yano Seiichi. *Rakugo: Nagaya no shiki*. Yomiuri shinbunsha, 1972.

Yano Takanori, ed. *Edo jidai rakusho ruiju*. Tōkyōdō shuppan, 1984.

Yasunaga, Toshinobu. *Ando Shoeki: Social and Ecological Philosopher of Eighteenth Century Japan*. New York: Weatherhill, 1992.

Yiengpruksawan, Mimi. "Monkey Magic: How the 'Animals' Scroll Makes Mischief with Art Historians." In *Orientations*, vol. 31, no. 3 (March 2000), pp. 74–83.

Yokoyama Shigeru and Matsumoto Ryūshin, eds. *Muromachi jidai monogatari taisei 5*. Kadokawa shoten, 1977.

Yonemoto, Marcia. *Mapping Early Modern Japan: Space, Place and Culture in the Tokugawa Period (1603–1868)*. Berkeley: University of California Press, 2003.

Yōrō Takeshi. *Suzushii nōmiso*. Bungei shunjū, 1991.

Yoshida, Kogorō. *Tanrokubon: Rare Books of Seventeenth-Century Japan*. New York: Kodansha International, 1984.

Yoshikawa Kōjirō and Ogawa Tamaki, eds., and Imataka Makoto et al., trans. *Tōshisen*. In *Chikuma sōsho 203*. Chikuma shobō, 1973.

Yumoto Kōichi. *Edo mangabon no sekai*. Kinokuniya shoten, 1997.

Zolbrod, Leon M. "The Vendetta of Mr. Fleacatcher Managoro, The Fifth (*Katakiuchi Nomi-tori Manako*)." In *MN*, vol. 20, nos. 1–2 (1965), pp. 121–134.

Manga
from the
Floating
World

Comicbook
Culture and
the *Kibyōshi*
of Edo Japan

Part II

Translations

A Note on Reading Backwards

This book is divided into two major parts. The first, consisting of prefatory materials, introductory chapters, and reference matter (Works Cited and Index), begins from the front cover and unfolds from the left page to the right, in the usual English-language order of reading. Part II of the book, consisting of three translations of *kibyōshi* with accompanying essays, annotation, and notes to the reader (including this one), begins here, from the "back" cover, and unfolds from the right page to the left, in the traditional Japanese (and Asian) order.

Casting the second part of the book "backwards" this way is intended both to honor the visual logic of the *kibyōshi* translated herein, which compels the eye from right to left, and, thereby, to approximate as closely as possible the original reading experience. Granted, some translators seek to naturalize Japanese comicbooks, reversing the traditional Japanese reading order by inverting the pictures into mirror images of themselves (as with at least one English-language version of Ōtomo Katsuhiro's *Akira*). Yet this method too often results in a distorted reflection of the original aesthetics and, therefore, is rejected in the present volume.

Many Western readers will undoubtedly find that reading this second part backwards feels unnatural, at least initially, though perhaps even ultimately. Nevertheless, precedent for having readers turn pages to the right instead of to the left can actually be found not only in the recent deluge of *manga* translations into English—the titles issued by Tokyopop and Dark Horse Comics come to mind—but also in a trickle of academic works. To wit, there is Thomas D. Conlan, trans., *In Little Need of Divine Intervention: Takezaki Suenaga's Scrolls of the Mongol Invasion of Japan*. Conlan's introductory essay is brief enough to be read backwards without much strain. The length of the first part of the present volume, however, would make such a backwards reading of that part, at least, irredeemably off-putting.

Consequently, a rather unorthodox dual pagination scheme is observed here, commencing from the front but continuing from the back. This means that, reading the pages in sequence, one will reach the end of this book only by getting stuck in the middle.

A Note on Translating the *Kibyōshi*

In his pioneering article over three decades ago, James T. Araki rendered a few *kibyōshi* into English employing what can be described as an illustrated playscript format with reduced reproductions of the original *kibyōshi* leaves interspersed strategically between stretches of translated text.[1] Subsequent translators by and large have followed suit, including Chris Drake, Sumie Jones, Scott Miller, and Wolfgang Schamoni, not to omit the present author. Although Araki provided no rationale for his choice, a clue can be found in an even earlier article of his in which, writing on one of the *kibyōshi*'s kindred genres, he observed that "the format of the *sharebon* is essentially that of the dramatic text."[2] Araki must have felt justified in retaining the playscript format for his *kibyōshi* translations, then, for aside from the genre's indebtedness to the stage, at the time of his writing the playscript format itself was the method of choice in the standard Japanese anthologies.

This is not to imply that the playscript format works perfectly in Japanese. In the original texts, dialogic utterances tend to float indiscriminately in the spaces between the figures of two or more fictional characters, making attribution sometimes tricky, though the playscript format customarily assigns definitive identities to speakers. Granted, clues as to the identity of the speaker are to be detected in such things as narrative context, vocal register, gendered pronouns, and the use of polite or humilific language. However, readers are left to draw their own conclusions, which means that in those instances when the speaker is ambiguous, even eminent annotators have provided drastically varying attributions. This would be fine were it not

---

1. Araki published "The Dream Pillow in Edo Fiction" in 1970. Granted, there were earlier translations: Zolbrod rendered Bakin's *kibyōshi* "The Vendetta of Mr. Fleacatcher Managoro" as a short narrative story in 1965, and Akimoto used a similar style even earlier. However, it is Araki's format that has endured.

2. Araki, "*Sharebon*: Books for Men of Mode," p. 32.

for the fact that none of the complexity of the various elements of the physical layout of the texts comes across in the playscript format, which perforce cleans up the jagged edges of the original texts.

Accordingly, by imposing a set, narratological sequence that was never present in the original, the playscript format gives the false impression that the reading process is straightforward, as if to imply that all readers would have read a *kibyōshi* the same way. The very linearity of the playscript, in other words, misleadingly suggests that there is an unambiguously "proper" way of reading. Granted, readers who are able to match the words transliterated into modern typescript with the original Japanese in the reproductions may be able to compensate for this effect. Yet even some Japanese readers today find the original Edo-period script too obscure to perform this matching process effortlessly or even correctly—particularly when the reproductions are diminutive, as is too often the case.

Most significantly, in my opinion, the playscript format easily lulls one into the mistaken impression that the visual and verbal texts are *separable*. Since it is this visual-verbal dynamic that largely commends the *kibyōshi* for attention in the first place, to subordinate the pictures in any way seems unsatisfactory. By deracinating the verbal text from its visual environment, the playscript format reduces the messy visual-verbal anarchy of the original to an artificial tidiness. In so doing, it effaces one of the unique, defining features of the *kibyōshi*. Simply put, the playscript format presents a rather canned experience.

As a vehicle of translation, the playscript format suffers from these drawbacks, for readers must rely solely upon the linear order of the translated text, and this order does not necessarily reflect the narrative order of the original, if one can even be said to exist. Furthermore, readers not fluent in Japanese cannot match the modern typescript transliterations of the original curvilinear script to that writing within the reproduced originals. Nor should they be expected to do so, for a translation that demands fluency in the original language is less a translation than a charade. Additionally, in light of the *kibyōshi*'s close affinity to the popular stage, the playscript format may inadvertently engender the misconception that a *kibyōshi* is a kind of illustrated performance text for a kabuki or puppet play.

One apparent benefit of the playscript format is that by including reproductions, even diminutively sized ones, it preserves, and thereby dignifies, something of the aesthetic appeal of the original *kibyōshi*. In practice, however, this has too often ended up having the opposite of the intended effect, since neither the translations nor the exegesis in any of the major Japanese anthologies are keyed to the pictures. Thus, the playscript format has perpetuated a tendency within literary studies in Japan to focus on the verbal text to the exclusion of the pictorial one, as though the latter were merely incidental or negligible. Regardless of whether the playscript format is mobilized to present the *kibyōshi* to a modern Japanese audience or to render the *kibyōshi* into another language, then, the pictures end up getting lost in translation.

Fortunately, there have been positive developments in recent years. Some works in the playscript format have begun to include slightly larger reproductions of the originals (as with the few books published by Kawade shobō shinsha). This makes it easier for Japanese readers, at least, to match the transliteration with the position of the original text. More promising is Koike Masatane's six-volume collection of transliterated and annotated *kibyōshi*, which provides some scholarly illumination of the pictures as well as the words.[3] One of the standard anthologies of premodern Japanese literature that has been updated within the past few years now also includes some annotation to pictorial aspects of the *kibyōshi* contained therein.[4]

Be that as it may, the playscript format is hardly the only way of rendering the *kibyōshi*. As far back as the 1920s, the scholar of Edo literature Yamaguchi Takeshi—in what could be dubbed the "dubbed format"—simply replaced the squiggly-looking cursive scrawl of original texts with a modern typescript (**Figure II.1**).[5] Regrettably, the mechanical regularity of Yamaguchi's straight-edged typescript did not adequately convey the flowing sensuality of the original handwritten "grass" script (*sōsho*). "Typesetting," as cartoonist Will Eisner has observed of the tendency to retain hand lettering in Western comicbooks, "does have a kind of inherent authority but it has a 'mechanical' effect that intruded on the personality of free-hand art."[6]

If only Yamaguchi had had at his disposal a curvilinear typescript that mimicked freehand lettering, one wonders if the playscript format would ever have become entrenched at all. Many translations of modern Japanese *manga* into other languages employ a straight-edged font, to be sure, though this is largely in keeping with the originals themselves. Perhaps the modern *manga* provides the cue for Stella Bartels-Wu, whose dubbed-format translation of a *kibyōshi* by Bakin into German likewise employs such an impersonal typeface.[7]

Award-winning *manga* artist Sugiura Hinako was, in contrast, able to avoid such antiseptic effect by replacing, in her relatively recent rendition of *Master Flashgold*, the original grass script with her own only slightly less curvaceous modern Japanese handwriting (**Figure II.2**).[8] What aesthetic beauty Sugiura sacrifices with freehand lettering may at least be compensated for by increased legibility. As irritating as some people find this sort of dubbing—especially the happy few who can appreciate the nuances of the original Edo-period Japanese scrawl—at least it allows one to become immersed in something approaching the visual-verbal pleasures of the original text.

---

3. See Koike, *Edo no gesaku ehon.*

4. Tanahashi, *SNKBZ 79.*

5. Yamaguchi, *Kibyōshi nijūgoshū.*

6. Eisner, *Comics and Sequential Art*, p. 27.

7. See Bartels-Wu, *Mitatemono und kibyōshi.*

8. See Sugiura, *Edo e yōkoso*, pp. 151–182. Sugiura won the Japan Cartoonists' Association Award in 1984 and the Bunshun Manga Award in 1988.

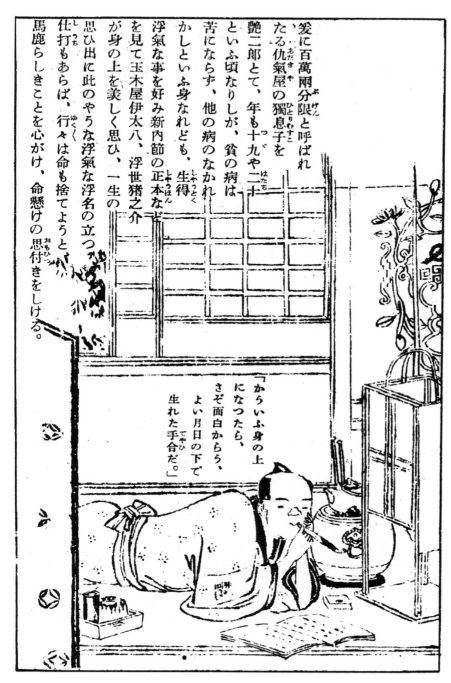

Fig. II.1 Yamaguchi Takeshi's typescript version of Kyōden's *Playboy, Roasted à la Edo* (*Edo umare uwaki no kabayaki*, 1785). In Yamaguchi, *Kibyōshi nijūgoshū*, p. 153.

Another drawback of the dubbed format is that, thus far, it has tended to deter sustained annotation. This is primarily an issue of space. The bare minimum of requisite exegesis often cannot be squeezed into the margins around the pictures. Thus, Sugiura's dubbed version dispenses with annotation entirely, which hardly aids the reader who lacks perfect fluency in Edo-period Japanese.

Fig. II.2 Sugiura Hinako's
handwritten version of
Harumachi's *Master Flashgold's
Splendiferous Dream* (*Kinkin
sensei eiga no yume*, 1775). In
Sugiura, *Edo e yōkoso*, p. 165.
Courtesy of Chikuma shobō.

A possible solution to these sorts of issues resides in the "hypertext" of electronic media, which would allow one to switch among grass-script original, modern typescript Japanese, and English translation at the push of a button without changing the pictorial frame. Such would have obvious pedagogical application.[9] It might be objected that the only thing electronic

---

9. Here I take my cue from X. Jie Yang, whose electronic primer *kanaCLASSIC* allows one to alternate between anomalously cursive *kana* (*hentaigana*) and modern typescript Japanese.

media cannot translate as well as paper is the materiality of the *kibyōshi* itself. Although the touch of Edo-period ragpaper would somehow feel closer to someone holding a modern book than someone viewing a computer screen, both modern media nonetheless remain translations of the original materiality. The principal stumbling block at the time of this writing, though, is that the use of electronic media has not yet become entirely feasible for academic publishing.

The present volume, in the meantime, employs a format that might be described as an amalgam of the dubbed method buttressed by extensive annotations of the pictures as well as the words. Although dubbing as a technique of rendering foreign films has its sworn enemies, here the idea is to enable the reader to encounter the *kibyōshi* as a visual-verbal text without having to long jump back and forth between playscript and pictures—which one doubts most readers actually do when using the playscript format—and without having to resort to translator's notes unless one wants to.

In lieu of Yamaguchi's square typescript or Sugiura's handwritten scrawl, the present volume as a rule employs a curvilinear typeface in the hopes that it conveys some semblance of the original cursive grass script, which the *kibyōshi* uses for both narrative and dialogic texts. For those cases in which a seal script (*tenshoji*) or a block script (*kaisho*) is employed to render signboards or title strips, for instance, a more appropriate square typescript is used.

In light of the extreme allusivity, topicality, and puzzle-like nature of the visual and verbal texts in the *kibyōshi*, I resort to "thick" translation, employing such apparatuses as an introductory essay, pictorial exegesis, and detailed annotation including comments on Edo-period Japanese, of course buttressed by bibliographic and other miscellaneous notes. The purpose of this strategy is to supply some of the information a contemporary reader (to say nothing of the ideal reader) might have had at his disposal. However, such thick translation can be off-putting to the informed general reader—and can seem like a "cop-out" to some no doubt better informed specialist translators. Thus, I have aimed for a more or less self-contained surface translation, downplaying the annotations by withholding reference marks within the texts themselves, while nonetheless retaining some of the inevitable—and desirable—jaggedness. The annotations are keyed to the translated text by their arrangement into sections following each translated piece and by highlighting those words appearing within the text that would seem to warrant elaboration.

To reiterate, each translation is layered, for the convenience of the reader, from broad strokes to minutiae as follows: (1) a general introductory essay, providing some useful contextualization, discussion, and bibliographic notes; (2) the translation proper, which bears no reference marks (so as not to impinge upon the visual field of the text any more than necessary), and which can perhaps be read—superficially, at least—without recourse to further annotation; (3) the annotations to both the pictorial as well as the ver-

bal texts, keyed to the translation by section number and boldfacing for quick identification, which might appeal less to the general reader than to the student of Japanese literature and culture; and (4) footnotes to all of the above, containing mostly scholarly citation but also some additional information that will no doubt appeal only to the inveterately curious.

Two final notes. Although it is often said that poetry and humor freight the translator with the heaviest demands, by far the most daunting aspect of annotating the *kibyōshi* is not the dense wordplay. Nor is it the visual-verbal play, the words of which can, after all, be tweaked in order to compensate for what the pictures cannot communicate in English. Rather, it is the many unidentified pictorial objects that cannot be hinted at (much less explained) in the verbal translation.

Although most practicing translators blithely ignore the school of thought holding that translation is by definition impossible, when it comes to such pictorial objects, the issue of untranslatability rears its head. How can one "read," let alone *translate*, an unfamiliar depicted object? This is not as ridiculous a query as it may seem. Although the object can always be explained within the annotations, the larger issue resides in differences in extralexical competency. The *kibyōshi* may be virtually untranslatable, in other words, the theory of untranslatability notwithstanding, not simply because its pictures render it unreadable, but because the visual-verbal imagination of eighteenth-century Japan is itself not readily transplantable.[10] Annotation alone surely cannot compensate for this disjunction.

That said, the annotations and notes in the present volume sometimes err on the side of excessiveness. To annotate the *kibyōshi* this way, as though it were a highbrow work of classical literature, no doubt will strike some readers as an exercise in absurdity. However, doing so helps demonstrate the remarkable allusive play of these pieces while paying due respect to the genre and the language of the mid-Edo period. Thus, these are specialized annotations intended slightly more for the student of Edo-period culture than for the informed general reader.

Finally, these annotations are offered in the spirit of treating the visual as well as the verbal texts as an open-ended interpretive occasion. They are not meant to foreclose all possible interpretations. Still, the only thing worse than annotations chasing wildly after allusive geese is a translation where the dynamic polyvalence of the original gets flattened out into a uniformly tasteless entity. To paraphrase Churchill on democracy, annotated translation is the worst form of translation, except for all the others.

---

10. I follow the lead here of Barbara C. Bowen, who describes Rabelais's books as being "probably less accessible to the general educated reader, Anglo-Saxon or French, than they were a generation ago. They have become, to put it bluntly, unreadable. . . ." In Bowen, "Rabelais's Unreadable Books," p. 742.

Chapter 5

Those Familiar

Bestsellers (1782)

Naturally, one does not laugh, move about
or leave the room while engaged in reading.
—Neo-Confucianist Kaibara Ekken

Santō Kyōden had his first commercial and critical success in the *kibyōshi* genre with *Those Familiar Bestsellers*, which he wrote and illustrated under the pseudonym Kitao Masanobu in 1782, at the tender age of twenty-one. At this point in his career, Kyōden was a less experienced author than illustrator, so commentators have tended to favor his pictures over his verbal story. Contemporary reviewer and author of popular fiction Ōta Nanpo raved, ranking *Familiar Bestsellers* "the great crème de la crème" (*dai jō jō kichi*) in the category of *kibyōshi* artwork for that year (**Figure 5.1**).[1] Among modern scholars, Mizuno Minoru has extolled the "realistic portrayal" evident in the expressiveness of the lines, the nuance of mannerisms, and the minor details of such things as a rosette hanging from a transom. For him, *Familiar Bestsellers* is the sole dividing line between Kyōden's juvenilia and mature oeuvre. Likewise, Koike Masatane feels the work captures contemporary life down to the smallest of details. And Tanahashi Masahiro, praising the graphic realism, hails the piece as representative of the genre.[2]

Nonetheless, the story itself holds a particular fascination. If the plot in most *kibyōshi* serves as a convenient frame upon which to hang numerous visual and verbal gags, then the one in *Familiar Bestsellers* is no exception, as it occasions a literary pastiche (*fukiyose*), collocated with the predictable strings of puns (*monozukushi*) and associative words (*engo*), centering on the world of contemporary publishing. Analogous perhaps to Swift's *Battle of the Books*, which pits "ancients" against "moderns," it describes the effort of a clique of out-of-date published material from the Kamigata (Kyoto-Osaka) region to defame another clique: the witty, sexy, and trendy comicbooks (*kusazōshi*) and woodblock prints of Edo. Naturally, the protagonist of this

---

1. For a transcribed version of Nanpo's *Bystanders See it Better* (*Okame hachimoku*, 1782), see Hamada, *Ōta Nanpo zenshū 7*, pp. 252–273.

2. Mizuno, *Santō Kyōden no kibyōshi*, pp. 11–12; Koike, *Hankotsusha Ōta Nanpo to Santō Kyōden*, p. 96; and Tanahashi in Koike, *Edo no gesaku ehon 1*, p. 216.

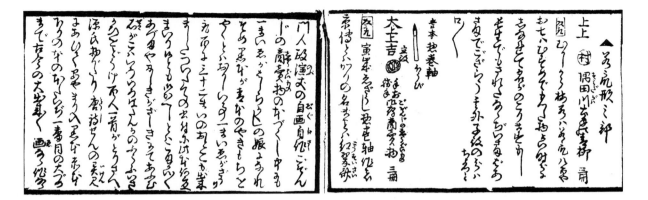

kibyōshi is himself a *kibyōshi* (though it should be kept in mind that the contemporary term was "bluebook"). Similarly, the narrator is a comicbook artist by the name of Kitao Masanobu. This deliberate self-reflexivity, humorously drawing attention to the genre and to the author, is a pervasive aspect of this and others of Kyōden's *kibyōshi*.

The Kyoto-Osaka clique is led by Reading Book and Glossy Book, genres long associated with the dominant publishing house in the region, the Hachimonjiya. No longer at the pinnacle of pop literature, these two books find themselves far from home, languishing at a flea market in Edo, where the best-selling genre of the day is Bluebook. Determined to recapture their erstwhile glory (not to mention their share of the market), they hatch a scheme to ensnare Bluebook in scandal by turning Edo genres against each other. In the end, the culpable parties are admonished by *The Tale of Genji* and *Tang Poetry Anthology*, as though contemporary literature must somehow inevitably answer to the authority of the classics.

No doubt reflecting the significance historically attached to honor in Japan, the theme of gossip-mongering runs throughout much of the literature, from at least the time of early classical poetry and the world of the Shining Prince Genji, where it lurks as a nagging apprehension. As Yoshida Kenkō observed in his fourteenth-century miscellany *Essays in Idleness*—a work that also figures in *Familiar Bestsellers*—"Indeed, it is a high reputation that lays the foundation for slander."[3] That a smear campaign could become the stuff of a humorous story by the Edo period probably indicates how much more the extended reach of mass printing must have heightened anxiety over the effect of a malicious rumor upon one's reputation.

This conflict between two groups of printed matter broadly spoofs the "feudal-house piece" (*oiemono*) of kabuki and puppet plays, which is merely one way that *Familiar Bestsellers* pays homage to the popular stage. To this well-known formula, in which rival factions lay claim to the succession rights of a single clan, Kyōden adds the twist of personification: woodblock-

Fig. 5.1 Ranking of Kyōden's *Familiar Bestsellers* as "the great crème de la crème" (*dai jō jō kichi*) in the category of *kibyōshi* artwork (indicated by the brush icon). From *Bystanders See it Better* (*Okame hachimoku*, 1782), a *kibyōshi* reviewbook by Ōta Nanpo. Courtesy of Tokyo Metropolitan Central Library, Special Acquisitions Collection.

3. McCullough, *Classical Japanese Prose*, p. 401.

printed pictures and books spring to life before the reader's eyes in concrete human form, their generic affiliation pictured as worn on their sleeves. Less well-studied specimens of popular culture are also represented, such as lottery tickets, board games, sheet music, landscape cards, and protective amulets. There are even "urinating forbidden" signs, which, judging by how frequently they appear within *kibyōshi* pictures, must have been a lucrative side-business for printers. As a kind of popular imagining of a publisher's catalogue of best-selling merchandise, *Familiar Bestsellers* speaks volumes, complementing recent forays by Mary Elizabeth Berry, Peter F. Kornicki, and others into the highly diversified world of eighteenth-century mass publishing.[4]

The anthropomorphic "creature battle" (*irui gassen*) has a long literary pedigree in Japan, by no means originating with Kyōden. Creatures were assaulting each other regularly in the companion booklets of the preceding several centuries, if not in earlier genres.[5] *The Cat's Tale* (*Neko no sōshi*, ca. 1602), for instance, comically pits feline against rodent[6]—a bit like Spiegelman's Cat-Nazis vs. Rat-Jews in *Maus*. In the syllabary booklets of the early Edo period, there was *The Tale of Chickens and Rats* (*Keiso monogatari*, ca. 1636), whose critters vie for rice rations in contemporary Kyoto. By the mid-eighteenth century, the creature battle royal had become the stuff of redbooks and blackbooks, the comicbooks from which the *kibyōshi* materialized. The redbook *We Now Present Those Storied Spooks* (*Kore wa gozonji no bakemono nite gozasōrō*), for instance, may even have provided Kyōden with a hint for his title.[7] The perennial favorite *Monkey vs. Crab* (*Saru kani gassen*), a redbook illustrated by Nishimura Shigenaga but of unstipulated authorship, retold the title's legendary grudge match, only to be recast as a *kibyōshi* in Koikawa Harumachi's *The Age-Old Yarn of Monkey vs. Crab* (*Saru kani tōi mukashibanashi*, 1783).

Harumachi also composed one of the most imaginative and influential creature battles to date, *New Roots of Verbal Jousting* (*Kotoba tatakai atarashii no ne*, 1778), involving personified slang expressions and words popular in Edo (**Figure 5.2**).[8] *New Roots* helped inspire Kyōden to issue *A Domestic Tale of Fruits in the Flesh* (*Kudamono: Mitate osewabanashi*, 1780), about a humorous struggle between unfriendly species of fruit (**Figure 5.3**).[9] It also exerted a profound influence upon *Familiar Bestsellers*, providing a model of patent self-reflexivity, not to mention contributing many of its vogue phrases. And

---

4. See Berry, *Japan in Print*.

5. For more on the history of the creature battle, see Koike, *Edo no gesaku ehon 1*, pp. 109–112; and Koike, *Edo no ehon 1*, pp. 17–18.

6. Skord, *Tales of Tears and Laughter*, pp. 33–46.

7. Reprinted in Koike, *Edo no ehon 1*, pp. 9–16.

8. Reprinted in Koike, *Edo no gesaku ehon 1*, pp. 87–112.

9. Mentioned in Koike, *Edo no gesaku ehon 1*, p. 247.

Fig. 5.2 Personified slang expressions. From *New Roots of Verbal Jousting* (*Kotoba tatakai atarashii no ne*, 1778), a *kibyōshi* written and illustrated by Koikawa Harumachi. Courtesy of Tokyo Metropolitan Central Library, Kaga Collection.

the young Kyōden was able to demonstrate in *Familiar Bestsellers* his uncanny expertise in the compositional tactics of creature-battle warfare.

Kyōden was also adept at embedding meaningful hidden references and allusions on the visual and verbal levels. His puzzles range from relatively simple puns, as when Pillar Print declares her pining (*matsu*) for Portrait Print while sitting beneath the shade of a pine tree (*matsu*), to a complex optical allusion (*mitate*) to a pair of playing cards (*karuta*) used in the matching game associated with the classic collection *A Hundred Poems by a Hundred*

Fig. 5.3 Personified species of fruit. From *A Domestic Tale of Fruits in the Flesh* (*Kudamono: Mitate osewabanashi* [*A Fanciful Tale of Fruits to the Rescue*], 1780), a *kibyōshi* written and illustrated by Kitao Masanobu (Santō Kyō-den), Japanese, 1761–1816. Woodblock printed book; ink on paper; 17.5 × 13.0 cm. Publisher: Tsuruya Kiemon (Senkakudō). Photograph © 2006 Museum of Fine Arts, Boston.

Poets (*Hyakunin isshu*). No direct reference is made to the matching-card game. The only verbal clue is a snippet of dialogue uttered by one of the characters, *A Hundred Buffoons*: "I shall look after my children / while getting merrily smashed." These are the last two lines of a madcap poem in Kondō Kiyoharu's (fl. ca. 1716–1736) picturebook *A Hundred Poems by a Hundred Buffoons* (*Dōke hyakunin shu*):

Aki no ta no	Without sojourning
Kario sumade ni	At that hut in autumn fields
Hiyori yoku	On fair-weathered days
Wa ga kodomora o	I shall look after my children
Raku ni sugosan.	While getting merrily smashed.

This bit of doggerel parodies a poem by Emperor Tenji, the very first in *A Hundred Poets*, replacing "my sleeves" (*wa ga koromode*) with "my children" (*wa ga kodomora*), and punning "to take care of" with the Edo slang "to get drunk" (*sugosu*):

Aki no ta no	In the autumn fields
Kario no io no	the hut, the temporary hut,
Toma o arami	its thatch is rough

Fig. 5.4 Workers in autumnal fields and the simple hut associated with Emperor Tenji's poem. Reprinted in Mostow, *Pictures of the Heart*, p. 143. Courtesy of the University of Hawaii Press.

Wa ga koromode wa   and so the sleeves of my robe
Tsuyu ni nuretsutsu   are dampened night by night with dew.[10]

Even if a reader recalls the particular *kyōka* in *A Hundred Buffoons* by its last two lines—no small feat in itself—he still needs to recollect the original poem from *A Hundred Poets*, then envision the twin pictures on the playing cards accompanying Emperor Tenji's poem: one depicting a rugged country hut (*io*); the other, some lackeys toiling outside (**Figure 5.4**). Each card contains only two or three lines of tastefully positioned verse, and this perhaps explains why the corresponding two panels in *Familiar Bestsellers* contain far less verbal text than any of its others. This scene, as in a game of matching cards itself, thus requires quick-witted matching of visual and verbal texts.

Although part of the challenge of reading any *kibyōshi* lies in such recondite cross-media play, much of the immediate fun of *Familiar Bestsellers* derives from the ways in which genres of literature and art are rendered. Bluebook dresses and speaks as the consummate sophisticate, displaying meticulous attention to the details of contemporary chic. One passage, if not a manifesto, has become the *locus classicus* of descriptions of the genre. Bluebook is described as a trendsetter, well versed in the finer points of social life, capable of bringing together members of different classes and of entertaining women and children. The corresponding pictures show an authentic dandy, nattily garbed in the latest silk halfcoat, hair done up in the modish Honda-style topknot, and grasping his long-stemmed pipe rakishly.

Redbook and Blackbook, by contrast, being two early genres of comicbooks now past their prime, dress in the frumpiest of fashions and babble in the worst clichés of yesteryear. "Thick as a big old tree stump" is this

---

10. Translated by Mostow, *Pictures of the Heart*, p. 141.

Blackbook—an expression appearing frequently in the by-then fusty black-books of preceding decades (not to mention in Harumachi's *New Roots of Verbal Jousting*), here additionally characterizing the genre itself as passé. "The slang of one generation," as Simon Dentith has observed, "becomes the target of parody in the next."[11] Similarly, the pictures portray Blackbook as dowdy, sporting an outmoded hairstyle, and gripping his long-stemmed pipe lumpishly.

The emphasis upon current sentiments being one of the hallmarks of the *kibyōshi*, Kyōden defines the bluebook as exhibiting a "keen insight into today's affairs." This is precisely what *Familiar Bestsellers* itself displays in its myriad references to authentic products on sale, actual commercial establishments, specific places and events, and real-life personalities, such as the kabuki star Ichikawa Danjūrō V, the comic raconteur Morikawa Bakoku, and the proprietor of the Ōgiya brothel Suzuki Uemon. The piece's "realistic portrayal" thus pertains to the contemporary pop culture scene as much as it does visual verisimilitude.

The eighteenth-century Edoite must have thrilled to see his own metropolis reflected this way. Kyōden manages to capture the *joie de vivre* of his city's ascendancy over Kamigata in terms of culture (if not in terms of economics and politics), particularly as manifested in mass publishing: "Until the end of the eighteenth century it was the publishers of Kyoto and Osaka that controlled [the] market and were the source of fiction consumed in Edo and elsewhere," writes Kornicki, "but the emergence of entrepreneurial publishers . . . and the development of new genres of fiction in Edo in the 1780s and 1790s, which daringly satirized official life or treated the world of the Yoshiwara pleasure quarter of Edo with only transparent disguises, signaled a shift to Edo."[12]

This shift is evident in the main battle lines of the story, even though the genres from Kamigata effectively turn those from Edo against each other—testament, no doubt, to the heated competition within Edo's own publishing world. Thus, beneath the *schadenfreude* of the portrayals of Blackbook as benighted and of the Kamigata genres as démodé lurks the sharp anxiety of literary obsolescence in an age of increased textual turnover. Still, the mere fact of Edo's newfound cultural centrality could never alone have vouchsafed the immense popularity of Kyōden's *kibyōshi*, even with the piece's "keen insight" into the affairs of the day. *Familiar Bestsellers*'s virtuoso implementation of the creature battle at the level of verbal as well as pictorial texts thus should not be sold short.

The present translation and notes are largely based on two annotated texts: Tanahashi Masahiro, in Koike Masatane et al., eds., *Edo no gesaku ehon 1*, in

---

11. Dentith, *Parody*, p. 2.
12. Kornicki, *The Book in Japan*, p. 139.

Gendai kyōyō bunko 1037 (Shakai shisōsha, 1980), pp. 215–248; and Mizuno Minoru, ed., *Kibyōshi sharebon shū*, in *NKBT 59* (Iwanami shoten, 1958), pp. 87–105. These are referred to below simply as Tanahashi and Mizuno. The pictures of this *kibyōshi* are reprinted by permission of the University of Tokyo.

Those Familiar

Bestsellers

You see before you a certain illustrator of those silly comicbooks published every New Year. Since you kids still might not be familiar with my works, I've been racking my brains about what to present here in order to earn your patronage. Hoping my New Year's dream would make a funny story, I'm off to my publisher, Mr. So-and-so, this very moment. How quickly I arrive at his gate! "Hello! Anyone home?!"

"Enough already, enough already! On with the show!"

...At the height of conversation, he shows his guests a review of bluebooks published the previous year. "Our popularity slump is due to this Bluebook—so it's up to you guys to sully his reputation!" Thus does Glossy Book entangle Redbook and Blackbook in his connivings without dirtying his own hands.

Those Kamigata types sure are crafty! Redbook and Blackbook look over the review for themselves, seething at Bluebook's good press:

"Used to be that all the Bluebooks in the world couldn't stack up to a few of us. But now we're discounted as angry demons, red-faced and black-hearted as hell!"

So one night, Glossy Book invites Redbook and Blackbook over and serves some of Mr. Sundry's Red Miso with pickled red snapper. It takes only a sip for Redbook to crimson. Next, Glossy Book sets out some gong-shaped rice cakes from Slander's Mill.

"What a shame!"

Now, Bluebook always delights the eyes of his readers regardless of their social standing. He knows just how to flatter, is ever stylishly composed, and displays a keen sense of insight into today's affairs. He possesses something of haiku's free spirit, yet without one jot of imprudence. On long, drizzly afternoons, women and children love browsing through him almost as much as snacking on tasty roasted beans. He devotes himself to dreaming up new ideas for his next issue with every paper fiber of his being. And being made of recycled stock, he naturally refrains from all extravagance.

"Zenkō's work is superb indeed. Kisanji's Dreamers the Winners also went over well. Lately, compared to theirs, my own ideas have been rather blah."

"The Unusual Treasure Ship was last year's success story."

"I may be a frail paper chrysanthemum, raised on the wild plain sheets, yet hoping to envelope you in my feelings, I seal my bond paper of passion for you before the gods, here on this stationery, ever green. You are, after all, the one for whom I pine. Please, do not tear my hopes to shreds; dismiss me not as some foolscap, scarcely cut out for you!"   Now, because Portrait Print is composed of neither stone nor wood, but flesh and pulp, a shiver of delight shoots down the nap of his neck. Soon he is enameled of her. The two of them draw up plans together so that their passion will never fade.

A slouch like Portrait Print's slipper valet, Penny Dreadful Print, comes a dime a dozen.

Bluebook decides to throw a New Year's bash. He invites all his friends and treats them to course after delectable course. Jokebook, lingering long after dinner to tell some amusing stories and anecdotes, has everyone bursting at the seams. This is why joking around on the job is forbidden —so it can be saved for after hours.

Borrowers are requested to return this book by the due date —The proprietor

Blackbook, thick as a big old tree stump, cannot quite imagine how to besmirch Bluebook's image, so he decides instead to get with the times. Outfitting himself in a trendy, pitch-black cowl, he accompanies Redbook through the pleasure quarter. Passing by Bluebook, they pretend not to notice him, then try to act inconspicuous, since heading the other way is Blackbook's boss, Chinese Paperback.

Bluebook feasts his eyes on her. "What a gorgeous piece!"

Yoshiwara Pleasure Quarterly Review: "Over there is Miss Brocade of the Eastern Salon!"

Redbook

Blackbook

And here is one of Edo's main attractions, a beautiful courtesan of the Eastern Salon, Brocade Print. Adorned in the finery of the pleasure quarters, Brocade cuts a pretty figure, careful not to skimp on the rouge. No wonder Edo woodblocks are admired throughout the land. It is on account of her that an elegant lady is said to be a "picture of perfection." Accompanied by attendants and trainees, Brocade is en route to pay her respects to the Goddess of Mercy at Asakusa.

"Hey, Karma Jizō's over there!"

BROWN BOOK

TRAVEL PARCHEESI

MISS LANDSCAPE CARD

BROCADE

CHINESE PAPERBACK

Courtesan trainees Travel Parcheesi and Sweet Sixteen Backgammon

Attendant courtesan Miss Landscape Card

Chinese Paperback

Blackbook and Redbook, determined to ruin Bluebook's reputation no matter what, summon Classic Math Problems, Yearly Annals, and A Hundred Poems by a Hundred Buffoons, among others, and conspire to tear apart Bluebook's and Portrait Print's friendship by abducting Pillar Print.

"Master Math, please double-check our scheme for mistakes."

With his sales slumping in recent years, Ogre Charm Print steals away from his hometown of Ōtsu in the middle of the night and comes to Blackbook's place. Blackbook's son, Junior Book, has been bawling all evening, so Ogre uses his charms to try and pacify the lad: "There, there, if you keep behaving like a spoiled brat, Uncle Ogre's going to turn into a real fiend—just like on my house crest—and that'd be really scary. Don't get on my donation shit list or you'll moxiburn in hell! You'd better not make so much as the hushed clang of a mallet on a gong!" And grumbling "Ugh, what a hassle!" he calms the boy down patiently. Hence the phrase "handling booklets with tender loving care."

Bluebook, feeling blue over his sister Pillar's disappearance, is afraid that Portrait has been cheating on her. Little does he suspect that Blackbook and Redbook are to blame. He worries that being called Pillar she has been pilloried by the gods—or, worse yet, has been swept off to the countryside in a souvenir-buying spree. So he hires Everybody's Horoscope to divine her fate.

"The signs are far from crystal clear, but try looking for her near Yushima or Shinmeimae, in one of the shop stalls."

...Saint Daishi's Tarot Cards, though without much luck."

"I've searched for Pillar Print in the busiest shopping centers of town, like Yokkaichi and Ryōgoku. Praying my chances would improve, I even resorted to

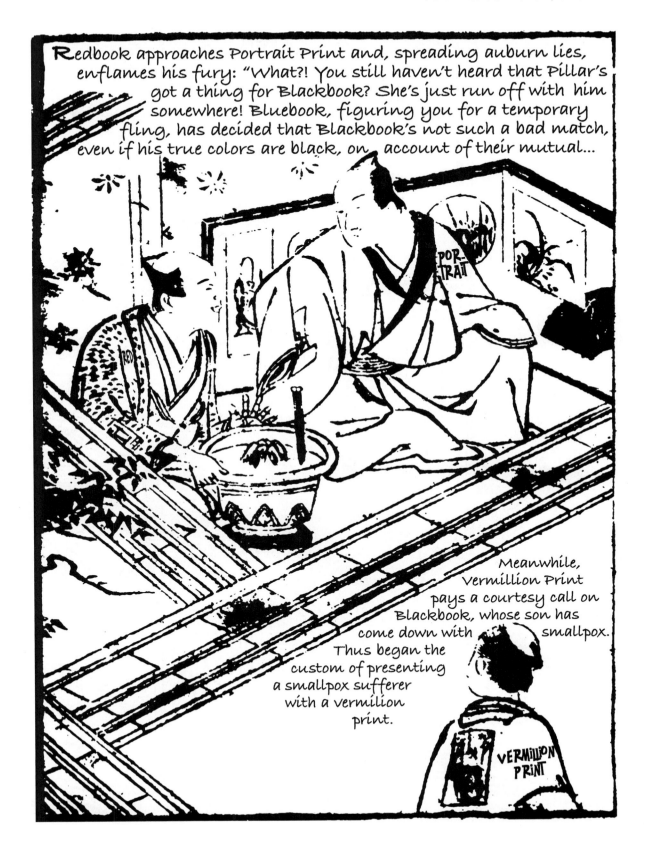

Portrait Print hears no more of the sordid details. Ascertaining Bluebook's whereabouts, he storms off toward the Yoshiwara to challenge him to a duel. Just then, Tang Poetry Anthology and The Tale of Genji emerge from a bordello in the Edochō section of the quarter, the House of Fans.

Observing Portrait Print's face discolored with rage, Genji and Tang listen to the particulars of his entire story, only to give him a good scolding.

Tale of Genji

Tang Poetry

"The frogs are croaking."

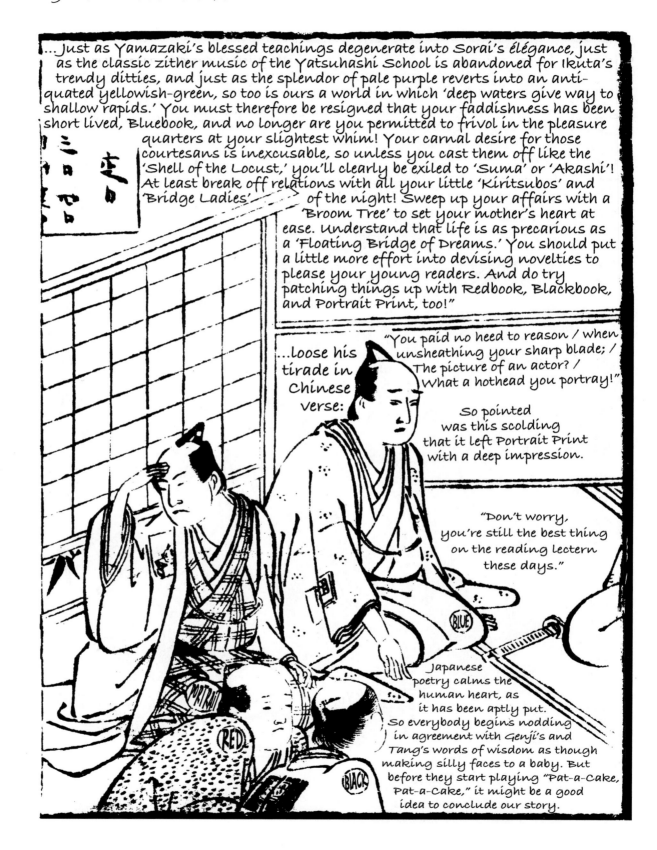

...Just as Yamazaki's blessed teachings degenerate into Sorai's élégance, just as the classic zither music of the Yatsuhashi School is abandoned for Ikuta's trendy ditties, and just as the splendor of pale purple reverts into an antiquated yellowish-green, so too is ours a world in which 'deep waters give way to shallow rapids.' You must therefore be resigned that your faddishness has been short lived, Bluebook, and no longer are you permitted to frivol in the pleasure quarters at your slightest whim! Your carnal desire for those courtesans is inexcusable, so unless you cast them off like the 'Shell of the Locust,' you'll clearly be exiled to 'Suma' or 'Akashi'! At least break off relations with all your little 'Kiritsubos' and 'Bridge Ladies' of the night! Sweep up your affairs with a 'Broom Tree' to set your mother's heart at ease. Understand that life is as precarious as a 'Floating Bridge of Dreams.' You should put a little more effort into devising novelties to please your young readers. And do try patching things up with Redbook, Blackbook, and Portrait Print, too!"

...loose his tirade in Chinese verse:

"You paid no heed to reason / when unsheathing your sharp blade; / The picture of an actor? / What a hothead you portray!"

So pointed was this scolding that it left Portrait Print with a deep impression.

"Don't worry, you're still the best thing on the reading lectern these days."

Japanese poetry calms the human heart, as it has been aptly put. So everybody begins nodding in agreement with Genji's and Tang's words of wisdom as though making silly faces to a baby. But before they start playing "Pat-a-Cake, Pat-a-Cake," it might be a good idea to conclude our story.

Once their sentences are served, and their recycling completed, Blackbook and Redbook will flourish as before.

Furthermore, Reading Book and Glossy Book are exposed as having ghostwritten the dastardly plot. Since old chapbooks get scrapped and used as wadding to fill holes, these two end up with graffiti on their facing pages, the eyes of their stitching gnawed out by small rodents, reduced to underlining in folding screens.

Essays in Idleness, carrying out instructions from Genji and Tang, supervises the local chapbooks.

handy reference work.

Blackbook: "I'm reformed already! I'm reformed already!"

This is why people start saying "red with shame."

Henceforth, bestsellers from all publishing houses will live in harmony, prospering for tens of thousands of years to come. And while even those obsolete slice-'em-and-dice-'em comicbooks will truly appreciate the ensuing reign of peace, peddlers out front are disruptive, barking in their passing voices: "We got portrait prints, comicbooks, treasure-ship pics, travel Parcheesi!" In fact, just as I was waking up from my dream, someone was exclaiming:

"Your publisher, Tsuruya Kiemon, here to bid you a happy New Year!"

KITAO

ILLUSTRATED AND WRITTEN BY KŌSUISAI DISCIPLE

MASANOBU

Annotations

FIRST FASCICLE

[Frontispiece] A scene from the ensuing fascicle, in which the protagonist's sister is about to sever a finger as a token of sincerity for her lover, here is contained within a picture atop a peepshow apparatus. The banner fluttering over the characters' heads bears the crane (*tsuru*) house crest of the publisher Tsuruya Kiemon. The panel at left bears the full title of the story, fascicle number, and author's attribution. The four apertures at bottom are eyeholes for the fictional viewer to see the peepshow accompanying a storyteller's performance, but here they serve as an invitation to the real-life reader to delve into the present story.

Those Familiar Bestsellers (*Gozonji no shōbaimono*). More literally, "The Merchandise You All Know." The term "familiar" (*gozonji*) plays on "chapbooks" (*gosōshi*), for when written in the historical orthography (*rekishiteki kanazukai*), these terms—*kosonshi* and *kosoushi*, respectively—appear visually similar. In light of how this orthographic gag is buttressed in the final section of the story by the term "booksellers' merchandise," the title might also be rendered *Those Storied Goods*.

Self-Serving New Publication (*Shinpan temaegatte*). The first hint that this work does not refrain from unabashed self-promotionalism.

Section 1

[Picture] A slightly mustachioed Kitao Masanobu appears humbly before the reader to introduce his *kibyōshi* as though he were the servant character Tarō Kaja (according to Tanahashi) of the noh or *kyōgen* stage delivering an opening prologue to a play. The house crests on the stiff shoulders of his formal coat (*kataginu*) together read "Masanobu." Those on his overskirt bear the logos of various Edo publishing firms through whom the real-life Masanobu actually published—the Tsutaya, Izumiya, Okumuraya, Tsuruya, Murataya, Marukoya, Nishimuraya, Iwatoya, Iseya, and Matsumuraya, to name most of them.[1] The decorative saké cask is associated with the New Year's festivities.

---

1. For a useful list of such publishers and their house crests, see Hamada, *Kibyōshi senryū kyōka*, p. 563.

illustrator of those silly comicbooks. Masanobu describes himself as "one who illustrates" (*ga o takumi suru*) frivolous chapbooks (*tawarezōshi*), not as an author. This must be because Masanobu was still an artist in the public eye and because actual children's books tended to be known by their illustrators.

you kids (*onko-samagata*). Addressing adult readers this way was a kind of running gag, found in other works, playing off the *kibyōshi* format's derivation from children's comicbooks.

my publisher (*hanmoto*). Tsuruya Kiemon (fl. ca. 1780s). Proprietor of the Senkakudō (fl. ca. 1760s–1860s) and one of Edo's foremost publishers of woodblock prints and comicbooks, including many of Kyōden's own early *kibyōshi*.

How quickly I arrive at his gate! (*Kore wa haya hanmoto no kado ni tsukite sōrō*). A spoof of the conventional stage line hurrying a journey along in the span of a few words.

On with the show (*tō tō hajime sōraeya*). "Let's begin already!" The identity of the speaker of this line is ambiguous.[2]

Section 2

[Picture] Masanobu, kneeling on a floor cushion, snoozes at his desk. The objects strewn about his studio—dishes, ink brushes, a tobacco pouch, a long pipe, a "pillar print" of a courtesan, a standing partition, and a "urinating forbidden" sign—find their way into the ensuing dream. The dream, encapsulated in a dream bubble, contains two scenes: in the right half, Reading Book and Glossy Book, sitting near a standing partition (*tsuitate*), conspire against Fashionbook and Bluebook; in the left half, dishes strewn about, Glossy Book (book in hand) enlists Redbook and Blackbook in a scheme to slander Bluebook. Many of the vogue phrases here were personified in Harumachi's *New Roots of Verbal Jousting*.

reading book (*yomihon*). A catch-all term for any kind of chapbook with few if any illustrations (as opposed to the highly pictorial genres of *kusazōshi*). The most successful publisher of reading books was the Hachimonjiya in Kyoto.[3]

book-lender's satchel . . . Yanagiwara Flea Market. The **book lender** (*kashihon'ya*) carried his merchandise in pack loads (*furoshiki*) and sometimes

---

2. Tanahashi attributes it to Masanobu; Mizuno to an unknown audience member.

3. By the early nineteenth century, the term *yomihon* would come to refer exclusively to a genre of lengthy, didactic works, epitomized by Bakin's *Nansō Satomi hakkenden* (1814–1832). For more on the Hachimonjiya, see "Kiseki and the Hachimonji-ya," in Hibbett, *The Floating World in Japanese Fiction*, pp. 50–64.

set up shop at places like the **Yanagiwara Flea Market** (*Yanagiwara no hoshimise*), located on the south bank of the Kanda River near Asakusa, close to the Yoshiwara.

out-of-towner . . . illustrated book (*kudari ehon*). A picturebook published in the Kyoto-Osaka region and imported to Edo.

Glossy Book (*kōzeibyōshi*). Books with a shiny, mica-paper cover, often in yellow or light gray. The Kyoto courtier Fujiwara no Kōzei (972–1027) used this kind of elegant paper for his poetry collections (notes Mizuno).

Bluebook (*aohon*). The contemporary term for what later would be called the *kibyōshi*.

Fashionbook (*sharebon*). A genre of urbane popular fiction that was a mainstay of Edo's publishing industry.

Local chapbooks (*jihon*). Works of popular literature issued in Edo, here referring to various comicbooks. Often used in contradistinction to "proper" books (*shomotsu*).

furrowing his brow (*hitae hachi no ji o yosete*). More accurately, "furrowing his brow into an eight." A droll likening of the graph "eight" (*hachi*) in the term Hachimonjiya ("Figure-Eight Shop") to a pair of knit eyebrows.

Redbook (*akabon*) and **Blackbook** (*kurohon*) are genres of children's comicbooks with characteristically monochrome covers. Although early redbooks were probably issued in Kamigata, by the time of *Familiar Bestsellers*, both genres had come to be mainly associated with Edo publishing.

Mr. Sundry's Red Miso (*yomo no aka*). A celebrated dish of reddish soybean paste, often consumed with **pickled red snapper** (*tai no misozu*). The phrase "Wash down a heap of red *miso* with pickled red snapper!" (*tai no misozu ni yomo no aka ippai nomikakeyama*), having appeared in innumerable blackbooks, was a cliché by the time of *Familiar Bestsellers*. *Yomo no aka* also puns on Yomo no Akara, a pseudonym of Ōta Nanpo, whose review book *Flowery Felicitations* is mentioned presently.

gong-shaped rice cakes from Slander's Mill (*Hikinoya no dorajirushi*). The *hiki* of Hikinoya, a shop specializing in gong-shaped rice cakes (*dorajirushi*), has at least three meanings: "mill," "reduction" (Redbook tries to remove the red from his face), and "slander."

review of bluebooks (*aohon no hyōbanki*). A reference to Nanpo's *kibyōshi* review book, *Flowery Felicitations* (*Kikujusō*, 1781).[4] Several of the four dozen new titles it reviewed—all of which were issued at the beginning of that same year—are mentioned below. *Flowery Felicitations* exerted more influence

---

4. For the complete text, see Hamada, *Ōta Nanpo zenshū 7*, pp. 220–252.

on *Familiar Bestsellers* than did other works (according to Hiyama Jun'ichi), even Harumachi's *New Roots of Verbal Jousting*.[5]

demons (*jigoku no oni*). Mizuno submits that these "demons from hell" had red and black faces.

Section 3

[Picture] Bluebook's monthly book club. From right to left: Bluebook, in a chic black halfcoat (*haori*); Pouch Book, holding a saké cup; Fashionbook, tobacco pouch in front of him; Portrait Print, with a slightly curled-up "single-sheet print" affixed to his sleeve; and Pillar Print, a fully rolled-up pillar print on her right shoulder, bearing a teapot. Her line of vision leads directly to Portrait Print's face, hidden from the reader's view. Bluebook and Fashionbook sport Honda topknots and suavely hold long-stemmed pipes. Since most of the books mentioned were issued by Tsuruya, the same publisher of the present *kibyōshi*, this discussion serves as a kind of product placement.

keen sense of insight into today's affairs (*tōsei no ana o sagashi*). More literally, "uncovers the discrepancies in contemporary society."

haiku's free spirit (*haiki*). Literally, "*haikai* spirit." Although this referred to the free-wheeling wit of what would come to be known as haiku, contemporary readers might also have thought specifically of those comic verses now called *senryū*.

recycled stock (*sukigaeshi no kami*). Prior to the widespread use of paper mulberry during the eighteenth century, genres of cheap literature such as comicbooks were typically printed on this rough, low-grade reprocessed paper.

Pouch Book (*fukurozashi*). Some comicbooks were sold in protective cloth pouches.

Portrait Print (*ichimaizuri*). A single-sheet woodblock print (also called *ichi-maie*), made in Edo, often a portrait of a kabuki star.

novel ideas (*shukō*). A play on the general meaning of the word as "conception" and on its specific literary use as "innovation."

The Unusual Treasure Ship (*Ōchigai takarabune*). Written by Shiba Zenkō and illustrated by Masanobu (Kyōden), this *kibyōshi* was published in 1781 by Tsuruya.

---

5. Hiyama, "*Gozonji no shōbaimono* to hyōbanki," p. 67.

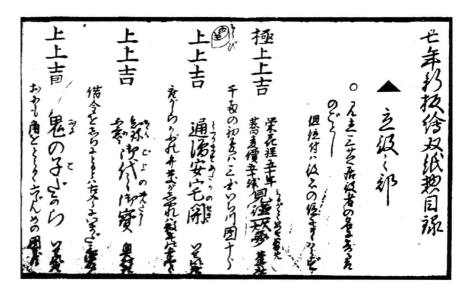

Fig. 5.5 Ranking of Hōseidō Kisanji's *Dreamers the Winners* (*Miru ga toku issui no yume,* 1781) as the "ultimate crème de la crème" (*kyoku jō jō kichi*) of *kibyōshi* to date. From *Flowery Felicitations* (*Kikujusō,* 1781), a *kibyōshi* reviewbook by Ōta Nanpo. Courtesy of Tokyo Metropolitan Central Library, Special Acquisitions Collection.

Dreamers the Winners (*Issui no yume*). Written by Kisanji and published by Tsuruya. Nanpo, in *Flowery Felicitations*, ranked this 1781 work (fully titled *Miru ga toku issui no yume*) as the "ultimate crème de la crème" (*kyoku jō jō kichi*) of *kibyōshi* to date (**Figure 5.5**).[6]

Gratuitous Account (*Mudaiki*). Harumachi's *kibyōshi* of 1781.[7] Thought to have been published by Tsuruya.[8]

Greasy Sweat (*Abura tsūe*). A fashionbook, published in 1781, fully titled *Zekkō abura tsūe*, written by Nandaka Shiran (née Kubota Yasuei, 1757–1820) and illustrated by Harumachi.[9]

Ichiba **Tsūshō** (1739–1812) and Iba **Kashō** (1747–1783) both were *kibyōshi* authors of some note.

Pillar Print (*hashirakakushi*). A woodblock print of a courtesan, or an actor in a woman's role, the long, slender format of which (averaging 13 × 67 cm) allowed it to fit on the alcove pillar (*hashira*).

Kinpira tomboy (*Kinpira na musume*). Pillar Print is an elegant lady, not some female version of Kinpira, the strong-willed warrior who appeared in comicbooks (one of which was mentioned in *New Roots of Verbal Jousting*).

Peach Boy . . . Urashima Tarō Many early comicbooks (especially redbooks) retold the legends of the Herculean "Peach Boy" Momotarō and of Urashima Tarō, whose centuries of living underwater with the sea god's

---

6. For an annotated version, see Mizuno, *NKBT 59*, pp. 69–86.

7. For an annotated version, see Koike, *Edo no gesaku ehon 1*, pp. 113–148.

8. See Tanahashi, *Kibyōshi sōran 1*, p. 282.

9. A transcribed, though unannotated, version can be found in Mizuno, *Sharebon taisei 11*, pp. 11–23.

daughter caught up with him abruptly when he opened a jeweled box against her instructions.

lacquer prints (*urushie*). The lacquer print, so named for its adoption of the hand-coloring technique of lacquer ware, became popular during the early part of the eighteenth century, only to be surpassed mid-century by other genres—most notably Edo's pillar print and brocade print. A pun on lacquer (*urushi*) and **tickled** (*ureshikatta*) is embedded within the phrase "looked pleased" (*urushigatta ge*).

Section 4

[Picture] Pillar Print, poised to slice off her little finger on a stone fountain as a "demonstration of sincerity" (*shinjū*) of her love for Portrait Print, bites a kerchief to stifle a scream, as Portrait Print stands by. A scabbard rests on the floorboards. Tanahashi suggests that this picture alludes to a particular finger-slicing scene from the kabuki play *A Beginner's Version of the Rise and Fall of the Heike and Genji Clans* (*Hiragana seisuiki*, first performed in 1739). Penny Dreadful Print slouches over his knees, off to the side of the veranda (*engawa*), not far from a stone lantern. A good-luck charm (*gofu*) is posted above the doorway and a rosette (*kusadama*) hangs from the transom. The pine tree is the pictorial analogue of Pillar Print's professed pining.

paper chrysanthemum . . . cut out for you. Perhaps taking its cue from a passage in Chikamatsu's play *Love Suicides at Amijima*, this passage consists of a string of puns on paper (*kamizukushi*).[10] A more literal rendition: "Frail chrysanthemum paper that I am (*kogiku no watashi*), raised on the wild plain sheets (*nobe ni sodachishi*), my situation unbearable (*tsurai kono mi*), I seal a Mino paper bond to the gods (*minogamisan kakete*). Deciding to make my feelings transparent paper to you (*nushi ni kokoro o misugami to*), I write on this roll of stationery, edges pasted together (*tsugiawasetaru makigami*); all I do is pine-patterned paper (*matsubagami*) to see you again, so do not think our relationship foredoomed, something impossible to cut off—like rotten veranda boards (*kusareta en no hashi kirazu*)!"

flesh and pulp (*shobōsho no yotsugiri*). A kind of high-quality paper stock.

shiver of delight . . . nap of his neck (*erimoto kara zotto suru hodo kebatatte*). The hairs on the nape of one's neck are likened here to the nap on ragpaper.

enameled (*irogoto to nari*). The pun here is on the "color" (*iro*) of "passion" (*irogoto*).

Has such a picture . . . in prints. This closely parodies a line from a popular ballad (*meriyasu*)—"Could such loving affinity exist even in China?"

---

10. Shively, *Love Suicides at Amijima*, p. 67.

(*konna enishi ga Kara ni mo arō ka*)—replacing "loving affinity" (*enishi*) with "in pictures" (*e ni shi*), and "China" (*Kara*) with "paper" (*kami*).

Penny Dreadful Print (*sanmon'e*). A crudely composed, inexpensive print worth the pittance of three copper *mon*. The implication is that Portrait Print's **slipper valet** (*zōritori*) is a cheap, uncouth fellow.

Section 5

[Picture] At the New Year's party, Jokebook, wielding a fan as prop as though he were a comic raconteur, provides lively entertainment, a candle and a jokebook not far away. Fashionbook, unable to keep his eyes off Jokebook, tries to fill his pipe bowl with tobacco from the open pouch lying before his knees. Behind him, the door to the serving room (black lacquered utensils barely visible) has been left slightly ajar, suggesting brisk activity. Pillar Print shields her mouth, opened in laughter, with her sleeve. Behind her hangs a *shamisen*, strings to the wall. Next to her, a standing lantern. Bluebook holds a book in one hand and what appears to be a toothpick in the other. Behind him, an unusual triangular alcove.

Jokebook (*hanashibon*). A collection of humorous short stories, including those used in comic storytelling (*rakugo*).

Borrowers . . . proprietor (*kono hon izugata e mairi sōrōdomo sōsō okaeshi kudasarubeku sōrō kono nushi sora*). Book lenders affixed such notices on the back covers of their rental items (according to Tanahashi). Other notices requested that borrowers neither scribble in books nor lend them to third parties.[11]

Section 6

[Picture] Bluebook and Stone Rubbing in the Edo version of a seedy alley. On the bamboo fence, above the water barrel (*tensuioke*), one sign advertises a potion (called *gessui hayanagashi*) used to induce early abortion, and another announces a performance by the comic storyteller Bakoku. This must be Morikawa Bakoku (1714–1791), who collaborated with Kyōden on several works of popular fiction. Next to the barrel, above the weeds, another sign prohibits public urination. A picture of a pair of scissors graced the obverse side of such signs, apparently as a symbolic warning that any man breaking the prohibition was subject to castration (**Figure 5.6**).[12] A last sign, concluding this, the first fascicle, appears in the bottom right-hand corner of the panel: "A frivolous work by the illustrator Kitao Masanobu" (*gakō Kitao Masanobu gesaku*).

---

11. Kornicki, *The Book in Japan*, pp. 392–393.
12. For more on this, see Hanasaki, *Edo kawaya hyaku sugata*, p. 26 and passim.

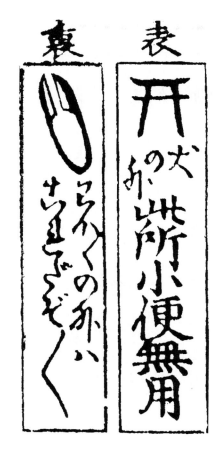

Fig. 5.6 A sign prohibiting urination. The pair of Japanese-style scissors on the back side (at left) may have served as a symbolic threat. Reprinted in Hanasaki, *Edo kawaya hyaku sugata*, p. 26. Courtesy of Miki shobō.

Stone Rubbing (*ishizuri*). A picture (also called *ishizurie*) made by assiduously rubbing paper over a carved image, this was a common souvenir of Edo.

Asakusa Kannon . . . Yoshiwara (*Hokkoku*). Since the Sensōji—a temple housing a well-known statue of the Goddess of Mercy (Kannon)—was located in Asakusa near the Yoshiwara, "to make a pilgrimage to the Asakusa Kannon" was a euphemism for visiting the pleasure quarter.

MIDDLE FASCICLE

[Frontispiece] In another scene framed within a picture atop a peepshow, Blackbook, paddle in hand and looking cross, grabs a woman by the hair.

Section 7

[Picture] Drumming up business—and drawing readers into the second fascicle—**Perspective Print** (*ukie*), seated, explicates a full vanishing-point

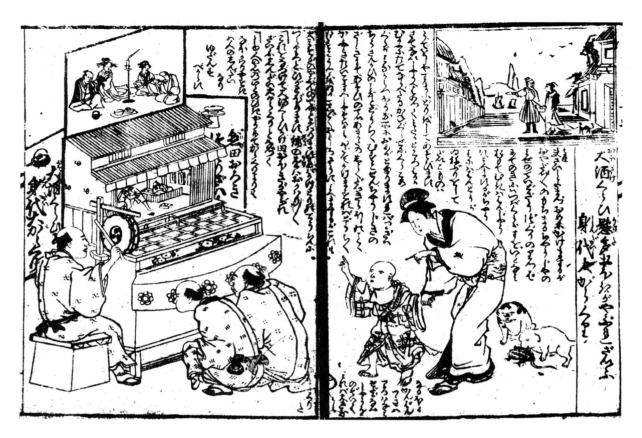

Fig. 5.7 A peepshow. The insert in the upper right-hand corner reveals a fanciful Western scene that the two squatting customers perceive through apertures. The storyteller accompanies himself on a handheld drum. From *Some Strange Sideshow and Tales of Ise* (*Kowa mezurashii misemonogatari*, 1801), a *kibyōshi* written by Santō Kyōden and illustrated by Kitao Shigemasa. Courtesy of Tokyo Metropolitan Central Library, Kaga Collection.

perspective print within his peepshow apparatus (*nozoki karakuri*), here identified as a "Grand Dutch Peepshow" (*Oranda daikarakuri*).[13] Atop the peepbox is an exotic-looking screen print depicting the arches of European architecture, birds flying toward the horizon, and Western-styled figures, one of whom is walking a dog on a leash. In front of this screen, a goofy-looking, long-necked goblin (*rokurokubi*) prop has popped out of a box to attract attention. Little Bean Print (*mamee*), with his bean-patterned robe, peers through a peephole at an internal print, magnified by a hidden lens. Lottery Ticket (*monzuke no kami*), passing by, looks on, amused. On his sleeve, two house crests of kabuki actors (one, the concentric-squares design of Ichikawa Danjūrō) are visible, reflecting the contemporary practice of integrating actors' crests into the design of lottery tickets (according to Tanahashi). A similar scene would appear in Kyōden's *Some Strange Sideshow and Tales of Ise* (*Kowa mezurashii misemonogatari*, 1801) (**Figure 5.7**).

Old Capital (*miyako*). This suggests a contrast between the banquet held in Kyoto (within an unseen picture in the Dutch-style peepshow?) and Bluebook's New Year's party in Edo.

---

13. For more on the peepshow, see Fukuoka, "Contextualising the Peep-Box in Tokugawa Japan."

Section 8

[Picture] A veritable *tableau vivant* of printed matter, set in front of a tea-shop on a bustling street near the Asakusa Kannon. At right, Bluebook (elegantly attired in a black halfcoat), Stone Rubbing (head shaved, sitting behind Bluebook in the same teashop stall, smoking a pipe), and *Yoshiwara Pleasure Quarterly Review* (*Yoshiwara saiken*), who points out Miss Brocade, whom Bluebook strains to observe.[14] Among those accompanying Brocade in her procession at left are the attendant courtesan (*shinzō*) Miss Landscape Card (*ebankiri*); the two young courtesan trainees (*kaburo*), Sweet Sixteen Backgammon (*jūroku musashi*), and carrying what appears to be an oversized backgammon piece, Travel Parcheesi (*dōchū sugoroku*); and Brown Book (*chabyōshi*). Immediately in front of Bluebook, on the other side of a partition, stand the uncouth poseurs Redbook and Blackbook (wearing a black cowl), trying desperately to cut fashionable figures while escaping notice by the elderly Chinese Paperback who, glancing backwards, ambles forth with a cane in one hand and a Buddhist rosary in the other. A samurai, two swords sheathed at his side, holds a fan to his face as if to hide his identity. The teashop is executed in fine detail, replete with shop curtain, hanging lantern, the bottom portion of a placard (presumably bearing the teashop's name), partitions between booths, tobacco tray, and, of course, tea cups. In front, lanterns on tall shafts, bamboo-thatched gates rolled to their respective sides, and, barely visible at left, the trunk and leaves of a gingko tree.[15]

thick as a big old tree stump (*taiboku no kirikuchi*). The clipped form of the expression "a root as thick as the stump of a gigantic tree" (*taiboku no kirikuchi futai no ne*), which appeared frequently in the blackbooks of at least a decade earlier (according to Mizuno). It also appeared in Harumachi's *New Roots of Verbal Jousting* (**Figure 5.8**).

pitch-black cowl (*makkuro kurojitate*). Apropos of Blackbook, but a current fashion statement (according to Mizuno).

Chinese Paperback (*karakami byōshi*). Printed on "Chinese paper," this genre of puppet plays in illustrated booklet format was a precursor to early comicbooks, a major source of literary material for the blackbook, and mentioned in *New Roots of Verbal Jousting*.

Brocade Print (*nishikie*). The multicolored print depicting high-ranking courtesans was typically sold within the Yoshiwara itself, at outlets such as the well-known **Eastern Salon** (*Azumaya*). Purportedly invented by the

---

14. Here I depart from the more literal rendering of *The Yoshiwara, Detailed* for the sake of the humor.

15. Jones identifies the bamboo-thatched gates in her dissertation, "Comic Fiction in Japan During the Later Edo Period," p. 63.

Fig. 5.8 The personified slang expression "thick as a big old tree stump" tormenting the fictional author Harumachi (though his sleeve bears the graph for "artist"). From *New Roots of Verbal Jousting (Kotoba tatakai atarashii no ne,* 1778), a *kibyōshi* written and illustrated by Koikawa Harumachi. Courtesy of Tokyo Metropolitan Central Library, Kaga Collection.

ukiyoe master Suzuki Harunobu (1725?-1770) and derived from the rose-hued print (*benizurie*), the brocade print made significant use of **rouge**.

gorgeous piece (*utsukushii mono*). A play on both meanings of *mono*— "thing" and "person."

Karma Jizō (*inga Jizō sama*). A reference to a landmark near the Asakusa Kannon, a stone statue of Jizō (the Bodhisattva or "patron saint" of souls lost in Hell), just at its peak of popularity (according to Mizuno).

Section 9

[Picture] Entertainers (*geisha*) performing by candlelight before Bluebook and Brocade at her parlor in the Eastern Salon. Courtesans were ensconced in boudoirs on the bordello's second floor, so in the right panel, through the lattice window, the top of a tree and the roof of an adjacent building (the round hole serving for ventilation) are visible below. *Parroting the Kabuki Stars*—his profile resembling that of a parrot (*ōmu*) (as in **Figure 3.10**)— imitates Ichikawa Danjūrō (note the actor's concentric-squares design on the fan) as Stage Melodies tunes her *shamisen*. Various dishes and cups are

scattered about. In the left panel, Bluebook, pipe in mouth, and Brocade, standing, watch the performance. Puppet Scorebook—in the stance of a puppeteer—molests Sweet Sixteen Backgammon.

Stage Melodies (*nagautabon*). A book of music and lyrics from the kabuki stage of Edo.

Puppet Scorebook (*gidayū no nukihon*). A book of excerpts of *gidayū jōruri*, the music originated for the puppet theater by Takemoto Gidayū (1651–1714).

Parroting the Kabuki Stars (*Sanshibai ōmuseki*). More literally, "Parroting Echo-Stones of the Three Stages." This book (and its namesake genre) contained excerpts of dialogues by celebrated actors from Edo's Morita, Nakamura, and Ichimura theaters, replete with instructions for vocal impersonation (*kowairo*).

toasted (*moteru*). In Edo parlance this had the particular meaning of being received by a courtesan in her bordello.[16]

spirited (*ippai ni*). A pun on "tremendously" and "one cup of saké."

flattering picture (*esoragoto*). This has the double sense of a put-on as well as an artistic construction.

kiddy pantomime books (*kodomo no kyōgenbon*). Picturebooks of kabuki and puppet plays for younger readers. Yoshiwara bordellos sometimes offered skits performed by children (*kodomo no kyōgen*) for the entertainment of their customers.

Now that's childish (*aa tsugamonee*). A line of dialogue associated with Ichikawa Danjūrō.

The young master would be grateful (*musuko wa arigataesama yo*). Probably a line from a kabuki play, though which one remains obscure.

Bring more saké, allegro non troppo (*ochōshi o hayaku*). A pun meaning "Pick up the rhythm (*chōshi*)!" as well as "Bring a bottle of saké (*chōshi*), quick!"

♪ Twang, twang, twang ♪ (*chin chin chin*). The sound of *shamisen* strumming.

really sixteen . . . hair down there. Although courtesan trainees worked until their early teens, this one is mistaken as older on account of her nickname "Sixteen Musashi." A related saying at the time asserted, "Only thirteen but with the pubes of a sixteen-year old" (in Mizuno)—that being the proverbial age of sexual awakening, as implied by the following comic haiku (in Tanahashi):

---

16. Ōkubo and Kinoshita, *Edogo jiten*, p. 1139.

Jūroku de

Musume wa dōgu

Sorou nari.

By sixteen

Girls are already

Fully equipped.

Section 10

[Picture] Blackbook's abode. At left, Redbook and Blackbook (who holds his pipe awkwardly), conspiring with their goons *Yearly Annals*, *A Hundred Buffoons*, and *Classic Math Problems* (an abacus on his sleeve). A candle sets the time as night. At right, Ogre Charm Print, gong and mallet on the floor in front of him, tries to mollify Blackbook's son, Junior Book, who has stayed up crying past his bedtime.

Classic Math Problems (*Jinkōki*). A well-known textbook (and the genre it inspired) of basic mathematics, teaching practical problem-solving related to everyday situations (such as buying rice), written by Yoshida Kōyū (d. 1672).

Yearly Annals (*Nendaiki*). Yoshida Kōyū is known to have compiled several works in this genre of historical events listed by year.

A Hundred Poems by a Hundred Buffoons (*Dōke hyakunin shu*). The generic title to several books of madcap verse closely spoofing the poems in the venerated anthology *A Hundred Poems by a Hundred Poets* (*Hyakunin is-shu*; compiled by Fujiwara Teika, 1162–1241), the most well-known of which being by comicbook author Kondō Kiyoharu (fl. ca. 1716–1736).[17] The irregular reading *shu* for *isshu* is not incorrect.[18]

Ogre Charm Print (*Ōtsue*). A folksy genre of ink painting (*sumie*), executed with thick black lines and then colored in, and typically depicting an ogre (*oni*) holding a *gong* (*kane*), a *mallet* (*shumoku*), and a *list* of temple donors (*hōgachō*). Long associated with the town of *Ōtsu* near Kyoto, with the establishment in the seventeenth century of the East-Sea Highway the "Ōtsu print" became a popular Kamigata souvenir for travelers. It was also frequently used as a children's amulet against nighttime crying (**Figure 5.9** and **Color Figure 10**).

Junior Book (*kobon*). Any small-format book, though literally, "child book."

---

17. For a discussion and facsimile reproduction of Kiyoharu's spoof, see Asano, *Kondō Kiyoharu gasaku* Dōke hyakunin shu *sanbu saku*, pp. 44–46 and 65–116, respectively.

18. Both Mizuno and Tanahashi sanction this reading, in spite of the fact that innumerable other titles retain the reading *isshu* of *Hyakunin isshu*, such as: *A Hundred Poems by a Hundred Dogs* (*Inu hyakunin isshu*, 1669); *A Hundred Poems by a Hundred Courtesans* (*Keisei hyakunin isshu*, 1703); and *A Hundred Poems by a Hundred Kyōka Poets* (*Kyōka hyakunin isshu*, 1843). In Mutō, *Mojiri hyakunin isshu o yomu*, pp. 217–229.

巡の中ゆ立へて志
仏乃弟く里せは
哭の心葦れとも
ろ海ー

雪縁粉

Fig. 5.9 Ōtsu print (*Ōtsue*) of a demon with mallet, gong, and list of temple donors. From *Souvenirs of Ōtsu (Ōtsu miyage*, 1780), a madcap-poem picturebook (*kyōka ehon*). Reprinted in Kisho fukuseikai, *Kisho fukuseikai sōsho 1.*

hushed clang (*chanto damanna*). Kyōden (according to Mizuno) puns "perfectly" (*chanto*) on "clang" (*chatto*), an onomatopoeia for the soft tap of a mallet on a gong in quiet musical passages.

"handling booklets with tender loving care" (*kobonnō*). Alternatively, "mollycoddling a juvenile." The word "booklet" (*kobon*) pivots into the phrase "child doting" (*kobonnō*).

Section 11

[**Picture**] A pictorial allusion to two matching cards (*karuta*) from the game associated with *A Hundred Poems by a Hundred Poets*. The three goons, from behind a fence, spy on Pillar Print and Portrait Print, who embrace in a kabuki-style love scene (*nuregoto*) on an open veranda (*nureen*) (on the stepping stone to which rests a pair of wooden flip-flops). The black-based pillow at right suggests some sort of amorous activity. Voyeuristic peeping (*kaimami*) is a standard trope running throughout Japanese drama and literature at least as far back as the tenth-century *Tales of Ise.*

Fig. 5.10 Illustration from *ABCs of Short Verse* (*Iroha tanka*, ca. 1736–1740), a red-book by Kondō Kiyoharu. Courtesy of Tokyo Metropolitan Central Library, Kaga Collection.

"**to provide for his children**" (*waga kodomora o raku ni sugosan*). A line from the poem in Kiyoharu's *Hundred Buffoons* parodying Emperor Tenji's opening poem of *A Hundred Poets*.

dye (*iro no sameru*). An indelible pun, meaning "colors fade" and "passions die."

trivial outcome (*ketai no wari sensaku*). A reference to an unwanted result in divination (according to Mizuno), here applied to mathematics.

literally or figuratively? (*hon no koto kae*). Two puns are embedded in this phrase: (1) *hon no koto*, a slang abbreviation for "true," can also mean "book matters"; and (2) *kae*, a colloquial interrogative, is written here with the graph for "picture" (*e*).

Section 12

[Picture] The squabble between Blackbook (paddle in hand) and wife, *ABCs of Short Verse*. Tanahashi and Mizuno suggest that this scene alludes to a picture in Kondō Kiyoharu's work by that title (**Figure 5.10**).[19] However, the "quarreling couple" (*fūfugenka*) was a standard pictorial trope appearing throughout eighteenth-century popular literature (if not actual life), as in the aforementioned *Hundred Buffoons* itself (**Figure 5.11**). Kyōden also appropriated elements from other works. The broken pot on the floor behind Blackbook, for instance, though thrown by the wife in Kiyoharu's *Short*

---

19. For an annotated version, see Suzuki and Kimura, *Kinsei kodomo no ehonshū*, pp. 346–351.

Fig. 5.11 Quarreling couple from *A Hundred Poems by a Hundred Buffoons* (*Dōke hyaku-nin shū*), a madcap-poem picturebook (*kyōka ehon*) illustrated and presumably written by Kondō Kiyoharu. Reprinted in Kisho fukuseikai, *Kisho fukuseikai sōsho 4.*

Verse, appears on the floor in front of the husband in the anonymous red-book *ABCs of Songs* (*Iroha uta*, ca. 1770) (**Figure 5.12**). And *Short Verse* in *Familiar Bestsellers* assumes the pose of the wife in *ABCs of Songs*, but wears the same face of a female demon mask (*hannya*), associated with the spurned wife, as the wife in the jokebook *A Good Listener* (*Kikijōzu*, 1773) (**Figure 5.13**).

The comb and bodkin in *Familiar Bestsellers*, having been dislodged from *Short Verse's* hair during the fracas, seem to be Kyōden's touch, along with the overturned teacup. The cartouche in the bottom right-hand corner, reading "a frivolous work by the illustrator Kitao Masanobu," terminates the second fascicle.

ABCs of Short Verse (*Iroha tanka*). A children's primer of the historical syllabary order (*iroha*) consisting of short poems (*tanka*) arranged "alphabetically" hovering above a simple illustrated story. Published by Kondō Kiyoharu sometime during the Genbun era (1736–1740).

"Flocks of sparrows . . . heart of a Phoenix" (*shūjaku nanzo taibō no kokoro o shiran*). A line from Sima Qian's classic *Records of the Grand Historian* (second century BCE) meaning that the ways of the sage defy comprehension by mere mortals.

snake eyes (*yoake no pinzoro me*). The side of a die indicating the number one, this also conjures up a jealous wife waiting up late at night for her husband to return (according to Mizuno).

don't get short . . . longest of poems (*sore wa anmari tanka ja*). The "short poem" (*tanka*) here plays on the term "short tempered" (*tanki*).

Fig. 5.12 Pot broken by a quarreling couple. From the anonymous redbook *ABCs of Songs* (Iroha uta, ca. 1770). Courtesy of Tokyo Metropolitan Central Library, Kaga Collection.

Don't block my way, you blockhead (*ee jama suna soko dōke*). This puns "buffoon" (*dōke*) and "get out of the way" (*doke*).

FINAL FASCICLE

[Frontispiece] In the final peepshow scene, Portrait Print strikes a dramatic pose, not unlike the way a vengeful kabuki actor would be portrayed in actual portrait prints.

Section 13

[Picture] *Everybody's Horoscope*, soothsaying sticks and paper lots strewn before him, advises Bluebook on where to find Pillar Print. Bluebook sits between a standing partition in the foreground and an alcove, with a hanging scroll of a plant in a woven basket, in the background.

being called Pillar . . . pilloried by the gods. There is a loose pun here between "pillar-concealed" (*hashirakakushi*) and "spirited away" (*kamikakushi*).

Everybody's Horoscope (*Nannyo ichidai hakke*). "Lifetime Horoscope for Men and Women." A book, of unknown authorship, consisting of astrological charts arranged by the date and time of birth.

Fig. 5.13 Spurned wife whose face resembles a demon mask. From *A Good Listener* (*Kikijōzu*, 1773), a jokebook by Komatsuya Hyakki. Courtesy of Hirosaki City Library.

Yokkaichi and **Ryōgoku**. Two of Edo's most popular commercial "bustling places" (*sakariba*), located near Edobashi and Ryōgokubashi, respectively.

Praying my chances would improve. A parody of a *shamisen* song (*shinnaibushi*) popular at the time (according to Mizuno), punning "fortune" (*hakke*) and "selfish" (*katte*).

Saint Daishi's Tarot Cards (*Daishi sama no omikuji*). A type of cartomancy, specifically augury, performed by drawing slips of paper upon which are written Chinese verse. The best known practitioner at the time was one Gansan Daishi of the Kan'ei Temple in Ueno.

signs are far from crystal clear (*hakke gaten no ikanu eki*). Kyōden loosely puns "result" (*hate*) on "fortune" (*hakke*).

Yushima . . . Shinmeimae. Sections of Edo known both for their shrines—places to which one would most likely be "divinely" spirited away—as well as for their shop stalls selling a variety of goods, including souvenir woodblock prints.

Section 14

[Picture] The architecture in this scene adheres more to the demands of narrative than to any sensible configuration of real dwellings. At right, Vermillion Print (*benie*), en route to Blackbook's house, passes by Redbook (setting out a brazier), who feeds Portrait Print (in front of a screen with several pasted-on pictures) a pack of lies. At far left, *Yoshiwara Pleasure Quarterly Review* (pipe in hand, the mountain-and-ivy insignia of the publisher

Tsutaya Jūzaburō on his sleeve) informs Bluebook of Redbook's sinister plot. A pair of flip-flops is placed haphazardly on the stepping stone, suggesting the urgency with which *Yoshiwara* has rushed to Bluebook's home.

auburn lies (*makkana uso*). Literally, "deep red lies." *Makkana* (also *maakana* or *makkaina*) figuratively means "outright." **enflames** (*taki tsukeru*) is an associative term. The same pun informs the following comic haiku, which suggests the preponderance of redbooks among the often preposterous *kusazōshi*:

Hyōshi made	Deep red lies
Maakana uso no	Down to their very covers—
Kusazōshi	Those comicbooks![20]

temporary fling (*ikka no hayarigi*). This "momentary popularity" refers both to the brief vogue of the portrait print genre as well as to Portrait Print's short-lived affair with Pillar Print.

even if his true colors are black (*iro wa kurokutemo*). *Iro* here refers both to the "color" black and to Blackbook's dark "passions."

presenting a smallpox sufferer with a vermilion print. It was customary to give someone afflicted with smallpox (*hōsō*) either a vermilion-colored print (*benie*) or a "smallpox picturebook" (*hōsō ehon*) as a kind of good luck charm for recovery (**Figure 5.14** and **Color Figure 9**).[21]

Section 15

[**Picture**] Portrait Print strikes the dramatic pose (*mie*) of a kabuki character bent on revenge: hair let down, body contorted, overskirt tucked up for action, fists clenched, teeth clutching a long sword. In the distance, *Tang* and *Genji*—who, with two swords each, are depicted as samurai—emerge from the Main Gate (*Daimon*) of the Yoshiwara, where they have been carousing at one of the most well-booked of pleasure-quarter establishments. Placards (*kōsatsu*) to the right of Portrait stipulate proper deportment in the quarter.

Tang Poetry Anthology (*Tōshisen*). This collection (Ch. *Tangshi xuan*), though not at the head of the canon in China, was a major part of the traditional Japanese curriculum of Chinese studies during the Edo period.[22]

---

20. Noted in Inoue, *Edo gesaku no kenkyū*, p. 22.

21. Such talismans were to be burned along with other potentially contagious belongings, so hardly any remain. A few therefore exceedingly rare smallpox picturebooks have been reprinted—in vermillion, no less—in Hanasaki, *Hōsō ehon shū*.

22. See Yoshikawa and Ogawa, *Tōshisen*.

Fig. 5.14 In a scene from one of the only known surviving "smallpox picturebooks" (*hōsō ehon*), a child performs an inspiring feat. Since such books were presented to children in their sickbeds as protective amulets—the vermillion color of the ink being believed to fend off all manners of evil as well as illness—they were normally burned after use. From *Children's Acrobatics to Keep Safe from Smallpox* (*Hōsō anzen kodomo no karuwaza*, date unknown). Written by Tamenaga Shunsui (1790–1843) and illustrated by Sadashige. Reprinted in Hanasaki, *Hōsō ehon shū*, p. 27.

The Tale of Genji (*Genji monogatari*). Murasaki Shikibu's classic tale (ca. 1000) of the life, loves, and progeny of the Shining Prince Genji.

House of Fans (*Ōgiya*). One of the Yoshiwara's premier bordellos, located in **Edochō**, boasting top-notch courtesans like Hanaōgi. Its proprietor Suzuki Uemon and his wife Okane were well-known students of the arts and poetry. One comic haiku (*Yanagidaru 20*) even quipped:

> Ōgiya e   House of Fans—
> Iku node *Tōshi*   Better study *Tang Poetry*
> *Sen* narai   Before visiting!

Kyōden and Uemon were good friends, participating in both the same amateur kabuki circle (according to Mizuno, in his annotations to *Playboy*) and madcap poetry coterie, the Yoshiwara Clique (*Yoshiwara ren*).

frogs are croaking (*kawazu ga nakimasu*). The croaking frog (*kawazu*) being long celebrated in Japanese poetry, this line may set the poetic mood of

the Yoshiwara (as Mizuno proposes) if not call to mind the Ōgiya's famously cultured proprietor. It also may well be a veiled reference to a vendetta scene from one of the Soga plays, since the brothers' father was none other than "Kawazu" Saburō.

Section 16

[Picture] A spoof of an admonishment (*iken*) scene from the stage. *Tang Poetry* (wearing a black halfcoat, sword removed) and *The Tale of Genji* (sword by his side, seated near a Tang desk and an alcove with its hanging scroll partially visible) chastise the principals: Bluebook (opposite *Genji*), Portrait Print (hand to forehead, glancing away), and Redbook and Blackbook (cowering in the bottom corner). Since *Genji* and Bluebook physically resemble each other in pose and dress, it has been suggested that this picture humorously juxtaposes the classic tale with the genre of *kibyōshi*.[23] The peacock feather is probably part of a writing quill that sits, with other implements, on the Tang desk.

Woodblock prints and comicbooks (*ezōshi*). During the Edo period, this word referred to a wide spectrum of illustrated prints, from woodblocks (*ukiyoe*) to picturebooks (*ehon*) and illustrated books (*eiribon*).

Alcoves and Tang desks (*tokonoma ya tōzukue*). Places where pictures were displayed and books perused. The Tang desk was a low, fancy, Chinese-style table, often made of rosewood, for reading as well as writing.

Yamazaki's blessed teachings degenerate into Sorai's *élégance*. Yamazaki Ansai (1618–1682) and Ogyū Sorai (1666–1728) were two major thinkers of the Edo period. The former founded the Suiga School of Shinto. The latter, by contrast, was primarily interested in Neo-Confucianism, and his "elegance" (*fūga*) was markedly alien—meaning Chinese (suggests Mizuno).

Yatsuhashi School . . . Ikuta's trendy ditties. The schools associated with Yatsuhashi and Ikuta symbolized the tension between the classical and the radically contemporary style of *koto* music. The former school, established in Kyoto during the late seventeenth century, was known for its graceful traditional scores and lyrics drawn from classical Japanese poetry. The latter, though founded not long afterwards (in the first decade of the eighteenth century), largely ignored the classical tradition, boldly imitating contemporary *shamisen* songs and employing colloquial language. It was not long before the Ikuta surpassed the Yatsuhashi in popularity.

'Deep waters give way to shallow rapids.' A reference to a poem in *Japanese Verse Old and New*:

---

23. Togasaki suggests this in her dissertation, "Santō Kyōden's *Kibyōshi*," p. 135.

Yo no naka wa	In this world of ours
Nani ka tsune naru	what is there of constancy?
Asukagawa	Yesterday's deep pool
Kinō no fuchi zo	in the River of Tomorrow
Kyō wa se ni naru	today becomes a rapid.[24]

unless you cast them off . . . 'Floating Bridge of Dreams.' This passage, in which *Genji* insists that Bluebook take a page from his book, consists of a string of puns on chapter titles from the classic tale: **'Shell of the Locust'** (*utsusemi*) pivots from the phrase "cast off your carnal desire for those courtesans" (*keisei ni mi o utsu*). Referring to the locales of Genji's self-imposed banishment, **'Suma'** hints both at **inexcusable** (*sumanai*) and to live (*sumu*) in **exile**, and **'Akashi'** plays on **clearly**. **'Kiritsubos'** emerges as a pivot from the phrase **break off relations** (*en o kiri*), and likewise **'Bridge Ladies'** (*hashihime*) from "the end of a weak pledge" (*usui chikai no hashi*). **'Broom Tree'** (*hahakigi*) and **mother's heart** (*haha no kokoro*) are conflated into a single phrase (*hahakigi no kokoro*). And the cliché **life is as precarious** (literally, "this world is a dream," *kono yo wa yume*) pivots into **'The Floating Bridge of Dreams'** (*yume no ukihashi*).

Chinese verse (*gogon zekku*). More specifically, the *wuyan jueju*, one of the major forms of Tang verse. Both Mizuno and Tanahashi suggest that this term plays on "crisis in battle" (*koko o sendo*).

"You paid no heed . . . a hothead you portray!" Less loosely: "Portrait Print, impetuously drawing your sword makes you a hothead (*tankimono*) who, though an actor's profile print (*nigaoe*), resembles nobody at all!"

deep impression. This line plays "was scolded" (*kimerarekeru*) with the name of a method of woodblock carving (*kimedashi*).

Chiding Prince (*Shikaru Genji*). A play on "Shining Prince" (*Hikaru Genji*).

Japanese poetry calms the human heart. A conflation of two lines from the acclaimed opening passage of the "Kana Preface" to *Japanese Verse Old and New*: "Japanese poetry has the human heart as seed and a myriad of words as leaves . . . It is song that moves heaven and earth without effort, stirs emotions in the invisible spirits and gods, brings harmony to the relations between men and women, and calms the hearts of fierce warriors."[25] This passage also famously introduces the croaking frog into Japanese poetics.

making silly faces to a baby (*shōchi shōchi awawa o suru*). This phrase puns a description of an adult mollifying an infant (*chōchi chōchi awawa*) to

---

24. Translated by McCullough in *Kokin Wakashū*, p. 205.
25. McCullough, *Kokin Wakashū*, p. 3.

express a term of consent (*shōchi shōchi*). **Pat-a-Cake** (*atama tenten*) is the attendant hand-clapping (according to Mizuno).

Section 17

[Picture] The recycling of trashy fiction in a slapstick mêlée. At left, two works of collective wisdom—*Essays in Idleness* (standing, fan in hand) and (seated behind him) *Encyclopedic Dictionary* (*Setsuyōshū*)—direct their subordinates. Redbook and Blackbook, squished beneath a plank, are about to get chopped up. Various tools, including a whetting stone, are visible on the floor. *Style Manual* sticks an ink brush in the eye of a Glossy Book. *Reading Primer* (*Teikin ōrai*), large brush in mouth, pins Reading Book to the ground. *Business Manual* (*Shōbai ōrai*) and, with a cleaver, *Classic Epistles* (*Kojō soroe*) help.

This rough treatment, incidentally, stands in stark contrast with Neo-Confucianist Kaibara Ekken's (1630–1714) stern warning, in a tract on educating children, about how to handle books properly:

Readers should wash their hands beforehand, adopt a reverent attitude, kneel formally before their desk with good posture and place the book properly on the desk in front of them. Books should not be thrown about, stepped over, used as pillows, have their pages folded back or turned with fingers moistened with spittle. Pages from discarded books with the words of the sages upon them should be disposed of with respect and not put to humiliating uses. Naturally, one does not laugh, move about or leave the room while engaged in reading.[26]

No doubt Ekken would also have disapproved of the scene in Kyōden's fashionbook *Behind Silk Brocade* (*Nishiki no ura*, 1791) in which lower-ranking women use a renowned commentary on *The Tale of Genji* (the *Kogetsushō*) as a trivet for their teapot.

live happily ever after (*medetaku osamarishi*). A formulaic closing, literally "ended felicitously."

shoddy construction (*hon no shitate ga warui*), **twisted plots** (*warudakumi*), and **warped characters** (*konjō ni hizumi*).

thousand-sheet piercing awl (*senmaidōshi*). A heavy-duty tool used to perforate thick stacks of paper.

totally recycled (*konjō o tojinaosareru*). "Have their nature reformed."

balance their books (*kure no shikomi*). Although a general term for year-end account settling, here it refers to the way that authors, illustrators, and publishers would scramble to meet deadlines for issuing works by the New Year.

---

26. From *Wazoku dōji kun* (1710). Translated in Kornicki, *The Book in Japan*, p. 261.

wadding (*koshibari*). Paper scraps were reused for such things as wall caulking.

facing pages (*kao*). Literally "faces."

eyes (*tojime*). The pun here is between "seam" and "corner of the eye."

"red with shame" (*akahajikaku*).

Essays in Idleness (*Tsurezuregusa*). Yoshida Kenkō's (1283–1350) celebrated miscellany (ca. 1331). It was the subject of some controversy during the Edo period, for although Neo-Confucian moralists like Hayashi Razan (1583–1657) had criticized the work as injurious to public morals, the Mind Study leader Teshima Toan (1718–1786) recommended that even young girls read it in their spare time for edification.[27]

Style Manual (*Yōbunshō*). A popular handbook of writing for everyday occasions.

Section 18

[Picture] The scene outside Masanobu's house, identifiable by his name-plate on the frame of the doorway, with its shop curtain and New Year's pine decoration (*kadomatsu*). Tsuruya, in costume befitting a formal seasonal visit—though here, no doubt, to collect the story Masanobu owes him—crouches down to examine a patched-up hole in the wall, ostensibly the final resting place of Glossy Book or Reading Book. Behind him, a young boy and a book peddler are bearing a load. The final placard reads "Illustrated and written by Kōsuisai disciple Masanobu" (*Kōsuisai monjin Masanobu gasaku*)—Kōsuisai being one of the pseudonyms used by Kyōden's artistic mentor Kitao Shigemasa.

bestsellers from all publishing houses (*sōshi doiya* [sic] *no shōbaimono*). Literally, "booksellers' merchandise."

obsolete slice-'em-and-dice-'em comicbooks (*kittari hattari no kusazōshi no sutarishi*). More literally, "the discarded of cut-and-slice comicbooks," referring both to the action-packed blackbook genre as well as to Blackbook's fate in this story.

treasure-ship pics (*takarabune*). Placed under the pillow to inspire auspicious dreams at the New Year.

travel Parcheesi (*dōchū sugoroku*). A board game popular during An'ei-Tenmei.

---

27. Mentioned in Sawada, *Confucian Values and Popular Zen*, p. 114.

Chapter 6

Playboy, Roasted

à la Edo (1785)

Is that what the quality do?
Then I'll do it too!
—M. Jourdain

Of the treasure trove of perhaps some twenty-five hundred *kibyōshi*, Santō Kyōden's *Playboy, Roasted à la Edo* is widely considered to be the crown jewel. A bestseller when first published in 1785, and alleged to have raised the price of paper, it was reissued over the following decade not once, but twice, with newly illustrated frontispieces gracing the covers (**Figure 6.1** and **Color Figure 2**).[1] This was something that was all but unheard of at the time. In fact, the piece was the first of only three by its author-illustrator to enjoy multiple editions.[2] More immediately, its success helped catapult the twenty-five-year-old Kyōden into the role of master. Among the dozen or so would-be disciples who began flocking to his gate, some went on to become prominent authors of late-Edo popular literature, including Shikitei Sanba, Santō Kyōzan, and Takizawa Bakin.[3] Scholars have long regarded *Playboy* as epitomizing Kyōden's *kibyōshi*, if not the genre itself. Little wonder it is the best studied, most often cited example, with the possible exception of Harumachi's *Master Flashgold's Splendiferous Dream*.

If *Familiar Bestsellers* tells the story of a smear campaign gone awry, *Playboy* describes the misadventures of a young man who has himself smeared

---

1. The plush frontispiece in this figure is from one of the two editions published in 1793. Reprinted in Kisho Fukuseikai, *Shinseiki 35–37*. The frontispieces in the translation proper come from the first edition, published at the beginning of 1785. Different editions of *Playboy* employ slightly different graphs in the title, as mentioned in Nakano, "*Edo umare uwaki no kabayaki*," pp. 80–81 and in Mizuno, *Santō Kyōden no nenpukō*, p. 49. For smallish reproductions of the frontispieces to all three editions, see Tanahashi, *Kibyōshi sōran 5*, pp. 286, 389, and 390. For a discussion of the second and third editions, see Tanahashi, *Kibyōshi sōran 2*, pp. 299–300.

2. The other two *kibyōshi* by Kyōden to enjoy more than one edition were *One Spring Night in Edo, One Thousand Gold Pieces* (*Edo no haru ichiya senryō*, 1786) and *Triple-Striped Ueda Silk, Woven with Playboy's Whims* (*Misujidachi kyaku no ki Ueda*, 1787). This does not include those of his *kibyōshi* reissued under starkly different titles: *Enma's Crystal Mirror* (*Kagami no jōhari*, 1790), for instance, was republished some years later as *Ono no Takamura's Pilgrimage Through Hell* (*Ono no Takamura jigoku ōrai*).

3. Miyatake, *Santō Kyōden*, pp. 62–64.

Fig. 6.1 Frontispiece to the deluxe second edition of Kyōden's *Playboy, Roasted à la Edo* (*Edo umare uwaki no kabayaki*), published in 1793. Reprinted in Kisho fukuseikai, *Shinseiki 35.*

intentionally. This young man—named Enjirō—does so out of the comically misguided conviction that infamy is the better part of fame. The gauche, odd-looking, sheltered son of a wealthy import-shop owner, Enjirō resolves to buy himself a reputation as a great philandering playboy, like the ones about whom he dreamily reads. He thereupon sets out on a series of fashionable though utterly shammed debaucheries designed to afford himself maximum publicity. Enjirō tattoos his arm with the names of fictitious lovers, painfully burning a few off to make his list appear authentic; pays a small fortune to have a geisha publicly beg his parents for permission to marry their son the heartthrob; and employs gazetteers to canvass Edo with the breaking news of his most recent peccadilloes.

The increasingly outrageous ruses culminate in an elaborate kabuki-style staging of a fake elopement and double suicide with a famous high-ranking courtesan named Ukina. This is a massive undertaking, an extravaganza, really, involving playwrights, actors, dancers, musicians, crooners, the staff of a bordello, even a cast of extras. Yet for all his efforts, the charade fails

when two masked marauders ambush the couple, stealing everything save their loincloths. Typically, at this point in a real kabuki play, there would be a long, sentimental travel song recapitulating the mournful journey of the lovers en route to meet their fate. Instead, *Playboy* burlesques such a song, describing the couple's demoralized race homeward, *en déshabillé*. This full-length tour de force is replete with associative words, allusions to classical poetry, and *double entendres* on everything from nakedness to the Nakanochō, the Yoshiwara's main strip.

The humor of *Playboy* nonetheless emanates in large measure from the deep chasm between Enjirō's craving to become a playboy on the one hand, and his uncouth nature on the other. Such is often the case with the uninitiated youth (*musuko*) and the out-and-out poseur (*hankatsū*), whose antics in the pleasure quarters are the stuff of the comedy of manners. As has been observed of the fashionbook, like so much Edo popular literature, the humor derives from how ridiculously its characters fall short of the ideal of sophistication. These characters are laughably inexperienced, pretentious, superficial. In contemporary terms, they were incapable of discerning the loopholes in the surface of things, the ability to do so being the *sine qua non* of the true sophisticate.

What blinds Enjirō to his own particular shortfall is his unbridled romanticism. Although not an abnormal condition of youth, Enjirō's particular wistfulness sweeps away what little common sense he might otherwise possess, turning him into an absurdly literal reader. In short, Enjirō takes everything at face value—everything, ironically, except his own face, which, with its quirky little nose, is hardly that of a great paramour. He may well be thought of as a kind of Edo counterpart to Austin Powers, who fancies himself a handsome swinger in spite of his unfashionably thick glasses and crooked teeth. Enjirō's otherwise intact literalism becomes apparent in the opening scene, where he is depicted poring over sentimental stage songs as though they were realistic guidebooks to proper etiquette, which of course they are not. Clearly smitten by the romance of the heroes of these songs (much like Don Quixote with his *roman de chevalerie*), Enjirō vows to live up to their example—even if it means dying in the process. An equally absurd paradox lies at the heart of Enjirō's quest, for indifference being integral to sophistication, his is the story of desperately seeking nonchalance.

Enjirō's idiosyncratic overzealousness aside, this confusion of fiction for real life may well have been salient to the many readers at the time who were encountering the jolting discrepancy between live theater and its representation in printed form. The relatively recent mass publishing of theatrical libretti of the sort Enjirō pores over, which extended for the first time to a significant degree the popular theater beyond the purview of the theatergoer, represents an important moment in the cultural history of Japan. Kabuki, one of the most pervasive forms of popular entertainment in the major cities, was essentially being dislocated from its primary *mise en scène* of

the public stage and relocated to the secondary—though no less dramatic—venue of the private boudoir.

Still, the fact that Enjirō casts himself as the star of his own kabuki spectacular suggests that he is seduced not merely by romantic stage songs, or their representation in printed form, but by the underlying allure of the theater itself—its Pineroticism, as George Bernard Shaw formulated it, that "compulsive whirl of furs, fans, and . . . flesh."[4] Enjirō epitomizes the stage-struck fan, without whom the rise of the cult of the kabuki idol during the late seventeenth century would never have been possible.[5] "Captivated by some delicious love story, or deluded by the latest dramatic productions of Dotombori," as the narrator of one of Saikaku's stories puts it, waxing moralistic about those crazed fans who lose themselves in Osaka's theater district, "their souls are caught up in giddy corruption."[6] Over the next century, the kabuki fanatic would be subdivided into set character types, such as the "play-crazed oaf" (kyōgenzuki yabo) or the "actor's mimic" (yakusha kidori), whom Sanba astutely characterized as "a pretentious fellow [who] flatters himself as a handsome man and a lady-killer [though] he is foppish and ugly."[7] Enjirō falls squarely within this tradition—his very name echoic of "performing" (enjiru) some make-believe role.

In broader strokes yet, Enjirō is swept away by the romance of highbrow literature, seemingly fancying himself as a latter-day version of the great ladykillers of the classical tradition. This is evinced pictorially. In one scene Enjirō is shown sitting smugly before a bookcase that houses his copies of The Tales of Ise and The Tale of Genji. The mental juxtaposition of the handsome visages of the heroes of these two tales against Enjirō's cartoonish mug amounts to a sly visual gag. In more literary terms, though, while Narihira and Genji manipulated language to have their way with women, Enjirō can hardly penetrate the surface of any utterance, let alone discern figurative from literal levels of meaning.[8]

At the level of language, then, Playboy—as is true of the best kibyōshi—is a veritable mélange of speech genres. Yet many of these utterances can be said to fall into one of two contrasting modes. The first is the romantic mode, to be found in the story's alluded-to sentimental ballads, classic

---

4. Shaw coined this neologism to describe the plays of Arthur Wing Pinero. Quoted in Kaplan and Stowell, Theatre and Fashion, p. 48.

5. For more on the figure of the kabuki star, see Kominz, The Stars Who Created Kabuki.

6. De Bary, Five Women Who Loved Love, p. 105.

7. For instance, there was Kishida Tohō's kibyōshi, The Kabuki-Crazed Uncouth Grandee (Kyōgenzuki yabo na daimyō, 1784). Also see Sanba's Critique of Theatergoers (Kyakusha hyōbanki, 1811). In Raz, "The Audience Evaluated," p. 214.

8. In The Tales of Ise, Narihira rebuffs several uncouth women who try to initiate romantic affairs with him by composing punning verse that deftly plays off their inability to fathom his meaning beneath the surface. In Chapter 14, for instance, a rustic woman interprets Narihira's poem as a vow to bring her back to the capital as his keepsake. His real message, though, is more along the lines of "You're no great beauty—get lost!"

works, lyrical travel poem, even love tattoos. In a sense, this mode itself seduces Enjirō, just as Narihira and Genji seduced their various inamorata.
For those readers familiar with the companion-booklet story *A Discretionary
Tale* (*Otonashi sōshi*, ca. 1570), Enjirō must have seemed closer to the sweet-
talked married woman than to the sweet-talking ladies' man who gleans his
verbal strategies right out of *Ise* and *Genji*.[9] And it is the romantic mode that
is employed by those addressing Enjirō directly in order to take advantage
of him, but which is dropped when addressing others. Then the idiom assumed is that of commerce, of pragmatism, of the quotidian. This second
mode is audible in the down-to-earth asides and dialogue of characters
negotiating with each other behind Enjirō's back. The disparity between
the two modes is sharply audible when the hired mistress switches—
mid-speech—from neglected lover to hard-bargaining businesswoman.

The characters who most readily apprehend how Enjirō's susceptibility
to the romantic mode qualifies him as an easy mark are Warui Shian and
Kitari Kinosuke. These opportunistic "drumbearers" (*taikomochi*)—sidekicks
for hire as ego-stroking guides to the pleasure quarters—sponge off their
gullible employer on top of the fees they charge him for their services. The
stratagems they recommend to Enjirō repeatedly backfire, bringing him
widespread ignominy but them financial gain. It never occurs to Enjirō that
(like Monsieur Jourdain in Molière's *Le Bourgeois Gentilhomme*) his tutors in
bamboozlement might also be bamboozling him, even though there are
several clues, which can be read merely by penetrating the façade of visual
and verbal texts.

Shian, for instance, warns Enjirō not to be taken in by the outward deportment of women, but to pay special attention to their physical appearance, especially calluses behind the ears—supposedly the irrefutable sign of
a hardened prostitute. This line itself was so clichéd as to be the weary
spoof of advice doled out too freely (not unlike Polonius' counsel to Hamlet, "to thine own self be true"), though Enjirō fails to realize even this.[10]

And it is through the ear that Kinosuke, for his part, persuades Enjirō is
the way to a woman's heart. He rattles off a list of romantic ballads guaran-
teed to do the trick. This list serves as a *mise en abyme*, a kind of cryptic table
of contents to the story, since many of its titles in one way or another bear
upon what ensues (as the objects surrounding the slumbering author in *Familiar Bestsellers* make their way into his dream).[11] The flagrant length of this
list gives body, in tangible space upon the page, to Enjirō's acceptance of

---

9. Skord, *Tales of Tears and Laughter*, pp. 17–32.

10. These lines were frequently mentioned in fashionbooks, as Jones points out in "William Hogarth and Kitao Masanobu," p. 72, n. 8.

11. The term *mise en abyme* derives from medieval heraldry, where it denoted a small coat-
of-arms identical in design to the larger coat-of-arms in which it was embedded. André Gide
appropriated the term to literary ends. For more on this, see Dällenbach, *The Mirror in the
Text*.

the unrealistic notion that sophistication can be boiled down to a formula, like a recipe for some glazed-and-grilled delicacy.

Following the self-serving advice of his sidekicks, Enjirō proceeds to have himself ambushed, kidnapped, thrashed about the face and neck, kicked in the ribs, scorched by the sun, cauterized with moxa, pricked by the tattooer's needle, disinherited, and publicly humiliated. Far from losing heart after each agonizing outcome, he redoubles his efforts, unflinchingly throwing himself into equally perilous, more harebrained (though he hopes more promising) schemes—all with what Sontag has identified in the comic hero as a kind of "cheerful dumbness."[12] Enjirō certainly displays no intellectual development, no emotional incrementation, no potential for ever budding into the hero of a *Bildungsroman* of a later era, let alone a Japanese "I-novel." There is something charming about his dogged determination, though. Simply put, he has heart.

On the other hand, Enjirō gets so carried away, at times losing sight of his ultimate goal of becoming a great rake, and taking his own propaganda seriously, that one suspects this is less a matter of his "phlegmatic" temperament (as Koike has characterized it) than a fetish for pain.[13] Such "anesthetization," though, or at least the blissful amnesia between episodes, resists earnest psychologizing. Aside from the fact that real Edo-born playboys preferred pleasure (if not deriving it from other people's pain), unadulterated masochism makes for good slapstick.[14] And although scholar Enoyama Jun'ichi is right in observing that unlike a great many *kibyōshi*, *Playboy* does not put any of its characters asleep to dream, Mutō Motoaki has submitted that Enjirō acts as though he were dreaming—not the literal dream of Master Flashgold, but a kind of romantic delirium nonetheless.[15]

To the extent that Enjirō's stupefying fantasy presumes the possibility of instant sophistication, *Playboy* may well satirize not just the romantic mode, or those who fall prey to it, but the hyper-affectations, materialism, gleeful optimism, and even the instructional texts (including kabuki plays as well as fashionbooks) of the *nouveau riche*, that set of mostly townsmen merchants whom Enjirō unmistakably emblemizes. The futility of his publicity campaign, then, becomes a wry comment upon the frenzied struggle to parlay newfound wealth into respectability.[16] *Playboy*, at this level, turns the psychodrama of bourgeois society into farce.

---

12. Sontag, "The Death of Tragedy," in *Against Interpretation and Other Essays*, p. 136.

13. This is Martin's translation of a term used by Koike (*Kenkyū*, pp. 227–228). In Martin, "Santō Kyōden and His *Sharebon*," p. 116.

14. Following Henri Bergson's opinion that "the comic demands something like a momentary anesthesia of the heart." In Sypher, *Comedy*, p. 64.

15. Enoyama, "Yume no shukō to *Edo umare uwaki no kabayaki*." Mutō argues that Enjirō shares much in common with Master Flashgold. See Mutō, "Futari no Enjirō."

16. Mutō suggests as much in "Futari no Enjirō," p. 9.

And it seems to do so at the expense of certain individuals. Ever since its publication, *Playboy* has led readers and scholars to contend that it directly spoofs one or more contemporary figures. In fact, there are some half-dozen such theories, some more plausible than others.[17] One holds that Enjirō was modeled on Izumiya Jinsuke (a.k.a. Taishin), a merchant of extravagant tastes who dabbled in imported goods and whose self-promotional activities were legendary.[18]

An interesting though improbable proposition—aside from the one that Enjirō parodies the hero of the first *kibyōshi*, Master Flashgold—is that Enjirō stands for none other than Kyōden himself. The chief indication being that just as Enjirō wins the girl in the end, Kyōden married a celebrated courtesan.[19] And why is it that Enjirō's most distinctive feature came to be called the "*Kyōden* nose" (*Kyōden-bana*) and not the "*Enjirō* nose"? This conflation would have profound implications for Kyōden as a professional author, for it became his most imperishable trademark; yet in terms of hard evidence, it would seem to bear all the validity of a conspiracy theory.

By far the most widely accepted view is that Enjirō is based on the entrepreneur Kishimoto Eijirō of the Asadaya. Aside from the close resemblance in merchant appellations—Asadaya Eijirō and Adakiya Enjirō—this Eijirō attained notoriety by ransoming a celebrated Yoshiwara courtesan whom he barely knew, Segawa of the Matsubaya, who has her fictional counterpart in *Playboy*'s Ukina.[20] Also, Eijirō purportedly collected works of literature he could scarcely fathom.[21]

Of course, these theories need not be mutually exclusive. Nakamura Yukihiko believes that *Playboy* is an intertwining (*naimaze*) of the worlds of two well-known contemporary couples: the first part of the story focusing on Asadaya Eijirō and Matsubaya Segawa, and the second on the samurai Abe-no-Shikibu Masaakira and his courtesan Ōgiya Hanaōgi. The dividing line apparently runs through the scene set in Ukina's boudoir and toilet, which contemporaneous sophisticates in the know would have recognized by several visual clues, according to Nakamura, as belonging to Hanaōgi.

---

17. Tanahashi, in his introductory essay to *Playboy*, estimates that at least four real-life models have been suggested.

18. Mentioned in Furuhashi, *Hyōgen no nagare*, p. 281. For more on Izumiya Jinsuke, see Kitahara, *Edo fūkyōden* and Katō, *Edo no fūryūjin*, pp. 103–139.

19. Koike relates this theory in *Hankotsusha Ōta Nanpo to Santō Kyōden*, p. 131. While it is true that Kyōden was involved with Kikuzono (b. 1764), an attendant courtesan (*furisode shinzō*) to the courtesan Hanaōgi of the Ōgiya, Koike fails to mention that Kyōden would not marry her until 1790—some five years after *Playboy* was published. Still, Kyōden was famous among authors of playful literature as a playboy.

20. Mentioned in both Koike, *Santō Kyōden no kenkyū*, p. 225, and Yamaguchi, "Kibyōshi ni tsuite," in *Yamaguchi Takeshi chosakushū 3*, pp. 326–327.

21. Koike, *Edo no gesaku ehon 2*, p. 148. The Asadaya Eijirō theory is articulated in several other places, too, such as Tanahashi, *Kibyōshi sōran 1*, p. 601, and Yamaguchi, *Edo bungaku kenkyū*, p. 409.

Thereupon, the story shifts to a spoof of the actual elopement and failed double-suicide attempt of Hanaōgi and Abe, which was the scandal *du jour* in Edo at the time *Playboy* was being cooked up.[22]

Nakamura's theory goes a long way toward explaining several seemingly unrelated minor points, such as: an aside about Bokuga, the proprietor of the bordello where Hanaōgi worked; the chain-patterned robe Enjirō dons, associated with Abe-no-Shikibu *Nobumitsu*, whom Nakamura opines was erroneously conflated (either in the popular imagination or in Kyōden's head) with Abe-no-Shikibu *Masaakira*; and, most provocatively, the lavatory sign urging vigilance against fire, which Nakamura suggests is a cheeky allusion to Masaakira's post as Fire Marshal of Edo Castle—if not to an infamous conflagration that occurred there on his watch. If true, then *Playboy* may have taken indirect aim at the Tokugawa shogunate by poking fun at the indiscretions of one of its public functionaries. After all, *Playboy* was published during the dawn of the so-called protest *kibyōshi*.

Yet Nakamura's theory feels strained in its explanation of the mysterious phrase "shared palanquin" (*dōyo*), which appears on the suicide mat in the final scene of the story, where Enjirō is scolded for his lowdown ways. This is one of the "puzzlers" that annotators have glossed over, though to their credit they correctly identify Kyōden's clever pictorial pun—"to wear a mat" (*mōsen o kaburu*), meaning something along the lines of "to eat humble pie." Nakamura claims that this was a vogue expression referring to a failed suicide attempt, and here, *specifically* to the disastrous Abe-Hanaōgi affair. Furthermore, the collar-like border on Enjirō's suicide mat—a highly irregular feature—derives from the ceremonial robe (*hoi*) of the sort that would have been worn by Abe in his official capacity as Fire Marshal (*jō-bikeshi yoriki*).[23] The truly sophisticated reader, Nakamura avers, would very likely have recognized the nonstandard graph *yo* of the word *dōyo* on Enjirō's suicide mat as being the standard *yo* of *yoriki* on Abe's robe.

Whether or not one accepts the particulars of Nakamura's dual-model theory, which at times pushes the limits of credulity, the presumption that there may be multiple real-life models for Enjirō has sparked new approaches to analyzing the work. Mutō maintains that *Playboy* is a kind of literary pastiche (*fukiyose*) of various existent playboys, interlaced with associated strings of puns (*uwakizukushi*). Enjirō probably *is* an amalgam of Eijirō and other actual personages, then, though who in particular is almost beside the point.

---

22. Nakamura's argument is more complex than this brief summary would imply. He pieces together fictional and nonfictional accounts suggesting that Abe-no-Shikibu Masaakira's failed suicide attempt took place in 1784. He also admits the possibility that there are still *other* models for Enjirō. See Nakamura, "*Edo umare uwaki no kabayaki* sadan," pp. 35–41.

23. Nakamura points out that Masaakira is known to have received the ceremonial robe whereas Nobumitsu did not.

That said, there is an indisputable model for the visual depiction of En-jirō, one that may also cast light on several of the lingering mysteries of the story. Enjirō made his début as a nameless illustration in another work compiled and illustrated by Kyōden that was issued the year prior to *Playboy*. Strictly speaking, though, Kyōden did not devise this nameless Enjirō. That particular distinction goes to one Kamo no Muchikage, an attendee of the "Handtowel Competition" held in the summer of 1784.[24] This was in essence a playful banquet, no doubt enlivened by vast quantities of saké, in which each participant submitted a fanciful handtowel (*tanagui*) of his or her own design involving some kind of imaginative visual-verbal pun or far-fetched explanation of familiar cultural icons.[25] In attendance at this gala gathering were many of the beautiful people of the day, such as: leading comic poet Ōta Nanpo and members of his *kyōka* circle; famed woodblock artist Utamaro; kabuki stars Ichikawa Danjūrō V and Segawa Kikunojō III; Ōgiya proprietor Suzuki Uemon (Bokuga); and high-ranking courtesans Segawa VI and Utahime of the Matsubaya. Kyōden recounted the gathering, replete with his renditions of the actual entries in the contest, in his humorous picturebook *The Handtowel Competition* (*Tanagui awase*, 1784).[26] This included his version of Muchikage's as-yet unnamed pug-nosed character (**Figure 6.2** and **Color Figure 3**). Thus, the original model for Enjirō's face was devised by Muchikage, then rendered by Kyōden.

Moreover, many of the places, patterns, and beautiful people associated with *The Handtowel Competition* appear in *Playboy*, even if only obliquely: Hanaōgi's double-cherry crest adorns a tobacco tray; Segawa's name is mentioned in passing; Utahime's name graces a lantern; Bokuga's part is said to be taken by another actor; Rokō is slated to dance the final number; a kerchief bears Danjūrō's easily recognizable pattern of triple concentric squares (*mimasu*);[27] and the robes hanging on the family garment rack in the last scene may be read as a hint to the reader to look to *The Handtowel Competition*, which opens with a series of pictures of draped fabrics. Finally, Enjirō's irregular suicide mat, with its odd border lines and the mysterious phrase "shared palanquin," likewise appeared in the earlier work (**Figure 6.3**).

---

24. Probably the poet and National Learning scholar Katō Chikage (1734–1808). His pseudonym "Kamo no Muchikage" is believed to have been a conflation of his own name with that of Kamo no Mabuchi (1697–1769), under whom he studied. See Suzuki, *Tachibana Chikage no kenkyū*, pp. 83–87.

25. The term *tanagui* was Edo slang for *tenugui*.

26. Published toward the end of 1784, *The Handtowel Competition* is a "picturebook of humorous iconographic allusions" (*kokkei mitate ehon*). For both a color reprint of the text and a transcribed version, see Tani, *Share no dezain*. For a discussion in English, see Iwasaki, "The World of *Gesaku*," pp. 308–311.

27. Representing three square cups stacked upon each other in order to cascade saké, used especially during festive occasions.

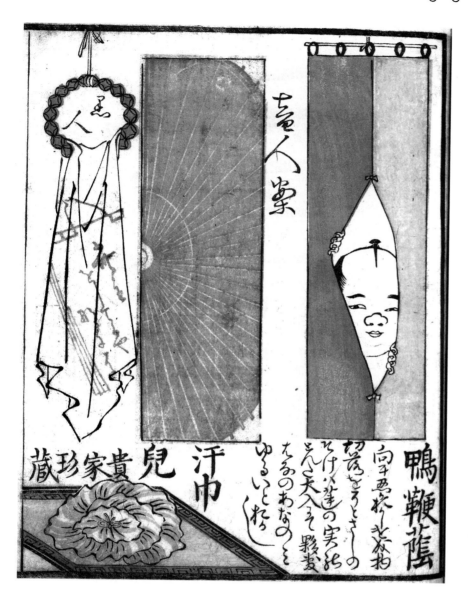

Fig. 6.2 Kamo no Muchikage's unnamed pug-nosed character who would become the model for Enjirō. From *The Handtowel Competition* (*Tanagui awase*, 1784), a humorous picture-book (*kokkei mitate ehon*) written and illustrated by Santō Kyōden. Courtesy of the National Institute of Japanese Literature.

It seems likely, then, that while Kyōden's *Playboy, Roasted à la Edo* serves as a kind of literary roast of assorted playboys—Asadaya Eijirō and perhaps Abe-no-Shikibu Masaakira foremost among them—it is more fundamentally an imaginative animation of *The Handtowel Competition*. Just as the contestants of the actual gathering spun whimsical yarns out of fanciful handtowels, *Playboy* utilized *The Handtowel Competition* as its basic cloth.

And so to the question "What if Muchikage's nameless face were the hero of a *kibyōshi*?" Kyōden responds with Enjirō. The clash between this reconceived character's homely looks and grand aspirations is captured visually; for his squat head, drowsy eyes, flaccid neck, droopy shoulders, and hunched-over, seemingly spineless posture portray him as a resolutely

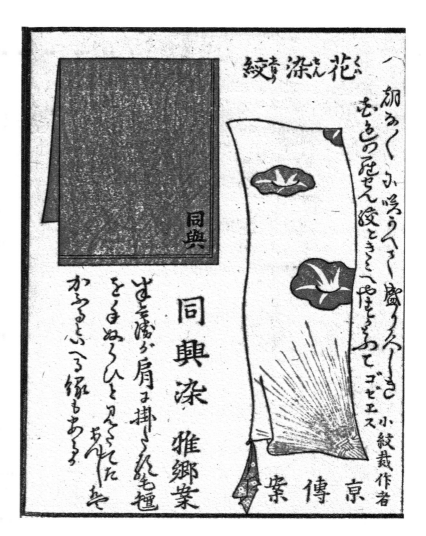

Fig. 6.3 Robe bearing the mysterious phrase "shared palanquin" (*dōyo*). This would become the model for Enjirō's unconventional suicide mat. From *The Handtowel Competition* (*Tenugui awase*, 1784), a humorous picturebook (*kokkei mitate ehon*) written and illustrated by Santō Kyōden. Reprinted in Kisho fukuseikai, *Shinseiki 31*.

uncouth slouch, though his expression of delighted gusto nonetheless betrays his philandering fantasies.[28] The figure of Enjirō therefore qualifies as a genuine cartoon, the essence of which, according to Gombrich, is "the condensation of a complex idea into one striking and memorable image."[29]

By far the most conspicuous feature of Enjirō's comic disparity, though, is as plain as the nose on his face. Since in the Japanese context the size of one's nose is proverbially correlated with the degree of one's hauteur, his haughty ambitions are sabotaged by that humble little snout of his. Although the other characters recognize this instantaneously, Enjirō's obliviousness

---

28. The rendering of the face, more so than body posture, is of course indispensable to comic art, for, "[u]nlike the body," as Eisner puts it, "its gestures are more subtle but more readily understood. It is also the part of the body that is most individual." Eisner, *Comics and Sequential Art*, p. 111.

29. Gombrich, *Meditations on a Hobby Horse*, p. 130.

to the fact transforms his nose into a cipher of his own self-delusion. Henri Bergson, in the Platonic vein of regarding comedy as emanating ultimately from the refusal to "know thyself," maintains, "A comic character is generally comic in proportion to his ignorance of himself."[30] Many of the great comic figures possess some physical characteristic that condenses their character into a visible sign conspicuous to everyone save themselves: Charlie Chaplin has his funny little shuffle; Charlie Brown, that wishy-washy curl of hair. To the extent that Enjirō's short, stubby nose captures the essence of his comic flaw in a way that makes him stick out among *kibyōshi* characters, he might be counted—along with Sharaku's caricatures of actors, or the figures in Hokusai's sketchbooks[31]—as one of the high accomplishments of Edo-period comic art.

As a well-trained artist, Kyōden was no doubt aware that Muchikage's nameless face derived from the rustic, goofy-looking mug of a particular type of caricature. The connection is acknowledged in *Playboy* when a woman quips that Enjirō, who looks even more ludicrous pretending to be a gigolo in the disguise of a traveling salesman of fan paper, is the spitting image of a "Toba picture" (*Tobae*). Annotators have traditionally taken this line as referring to the comic *Frolicking Critters* scrolls, attributed to the late Heian-period abbot Toba Sōjō, which humorously depicted rabbits, monkeys, and so forth engaged in human activities, such as reciting sutras and sumo wrestling.[32] And when compared to an anthropomorphized frog, Enjirō's face may indeed appear faintly amphibian.

However, eighteenth-century readers were presumably far less familiar with twelfth-century scrolls than with the widely disseminated cartoons of their own day. The "Toba cartoons" (as they ought to be called to avoid confusion), while admittedly deriving stylistic inspiration from Toba Sōjō's scrolls (which had begun to be reprinted during the seventeenth century), were a different animal. The Toba cartoons began appearing in the Kyoto-Osaka area during the early part of the eighteenth century—particularly in the works of Ōoka Shunboku (1680–1763)—and continued to be produced during the time of *Playboy*, as with Matsuya Nichōsai's (fl. 1781–1788, a.k.a. Jichōsai) collection of actor caricatures *Picturebook of Water and Sky* (*Ehon mizu ya sora*, 1780). Enjirō thus bears an unmistakable likeness to the homunculus, little human figures of these hastily sketched comics that often featured round heads, squinty eyes, and triangles for noses (**Figure 6.4**).

---

30. Bergson, "Laughter," p. 71.

31. For more on Hokusai as comic artist, see Rosenfield, "The Anatomy of Humor in Hokusai's Instruction Manuals."

32. Each of the three major annotated editions mentions Toba Sōjō but not the Edo-period Toba cartoons. See *NKBZ*, p. 131 n. 9; *NKBT*, p. 150, n. 1; and Tanahashi, in Koike, *Edo no gesaku ehon 2*, p 169, n. 2.

Fig. 6.4 Cartoon characters shooting handheld fireworks. From *Toba Caricatures of the Three Kingdoms* (*Tobae sangokushi*), by Ōoka Shunboku (1680–1763). Courtesy of Tokyo National University of Fine Arts and Music Library.

Furthermore, these Toba cartoon figures were increasingly coming to be printed on various sorts of commercial goods—an Edo forerunner, maybe, of "cute" merchandising. So, they would have been associated in the popular imagination with the sort of fan Enjirō pretends to peddle: "Recently, anywhere one looks," one work noted with delight, "from paper fans to crepe-silk wrappers, one sees Toba cartoons everywhere, their faces, forms, and limbs not quite human, a veritable pageant of hobgoblins!"[33] This is why, at the end of *Playboy*, an account of the failed suicide attempt is depicted and disseminated widely *not* on broadsheets (*kawaraban*) or illustrated leaflets (*ezōshi*), as was *de rigueur*;[34] but rather, on inexpensive, persimmon-varnished paper fans. This amounts to a farfetched explanation (*kojitsuke*) reversing cause and effect (not unlike the gag of Enjirō hiring Kyōden as his amanuensis); for in real life, the picture of Enjirō's face ultimately derives from Toba cartoons of the sort found on fans, though in *Playboy*

---

33. From *Kankatsu heike monogatari* (1710). Quoted in Shimizu, *Manga no rekishi*, pp. 167–168.

34. Kamiya Jihei's love suicide, for instance, was disseminated this way, at least according to Chikamatsu's *Shinjū ten no Amijima* (1721). See Shively, *Love Suicide at Amijima*, p. 91 and n. 217 on pp. 125–126.

Fig. 6.5 Enjirō, Warui Shian, and Kitari Kinosuke. From *The Stylishly Slangy Latticed Bordello (Tsūgen sōmagaki*, 1787), a fashionbook written and illustrated by Santō Kyōden. Courtesy of Yamaguchi University Library.

it is the Toba cartoons on fans that are said to derive directly from Enjirō's face.

Whatever Enjirō's artistic heritage might have been, the destiny of his character continues to be rewritten. Kyōden himself revisited Enjirō and his sidekicks in the celebrated *Stylishly Slangy Latticed Bordello (Tsūgen sōmagaki)*, a fashionbook published two years after *Playboy*, though by no means a sequel per se to it (**Figure 6.5**).[35] There is even a story about Enjirō's progeny Unutarō, who bears obvious physical resemblance to his literary progenitor (**Figure 6.6**).[36] Other authors have drawn inspiration from *Playboy*, too. The contemporary writer Jitōkan Shujin modeled Kinkei, the protagonist of his *kibyōshi* titled *Yobitsugi kogane no naruki* (1790), after Enjirō.[37]

More recently, Inoue Hisashi (1934–) has written less a takeoff than an imaginative pastiche of sorts, the Naoki Prize–winning *Shackled Love Suicide (Tegusari shinjū*, 1972), about a rich kid named Izumiya Eijirō who sets out on

---

35. For an annotated edition, see Mizuno, *NKBT 59*, pp. 353–386. Although the Enjirō of *Latticed Bordello* visually resembles the one of *Playboy*, their characters are drastically different, as Mutō observes in "Futari no Enjirō," pp. 9–10.

36. For a transcribed edition of this work, a *kibyōshi* titled *Himon yari shō no yotsudakebushi* (1789), see Mizuno, *SKZ 2*, pp. 29–41.

37. Mentioned in Tanahashi, *Kibyōshi sōran 2*, pp. 163–164.

Fig. 6.6 Enjirō's progeny Unutarō. From *Himon yari shō no yotsudakebushi* (1789), a *kibyōshi* written and illustrated by Santō Kyōden. Courtesy of Tokyo Metropolitan Central Library, Tokyo Collection.

a propaganda campaign to pass himself off as a great writer of playful literature. This Eijirō consorts with the narrator Jippensha Ikku, Shikitei Sanba, Tsutaya Jūzaburō, Ōta Nanpo, Takizawa Bakin, Tōshūsai Sharaku, and Santō Kyōden himself (who, it will be remembered, in real life was manacled).[38] So many characters, places, incidents, and phrases overlap between the two stories that it may be possible to read *Shackled Love Suicide* as a kind of humorous etymology of *Playboy* itself (a little like the way that the Oscar-winning film *Shakespeare in Love* playfully explains the supposed origins of some of the Bard's oft-quoted lines). Even the many discrepancies are playfully suggestive. The "Kyōden nose," for instance, is recast as a sign of Kyōden's own snobbishness. And the protagonist "Izumiya Eijirō," rather than merely harking back to Enjirō himself, conflates two of his

---

38. For a discussion of Inoue's piece, see Cohn, *Studies in the Comic Spirit in Modern Japanese Fiction*, pp. 136–141 *passim* and 164–165. My gratitude to Christopher Robins for sharing his unpublished translation with me.

supposed real-life models—*Izumiya* Jinsuke and Asadaya *Eijirō*—Inoue's own studious joke for those in the know.

In closing, *Playboy* no doubt appealed to contemporary readers for many reasons, not the least of which is that the story delights in the eternal theme of romantic youth. Yet it also contains enough in-group references and local color to have satisfied even the most discriminating of sophisticates. *Playboy*'s satirical guns likewise point in all directions. The piece can be read as a conservative satire, policing the boundaries of the literary and dramatic arts by lampooning kabuki plays, the fashionbook tradition, and the rise of the *nouveau riche* as a class, if not as specific individuals. It can also be read as a progressive satire, taking a swipe at the government through the proxy of Edo Castle's Fire Marshal, thereby emboldening others, perhaps, to try their hand at such nose-thumbing. Admittedly, any reading of a story about misreadings is by definition a perilous undertaking. In the final analysis, then, the object of *Playboy*'s satire may prove as slippery to get hold of as an unglamorously live eel.

The present translation and annotations rely heavily on the work of four annotated editions: (1) Mizuno Minoru, *Kibyōshi sharebon shū*, in Mizuno, ed., *NKBT 59* (Iwanami shoten, 1958), pp. 135–156; (2) Hamada Giichirō, in Hamada et al., eds., *Kibyōshi senryū kyōka*, in *NKBZ 46* (Shōgakukan, 1971), pp. 117–137; (3) Nakano Mitsutoshi, "*Edo umare uwaki no kabayaki*: Sakuhin kanshō," in *Kyōden, Ikku, Shunsui*, in Jinbō Kazuya et al., eds., *Zusetsu Nihon no koten 18* (Shūeisha, 1980), pp. 80–91; and (4) Tanahashi Masahiro, in Koike Masatane et al., eds., *Edo no gesaku ehon 2*, in *Kyōyō bunko 1038* (Shakai shisōsha, 1981), pp. 147–182. To complicate matters slightly, Tanahashi updated the *NKBZ* version (*not* the *Edo no gesaku ehon* one), also entitled *Kibyōshi senryū kyōka*, but published it in *SNKBZ 79* (Shōgakukan, 1999), pp. 85–108. Use was made, too, of the unannotated text in Mizuno Minoru et al., eds., *Santō Kyōden zenshū 1* (Perikansha, 1992), pp. 183–201.

A preliminary version of this translation, in playscript format with extensive annotation of both the visual and verbal texts, appeared in my dissertation, "Blowing Smoke: Tobacco Pouches, Literary Squibs, and Authorial Puffery in the Pictorial Comic Fiction (*Kibyōshi*) of Santō Kyōden (1761–1816)" (Harvard University, 1997), pp. 300–364. Chris Drake's translation—to which Haruo Shirane has had pictorial annotation added—is published in Shirane, ed., *Early Modern Japanese Literature* (New York: Columbia University, 2002), pp. 687–710. Among the essays in English on *Playboy*, I benefited the most from Sumie Jones, "William Hogarth and Kitao Masanobu: Reading Eighteenth-Century Pictorial Narratives," in *Yearbook of Comparative and General Literature*, no. 34 (1985), pp. 37–73.[39]

---

39. For more on *Playboy* in English, see: Jones, *Edo Pop* (forthcoming); Keene, *World Within Walls*, pp. 405–406; Lane, "The Young Man from Edo Who Was Punished for Loving

The illustrations of this *kibyōshi* are from the deluxe second edition, published in 1793, as reprinted in Kisho fukuseikai, *Shinseki 35*. The frontispieces, from the original 1785 edition, are courtesy of Hōsa bunko.

Too Daringly"; Miner, "The Grounds of Mimetic and Nonmimetic Art"; Seigle, *Yoshiwara*, pp. 198–200; and Akimoto, *Twilight of Yedo*, pp. 156–171.

Playboy, Roasted

à la Edo

Here is Enjirō, only son of the tycoon owner of the D. Bauchery Shop. Twentyish, without ever having contracted poverty or any other disease, thank you very much, Enjirō is congenitally pre-sensual pursuits. How he envies those who, in the romantic ballads he reads, kill themselves for love, like Tamakiya Itahachi or Ukiyo Inosuke.

disposed toward playbooks of

"Why, for a lifetime of memories, I'd kill myself too!"

Having got this prepos-terous idea into his head, Enjirō schemes perilous schemes.

"What fun to end up like these guys— they must've been born under a lucky star!"

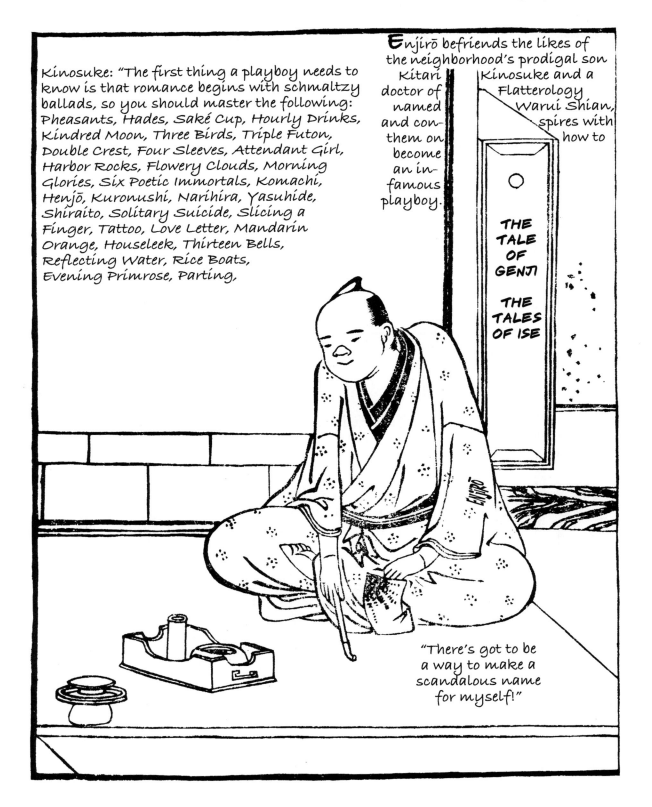

Kinosuke: "The first thing a playboy needs to know is that romance begins with schmaltzy ballads, so you should master the following: Pheasants, Hades, Saké Cup, Hourly Drinks, Kindred Moon, Three Birds, Triple Futon, Double Crest, Four Sleeves, Attendant Girl, Harbor Rocks, Flowery Clouds, Morning Glories, Six Poetic Immortals, Komachi, Henjō, Kuronushi, Narihira, Yasuhide, Shiraito, Solitary Suicide, Slicing a Finger, Tattoo, Love Letter, Mandarin Orange, Houseleek, Thirteen Bells, Reflecting Water, Rice Boats, Evening Primrose, Parting,

Enjirō befriends the likes of the neighborhood's prodigal son Kinosuke and a Flatterology Warui Shian, spires with how to

Kitari doctor of named and con- them on become an in- famous playboy.

THE TALE OF GENJI

THE TALES OF ISE

ENJIRŌ

"There's got to be a way to make a scandalous name for myself!"

...Lingering Leaves, Temporary Pillow, Summer Clothes, Spring Nights, Autumn Evenings, Gleaming Mirror, Midnight Bell, Hazy Moon, Vernal Mists, Scattered Birds, River of Burning Passion, Shrine Virgins Three, Coming of Age Ceremony, Myriad Chrysanthemums, Autumn Mosquito Net, Grasses of Yoshino, Summer Moon, Morning Crow, Village Cock, Folding Flower-Viewing Banquet, Lingering Warmth, Everlasting Bond, Dyed Threads, Bird of Hades, Two-Stroke Character, Left-Handed Writing, Robe of Edo, Tatami Divination, Nothings.

Fan, Blossom Fragrance, Bodkin, Rendezvous Peak, Loving Cherry, Seven Herbs, This Heart of Mine, Summer Single Crevice, and Sweet

There are many, many others, though these should do for now. Ouch, my jaw aches! Secret teachings abound on the art of love letters. If her envelope isn't sealed, you've been dumped. If she starts signing her childhood name at the end, you've got problems!"

Shian: "A missive with lipstick-smudged creases is a telltale sign she's no amateur.

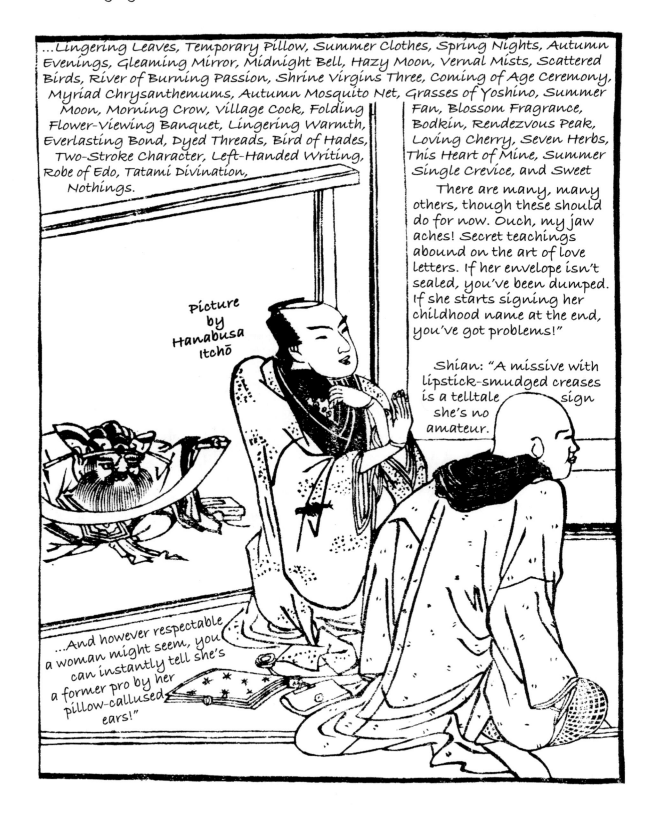

Picture by Hanabusa Itchō

...And however respectable a woman might seem, you can instantly tell she's a former pro by her pillow-callused ears!"

Enjirō, jealous of the philanderings of kabuki stars into whose homes beautiful young women would scamper as groupies, decides to hire

...a locally popular geisha, a dancing girl named Oen, and for fifty gold pieces have her come scampering. He sends Warui Shian to pay a visit.

"If all I have to do is scamper, I'm more than game!"

"That's his request. Anyway, my plan's to cash in

...on your good fortune."

The housemaids, peeking in, whisper among themselves: "It doesn't matter if she's from the Senke, Koryū, or Enshū school of tea—anyone falling for our Enjirō has got to be steeped in eccentricity!"

Clerk: "I never dreamed a lady would fall for someone with the mug of our young master. You're certain you don't have the wrong gate, ma'am?"

Oen delivers her lines perfectly: "I'm an unattached working girl, accustomed to living in the back alleys, a dancer who seduces men. One night, during one of those singles' parties at Yakushi Hall in Kayabachō, from behind some potted plants I spotted your Enjirō here, and it was love at first sight! If you won't let me marry him, at least let me cook rice for him as his kitchen maid! Turn me down and I'll take my life!"

"Wow! We playboys never know what sort of trouble we'll get ourselves into! Grumble loud enough to be heard next door and I'll throw in an extra ten gold!"

Enjirō's father Yajiemon, unaware of Oen's being in Enjirō's employ, feels sorry for her and sends her away with all sorts of advice.

Although Enjirō firmly believed that everyone would be gabbing about his exploits with Oen, nobody hears a peep, not even his next-door neighbors. Disappointed, he commissions a tabloid press, sets his story to print, and, paying one gold per peddler up front, has copies distributed throughout Edo.

...Not worth reading, even if it is free!"

"What's this? Poppycock! Baseless rumors!"

"Extra! Extra! Beautiful geisha falls for playboy Enjirō, son of D. Bauchery Shop owner, throws herself at his feet! Breaking news! Breaking news! Read all about it! This edition complimentary!"

Enjirō is convinced that every time he sneezes it means the world is gossiping about him, though nobody in town gives the slightest hoot. So he begins consorting with prostitutes, hoping to improve his image. All snazzed up, he is escorted by Warui Shian and Kitari Kinosuke to the Wanton Pines teahouse, located on the Yoshiwara's main boulevard, the Nakanochō.

Woman: "The man we've sent to inquire about the availability of Miss Segawa or Miss Utahime just ran into Konomo, Utahime's attendant, at the Petite Pines teahouse, so she must be presently indisposed."

"I hear Kōraiya's going to take Bokuga's part at the Kobikichō Playhouse."

Sōri

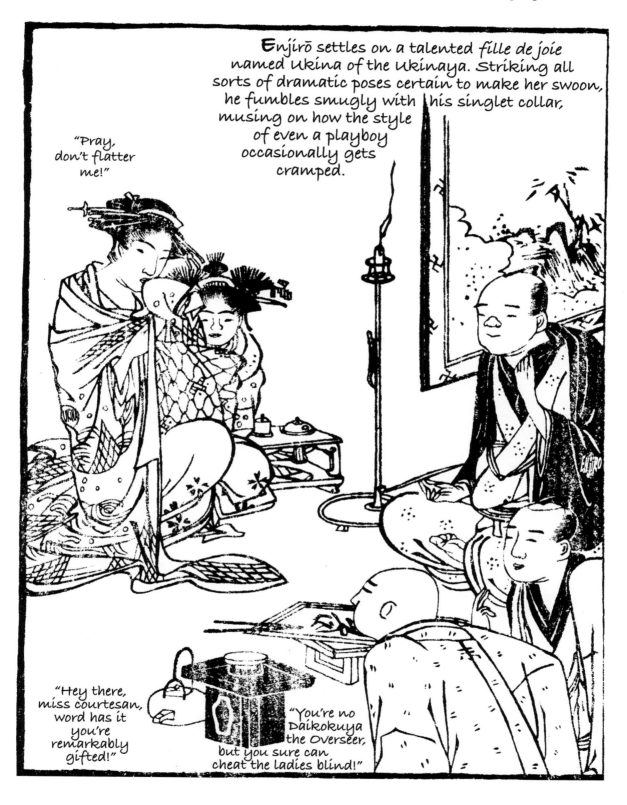

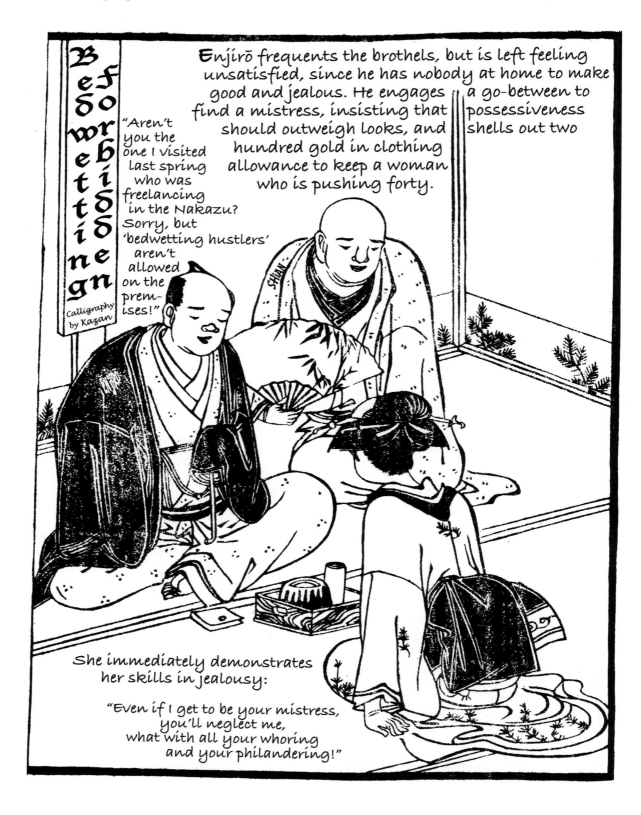

Bedwetting Forbidden

Calligraphy by Kazan

Enjirō frequents the brothels, but is left feeling unsatisfied, since he has nobody at home to make good and jealous. He engages a go-between to find a mistress, insisting that possessiveness should outweigh looks, and shells out two hundred gold in clothing allowance to keep a woman who is pushing forty.

"Aren't you the one I visited last spring who was freelancing in the Nakazu? Sorry, but 'bedwetting hustlers' aren't allowed on the premises!"

She immediately demonstrates her skills in jealousy:

"Even if I get to be your mistress, you'll neglect me, what with all your whoring and your philandering!"

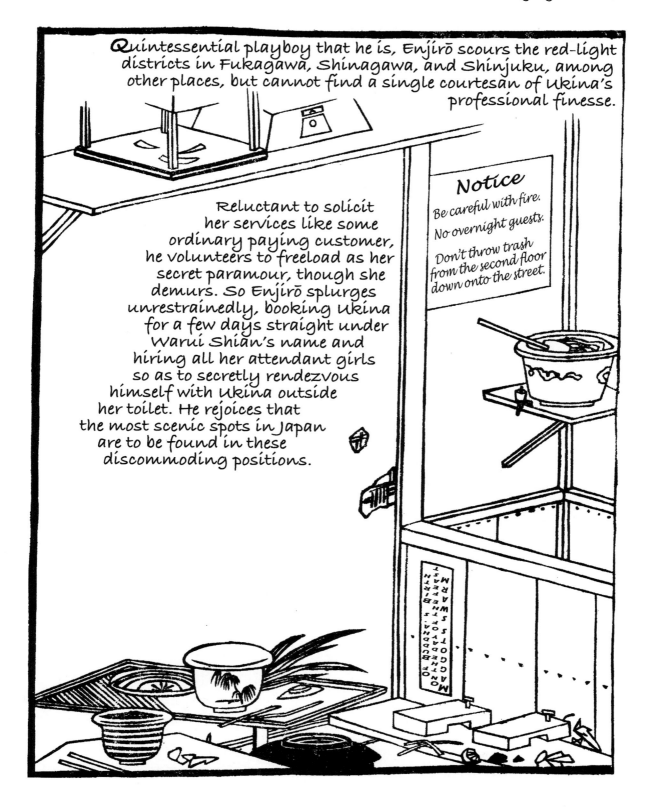

Quintessential playboy that he is, Enjirō scours the red-light districts in Fukagawa, Shinagawa, and Shinjuku, among other places, but cannot find a single courtesan of Ukina's professional finesse.

Reluctant to solicit her services like some ordinary paying customer, he volunteers to freeload as her secret paramour, though she demurs. So Enjirō splurges unrestrainedly, booking Ukina for a few days straight under Warui Shian's name and hiring all her attendant girls so as to secretly rendezvous himself with Ukina outside her toilet. He rejoices that the most scenic spots in Japan are to be found in these discommoding positions.

Notice

Be careful with fire.

No overnight guests.

Don't throw trash from the second floor down onto the street.

Enjirō, recalling the lyrics of "Garden Cherry," envies the two-timing customer who gets dragged back to his courtesan: ♪The bark of the dogcherry / Declares he is heading out / Squabbles bloom in the grass-ping hands / Of attendant girls at his sleeve yanking / His hair carelessly back / To Paulownia Valley he goes!♪

"Getting kidnapped like this is great for my image!"

"Hey! What's happening? Let go of me!"

So he pays some attendant girls and trainees to jump him at the Yoshiwara's Main Gate and whisk him back to Ukina, even if it means ripping his jacket. The girls, getting dolls in the bargain, chatter away as they drag Enjirō off.

"There you are! You've been neglecting me! Really, why are men so cruel? If you can't stand being adored, you shouldn't've been born such a heartthrob! And those

Love Letters

whores—the nerve of them! Keeping another lady's man out all night! You of all people—then again, I guess that's just the way you are!"

No sooner does Enjirō come home after some five or six days away than his mistress, who was being paid to wait, launches into her well-rehearsed litany of grievances:

"This is the first time I've ever been gotten jealous over, I'm ashamed to say, and it feels in-de-scrib-ably grand! I'll buy all the clothes you want—just complain a wee bit more. Pretty please!"

"All right, that wraps it up for today. Gimme the Hachijō silk and chirimen striped crepe you promised, and I'll continue bitching."

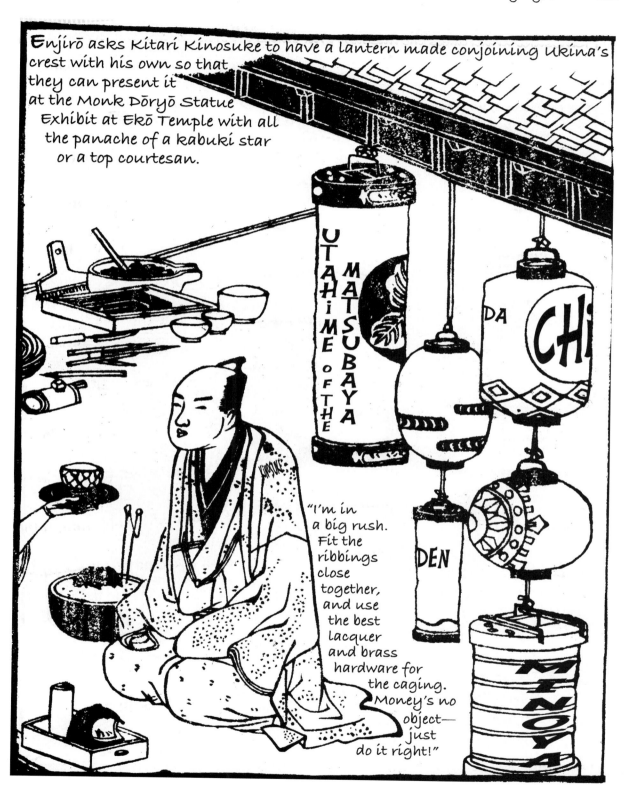

Enjirō asks Kitari Kinosuke to have a lantern made conjoining Ukina's crest with his own so that they can present it at the Monk Dōryō Statue Exhibit at Ekō Temple with all the panache of a kabuki star or a top courtesan.

"I'm in a big rush. Fit the ribbings close together, and use the best lacquer and brass hardware for the caging. Money's no object—just do it right!"

Kinosuke undertakes the mission and places an order with a lanternmaker at Tamachi. Enjirō then has the Nakaya design some handtowels incorporating the conjoined crest and donates them, in the most conspicuous way, to fashionable shrines everywhere—and at such exorbitant expense!

The offerings, while made not in the service of holy vows, nonetheless contribute to Enjirō's scandalous reputation.

YE OLDE LANTERNMAKER

"I won't be able to get to it for a while. This time of year I'm swamped with orders for the evening cherry-viewing festival in the Yoshi-wara."

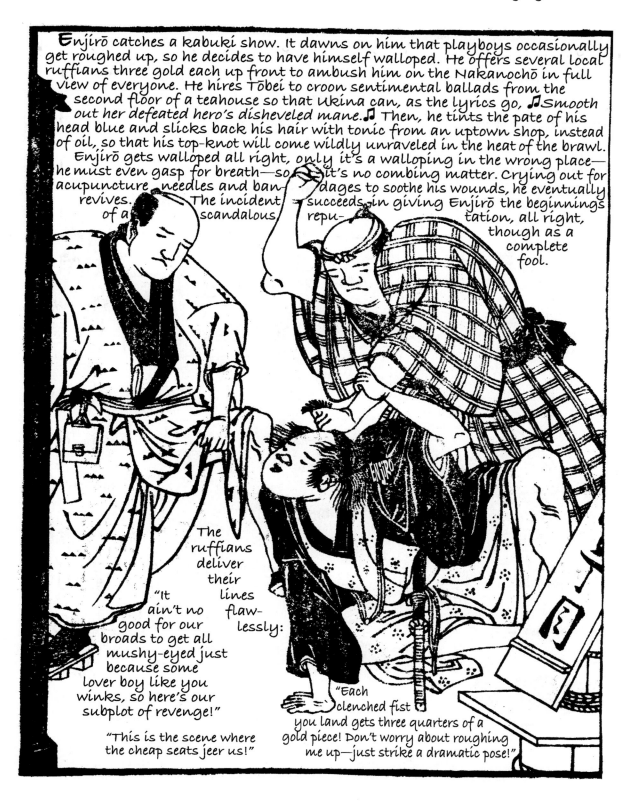

Enjirō catches a kabuki show. It dawns on him that playboys occasionally get roughed up, so he decides to have himself walloped. He offers several local ruffians three gold each up front to ambush him on the Nakanochō in full view of everyone. He hires Tōbei to croon sentimental ballads from the second floor of a teahouse so that Ukina can, as the lyrics go, ♫Smooth out her defeated hero's disheveled mane.♫ Then, he tints the pate of his head blue and slicks back his hair with tonic from an uptown shop, instead of oil, so that his top-knot will come wildly unraveled in the heat of the brawl.

Enjirō gets walloped all right, only it's a walloping in the wrong place— he must even gasp for breath—so it's no combing matter. Crying out for acupuncture needles and ban- dages to soothe his wounds, he eventually revives. The incident succeeds in giving Enjirō the beginnings of a scandalous repu- tation, all right, though as a complete fool.

The ruffians deliver their lines flaw- lessly:

"It ain't no good for our broads to get all mushy-eyed just because some lover boy like you winks, so here's our subplot of revenge!"

"This is the scene where the cheap seats jeer us!"

"Each clenched fist you land gets three quarters of a gold piece! Don't worry about roughing me up—just strike a dramatic pose!"

Enjirō becomes the toast of the town, though when he discovers that this is only because people want to ingratiate themselves with him, he quickly loses interest in riches. Aspiring to be cut off financially at any cost, he pleads with his parents, who refuse to renounce their only son.

At length, through the intercession of his mother, he settles for seventy-five days of temporary disinheritance, after which time he is to be taken back without delay.

"If that's what you want, fine. Get out of my sight this instant!"

"Am I really disowned? Whoopee! Yahoo! Of the four hundred and four afflictions, none's as cruel as wealth! Why do nice guys always finish rich?"

"I can't condone the young master's decision."

Although Enjirō obtains his hard-earned disinheritance, he manages to survive on a secret allowance from Mommy. Desperate to find some debonair line of work, he supposes that a traveling salesman of fan paper would afford a playboy all sorts of amorous opportunities. And so Enjirō sets out peddling his goods, even before the arrival of summer. He spends the live-long day on his feet, develops huge blisters, and becomes calloused to the entire business. Finally, he has established a scandalous reputation for himself, all right, though as a big kook.

"Hey, someone with the goofy face of a Toba cartoon's passing by! Everybody, come take a look!"

LOTTERY TICKETS SOLD HERE

"Seems like another beauty's fallen for me! Ah, what we playboys must put up with!"

"I'm shocked—walking outside, you can actually get burned by the sun! What agony!"

Enjirō is anything but discouraged, and his seventy-five days pass before he knows it. Although his parents offer daily to pardon him, not having had his fill of infamy, he pleads through some relatives for a twenty-day extension. Reckoning that nothing is more romantic than a pair of lovers killing themselves, he inquires if Ukina would mind throwing away her life for his sake, but she minds, so Enjirō hits upon the ⚜ scheme of staging a phony double suicide.

"Having Karan design a super-sized intaglio print of a lotus blossom was a nice ⚜ touch!"

...He arranges for Kinosuke and Shian to lie in wait and, on the cue of the nenbutsu prayer, to prevent him and Ukina from actually shedding blood. First, Kinosuke and Shian ransom Ukina for fifteen hundred gold. Then they purchase some necessary props, including two padded silk robes with matching patterns inspired by the familiar lyrics: ♫A crowbar on the shoulder, an anchor at the skirt, even in hock, these robes just float along♫ These they get on sale at the Nakaya and at Yamasaki Fabrics. Enjirō orders deluxe prints commemorating his farewell verse and has them distributed at all the Nakanochō teahouses.

"For your suicide sword
we've requisitioned a
stick covered in tinfoil."

Ukina at first protests, anxious that her own reputation would suffer, pseudo-suicide or not. She eventually acquiesces, though, after Enjirō, reciting Yuranosuke's line, promises "to reunite her with the man she loves!" if only she plays her part competently. Enjirō secures interest-free backing to stage their autumnal tragedy, employs a theater manager, commissions the great playwright Sakurada to come up with a script, and arranges for the star actors Monnosuke and Rokō to dance the final number. Even so, the show seems destined to flop. It occurs to Enjirō that real playboys don't ransom courtesans decorously, so he smashes through the latticework, props up a ladder to the second floor of Ukina's brothel, and spirits her away in grand elopement-scene style.

"I've heard the saying 'eyedrops from two floors above' before, but ransoming a courtesan from the second floor— that's a first!"

One's finale should be played out in a conspicuous, fashionable locale, so Enjirō chooses the Mimeguri Embankment. Late nights being spooky there, his cast of extras—teahouse personnel, water cabbies, professional and dilettantish sidekicks, geisha—assembles much earlier, at dusk. Formally attired in overskirts and halfcoats, they accompany the two lovers as far as the Ōkawa Bridge, as though seeing off the lucky winners of a raffled pilgrimage to the Grand Shrines at Ise. The crowd then...

"Hey there, not so fast—we're not actually dying to kill ourselves! Someone's supposed to be here any moment to stay our hand! I . . . er . . . I wonder what's keeping them? Take our clothes, but spare our lives—we've learned our lesson already!"

shared palanquin

"Somehow I figured it'd end up like this."

UKINA

Dramatis Personae: Enjirō of the D. Bauchery Shop, Ukina of the Ukinaya

Lovers' Suicide Journey: "Goose Pimples Spoil the Fun"

♫Scandalous indeed / Is the saying: / "If a man makes love / In the morning, / He can die in the evening / Without regret"! / For that stiff line from the Analects, / Here's one from a stage song, / As supple as the flesh of nude lovers: / ♪Alone she can't loosen / The sash they tied together♪ / Just as our heroes / Can't lose those treacherous thugs / Looming on the heights / Of the unfinished embankment, / A slippery slope, / Whence ♪If a woman stumbles / Into the demimonde, / Will her reputation improve?♪ / Which fallen woman / Binds to herself a lice collar / Like our lovers bound / Even by the trysting god / Would they be turned away / To face Mt. Peppersoy / Sauce on cuttlefish, / Fried to a crisp is their relationship of / Long ago Ukina / Used to promenade / Down the Nakanochō / In an Outward Eight Sashay, / Yet nowadays / It's an Inward Seven Stumble, / Without sleeves for / Their tears and snivel to wet, / The lovers have only / Their loincloths to wring dry, / Ukina's bare skin / In the bone-chilling easterly wind / Breaks out in goose pimples / Enjirō's face turns the inky gray / Of those geese in the verse / About "the lines of a letter" / Asking for tidings, / In lettering black as the "Crow- / Bar-patterned shoulders" / And their / "Anchor-patterned hems" / On passionate purple / Robes in hock at some pawnshop / By the River Sumida /

...Whose fame flows far and wide / Near Iozaki /
Where couples haggle at the Livelong Day- /
Shop until the bells / Of Longevity
   Temple chime in / "Ten o'clock
and all's well!" / Since by sunrise,
   tomorrow / Enjirō and Ukina / Will
both bare their breasts, / On a spring day, /
   Long as their loincloths / Fresh as scarlet silk crepe, /
   Then vanish forever / At Sunhigh Temple, /
      A stark-naked couple /
         Streaking to their destiny! ♫
            **Shamisen flourish
               and exeunt**

Just as the ox has but itself to blame
   for the ring in its snout,
Enjirō has but himself to fault
for his poorly executed suicide attempt
   becoming a huge scandal
      and getting depicted on
         tawdry round fans.

"For most folks,
a suicide journey's a kimono-clad trek
to their final destination, whereas for us,
   it's a trip in the buff back home. Now that's
      what I call ass-backwards! And flashing
      our scarlet silk loincloths in this place
            is clearly indecent!"

"I acted on a whim,
so I deserve this.
But you—you must
be freezing!"

"Such misery
for getting barely
involved!"

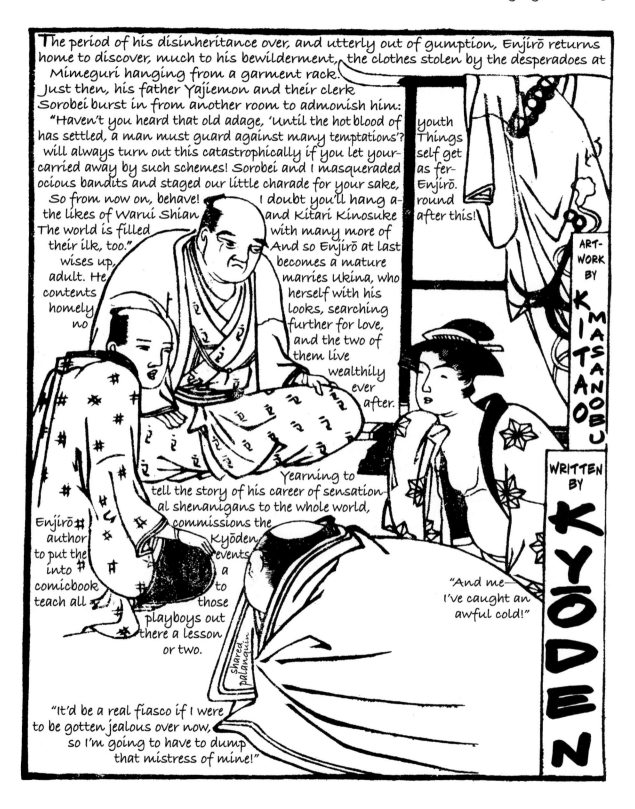

The period of his disinheritance over, and utterly out of gumption, Enjirō returns home to discover, much to his bewilderment, the clothes stolen by the desperadoes at Mimeguri hanging from a garment rack.

Just then, his father Yajiemon and their clerk Sorobei burst in from another room to admonish him:

"Haven't you heard that old adage, 'Until the hot blood of youth has settled, a man must guard against many temptations'? Things will always turn out this catastrophically if you let yourself get carried away by such schemes! Sorobei and I masqueraded as ferocious bandits and staged our little charade for your sake, Enjirō. So from now on, behave! I doubt you'll hang around the likes of Warui Shian and Kitari Kinosuke with many more of after this! The world is filled with their ilk, too."

And so Enjirō at last wises up, becomes a mature adult. He contents marries Ukina, who herself with his homely looks, searching no further for love, and the two of them live wealthily ever after.

Yearning to tell the story of his career of sensational shenanigans to the whole world, Enjirō commissions the author Kyōden to put the events into a comicbook to teach all those playboys out there a lesson or two.

"It'd be a real fiasco if I were to be gotten jealous over now, so I'm going to have to dump that mistress of mine!"

"And me—I've caught an awful cold!"

shared palanquin

ART-WORK BY KITAO MASANOBU

WRITTEN BY KYŌDEN

Annotations

FIRST FASCICLE

[Frontispiece] A partially unfurled picture scroll, bearing the title, the fascicle number, a fastening cord, a backing of mountain-cherry design, and the mountain-and-ivy logo of publisher Tsutaya Jūzaburō. The scene depicts the protagonist Enjirō getting tattooed, as a woman peeks in curiously from the other side of a window. Enjirō conspicuously lacks the pug nose he wears throughout the story proper. None of the figures in the three frontispieces closely resemble their corresponding characters within, for that matter. While this discrepancy may suggest that someone other than Kyōden executed the cover art, more likely it provides pictorial clues to the identity of real-life models for the characters. Here, this would be Asadaya Eijirō.

Playboy, Roasted à la Edo (*Edo umare uwaki no kabayaki*).[1] This title wittily juxtaposes two phrases: (1) "Edo-born playboy" (*Edo umare uwaki*), which exploits the clipped form of "profligate" (*uwakimono*); and (2) "Edo-style spitchcock of eel" (*Edo-mae unagi no kabayaki*), a wildly popular glazed-and-grilled delectable—and purportedly an aphrodisiac. The pivoting effect of this title can be approximated in English, albeit somewhat unappetizingly, as *Edo-Born Playboiled Eel.*

Section 1

[Picture] The caricature of an idle rich kid, this picture shows a pug-nosed Enjirō lolling about at home, casually attired, pipe to mouth, engaged in lantern-lit solitary perusal of sentimental narrative songs. His legs are obscured by a folding screen near his tobacco tray. At right, two fire-prongs stick out of a brazier, upon which rests a kettle. The crossed-through zero Ø on the flowery design of the shop curtain (positioned behind the lantern and divided in two by a slit) is actually the "O" and part of the overlapping upside-down "V" of "VOC," the acronym of the Vereenigde Oostindische Compagnie (**Figure 6.7**). The Dutch East India Company (as it is also

---

1. The title on the frontispieces of all three editions observes the traditional orthography, glossing the graph for *umare* as *mumare*—though this would have been pronounced *umare* or even *n'mare.*

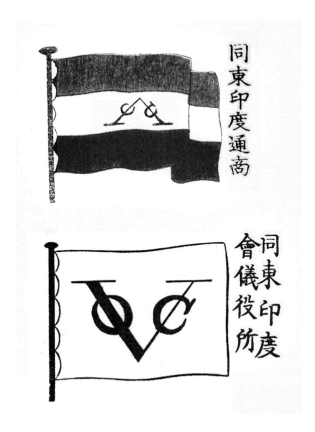

Fig. 6.7 Banners of the Dutch East India Company (Vereenigde Oostindische Compagnie). From *Bankoku haku kizufu* (1854). Reprinted in Jinbō, *Kyōden Ikku Shunsui,* in *Zusetsu Nihon no koten 18,* p. 83. Courtesy of Shūeisha.

known) maintained a trade post on the man-made island of Deshima in Nagasaki harbor. Owners of import boutiques even in Edo sometimes incorporated this easily recognizable foreign design into their shop curtains to signify the exotic nature of their business.[2]

Enjirō. This name, echoic of the real-life mogul Eijirō, plays on "to enact" (*enjiru*). The graph for *en* means both "luster," alluding to the glazed finish on the roasted eel of the title—if not the superficial veneer of the arriviste— and "charm," denoting the protagonist's imagined sexual charisma.

D. Bauchery Shop (*Adakiya*). A conflation of Eijirō's shop name, the Asadaya, and "flirtatious spirit" (*adana ki*).

Twentyish (*tsuzu ya hatachi*). "Nineteen or twenty" was a common expression for a young adult.

without ever having contracted poverty . . . thank you very much (*hin no yamai wa ku ni narazu hokano yamai no nakare kashi*). A line from a

---

2. Nakano, "*Edo umare uwaki no kabayaki*," pp. 82–83.

popular song of narrative music known as *katōbushi*.[3] No doubt "**disease**" (*yamai*) insinuates something sexually transmitted. Syphilis in particular was a relatively common fact of life for visitors to Edo's pleasure quarters. One study claims that as many as half of all frequenters there had contracted it.[4] Its classic sign at the time was considered to be a "squished nose" (*hana-kuta*)—not completely unlike Enijrō's.[5]

romantic ballads (*shinnaibushi*). These sentimental narrative songs of the theater often thematized love suicides and were vastly popular during An'ei-Tenmei. Unabridged, officially authorized **playbooks** (*shōhon*) of these ballads frequently included musical scores.[6]

Tamakiya Itahachi . . . Ukiyo Inosuke. One of the great popularizers of romantic ballads, Tsuruga Wakasanojō (1717–1786) describes in his compositions the love suicides of these two characters.

Section 2

[Picture] Kitari Kinosuke and Warui Shian (head shaved) advising Enjirō in the ways of *savoir-faire*. Kinosuke and Shian cut sophisticated figures—attired in the latest fashions, chic long-stemmed pipe, tobacco pouch and stylishly patterned tissue-paper at hand, and black ascots draped rakishly around their necks. Enjirō's baggy outfit, stodgy pipe, and bare neck betray his boorishness. In the alcove behind him stands a covered bookcase (*hon-bako*) bearing the titles *The Tale of Genji* and *The Tales of Ise*. The respective protagonists of these classic stories, Prince Genji and Ariwara no Narihira, were two infamously charismatic womanizers, which is presumably how Enjirō wants himself to be seen.

Behind Kinosuke and Shian stands a screen painting, bearing the signature of the artist **Hanabusa Itchō** (1652–1724) and depicting Enma, King of Hell. Enma reads a list of names of sinners so that he can sort out the liars (to have

---

3. *Katōbushi* is a genre of *shamisen*-accompanied recitative song in the kabuki and puppet theaters. Characterized by a forceful striking of the strings producing a clear, crisp sound, and by vocal techniques borrowed from the noh, it was influenced by a variety of earlier narrative styles as well as by music performed in the Yoshiwara. The particular song here is titled *Kyūsue ganjō yogi*. For a discussion of *katōbushi*, see Koyama, *Jōkyoku no shinkenkyū*, p. 734 and passim.

4. Suzuki, *Palaeopathological and Palaeoepidemiological Study of Osseous Syphilis in Skulls of the Edo Period.*

5. If left untreated, syphilis often leads to a deterioration of the septum resulting in a collapsed-looking nose. The term "squished nose" thus came to refer to a syphilitic person, and Kyōden used it this way in his other *kibyōshi*, such as the politically incorrect *Buffing Up Aoto's Loose Coins* (1790).

6. Koyama is careful to distinguish between two kinds of playbooks: the first, a full script, contains everything from dialogue and stage directions to details of actors' wardrobes and stage properties; the second, a libretto, is replete with musical annotation for *shamisen* players and lyrics for reciters. In Koyama, *Jōkyoku no shinkenkyū*, p. 21 and passim.

their tongues pulled out with searing-hot prongs). The superimposition of Shian and Kinosuke in front of this list colors them as con artists.[7]

The overall scene here may also allude pictorially (according to Tanahashi) to a passage in the *Analects* in which Confucius expounds on three kinds of deleterious relations: "Friendship with the man of specious airs; friendship with the insinuatingly soft; and friendship with the glib-tongued—these are injurious."[8]

Kitari Kinosuke. A name that puns on "North Village" (*Kitari*), a slang term for the Yoshiwara pleasure quarter (located in the northern part of Edo). It can also mean something like "Mr. He's Come Yet *Again*!"—an appropriate epithet for an unwelcome though frequent visitor.[9]

doctor of Flatterology (*taiko isha*). "Drum doctor" was an alternative term for a "drumbearer," the ego-stroking hired sidekick.

Warui Shian. Literally, "bad plan." Parodies the Chinese-sounding name physicians typically assumed. An English equivalent might be "Mel Practice, M.D."

how to become an infamous playboy (*iyoiyo uwaki na koto o kufū suru*). Literally, "He plots all sorts of philandering things."

schmaltzy ballads (*meriyasu*). A type of soulful lyric song, literally "embroidered ballad," originally sung to dance numbers on the kabuki stage.[10] Brandon notes that the *meriyasu* typically accompanied "tender scenes in which a female character mimes, without dialogue, her state of mind."[11] By An'ei-Tenmei, however, it had come to be widely performed offstage as well. In either case, its cloying sentimentality reputedly catered to the tastes of women. As one comic haiku (*Yanagidaru shūi* 2:26) put it:

> Meriyasu wa   Embroidered ballads—
> Onna no guchi ni   Women's idle grumblings
> Fushi o tsuke   Set to sweet music.

"Pheasants . . . Sweet Nothings" (*Kigisu, Muken, Sakazuki, Tokizake, Yukari no tsuki, Mitsu no tori, Mitsu buton, Futatsu mon, Yotsu no sode, Kaburodachi, Oki no ishi, Hana no kumo, Asagao, Rokkasen, Komachi, Henshō, Kuronushi, Narihira, Yasuhide, Shiraito, Hitori shinjū, Yubikiri, Irebokuro, Kishō, Mukashigusa, Mannensō, Jūsangane, Mizukagami, Inafune, Matsuyoi, Wakare, Nagori no momiji,*

---

7. Nakano, "*Edo umare uwaki no kabayaki*," p. 82.

8. The passage is from Book 16 (*Ji Shi*), Chapter 4. Translated in Legge, *Confucius*, p. 311.

9. Jones suggests this in "William Hogarth and Kitao Masanobu," p. 65.

10. The word *meriyasu* derives from the Spanish *medias* or the Portuguese *meias*, meaning "knitwork," supposedly reflecting the form's expandability to suit the particular needs of the reciter during a performance. According to a different etymology (no doubt tongue-in-cheek), a Yoshiwara geisha coined the word by quipping that listening to such songs could easily make one "feel depressed" (*ki ga meiriyasu*). In Koyama, *Jōkyoku no shinkenkyū*, p. 310.

11. Brandon, *Kabuki*, p. 365.

Kari makura, Natsugoromo, Haru no yo, Aki no yo, Masukagami, Yowa no kane, Oborozuki, Harugasumi, Midaredori, Omoigawa, Onnasangū, Genbuku, Mangiku, Kugatsugaya, Yoshinogusa, Natsu no tsuki, Akegarasu, Muragarasu, Ōgi, Hana no ka, Hana no en, Nokoru atusa, Sashigushi, Ai no yama, Tokezu, Someito, Meido no tori, Koizakura, Aki no shichikusa, Futatsu moji, Hidarimoji, Wagakokoro, Edo yukata, Tatamizan, Hitotsu mizo, Koibanashi). These were authentic titles of *meriyasu* popular around the time.[12]

Houseleek (*mannengusa*). A kind of plant with whorled leaves and a white, pink, or yellow flower.

Tatami Divination (*tatamizan*). The practice of prognosticating that certain someone's feelings by tossing a hair pin onto a straw mat. One adds up the number of strands between the spot where the pin lands and the crevice dividing mats, not unlike counting out "he loves me, he loves me not" with flower petals. Note the following comic haiku (*Yanagidaru shūi* 7:6):

Shimai o ba	"He loves me!"—
Kuru ni shite oku	The conclusion of her
Tatamizan	Tatami divination.

Secret teachings (*denju*). Esoteric discourse on art or poetry that normally can only be passed on by the master of a school to his disciples.

childhood name (*osana*). Given at birth.

creases (*hitsu sakime*). After writing a letter on a roll of stationery paper, one makes a "tearing crease," wets it with the mouth, and rips off the portion to be sent.

pillow-callused ears (*mimi no waki ni makuradako*). Resulting from the chaffing against the wooden pillow-stand during vigorous amorous activity to which the earlobes of a **former pro** (*shōbai agari*) had ostensibly been subjected.

Section 3

[Picture] Kinosuke tattooing Enjirō behind a screen for privacy. A typical display of sincerity (*shinjū*), the **tattoo** (*horimono*) was made by etching the name of one's lover into the skin with a needle, then applying ink (note the black inkstone next to the tobacco tray on the floor) into the wound to proclaim the supposed indelibility of the affection.[13]

---

12. Hino Tatsuo has identified the contemporary collections in which most of these songs appeared. In Hino, "*Edo umare uwaki no kabayaki*: Kaisetsu," pp. 187–188.

13. Although the modern Japanese for tattoo is *irezumi*, during the Edo period this term referred to the branding of convicts as a kind of painful punishment as well as a form of public humiliation (not unlike the way French inmates in the eighteenth century were marked with the letters *GAL* for *galérien*, "galley prisoner"). See Sugiura, *Edo e yōkoso*, p. 23.

the 'till-death-do-us-part' spot (*inochi*). Literally "vital" (derived from the word's basic meaning of "life"), this term was also commonly used in a love-pledge tattoo, such as "Enjirō and Ukina, for life!"

moxa (*kyū*). Two principal methods for removing tattoos were advocated in the Yoshiwara at the time: burning them off with the bowl of a tobacco pipe, or burning them off with moxibustion.[14] Although either method would hurt a great deal, if a passage from a popular book is any indication, the pain must have been worth enduring, especially if it enabled a courtesan to deceive her client into believing that he was her one-and-only:

"Show me proof you haven't had any serious lovers before," the john demands, searching for tattoos. "There's never been anyone but you," she avows, presenting her right arm for inspection. "Just look—I'm clean!" "You trying to pull a fast one on me?" Poring over her left arm, he discerns the vestiges of several burned-off names. "What about these?!" "These? They've all been removed!" "How could you have done such a thing! Now even when you die, there'll be evidence you were a whore!" "So what's the big deal?" "They burn people alive for less, that's what!" "Well, you men expunge tattoos all the time, too—so we're even!"[15]

Section 4

[Picture] Shian making arrangements with Oen, whose drawn-up knees (*tatehiza*) and elegantly long-stemmed pipe (*nagagiseru*) help portray her as a seasoned coquette. The black *shamisen* case on the shelf locates this scene in a geisha's room. The annotators remain mute about the object in Shian's mouth, though Koike Masatane suggests that Shian is biting down onto a handtowel in the manner of a female impersonator in kabuki.[16] This would be more plausible were the object not to appear too stiff for cloth.

Oen. A famous contemporary geisha (*odoriko*) whose name is written with the same graph for *en* as in Enjirō.[17]

plan (*suji*). Literally "plot," this plays off of the "plan" (*shian*) of Warui Shian's name.

Section 5

[Picture] Oen, sleeve to her face, bursting into crocodile tears one night in the foyer to Enjirō's family shop. Enjirō's father, holding a lantern and

---

14. Moxibustion is the cauterization any of the body's vital points with a cone-shaped concoction of gauze and medicinal herbs.

15. From *How to Procure a Courtesan* (*Keiseikai kokoroe*, 1799), a fashionbook by Umebori Kokuga (1750–1821). Quoted in Mitani, *Edo Yoshiwara zushū*, p. 251.

16. Koike, *Hankotsusha Ōta Nanpo to Santō Kyōden*, p. 118.

17. Although *odoriko* originally meant "dancing girl," during the eighteenth century it came to be applied to female geisha.

standing in front of Enjirō's mother, tries to calm the groveling geisha. Housemaids, their silhouettes visible against the backlighting, steal a glance from between sliding paper doors. Enjirō watches with his odd-looking face in plain view of the reader, but not entirely visible to the shop clerk Sorobei, who is seated behind Oen with a perplexed look on his face. "Sorobei" is an apt name for a clerk, since it echoes both the courteous verbal suffix (*sōrō*) used toward customers, as well as the main tool of the trade, the abacus (*soroban*).

steeped in eccentricity (*chajin*). A play on "tea master" and "unusual person." The schools mentioned were active during An'ei-Tenmei.

I'm an unattached working girl . . . seduces men. This line parodies a contemporary song (*katōbushi*) entitled "Dōjōji" (as Mizuno notes) which runs: "Now, I'm an unmarried mistress, accustomed to living deep in Kinoji, a lady entertainer who amuses men."

singles' parties at Yakushi Hall in Kayabachō (*Kayabachō no yūyakushi*). Held bimonthly at the Yakushi Hall in Kayabachō (near Nihonbashi), this temple fair served as a meeting place for singles. The phrase "**love at first sight**" (*misomemashita*) plays off the association of Yakushi with eyes, since votive tablets with the graph for "eye" were offered to the statue of the Buddhist saint Yakushi—the so-called "Physician of Souls"—to pray for relief from ocular ailments.

Section 6

[Picture] A tabloid peddler spreading the word about Enjirō's latest conquest, as a woman rightly looks on in disbelief from within her house. The absence of musical notation suggests that this particular peddler was not "singing the news" (as others were wont to do). He has traveled some distance, since the sort of residence depicted here was located in the daimyo's section of Edo proper. The covered head, sturdy walking sandals, kimono tucked-up for mobility, and printed paper in hand are all distinctive features of such peddlers. The pile of sand (*morizuna*) visible in the bottom left-hand corner was typically placed near the door as a sign welcoming visitors, here perhaps suggesting that the woman longs for company in a kind of Edo version of the desperate housewife—though not so desperate as to fall for the likes of Enjirō based on his peddler's propaganda.

tabloid press (*yomiuri*). The broadsheet (*kawaraban*), as it was also known, contained just as much current gossip as actual earthshaking news, typically purveying hearsay about such things as double suicides, vendettas, earthquakes, volcanic eruptions, fires, riots, crazed kabuki stars, freaks, even sightings of monsters (not unlike today's scandal rags). Woodblock printing technology had, by An'ei-Tenmei, advanced to the point where thousands

of copies could be made within days of a current event, circulated widely, and sold for a pittance (see **Figure 1.1**).[18]

Extra! Extra! (*hyōban*). "Hot news!" Strictly speaking, broadsheets were not actually issued on a regular basis.

Baseless rumors (*kata mo nai koto*). This line—as might be expected of one who resides in a daimyo's mansion—parrots the language of the sporadically issued official prohibitions against broadsheets.[19]

Section 7

[Picture] Enjirō, Kitari Kinosuke, and Warui Shian, conversing with a hostess (*joshō*) over a light snack at a so-called **teahouse**. Having nothing to do with the serious pursuit of the "way of tea" (*chadō*), the "teahouse of assignation" (*hikitejaya*), as it was properly called, was an establishment where a client paid to bide his time while having a courtesan summoned. From there, she might agree to take him to her private bordello quarters.

Kyōden displays close attention to detail here: the unusual hexagonal lantern (*shokudai*); the pine-needle pattern (apropos of the name of the teahouse) on the sliding door (*fusuma*) on the left side of the page; the small Buddhist altar (*butsudan*) on the "god shelf" (*kamidana*); on the wall opposite it, the letter-holder (*jōsashi*); and, beneath that, on the illustrated screen (*tsuitate no e*), the signature of Tawaraya **Sōri** (a member of the Kōrin School and thus a pupil of Sumiyoshi Hiromori, who flourished during the late eighteenth century).

sneezes . . . gossiping (*kushami o suru tabi seken de ore ga uwasa o suru darō to*). This seems to have been an actual folk belief and not merely another of Enjirō's half-baked notions.[20]

escorted (*kami ni tsure*). One or more hired sidekicks would typically accompany a wealthy patron during his carousing in the Yoshiwara.

Wanton Pines (*Uwakimatsuya*). The name of this Yoshiwara establishment, when reread in the present context, can mean something like "pining for profligacy."

Kōraiya's going to take Bokuga's part at the Kobikichō Playhouse. Kōraiya is the house name of actor Matsumoto Kōshirō IV (1737–1802). **Bokuga** is a pseudonym of Suzuki Uemon, proprietor of the Yoshiwara's

---

18. For more on this, see Kornicki's account of various sorts of "works dealing with matters too indiscreet to be published" (*jitsuroku*) in his "The Enmeiin Affair of 1803."

19. Edicts against "groundless" and "false" hearsay in *yomiuri* are mentioned in passing in Groemer, "Singing the News," p. 243.

20. Ishikawa, *Edo bungaku zokushin jiten*, pp. 112–113.

"House of Fans" (Ōgiya) and one of the quarter's colorful figures.[21] Bokuga had played the role of Kudō Suketsune in the 1784 spring production of *Hatsugoyomi nigiwai Soga* in Kobikichō at the Morita Playhouse (the present-day Kabukiza).

Section 8

[Picture] Enjirō converses with the courtesan Ukina in her private quarters at the bordello. Sidekicks Kitari Kinosuke and Warui Shian provide light banter. A young trainee sits flanking Ukina. Enjirō fiddles with his collar in affectation of a dandy. Ukina puts sleeve to mouth in an apparent gesture of modesty—though judging by her line of sight, this may actually serve to suppress a chuckle over Enjirō's odd little nose.

fille de joie (*jorō*). "Prostitute." Here the term is used to refer to an upper-ranking courtesan (*oiran*).

Ukina of the Ukinaya (*Ukinaya no Ukina*). Ukina means something like "tarnished name" or "naughty reputation."

dramatic poses (*mie*). In kabuki, an actor's dazzling stance held for several seconds to maximal theatrical effect.

singlet collar (*jiban*). This word (typically rendered in phonetically equivalent graphs) derives from the Portuguese for "underclothing" (*gibão*).

Daikokuya the Overseer (*Daikokuya*). Established and ran the Yoshiwara registry for geisha. His personal name, Sōroku, was also homophonous with the official title of a manager of blind musicians. Kinosuke thus puns while complementing Warui Shian on his ability to sweet-talk Ukina into getting involved with the likes of Enjirō.

Pray (*ogaminsu*). Courtesan-speak for "please," derived from the verb "to pray" (*ogamu*).

MIDDLE FASCICLE

[Frontispiece] Warui Shian, lying belly-down on five futons, as Enjirō and Ukina cavort in an adjacent room. If Nakamura's theory is correct, this Enjirō may be drawn to resemble the real-life samurai Abe-no-Shikibu Masaakira.

---

21. As mentioned in the preceding chapter, Uemon was active in the same *kyōka* and amateur kabuki circles as his friend Kyōden.

Section 9

[Picture] Enjirō (with pipe) and Warui Shian (with fan) interviewing a prospective mistress. Note the tobacco pouch and tray on the floor between them. The formal square script (*kaisho*) of the pillar tablet (*hashirakake*) behind Enjirō clashes conspicuously with its quotidian message.

make good and jealous (*yakimochi o yaku*). "To roast rice-cakes" is an idiomatic expression meaning "to burn with envy."

freelancing (*jigoku*). Here referring to a woman who prostitutes herself on the sly.

Nakazu. One of Edo's unlicensed quarters.

bedwetting hustlers (*shōbengumi*). The perpetrators of a supposedly notorious scam during An'ei-Tenmei.[22] A woman would become mistress to a wealthy—though not necessarily attractive—man, accept his gifts and money, and then, in order to avoid sexual consummation, feign incontinence, deliberately urinating in bed. Among the many associated comic haiku is one (*Yanagidaru* 54:5) that alludes to the fact that certain insects are known to answer the call of nature:

Shōben o	Those who piss and run—
Shite nigeru no wa	Kept women
Mekake to semi	And cicadas.

Bedwetting Forbidden (*shōben muyō*). Mention of both the prohibition against urination and the signature of *Kazan*—whose name is written with the graphs for "flower" and "mountain"[23]—amounts to a playful allusion to a haiku (*hokku*) by one of Bashō's major disciples, Enomoto Kikaku (1661–1707):

Kono tokoro	In this place
Shōben muyō	Urinating forbidden—
Hana no yama	Flowery Mountain.

Section 10

[Picture] Enjirō, Warui Shian, and Ukina at the Ukinaya bordello. In a ploy to become Ukina's clandestine lover, Enjirō trades places with Warui Shian, who, assuming the position of a rich client, luxuriates on a five-layered futon and enjoys a pipe and fancy tobacco tray. Enjirō, chin in hand, pipe before him, stretches out on the barest of bedding (*senbei-buton*) just outside the lavatory, with its characteristic wooden flip-flops and washbasin (*chōzubachi*). As though to heed the letter but not the spirit of the rules posted

---

22. See Hanasaki, *Edo kawaya hyaku sugata*, pp. 85–87.

23. Not to be confused with a famous painter by that name who had yet to become active.

on the wall above the basin (with bowl of water and dipper), someone has left a tray, serving vessels, and rubbish strewn about the floor. An amulet to ward off bugs is posted upside-down for efficacy. Many of these realistic pictorial details, together with the double cherry-blossom crest on the tobacco tray, have led Nakamura to conclude that this scene visually alludes to the real-life courtesan Hanaōgi and her apartments at the Ōgiya.[24]

ordinary paying customer (*hitotori*). As opposed to a non-paying **secret paramour** (*mabu*).

under Warui Shian's name (*Warui Shian ga naate nite*). "By the alias Naughty John." In addition to meaning "scheme," *shian* was a vernacular term for a male client of a female entertainer or prostitute.

hiring all her attendant girls (*shinzōkai*). A standard ruse whereby a client procures assistant courtesans (*shinzō*) in order to meet secretly with their "elder sister" (*ane jorō*), a high-ranking courtesan (*oiran*) with whom he would otherwise not be able to rendezvous.

most scenic spots in Japan . . . discommoding positions (*fujiyū na tokoro ga Nihon da*). The "inconvenience" (*fujiyū*) refers specifically to that of seeing a courtesan on the sly—and here, in this picture, of doing so next to a commode (**outside her toilet** is my addition). The term "Japan" (*Nihon*) was a popular abbreviation for "best in Japan" (*Nihon ichi*).

Mr. Big Spender . . . burn with envy. A rich patron (*daijin*) might understandably get upset if the high-ranking courtesan, whom he had maneuvered to meet by expensively buying up her attendants, was spending the night with another client free of charge.

quintuple-layered futons (*itsutsu-buton*). Most clients in the Yoshiwara slept on three layers of futon, so five was a luxury only the wealthiest of clients could afford.[25]

killing time . . . pain in the butt (*ji ni naranee*). Puns "isn't a long wait" and "doesn't get hemorrhoids."

Maggots swarm . . . Buddha's birth. The first half of a poem (*tanka*) written as a talisman to ward off coprophagic insects:

Chihayaburu	Swarming mightily,
Uzuki yōka wa	On the day of the Feast
Kichinichi yo	Of Buddha's Birth,
Kamisagemushi o	Those godmaggots
Seibai zo suru	Will be punished!

---

24. Nakamura, "*Edo umare uwaki no kabayaki* sadan," p. 37 and passim.

25. Actually, daimyo customarily slept on six layers, according to Mitani, *Edo Yoshiwara zushū*, p. 199.

The eighth day of the fourth month (*uzuki no yōka*) was the annual observance of the Feast of the Buddha's Birth (*kanbutsue*). The poem implies that a second feast will take place after the first.

A related comic verse (*Yanagidaru* 106:24) poses a dilemma between the desire to uphold the Buddhist injunction against taking the life of any sentient being and the urge to crush even those bugs with a holy-sounding name:

Kamisagemushi o	Retaliation against
Seibai wa	Godmaggots
Shaka hakai	Breaks religious law.

Another comic haiku (*Yanagidaru* 114:12) underscores the belief in the efficacy of abracadabras:

Kuso no soba	Poop-teeming
Chihaya no uta de	Mighty godmaggots—
Mushi o yoke	Recite 'em away!

Section 11

[**Picture**] Enjirō's fake ambush at the entrance to the Yoshiwara. A couple of trainees and an attendant courtesan grab Enjirō's person to physically force him back to their bordello like some disloyal client. The logo on the lantern of the passerby is that of the Nakaya, a fabric store mentioned presently. Enjirō's "eyes-only hood" (*mebakari zukin*), normally used to hide one's face, has been put on incorrectly (according to *SNKBZ*) to deliberately reveal his identity.

gets dragged back (*tsukamaru*). A courtesan who discovered that one of her clients had left her or was secretly frequenting a rival bordello often had her **attendant girls** (*shinzō*) and **trainees** (*kaburo*) lie in ambush at the **Main Gate** (*Daimon*) in order to intercept him. This strategy seems to have become a standard excuse for tardiness used at least by those given to vanity (*Yanagidaru* 6:36):

Tsukamikomi	The poseur who claims
Mashita to teishu	"My courtesan had me ambushed!"—
Hana no miso	Florid self-flattery!

Garden Cherry (*Iezakura*). The title of a song (*katōbushi*) popular at the time. The excerpt here is full of wordplay, especially about plants: **bark of the dog** (*tsugeru inu*) pivots into **dogcherry** (*inuzakura*); **squabbles** (*kuzetsu*) **bloom** (*tsubomi hokorobishi*); **grassping hands** (*chikaragusa*) contains the word "grass" (*kusa*); and **Paulownia Valley** (*Kirigayatsu*), in Kamakura, is named for its deciduous tree.

Section 12

[Picture] Enjirō, in a posture of bemused embarrassment, and his mistress, pretending to be extremely jealous. The object on the wall is not a typical letter holder, but a special container for **Love Letters** (*kishōsashi*). Playboys were known to collect written pledges of devotion as trophies of their amorous conquests.

You've been neglecting me (*koko zo hōkō no shidokoro*). Literally, "Far from fulfilling your duties here," implying "you've been away from home fooling around!"

Hachijō silk . . . *chirimen* striped crepe (*hachijō . . . shima-chirimen*). Extravagant fabrics. The latter is a silk crepe made of tussah.

ashamed to say (*hazukashii kotta ga*). The *kotta ga* here is a contraction of *koto da ga*.

Section 13

[Picture] At a lantern shop, Kinosuke waits patiently as the lanternmaker, spectacles hanging from an ear, glances at Enjirō's written order incredulously (according to Tanahashi) because of the unreasonableness of the request. A shop boy hospitably offers Kinosuke a cup of tea. A brazier, a stiff brush, an inkstone with case, a small knife, brushes, pieces of bamboo, and incomplete lanterns lie strewn about. The finished lanterns hanging from the eaves are presumably awaiting pickup. One bears the name of the Minoya, a Yoshiwara bordello. Another has the *den* of Kyōden (or of his merchant designation Denzō). Yet another reads "Utahime of the Matsubaya."

conjoining Ukina's crest with his own (*Ukina to temae no mon o hiyoku-mon ni tsukesaseru*). Combining one's house crest with that of another served as an open announcement of romantic commitment.

the Monk Dōryō Statue Exhibit at Ekō Temple (*Ekōin Dōryō no kaichō*). Monk Dōryō was the guardian deity of the Ekōin, a Pure Land Buddhist temple, situated near the Ryōgoku Bridge.[26] A statue of him was displayed there in 1784—the year before the issuance of *Playboy*—at a famously well-attended temple exhibition (*kaichō*) of feretory treasures.[27] Thus, Enjirō advertises his supposed love affair with Ukina at an event with maximum public exposure.

Nakaya. Fabric store to the Yoshiwara.

---

26. Built for the victims of the great Meiwa fire of 1657, the Ekōin would come to house the memorial tablet for Kyōden.

27. For more on temple exhibitions, see Akai, "The Common People and Painting," pp. 175–179.

handtowels (*chōzu tenugui*). For use at ablution basins at temples and shrines.

Section 14

[Picture] Enjirō, hair tousled loose, getting kicked and pummeled with great bravado by two local thugs. A sheathed tobacco pipe and "hanging pocket" (*inro*) dangle from one thug's sash. A street sign leans against a water barrel in the front right corner. Hamada criticizes the composition as having too much text and not enough room for the picture to convey detail.

Ōgie **Tōbei** was a famous male geisha. His name appears in the spring edition of *The Yoshiwara, Detailed* for 1785 (**Figure 6.8**).

second floor of a teahouse (*chaya no nikai*). Teahouses in the Yoshiwara overlooked the Nakanochō, so Tōbei's sentimental ballads would have been audible from Enjirō's position.

♪ **Smooth out . . . disheveled mane.** ♪ As a courtesan does for a defeated playboy in a ballad.

uptown shop (*ageyamachi*). A section within the Yoshiwara noted for its hair salons.

subplot of revenge (*yakimochi no suji*). A "jealousy plot."

scene where the cheap seats jeer us (*kiriotoshi kara bachi ga ataru to iu ba*). The unpartitioned area in front of the stage reserved for groundlings who could not afford box seats was known as the "crush" (*kiriotoshi*).[28] Members of the kabuki audience would shout "Damn you!" (*bachi ga ataru*) during scenes in which villains beat up the hero (*chōchaku*).

Section 15

[Picture] In an inversion of an admonishment scene of the prodigal son, Enjirō pleads humbly (kneeling, eyes downcast) to be disinherited. Not until his mother intervenes on his behalf does his father, enthroned on a floor cushion and eyeballing Enjirō menacingly, grant his begrudging consent. The clerk Sorobei looks on dutifully.

seventy-five days. Gossip proverbially lasted this long.

---

28. By the 1780s, the term *kiriotoshi* had come to refer to a part of the parquet (*doma*) extending from the general entrance, or "mouse door" (*nezumi kido*), to the forestage. Eventually, the gangway, or "flower ramp" (*hanamichi*), would come to run through this area.

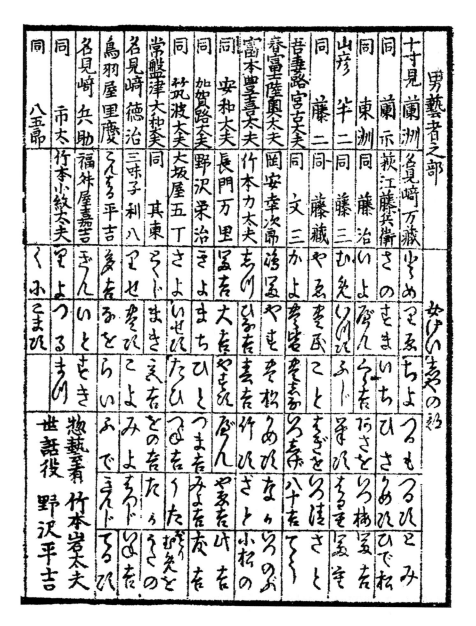

Fig. 6.8 List of major geisha indicating men (top two rows) as well as women (bottom six). The name of the celebrated male geisha Ōgie Tōbei appears second row down, second from right. From the New Year's edition of *The Yoshiwara, Detailed* (*Yoshiwara saiken*, 1785). Reprinted in Hanasaki, *Tenmeiki Yoshiwara saiken shū*.

four hundred and four afflictions . . . wealth (*yonhyakuyon byō no yamai kanemochi hodo tsurai mono wa nai no sa*). A travesty of the adage "Of the four hundred and four afflictions, none's as cruel as poverty!"

Section 16

[Picture] Three geisha on one of their pilgrimages to the **Goddess of Mercy** (Kannon) Temple in **Asakusa** near the Yoshiwara. The shop sign for **toothpicks** (*yōji*) and the fallen leaves of the ginkgo tree pinpoint this scene to the Okuyama section. Each geisha holds a hundred-stranded tally

made of straw, one strand of which is discarded after every trip to keep count.

Yagenbori. The area around the Ryōgoku Bridge where many geisha resided.

barefoot pilgrimages (*hadashimairi*). The **customary hundred** is my addition.

So that's how barefoot pilgrims got to be so footloose (*naruhodo hadashimairi to iu yatsu ga ōkata wa uwaki na mono nari*). This line plays off the notion that faith is born of capriciousness (according to Mizuno).

Arrow Range (*dokyūba*). Many such shooting galleries fronted for prostitution booths.

FINAL FASCICLE

[Frontispiece] Enjirō, dressed as a fan-paper vendor, tries to seduce a refreshment-stand woman.

Section 17

[Picture] The sun-roasted playboy manqué Enjirō, trying to appear suave, decked out as a fan-paper vendor (flashy robe, folding fan, and a stack of boxes on his shoulder). His kerchief, bearing the concentric-squares crest of the actor Ichikawa Danjūrō, comes straight out of *The Handtowel Competition* (**Figure 6.9**). The pattern on his fan appears in a related piece, *Record of the Treasure Competition* (*Takara awase no ki*, 1783) (**Figure 6.10**).[29]

A refreshment-stand (*mizuchaya*) woman tries to stifle a laugh with a saucer in hand as she looks at the fellow who reminds her of a **Toba cartoon** (*Tobae*). A marsh-reed screen (*yoshizubari*) shields the stand from the presumably sweltering sun. **Lottery tickets** were sold as a side business at shops throughout Edo.

secret allowance from Mommy (*haha no kata yori kane*). Less liberally, "money from his mother." A related comic poem (*Yanagidaru shūi* 9:16) describes an overprotective woman who daydreams about sending her disinherited boy some clothes on the sly:

Kandō ni	The disowned son;
Yuki take haha no	His mother estimates measurements
Kara-zumori	In her mind.[30]

---

29. This book helped inspire the handtowel gathering of 1784, as per Tani, *Share no dezain*, p. 225. Reprinted in Kisho Fukuseikai, *Kisho fukuseikai sōsho 6*.

30. Translated in Blyth, *Edo Satirical Verse Anthologies*, p. 302.

見増染

市川三升案

惟一案

Fig. 6.9 Handtowel bearing the concentric-squares crest of actor Ichikawa Danjūrō. From *The Handtowel Competition* (*Tanagui awase*, 1784), a humorous picturebook (*kokkei mitate ehon*) written and illustrated by Santō Kyōden. Reprinted in Kisho fukuseikai, *Shinseiki 31*.

traveling salesman of fan paper (*jigami-uri*). Typically garbed for traveling during the hottest months of the year, these itinerant vendors would sing, mimic kabuki stars, and perform variously to ply their wares. The occupation served aptly as a cover for a gigolo.

becomes calloused to (*korikori to suru*). The original puns "gets fed up with" and "gets stiff muscles."

Section 18

[Picture] Enjirō and Ukina, seated before mirrored vanities in a kabuki-style backstage dressing room, preparing themselves for their bogus double suicide. The anchor-and-crowbar design on their matching kimono comes from *The Handtowel Competition* (**Figure 6.11**). Enjirō arranges his topknot (*hakesaki*) while his coiffeur (pictured standing behind him) wipes the hair

Fig. 6.10 Lady Han's fan (*Hanjo no ōgi*). From *Record of the Treasure Competition* (*Takara awase no ki*, 1783), a humorous picturebook (*kokkei mitate ehon*) attributed to Hezutsu Tōsaku and Moto no Mokuami. Illustrated by Kitao Masanobu and Kitao Masayoshi. Courtesy of Tōyō bunko.

tonic from his hands. Ukina adjusts her collar. Her two trainees look on in apparent disbelief. Kinosuke inspects the props before him against the ledger (*chōmen*), as is the duty of the stage manager, while Shian assists. The props include: a paper parasol with a bull's-eye design (*janome-gasa*); collapsible paper lanterns (*odawara-jōchin*); a Buddhist rosary (*juzu*); the tinsel-covered wooden sword (*hakuoki*); "death wear" (*jisei no orimono*); a sprig of Japanese star anise (*shikimi*), typically placed before a grave marker to honor the dead; and, in the bottom right-hand corner, a rolled-up carpet or "suicide mat" (*mōsen*) upon which to kill oneself—also used in kabuki to remove actors from the stage after their characters have expired.

anything but discouraged (*iyoiyo nori ga kite*). Playboys might feel this way for amorous reasons (*Yanagidaru* 5:25):

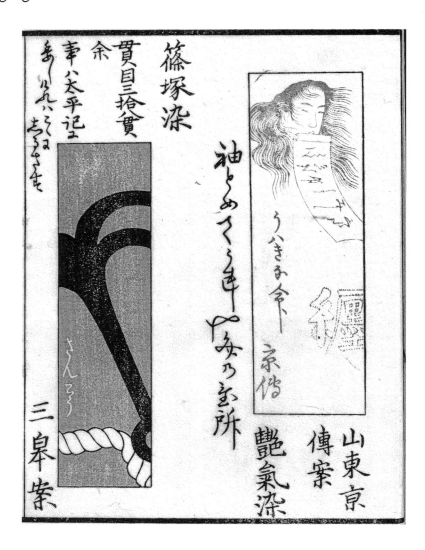

Fig. 6.11 Anchor-and-crowbar design. From *The Handtowel Competition* (*Tanagui awase*, 1784), a humorous picturebook (*kokkei mitate ehon*) written and illustrated by Santō Kyōden. Reprinted in Kisho fukuseikai, *Shinseiki 31*.

Kishō nado	The young dilettante,
Moratte musuko	Sweet promises extracted,
Nori ga kuru	Spunkier than ever.

phony double suicide (*uso shinjū*). Edo-period stories of people faking their deaths were not unknown—Saikaku's Moemon and Osan, for instance, hire body doubles to plunge into the ocean from a cliff.[31] However, Enjirō seems to be the first and only to stage his suicide as a full-blown kabuki play.

♪ *A crowbar on the shoulder . . . float along* ♪ From a popular song, this line puns "forfeited" (*nagare*) with the rank of a courtesan.

---

31. De Bary, "What the Seasons Brought the Almanac Maker," pp. 140–141, in *Five Women Who Loved Love*, pp. 115–156.

deluxe prints (*surimono*). Lavishly produced woodcuts on the finest paper, custom-made for special occasions, often containing a poem.

farewell verse (*jisei no hokku*). Written on the cusp of one's death.[32]

Karan. Another artistic sobriquet for Kitao Shigemasa (1739–1820), head of the Kitao School of woodblock printing and Kyōden's artistic mentor.

super-sized intaglio print (*ōbōshoe karazuri*). A large-format (*ōbōsho*) print (*e*) of high-quality ragpaper onto which a design is embossed (*karazuri*).

lotus blossom (*hasu*). Lovers were said to be reborn together on the same one.

Section 19

[Picture] The oxymoronic prearranged elopement, staged with the full co-operation of the bordello staff. Two servants and a trainee see off Enjirō and Ukina safely, holding portable lanterns to illuminate the way.

"to reunite her with the man she loves" (*suita otoko to sowasete yarō*). The long-suffering hero Yuranosuke's line from the perennially favorite play about the forty-seven loyal retainers (*Kanadehon chūshingura*, 1748).[33]

autumnal tragedy (*aki kyōgen*). Gloomy, sad kabuki plays—especially double-suicide pieces—were often performed in the fall.

Sakurada Jisuke I (1734–1806). Kyōden's friend and one of the most popular playwrights in late eighteenth-century Edo (along with Namiki Go-hei, 1747–1808), as per the following comic haiku (*Yanagidaru* 63:29):

Sakurada wa	Sakurada's
Namiki ni tsuzuku	The playwright second only
Sakusha nari	To Namiki.

Monnosuke and Rokō. Monikers of the kabuki idols Ichikawa Monno-suke II (1743–1794) and Segawa Kikunojō III (1751–1810). Wildly popular during the 1780s, they often worked with Sakurada Jisuke. Kyōden alludes to them not infrequently in other works—such as *The Handtowel Competition* and *Swingers*. Enjirō of course flatters himself to think that he will be played by the dashing Monnosuke. And who better to portray Ukina, a character openly associated with real-life courtesan Matsubaya Segawa, than the great actor of women's roles with a similar name?

smashes through the latticework, props up a ladder (*renji o kowashite hashigo o kake*). In an ordinary elopement, one props up the ladder to break through the latticework on the second floor. In his staged version, however,

---

32. For a collection in English, see Hoffmann, *Japanese Death Poems*.

33. For an English translation, see Keene, *Chūshingura*.

Enjirō does just the opposite, breaking through the latticework first, *then* placing the ladder.

eyedrops from two floors above (*nikai kara megusuri*). A metaphorical expression for something futile (like Enjirō's entire undertaking).

Section 20

[Picture] Two desperadoes ambush the couple by the light of a gibbous moon. Enjirō, candle at his side, hand raised to protect himself, pleads for their lives. Ukina, small branch of star anise protruding from her sash, likewise shields herself with her sleeve. The desperadoes have their leggings tucked up, exposing their flanks (*shirihashori*), and wear stylish black hoods. Across Enjirō's shoulder is slung the suicide mat.

finale (*saigo no ba*). "Place of death" as well as the "final curtain" of a play.

Mimeguri Embankment (*Mimeguri no dote*). The banks of the Sumida River near Mimeguri Inari Shrine in Mukōjima, located to the southeast of the Yoshiwara.

extras (*Enjirō ni tsutometaru*). Literally, "those employed by Enjirō." *Tsutometaru* also means to enact a role.

water cabbies (*funayado*). A reference to the operators of riverboat taxis (*chokibune*) and their rental shops on the Sumida at San'yabori (near Mimeguri Inari Shrine). These light vessels provided the fastest of the three major modes of transportation between Edo and the Yoshiwara (riding either a palanquin or a horse via the Sensōji and up the Nihonzutsumi path to the main entrance being the other two). The riverboat taxi was also the most expensive of these and therefore the vehicle of choice for rich patrons like Enjirō, eager to make a grand entrance or otherwise flaunt their wealth.[34]

dilettantish sidekicks (*massha*). Mere amateurs compared to **professional** ones (*taiko*).

geisha. Here, probably the female variety.

Ōkawa Bridge (*Ōkawabashi*). Spanned the main branch of the Sumida, connecting Asakusa and Honjo.

lucky winners of a raffled pilgrimage to the Grand Shrines at Ise (*Daidaikō*). Less long-windedly, "sacred music and dance clubbers," referring to those few members of a religious association (*kō*) fortunate enough to win a fund-raising raffle for a free trip to the shrines that, among other things, were known for performances of "sacred music and dance" (*daidai kagura*).

---

34. See Mitani, *Edo Yoshiwara zushū*, pp. 33 and passim.

Tada's statue of Yakushi (*Tada no Yakushi*). Located at a temple east of the Sumida River, this celebrated statue was sculpted by Eshin Sōzu (942–1017) and commissioned by Minamoto Mitsunaka (912–997), who was also known as Tada no Manjū.[35]

journey to death (*michiyuki*). In the kabuki and puppet theaters, a poetic passage reiterating key moments of the play and describing the emotions of the two protagonists en route to their lovers' suicide. Characterized by complex wordplay involving pivot and associative words, often in terms of Buddhist teachings on impermanence, the *michiyuki* is performed to the accompaniment of the full stage ensemble (*hayashi*) and tends to culminate in a vigorous dance.

coup de grace (*kaishaku*). In a ritual suicide, the "accomplice" who kindly chops off the head.

Section 21

[Picture] The denuded lovers, under a parasol, returning from their botched attempt at fake suicide. Enjirō, his loincloth trailing behind conspicuously, has been allowed to keep the suicide mat and tinfoil sword. The scene is set just southeast of the Yoshiwara, near Mimeguri Inari Shrine, one of Edo's notable scenic spots, recognizable by the way the Sumida embankment conceals all but the top part of the shrine gate. This view is glamorized in innumerable guidebooks and comic poems, such as the following (*Yanagidaru* 36:32), in which the upper rung is obliquely compared to a water taxi:

Dote e torii ga	The shrine gate
Merikonda	Looks like it's sunk
Yō ni mie	Into the bank.

Goose Pimples Spoil the Fun (*kyōgasamehada*). The title of this spoof of a lovers' travel poem pivots "fun spoiling" (*kyōgasame*) and shivery "goose bumps" (*samehada*). *Playboy* is not the only Edo-period work, incidentally, to tweak the standard *michiyuki* formula: Akinari presents an underwater fish-eye's view of one in *Tales of Moonlight and Rain*; Tsuruya Nanboku makes a mockery of it in *Scarlet Princess of Edo* (*Sakurahime azuma bunshō*, first performed in 1817) when Zangetsu and Nagaura get ousted from the temple.

"If a man makes love . . . without regret." A travesty of a passage in the *Analects*: "If a man in the morning hear the right way, he may die in the evening without regret."[36]

---

35. The temple was the Tendai-sect Tamajima-zan Myōjō-in Tōkōji.
36. Legge, *Confucius*, p. 168.

stage song (*bungobushi*). A kind of kabuki ballad named for the reciter who invented it (Miyakoji Bungonojō, ca. 1660–1740). Essential to double-suicide pieces, *bungobushi* was said to be supple as the flesh (*yawarakana hada*).[37]

♪ Alone she can't loosen/the sash they tied together ♪ A reference to a poetic exchange from *The Tales of Ise* (episode 37):

Long ago a man began seeing a promiscuous woman. Doubting her fidelity, he wrote:

Ware narade	Do not untie
Shitahimo tokuna	Your undersash, my flower,
Asagao no	Except for me;
Yūkage matanu	Though like the Morning Glory,
Hana ni wa ari tomo	Await not evening's shadows.

Her response:

Futari shite	This sash
Musubishi himo o	The two of us once tied—
Hitori shite	Never by myself
Ai miru made wa	Shall I let it be undone
Tokaji to zo omou	Until we meet again.

heights *(takami)*. The following passage contains other references to and associative words of elevation.

unfinished (*fushin*). This puns on the treacherous-looking (*fushin na*) desperadoes who have just robbed Enjirō and Ukina.

♪ if a woman stumbles . . . trysting god. A spoof of a line from the *katōbushi* ballad "Among the Pines" (*Matsu no uchi*): "Will one's reputation improve if one falls from the embankment into the Sumida River? Such is the intention of the gods in fastening the undersashes of prostitutes everywhere!" Kyōden's version substitutes the two phrases "Nobody knows whence the whores come" (*doko no jorōshū ka shirazu*) and "to fasten a lice collar" (*shiramihimo musubu*) for the line "to fasten the undersashes of whores everywhere" (*doko no jorōshū no shitahimo o musubu*).

To face Mt. Peppersoy/Sauce on cuttlefish (*mukasansho jōyu no yakizurume*). Following the stem of the verb "to proceed toward" (*mukau*) is the suffix "let us" (*sansho*, a clipped form of *shimashō*), which pivots into "pepper" (*sansho* or *sanshō*), which then flavors the "roasted cuttlefish with soy sauce" (*jōyu no yakizurume*).

---

37. Both Mizuno and Hamada note a popular saying, spoofing a line from the "Kana Preface" to *Japanese Verse Old and New*, that likens the musical quality of the major types of recitative music to different articles of clothing: "*Katōbushi* resembles a stiff ceremonial garb; *gekibushi*, a divided skirt; *handayūbushi*, a halfcoat; and *bungobushi*, soft, exposed skin."

Fried to a crisp (*bin to hizoru*). The cuttlefish "shrivels up" as love "withers" after the argument.

Outward Eight Sashay (*soto-hachimonji*). The name of a fancy step executed by high-ranking Yoshiwara courtesans in formal processions, describing the movement of both feet shuffling alternately forward, then laterally in a semicircle backwards to the original position, and finally forward again one pace. The maneuver was tricky to perform in tall clogs and multilayered kimono—and some courtesans occasionally tripped. There was an easier step, known as the "Inward Eight" (*uchi-hachimonji*).[38] The **Inward Seven** (*uchi-shichimonji*)—no doubt Kyōden's invention—would have been more of a **stumble** than a sashay, since the corresponding graph is not easily traced by the foot.

turns the inky gray (*kao wa usuzumi ni*). "To become livid." The **geese** who look like **the lines of a letter** are from the poem (*Goshūishū* 71):

Usuzumi ni	How they resemble
Kaku tamazusa to	The lines of a letter
Miyuru ka na	Written in light grays—
Kasumeru sora ni	Those geese returning homeward
Kaeru karigane	Through the darkening sky.

Crowbar-patterned shoulders (*kanade kanateko*). This plays with the *kana* **lettering** (*kanade*) and the "crowbars on the shoulders" (*kata ni kanateko*) that Enjirō had previously commissioned. Likewise, the "anchor at the hem" (*suso ni wa ikari*) mentioned earlier appears here as **Anchor-patterned hems** (*suso moyō*).[39]

passionate purple (*yukari no iro*). The color of "ardor" (*yukari*) puns on "anchor" (*ikari*).

pawnshop (*nanatsuya*). The embedded "seven" (*nana*) plays with the other reading of the graph for seven (*shichi*) of the Inward Seven footwork. It may also be euphonic (as Mizuno suggests) with the clause "to achieve **fame**" (*na ni nagare*), though more likely, pawnshops are associated with "selling off" (*nagare*), which, in turn, in its other meaning of **flows**, is an associative word of **River Sumida**.

Iozaki. An old name for Mukōjima, near the Mimeguri Embankment of the Sumida.

Livelong Day-Shop . . . Ten o'clock. The "fourth bell" (*yotsu no kane*) that sounds **ten o'clock** in the morning puns on the **Livelong Day-Shop**

---

38. Performed in the Old Yoshiwara and in the Shimabara, according to Mitani, in *Edo Yoshiwara zushū*, p. 214.

39. Nakamura claims this is the conjoined-coins pattern of Abe-no-Shikibu Nobumitsu.

(*Yotsumeya*). This establishment, located near Mimeguri Shrine, was especially renowned for both its elixirs (with which the failed pseudo-suicide contrasts ironically) and its aphrodisiacs (with which the grilled eel alluded to in the story's title is associated). The proprietor's personal name Chōmeigan is partially echoed in **Longevity Temple** (*Chōmeiji*). The related phrase **bare their breasts** (*mune o aku*) pivots into **tomorrow** (*akuru hi*).

spring day,/Long as their loincloths (*fundoshi nagaki haru no hi*). "Long" (*nagaki*) pivots between "loincloths" (*fundoshi*) and "spring day" (*haru no hi*).

Fresh as scarlet silk crepe. Being well "past the four bells" (*yotsu sugi*) of morning, Enjirō and Ukina feel "late-morning fresh" (*yotsusugi no*), a phrase that pivots into "morning sun" (*yotsusugi no hi*), which then leads into "silk crepe" (*hijirimen*).

Sunhigh Temple (*Hidaka no tera*). Affiliated with "long spring day," this temple (better known as Dōjōji) housed a legendary bell (associated with "fourth bell"). The name of the temple echoes **stark-naked couple** (*hadaka no teyai*).

Shamisen flourish (*hiki sanjū*). Stage directions prompting the *shamisen* players to sound the play's finale.

Just as the ox . . . ring in its snout (*ushi wa negai kara hana o tōsu*). A proverb, admonishing a complainer to search for the cause of his grievance in himself. Along with the earlier remark about Enjirō sneezing, and the implied reference to the ravages of syphilis, and possibly the homophonous mentioning of flowers (*hana*), this is one of the verbal comments drawing attention to Enjirō's nose.

tawdry round fans (*shibu-uchi*). Cheap, oblong, persimmon-varnished paper fans, sometimes bearing Toba cartoons depicting contemporary events.

ass-backwards (*urahara*). "Backside and belly."

indecent (*okashii*). A pun on "fun" and "improper."

Section 22

[Picture] Enjirō's father and the clerk Sorobei chastising Enjirō and Ukina, whose clothes are draped over the family garment rack. There is a visual-verbal pun here: Enjirō has wrapped the suicide mat around himself to warm up, calling to mind the phrase "to shroud oneself in a carpet" (*mōsen o kaburu*), an idiomatic expression meaning "to catch a scolding."

'Until the hot blood of youth . . . many temptations' (*Wakaki toki wa ketsuki imada sadamarazu imashimuru koto iroiro ari*). Another travesty of a line

from the *Analects*: "In youth, when the physical powers are not yet settled, [the superior man] guards against lust."[40] Kyōden puns "lust" (*iro*) and "many" (*iroiro*).

comicbook (*kusazōshi*). That is, the present *kibyōshi*.

---

40. Book 16 (*Ji Shi*), Chapter 7. In Legge, *Confucius*, p. 312.

Chapter 7

The Unseamly

Silverpiped Swingers

(1788)

*In the absence of an Archimedean point in the
body that assumes the stability and nature of
sexual difference, one sex is, and has always been,
in tension with two: stark polarities poised on
the edge of chiaroscuro shadings.*
—Thomas Laqueur[1]

Lovers in eighteenth-century Japan unable to be united in this life might perhaps commit double suicide in the hopes of joining each other in the next. If fate did not smile upon them, however, such lovers risked rebirth not on the same lotus blossom, but on the same chromosome, as identical, or even conjoined, twins. Congenital anomalies, in contemporaneous terms, were regarded as object lessons in the Buddhist doctrine of karmic causation, as retribution either for one's own moral and sexual transgressions in a previous existence, or for those of one's relations—the sins of the parents visited upon the child. The birth of freakish progeny to a hunter and his wife, for example, would be attributed either to the defilements of his occupation, which is to say the handling of animal flesh, or, in a kind of "maternal impression theory" version, to some unseemliness on her behalf. An ordinary woman was doomed to bear twins, according to this logic, merely by slicing vegetables accidentally on the lid of a saucepan, naively chomping on a bifurcated turnip, even conceiving while making love inadvertently on the crevice between tatami mats.

The present story, Santō Kyōden's *Unseamly Silverpiped Swingers*, imbibes deeply of such religious and folk beliefs, comically describing the lives, loves, and vicissitudes of a pair of conjoined twins. These are not just any conjoined twins, but the rarest kind, "bicephalous" twins, beings with two heads but a common, single torso. As it happens, one of these heads is male, the other female.

---

1. Laqueur, *Making Sex*, p. 114.

Fig. 7.1 Twins fused at the spine. From *Tale of Koyasu* (*Koyasu monogatari*, 1661). Reprinted in Yokoyama and Matsumoto, *Muromachi jidai monogatari taisei 5*, front matter. Courtesy of Kadokawa shoten.

There has never been a case of differently sexed conjoined twins on record, nor could there be, for such is a medical impossibility. Conjoined twins are identical twins, and emanating from the same egg, by definition have the same sex, even if hermaphroditic. Still, this did not prevent differently sexed conjoined twins from inhabiting earlier works of Japanese literature. One particularly enduring story, which appeared under alternative titles in different genres—such as the short-story collection (*setsuwa*) and the companion booklet (*otogizōshi*)—during the fifteenth to seventeenth centuries, describes a brother and sister whose torsos are fused together at the spine (**Figure 7.1**). The pair, described as "two-headed, eight-limbed" (*nimen hassoku*) twins, turns out to be a manifestation of the matchmaking de-

ity at Kyoto's Kiyomizu Temple, Koyasu Jizō, from whom the best-known version of the story gains its title, *Tale of Koyasu* (*Koyasu monogatari*).[2]

None of the versions of *Tale of Koyasu* appreciably influences *Swingers*, in which the twins share the same two-legged, two-armed torso. More crucially, Kyōden's twins are linked to their lovers from disparate contemporary stories. That is, the dichotomous condition of the male head—named Hanbei—and of the female head—Onatsu—is the humorous gimmick by which Kyōden performs a classic intertwining (*naimaze*) of two well-worn, though unrelated, "worlds" (*sekai*) that were based on two sensational real-life incidents.

The first concerns the beauty Onatsu and her man Seijūrō, youthful lovers whose double suicide attempt in Himeji circa 1660 was narrowly thwarted. Their nonetheless tragic fate—execution for him, full-blown madness for her (according to some accounts)—has been retold in myriad works across the spectrum of genres. One scholar lists over a hundred titles from the last two centuries of the Edo period alone.[3] Praise for the lovers has been sung in popular ballads (*utazaimon*), like *Onatsu and Seijūrō* (*Onatsu Seijūrō*), and touched upon in novellas, such as Nishizawa Ippū's *Adultery's Triple Revenge* (*Midare hagi sanbon yari*, 1718).[4] Their names in fact survive beyond the Edo period: modern playwright Mayama Seika would pen *Onatsu and Seijūrō* (*Onatsu Seijūrō*, 1940);[5] and Tsubouchi Shōyō, who dismissed much Edo popular fiction as damagingly frivolous, would himself compose a dance drama (*butōgeki*), entitled *Onatsu Deranged* (*Onatsu kyōran*, 1908).[6]

Their story is perhaps best known in English as the "Story of Seijuro [*sic*] in Himeji," in William Theodore de Bary's widely accessible and standard translation of Saikaku's masterpiece *Five Women Who Loved Love* (*Kōshoku gonin onna*, 1686).[7] Yet the most celebrated Seijūrō-Onatsu yarn during the Edo period itself, by all accounts, was Chikamatsu's puppet play, *A Prayer-Song to Buddha on the Fiftieth Anniversary* (*Gojūnenki utanenbutsu*, 1709), which has been called one of the base texts of the present piece.

The second world entwined into *Swingers*, describing the successful double suicide in 1722 of husband and wife Hanbei and Ochiyo (spurred by the mother-in-law), also consists of copious versions, two of which were brought to the puppet stage the same year as the actual events. Ki no Kaion's

---

2. Two different versions of *Koyasu monogatari* are reprinted in Yokoyama and Matsumoto, *Muromachi jidai monogatari taisei 5*: a Muromachi-period tale (also included in the early Edo publication of *Issun bōshi*), pp. 142–162, and an early Edo-period version, dated 1661, pp. 163–178.

3. See Takeno, "Tajimaya Onatsu no zōkei." Takeno covers works issued between the years 1664 and 1868 in the related article, "Onatsu Seijūrō mono no rinkaku."

4. See Richard Lane, "Saikaku's *Five Women*." Lane cites two nonfictional sources (a 1664 entry in *The Diary of Matsudaira, Lord of Yamato* and a note in the 1760 semi-historical manuscript *Shoki shishūki*) attesting to the fame of the Onatsu-Seijūrō legend.

5. Mayama, *Mayama Seika zenshū 3*, pp. 1–100.

6. Inagaki, *Tsubouchi Shōyō shū*, pp. 353–357.

7. See de Bary, *Five Women Who Loved Love*, pp. 39–72.

(1663–1742) *Love Suicides and the Double Maternal-Sash* (*Shinjū futatsu haraobi*) is thought to have barely preceded Chikamatsu's *Love Suicides on the Eve of the Kō-shin Festival* (*Shinjū yoigōshin*). However, no end to the debate is in sight, for the margin between first runs of these plays can be measured in terms of weeks, if not days.[8]

The few scholars who have written on *Swingers*, albeit only briefly, invariably view it as a relatively straightforward combination of these two dramas by Chikamatsu, probably on account of the playwright's prestige, even to the point of ignoring other manifestly germane works. Yet the notion that Kyōden was *exclusively* beholden to Chikamatsu's *Prayer-Song to Buddha* and *Eve of the Kōshin Festival* is overdetermined. In order to demonstrate as much, a précis of Kyōden's story is in order.

Although most *kibyōshi* set in the past are transparently disguised allegories of the-then Edo present—and this certainly pertains to *Swingers*—the setting of sixteenth-century Yamashiro province is, nonetheless, not exactly arbitrary. According to historical records, bicephalous twins actually were born there in the twelfth year of Tenshō (1584). Kyōden's readers some two centuries later would have been familiar with this event through contemporary accounts, such as the widely circulated *Fully Illustrated Yearly Annals* (*Nendaiki ōeshō*, 1781) (**Figure 7.2**). The Yamashiro twins gripped the imagination, and references to them persisted throughout the Edo period.[9]

Kyōden's story commences when the wife of a poor hunter has an enigmatic dream in which she devours a legendary two-headed creature from Hell. Little does the hunter's wife suspect that this dream portends the birth of two-headed conjoined twins. Unable to support the extra mouth, the hunter and wife sell their offspring—upon whom they have provisionally bestowed the collective name Oinosuke—into a Kyoto sideshow. Oinosuke eventually attains a modicum of success and assumes the adult names Hanbei and Onatsu. The two of them move to Edo, where they rise to the rank of *bona fide* geisha. Before long, Hanbei and Onatsu each take lovers—the greengrocer's daughter Ochiyo and the playboy Seijūrō—though after some logistical complications, all four of them consent to a *double* double suicide. A fittingly whimsical travesty of the classic travel poem from the stage ensues (not unlike the one found in Kyōden's *Playboy*), but in the end, a doctor trained in Western medicine happens upon the two-headed protagonists and offers to separate them surgically.

Head transplants in eighteenth-century Japan were a medical impossibility, of course, so the story's ending is farcical contrivance. And yet there were contemporary attempts at corrective surgery of anomalously bodied

---

8. Chikamatsu's play can be found in Matsuzaki, *Chikamatsu jōrurishū 2*, pp. 305–353. For a translation into English, see Gerstle, *Chikamatsu*, pp. 278–324.

9. The latest example I have been able to locate comes in the *Wakan nendai chōhōki* of 1848, in the holdings at Tsukuba University.

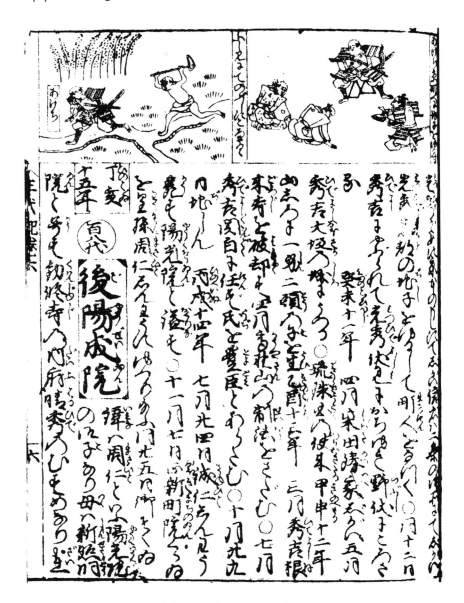

Fig. 7.2 Textual affirmation (sixth line from right) of a "Two-headed, one-bodied child born in Yamashiro" (*Yamashiro ni ittai nitō no ko o umu*). From *The Fully Illustrated Yearly Annals* (*Nendaiki ōeshō*, 1781). Courtesy of the Kariya Central Library, Murakami Collection.

people. The so-called testicle girl died on the table in 1806, and one wonders if the misbegotten endeavor had been undertaken by physicians even only remotely inspired by *Swingers*. Their attempt was not completely without precedent, or at least counterpart, for the first successful separation of conjoined twins in the West is supposedly documented as having taken place as early as 1690.[10]

One of the delightful conundrums of Kyōden's story—if not its central one—concerns the precise nature of the twins' shared genitalia. The narrator remarks early on that the hunter's children are not equipped with the

10. Grosz, "Intolerable Ambiguity," p. 62.

Fig. 7.3 Bearded hermaph-
rodite with a vaginal opening at the stem of his—or
her?—erect penis. From
*The Illness Scrolls (Yamai no
sōshi*, ca. twelfth century).
Courtesy of Kyoto Na-
tional Museum.

usual "gun." This comment, which is hard not to read in Freudian terms,
becomes the more titillating retrospectively, after the full-grown Hanbei and
Onatsu have, with their single torso, consummated their desires with members of both sexes. Kyōden thus plays with the conspicuously absent phallus (as does Edward Gorey in *The Curious Sofa*)—which is *not* to say that he
withholds subtle pictorial clues. The superabundant references to heads, for
instance, may serve as a kind of compensatory fantasy against an undisclosed emasculation. Pipes and tobacco pouches can be found throughout
the pictures, symbolizing male and female sex organs. In an early scene, a
pouch envelops a pipe, as though to suggest that the infants' genitalia have
not yet become fully differentiated. In another scene, there blooms a bunch
of sweetflag irises—a classic symbol of hermaphroditism owing to the
synecious coexistence of stiff "male" leaves and supple "female" blossoms.
Images of double genitalia would have been familiar to most readers
through a variety of texts, beginning with the classic *Illness Scrolls (Yamai no
sōshi*), a late Heian-period illustrated study of deformities and disease that
contained a scene of a bearded hermaphrodite with a vaginal opening at the
stem of his erect penis (**Figure 7.3**). Such images inhabited the new popular culture, too, as with the carved figurine depicting an infant emerging
from a vagina located at the base of a phallus (**Figure 7.4**).

Kyōden's hints of hermaphroditism would seem to belie the narrator's
statement, at story's end, that Hanbei's head gets transplanted onto another

Fig. 7.4 An infant emerging from a vagina on the back of a phallus. This unsigned *netsuke* (retrospectively titled "Genitalia and Child") possibly doubled as a dildo. In the private collection of Dr. Joseph Kurstin. Stained wood, 19th century. 12.2 × 5 × 3.5 cm (4 13/16 × 1 15/16 × 1 3/8 in.). Photograph © 2006 Museum of Fine Arts, Boston. Courtesy of Museum of Fine Arts, Boston.

body while Onatsu's head retains its own female body, for nothing has altered their shared torso's vaguely hermaphroditic, intersexed nature. Yet such discrepancies are perhaps best written off to comic license. Overall, the story undeniably partakes in the gender-bending mode of the male performer of female roles (*oyama* or *onnagata*) on the kabuki stage, whose allure resides in the taut androgyny between the apparent female-costumed body and the actual "male body beneath."[11] As much as *Swingers* in this vein plays with the alignment of gender with sex, its purpose seems less to seriously challenge the strict binary logic of "stark polarities" than to entertain.

11. Mezur uses this phrase in "Undressing the *Onnagata*."

Although Onatsu and Hanbei fail to carry out their suicides in an effort to become unambiguously uncoupled, their plan comically inverts the belief in joint rebirth upon the same lotus blossom. Similarly, one scene, in which Hanbei and Onatsu are mistaken through a window for a couple making love, puckishly reverses the conventions in contemporary erotic prints of segmenting body parts and of portraying lovers as twins. This is more than Kyōden turning *shunga* clichés on their heads: the humor of the story largely derives from an adroit, albeit inevitable, tropic economy of inversions, reversals, chiasma, duplications, uncanny similarities, repeated onomatopoetic and mimetic phraseology, parallel syntax, and his-and-hers matching subplots. The phenomenon of twinned embodiment practically necessitates the frenzied unleashing of linguistic, narrative, even imagistic couplings (optical illusions as well as visual echoes).[12] Inseparable twins are compared and contrasted incessantly, their personalities delineated as either perfectly identical or exactly opposite, with little wiggle room in-between. This is true of conjoined twin narratives in general, incidentally, such as the classic biographies of Chang and Eng Bunker, and the late twentieth-century American film by the Polish brothers, *Twin Falls Idaho*.

The most pervasive form of doubling in *Swingers*, though, is the pun, including its sexualized variety, the *double entendre*. Although such wordplay pervades most *kibyōshi*, it takes on especial significance in this one, for like conjoined twins themselves, the pun represents the cohabitation of multiple identities within a single space. Strings of puns (*monozukushi*) and associative words (*engo*) related to heads, necks, twins, couplings, bifurcations, freaks, and so forth twine Kyōden's story together giddily—as do references to the underworld (associated with the two-headed creature from Hell) and karma. The hunter's past slaughter of animals also engenders bestial imagery, which likewise is related to the fact that twins were said to emanate from a "beast belly."

Fish and boats are never far from the surface of many passages, too. In some versions of the Onatsu-Seijūrō tale, the lovers are apprehended when the vessel on which they are fleeing is turned back. Fish, on the other hand, are associated with Sniffing Nose (one of the two heads from Hell), as evidenced in a comic poem that plays on her ability to sniff out rotting flesh. The fish and the boats therefore are not connected directly to one another, let alone to the bestial imagery. Still, Kyōden is capable of squeezing double duty out of the components of his story, such as with the visual comparison of the twins to a dish of dried fish served split down the middle (*aji no himono*), which also happened to be the stuff of a notoriously shammed freak spectacle in Edo, circa 1777.

---

12. This was not Kyōden's first time illustrating a *kibyōshi* in which a woman bears a freakish child to the father's astonishment, for he provided the pictures (under the Masanobu pseudonym) to Kishida Tohō's *Japan's Daemon* (*Nippon Daemon*, 1783), in the collection of Kaga Bunko.

This term "freak," it might be objected, smacks of insensitivity, political incorrectness, even bad taste. The Japanese term *katawa*, though, was hardly less offensive.[13] Nonetheless, the act of writing about freaks itself may invite the charge of pandering to what one disability activist has aptly termed a "pornography of the disabled." To the extent that Kyōden's story exploits the image of freaks in Japan, the present chapter could easily be misperceived as complicit in a kind of Orientalism, with its ignoble tradition of narrativizing freaks as exotic "Orientals"—Chinese Giants, Fijian Mermaids, Laotian "Missing Links," Hottentot Venuses, and Circassian Beauties, let alone Siamese Twins.[14] Yet the word "freak" has actually been appropriated recently by freaks themselves as a kind of manifesto of self-determination, an act of political defiance, in much the same way that "queer" has been appropriated by "Queer Theory," as well as by queers themselves.[15] Most importantly, "freak" is blunter, more powerful, less euphemistic than polite monstrosities, like "differently physiognomied individual."

Be that as it may, the commercial street spectacle (*misemono*)—of which the freakshow was a major subgenre—was more than a curiosity in late traditional Japan. It constituted a vibrant facet of urban life.[16] So much so that it should perhaps be considered just as much a part of the Floating World as the pleasure quarters and the kabuki stage. Surely it is no coincidence that spectacles were located next to the theater district in each of the chief metropolises—Edo's Nihonbashi, Osaka's Dōtonbori, and Kyoto's Shijō-gawara. Kawazoe Yū has even opined that the enjoyment of fake or "gaffed" freaks was a defining feature of Edo culture.[17] So established was the public display of freaks that it is surprising that relatively little has been written on the subject in English.[18] Freaks were part of much broader discourses on the body and on alterity, or the corporeal and cultural Other. Sightless people, legless beggars, armless wonders, bearded ladies, dwarves, and many others posing a threat to the illusion of normalcy—not to omit foreigners, especially of the Western persuasion—overrun the popular literature and art of the day.[19] Those wonderful oddballs of *Tales of Modern*

---

13. In fact, Teshima Toan (1718–1786), thinker and disciple of Mind Study founder Ishida Baigan, even went so far in his book *Zenkun* as urging children against making fun of those with physical disabilities. Mentioned in Sawada, *Confucian Values and Popular Zen*, p. 112.

14. It makes little difference that Circassia lies in the Caucasus, for as a sideshow attraction Circassian beauties were billed as having been rescued from Turkish harems.

15. Here I follow the lead of Grosz, "Intolerable Ambiguity," p. 56.

16. The classic study on Edo-period sideshows is that of Asakura, *Misemono kenkyū*, though see also Gunji and Sekiyama, *Misemono zasshi*, as well as Kawazoe, *Edo no misemono*.

17. Kawazoe, *Edo no misemono*, p. 80.

18. The exception that proves the rule being a lone article by Markus, "The Carnival of Edo."

19. Even broadsheets catered to the public's appetite for freaks: "Although *kawaraban* for the most part avoided dealing with explicitly political events, they did feature news and current events of a non-political nature, such as love suicides in the early eighteenth century,

Eccentrics (*Kinsei kijinden*, 1790) can be regarded as case studies in aberrant personality.[20] So, too, the shape-shifting monsters (*bakemono*), such as the long-necked goblin (*rokurokubi*) or the goofy water sprite (*kappa*), who frequent a significant portion of *kibyōshi*. These turn out to be benignly mischievous, almost lovable creatures, more of the friendly Casper, than the fiendly *Kwaidan*, variety.

Whereas the cultural context of the freakshow is crucial to the present story, so too are the texts that Kyōden spoofed. Scholars have argued that Kyōden based *Swingers* almost exclusively on the previously mentioned plays by Chikamatsu.[21] Kyōden was intimately aware of these plays and alludes to them occasionally. More profoundly influential, however, were the two dance dramas (*tomimotobushi*) written by one of the major playwrights of the day and Kyōden's friend Sakurada Jisuke I (1734–1806): *Onatsu's and Seijūrō's Travel Poem: Conjoined Crests of Chrysanthemum and Butterfly* (*Onatsu Seijūrō michiyuki: Hiyoku no kikuchō*); and *Ochiyo's and Hanbei's Travel Poem: The Hedgerow's Pattern* (*Ochiyo Hanbei michiyuki: Kakine no yuiwata*).[22] Both premiered at the Ichimura Theater in 1781 as part of a legendary three-day performance (*mikkagawari*) of plays about the Soga brothers through the ages (*bandai Soga*). Several of the leading actors of the day took the roles: Segawa Kikunojō III (1751–1810), at the time ranked as one of the best actors of female roles, played both Onatsu and Ochiyo; Ichikawa Monnosuke II (1743–1794) played Seijūrō; and Bandō Mitsugorō I (1766–1782) took the role of Hanbei. Textual analysis strongly suggests that, contrary to the received wisdom, Kyōden closely parodies the plays by Sakurada and not those by Chikamatsu.[23]

More elusively, non-textual or "performative" aspects of Sakurada's pieces are incorporated into *Swingers*. Kyōden alludes to the written libretto, of course, but also to features of the three-day Soga performances themselves, such as the house crests of the actors and their poses in particular scenes. One of Kyōden's lines, about binge eating, plays off the childhood nickname of the kabuki star Ichikawa Danjūrō. Another scene, in which Seijūrō comes to the aid of Onatsu (who has been abducted by Hanbei), puns visually on the elements of the corresponding scene in Sakurada's play, such as Seijūrō's sword and lantern. Kyōden's Seijūrō is not simply Seijūrō, then, but the actor Ichikawa Monnosuke in the role of Seijūrō.

---

vendettas, natural disasters such as fires and floods, and the appearance of supposed freak animals." In Kornicki, *The Book in Japan*, p. 65.

20. See Rosenfield with Cranston, *Extraordinary Persons*.

21. Yamaguchi, Koike, Mori, and Tanahashi each makes this claim (in works quoted at the end of this essay).

22. Reprinted in Takano, *Nihon kayō shūsei 10*, pp. 472–474 and pp. 474–476, respectively.

23. Kern, "Santō Kyōden gasaku no kibyōshi *Sogitsugi gingiseru* no saikō to shichū."

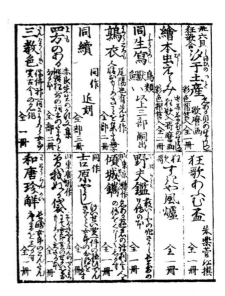

Fig. 7.5 Colophon from *The Yoshiwara, Detailed* (*Yoshiwara saiken*, 1788). No mention is made of *The Unseamly Silverpiped Swingers*. Reprinted in Hanasaki, *Tenmeiki Yoshiwara saiken shū.*

The influence of extra-textual elements in *Swingers* suggests a similar dynamic in other *kibyōshi*. Could it be that actual kabuki performances are even more pivotal to the *kibyōshi* genre than anyone has thus far acknowledged? It is possible that had previous commentators on *Swingers* been aware of these performative aspects, they might not have argued for the primacy of Chikamatsu's versions of the Onatsu-Seijūrō and Ochiyo-Hanbei tales. Perhaps even contemporary readers too, separated from the original 1781 performance of Sakurada's dance pieces by at least a half dozen years, were at pains to recognize their significance?

This might help explain why *Swingers* enjoyed no particularly grand success. None of the contemporary review books mentions it. Nor was it reissued in multiple editions or announced in that year's *The Yoshiwara, Detailed,* as were the really big hits (**Figure 7.5**). Only Kyōden and his protégé Shikitei Sanba seem to have alluded to *Swingers* within their *kibyōshi.*[24] The fact that the Kansei Reforms banned silver pipes the year after *Swingers* was published is mere coincidence—surely Matsudaira Sadanobu did not take his cue from the present piece in particular.[25] Why, then, was Kyōden so slow in bringing *Swingers* to publication? Was there some illustrated playbook of Sakurada's plays published closer to the issuance of *Swingers,* though now lost to posterity? Or was Kyōden's text exceedingly obscure for general readers, its homage to performative aspects too clever by half?

---

24. As Koike points out in *Santō Kyōden no kenkyū,* p. 273 and passim, Sanba based his *kibyōshi* of 1805, *Naburumoyomi to utaizukushi,* largely on *Swingers.* And Kyōden himself recycled some material in works such as *Tadagokoro oni uchimame* (1792) and *Ryōtō fude zen'aku nikki* (1799), which can be found in Mizuno, *SKZ 3,* pp. 129–153 and *SKZ 4,* pp. 311–331, respectively.

25. Noted in Mizuno, *SNKBT 85,* p. 52, n. 5.

The present translation is based on, and its pictures culled from, the *kibyōshi* in the collections of the Matsuura Museum of History (all of the interior pictures except for the last one) and Tōyō bunko (frontispieces and the last picture). Use was also made of the versions in the collections at Kaga bunko and the Museum of Fine Arts, Boston.

Annotations are my own and follow my article, "Santō Kyōden gasaku no kibyōshi *Sogitsugi gingiseru* no saikō to shichū," in *Chōsa kenkyū hōkoku 22* (Kokubungaku kenkyū shiryōkan, 2001), pp. 17–62. A modern typescript version—though unannotated—can be found in Mizuno Minoru et al., eds., *Santō Kyōden zenshū 1* (Perikansha, 1992), pp. 383–400. Previous scholarship is limited to the occasional passing comment and a few brief précis, most notably in the following: Koike Tōgorō, *Santō Kyōden no kenkyū* (Iwanami shoten, 1935), pp. 272–273; Yamaguchi Takeshi, *Yamaguchi Takeshi chōsakushū 3* (Chūō kōronsha, 1972), pp. 472–476; Mori Senzō, *Zoku kibyōshi kaidai* (Chūō kōronsha, 1974), pp. 142–144; and Tanahashi Masahiro, *Kibyōshi sōran 1* (Seishōdō, 1986), pp. 744–745.

The Unseamly

Silverpiped Swingers

Spotting Eyes observes: "Here comes a real beauty. Too flashy for a respectable woman, though. Must be an Edo geisha."

"Hmmm," says Sniffing Nose, "smells like an eel shop's nearby. How yummy! I'll bet someone 'round here's hosing a potted flower."

Once upon a time, perhaps back in the Tenshō era, there lived a certain huntsman who eked out his existence deep in the mountains of Yamashiro. One day the wife of this huntsman had a mystifying dream:

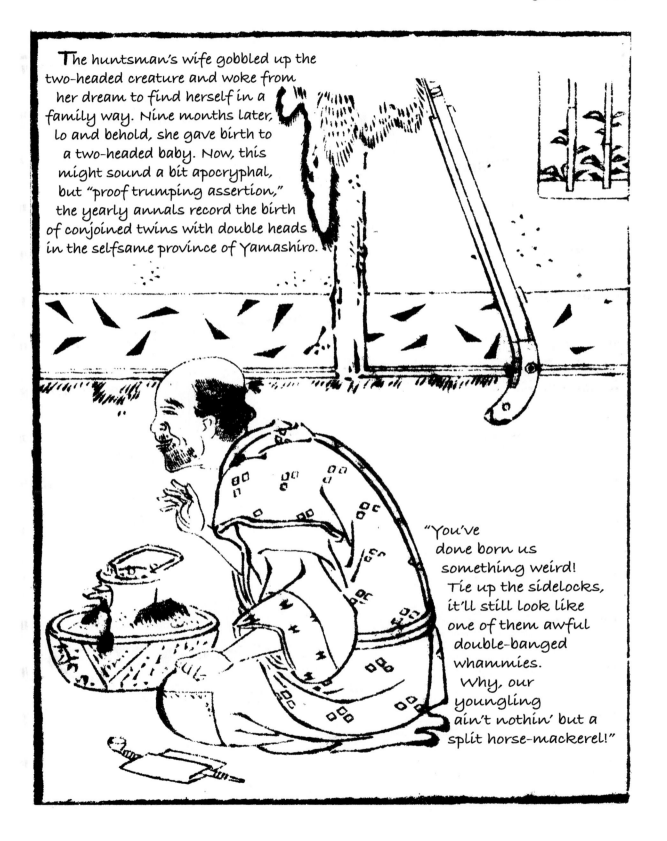

The huntsman's wife gobbled up the two-headed creature and woke from her dream to find herself in a family way. Nine months later, lo and behold, she gave birth to a two-headed baby. Now, this might sound a bit apocryphal, but "proof trumping assertion," the yearly annals record the birth of conjoined twins with double heads in the selfsame province of Yamashiro.

"You've done born us something weird! Tie up the sidelocks, it'll still look like one of them awful double-banged whammies. Why, our youngling ain't nothin' but a split horse-mackerel!"

The father was a huntsman,
as you know, yet his child
was hardly equipped
with the usual gun.

"Heard of a
white-headed pig before.
But never
a two-headed kid."

"Ga! Ga!"
mewls the infant,
in two-part
harmony.

The huntsman and his wife, despondent over the birth of such prodigious progeny, bemoaned whatever past karmic misdeeds had incurred this wretched fate. Rather than ditch in the mountains their kin, whom they of course nonetheless adored, they reared it, and as it grew, one head gradually began looking male, and the other, female. At age seven or eight,

"Gettin' born like that ain't so bad. But what we gonna sell it off as, callgirl or callboy?!"

...their facial features bore such jewel-like luster that the parents cursed the deformity all the more.

"What with rice so costly, and one too many mouths to feed, we're in deep trouble!"

At a loss what to call their offspring, they consulted Ono no Takamura's Lyrical Character Dictionary and settled on Oinosuke—"Girlboy."

"It's an act of mercy, really, putting your kids on public display. Of course, it would also make up for past sins . . . So how about calling it a done deal at twenty silvers?!"

Just as a serpent recognizes a snake's path, sure enough around that time a sideshow huckster, having heard of the little two-headed monster, comes charging up the mountain, Lord Raikō-like, corners the parents, and makes his sales pitch:

"There's a case of this in *The Illustrated Encyclopaedia of Edification*, which says: 'The god of Mt. Yangling, who in form resembles a human—though with two noggins!—is termed *Monstre Double*.'"

And so Oinosuke came of age and, at the Shijō riverbank in Kyoto, made a timely debut. People of every station and class, from all over the capital and beyond, queue up to catch the show.

"I hear the father's some backwoods hunter."

FLEDGLINGS of the SHARED WINGS

Time flew until Oinosuke, already eighteen, left the Shijō riverbank for a succession of sideshow appearances in hotspots here and there, making a fortune. In a world where it is hard enough for an ordinary person to squeak by solo, Oinosuke manages spectacularly as a duo.

Man that he was, the male half of the act constantly had lust on the brain, and longed to head for Edo. Being part of a joint effort, though, there was no getting his way without consulting his feminine side.

"What do you think, dear?"

Bright moon illumines the river ahead

"What do you think, dear?"

This was more tête-à-tête than head-on confrontation.

"How about adopting new names? We were born in midsummer, so I'll be 'Mid'—Hanbei— and you be 'Summer'—Onatsu."

They appear in the Nakazu district as a two-bit performer and —certainly not on account of their two necks—become an unexpected sensation. Thus was coined the "double header."

Having heard that only the trendy prosper in Edo, Hanbei quits the sideshow to take up vocal impersonation, and Onatsu shamisen playing.

"Oh, you're still working on that wasabi plum appetizer. How about another drink?"

"Thank goodness for Takinoya!"

"How ho-hum da-doo dumb!"

In a world full of debauchery, no place is as scandalous as Edo, where even the malformed do not get by unscathed. Thus did Ochiyo, the daughter of the greengrocer next door, fall for Hanbei's handsome visage, plying him with love letters.

"Joined at the hip with lovely Miss Onatsu here, you must get lots of necking!"

"How? With only one bod between us, even foreplay's out!"

Onatsu's head sleeps like a top.

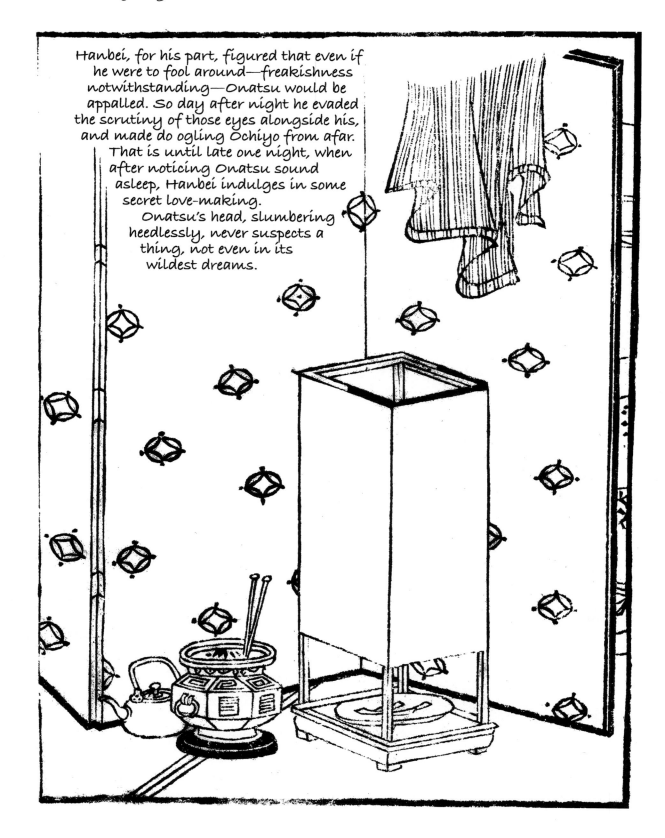

Hanbei, for his part, figured that even if he were to fool around—freakishness notwithstanding—Onatsu would be appalled. So day after night he evaded the scrutiny of those eyes alongside his, and made do ogling Ochiyo from afar.

That is until late one night, when after noticing Onatsu sound asleep, Hanbei indulges in some secret love-making.

Onatsu's head, slumbering heedlessly, never suspects a thing, not even in its wildest dreams.

Curiosity seekers never being in short supply, there was in the neighborhood a certain Tajimaya Seijūrō who came on to Onatsu, allured by her sightly neck. Despite her own heartfelt attraction to this rake Seijūrō, Onatsu, in deference to Hanbei, had always resisted temptation. No sooner has Hanbei fortuitously dozed off, though, than Onatsu sneaks out of the bedroom, ever so daintily, to meet Seijūrō for a little hanky-panky.

Hanbei, conked out from his own dalliances, comes along for the ride unprotestingly, oblivious—like a passenger on the Shirakawa night boat—to Onatsu's single-mindedness, though mumbling in his sleep:
"Yeah, that's it! His pestle slips into her drain! Bang, bang! Pant, pant!"

Ochiyo collapsed softly in Hanbei's embrace, though when she came to, he was nowhere to be found. Incensed that he might be two-timing her, she searches high and low, only to gallop into the midst of Onatsu and Seijūrō horsing around. Ochiyo grabs Hanbei's arm to drag him back to her boudoir. Seijūrō informs Onatsu they have some things that need discussing too, and as the ever-so-popular Onatsu and Hanbei are practically tugged apart like so much dried octopus, Hanbei wakes up, eyes meeting Onatsu's, embarrassment flushing both faces red.

"I'm so ashamed, Hanbei!"

"I'm so ashamed, Onatsu!"

"We still have some talking to do! Stay put!"

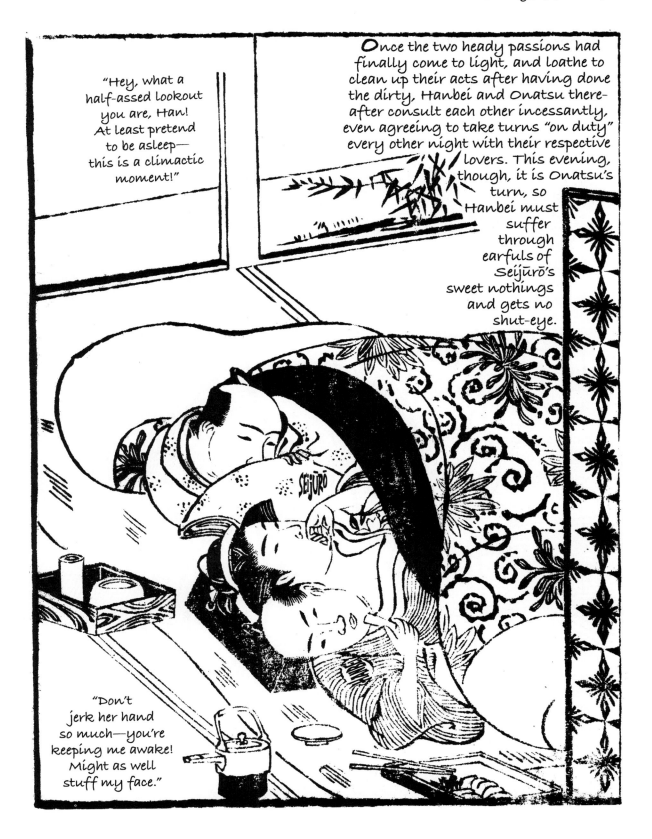

"Hey, what a half-assed lookout you are, Han! At least pretend to be asleep—this is a climactic moment!"

Once the two heady passions had finally come to light, and loathe to clean up their acts after having done the dirty, Hanbei and Onatsu thereafter consult each other incessantly, even agreeing to take turns "on duty" every other night with their respective lovers. This evening, though, it is Onatsu's turn, so Hanbei must suffer through earfuls of Seijūrō's sweet nothings and gets no shut-eye.

"Don't jerk her hand so much—you're keeping me awake! Might as well stuff my face."

After their scuffle, they pestered one another relentlessly. When Onatsu was about to grab a bite, Hanbei would make for the bath. If, feeling chilly, Hanbei tried to throw on another layer of kimono, Onatsu would disrobe, remarking how the evening had turned into a real scorcher. Just as Hanbei lay down to nap, Onatsu would snap him up to read, if only a puppet play.

"Hey, you can't do that!"

Of two minds about everything, nothing they did was whole-hearted. And while they could hardly go on living together hungry, cold, and tired, neither would budge, each putting up a bold front.

"How infuriating!"

Seijūrō takes stock of the strange sight.

...pulled a warm hood over her head, and was sneaking off when spotted by Seijūrō who, coming to Onatsu's rescue, gives Hanbei such an awful thrashing even Onatsu's side aches.

Some time having passed since his last rendezvous, Hanbei longed to see Ochiyo, but was thwarted by Onatsu. So he tied up her hand, stuffed a monkey gag in her face,

"Don't mind the gawkers—just keep up the pace!"

Quadruple Suicide Poem:
"Up to Conjoined Necks in Love's Deep Waters"

♫The snowy white / Of the deutzia blossom:
As evanescently / As it assumes flowery shape
In a potted plant / Which onto a hedge tree
Does bamboo graft, / So, too, in the narrow gap
Between two hearts / Do moored-together lives
Head off to vanish, / Their finale to be played out
At the River Galguy, / Joined together at the neck,
So very gaunt-faced, / My hand in your hand
On this body of ours / Our own to do with as we please—
But how's that possible?!— / ♪Isn't that Seijūrō
Passing by over there? / That sedge hat sure looks like his,
That maple-leaf parasol / A twilight crimson and yet...♪
That suicide mat! / It's slung over the shoulder
Of Hanbei! / This couple of lovers here
Will spread it out, / So the couple next to them
Must use the ground / As the final resting place
For life's brief dew, / And of the hem pattern to rest
With Seijūrō / Could anything else remain
Save the word "Girlboy"?!♫

Hanbei and Onatsu, keenly aware they would always be of two souls but one body, forever incapable of joining their respective lovers, decide to commit suicide in the hopes that Enma, King of Hell, would separate them so that in the next life they might be reunited as man and wife. Together with Seijūrō and Ochiyo, they muster their resolve, and set out on their suicide journey— three-bodies and four-heads—toward the burial grounds at Toribe.

"Don't get so close to Hanbei, there, Onatsu. You two get hitched up again and we'll be in a real double-bind!"

The doctor amputated Hanbei's head, reattaching it, through the miracle of surgery, to the torso of some poor soul whose time had come, the result being that Hanbei occupied his own male body, and Onatsu, her own female body. After a hundred or so days complication-free, Hanbei and Ochiyo tie the knot, as do Onatsu and Seijūrō, and everyone lives happily ever after, even the old huntsman and wife from Yamashiro, who shuttle back and forth between the new households.

ILLUSTRATED BY MASANOBU

WRITTEN BY KYODEN

Annotations

FIRST FASCICLE

[Frontispiece] The text here indicates the title, subtitle, edition, and publisher, though not the author, illustrator, or date of publication. The year can nonetheless be inferred by a pictorial pun: the innumerable objects resembling jingle bells in the upper third of the picture are "monkey fasteners" (*kukurizaru*), children's bedding ornaments used by courtesans as talismans to retain their customers in the coming new year, and suggest that the piece was issued at the beginning of the year of the monkey (*sarudoshi*), 1788.[1] The illustration of a napping woman and her bubble-encapsulated dream is gleaned from a scene in the first of the three fascicles and serves to pique the reader's curiosity.

Unseamly Silverpiped Swingers (*Sogitsugi gingiseru*). Originally, in Japanese wood joinery, *sogitsugi* referred to the dovetailing of "male" and "female" pieces of wood.[2] This gave rise to slang meanings of "incongruously joined" (as in *haikai* criticism) and, by extension, "indecent," or even "obscene." *Gingiseru*, literally "silver pipe," came to signify, in the Edo vernacular, the sophisticate himself—a "silverpipe"—who wielded this conspicuous emblem of extravagance.[3] This double sense is attested to by the following comic haiku, a parental rebuke of a prodigal son:

Gingiseru	Silverpipe—
Kore mo iken no	Even this figures
Kazu ni iri	In his scolding.[4]

One Body, Two Heads (*Ittai funjin*). More accurately, "one body, multiple forms." A slogan asserting the Buddha's wondrous capacity to assume different guises (as with Koyasu Jizō in *Tale of Koyasu*) in order to save sentient beings. Here, the phrase plays on the dichotomous condition of the story's protagonists.

---

1. Satō, *Seirō wadan shinzō zui*, pp. 205–206.

2. For more on this—what is technically termed a "simple-scarf joint"—and others, see Kiyoshi, *The Japanese Art of Joinery*.

3. Mori concurs with *Shōsetsu nenpyō*'s reading of *gingiseru*, as opposed to *ginkiseru*. For more on pipes, see Tabako to shio no hakubutsukan, *Kiseru*. The silverpipe was exalted in the influential fashionbook, *Today's Fashionable Chic* (*Tōsei fūzoku tsū*, 1773).

4. From *Yanagidaru shūi*, 40:12, in Kasuya, *Senryū daijiten*, p. 223.

Nishimiya Shinroku (fl. ca. 1780s) was the proprietor of the Kangetsudō publishing house in Edo, which specialized in popular fiction, and the issuer of a handful of Kyōden's *kibyōshi*.[5]

Section 1

[Picture] The wife of the hunter, in their backcountry hovel, leaning over her rice tub (*ohitsu*), weary from toiling (note the rag thrown over the screen), during a midday nap (corroborated by the fan on the floor next to her). Some things mentioned in her bizarre bubble-encapsulated dream of Spotting Eyes and Sniffing Nose appear later in the story, such as potted plants, water, Hell, and geisha, not to mention two-headed creatures.

Tenshō era. 1573–1592.

Yamashiro. A province located in the Kinki region, near Kyoto.

Sniffing Nose (*Kaguhana*) and Spotting Eyes (*Mirume*). The female and male heads of a two-headed creature (called Ninzudō) with a pole for a body, who according to popular belief assists King Enma in assigning sinners to their proper level in Hell (not unlike Minos in Virgil's *Aeneid*). Sniffing Nose is not infrequently associated with fish because her olfactory senses are adept at detecting more than that which is morally rotten, as is evident in the following comic haiku (from *Yanagidaru shūi*):

Kaguhana o	Lord Enma
Yonde Enma wa	When shopping for mackerel
Saba o kai	Beckons Sniffing Nose.

Numerous associative words connecting Sniffing Nose and fish follow below, such as the eel shop (*unagiya*), a reference to the contemporary popularity of soy-broiled eel (if not a playful autocitation to Kyōden's *Playboy*).

How yummy (*Ki ga aji ni natta*). Literally "tasty," *aji* is homophonic with "horse mackerel." It was also Edo slang for something sexually arousing.

hosing a potted flower (*ueki e mizu o kakeru*). More accurately, "pours water on a potted plant." A euphemistic expression for the consummation of sexual desire.

Edo geisha. Mori suggests that this line quips about the professionalism of Edo's pleasure-quarter entertainers.

---

5. Nishimiya should not be confused with the place name Nishinomiya.

Fig. 7.6 In the Land of Butt-gas (*Hōhi no kuni*), a mother (behind a maternity screen) and a father hold their noses in response to the awful fart of their newborn—"a lad as stout as a sweet potato" (*satsumaimo no gotoku futoritaru otoko*). From *The Proverbial Crude Exegesis* (*Kotowaza gesu no hanashi*, 1796), a *kibyōshi* written by Santō Kyōden and illustrated by Kitao Shigemasa. Courtesy of Tokyo Metropolitan Central Library, Kaga Collection.

Section 2

[Picture] The hunter (unshaven, pipe and tobacco pouch at his side, flint-lock musket near an animal pelt on the wall in the background), his wife (under a blanket, behind a maternity screen, hair done up with some kind of cheap straw accessory), and their bicephalous newborn (looking very much like a split horse-mackerel). Such maternity screens appear in many other stories, too (**Figure 7.6**). The children's bedding sports a mountain cherry (*yamazakura*) pattern, here perhaps reinforcing the mountainous setting.

Nine months (*totsuki*). Actually, the period of pregnancy (*totsuki tōka*) concludes in the tenth month by the Japanese count.

two-headed baby (*kashira futatsu aru ko*). Popular belief held that a woman who consumed something bifurcated, such as a two-branched turnip (*futa-ware daikon*) or a double-yoked egg (*futago no tamago*), was destined to give birth to twins.[6]

"proof trumping assertion" (*ron yori shōko*). A line from the Confucian *Analects*.

yearly annals (*nendaiki*). Those of Kyōden's day, such as the *Nendaiki ōe-shō* (1781), indeed mention the birth of bicephalous twins in Yamashiro in 1584.

hardly equipped with the usual gun (*teppō nite wa nashi*). This phrase contains several puns. *Teppō* means "gun," but was also Edo slang for: "blowfish" (*fugu*), an associative word of Sniffing Nose; "tall tale," as in the alternative reading *teppō hanashi* (which playfully undercuts the narrator's express claim of authenticity); and "pipe," as pictured next to the hunter. Nakano Eizō contends that *teppō* was an argot for the male sex organ, though none of the standard reference works substantiates this.[7] However, the following risqué haiku (from *Yanagidaru*), in which the word "bullets" (*tama*) puns on its well-known slang meaning of "testicles" (*kintama*), supports Nakano:

Teppō no	Beneath the gun
Shita ni furari to	Dangling aimlessly—
Futatsu no tama	Two metal balls.

white-headed pig (*ryōtō no inoko*) . . . **two-headed kid** (*ryōtō no akako*). The term *ryōtō* puns on "Liaodong" and "two headed." "Pig" (*inoko*) is substituted with "infant" (*akako*). In the "Biography of Zhu Fu," a man from Liaodong is said to discover a rare, partially albino piglet. Intending to present the oddity to his lord, he travels east, crosses the Yangzi River, and arrives at court only to be told that *all* pigs in the region have white heads. Thereupon, he returns home in shame.[8]

---

6. Little has been written on beliefs concerning conjoined twins in late traditional Japan, though see Ishikawa, *Edo bungaku zokushin jiten*, pp. 319–320. On the persistence of such beliefs into the modern period, Yoshiko Ikeda (citing a Monbushō report from 1952) notes that superstitions about twins abounded in all parts of Japan: "The popular belief seemed to be that mothers were destined to have twins as punishment for their sins, for disgraceful acts, or for violating taboos. To cite some examples, 'When a woman has sexual intercourse over the seams of the Tatami mats,' 'When a woman eats a two-branched turnip,' 'When a woman cuts vegetables on the lid of a saucepan,' 'When a pregnant woman pulls a piece of cloth or paper with another woman . . . then she is destined to have twins.' It was also reported that a woman with criminal ancestors is fated to have twins. Another well-known belief was that different-sexed fraternal twins who were especially disliked were 'reincarnations of men and women who committed double suicide'" (pp. 313–314). See Yoshiko Ikeda, "Paternal Attitude toward Twins in Japan," pp. 313–322.

7. Nakano, *Edo higo jiten*, p. 354.

8. From the *Hou han shu*. Quoted in Morohashi, *Daikanwa jiten II*, p. 190.

done born us something weird (*ten kochi mo nai ko*).[9] More exactly, "pre-posterous kids."

double-banged whammies (*itagoto*). This refers to a severe blow, but may pun on "to fry" (*itameru*), another associative word of fish (and thus of Sniffing Nose).

split horse-mackerel (*aji no himono*). A dish of "dried horse-mackerel," often served split down the middle, as though two identical fish were joined together. Mori calls this an especially good *kibyōshi*-esque imagistic gag (*mitate*).

Section 3

[Picture] The threadbare rustic couple, discussing the fate of Oinosuke over a downhome meal. The rice tub is situated to the right of the hunter, who has a wooden scoop (*hishaku*) in one hand and a rice bowl in the other. Oinosuke holds a bowl and chopsticks. In the brazier is a pair of tongs (*hibashi*) for handling the firewood (*takigi*) under the kettle, which sits on a stand (*gotoku*) black with soot. The homespun clothing bespeaks the family's impoverished, backwoods circumstances: the hunter wears a crudely woven straw "mountain cap" (*yamaoka zukin*) and sits cross-legged on a thatched mat, his rugged legging exposed; the wife wears a patchwork (*tsugihagi*) garment; and Oinosuke's kimono bears two different types of "tuck" (*nuiage*)—stitching (represented by the dotted lines) that could be readily let out to allow room for growth—a shoulder tuck (*kataage*) along the lapel, and a waist tuck (*koshiage*) below the sash.

Ono no Takamura's Lyrical Character Dictionary (*Ono no Takamura utajizukushi*). One of the major writing primers of the Edo period, in the form of a glossary of Chinese graphs supplemented by short mnemonic poems, reprinted frequently and disseminated widely.[10] Sanba would publish a spoof (in the funnybook genre) titled *Ono no Takamoron's Bogus Character Dictionary* (*Ono no Bakamura usojizukushi*, 1806). Takamura (802–852) was a Heian poet who is portrayed (in such works as *Takamura monogatari*) as a tortured figure unable to satisfy his love for—of all people—his half sister. He is frequently associated with Hell, and many *kibyōshi* depict his wanderings there.[11]

---

9. Mizuno, perhaps taking this line as some kind of play on orthography, seems to misread this as "not of heaven or earth" (*ten to chi mo nai*).

10. For more on primers, see Ishikawa Matsutarō's 100-volume *Ōraimono taikei*.

11. See Kyōden, *Enma's Crystal Mirror* (*Kagami no jōhari*, 1790) in Koike, *Edo no gesaku ehon 3*, pp. 213–248.

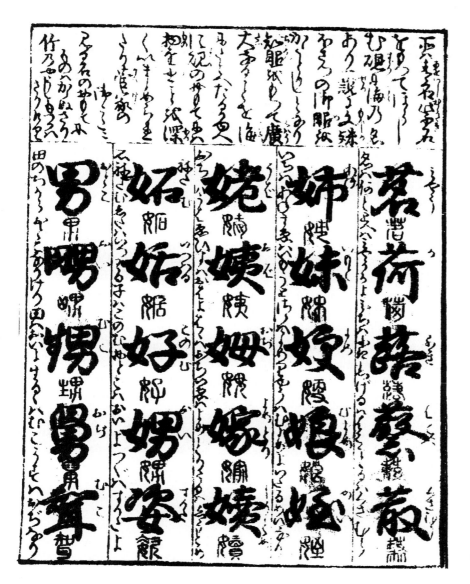

Fig. 7.7 The graph *oi* of Oinosuke (second column from left, second from bottom) as it appeared in *Ono no Takamura's Lyrical Character Dictionary* (*Ono no Takamura utajizukushi*, 1819), a major Edo-period primer employing mnemonic verses to help students memorize Chinese graphs. Authorship unknown. Courtesy of the Daté Historical Museum.

Girlboy (*Oinosuke*). Written by melding the graphs for "girl" (*onna*) and "boy" (*otoko*), the graph *oi* is drolly suited to this story's protagonists (in much the same was as "Joseph-Josephine" is to the "half-man, half-woman" sideshow spectacle in the West). Although this graph would come to mean only "to chatter" (*nan*), contemporary editions of *Ono no Takamura's Lyrical Character Dictionary* do in fact stipulate the *oi* reading (**Figure 7.7**).[12]

one too many mouths to feed (*futatsu no kubi de kuitaterarete*). Behind this rather blasé jest lurks a bitter irony, since at the time of publication Japan was experiencing the highest rice prices in its history—roughly triple the

---

12. For more on this, see Ishikawa, *Nihon kyōkasho taikei 7*, p. 426 and passim.

usual going rate (according to historical economist Sorenaka Isao).[13] Little wonder that impoverished families on the brink of starvation might actually sell their children into some kind of indentured servitude, such as the flesh trade in the pleasure quarters.

callboy (*kagema*). A young male prostitute, serving primarily male clientele.

Section 4

[Picture] The sideshow impresario, freshly arrived from his trek, still wearing his rain slicker (*kappa*) and sword, eagerly negotiating with the rural couple. The couple has set out a small portable brazier (*hiire*) so that he can light a pipe, which he smokes urbanely. At hand are his tobacco pouch (*tabakoire*) and rain hat (*kasa*). The log pillar (*marukibashira*), bamboo veranda, and pine tree all indicate a bucolic dwelling. The waterfall alludes pictorially to the story of Raikō, to whom the impresario is likened. Tucks are again visible on Oinosuke's kimono, implying continued bodily development.

Just as a serpent recognizes a snake's path (*Ja no michi wa hebi ga shiru to*). This proverb, implying that the wicked know the way of their own kind, characterizes the **sideshow huckster** (*misemonoshi*) as serpentine.

two-headed monster . . . Lord Raikō. Minamoto Raikō (948–1021) was a Heian-period general famed for going to the mountains of Ōe to quell the demon Shuten Dōji, to which the two-headed kids (*ryōtō dōji*) are compared. Some versions of *Tale of Koyasu* refer to the Raikō legend and its Ōe setting.[14]

make up for past sins (*tsumi o messuru*). Just as much a reference to the huntsman's offense of taking life as to some indiscretion on the part of his wife. An early nineteenth-century depiction of a barker's spiel about a "bear girl" similarly explains her freakish hirsuteness as resulting from her parents' occupation as hunters.[15]

twenty silvers (*nijū me*). A fitting sum for conjoined silverpipes, since *nijū* puns both on "dual" and, pictographically, on "twenty," which is written with the graphs for "two" tens (and can be orthographically represented as

---

13. "Social and economic disorder persisted because the existing agrarian economy proved vulnerable to the natural disasters which mercilessly hit Japan during this period, especially in 1783, 1785, and 1787. Crop failures in these years destroyed any equilibrium between supply and demand. This disruption in turn brought about acute shortages in urban centers and a consequent spiral of prices in Osaka, Edo, and other areas . . . the price of rice at the wholesale market in Osaka reached a record high in June of 1787, ranging from 181 to 187 *monme* of silver per *koku*, roughly three times the usual price." In Sorenaka, "The Kansei Reforms," p. 152.

14. Yokoyama and Matsumoto *Muromachi jidai monogatari taisei 5*, p. 171.

15. Markus, "Carnival of Edo," pp. 529–530.

nishū—"two heads"). The *me* (properly called *monme*) is a unit of measurement (approximately 0.1325 ounces) of silver currency.

Section 5

[Picture] Oinosuke, wearing a kimono with a crest of cherry blossoms and the graph *oi* on the right shoulder, performing a herky-jerky dance on a makeshift stage.[16] A showman, garbed in stiff-shouldered formal wear (*kataginu*), uses a folding fan to point at his spectacle while delivering his spiel. Showmen and their acts appear thus in several other pictures of sideshows from the period, as in the figure of Lady Hachikazuki in Kyōden's *Horned Words of the Dish-Bearing Demoness* (see **Figure 4.12**); or in Shikitei Sanba's *Spurious History of Comicbooks* (*Kusazōshi kojitsuke nendaiki*, 1802).[17] The audience is composed of gawking men, a few of whom appear to be dressed stylishly in striped and black halfcoats, and some women, probably courtesans. Apparently, mixed-sex crowds were not uncommon at sideshows.

Shijō riverbank in Kyoto (*Kyōto Shijō no Kawara*). Along the banks of the Kamo River at Shijō, Kyoto's hotbed of miscellaneous entertainment, such as sideshows, as well as the site of early kabuki—notorious for its burlesque dances, backstage prostitution, and cross-dressing.

Illustrated Encyclopaedia of Edification (*Kinmōzui*). A voluminous, liberally illustrated encyclopedia for the general reader, compiled by Nakamura Tekisai (1629–1702) in 1666. The Chinese classics and taxonomies of the human somatotype make up just some of its myriad sections. It was continuously revised and refined during the ensuing decades, and over the following century, scores of similar illustrated dictionaries were issued incorporating the term *kinmōzui* into their titles. Because the quote attributed to the *Kinmōzui* appears neither in the original 1666 edition nor in any of its subsequent reissues, Kyōden must have had one of the many other differently titled works in mind—such as Hirazumi Sen'an's *Illustrated Encyclopedia of Chinese Edification* (*Morokoshi kinmōzui*, 1719), where the quote, in fact, appears almost verbatim (**Figure 7.8**).

god of Mt. Yangling (*Yōrei sanjin*). Although this term appears in Hirazumi's *Illustrated Encyclopedia of Chinese Edification*, it is not to be found in any

---

16. "The setup for a *misemono* show was generally very simple: a few reed screens suspended from posts, a few benches, perhaps a platform for the attraction, and business could commence. The entire site could be dismantled (and often was) at closing time . . . Tall oblong banners fluttered above [exhibits, and] billboards and, where available, prints of the attraction decorated the outside of the booths." In Markus, "The Carnival of Edo," pp. 511–512.

17. Koike, *Edo no gesaku ehon 4*, pp. 229–266.

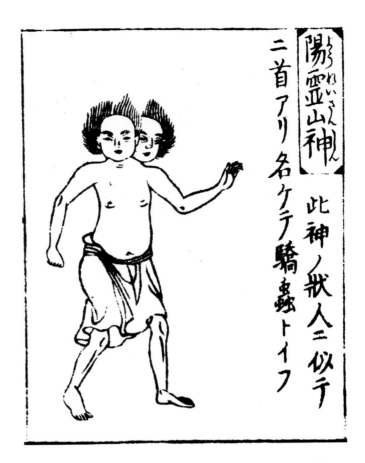

Fig. 7.8 Entry for the two-headed god of Mt. Yangling (J. Yōrei sanjin). From *The Illustrated Encyclopedia of Chinese Edification (Morokoshi kinmōzui,* 1719) by Hirazumi Sen'an. Hirazumi largely based his work on the Chinese encyclopedia *Assembled Pictures of the Three Realms (Sancai tuhui,* 1609). Courtesy of the Ueda Municipal Library, Kashun Collection.

of the standard reference works, contemporaneous as well as modern.[18] This is because there is apparently no such thing as *Yōrei sanjin.* Hirazumi (or one of his predecessors) must have slightly miscopied a poorly printed character from his main Chinese source, *Sancai tuhui* (J. *Sansaizue,* 1609) (**Figure 7.9** and **Figure 7.10**). By mistakenly writing "spirit" (*rei*) for "emptiness" (*kyo*), Hirazumi thereby inadvertently altered the place-name Yōkyo (Ch. Yangxu) to Yōrei (Yangling) (see **Figure 7.8**).[19]

Monstre Double (*Kyōchū*). A two-headed Chinese mountain deity (Ch. *Jiaochong*).[20]

Shinbōkōdai Temple Dancers (*Shinbōkōdaiji no odori*). Originally a song, popular in Echigo province during the latter part of the seventeenth cen-

---

18. Including everything from the *Wakan sansaizue* to Morohashi's *Daikanwa jiten.*

19. See Ming, *Sancai tuhui* 2, p. 878. Together with the *Kinmōzui,* Terashima Ryōan's 105-volume illustrated compendium of China and Japan, the *Wakan sansaizue* (1713)—essentially a translation of the *Sancai tuhui* into Japanese—was one of the principal texts from which images of the fantastic Other were generally culled in late eighteenth-century Edo.

20. Kyōden would use this again in *Tadagokoro oni uchimame.*

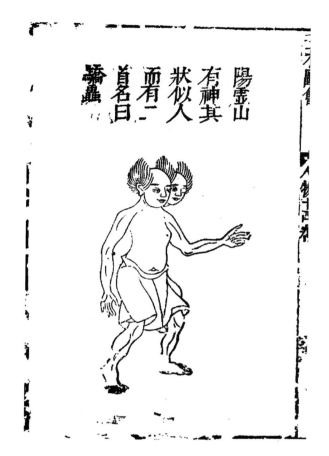

(*left*) Fig. 7.9 Entry for the two-headed god of Mt. Yangxu (J. Yōkyo sanjin). From *Assmebled Pictures of the Three Realms* (*Sancai tuhui,* 1609), compiled by Wang Qi. Courtesy of the Harvard-Yenching Library.

(*right*) Fig. 7.10 Detail from *Assmebled Pictures of the Three Realms* (*Sancai tuhui,* 1609) showing the poorly printed variant of the graph *kyo* 虚 that Hirazumi (if not others) would later miscopy as *rei* 霊. Courtesy of the Harvard-Yenching Library.

tury, this became a sensational dance in Edo during the 1770s (under the name *Shinbokōdaiji* [sic] *no odori* or *Otasuke odori*) connected to begging. Both the song and the dance crop up frequently in contemporary popular literature. There was even a *kibyōshi* by Sakuragawa Tohō, entitled *Shinbokōdai Temple Story* (*Shinbokōdaiji banashi,* 1787), published the year prior to *Swingers.*[21] The Edo performers (Mori notes) used a kind of puppet (*ichimatsu ningyō*), so the checked pattern (*ichimatsu*) of Oinosuke's sash may be a sly visual-verbal reference.

fake (*tsukurimono*). Although a special term for stage props, this had the more general meaning of gaffed freak (and pops up again and again in contemporary accounts of sideshows).

Shared Wings (*Hiyoku*). A couple of birds from Chinese legend, one male and the other female, whose wings were fused together emblematizing their eternal love for each other. Poet Bai Juyi appropriated the image as a

---

21. Tanahashi, *Kibyōshi sōran 1,* p. 711. Tanahashi fails to mention where he found this *kibyōshi.* I have been unable to locate a copy in order to check possible influences upon *Swingers.*

metaphor for the undying passion between Emperor Xuanzong (685–762) and his concubine Yang Guifei in his classic "Song of Everlasting Sorrow" (*Changhen ge*). This was also an infamous gaffed freak, put on display in Edo freakshows. The term *hiyoku* also alludes to the title of Sakurada's *Conjoined Crests of Chrysanthemum and Butterfly*.

Twitchity-twitch (*Yoiyoi*). Uttered in keeping time to music, this phrase was also a derogatory slang term for a loss of bodily motor control, especially of the legs (*locomotor ataxia*), or for such a spasmodic person.

Section 6

[Picture] Hanbei (the graph *han* on his sleeve) and Onatsu (the graph *natsu* on her sleeve) at home, respectfully at odds, arms crossed, eyes cast in opposite directions. Some pictorial gags reinforce the discord: the crest on the robe on the garment rack (in the upper right-hand corner) shows two identical symbols (perhaps sword guards?)—at opposing ends of the circle; likewise, the twins straddle the crack between tatami seams (*tatami no heri*), a pipe visible on his side, a tobacco pouch visible on hers. In the background, a short robe (*happi*) and a string with a key at the end are draped over a transverse pole. The sweetflags (*ayame*) at the bottom of the standing screen symbolize hermaphroditism as much as they do midsummer.

What do you think, dear? (*Omae dō omowashiyansue*). Courtesan-speak (*arinsu kotoba*). The gruff masculine "you" (*omae*) of modern Japanese was used by both sexes during the Edo period as a term of respect toward a superior.

This was more tête-à-tête than head-on confrontation (*Kore wa hiza tomo dangō de wa nai tsura to no dangō da*). Instead of the proverbial "knee-to-knee conference," Onatsu and Hanbei can only meet face to face.

midsummer (*gogatsu no hange*). By the old lunar calendar, "midsummer" falls in the "fifth month" (*gogatsu*)—when the conjoined twins in one version of *Tale of Koyasu* are said to have been born.[22] **Hanbei** derives from "mid" (*han*) and **Onatsu** from "summer" (*ge* being the Sinified reading of *natsu*).

Bright moon illumines the river ahead (*Meigetsu zensen ni mitsu*). The last line of a Chinese poem by Yang Jiong (J. *Yōkei*) from the *Tang Poetry Anthology* (*Tōshisen*). The connection to the present piece is obscure.[23]

---

22. Yokoyama and Matsumoto *Muromachi jidai monogatari taisei 5*, p. 147.

23. The full poem runs: "Your jade, Mr. Zhao, worth a row of cities / Has been passed through the world from the beginning / I see you off as you return to your old office / The bright moonlight illumines the river ahead." It is possible that Kyōden confused the term *liancheng bi* ("row of cities") with *lianbi*, two beautiful men who are lovers. For an annotated version of the poem, see Mekada, *Tōshisen*, pp. 598–599. For an An'ei-Tenmei-era commentary, see *Tōshisen kokujikai* (1782) in Hattori and Hino, *Tōshisen kokujikai*, pp. 405–407.

MIDDLE FASCICLE

[Frontispiece] Onatsu and Hanbei as adults, wearing a kimono with a mountain cherry design. They appear inside their home which, below, will be shown from the outside, from the point-of-view of two passersby.

Section 7

[Picture] Two pedestrians erroneously taking Onatsu and Hanbei for a couple in *flagrante delicto*—erroneously, but understandably, for several of the visual cues, if read against the conventions of contemporary pornography, reinforce a sexualized interpretation: the sleeve to Onatsu's mouth suggests a stifled moan;[24] the potted plant (*ueki*) on the windowsill near Onatsu and Hanbei is evocative of bodily limbs intertwined in the throes of passion;[25] and the graph for **water** (*mizu*) on the drainage barrel (*tensuioke*) calls to mind the "wet stuff" (sex) of the "water trade" (adult entertainment). The blossoms of "morning face" (*asagao*) set the time as mid-morning. Haga Tōru suggests that one of the main characteristics of Edo pornography is the depiction of spontaneously initiated, casual sex in locales barely shielded from public scrutiny. Included among such "precarious" (*kiwadoi*) places are verandas, balconies, baths, kitchens, staircases, and windows.[26]

tramp themselves to faraway Edo (*karada wa harubaru Edo e kudarikeru*). More literally, their "body left the capital for faraway Edo," which loosely plays on the phrase "to sell one's body" (*karada o haru*).

floozying around (*chiwatteiru*). Here, a slang term for seducing a woman.

Filthy beasts (*Chikushōme*). A pejorative word meaning something like "pervert!" There was also a strong contemporary association with differ-

---

24. "The link of the sleeve to sex was apt, for when a kimono was cast off the sleeve fell wide, leaving tempting openings, as is suggested by many *shunga*. . . . Since ancient times the sleeve was the recipient of flooding emotional outbursts, and the expression to 'wet one's sleeve' (*sode o nurasu*) described the culmination of high feeling in classical tales." In Screech, *Sex and the Floating World*, pp. 187–188.

25. "[In Edo *shunga*, certain] acts of love might be referred to via vegetal or animal types. . . . Symbols were used in pictures to expand the signification of the scene," notes Screech, who goes on to give an example from a print by Suzuki Harunobu: "a rock bamboo (*iwatake*) is seen just outside the screens . . . It is invisible to the woman, although like her it is upright, and it is held in place by a frame; its stems try to flop over but cannot. The man holds the woman in a similar way." In Screech, *Sex and the Floating World*, pp. 135–136.

26. "This type of hastiness and agitation are [*sic*] among the most apparent features of the erotic art of Tokugawa Japan, at least from the period of Suzuki Harunobu (1725–1770) down to the end of the regime." In Haga, "Precariousness of Love, Places of Love," p. 97. It should be noted that Haga omits from his list the ordinary bedroom—which becomes transformed into such a "precarious" place by the addition of a furtive third party. Many *shunga* contain scenes of this sort, depicting a rake, for example, taking his lover from behind as she lies quietly next to her obliviously sleeping husband.

ently sexed twins born of a "beast belly" (*chikushōbara*), which, in turn, had vague associations with incest.

Section 8

[Picture] Hanbei impersonating the singing and acting of kabuki idols, such as Ichikawa Monnosuke (who played Seijūrō), to Onatsu's *shamisen* accompaniment (*nagauta*). They perform in front of teahouse patrons and serving women in Edo's Nakazu district, famously located on the confluent branches of the Sumida River (hence the water pictured in the background)—an ideal setting for an imagistic pun on the bifurcation of the twins. Judging by the writing on the paper lantern (*chōchin*) in the upper-left hand corner, and by the box-like hanging lamp (*kakeandon*), this teahouse is the Azumaya. Hanbei's and Onatsu's joint left hand appears to oscillate between holding his fan and fingering her instrument. The image of a half-man, half-woman act may have called to mind the spectacle of a one-man show in which an actor simultaneously played two roles by garbing the left and right sides of his body as different characters (*katami kawari no mono-morai shibai*).

only the trendy prosper in Edo (*Oedo wa nandemo atarashiku nakereba hayaranu*). More accurately, "In Edo, whatever isn't new isn't popular," though to be "popular" (*hayaru*) specifically referred to a geisha retaining a large clientele.

vocal impersonation (*kowairo*). The vocal and gestural impersonation of kabuki stars that swept Edo as a fad in the 1780s.

Nakazu. One of Edo's unlicensed districts, celebrated for its teahouses, lantern-lit restaurants, firework displays, boat parties, and sideshows (and, as Enjirō discovered, decried for its bedwetting hustlers). The talented impersonator Matsukawa Tsuruichi famously performed *kowairo* routines there, imitating kabuki stars (such as Ichikawa Danjūrō V and Kikunojō III) sometimes in both male *and* female roles.[27] Located on reclaimed land—actually a sandbar augmented by landfill—on the west bank of the Sumida (between Eitaibashi and Shin'ōhashi), the Nakazu (sometimes also rendered Nakatsu) was the most popular place in Edo to enjoy the evening cool during summer. Built around 1772, it would be dismantled less than two decades later, in 1789. Soon after, a comic haiku (*Yanagidaru* 75:28)—playing off a famed verse by Bashō

Natsukusa ya	Summer grass—
Tsuwamonodomo ga	Of warriors' dreams
Yume no ato	All that remains.[28]

---

27. Clark, "The Rise and Fall of the Island of Nakazu," p. 79.
28. Translated by Edwin A. Cranston.

—waxed parodic:

Nakazu ima	Nakazu today—
Bakamonodomo ga	Of silly fools' dreams
Yume no ato	All that remains.[29]

double header (*nishu*). Kyōden puns "two-headed" (*nishu*) and "two-bit" (*nishu*), as in a "two-bit performer" (*nishu geisha*). A *shu* (half of one *bu*) was also the cheapest rate for procuring a low-ranking courtesan (*shinzō*).

♪ **Brothers, adopted at ages five and three . . .** ♪ Probably lines lifted from a confrontation scene (*taimen no bamen*) between the Soga Brothers and their father, Kawazu Saburō's murderer Kudō Suketsune, in one of the myriad Soga plays. The most likely candidate is *Nanakusa yosooi Soga* by Sakurada Jisuke, since Kyōden borrows heavily in the sections to come from the works of this playwright, and because the role of Soga Gorō was performed in the first run in 1782 by Takinoya (the actor Ichikawa Monnosuke), who is mentioned presently.[30] **Sukenobu** is the brothers' adoptive father.

♪ **Ah, these rainy nights, so very charming . . .** ♪ (*Ame no furu yo wa naa hitoshio yukashi*). Originally a line from a rather dated, though still popular, ballad (*kayō*) meant to be sung to shamisen accompaniment (according to Mori). Also mentioned in Sakurada Jisuke's *Hanakawado migawari no dan*, a dance piece first performed in 1783 featuring Ichikawa Monnosuke.

Takinoya is the hereditary stage-name (*yagō*) of the actor Ichikawa Monnosuke, who played Seijūrō in Sakurada's *Conjoined Crests of Chrysanthemum and Butterfly* (1781) as well as Gorō in the same playwright's *Nanakusa yosooi Soga* (1782).[31]

wasabi plum (*umeboshi ni wasabi*). Apparently a savory finger food to go with saké, though the connection here is unclear. Perhaps a metaphor for the mixing of opposites?

brilliant pieces (*tsū*). Although most often referring to a "sophisticate" of the pleasure quarters, *tsū* was also a stage term for money (no doubt because sophistication was associated with liberality). The line thus puns a musical "maestro" and the "money" associated with "two-bit geisha."

---

29. Kasuya, *Senryū daijiten*, p. 547.

30. Unfortunately, the only extant version of *Nanakusa yosooi Soga* is incomplete, being composed of extracts that do not include the obligatory confrontation scene. The extracts are contained in Atsumi, *Soga kyōgen gappeishū*, pp. 141–182.

31. Takinoya is identified as Monnosuke's house name in the second fascicle of *The Complete Writings on Actors* (*Yakusha zensho*, 1774), which is on p. 213 of the modern typescript edition in Geinōshi kenkyūkai, *Nihon shomin bunka shiryō shūsei 6*, pp. 199–241.

How ho-hum da-doo dumb! (*Yoppodo aryarii donno baka aru nō*). Gibberish, probably chanted in accompaniment to music, though clearly embedding the words "how" (*yoppodo*) and "dumb" (*baka*).

Section 9

[Picture] Ochiyo (sleeve to mouth) and Hanbei (blowing puffs of smoke) in intimate repose, as Onatsu lies fast asleep on a doubly-long honeymoon pillow. A tobacco pouch is tucked under the futon. Hanbei holds his pipe in an erect position. A few pictorial gags here are reminiscent of contemporary erotica: the bedclothes and folding screen obscure the view of the lovers' lower bodies (not unlike a scene from *Master Wetdream*—see **Figure 3.1**); a standing lamp (*andon*), its wick floating in a dish of oil, stands in for Hanbei's would-be erection; "twinned" prongs penetrate the depths of a brazier (*hibachi*); and the striped robe strewn over the folding screen, as well as Ochiyo's sash lying on the ground behind her, is evocative of lovers passionately disrobed. This sort of *liaison dangereuse*, in which a furtive third party makes love to someone whose partner is sleeping nearby, appears not infrequently in erotic prints of the time. Onatsu's head is on the right of their shared body, and Hanbei's on the left, in every picture except for the two amorous scenes.

Hanbei and Ochiyo were real-life husband and wife whose double suicide in 1722 was sensationalized in a number of plays, though Kyōden borrows mostly from Sakurada's version of the story.

freakishness notwithstanding (*katawamono no kuse ni irogurui seba*). More accurately, "if he could philander in spite of being a freak." This line puns "in spite of" (*kuse ni*) and "quirkily" (*kuseni*).

necking (*kuttsuite*). More literally, "coupling." This slang phrase refers to both the "fusing together" of necks as well as the physical union of lovers.

Section 10

[Picture] Seijūrō and Onatsu in the throes of passion, trying not to awaken the somniloquent Hanbei, who is apparently semiconscious of Onatsu's romantic escapade. The graph on the sleeve of Seijūrō's stylish black jacket can be read *Kiyo* (for his nickname *Kiyo-sama* in many versions of the story) as well as *Sei*. (This scene may call to mind a celebrated, if scandalous, passage from Saikaku's version, wherein Onatsu, on a picnic with several women from her family's shop, slips behind some screening to make love secretly to Seijūrō.) A handtowel is draped over the wardrobe stand (*emon-kake*), behind which hang a parasol (*karakasa*) and what appears to be a sedge hat (*amigasa*) decorated with a variety of crests. On the floor behind the wardrobe is a half-hidden vanity (*kyōdai*), its mirror obscured.

Curiosity seekers (*Monozuki na hito*). Literally "eccentric" people, here the "stuff" (*mono*) that Seijūrō "adores" (*suki*) is that of the sideshow (*misemono*).

Tajimaya Seijūrō and **Onatsu**. A pair of real-life lovers, whose tragic story has been retold variously, including a play by Chikamatsu and a short story by Saikaku. Kyōden draws liberally from the version by Sakurada.

Onatsu sneaks out of the bedroom . . . for a little hanky-panky. There is a similar passage in *The Illness Scrolls* about a hermaphrodite (*futanari*) stealing away at night for sexual shenanigans.[32]

Shirakawa night boat (*Shirakawa yobune*). Frequently abbreviated as "Shirakawa," this was a slang expression of ignorance. When asked about the sights of the capital, passengers who had fallen asleep on the nocturnal vessel would reply with the name of the boat, punning on "Don't know!" (*shiranu*).[33]

His pestle slips into her drain (*Nagashi e surikogi ga ochita*). Literally, "the pestle fell into the drain." Since "pestle" was a slang term for penis, parallelism dictates that "drain" refers to vagina.

Bang . . . pant (*Gōgō fūfū*). Onomatopoeia for something hard dropping and for deep breathing, respectively.

My, that was good for me—you're the tops! (*Yoi shubi ja. Umai umai*). More literally "That came off well! Very, very well!" Embedded in this expression of *jouissance* is the slight orthographic pun, "nice neck!" (*yoi shu*).

Section 11

[Picture] Seijūrō and Ochiyo in a fierce tug-of-war over Onatsu and Hanbei, who are said to resemble a dried octopus. The room is probably Seijūrō's, since he has stripped off his black halfcoat (worn in the previous scene) and insists that Onatsu remain where she is. Hanbei and Onatsu once again straddle opposite sides of tatami seams.

gallop into the midst . . . horsing around. Less literally, "Ochiyo bursts in on Onatsu and Seijūrō in a compromising position." During the Edo period "deliciousness" (*umakoto*) was a euphemism for sensual pleasure. "Horse" (*uma*) was also slang for an enormous "horse-sized" penis. "Gallop" (*kaketsuke*) is an associative word.

dried octopus (*hipparidako*). A culinary dish prepared by flaying and drying the legs of an octopus. By extension, the term came to be used in the eigh-

---

32. Tanaka and Ienaga, *Jigoku sōshi, gaki sōshi, yamai no sōshi*, p. 63.

33. Kyōden would publish a fashionbook by the title *Shirakawa yobune* in 1789 (a year after *Swingers*). It is reprinted in Mizuno, *Sharebon taisei 14* (1981), pp. 333–349.

teenth century to describe a celebrity—specifically a kabuki star—tugged this way and that by a mob of overzealous fans.[34]

Section 12

[Picture] Hanbei, unable to sleep during the curious *ménage à trois*, derives oral satisfaction by snacking on some finger food off a nearby tray (*suzuributa*). Onatsu has her hand to her lips, perhaps to muffle a moan, and Seijūrō has a sleeve over his mouth.

loathe to clean up their acts after having done the dirty (*nurenu saki koso tsuyu o mo itoe*). "One abhors the dew only until being dampened." A proverb implying that there is no turning back after having had a taste for something illicit or immoral. In the present context "dampen" has distinctly sexual overtones.

half-assed lookout (*bankō*). Kyōden plays on the graph for "duke" (*bankō*), which is used disparagingly toward a sentinel, writing it with the "half" (*han*) of Hanbei's name.

climactic moment (*kanjin no tokoro*). Less blatantly, "vital point."

Might as well stuff my face (*Ore wa gebizō demo shiyō*). The term for sloppy gourmandizing (*gebizō*) puns (according to Mori) on the childhood name of the actor Ichikawa Danjūrō (Ebizō).

FINAL FASCICLE

[Frontispiece] Hanbei, on drawn knee (*tatehiza*), mysteriously separated from Onatsu.

Section 13

[Picture] Matters having come to a head, Hanbei and Onatsu are locked in mortal combat, overturning a tobacco bin (*tabakobon*) and knocking out hair ornaments—a comb (*binrō no kushi*) and a bodkin (*mimikaki kanzashi*)—in the fray. The wood grain (*mokume*) in the background is bifurcated, perhaps visually echoing the antagonism between the protagonists?

heart divided in two (*kokoro ga wareware ni nari*). "Each their own" (*wareware*) read literally means "broken broken" (*ware ware*).

passenger boat (*noriaibune*). A floating omnibus for the masses without the financial means to reserve regular seating. Aside from serving as the setting

---

34. Kyōden would recycle the tug-of-war idea in *Ryōtō fude zen'aku nikki* (1799), in the scene where Jizō and a devil vie for a two-headed twin. Mentioned in Yamaguchi, *Yamaguchi Takeshi chōsakushū 3*, p. 473. See Mizuno, *SKZ 3*, p. 328.

Fig. 7.11 A wealthy man in a boatful of people holds up his coin purse that he egotistically believes has weighed them down. From the comic vignette "The Passenger Boat" (*Noriaibune*), in the anonymous jokebook *Karukuchi heso no yadogae* (ca. 1760s). Reprinted in Mutō, *Eiri kobanashi o yomu*, p. 31. Courtesy of Tōkyōdō shuppan.

for storytelling, gambling, and other such liminal activities, it figures prominently in most versions of the Onatsu-Seijūrō tale. One humorous story, in a jokebook popular a couple of decades earlier, describes such a boat *immobilized* by too many passengers, though one wealthy patron fatuously believes that it is his coin-filled purse—perhaps presaging Hanbei's carrying pouch in the next scene?—that is to blame for their predicament (**Figure 7.11**).[35]

wench (*hattsukeamame*). An invective for a woman.

─────────

35. The story, titled "The Passenger Boat," was included in *Karukuchi heso no yadogae*, an anonymously written and illustrated *hanashibon* published during the 1760s. Reprinted in Mutō, *Eiri kobanashi o yomu*, p. 31.

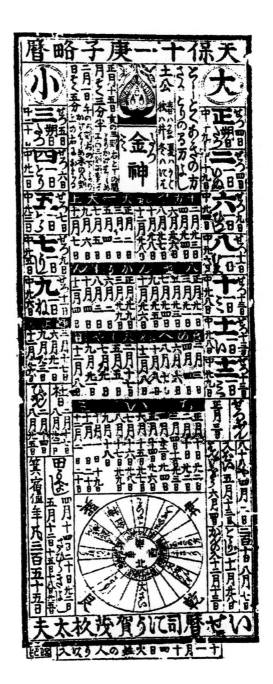

Fig. 7.12 Pillar calendar for the year Tenpō 11 (1840). Included are various noteworthy dates, a list of long and short months, and a circular zodiac. Reprinted in Nakamura, *Kogo daijiten 4*, p. 1065. Courtesy of Kadokawa shoten.

Section 14

[Picture] Hanbei, washcloth in hand and small carrying pouch (*nukabukuro*) in mouth, straining to leave for the bath, as Onatsu, chopsticks at the ready, attempts to eat. In front of her are a standing tray (with soup bowl and two cups), a large serving container, and a chopsticks box. Pasted to the wall at left are a pillar calendar (*hashiragoyomi*) with a circular Chinese zodiac (**Figure 7.12**), and a talisman reading "here's wishing for" (*kanau*) above a

picture of what looks like a two-handled saké keg (*tsunodaru*). The cross-hatch in the paper door (*shōji*) is a makeshift handle (*tegakari*). The sliding door (*fusuma*) on the floor of the right panel has come off its track (*shikii*), revealing the kitchen with its wood-paneled floor needed to support the heavy cooking hearth (*kamado* or *hettsui*). Firewood is stoked into the fuel hole (*takiguchi*), heating the wood-covered pot, which here has a colander (*zaru*) on it. A portable clay stove (*shichirin*), used to keep food warm, stands to the left of the hearth. Its coals can be blown with a bamboo tube put to the aperture toward the front bottom. On the altar shelf (*kamidana*) above the hearth stand a saké vessel (*tokkuri*) and a small votive tablet (*ema*). Near the basket (*kago*) are a utensil satchel nailed to the wall and a chopping knife (*hōchō*).

real scorcher (*tonda atsui*). The gag here—that Onatsu's feeling hot is apropos of her name ("Summer")—appears frequently in one shape or another, as in the following bawdy verse:[36]

Seijūrō	Seijūrō
Atsui onna to	And a hot woman
Chitsu tsukuri	Are getting it on.[37]

if only a puppet play (*jōruribon demo*). Apropos because Onatsu and Hanbei themselves were known to contemporary readers largely through puppet plays.

infuriating (*jirettei*). Literally, "tantalizing," this word was used mostly by women.

Section 15

[Picture] By cover of night Hanbei, foot pointing forward, abducts Onatsu, foot contorted in the opposite direction. Seijūrō, charging to the rescue, is the picture of an archetypical kabuki-style pose of revenge: robe hoicked up to facilitate mobility; thrusting a lantern (inscribed with his shop's name, Tajimaya) in front of him to light his way; eyes crossed (judging by his fretted brows and severe frown); about to draw his sword. That he is positioned to round a corner (*kado*) may be a visual pun on "kidnapping" (*kadowakashi*). No doubt this picture is a reenactment of a scene from Sakurada's dance drama, wherein Seijūrō, lantern raised, searches high and low for his Onatsu. Moreover, Seijūrō is drawn to resemble the actor who

---

36. Punning "hot" on Onatsu: Chikamatsu's play *Prayer-Song to Buddha on the Fiftieth Anniversary* (in Torigoe, *Chikamatsu Monzaemon shū 1*, p. 56); Saikaku's *Five Women Who Loved Love* (where Onatsu is garbed in *natsugoromo*—"summer clothes"); Suga Sensuke's puppet play of 1778 *Natsu yukata Seijūrō-zome* (in Tsuchida, *Suga Sensuke zenshū 5*, pp. 181–223); and so on.

37. In Kasuya, *Senryū daijiten*. This verse, which qualifies as a *bareku* by virtue of its inclusion of the vulgar term *chitsu* for vagina, dates from 1775.

Fig. 7.13 The actor Ichikawa Monnosuke in the play *Kachizumō uchiwa no ageha*. Detail from a multicolored woodblock print by Torii Kiyonaga, ca. 1783. Courtesy of Waseda University, Tsubouchi Memorial Theatre Museum (Object #201-0630).

played him, judging by contemporary portraits (*nigaoe*) of that actor, Ichikawa Monnosuke (**Figure 7.13**). Pasted to the wall is an advertising leaflet for an abortion-inducing concoction (*gessui nagashi*). Beneath it is a public urinal (*shōben-uke*), most likely installed by the owner of this private house as a preventive measure against the sullying of his nice wooden exterior walls.[38]

monkey gag (*sarugutsuwa*). Made of cloth and used on humans as well as on beasts.

warm hood (*sodezukin*). More properly, "sleeve-shaped cowl" (*sodenari-zukin*), this was an insulated hood ("warm" is my supplement), resembling a kimono sleeve, worn against the cold. Hanbei covers Onatsu's head with this as part of her abduction, but also possibly as his sarcastic comeback to her earlier complaint about feeling too hot.

Section 16

[Picture] In a travesty of the classic suicide journey for two, the four lovers, with many of the conventional implements: a suicide mat is slung over Hanbei's shoulder; Hanbei and Ochiyo clutch an opened maple-leaf parasol; Ochiyo holds a Buddhist rosary (*juzu*); and Onatsu and Seijūrō, hand in hand, wear kerchiefs folded into make-shift caps. Seijūrō carries his sedge hat (*sugegasa*) that is mentioned in most versions of his story. Ochiyo wears a waist sash (*koshiobi*) to prop up her large sash. Everybody's feet point in the same direction, suggesting unity of purpose.

---

38. Hanasaki Kazuo suggests this in his study of Edo-period toilets, where he further speculates that such privately installed public urinals were not an uncommon sight in Edo. See Hanasaki, *Edo kawaya zue*, pp. 29–32. For an updated and more accessible version, see his *Edo kawaya hyakusugata*.

reunited as man and wife. An inversion of the folk belief holding that a couple who commits a love suicide will be reborn as conjoined twins.

burial grounds at Toribe (*Toribeno*). Also known as *Toribeyama*, the site of love suicides in innumerable plays and ballads, most notably Sakurada's version of the Onatsu and Seijūrō tale.

Up to Conjoined Necks in Love's Deep Waters (*koi no fuchi moyai no kubitake*). The title of this travel poem sustains a good deal of wordplay. *Moyai* refers to "mooring" (an associative word of boats and "deep pool," *fuchi*) as well as to "shared" (as in "shared neck"). *Kubitake* (also *kubittake* or *kubidake*) can mean "depth" (as in fathoming the "depths" of love's waters), "up to the neck," "necks only," or even (taking *take* as "Mr." or "Mrs.") "Mr. and Mrs. Neck." A comprehensive rendering might be: "Mr. and Mrs. All Heads over Heels in Love's Deep Waters up to Their Moored-Together Necks." The phrase *koi no fuchi* is mentioned in Chikamatsu's play about Ochiyo and Hanbei.[39]

River Galguy (*Minanogawa*). A river in Ibaragi prefecture. Although one of the several different ways of writing *mina* includes the two graphs for man and woman, Kyōden reverses the order, conceivably to make this "groaner" of a pun (*dajare*) on the "woman" and "man" (*oi*) in the graph of Oinosuke.

♪ Isn't that Seijūrō . . . ♪ (*mukau tōru wa . . .*). Similar lines appear in many versions of the Onatsu and Seijūrō tale, though Kyōden's most closely follows Sakurada's play.[40]

maple-leaf parasol (*momijigasa*). An oblique reference to Ichikawa Monnosuke, the actor who played Seijūrō in Sakurada's play, and whose house crest (*kamon*) consists of four maple leaves (*momiji*) (**Figure 7.14**).

twilight crimson (*yūgurenai*). "Twilight" (*yūgure*) is fused into "crimson" (*kurenai*), yielding the pivot-word "night crimson" (*yūgurenai*).

suicide mat . . . life's brief dew (*kata ni kaketaru mōsen wa . . . inochi no tsuyu no okidokoro*). These lines follow Sakurada's version of the story instead of Chikamatsu's.[41]

---

39. See Torigoe, *Chikamatsu Monzaemon shū 1*, p. 15.

40. Koike Tōgorō claims the line parodies a line from Chikamatsu's *Prayer-Song to Buddha on the Fiftieth Anniversary*. In Koike, *Santō Kyōden no kenkyū*, p. 273. However, there are numerous lexical and orthographical differences. For a more detailed comparison of the two plays, see Kern, "Santō Kyōden gasaku no kibyōshi *Sogitsugi gingiseru* no saikō to shichū." For Chikamatsu's play, see Torigoe, *Chikamatsu Monzaemon shū 1*, pp. 13–57.

41. Koike claims that similar lines are to be found in Chikamatsu's *Eve of the Kōshin Festival*. See Koike, *Santō Kyōden no kenkyū*, p. 273. However, Kyōden follows Sakurada's lines nearly verbatim, as per Takano, *Nihon kayō shūsei 10*, p. 474.

Fig. 7.14 Entry for Ichikawa Monnosuke (second column from right), indicating his house name Takinoya and house crest of four maple leaves. From the second volume of *The Complete Writings on Actors* (*Yakusha zensho*, 1774). Reprinted in Geinōshi kenkyūkai, *Nihon shomin bunka shiryō shūsei 6*, p. 213.

of the hem pattern to rest . . . Girlboy (*Seijūrō to netaru susomoyō oi to iu ji ya nokoruran*). This is a close parody of a line from Sakurada's version of the Onatsu-Seijūrō tale, the only difference being that Kyōden has replaced Sakurada's "love" (*koi*) with the *oi* of Oinosuke.

Section 17

[Picture] The protagonists at their would-be death scene (*saigoba*), seated in front of bound-together stacks of hay, and the Dutch-style doctor, wearing Western-looking knickerbockers (replete with buttons) and Japanese-style string sandals (*zōri*). The Chinese-style lightening design (*raimon*) on his cloth sack enhances the air of exoticism.

nenbutsu. The prayer to Amitabha Buddha for rebirth in the world to come.

Nagasaki. Famed as the center of "Dutch Studies."[42]

---

42. Interestingly, a Dutch-style physician "cures" a long-necked goblin in Kyōden's *The Stage-Prop Fan's Prosperity* (*Kyōgen suehiro no sakae*), a *kibyōshi* published the same year as *Swingers*. See Mizuno, *SKZ 1*, pp. 415–432.

we won't have to kill ourselves. This plays off a well-known slogan-like line in many versions of the story, though first appearing in Saikaku: "If you kill Seijūrō, kill Onatsu too!" (*Seijūrō korosaba Onatsu mo korose*).

I'm more than willing . . . go-ahead (*Kono Hanbei wa zuibun shōchi naredomo futari moyai no inochi de gozareba tonari no kubi no ryōken o kiite de gorōjimase*). Literally, "This half Hanbei entirely consents, though our two lives being moored together, please ask the opinion of my adjoining neck." "This half" (*kono han*) pivots into "I, Hanbei" (*kono Hanbei*). The "same boat" and "go-ahead" of the translation reflect the "moored" (*moyai*) and "adjoining neck" (*tonari no kubi*) of the original.

Section 18

[Picture] The two happily coupled uncoupled couples.

Hanbei's head (*Hanbei ga kubi*). Since the "silverpipe" of the title refers to Hanbei and Onatsu, this line, playing off the fact that pipe bowls—"goose necks" (*gankubi*) as they were termed (and upon which *ga kubi* puns)—could be detached and transferred to other pipe stems, is the story's punning jackpot.

surgery (*ryōji*). More precisely, medical "treatment."

a hundred days (*hyaku nichi*). Related to the custom of making a pilgrimage to a temple once a day for a hundred consecutive days (*hyaku nichi mairi*) in order to pray for convalescence from some kind of illness.

Masanobu. Kyōden.